THE ROUGH GUIDE TO

Sardinia

written and researched by

Robert Andrews

ROUGH
GUIDES

roughguides.com

Contents

INTRODUCTION   4

Where to go   6   Things not to miss   12
When to go   8   Itineraries   18

BASICS   20

Getting there   21   Culture and etiquette   41
Getting around   26   Sports and outdoor activities   42
Accommodation   30   Shopping   43
Food and drink   32   Travelling with children   44
The media   37   Travel essentials   44
Festivals   38

THE GUIDE   52

1 Cágliari   52   5 Alghero and the northwest coast 164
2 The southwest   78   6 Sássari and around   198
3 Campidano, La Marmilla and   7 Gallura   226
   Sarrabus   110   8 Nuoro and Ogliastra   266
4 Oristano and around   134

CONTEXTS   306

History   307   Books   319
Sardinian wildlife   315   Italian   322

SMALL PRINT & INDEX   333

Introduction to
Sardinia

Undeniably and exuberantly Italian, yet expressing a unique regional identity, Sardinia presents a distinctive take on the Mediterranean island experience. Its position midway between the Italian mainland and the North African coast, and the traces left by the many invaders and settlers who shaped its history, have together forged a hybrid, fragmented character – "lost between Europe and Africa," as D.H. Lawrence put it, "and belonging to nowhere". In fact the Sard people reject the need to "belong" anywhere. While accepting their shared Italian culture, they are also passionately loyal to their island home in all its diversity, from the rocky headlands and secluded beaches on the coast to the forested mountains and pungent expanses of wilderness in the interior.

Together with these physical differences go deep cultural contrasts, often corresponding to the mosaic of smaller territories that make up the island. From Gallura and Logudoro in the north to Sulcis and Sarrabus in the south, each has its own traditions, dialects and historical roots. At a still more local level, each village celebrates its individuality at the many flamboyant **festivals** that take place throughout the year, ranging from rowdy medieval pageants to dignified religious processions, all helping to keep tradition alive in an island where the past is inescapable.

And yet, while Sardinia is big enough to accommodate this range of diverse faces – it's the Mediterranean's second-biggest island after Sicily (though with less than a third of Sicily's population) – it's small and manageable enough to allow you to travel from the sleek yachts and glistening beaches of the fabled Costa Smeralda to the granite *stazzi*, or farm dwellings, of the mountainous interior in less than an hour.

ABOVE COASTAL WATCHTOWER, SANTA MARIA NAVARRESE (P.303)

FACT FILE

• Sardinia (Sardegna in Italian) has a **population** of nearly 1.7 million, and nearly twice that number of **sheep**. The flocks have diminished significantly in recent years, but the Italian mainland's cartoon caricature of the Sards perpetuates the image of the wily shepherd, be-capped and in brown corduroys, or else swathed in hairy sheepskins. The local sheep's cheese, **Pecorino Sardo**, is one of Italy's most flavoursome cheeses.

• Sardinia's position on the chief Mediterranean trade routes has ensured that it has rarely been free of foreign intervention – though this has endowed the island with a rich **heritage** of archeological and artistic monuments. The most truly Sardinian remains, however, are prehistoric, notably the "fairy houses", "giants' tombs" and seven thousand-odd *nuraghi* (stone towers) dotted around.

• Despite the centuries of occupation, Sardinia has retained a fiercely **independent identity**. Since 1948 the island has had a degree of **regional autonomy**, but only a minority of the population supports the separatist cause.

• The official **Sardinian flag** is known as the Quattro Mori, for the four Moors depicted on a white background. Until 1999, the four were blindfolded and facing west – towards Spain, the former colonial ruler – but the flag was altered to show the heads unblindfolded and looking east: liberated, enlightened, and gazing steadily across to the Italian mainland.

Where to go

Sardinia's lively capital, **Cágliari**, is a microcosm of the island's diversity, with traces of every phase of the island's past, from the spindly statuettes of the prehistoric nuraghic culture to a Roman theatre and Pisan citadel. Some of the finest Roman and Carthaginian ruins are a short journey outside town at **Nora**, one of a number of sites that attest to Sardinia's former prominence in Mediterranean trade. Many of the powers that occupied the island were drawn to its mines, still visible throughout the regions of **Sulcis** and **Iglesiente**, west of Cágliari. Off the Sulcis coast, the islands of **Sant'Antíoco** and **San Pietro** provide more archeological remains, while the southern littoral and the Iglesiente's **Costa Verde** are among Sardinia's most scenic coastlines.

La Marmilla, a hilly region north of Cágliari, contains Sardinia's greatest nuraghic site, **Su Nuraxi**, while the rugged **Sarrabus** area east of the capital is fringed by some of the island's most spectacular beaches. Halfway up Sardinia's western side, the province of **Oristano** holds numerous nuraghic, Carthaginian and Roman remains, the most important of which, the ruins of **Tharros**, lie on the **Sinis peninsula**, whose lagoons and coasts attract aquatic birds and beach pilgrims respectively. North of here, the picturesque river port of **Bosa** is separated by a long, unspoilt stretch of rocky coast from the popular resort of **Alghero**, which retains its distinctive Catalan character, the result of intensive settlement five centuries ago. **Stintino**, on the island's northwestern tip, lies near some beaches of jaw-dropping beauty.

Inland, Sardinia's second city, **Sássari**, makes a good base for touring the Pisan churches scattered throughout the Logudoro area to the south and east. Strikingly situated on a promontory of the north coast, **Castelsardo** is the chief town of **Anglona**, a region indelibly

RIGHT THARROS, SINIS PENINSULA (P.151)

associated with the Doria family of Genoa – one of the Mediterranean's leading mercantile powers in the Middle Ages. Bordering it, **Gallura**'s jagged-peaked interior makes a dramatic backdrop to its famously beautiful granite coastline, where the **Costa Smeralda** remains an exclusive enclave for celebs and tycoons. This and other areas of the northeast coast hold some enticing stretches of rocky or sandy shore, with some of the best beaches clustered around **Palau**, embarkation point for trips to the beautiful **Maddalena archipelago**, and **Santa Teresa di Gallura** on Sardinia's northern tip, the chief port for connections with Corsica.

Below **Olbia** – the main entry point from the mainland – most of Sardinia's eastern coast is largely inaccessible, the sheer cliff walls punctuated by a few developed holiday spots such as **Cala Gonone** and **Santa Maria Navarrese**. The provinces of **Nuoro** and **Ogliastra** occupy most of the mountainous interior of this coast, and are the best places to encounter the last authentic remnants of the island's rural culture, particularly its costumes and village festivals. This is especially true in the central area known as **Barbagia**, where the sparse population is concentrated in small, insulated villages that provide an excellent opportunity to view the quiet life of the interior at

SARDINIA'S TOP 10 BEACHES

Sardinia has some of the Mediterranean's most gorgeous **beaches**. On the whole, they're clean and pollution-free, and many have facilities operating June–Sept – a bar or two, sun-loungers and parasols to rent, and often activities available such as wind-surfing and pedalo and canoe rental. Otherwise, seek out more remote sections without any of the paraphernalia, and bring your own shade.

Liscia Ruja, Costa Smeralda (see p.243)
Chia, south coast (see p.87)
Rena Bianca, Santa Teresa Gallura (see p.255)
Capo Carbonara, southeast coast (see p.127)
Cala Sinzias, Costa Rei (see p.129)

Piscinas, Costa Verde (see p.109)
Cala Corsara, Spargi, La Maddalena (see p.255)
Sa Mesa Lunga, Sinis peninsula (see p.153)
La Pelosa, northwest (see p.197)
Spiaggia Cartoe, east coast (see p.300)

first hand, and make useful bases for mountain rambles. If your image of Sardinia is all shaggy sheep and offbeat folklore – the kind of place depicted in films like *Padre Padrone* – then these mountain slopes will probably fit the bill.

When to go

The best advice that can be given regarding when to visit Sardinia is to avoid the month of **August** if at all possible. Travelling at this time is by no means impossible, but the negative factors include sweltering heat, crowds, increased prices, frayed tempers and scarce accommodation. June, July and September can also be oppressively hot, but there

ABOVE SU GIUDEU BEACH, CHIA (P.87) **RIGHT FROM TOP** SANT'EFISIO FESTIVAL, CÁGLIARI (P.40); NIGHTLIFE IN CÁGLIARI (P.75)

SARDINIA'S PISAN CHURCHES

Visitors to Sardinia who have spent any time in Tuscany may be surprised to discover a whole string of **Romanesque churches** scattered throughout the island which would look more at home in that mainland region. The odd juxtaposition is due to the close association of **Pisa** with Sardinia between the eleventh and fourteenth centuries. Religious orders were introduced and architects imported, leading to the construction of churches all over the island, with a particular concentration in the Logudoro and Anglona areas of northern Sardinia. You'll encounter the characteristic black-and-white pattern in the unlikeliest of places, sometimes in remote countryside, such as the marooned-looking **Santa Trinità di Saccargia**. Two of the most monumental examples, **San Gavino** and **San Simplicio**, seem lost among the quiet backstreets of Porto Torres and Olbia respectively. Most of the surviving specimens are in a good state of repair, but the interiors have little in the way of decoration – which helps to preserve their murky medieval atmosphere intact.

is nothing like the kind of holiday frenzy of the peak weeks. You can count on **swimming** fairly comfortably at any time between May and October, and you won't be considered excessively eccentric if you take dips during the winter months. There's much to be said for travelling in Sardinia in **winter** – the weather can be warm and clear and the tourist presence is refreshingly low-key, though the diminished daylight hours can limit your freedom of movement, and you may find many facilities (including most campsites) closed. Some of the **best festivals** take place in **spring**, and this is also the ideal period for walking, when the countryside is at its most vibrant, the air limpid and the wildlife abundant. **Autumn** is also an inspiring time for being outdoors, especially for the gradations of colour on the forested slopes of the interior.

AVERAGE DAILY TEMPERATURES AND MONTHLY RAINFALL

	Jan	Feb	Mar	Apr	May	Jun	Jul	Aug	Sep	Oct	Nov	Dec
CÁGLIARI (SEA LEVEL)												
Av temp (°C)	10	11	12.5	14.5	18	24	25	25.5	23	18.5	14	12
Av temp (°F)	50	52	54.5	58	64.5	75	77	78	73.5	65.5	57	53.5
Rainfall (mm)	4.4	4	3.9	3.5	3.5	0.8	0.5	0.8	3	5	6	7
NUORO (ALT 550M/1804FT)												
Av temp (°C)	4	5	7	10	14	19	23	22	19	15	9	6
Av temp (°F)	39	41	44.5	50	57	66	73.5	71.5	66	59	48	43
Rainfall (mm)	15.5	15	14	11.5	10	3.5	1.5	1.5	6	10.5	15	18

ABOVE SANTA TRINITÀ DI SACCARGIA, NEAR SÁSSARI (P.222)

MORTORIO, AN ISLAND OFF THE COSTA SMERALDA

Author picks

Sardinia is a place that constantly throws up new discoveries and experiences not always appearing in the tourist brochures. Here's a selection of personal favourites:

Church treasures You don't have to visit galleries to see great art in Sardinia – some of the smallest, most unprepossessing churches preserve some real gems of medieval art; the magnificent altarpiece in San Pietro Apostolo, Tuili (p.124), is well worth a detour.

Rides and drives The landscape of Sardinia is itself one of its greatest pleasures, best appreciated on long, meandering journeys through the mountainous interior. Favourite routes include the roads running through Gerrei (p.126), south of Dorgali (p.298) and west of Aggius (p.264).

Isles of wonder The island has its own sub-groups of islands, the most dramatic of

which is the archipelago of La Maddalena, off the northeastern coast; you can explore the pristine beaches and silky waters on boat trips – join a group or rent your own motor-dinghy (p.250).

Ancient towers Nuraghe-spotting is one of the classic pastimes when travelling through the island. Some of these prehistoric monuments are well restored and can only be visited with a ticket; others are mossy ruins in fields, free to enter. One of the most satisfying is the Nuraghe Mannu outside Cala Gonone (p.300).

Culinary pursuits You'll enjoy exquisite sea- and land-based dishes in restaurants throughout the island, but some of the best places, combining tasteful decor, friendly service and outstanding, reasonably-priced food, are off the tourist track, in such inland centres as Sássari (p.210) and Nuoro (p.277).

> Our author recommendations don't end here. We've flagged up our favourite places – a perfectly sited hotel, an atmospheric café, a special restaurant – throughout the guide, highlighted with the ★ symbol

17

things not to miss

It's not possible to see everything Sardinia has to offer in one trip – and we don't suggest you try. What follows is a selective taste of the island's highlights: historic monuments, dramatic landscapes and great beaches. All entries have a page reference to take you straight into the Guide, where you can find out more. Coloured numbers refer to chapters in the Guide.

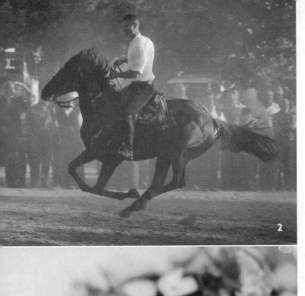

1 THARROS, SINIS PENINSULA

Page 151

Founded by the Phoenicians on a promontory jutting into the sea, this historic site retains extensive evidence of the Punic and Roman settlers who followed.

2 S'ARDIA, SÉDILO

Page 159

This manic horse race at dawn has ancient origins – it was originally held in honour of the emperor Constantine.

3 SEAFOOD IN ALGHERO

Page 177

Alghero's restaurants are renowned for their fresh seafood platters, with ingredients straight off the boat.

4 BOSA

Page 187

Explore the atmospheric lanes of this quiet riverside town overlooked by a hilltop castle, dine at its excellent restaurants and enjoy the enticing beaches nearby.

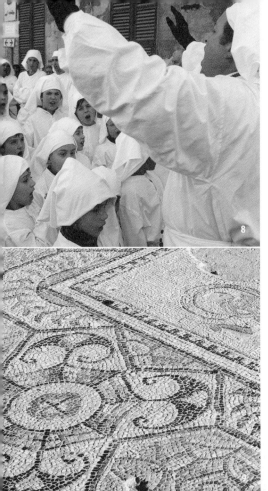

5 WALK TO TÍSCALI
Page 281

The climb to this nuraghic village – cunningly hidden within a huge cave in the Lanaittu valley east of Nuoro – makes a fabulous half-day hike.

6 ETHNOGRAPHIC MUSEUM, NUORO
Page 275

A visit to this extensive collection – crammed with masks, costumes, craftwork and musical instruments – offers intriguing insights into the local culture.

7 INLAND GALLURA
Page 260

Interspersed with thick groves of cork oaks, the granite rockscape of this scarcely populated mountainous zone offers unforgettable panoramas.

8 EASTER CELEBRATIONS
Page 40

Costumes, processions and intense drama are the main ingredients of Sardinia's various *feste* commemorating Easter.

9 NORA
Page 84

An important Phoenician, Carthaginian and Roman centre for more than a thousand years, Nora's splendid seaside position and fragmentary ruins still evoke its former glory.

10 CASTELSARDO OLD TOWN
Page 216

With historic churches buried among its steep lanes, and a castle/museum at its summit affording distant coastal views, this old Doria stronghold repays the uphill slog.

11 LA PELOSA
Page 197

The beaches and rocky backdrop of this beauty spot are postcard-perfect, with aquamarine water and mesmerizing views.

12 NURAGHE SANTU ANTINE
Page 224

One of the island's most imposing *nuraghi*, on the plains southeast of Sássari amid a cluster of these prehistoric monuments.

13 SA SARTIGLIA, ORISTANO
Page 146

Costumed hijinks and equestrian showmanship recall the medieval roots of this boisterous festival.

14 SÁSSARI'S OLD TOWN
Page 200

The compact old quarter of Sardinia's second city makes for an atmospheric wander through its medieval lanes.

15 NEPTUNE'S GROTTO, ALGHERO
Page 180

Stalactites, stalagmites and eccentric rock formations are the highlights of a tour through the Grotta di Nettuno, a cave complex set in towering cliffs by the sea.

16 MUSEO ARCHEOLOGICO, CÁGLIARI
Page 62

Sardinia's premier archeological collection includes grinning deities, nuraghic figurines and ancient Phoenician inscriptions.

17 BASTIONE SAN REMY, CÁGLIARI
Page 60

Part of the formidable city walls surrounding the old citadel, this offers stupendous views of the city and coast – especially recommended at sunset.

14

15

16

17

Itineraries

The following itineraries suggest a framework for enjoying the best that Sardinia has to offer. They dip into the island's historical treasures as well as allowing you to leg-stretch amid some of Sardinia's finest scenery.

ON THE CASTLE TRAIL

Whether they are prestige projects for bored aristocrats, eccentric family mansions or grim reminders of past oppression, Sardinia's castles come in all shapes and sizes. Often, however, they occupy lofty sites with unrivalled views over the landscape.

❶ Sanluri The compact Castello di Eleonora di Arborea is named after Sardinia's medieval warrior queen and holds an entertaining array of military and historical mementos. **See p.117**

❷ Bosa The shell of Castello Malaspina crowns this riverside town with 360-degree views. The walls are all that's left of the thirteenth-century construction, within which stands a frescoed medieval church. **See p.190**

❸ Burgos Completed in the fourteenth century, La Reggia dominates the Tirso valley from its high vantage point, and contains an exhibition on Sardinian castle-building. **See p.280**

❹ Castelsardo This Doria stronghold overlooking the sea was at the centre of political and military power struggles for centuries; these days, by contrast, it houses an innocuous museum of basketwork. **See p.217**

❺ Palau There's nothing dainty or self-effacing about the brutally functional fortress overlooking Palau and the Maddalena archipelago, dating from the nineteenth century – but it's still a fabulously panoramic spot. **See p.248**

❻ Posada At the top of this old village, the Castello della Fava stands sentinel over the coast, an atmospheric watchtower with superb views to reward your climb up ladders and through trapdoors to the parapet. **See p.295**

MOUNTAINS AND NATURE

Although most famous for its beaches, Sardinia is essentially a place of mountains and forests, the perfect terrain for cycling, hiking and getting up close to its natural marvels.

❶ Sette Fratelli The "Seven Brothers" are easily accessible from Cágliari, but it's one of the island's least-known ranges, sparsely populated and cut through by splashing streams. **See p.130**

❷ Giara di Gésturi Not exactly a mountain, this high plateau is nonetheless a secluded, uncontaminated area of forest and swampy meadows, where miniature wild horses, boars, migrating birds and goats are among the creatures to look out for. **See p.125**

❸ Gennargentu Sardinia's central Gennargentu mountains hold the island's highest peaks and remotest tracts. Largely covered with chestnut and oak forests, the area is rich with hiking possibilities and peppered with traditional communities – generally regarded as representing the "real Sardinia". **See p.288**

❹ Montes This high tableland south of Nuoro is empty and desolate but has a scenic splendour – ideal for relatively unstrenuous walking, biking and horseriding. **See p.283**

ABOVE THE VIEW FROM CASTELLO MALASPINA, BOSA

⑤ Supramonte Rising dramatically above Sardinia's east coast, this massif includes two of the island's most renowned hiking trails, leading through the Gorroppu gorge and to the nuraghic eyrie of Tíscali, both best explored on organized expeditions. **See p.280**

⑥ Monte Limbara The granite peaks of Gallura are perhaps the most breathtaking of Sardinia's highlands, a landscape of boulder-strewn slopes, tranquil lakes, cork forests and distant views to the sea. See **p.263**

NURAGHIC INVESTIGATIONS

From top to bottom, Sardinia is filled with the enigmatic remains of its nuraghic civilization, flourishing between around 1800 BC and 900 BC. The tapering, broad-stoned towers are in various states of dilapidation, and they're usually well worth checking out, but be careful – *nuraghe*-hunting can become an obsession.

❶ Arzachena Far in spirit from the nearby Costa Smeralda, this inland town has a rich concentration of *nuraghi*, "giants' tombs" (burial sites), shrines and stone circles within easy reach. **See p.244**

❷ Nuraghe Maiore Outside Tempio Pausania in Gallura, this *nuraghe* rises grandly above the cork woods and hosts a breeding colony of Lesser Horseshoe bats. There are wonderful views from the top. See **p.261**

❸ Santu Antine Probably a royal palace at one time, with walls nearly 18m high, this stands in an area dubbed "La Valle dei Nuragi" for its profusion of these monuments. **See p.224**

❹ Losa This mighty example of the nuraghic genre is perhaps the most aesthetically pleasing of all, with clean lines, neat stonework and a vivid growth of orange, yellow and green lichen adorning its sides. **See p.159**

Corsica

TYRRHENIAN SEA

ON THE CASTLE TRAIL
MOUNTAINS AND NATURE
NURAGHIC INVESTIGATIONS

❺ Su Nuraxi The granddaddy of all *nuraghi*, UNESCO-listed and the one that attracts most visitors, this is the biggest and most sophisticated of all the island's nuraghic complexes – an essential stop. **See p.122**

❻ Arrubiu Unique for its five-towered construction, this rust-red complex sits in isolated majesty in a forsaken tract of country. Sign up for one of the atmospheric night tours to experience it in torchlight. **See p.126**

PIZZA

Basics

21 Getting there

26 Getting around

30 Accommodation

32 Food and drink

37 The media

38 Festivals

41 Culture and etiquette

42 Sports and outdoor activities

43 Shopping

44 Travelling with children

44 Travel essentials

Getting there

Of the two ways to reach Sardinia – by air or by sea – flying is obviously the quicker, and prices compare well with the long rail/ferry option. Even so, arriving by sea has much to recommend it, helping to give a sense of Sardinia as an island, as well as being more fuel-efficient. Note, however, that the ferries can get uncomfortably congested in high season.

Most direct **flights** from the UK are seasonal, confined to the May–September period; other services are routed via the Italian mainland. Airfares usually depend on the **season**, with the highest being around July and August; prices drop during the "shoulder" seasons – April to June and September to October – and are cheapest November to March (excluding Christmas and New Year). The price ranges quoted below assume midweek travel during the high (but not peak) season. The main Sardinian **airports** are outside the towns of Cágliari, Olbia and Alghero.

You might also consider a **package deal** from a tour operator (see pp.25–26). Although Sardinia is not a particularly cheap package holiday destination, many operators offer rates as competitively as you could find on your own and also provide specialized tours, such as hiking or archeology.

Flights from the UK and Ireland

Direct flights from the UK take two to three hours. The **budget airlines** Ryanair (London Stansted and London Luton to Alghero), easyJet (London Stansted to Cágliari and London Gatwick to Olbia) and Jet2.com (Edinburgh and Leeds-Bradford to Olbia) usually offer the cheapest fares, with flight-only deals starting at around £40 one-way; some routes are operated between May and September only.

It may also be worth looking at cheap flights to **other Italian destinations** if your preferred dates are unavailable or if you want to combine Sardinia with a visit to somewhere else in Italy, making onward connections by air. We've provided a summary of flights from the Italian mainland (see p.22) and ferries from the Italian mainland and France (see pp.24–25).

Apart from a Ryanair connection between Dublin and Alghero, there are no **direct flights from Ireland** to Sardinia. Aer Lingus and Ryanair fly from Dublin to Rome, Milan and Venice; Ryanair also flies to Pisa and Palermo and Aer Lingus flies to Milan,

Bologna, Naples and Catania. Flights to Rome (around 3hr) and Milan (2hr 30min) are once or twice daily in summer, less frequent in other periods. Prices can be wildly erratic. Return fares from Dublin to Rome or Milan might cost around €200, according to availability.

Price-wise, it sometimes pays to get to London on one of the numerous daily flights and catch a Sardinia-bound plane from there.

Flights from the US and Canada

Although there are no direct flights **from North America** to Sardinia, you can fly to the Italian mainland from a number of cities. The main point of entry is Rome, though Alitalia, Delta and United also fly direct to Milan. There are plenty of connecting flights from both airports to Sardinia. You could also take advantage of well-priced routes available from all over North America to other **European cities** for onward flights to Sardinia.

Alitalia, the Italian national airline, offers the widest choice of routes between the US and Italy, flying direct from New York, Atlanta, Miami and Los Angeles to Rome and Milan. The **US airlines** Delta Airlines, American Airlines and United also fly to Rome and Milan from New York, taking around 8 hours 30 minutes; for the **connection to Sardinia** add another hour or two, depending on the service, plus any time spent waiting for the connection itself.

The basic round-trip **fares to Italy** vary little between airlines, though it's always worth asking about special promotions. Generally, the cheapest round-trip fare travelling from New York midweek in high season starts at around US$1200.

From Canada, Alitalia flies daily from Toronto to Rome, and Air Canada and Air Transat fly to Rome from Toronto and Montréal, all taking 8–9 hours. Air Transat also flies to Venice from the same cities. The return fare costs from Can$1250, to which you should add the fares for the onward flights.

Flights from Australia, New Zealand and South Africa

There are no direct flights **from Australia** and **New Zealand** to Italy or Sardinia, although many airlines fly from Hong Kong, Singapore, Beijing, Shanghai or a Middle Eastern hub to Rome or Milan, from where it's easy to pick up a connecting flight. Reckon on paying Aus$1500–2000 return. The best deals **from New Zealand** work out at around NZ$2500 return, and may involve a change at Los Angeles. With stops, flights to Europe from Australia or New Zealand may take 30–40 hours.

From South Africa, flights from Johannesburg or Cape Town to Rome or Milan usually involve a transfer at a European hub such as Frankfurt, Zürich or Paris, or at Istanbul or Abu Dhabi. Journey time is 12–20 hours including stops, and the high-season price starts at around ZAR7000 return.

Flights from the Italian mainland

There are plentiful flights to Sardinia **from the Italian mainland** connecting all three of Sardinia's airports with major Italian cities. The most frequent flights are between Rome and **Cágliari** (at least 10 daily; 1hr 10min), and Cágliari also has one or two flights daily from Bologna, Florence, Naples, Pisa, Turin, Venice and Verona. There are at least four flights daily from Rome and two from Milan to **Olbia** and 1–2 from Bologna; **Alghero** has at least four from Rome and three from Milan.

The main **carriers** are Air One, Meridiana and Ryanair. Flight time is about an hour from Rome to Cágliari and from Milan to Alghero. Fares vary seasonally and according to how far in advance you book: the cheapest fares are between Rome and Olbia, from €54 one-way.

Overland from the UK and Ireland

The **overland route** to one of the embarkation ports for Sardinia may prove quite an endurance test, whether you do it by coach, train or your own transport. Obviously, you can choose to make the journey at a more leisurely pace, with numerous stops en route, but this will add to the expenses.

By rail from the UK and Ireland

Travelling **by train** to Sardinia isn't usually cheaper than flying, but it is more climate-friendly, and in some ways less stressful. If you timed it well, you could hop onto a ferry within an hour of arriving at your port of embarkation for Sardinia (allow around 30min for a taxi across town).

From London, the fastest journey across the Channel (using Eurostar) and through France to the nearest port of Marseille, including at least one change of trains, will take around seven hours, costing from £190 return, while the journey time to Genoa, the nearest Italian port, is around sixteen hours (with two changes) and costs from £310 return. **Fares** vary according to availability and how far in advance you book (bookings may be made up to three months in advance); discounts apply to under-26s. The total fare sometimes works out cheaper if you buy each leg of the journey separately.

Eurostar trains go from St Pancras in London via the Channel Tunnel to Paris (about 2hr 20min), where passengers must change stations for onward travel, necessitating a Métro journey from the Gare du Nord to the Gare de Lyon; some journeys involve a change at Lille instead. You can get through-ticketing – including the tube journey to St Pancras – from Eurostar (see p.26), from most travel agents or from mainline train stations in Britain.

Rail passes

If you're planning to make Sardinia part of a longer European trip, it might be worth investing in a **rail pass** – InterRail and Eurail passes offer unlimited rail travel in European countries within a given period, and must be bought before leaving home. None of the passes available is likely to pay for itself if you're planning to stick to Sardinia or even just Italy, however. **Rail Europe** is the umbrella company for all national and international rail purchases, and its comprehensive website (see p.26) is the most useful source of information on which passes are available and current prices; tickets can be purchased from here or from one of the other agents listed on p.26.

The **InterRail** pass is only available to European residents, and you'll be asked to provide proof of residency of at least six months in order to buy one. Passes cover thirty European countries (including

---

PACKAGE HOLIDAYS

If you don't want to move around much, it's worth looking at travel-plus-accommodation **package holidays**. The major package destinations are Alghero and Stintino in the northwest, Santa Teresa Gallura and the Costa Smeralda in the northeast, Santa Margherita di Pula in the southwest and the area around Villasimius in the southeast. It's obviously cheapest to go out of season – something to be recommended anyway, as the resorts and sights are much less crowded, and the sea is often warm enough to bathe in as early as Easter and as late as October. Should you want to rent a car, check with the package company before you leave, as some **fly-drive deals** work out very cheaply.

Turkey) and are available as either one-country passes (for example Italy) or global passes, covering all countries. An **Italy pass** in standard class costs from £153 for three days in a month to £262 for eight days in a month. **Global passes** can be for either flexible or continuous periods: for five days in ten the cost in standard class is £225, for ten days in 22 it's £321, for 22 continuous days it's £416, and for one month it's £537. There are significant reductions for travellers aged 12–25. Although InterRail passes do not include travel between Britain and the Continent, pass-holders for zones covering England, Ireland, France or Belgium are eligible for a discount on some ferry services.

A **Eurail** pass, only available to non-European residents, allows unlimited free first-class train travel in Italy and 22 other countries and is available for continuous periods of fifteen days (€549), 21 days (€709), one month (€873), two months (€1231) and three months (€1518), and for flexible periods of any ten or fifteen days within two months (€648 and €850 respectively). Eurail also offers a **Select Pass** allowing travel in three, four or five bordering European countries, a **Regional Pass** covering groups of countries – both available for five–ten days within a two-month period – and a **one-country pass** for three–ten days within two months. There are reductions for under-26s

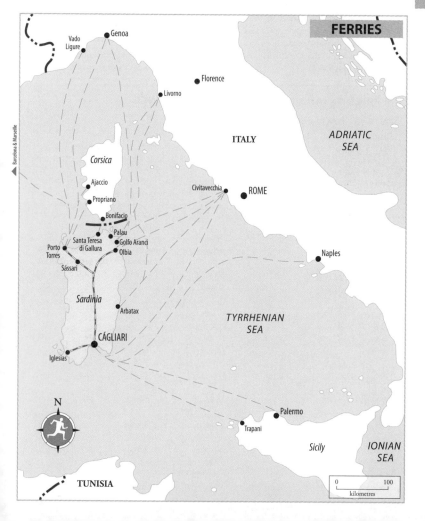

travelling in standard class and for two or more people travelling together.

The national rail companies of many European countries also offer their own passes, most of which can be bought in advance through Rail Europe or direct from the national rail company.

By bus from the UK and Ireland

There are currently no direct **bus services** from the UK or Ireland to the French or Italian ports, though **Eurolines** operates a daily service from London's Victoria Coach Station to Paris, from where, in summer, you can board a bus for Marseille (the nearest ferry port for Sardinia), taking around eighteen hours for the whole journey (May–Sept; return trip from London around £120), and to Milan (£120 return), taking about 24 hours, from where there are frequent connections to Genoa and Livorno. Buses use the Channel ferry crossing, which is included in the price.

By car and ferry from the UK and Ireland

If you're travelling with your **own vehicle**, the best cross-Channel options for most drivers will be the standard ferry/hovercraft links between Dover and Calais/Ostend or Newhaven and Dieppe. Crossing using Eurotunnel (24hr service, departures every 15min at peak periods) will speed up the initial part of the journey. From England's southwest, you can cut driving time by using the more expensive Portsmouth–Caen/Cherbourg routes operated by Brittany Ferries.

Bear in mind when calculating driving costs that **motorway tolls** can add around £65/€80 per car driving through France from Calais to Marseille (tolls are also charged on Italian *autostrade*).

By ferry from the Italian mainland and France

Ferries run year-round from **ports in mainland Italy** and **Sicily**, and there are also direct ferries

---

FERRIES TO SARDINIA FROM ITALY AND FRANCE

FROM THE ITALIAN MAINLAND

Tirrenia run most of the services to Sardinia from the Italian mainland and from Palermo and Trápani in Sicily. Daytime crossings take the shortest time, but may cost more. **Fares** also vary according to season, the day, availability and the speed of the vessel. The most expensive fares are at weekends in August. The prices given below are the cheapest one-way fares for deck class in high season – typically July (fares will be higher in August, cheaper in June or earlier). They're very approximate, as discounts and special deals may be in force. Reclining seats add at least €5 more, berths in shared cabins another €30 or so. The car fares given are for vehicles less than 4m in length; reckon on another €10–20 for cars longer than this.

FERRIES (TRAGHETTI) FROM ITALY

Route	Company	Frequency	Length of crossing	Single passenger	Car fare
Civitavecchia–Arbatax	Tirrenia	2 weekly	10hr 30min	€42	€84
Civitavecchia–Cágliari	Tirrenia	1 daily	15hr –17hr	€50	€96
Civitavecchia–Olbia	Moby	2–9 weekly (June–Sept)	5–8hr	€63	€24
Civitavecchia–Olbia	Saremar	1 daily (April to mid-Sept)	7hr	€40	€55
Civitavecchia–Olbia	Tirrenia	1–3 daily	5hr 30min– 7hr 30min	€44	€63
Civitavecchia–Porto Torres	Grimaldi	2–4 weekly	7hr 15min	€65	€60
Genoa–Arbatax	Tirrenia	2 weekly	16hr 30min– 20hr 30min	€63	€117
Genoa–Olbia	Moby	1–2 daily (late May to mid-Oct)	9hr 30min	€79	€30
Genoa–Olbia	Tirrenia	3–5 weekly	10–12hr	€70	€124

from Marseille and (occasionally) Toulon in France. From the Italian mainland, the shortest ferry **crossing to Sardinia** is from Civitavecchia (near Rome) to Olbia.

There are also numerous connections to Sardinia **from Corsica**. You can reach Bastia, in northern Corsica, from Italy on Corsica Ferries from Savona and Livorno, and on Moby Lines from Genoa and Livorno. Bastia lies 178km from the southern port of Bonifacio, from where it's a short hop to Santa Teresa Gallura in Sardinia. From France, Marseille, Toulon and Nice have regular connections with all the Corsican ports on SNCM and Corsica Ferries.

Any travel agent can provide up-to-date cross-Channel **schedules** and make advance bookings (essential in high season if you're driving). For the Italian crossings, contact the companies or their agents; we've provided a basic summary of all the routes (see box below). For the lowest prices, book ahead and watch out for **special offers** that

apply on certain dates, usually available when you're buying a return ticket on your outward journey and when you're travelling with a car; check with the agent.

AGENTS AND OPERATORS

Citalia UK ☎ 0844 415 1987, ⓦ citalia.com. Package holidays based in some of Sardinia's smartest resorts, including the Costa Smeralda and around Chia. Look for the regular special offers.

CIT World Travel Australia ☎ 1300 380 992, ⓦ cit.com.au. Italy specialists offering packages to hotels in the Villasimius area, plus car rental and rail passes.

Flight Centre UK ☎ 0844 800 8660, ⓦ flightcentre.co.uk; US ☎ 1 877 992 4732, ⓦ flightcentre.us; Canada ☎ 1 877 967 5302, ⓦ flightcentre.ca; Australia ☎ 133 133, ⓦ flightcentre.com.au; New Zealand ☎ 0800 243 544; ⓦ flightcentre.co.nz. Discount international airfares and holiday packages.

Headwater UK ☎ 0845 527 6228, ⓦ headwater.com. Guided walking holidays in the Barbagia region and around Cala Gonone, and cycling on the west coast around Sinis and Bosa.

Route	Company	Frequency	Length of crossing	Single passenger	Car fare
Genoa–Porto Torres	Tirrenia	1–2 daily	9–11hr 30min	€52	€62
Livorno–Golfo Aranci	Sardinia Ferries	4–9 weekly	6hr 30min–10hr 30min	€40	€45
Livorno–Olbia	Moby	1–2 daily	6–8hr 30min	€63	€51
Naples–Cágliari	Tirrenia	2 weekly	16hr 15min	€45	€92
Palermo–Cágliari	Tirrenia	1 weekly	13hr 30min	€48	€98
Trápani–Cágliari	Tirrenia	1 weekly	10hr	€45	€97
Vado Ligure–Porto Torres	Saremar	3 weekly (April to mid-Sept)	11hr 15min	€50	€75

FROM THE FRENCH MAINLAND AND CORSICA

There are numerous connections from mainland France and Corsica to Sardinia. The main departure point on Corsica is Bonifacio, on the island's southern tip, just an hour across the straits from Santa Teresa Gallura. SNCM and La Meridionale also sail from Propriano and Ajaccio to Porto Torres. Note, too, that the year-round ferry from Trápani (Sicily) starts in Tunis.

Route	Company	Frequency	Length of crossing	Single passenger	Car fare
Ajaccio (Corsica)–Porto Torres	SNCM/La Meridionale	0–2 weekly (April–June, Aug & Sept)	4hr	€33	€47
Bonifacio (Corsica)–Santa Teresa Gallura	Moby	4 daily (early April to Sept)	50min	€22	€6–27
Bonifacio (Corsica)–Santa Teresa Gallura	Saremar	2–3 daily	1hr	€18	€35
Marseille–Porto Torres	SNCM/La Meridionale	3–4 weekly	15–18hr	€87	€120
Propriano (Corsica)–Porto Torres	SNCM/La Meridionale	2–4 weekly	3hr 30min	€31	€43

Just Sardinia UK ☎ 01202 484 858, ⓦ justsardinia.co.uk.
Sardinian specialists offering tailor-made holidays and tours throughout
the island, with various accommodation options, flights and car rental.
North South Travel UK ☎ 01245 608 291, ⓦ northsouthtravel
.co.uk. Friendly travel agency offering discounted fares worldwide. Profits
are used to support projects in the developing world, especially the
promotion of sustainable tourism.
Sardatur UK ☎ 020 8940 8399, ⓦ sardinia-holidays.co.uk.
Hotels and self-catering villas and apartments on the southwest coast,
Villasimius, the Costa Smeralda, Santa Teresa Gallura, Oristano and
Cala Gonone.
Simply Travel UK ☎ 0871 231 4050, ⓦ simplytravel.co.uk.
Upmarket packages in Alghero and Ísola Rossa.
STA Travel UK ☎ 0333 321 0099, US ☎ 800 781 4040, Australia
☎ 134 782, New Zealand ☎ 0800 474 400, South Africa ☎ 0861
781 781; ⓦ statravel.com. Worldwide specialists in independent travel;
also student IDs, travel insurance, car rental, rail passes and more. Good
discounts for students and under-26s.
Student Flights US ☎ 1 800 255 8000 or ☎ 480 951 1177,
ⓦ isecard.com. Student/youth fares, student IDs and passes.
Tabona & Walford UK ☎ 020 8767 6789, ⓦ tabonaandwalford
.com. Eight-day coastal and mountain walking trips around Oliena and
Cala Gonone, taking in Cágliari, Nuoro and Su Nuraxi. Also bespoke tours.
Thomson UK ☎ 0871 231 4691, ⓦ thomson.co.uk. Charter flights
and accommodation in large and glitzy hotels, mainly in Alghero and the
northern coast.
Trailfinders UK ☎ 020 7938 3939, Ireland ☎ 01 677 7888;
ⓦ trailfinders.com. One of the best-informed and most efficient agents
for independent travellers, offering flights, hotels, insurance and car rental.
Travel Cuts Canada ☎ 1 800 667 2887, ⓦ travelcuts.com;
US ☎ 1 800 592 2887, ⓦ travelcutsus.com. Canadian and US
student-travel firms for flights, rail travel, tours, accommodation and
student cards.
USIT Ireland ☎ 01 602 1906, ⓦ usit.ie. Ireland's main student and
youth specialists for transport, tours, passes and insurance.

RAIL CONTACTS

CIT World Travel Australia ☎ 1300 380 992, ⓦ cit.com.au.
Eurail ⓦ eurail.com.
European Rail UK ☎ 020 7619 1083, ⓦ europeanrail.com.
Eurostar UK ☎ 0843 218 6186, ⓦ eurostar.com.
The Man in Seat Sixty-One ⓦ seat61.com. Comprehensive
information for rail travel in Europe.
Rail Dude ⓦ raildude.com. International train tickets and passes.
Rail Europe UK ☎ 0844 848 4078, US ☎ 1 800 622 8600, Canada
☎ 1 800 361 7245; ⓦ raileurope.com; ⓦ raileurope.co.uk.
Rail Plus Australia ☎ 03 9642 8644 or ☎ 1300 555 003, New
Zealand ☎ 09 377 5415; ⓦ railplus.com.au; ⓦ railplus.co.nz.
STA Travel UK ☎ 0333 321 0099, US ☎ 800 781 4040, Australia
☎ 134 782, New Zealand ☎ 0800 474 400, South Africa
☎ 0861 781 781; ⓦ statravel.com.
Trenitalia (Italian State Railways or FS) Italy ☎ 892 021,
ⓦ trenitalia.com.

BUS CONTACTS

Eurolines ☎ 0871 781 8178, ⓦ eurolines.co.uk.

FERRY OPERATORS AND UK AGENTS

Corsica Ferries ⓦ corsicaferries.com, in UK c/o Viamare
☎ 020 8206 3420, ⓦ viamare.com.
Enermar ⓦ enermar.it.
Grimaldi ⓦ www.grimaldi-lines.com, in UK c/o Viamare
(see above).
Moby Lines ⓦ moby.it, in UK c/o Viamare (see above).
Sardinia Ferries ⓦ sardiniaferries.com, in UK c/o Viamare
(see above).
SNCM ⓦ sncm.fr, c/o Southern Ferries in UK ☎ 0844 815 7785,
ⓦ southernferries.co.uk.
Tirrenia Line ⓦ www.tirrenia.it.

Getting around

**Touring Sardinia by car is the most
hassle-free option, though also the most
expensive. For shorter journeys on level
terrain, biking is ideal. Getting around
by public transport, while cheap, is not
always easy: the rail system is slow,
few buses run on Sunday, and route
information can be frustratingly difficult
to obtain, even from the bus and train
stations themselves.**

One thing to bear in mind is that travelling **by
train** is not the best way to see the island. Some
stations are miles away from the towns they serve,
while much of the east and centre of Sardinia is
accessible only by bus or car. In the event of strikes
(not that uncommon in Italy), a small number of
essential transport services are guaranteed to run
(though these can get packed).

As for the **roads**, drivers, bikers and pedestrians
alike are advised to keep their wits about them at
all times. Driving in Sardinia is not the competitive
sport that it can be in Rome, Naples or Sicily, but
neither is slow or indecisive behaviour at the
wheel or crossing roads much tolerated. Nonetheless,
anyone used to negotiating mainland Italy's roads
will find Sardinia a doddle, and pedestrians accus-
tomed to being treated as human skittles will be
pleasantly surprised to find that drivers actually
stop at pedestrian crossings and respect red lights.
Local pedestrians also respect signals, and especially
in Cágliari and Sássari, where traffic is heavy and
constant, it is sensible to do likewise.

If you're in a hurry, you can always travel around
Sardinia **by plane**; flights are frequent and it's

DISTANCES IN KILOMETRES

	Cágliari	Oristano	Alghero	Olbia
Cágliari	–	93	227	276
Oristano	93	–	135	184
Alghero	227	135	–	136
Olbia	276	184	136	–

usually possible to purchase your ticket at the airport and jump on the first flight (though prior booking is recommended).

By rail

Sardinia's **train network** connects all the major towns. The main lines are operated by Italian State Railways, **Trenitalia**, also known as Ferrovie dello Stato (**FS**), while a few local routes are run by the independent company, **ARST**, which also runs most of the buses. Trenitalia is responsible for services between Cágliari, Iglésias, Carbónia, Oristano, Sássari, Porto Torres and Olbia, while ARST operates routes between Cágliari and Mandas, Sássari and Alghero, and Nuoro and Macomer. ARST also runs a few very limited internal routes in summer (including the Trenino Verde), between Mandas and Arbatax, Ísili and Sórgono, and Tempio

Pausania and Palau. These can be steam- or diesel-powered, and are often noisy and slow, though they run through some spectacular countryside.

Generally, trains leave punctually and arrive within ten minutes or so of the scheduled time. All trains can get quite full at certain times – for example, the school runs in the morning and at lunchtime – and smoking is not permitted. **Tickets** can be bought from any train station, by telephone or through the Trenitalia website (see opposite), and from some travel agents. Fares are very reasonable, calculated according to the distance travelled; the longest trip you can make on the island, the 300km journey between Olbia and Cágliari costs around €17 for a second-class ticket. Note that all tickets must be validated – punched in machines scattered around the station and platforms – within six hours for distances of less than 200km, or 24 hours for distances over 200km. Failure to do this can land you with an on-the-spot fine. If you don't have time to buy a ticket, you can simply board your train and pay the conductor, though you'll be charged a *supplemento*.

A **rail pass** is worth considering if you plan to travel extensively around Italy or Europe, though it's not actually a lot of help once you've arrived in Sardinia, with its limited rail network. The Europe-wide InterRail and Eurail passes (see pp.22–24) give unlimited travel on the FS network, though you'll be liable for (small) supplements on the faster trains.

Timetables

Train **timetables** can be consulted on boards displayed at train stations, in booklets and CDs available for sale at the ticket desks of most main stations, online at the Trenitalia website (see opposite) and in daily newspapers. "Departures" are *Partenze*, "Arrivals" *Arrivi*, "Delayed" *In Ritardo*, "On time" *In Orario*. Pay close attention to the timetable notes, which may specify the dates between which some services run (*Si effetua dal…al….*), or whether a service is limited or seasonal (*periódico*), denoted by a vertical squiggle; *feriale* is the term for the Monday to Saturday service, symbolized by two crossed hammers, *festivo* means that a train runs only on Sundays and holidays, with a Christian cross as its symbol.

MAIN PUBLIC TRANSPORT OPERATORS IN SARDINIA

ARST ☎ 800 865 042, ⊕ arst.sardegna.it. The main regional bus company, also running a few train routes including the Trenino Verde tourist service.

Deplano ☎ 0784 295 030, ⊕ deplanobus.it. Private bus company operating between Nuoro and Olbia airport.

Digitur ☎ 079 262 039, ⊕ digitur.it. Private bus company operating a year-round service between Porto Torres, Bosa and Cúglieri, and a summer service between Alghero airport and Santa Teresa Gallura via Porto Torres and Castelsardo.

Redentours ☎ 0784 30 325, ⊕ redentours.com. Private bus company operating between Nuoro and Alghero's airport.

Sardabus ⊕ sardabus.it. Private bus company serving Castelsardo, Stintino, Santa Teresa Gallura and Tempio Pausania.

Saremar ☎ 199 118 877, or ☎ 02 3959 5016 from outside Italy, ⊕ saremar.it. Ferry company for crossings to San Pietro and La Maddalena.

Trenitalia (Italian State Railways, or FS) ☎ 892 021, ⊕ trenitalia.it. State railways.

Turmo ☎ 0789 21 487, ⊕ gruppoturmotravel.com. Private bus company operating services linking Olbia with Santa Teresa Gallura, Nuoro, Sássari and Cágliari.

By bus

Sardinia is served by an extensive network of **buses** (*autobus* or *pullman*) covering every town, most villages and a good number of beaches too, though schedules can be sketchy and are much reduced on Sundays. Prices are marginally more expensive than trains, with a Cágliari–Sássari trip, for example, costing around €19 and taking 3hr 40min, as opposed to €16 by train with a journey time of 2hr 50min–4hr.

The main regional bus company, **ARST** (Azienda Regionale Sarda Trasporti), covers local and long-distance routes from the main cities of Cágliari, Oristano, Sássari, Nuoro and Olbia. Smaller companies such as Digitur, Deplano and Turmo run services connecting the island's airports and tourist resorts to various towns and cities, mainly in summer. Note that some ARST services covering beach areas and archeological zones only operate during the summer, while others are linked to school/market requirements – sometimes meaning a frighteningly early start, and last departures as early as 1 or 2pm. Occasionally there are no buses at all during school holidays. **Schedules** are summarized in the Guide, but the companies' websites (see box, p.27) have fuller information. Timetables are rarely available to be given out, but are usually posted up at the bus stops and stations, and local tourist offices can usually help out too.

City **bus terminals** are all very central, and most buses make stops at the local train station – if you want the bus station, ask for the *autostazione*. Wherever possible, you should buy **tickets** before boarding, from ticket offices and local bars and *tabacchi*, though if everywhere is closed you can buy tickets on board (for which a small supplement is usually charged). For longer hauls (and if you want to be sure of a place), it's worth buying them in advance. Bus stops are often quite difficult to track down; if you want directions, ask: *Dov'è la fermata dei pullman?* ("Where's the bus stop?") If you want to get off a bus, ask *posso scéndere?* ("Can I get off?"); "the next stop" is "*la próssima fermata*".

City buses, usually charging a flat fare of €1, are good for quick rides across town. It's best to purchase tickets before boarding from bars and shops that display the bus company sticker, or from the kiosks and vendors at bus terminals and stops, but, again, you can buy them directly from the driver for which you'll generally be charged a 50 percent supplement. Once aboard, you must punch the tickets in the machine or they're invalid; checks are occasionally made by inspectors, who can charge spot fines. Smoking is strictly prohibited.

By car

Car travel across the island can be very quick as long as you follow the main roads. Minor roads can be narrow, very bendy and often confusing, though they can also be the most spectacular routes. The island has no motorways or autostradas, and therefore no tolls; instead, good dual carriageways, or **superstradas**, run for most of the way between Cágliari, Oristano, Olbia, Sássari and Nuoro. The straightest and fastest is the **SS131**, aka the **Carlo Felice highway**, named after the king who commissioned it. Extending the length of the island, from Cágliari via Oristano and Sássari as far as Porto Torres, it is rarely congested, though occasionally poorly lit and surfaced; beware of tricky junctions. Other superstradas branch off east to Nuoro and Olbia, and link Cágliari with Iglésias, Carbónia and Sant'Antíoco.

Sardinia's **secondary roads** are the most rewarding to explore, though these may increase your journey time, and you'll need to exercise maximum caution in negotiating their twists and turns. The going can be especially slow along the coasts in summer.

At all times while driving in **rural areas**, be prepared for the sudden appearance of a flock of sheep, wild pigs or a panniered horse on the road. In remoter parts, there are *strade bianche*, or "white roads" – little more than rough tracks which can continue for hours, seemingly going nowhere; these can become very rocky, and should not be attempted with a low axle. Signposting on these lanes is nonexistent, and it's easy to lose one's direction. Nonetheless, they're perfect for spontaneous detours, and can lead to excellent spots for a walk or picnic, not to mention the splendid beaches often lying at the end of them.

Fuel

Italy is one of the most expensive countries in Europe in which to buy **fuel**: it's around €1.80 per litre for unleaded (*senza piombo*), €1.72 per litre for diesel (*gasolio*), though gas (*PLG*) is more reasonable at .about €0.86 per litre. Fuel stations are spaced at fairly regular intervals along the superstradas, and there are pumps in most towns and villages. Although most are closed 12.30pm to 3.30pm and after 7.30pm, and often on Sunday or one other day of the week, the majority have self-service dispensers which take euro notes and (sometimes) credit cards. Make sure your notes aren't dog-eared, or the machines won't accept them. If your tank is filled before all your prepaid fuel is dispensed, you can punch a button for a receipt and ask for a refund when the station opens. All stations accept major credit cards.

Legal requirements

As for **documentation**, you need a valid driving licence and, if you are a non-EU licence holder, an international driving permit. It's compulsory to carry your car documents and passport while you're driving in Italy, and you'll be required to present them if stopped by the police. You are also required to carry a portable triangular danger sign and a fluorescent jacket in case of an accident or breakdown, supplied in rented vehicles and available in most car accessory shops (for other local regulations, consult Ⓦ theaa.com). If bringing your own car, you should contact your insurance company prior to departure to request cover for outside your home country.

Rules of the road

The **rules of the road** are straightforward: drive on the right; at junctions, where there's any ambiguity, give precedence to vehicles coming from the right; and observe the speed limits (50kph/30mph in built-up areas, 90kph/55mph on country roads or 110kph/70mph on dual carriageways). Note that some road customs are markedly different from what you may be used to: flashing headlights, for example, mean: "Get out of my way!"

Traffic restrictions

In towns, keep your eyes peeled for signs indicating a ZTL (*Zona di Tráffico Limitato*), where restrictions are in force for parking or even passing through. The red-rimmed signs give details of which restrictions are in force and when. Where there are no *vigili* (local policemen) visible, there will usually be a camera recording numberplates, and fines will invariably find their way to you (car rental agencies will take the sum using your credit card details and impose a hefty admin charge on top).

Parking

Parking can be a real headache in Sardinia. The task of finding a space is easier in the early afternoon, when towns are quiet, or at night. At all other times, strictly enforced restrictions operate, allowing you to leave your vehicle only in designated areas – usually between blue lines. Seek out the parking attendant and buy a ticket for as long as you think you'll be parked; it's not expensive, usually around

€0.50–1 for the first hour, €1–2 for every subsequent hour. If you park in a *zona di rimozione*, your car will most likely be towed away; and if you've chosen a street that turns into a market by day, you'll be stuck until it closes down.

Breakdown

If you break down, dial ☎116 and tell the operator where you are, the type of car and your registration number. The nearest office of the **Automobile Club d'Italia** (ACI) will send someone out to fix your car, though it's not a free service, and you'll pay a further hefty bill if you need a tow. Temporary membership of ACI (☎803 116, Ⓦaci.it) gives free or discounted tows and repairs; alternatively, arrange cover with a motoring organization in your country before you leave. Any ACI office in Sardinia can tell you where to get **spare parts** for your particular car.

Security

Although **car crime** is rarer than in most of mainland Italy, it's prudent not to leave anything visible in the car when you park it, including the radio. If you're taking your own vehicle, consider installing a detachable car-radio, and always depress your aerial and tuck in your wing mirrors. The main cities and ports have **garages** where you can leave your car, a safe enough option. The car itself is unlikely to be stolen if it's got a right-hand drive and a foreign number-plate: they're too conspicuous to be of much use to thieves.

Car rental

Car rental (*autonoleggio*) in Sardinia can be expensive, from around £70/€86 to £136/€168 per week for a Fiat 500 or similar plus fuel when booked in advance from one of the major international firms, usually more from local companies (contact details are given in the city listings). In August, many companies charge an extra ten percent. Some rental deals cost less per day, but involve an additional charge for every kilometre driven over, say, 100km. Your best plan, however, is to arrange car hire in conjunction with your flight/holiday – most travel agents or tour operators can provide details. The major **rental companies** have offices at each of the main airports. You can also check local and national companies on the website Ⓦ autonoleggi.sardegna.it. Note that, apart from its fuel efficiency, choosing a smaller car is preferable both for negotiating narrow alleys and for easier parking. Most rental companies offer **GPS** (Sat Nav) equipment for a supplement of €10–15 per day.

CAR RENTAL AGENCIES

Auto Europe ⓦ autoeurope.com.
Avis ⓦ avis.com.
Europcar ⓦ europcar.com.
Hertz ⓦ hertz.com.
Holiday Autos ⓦ holidayautos.co.uk.
Maggiore ⓦ maggiore.it.
Sardinya ⓦ autonoleggiosardinya.it.
Sixt ⓦ sixt.com.
Thrifty ⓦ thrifty.com.

Hitchhiking

Hitchhiking (*autostop*) is not widely practised in Sardinia and is not recommended as a means of getting around. It's definitely not something that women should do alone, particularly in the more out-of-the-way places; also be warned that cars will sometimes stop to offer a lift to a woman standing alone at a bus stop. Women hitching should travel in pairs and always ask where the car is headed before accepting a lift (*"Dov'è diretto?"*). If you want to get out, say: *"Mi fa scéndere?"*

By ferry

You'll use **ferries** to get to the inhabited offshore islands: from Palau for La Maddalena, and Calasetta or Portovesme for San Pietro. The main company is Saremar. Departures are at least hourly, with more in high season, and there's a night-time service every two hours or so. All take vehicles, and if you are transporting yours it makes sense to get to the port early to be sure of a place (things can get quite congested, especially in August); some offices are only open twenty minutes before departure. Frequencies are listed in the Guide. Saremar and Moby Lines also operate daily services between Santa Teresa Gallura and Bonifacio in Corsica, while most seaside holiday centres offer boat tours of the coast and islands.

Accommodation

On the whole, accommodation in Sardinia is cheaper than in the rest of Italy. The main problem is lack of availability, as the various options can be fully booked in summer. Even outside the high season, it's advisable to book as early as you can.

As well as hotels, there are hostels, B&Bs, *agriturismi* (rural accommodation), self-catering units and campsites with bungalows or caravans to rent. Several of the general websites (see pp.25–26)

ACCOMMODATION PRICES

The **prices** of all serviced accommodation should be listed in the local booklets provided by the tourist office, and all the lodgings listed in this guide have been given an approximate rate, representing the **cheapest** available option for two people sharing a room or pitch in high season – typically July, as opposed to peak season (Aug) – or for single dormitory beds in hostels. Outside high season, you'll usually pay much less; in peak season you'll pay the top whack. Be prepared to treat all prices as flexible – even the rates provided by the establishment itself are fluid, varying according to demand. It's always worth trying to negotiate a lower price than the "official" rate, especially in low season, and always if you're staying more than a couple of nights (ask: *c'è uno sconto per tre/quattro/cinque notti?*). Campsite and hostel rates, however, are more rigid.

---

have links to accommodation options with online booking, as have the dedicated accommodation sites (see opposite).

Nearly all hotels and B&Bs include **breakfast** in the price, whether you want it or not. Cheaper places may have shared bathrooms, though many also have a few en-suite rooms. Increasingly, the owners and staff of most establishments have a smattering of English, otherwise the phrases provided in our Language section (see p.325) should help you overcome the linguistic barriers.

Hotels

There's a vast range of **hotel** accommodation in Sardinia, officially graded from one to five stars, and taking in everything from small, family-run places to large, impersonal establishments with sports facilities, private parking and restaurants on the premises.

Prices vary according to grading, location, season and availability. When demand is high, many establishments require that you take **half- or full board**, and there may also be a **minimum stay** of three nights or a week. In practice, if you call on spec, you'll often be given a room for just a night or two if there's availability. In all cases, always ask to see the room before you agree to stay: *posso vedere?* ("May I see?").

There are few **single rooms** available, and these are often occupied during the week by workers and commercial travellers. In high season especially, lone travellers will often pay most (if not all) the price of a double. Three or more people sharing a room should expect to pay around 35 percent on top of the price of a double room.

B&Bs and agriturismi

Recent years have seen a huge growth in **B&Bs** in Sardinia, mostly in towns. These can vary a lot, but are generally clean and comfortable, and set apart from the host family's living quarters. Increasingly, rooms have private **bathrooms**, either en suite or close by. Some places can be fairly luxurious, with all the facilities you might expect in a three-star hotel, but with better breakfasts. The quality of the accommodation isn't always reflected in the price; most charge €30–40 per person per night, depending on the season and location. Ask at the local tourist office for a list of B&Bs; alternatively, consult the websites of B&B associations (see below), and watch for "B&B" or "*cámere*" (rooms) signs. An *affittacámere* (rented room) is simply a bureaucratic name for a B&B with more than three rooms – otherwise there's little difference between the two categories.

Outside towns, you might consider a night or two in an **agriturismo**, a cottage or farmhouse offering informal dinner, bed and breakfast. Many also have various activities available, such as escorted walks and excursions, horseriding, hunting and mountainbiking. Some of these places are relatively remote, but if you want to get close to nature, or to isolated beaches, they're ideal. Although some *agriturismi* have expanded and standardized their facilities, detracting from one of the main reasons to stay in them in the first place, others retain a homely feel, and often offer more authentic country cooking than most restaurants – indeed, some are renowned for their cuisine. They tend to be pricier than B&Bs, charging around €70–100 for a double room, and another €25–30 a head for a three-course dinner. Some *agriturismi* are detailed in the Guide, and local tourist offices can tell you of all the suitable places in the area. *Agriturismo* associations, from which you can get details of properties and book online, are listed below.

B&B ASSOCIATIONS

BB Planet Ⓦ bbplanet.com.
Bed and Breakfast Ⓦ bed-and-breakfast.it.
Domus Amigas Ⓦ domusamigas.it.
In Sardegna Ⓦ insardegnabb.it.
Sardegna B&B Ⓦ sardegnabb.it.

AGRITURISMO ASSOCIATIONS

Agriturismo di Sardegna Ⓦ agriturismodisardegna.it.
Agriturismo Online Ⓦ agriturismo-on-line.com.
Agriturismo.com Ⓦ agriturismo.com.
Agriturismo.it Ⓦ agriturismo.it.
Agriturismo.net Ⓦ agriturismo.net.

Rented apartments and villas

For longer-term stays in resorts, you might consider renting a **villa** or **apartment**. This can be horrendously expensive in high summer – €800–1000 a week for a one-bedroom place in Alghero, for example – but there are real bargains to be had in May, June and September, not to mention the winter months; ask in the local tourist office or estate agency (*agenzia immobiliare*), and keep an eye out for local advertisements.

APARTMENT AND VILLA RENTALS

Affitto.it Ⓦ affitto.it.
casa.it Italy Ⓣ 0422 5944, Ⓦ casa.it.
Interhome UK Ⓣ 020 8877 6370, Ⓦ interhome.co.uk.
Owners Direct Ⓦ ownersdirect.co.uk.
Rent Sardinia Italy Ⓣ 070 684 545, Ⓦ rent-sardinia.com.
Rural Journey Ⓦ ruraljourney.com.
Sardinian Places UK Ⓣ 0845 330 2049, Ⓦ sardinianplaces.co.uk.

Hostels

Sardinia has five official Hostelling International (HI) **youth hostels**: two in the north of the island – in Fertilia (near Alghero) and Lu Bagnu (near Castelsardo) – one at Lanusei (near Arbatax), one in the southeast, at San Priamo (near Muravera) and one in Cágliari. There are also unofficial hostels, for example at Oristano (see p.145) and Bosa (see p.192). For the official ones, you need to have HI membership, and booking in advance is essential, either over the phone or on the websites of AIG (the Italian Youth Hostel Association; Ⓦ aighostels.com), or the Hostelling International (Ⓦ hihostels.com). Availability is limited at all times, and in the summer months hostels are almost permanently full. **Charges** for HI or AIG members are around €20 for a dormitory bed, €10 for an evening meal and €2 for breakfast (if this is not included in the overnight rate). AIG membership costs €5, valid for a year, and comes with a few perks such as discounts on car rental, student cards and travel insurance. For HI membership, contact your home hostelling organization (see p.32).

YOUTH HOSTEL ASSOCIATIONS

US and Canada

Hostelling International USA ☎ 1 301 495 1240,
Ⓦ hiusa.org.
Hostelling International Canada ☎ 1 800 663 5777,
Ⓦ hihostels.ca.

UK and Ireland

Youth Hostel Association (YHA) England and Wales
☎ 0800 019 1700, Ⓦ yha.org.uk.
Hostel Association ☎ 0845 293 7373, Ⓦ syha.org.uk.
An Óige (Irish Youth Hostel Association) ☎ 01 830 4555,
Ⓦ anoige.ie.
Hostelling International Northern Ireland ☎ 028 9032 4733,
Ⓦ hini.org.uk.

Australia and New Zealand

YHA Australia Ⓦ yha.com.au.
YHA New Zealand ☎ 0800 278 299, Ⓦ yha.co.nz.

Camping

Sardinia has about ninety officially graded **campsites** dotted around its coasts and the islands, but there are no official sites in Sardinia's interior apart from the occasional field attached to a hotel or *agriturismo*. Facilities range from very rudimentary to the full gamut of shops, disco, pool and diving tuition. Campers can expect to pay €15–35 per pitch in high season, sometimes with an extra charge per person, and a car may cost an extra €5 per day or so, a campervan €10–15. Many sites also offer **bungalows**, **caravans** or **cabins** with cooking facilities at reasonable rates – €30–80 a night for a bungalow or caravan for two people in high season. Electricity and gas are included in the price; extras may include bed linen (around €10) and final cleaning (€20–30).

Months of opening are detailed in the Guide – though these periods are very flexible, and campsites generally open or close whenever they want, depending on business. Only a handful of campsites stay open between October and April. Don't assume there will always be availability in summer: the better sites fill up quickly (particularly in August), so always phone first. More details of Sardinia's campsites can be found on the websites Ⓦ camping.it and Ⓦ campeggi.com.

By and large, **camping rough** is a non-starter: it's frowned upon in the tourist areas and regarded with outright suspicion in the interior (locals are especially wary of the danger of forest fires).

Food and drink

Eating and drinking are refreshingly good value in Sardinia, and the quality is usually high. Often, even the most out-of-the-way village will boast somewhere you can get a decent lunch, while towns like Cágliari and Alghero can keep foodies happy for days. A full meal with local wine averages at around £25/€30 a head, though there are often much cheaper set-price menus available.

The summary below and the food glossary in the Language section (see pp.326–331) will help you find your way around supermarkets and menus, and point out some of the specialities that are found in nearly every restaurant.

Sardinian cuisine

Historically, the twin pivots of traditional **Sardinian cuisine** have been land- and sea-based local produce, and this continues to be the principal distinction today. Mutton, beef, game, boar, horsemeat and donkeymeat are the staples of the cooking in the interior, while the coasts rely on fish – tuna, sea bass and sardines all figure heavily. Add to these the essential components of Italian gastronomy – pasta, tomato sauce, olives and fresh vegetables – and a choice of seasonal fruit and sheep's cheese. Some of the most famous Italian wines hail from Sardinia – wine was already being made on the island at the time of the Phoenicians – and a meal is often rounded off with traditional biscuits of almonds and honey.

The mild winters and long summers mean that **fruit** and **vegetables** have longer seasons than in northern Europe, and are much bigger and generally tastier: strawberries appear in April, oranges are available right through the year, and even bananas are grown on a small scale. Unusual and unexpected foods are a bonus too, such as prickly pears (introduced from Mexico by the Spanish), wild asparagus and wafer bread (*pane carasau*), while foreign elements have been introduced to specific areas – couscous on the island of San Pietro, and Catalan dishes in Alghero.

> ### NO SMOKING
> Note that, unless you're sitting outside, **smoking** is not permitted in Italian bars or restaurants.

Breakfasts and snacks

Most Sardinians start the day in a bar, their **breakfast** (*prima colazione*) consisting of an espresso and the ubiquitous *cornetto* – a croissant, either plain or filled with jam, custard or chocolate, which you usually help yourself to from the counter; bigger bars and patisseries (*pasticcerie*) will have more choice. Hotel breakfasts may be limp, forgettable affairs, but you'll often find a truly impressive spread at B&Bs and *agriturismi*, including home-made jams, fruit and yoghurt.

At other times of the day, **rolls** (panini) can be pretty substantial, packed with any number of fillings. Numerous bars sell these, though you may find fresher fare by going into an *alimentari* (grocer's shop) or supermarket and asking them to make you one from whatever's on offer, for which you'll pay €2–4, depending on what and how much you choose for the filling. Bars may also offer *tramezzini*, ready-made sliced white bread sandwiches with mixed fillings – lighter and less appetizing than your average *panino*. Toasted sandwiches (*toste*) are common too: in a sandwich bar you can get whatever you like put inside them; in bars which have a sandwich toaster you're more likely to be limited to cheese with ham or tomato.

Apart from sandwiches, other prepared takeaway food is pretty thin on the ground. You'll get small pizzas, portions of prepared pasta, chips, even full hot meals, in a **távola calda**, a snack bar that's at its best in the morning when everything is fresh. The bigger towns have them, often combined with normal bars.

You'll get more adventurous ingredients in **markets** – good bread, fruit, pizza slices and picnic food, such as cheese, salami, olives, tomatoes and salads. Some markets sell traditional takeaway food from stalls, such as boiled artichokes, cooked octopus, sea urchins, mussels, and *focacce* – oven-baked pastry snacks either topped with cheese and tomato, or filled with spinach, fried offal or meat. For picnics, look out for sweet peppers (*peperoni*), baby squid (*calamari*), seafood salad (*insalata di mare*) and dry-roast tomatoes or aubergines in oil, all of which can also be found in the **supermarkets** present in most towns and larger villages.

Pizza

As elsewhere in Italy, **pizza** in Sardinia comes flat and not deep-pan, and the choice of toppings is fairly traditional. It's still common to find pizza cooked in wood-fired ovens (*forno a legna*), rather than squeaky-clean electric ones, so that the pizza arrives blasted and bubbling on the surface, with a distinctive charcoal taste. However, because of the time it takes to set up and light the wood-fired ovens (and the sweltering heat they generate), these pizzas are usually only served at night, except in some resorts in summer.

When served at table, a basic cheese and tomato pizza costs around €6/£5, something a bit fancier between €7 and €10 (£5.70–£8). It's quite acceptable to cut it into segments and eat with your hands, washing it down with a beer or Coke rather than wine. Most sit-down outlets are hybrid pizzeria-*ristoranti*, which serve full meals too, and most places will also sell pizzas to **take away** (*pizza d'asporto*). Check our list of pizzas (see p.327) for what you get on top of your dough.

Full meals: lunch and dinner

Full meals can be elaborate affairs. These are generally served in a trattoria or a ristorante, though these days there's often a fine line between the two: traditionally, a **trattoria** is cheaper and more basic, offering home cooking (*cucina casalinga*), while a **ristorante** is more upmarket (tablecloths and waiters). There may not be a written menu in a trattoria, in which case the waiter will simply reel

---

ICE CREAM

You'll probably end up with an **ice cream** (*gelato*) at some point during your stay: many people eat a dollop of ice cream in a brioche for breakfast, and in summer, a cone (*un cono*) is an indispensable accessory to the evening *passeggiata*. Many bars have a fairly good selection, but for real choice go to a **gelateria** (ice cream parlour) where the range is a tribute to the Italian imagination and flair for display. If they make their own on the premises, there'll be a sign saying *produzione propria*. As for **flavours** (*gusti*), you'll have to go by appearance rather than attempt to decipher their exotic names, many of which don't mean much even to Italians; you'll find it's often the basics – chocolate (*cioccolato*), lemon (*limone*), strawberry (*frágola*) and coffee (*café*) – that are best. There's no trouble in identifying the finest gelateria in town: it's the one that draws the crowds.

off a list of what's on that day. There will almost always be a proper menu in a ristorante, and you'll find more choice. In either, a plate of pasta, a meat or fish course, fruit and a drink should cost €20–40/£16–32 (though seafood usually pushes up the price). Watch out for signs saying *menu turístico*, *pranzo turístico*, *pranzo completo* or *prezzo fisso* – a limited set menu with or without wine, which can cost as little as €15/£12, but is usually more in the region of €20–25/£16–20 (less at lunchtime). Classier *ristoranti* will charge around €40–80/£32–65 per head, including quality wine. Many of these are worth blowing the budget and going out of your way for.

Other eateries usually found in tourist resorts include the hybrid trattoria-ristorante-pizzeria; the *spaghetteria*, which specializes in pasta dishes; and the *birreria* – a pub with snacks and music, often the haunt of the local youth. Lastly, if you ever tire of the Sardinian diet you might try out one of the many **Chinese**, **North African** and **Indian restaurants** that have sprouted in the bigger towns in recent years – they're mostly as good as or better than the ones at home, and significantly cheaper than most Italian restaurants. Many eating places close for three or four weeks in November or February.

Traditionally, a **meal** (lunch is *pranzo*, dinner is *cena*) starts with an **antipasto** (literally "before the meal"), at its best when you circle around a table and pick from a selection of cold dishes, main items including stuffed artichoke hearts, olives, salami, anchovies, seafood salad, aubergine in various guises, sardines and mixed rice. A plateful will cost around €10/£8. If you're moving on to pasta and a main course, however, you'll need to pace yourself.

The main **menu** starts with **primi**: soup, pasta or rice, usually costing €7–12/£5.50–10. **Secondi**, meat or fish dishes costing roughly €12–18/£10–15, are generally served alone except for perhaps a wedge of lemon or a tomato. **Side dishes** (*contorni*) and **salads** (*insalate*) are ordered and served separately, and often there won't be much choice: potatoes will usually come as chips (*patatine fritte*), but you can also find them boiled (*lesse*) or roast (*arroste*), while salads are simply green (*verde*) or mixed (*mista*), usually with tomato. **Bread** (*pane*), which in Sardinia comes in a variety of forms – though rarely brown (*integrale*) – will be served with your meal. Used in ceremonies as well as for everyday needs, Sardinian bread can be thin and crispy or soft, floury and delicately shaped, and differs markedly from place to place.

If there's no menu, the verbal list of what's available can be a bit bewildering, but if you don't hear anything you recognize just ask for what you want: everywhere should have pasta with tomato sauce (*pomodoro*) or meat sauce (*al ragù*). When **ordering fish**, bear in mind that it is usually priced by weight (usually per 100g, *all'etto*) – if you don't want the biggest one they've got, ask to see what you're going to eat and check the price first.

Afterwards, you'll usually get a choice of **fruit** (*frutta*) or other **desserts** (*dolci*). Sardinia is renowned for its almond-based sweets, though they're not always available; most restaurants will only have fresh fruit salad (*macedonia*) and fresh or packaged ice cream and desserts – in common with the rest of Italy, Sardinia has embraced the mass-produced, packaged sweets such as *tiramisù*, *tartufo* and *zuppa inglese*; some of them aren't bad, but they're a poor substitute for local desserts.

It's useful to know that you don't have to order a full meal in trattorias and restaurants. Asking for just pasta and a salad, or the main course on its own, won't outrage the waiter. Equally, asking for a dish listed as a first course as a second course, or having pasta followed by pizza (or vice versa), won't be frowned upon.

Special diets

Vegetarians may find their food principles stretched to the limit in Sardinia. If you're a borderline case, the abundance of excellent fish and shellfish and the knowledge that most meat is free-range might just push you over the edge. On the whole, though, it's not that difficult if you're committed. Most pasta sauces are based on tomatoes or dairy products, and it's easy to pick a pizza that is meat- (and fish-) free. Note, however, that even "vegetarian" minestrone and risotto are cooked with meat or fish stock. To be sure, state clearly your position ("I am vegetarian" = *sono vegetariano/a*) and ask whether the dish has meat in it (*c'è carne dentro?*). The majority of places can be persuaded to cook egg dishes or provide you with a big mixed salad.

If you're a **vegan**, you'll be in for a hard time, though pizza without cheese is a good stand-by, and the fruit is excellent. **Coeliacs** and others on a **gluten-free** diet will find similar difficulties, though the condition is generally more widely understood and catered for than in Britain. The best solution may be to stock up with food items to prepare yourself: many bigger stores and independent shops in the main towns will have vegan-friendly and gluten-free products as well as other foods suitable for special diets.

TOP 5 RESTAURANTS

Throughout the Guide, we've marked restaurants that especially appeal as "Author picks", but these are a few places that deserve special mention, worth going out of your way for.

Il Pórtico Nuoro. Few places combine tasteful decor, friendly service and outstanding, reasonably priced food so convincingly. The cuisine is traditional but inventive, every dish a revelation (see p.277).

Dal Corsaro Cágliari. An oasis of old-fashioned, formal elegance, but offering decidedly fresh, gourmet-quality food, this restaurant upholds its venerable values (see p.74).

Mabrouk Alghero. It's a miracle how this tiny, backstreet place can produce its culinary delights, but it succeeds brilliantly. Don't look for a menu, go with the flow

– and you're guaranteed a feast to remember (see p.178).

Antica Dimora del Gruccione Santu Lussurgiu. Genuine country cooking at its best, tackled with enthusiasm and charm, which you can enjoy in eighteenth-century surroundings, and there's a courtyard garden (see p.161).

Da Lucio Marceddì. The food is marvellous, the service friendly and professional, but what really marks out this seafood restaurant is its remote location steeped in atmosphere (see p.155).

The bill

At the end of the meal, ask for **the bill** (*il conto*). In many trattorias this doesn't amount to much more than an illegible scrap of paper, and if you want to be sure you're not being diddled, ask to have an official receipt (*una ricevuta*), something they're legally obliged to give you anyway. Nearly every-where, you'll pay cover (*pane e coperto*), which amounts to €1–2 per person; **service** (*servizio*) will be added as well in some restaurants, another ten percent – though up to fifteen percent or even twenty percent in some places. If service is included, you won't be expected to **tip**; otherwise leave 10–15 percent, though bear in mind that the smaller places – pizzerias and trattorias – won't expect this.

Drinks

Although Sard children are brought up on wine, there's not the same emphasis on dedicated **drinking** here as there is in some other countries. You'll rarely see drunks in public, young people don't make a night out of getting wasted, and women especially are frowned upon if they're seen to indulge. Nonetheless, there's a wide choice of alcoholic drinks available in Sardinia, at low prices; soft drinks come in multifarious hues, thanks to the abundance of fresh fruit and there's also mineral water and crushed ice drinks.

Coffee, tea and soft drinks

One of the most distinctive smells in a Sardinian street is the aroma of fresh **coffee** wafting out of a bar (many trattorias and pizzerias don't serve hot drinks). It's usually excellent: the basic choice is

either small, black and very strong (espresso, or just caffè), or white and frothy (cappuccino), but there are other varieties, too. A caffelatte is an espresso in a big cup filled up to the top with hot milk. If you want your espresso watered down, ask for a *caffè lungo*; with a shot of alcohol – and you can ask for just about anything in your coffee – is *caffè corretto*; with a drop of milk is *caffè macchiato* ("stained"). If you want to be sure of a coffee without sugar, ask for *caffè senza zúcchero*, though in most bars you serve yourself with sugar. Most places also sell decaffeinated coffee (ask for Hag, even when it isn't). In summer you may prefer your coffee cold (*caffè freddo*). In some holiday centres, you'll find *granita di caffè* in summer – cold coffee with crushed ice and topped with whipped cream (*senza panna* if you prefer it without).

Tea is available in all bars, and is especially popular in summer, when you can drink it iced (*tè freddo*) – usually sweet and mixed with lemon (it's also available in tins with lemon or peach), it's an excellent thirst-quencher. Hot tea (*tè caldo*) comes with lemon (*con limone*) unless you ask for milk (*con latte*). **Milk** itself is drunk hot as often as cold, or you can get it with a dash of coffee (*latte macchiato*), and in a variety of flavoured drinks (*frappé*) too.

Alternatively, there are various **soft drinks** (*analcóliche*) to choose from. A **spremuta** is a fresh fruit juice, squeezed at the bar, usually orange, occasionally also lemon and grapefruit. You might need to add sugar to a lemon juice (*spremuta di limone*), but orange juice (*spremuta di arancia*) is usually sweet enough on its own, especially the crimson-red variety, made from blood oranges. You can also have orange and lemon mixed (*mischiato*).

A **frullato** is a fresh fruit shake, often made with more than one type of fruit. A **granita** (a crushed-ice drink) comes in several flavours including coffee. Otherwise, there's the usual range of fizzy drinks and bottled juices; Coke is prevalent, but the home-grown Italian alternative, Chinotto, is less sweet – good with ice and a slice of lemon. As for **water**, mineral water (*acqua minerale*) is the usual choice in bars and restaurants, either still (*senza gas* or *naturale*) or fizzy (*con gas*, *gassata* or *frizzante*). Tap water (*acqua normale*) is drinkable almost everywhere and you won't pay for it in a bar. Water is especially prized when it comes from mountain springs, of which you'll see a great many as you travel around the island. Avoid water wherever you see a sign saying "*acqua non potabile*" (unsafe for drinking), and always ask a local if you're unsure about the water in a public fountain.

Beer and spirits

Beer (*birra*) is usually a lager-type brew which comes in a third of a litre (*píccola*) or two thirds of a litre (*grande*) bottles: commonest (and cheapest) are the Italian brand, Peroni, and the Sardinian Ichnusa (brewed in Assémini, near Cágliari). A small (33cl) bottle of Ichnusa beer costs about €4 in a bar or restaurant, a larger (66cl) bottle €6; if this is what you want, ask for *birra nazionale*, otherwise you'll be given the more expensive imported beers, like Carlsberg and Becks. In some bars and bigger restaurants and in all *birrerias* (pubs) you also have a choice of draught lager (*birra alla spina*), sold in units of 25cl (*píccola*) and 50cl (*media*), measure for measure more expensive than the bottled variety. In some places you might find so-called "dark beers" (*birra nera*, *birra rossa* or *birra scura*), which have a slightly maltier taste, and in appearance resemble stout or bitter. These are the most expensive of the draught beers, though not necessarily the strongest. As in the rest of Italy, Sardinia is enjoying a revival of interest in quality, locally produced beers (*birra artigianale*, or ("artisan beer") – a couple of places specializing in these are noted in the Guide (see p.76 & p.91).

All the usual **spirits** are on sale and known mostly by their generic names – except **brandy**, which you should call *cognac* or ask for by name. The best Italian brandies are Stock and Vecchia Romagna; for all other spirits, if you want the cheaper Italian stuff, again, ask for *nazionale*. A generous shot costs around €3–5. Among the **liqueurs**, favourite in Sardinia is *mirto*, made from the leaves and berries of wild myrtle, which you should drink chilled; the more common red is rated more highly than the white. There's also the standard selection of **amari** (literally "bitters"), an after-dinner drink served with (or instead of) coffee. It's supposed to aid digestion, and is often not bitter at all, but can taste remarkably medicinal. Favourite brands include Averna and Ramazzotti, but there are dozens of different kinds.

Other **strong drinks** available are *grappa di mirto*, almost pure alcohol, from distilled myrtle husks; *Fil'e Ferru*, a fiery grappa-like concoction brewed in the interior; and, though not especially Sardinian, *sambuca* – a sticky-sweet, aniseed liqueur, traditionally served with one or more coffee beans in it and set on fire (though only tourists are likely to experience this these days).

Wine

With just about every meal you'll be offered **wine** (*vino*), either red (*rosso*) or white (*bianco*), labelled or local. If you want the local stuff, ask for *vino locale* or *sfuso*; on the whole it's fine, often served straight from the barrel in jugs and costing as little as €5 a litre (a *caraffa*, or carafe, is a litre, *mezza caraffa* a half-litre).

Bottled wine is much more expensive, though still good value; expect to pay from around €8 for a mid-quality wine in a restaurant, more like €12–18 in places like Alghero.

Sardinia also produces delicious **dessert wines**, the most famous being **Vernaccia**, sweet or dry, honey-coloured, with a bitter-almond taste, from the Tirso river area around Oristano. If you're heading to Bosa, watch out for mellow **Malvasia**, also served as a table wine, and also produced around Cágliari. Sweet white **Moscato** comes from Cágliari, Sorso-Sénnori and Tempio Pausánia, while the Alghero territory produces **Anghelu Ruju**, one of the strongest and best dessert wines, a sweet red with cherry and cinnamon aromas.

Fortified wines are fairly popular too: Martini (red or white) and Cinzano are nearly always available; Cynar (an artichoke-based sherry) and Punt'e Mes are other common aperitifs. If you ask for a Campari-Soda you'll get a ready-mixed version in a little bottle; if you want the barman to mix you one, ask for a Campari bitter. A slice of lemon is *uno spicchio di limone*; ice is *ghiaccio*.

Where to drink

Bars in Sardinia are either functional refuelling stops – good for a coffee in the morning, a quick beer or cup of tea – or social centres, which have tables and

SOME CLASSIC SARDINIAN WINES

Rich and fruity, cool and refreshing, Sard wines rank among Italy's finest. The following are ones to look out for.

Cannonau Robust, ruby-coloured red, quite dry, and ubiquitous in Sardinia. Nepente di Oliena and Cannonau di Jerzu are two of the best.

Carignano Full-bodied red largely from Sulcis in the southwest, good with starters, meat and cheese.

Malvasia From Bosa or Cágliari, a delicious, golden dessert wine.

Mandrolisai Fruity dry red or rosé, produced around Sórgono.

Monica Light, slightly cherry-ish red, mainly from the southern half of the island.

Moscato Velvety, sweet white, drunk with desserts.

Nasco Fashionable among aficionados, a dry or sweet amber-coloured white from around Cágliari.

Nuragus A light white from the Cágliari area, whose origin dates back to pre-Roman times. Great with seafood.

Torbato Cool and dry white wine from Alghero.

Vermentino A dry, light, white wine from Gallura or Alghero – good with fish or as an aperitif.

Vernaccia From Oristano, a strong, sherry-like dry white, often drunk as an aperitif, and a perfect accompaniment to *dolci*.

a greater range of snacks, and are conducive to whiling away part of a morning or afternoon, reading or people-watching. Many bars don't stay open much after 9pm, though this varies from place to place, and hours are extended in summer, sometimes to midnight or 1am. As in bars throughout the Mediterranean, there are no set licensing hours and children have free access. All have toilets, and most won't object to you using their facilities even if you're not drinking there.

If you're just having a drink at a stand-up bar, pay first at the cash till (*la cassa*), present your receipt (*scontrino*) to the bar person and give your order. If there's no cashier, pay either before or after being served. If you're sitting down, wait for someone to take your order, and there'll usually be a 25–35-percent service charge (shown on the price list as *távola*); you're often expected to pay the bill on being served. If you don't know how much a drink will cost, there should be a list of prices (*listino prezzi*) behind the bar or *cassa*. When you present your receipt, it's customary to leave an extra €0.50 or so on the counter – though no one will object if you don't.

For more serious drinking, you can repair to a pub or **birreria**, where people go just to drink and socialize, though often these places sell snack food too. You'll usually find a younger crowd here, and there's often a music soundtrack. Other places to get a drink are an **enoteca**, a rudimentary wine bar selling cheap local wine by the glass; a **bar-pasticceria**, which sells wonderful cakes and pastries too; and a **távola calda**, which, in a train station, always has a bar.

Note that, as with restaurants, bars are **non-smoking** (in rare cases there is a separate smoking room), but you can still smoke at tables outside.

The media

Sards are among Italy's most avid readers of newspapers and magazines, which are readily available on every shopping street and in train stations. Foreign-language publications are sold in the same outlets in all the main centres, though at a considerable mark-up (so it is cheaper to read them online).

Television and **radio** are provided in most hotel and some B&B rooms. You'll need your own short-wave receiver to pick up non-Italian radio stations. To keep in touch with Italian news in English go to Ⓦlifeinitaly.com.

Newspapers and magazines

You'll find the main **national newspapers** on any newsstand: *La Repubblica* (Ⓦrepubblica.it), centre-left, with a lot of cultural coverage; *Il Corriere della Sera* (Ⓦcorriere.it), authoritative and rather conservative; *L'Unità* (Ⓦunita.it), the former Communist Party organ, also strong on culture; *Il Manifesto* (Ⓦilmanifesto.it), a more radical and readable left-wing daily; and the pink *Gazzetta dello Sport* (Ⓦgazzetta.it), essential reading for the serious sports fan.

Most people, however, prefer Sardinian **local papers**, which offer non-Sards good insights into local concerns as well as being useful for transport timetables, entertainment listings, festival announcements and local chemists, hospitals, internet cafés, etc. There are two main ones: *L'Unione Sarda* (Ⓦ unionesarda.it), most read in Cágliari and the south of the island, and *La Nuova Sardegna* (Ⓦ lanuova sardegna.it), also called "La Nuova", favoured in Sássari and the north. There's little to tell between them in terms of content, and each has local editions for the island's main towns. Note that Monday editions of all national and regional newspapers are almost exclusively devoted to sport, with very slim coverage of any other news.

English-language and other **foreign-language newspapers** can be found at kiosks and newsagents in Cágliari, Sássari, Oristano, Nuoro, Olbia, Porto Cervo and Alghero, usually available the same day in thinned-down editions, though costing more than at home.

Television

Surprisingly, for such an outdoor society, Italians are among the most dedicated **TV**-watchers in the world. The three state-run channels, RAI 1, 2 and 3, have got their backs against the wall in the face of the domination of the numerous private channels by Silvio Berlusconi's Mediaset corporation, which includes Rete 4, Canale 5 and Italia 1 – three of the biggest in the **independent sector**. On the whole, the output is fairly bland, with a heavy helping of soaps, sitcoms, cabaret shows and films, though the **RAI channels** have less advertising and mix some good reporting in among the dross. RAI 3 has the most intelligent coverage, and broadcasts Sardinian news programmes. Of the **local channels**, *Videolina* is most popular in Cágliari, *Sardegna Uno* in the north, *TeleSardegna* around Nuoro and *Tele Regione* transmits everywhere; advertising is constant on all of these. **Satellite TV** is increasingly available in hotels.

Radio

The situation in **radio** is even more anarchic than the TV scene, with the FM waves crowded to the extent that you can pick up a new station just by walking down the corridor. The myriad of **commercial stations** broadcast virtually undiluted chart music. Again, the RAI stations are generally more sober, with far less advertising: **RAI 1** and **RAI 2** include serious news programmes among the phone-ins and pop, while for higher-brow culture, including literature and classical and jazz music, tune into **RAI 3**, which devotes afternoons and late evenings to themes such as Brazilian or Celtic music. Frequencies vary according to where you are, so be prepared for regular retuning.

With a short-wave radio, you can also pick up programmes of the **BBC World Service** and **Voice of America**: check the websites Ⓦ bbc.co.uk/world serviceradio and Ⓦ voanews.com for schedules and frequencies.

Festivals

Sardinia's festivals – *feste* and *sagre* – are high points of the island's cultural life, and excellent opportunities to view traditional costumes and dancing and to hear local music. While many are religious in origin – mostly feast days for saints having a special role for a particular locality – others are purely secular, celebrating harvest or some other event, or simply perpetuating ancient games and competitions. These are still basically unchanged in the smaller towns and villages, though some have evolved into much larger affairs spread over three or four days, while others have been developed with an eye to tourism.

In all, **masks** and **costumes** play a prominent role, emblems of local identity representing a variety of functions and traditions, and injecting an eerie theatricality into the proceedings. **Horses**, too, are often present, and may be the main protagonists. Many *feste* attract groups of singers and dancers from surrounding villages, and special food and sweets are available from stalls. Local people spend months preparing for the occasion, and they're well worth scheduling into your visit.

Carnival

Traditionally, the **Carnival** season starts with Sant'Antonio's day on January 17, but in practice most of the action takes place over three days climaxing on Shrove Tuesday, usually in February. Although the occasion is intended as a prelude to the abstinence of Lent, most Carnival celebrations smack of paganism. Children wear fancy dress, and impressive masks are commonly worn, producing a somewhat sinister effect.

In Mamoiada, south of Nuoro, the three-day festival features music, dancing and the distribution of wine and sweets, climaxing in the ritual procession of the *issohadores* and *mamuthones* representing respectively hunters and hunted. The latter are clad in shaggy sheepskin jerkins, their faces covered in chilling black wooden masks, their backs hidden beneath dozens of sheep-bells with which they create a jangling, discordant clamour. Meanwhile the "hunters" lasso bystanders who are supposed to appease them with gifts of wine (but rarely do).

Oristano's **Sa Sartiglia** is wildly different, a medieval pageant involving much horseback racing and a jousting competition in which masked and mounted "knights" attempt to ram their swords through a hanging ring, called *sartija* – a Spanish word which gives its name to the festival.

Various other strange goings-on take place during this period: a six-day festival at Bonorva, between Oristano and Sássari, includes masked processions, dances and ritual burnings of puppets; Bosa, south of Alghero, holds another six-day event, with theatrical funeral processions and costumed searches for the *Giolzi*, spirit of Carnival and sexuality; the normally taciturn mountain town of Tempio Pausania, in Gallura, bursts into life with masks and floats as another symbolic puppet is incinerated; while frenetic horse races are held at Santu Lussurgiu, in the mountains north of Oristano.

Ferragosto

August is the month when tourists flood into the island, emigrés return for the summer and all the resorts devote every last euro to entertainment. The high point comes in the middle of the month with **Ferragosto**, officially the Feast of the Assumption, or *Assunta*, though in practice stripped of its religious aspects by most people. The national holiday is celebrated all over Italy more exuberantly than Christmas, with towns and villages erupting with dazzling fireworks displays. Some of Sardinia's Ferragosto celebrations are coupled with another festival, as in Sássari's spectacular **I Candelieri**. This event – which had its origin in the fifteenth century when plague was apparently averted by divine intervention – starts on August 14, and takes its name from the huge candles carried through thronged streets amid delirious dancing.

A similar festa is held in the nearby village of Nulvi, also starting on August 14, but with just three candles (here representing shepherds, farmers and craftsmen), which are preceded by twelve monks – representing the apostles – singing medieval hymns. The Madonna herself is wheeled around town on August 15, and there follows some sort of religious ceremony every day until August 22.

Religious festivals

The vast majority of Sardinia's festivals are related to religion, though sometimes in the loosest possible way. The saints' days, of course, always have a religious element, but the most dramatic scenes are usually to be seen at Easter. Most towns and villages feature events on **Good Friday**, when silent processions carrying a statue of Jesus on the cross file through the streets and into the main church, where the image may be ritually taken down from the cross before being laid in a coffin. On **Easter Sunday**, the image is again paraded through the streets, to meet a statue of the Madonna in a symbolic encounter known as *Su Incontru*, amid much celebration and gunfire. One of the most dramatic Easter celebrations takes place in Iglésias, where there are almost daily processions for a week, beginning on the Tuesday of Easter week and culminating in a re-enactment of the Passion, with all the local guilds represented.

On the first Sunday after Easter, more religious processions and musical events take place in Alghero and Valledoria (near Castelsardo).

Fifty days after Easter, **Pentecost** sees a prolonged series of events at Suelli, north of Cágliari. In fact, the festival kicks off the Friday before, when the entire population exits from the village and spends the night in the fields gathering wood, singing songs and dancing. The wood collected is brought into the town, and a bonfire is lit on Pentecost Sunday, amid costumed processions and games. In Porto Torres, statues of the local martyrs are borne ceremonially to the basilica of San Gavino, and on the following day transported to the sea. There's a boat race, a costumed parade and a huge fish fry-up.

Sardinia has a number of *chiese novene*, remote churches open only for nine days a year when **pilgrimages** take place. The best-known of these are Sant'Antine, outside Sédilo, and San Salvatore, on the Sinis peninsula, where pilgrims gather at the beginning of July and the beginning of September respectively – both places are in Oristano province.

Cultural events

Aside from the festivals, there's a range of **cultural events** throughout the year. Concerts and dramatic performances are sometimes held at outdoor venues in summer, and films, too, can be enjoyed under the stars. Any of the provincial tourist offices can tell you about forthcoming events, and see also Ⓦ sardegnacultura.it and Ⓦ sardegnaturismo.it.

A festival calendar

Festivals marked ★ are especially worth checking out.

JANUARY

Festa di Sant'Efisio Jan 14–15. The martyrdom of Sant'Efisio is remembered in Pula and Nora by costumed processions of marching bands, praying women and traditional musicians, followed by fireworks.

Festa di Sant'Antonio Jan 16–17. St Anthony's day is celebrated in dozens of Sardinian villages, usually with bonfires, since the saint is supposed, Prometheus-like, to have given the gift of fire to men after he stole it from hell. The liveliest celebrations are at the villages of Abbasanta, near Oristano, and Mamoiada, Bitti, Lodè, Orosei and Lula, all located around Nuoro.

Festa di San Sebastiano Jan 19–20. Among the villages commemorating this day are Turri and Ussana, both in Cágliari province, and Bulzi, inland from Castelsardo. Again, bonfires, processions and hymns are the order of the day, usually ending up with wine and food all round.

FEBRUARY

Su Sessineddu Feb 3. San Biagio's day in Gergei (north of Cágliari) is the occasion of this bucolic event, which is named after the reed frames that are hung with sweets, fruits and flowers and attached to the horns of oxen. This is primarily a children's festival, which involves seeing who can scoff the most goodies before staggering home.

★ **Carnival** Weekend preceding Shrove Tues. Processions, fancy dress and festivities just about everywhere, with especially theatrical events in Bonorva, Bosa, Mamoiada (see p.284), Oristano, where Sa Sartiglia is the big draw (see p.146), Santu Lussurgiu (see p.161) and Tempio Pausania (see p.262).

MARCH

★ **Sagra degli Agrumi** March is traditionally bereft of merry-making on account of Lent, though Muravera (on the coast east of Cágliari) enthusiastically marks the citrus fruit (*agrumi*) harvest. Traditional Sardinian dances are performed as peasant carts trundle through town (see p.132). It's always held on a Sunday, though the date varies, and may occur in April.

APRIL

Festa di San Giorgio April 23. Several villages on the island celebrate St George's day: Bonnanaro, southeast of Sássari, is the scene of religious processions and prayers conducted entirely in Sard; Bitti, a mountain village north of Nuoro, has a horseback procession in traditional costume and renditions of mournful shepherds' songs; and Onifai, near Orosei, holds horseback processions, dances and poetry competitions.

★ **Easter** The most significant religious festival of the year sees holy processions and events throughout the island. Some of the most distinctive rites can be seen at Alghero, Castelsardo, Iglésias (see p.105), Sássari, Oliena (near Nuoro), Santu Lussurgiu (north of Oristano) and Valledoria (near Castelsardo).

Festa di Sant'Antíoco Second Sun after Easter. Three days of events commemorate the feast day of this North African-born saint – most exuberantly in the town named after him (see p.95), but also impressive in Dolianova (outside Cágliari), Gavoi, in the Barbagia region southwest of Nuoro Mogoro (south of Oristano), Ulassai, south of Lanusei on the east coast, and Villasor (northwest of Cágliari).

MAY

★ **Festa di Sant'Efisio** May 1–4. Cágliari's feast day in honour of its Roman martyr is the city's biggest event (see p.67), commemorating the saint's delivery of the city from plague in 1656. Costumed delegations from dozens of the island's towns and villages participate, making the opening and closing ceremonies excellent opportunities to view Sardinia's diverse costumes.

Festa dei Mártiri Turritani May 3. The first part of Porto Torres' major festival sees an impressive procession accompanying plaster images of the town's martyred saints from the Pisan basilica of San Gavino to the clifftop church of Balai, where they remain until Pentecost.

Festa di San Simplicio May 15. Olbia's yearly extravaganza commemorates its patron saint, and consists of fireworks, the distribution of sweets and wine, and various games and water competitions.

La Cavalcata Penultimate Sun. Costumed revelry takes over Sássari for this pageant (see p.207), which, as its name suggests, has a distinctly horsey flavour to it, culminating in grand equestrian stunts in the afternoon.

Festa di San Bachisio May 29. In the countryside outside Onanì, northeast of Nuoro, traditional Sardinian dances take place for three consecutive days and nights.

Pentecost Fifty days after Easter. Celebrations at Suelli, north of Cágliari, and Porto Torres, with costumed processions and games.

JUNE

Girotonno Ⓦ girotonno.org; first week. Carloforte, on the isle of San Pietro, celebrates the annual tuna catch with four days of eating, drinking, concerts and dance performances.

Fiera di San Leonardo Ⓦ cavallinfiera.it; June 2–3. The island's most important horse fair takes place around the Romanesque church of San Leonardo de Siete Fuentes, near Santu Lussurgiu, north of Oristano.

Festa della Beata Vérgine dei Mártiri Second Sun. Fonni, south of Nuoro, hosts a festival devoted to the "Blessed Virgin of the Martyrs", featuring costumes and processions on horseback.

Festa di San Vito June 15. The village of San Vito, outside Muravera (on the coast east of Cágliari), honours its saint with three days of spirited feasting.

Festa di San Giovanni Battista June 24. A pre-Christian feast day marking the summer solstice coincides with St John the Baptist's day, is celebrated in more than fifty villages all over Sardinia, with processions, dances, songs and poetry competitions. Among the villages are Bonorva (between Oristano and Sássari), Buddusò (in the Galluran mountains between Olbia and Nuoro), Escalaplano (a mountain village between Cágliari and Lanusei), Fonni and Gavoi (both near Nuoro).

Festa di San Pietro e San Paolo June 29. Saints Peter and Paul are commemorated in a score of Sardinian villages, notably Ollolai and Orgósolo (both south of Nuoro), Terralba (south of Oristano) and Villa San Pietro (on the coast south of Cágliari). On the island of San Pietro, there's music, dancing, a procession of boats and spectacular fireworks.

JULY

⭐ **S'Ardia di Costantino** July 6–8. Locals at Sédilo, between Oristano and Nuoro, indulge their passion for horses with characteristic gusto in this three-day event (see p.159), in honour of the Roman emperor (and saint) Constantine. The reckless horse-racing guarantees plenty of thrills and spills and attracts thousands of fans.

Gara di Poesia July 25. Orosei, on the coast east of Nuoro, stages one of the most important of the island's many poetry competitions, in which contestants recite or sing verses in *sardo*.

Festa di Sant'Ignazio Nearest Sun to July 31. Three days of merriment – with all the usual festival paraphernalia – take place at Musei, just off the Iglésias–Cágliari road, in honour of the founder of the Jesuit order, St Ignatius of Loyola.

AUGUST

Festa di Santa Maria del Mare First Sun. Bosa hosts various events in honour of its patron saint, with an emphasis on water, including a river procession and various watersports.

Ferragosto Aug 15. This mid-summer jamboree to mark the festival of the Madonna is celebrated with displays of dazzling fireworks. In Sássari, the event is combined with the rough and tumble of I Candelieri (see p.207). Other places worth mentioning are Dorgali, near Nuoro, Golfo Aranci, north of Olbia, Guasila, north of Cágliari, Nulvi, near Sássari, and Orgósolo, also in the Nuoro region.

Sagra del Redentore Last ten days. The most colourful event in Sardinia's mountainous Barbagia region, Nuoro's famous festival (see p.278) includes traditional music and the most important of the island's costume competitions. The second, religious part features a procession up to the statue of Christ the Redeemer on top of nearby Monte Ortobene.

Festa di San Giovanni Battista Aug 29. St John the Baptist has a second holy day, celebrated in several villages, notably Orotelli, west of Nuoro, and San Giovanni di Sinis, west of Oristano.

SEPTEMBER

⭐ **La Corsa degli Scalzi** First Sun. The lagoon town of Cabras, near Oristano, re-enacts the rescue of its statue of San Salvatore from raiders in the sixteenth century: an army of barefoot young men dressed in white sprint the 8km from the saint's sanctuary into town with the saint borne aloft (see p.149).

Sagra Campestre di Santa Maria de Sauccu Sept 7–17. Two separate processions take off from Bortigali, near Macomer, to Santa Maria de Sauccu, a sanctuary 10km away in the mountains, the venue for dances, picnics and poetic competitions over the next nine days.

Festa di Santa Maria Sept 8. The Madonna is venerated in Ales, a village southeast of Oristano, when her statue is brought out amid much fanfare no fewer than six times in three days.

Festa di Nostra Signora di Regnos Altos Second Sun. Not for the first time in the year, banners and bunting are strung across the narrow lanes of Bosa's old centre. Once the religious formalities are out of the way, tables are laid, food is guzzled and drink quaffed.

Festa di Santa Greca Last Sun. More than a hundred thousand devotees every year come to pay their tributes to Santa Greca, in five days of festivities at Decimomannu, outside Cágliari.

OCTOBER

Festa di San Francesco Oct 4. Nestled in the mountains between Nuoro and Olbia, the village of Alà dei Sardi takes to the fields and spends two days attending open-air Masses, eating and feasting in honour of St Francis.

Sagra delle Castagne Last Sun. This chestnut fair is held at Aritzo in the heart of the Barbagia mountains (see p.290). The smell of the cooking nuts permeates the air for days.

NOVEMBER–DECEMBER

Tuttisanti (or Ognissanti) Nov 1–2. All Saints' Day is a public holiday and is followed by I Morti, the Day of the Dead, a time of mourning observed all over the Catholic world. Families troop en masse to the local cemetery where loved ones are buried; in parts of Sardinia, the table is laid and the favourite dishes of the deceased are served up and left overnight – apparently, just the odours are enough to satisfy them.

Christmas Dec 24–25. Not the big commercial hoo-ha it is in some countries, Christmas is primarily a family event. Fish is normally eaten on Christmas Eve, and lamb is the traditional fare on Christmas Day, followed by *panettone*, a dry, sweet cake.

Culture and etiquette

Broadly speaking, Sardinia shares many of the cultural characteristics you'll be familiar with if you've travelled elsewhere in Italy. Sards are a mainly Catholic, family-centred, food-loving people who largely share the Italian devotion to sun, style and good living. There are also, however, differences, that become apparent to anyone who has spent time both here and on the Italian mainland.

As an island with its own separate language, Sardinia has a slightly less accessible feel, the people are marginally more standoffish, their traditions more esoteric. Perhaps because of the island's comparatively low density of population, personal space is more valued here – Sards have a subtle sense of dignity in themselves and their relations with others. As a result the island can sometimes have a distinctly muted feel in comparison with some of Italy's more buzzing hotspots – less extrovert and less showy.

Most Sards are polite and approachable. Even in obscure rural spots, where suspicion of outsiders is ingrained, basic decorum is always observed. The **Church** may not wield as much influence as in former times, but the institution remains at the centre of community life and commands respect locally. The rules for **visiting churches** are much as they are all over the Mediterranean: dress modestly (which usually means no vests, shorts or short skirts, and covered shoulders), and avoid wandering around during a service.

Sardinia's attitudes on **gender issues** show few traces of the prejudices prevailing in much of the Italian south, perhaps due to the greater tolerance required to deal with the regular flow of tourists. The importance placed on good manners alone will mean that abuse and discrimination are rarely encountered. The sexual harassment of **women** for which Italy was once well known is a rare event nowadays, and while women can expect to attract occasional unwelcome attention in bars, restaurants and on the beach, such intrusion is increasingly frowned upon. If you are pestered, however, it can usually be stopped with a loud *Lasciátemi in pace!* ("Leave me alone!"), though stronger language is not advised. And in a place where the sanctity of the family is still paramount, the best protection of all is to flaunt a wedding ring.

Sports and outdoor activities

In spite of the traditional stereotype of a holiday in Sardinia as a passive, beach-lounging affair, the island is becoming increasingly popular for hiking, biking, riding and watersports. There is also growing interest in such pursuits as free climbing, caving and kayaking. The island has one ski run, in the Gennargentu mountains near Fonni (see p.287), with a season extending from December to March. There are public tennis courts in most towns and attached to hotels, with racquets sometimes available for rent.

Biking

Increasing numbers of people in Sardinia are using **bicycles**, either for long-distance pedalling or for getting around locally. Most big towns have rental facilities, as do seaside resorts like Alghero and Santa Teresa Gallura and some of the offshore islands, and bikes are also available at some hotels. Outlets are given in the Guide; the charge is usually €12–15 per day, less in low season. If you use a bike, take care to make yourself conspicuous, especially outside towns, where the relative rarity of cyclists means people won't be expecting you. Prepare too for some arduous uphill pedalling.

The roads are perfect for petrol-assisted cruising, however, and have become a favourite touring ground for squads of bikers from Germany and Switzerland. **Motorbike** rental is rare, though most places that rent out bicycles also rent out scooters. If you opt for one of these, remember that the smaller models are not suitable for any kind of long-distance travel, though they're ideal for buzzing around towns and beaches; expect to pay from €40 a day in high season. Crash helmets are compulsory.

BIKE INFORMATION, TOURS AND ITINERARIES

Dolce Vita Bike Tours ☏ 070 920 9885, ⓦ dolcevitabiketours.com. Group and self-guided biking tours all over the island, including an eight-day trip from Olbia in the north to Pula in the south. Accommodation, food and luggage transport arranged.

Federazione Ciclistica Italiana ☏ 06 3685 7813, ⓦ www.federciclismo.it. Italy's main cycling organization.

IchnusaBike ☏ 070 857 0370 or ☏ 329 448 2419, ⓦ ichnusabike .it. Various organized tours, including week-long trips on the Transardinia route between Cágliari and Olbia, with accommodation, food and luggage transport arranged. Bike rental too, with delivery and collection anywhere on the island.

Sardinia Mountain Bike ⓦ sardiniamountainbike.com. Events, itineraries and excursions, mainly in central and southern Sardinia.

Climbing

Sardinia offers some of the best year-round **climbing** terrain in Europe. With its inland peaks and sea-cliffs on every coast, it is becoming increasingly known, attracting enthusiasts to the areas around Ísili and Domusnovas in the south, and Dorgali, Baunei, Jerzu and Cala Gonone on the eastern coast. See ⓦ climb-europe.com/sardinia .htm for areas, routes and local accommodation, and ⓦ sardiniaclimb.com for popular climbs and climbing news. Local tourist offices can put you in touch with climbing clubs, some offering courses, while *The Lemon House* guesthouse (**W**peteranne.it) is a well-known reference point for climbers – as well as bikers, walkers and kayakers – in the Ogliastra region. See also Books (p.320).

Hiking

Hiking was until recently a fairly rare phenomenon in Sardinia, and there are no long-distance paths and few marked and maintained routes (though the situation is improving). Nonetheless, the island can boast some of the most magnificent walking country in Europe, including the Gorroppu canyon (see p.298); Supramonte, south of Nuoro (pp.280–282); and the Gennargentu mountains of the interior (see pp.287–291). In fact almost every part of Sardinia offers scope for serious or casual hikes, and there are scores of hiking cooperatives that will supply **guides** for walks of all levels of difficulty. Phone numbers for some of these are given in the Guide; others may be contacted through local tourist offices, such as that at Oliena (see p.281), which can also supply itineraries and rough maps, or else through the Sardinian branch of the Associazione Italiana Guide Ambientali Escursionistiche (AIGE **T**340 676 8153 or **T**0426 200 700, **W**aigae.org), which has a database listing nearly sixty guides on the island.

We've outlined in the Guide some of the island's most memorable hikes (see p.131, p.281 & p.299). Remember to bring suitable footwear, a sun hat (for some stretches, a helmet is advised) and a good supply of water. Always inform somebody (for example, the hotel or local tourist office) where you're heading. Longer hikes are inadvisable without an experienced guide. We've recommended a few maps for general use (see p.48), though large-scale hiking maps are thin on the ground.

Riding

Horses and Sardinia have been an item for centuries, and Sards have long been acknowledged as among Italy's finest riders. There's ample evidence of this on display in the festivals featuring equestrian skills, notably in Oristano province, and in the **riding courses** and **excursions** available throughout the island. The largest of the riding operations is outside Arborea, south of Oristano (see p.155); it organizes courses and a range of treks through pinewoods and on the nearby beaches, and can provide information on riding activities over the whole island. The Barbágia, too, provides myriad possibilities for riding

in the hills, for example from Su Gologone, near Oliena and Nuoro (see p.280). Rates depend on the length of the excursion and whether or not you're part of a group.

Watersports

You'll find a full range of **watersports** available on most coasts from Easter on. Apart from the dedicated operators, facilities are often offered at the bigger hotels, even for non-residents, and from some campsites. **Waterskiing** has largely been supplanted by **windsurfing**, of which the favourite spot is Porto Pollo, near Palau (see p.250) – the place for **kite-surfing**, too. **Surfers** tend to congregate on and around the Sinis peninsula, near Oristano, especially at Capo Mannu (see p.153).

Sailing is another favourite summer pastime, particularly around Alghero, the Costa del Sud, the Costa Smeralda and the Maddalena archipelago. This is a high-spending pursuit in Sardinia, however, and most enthusiasts will have to make do with joining a group with a full crew to do the actual sailing. Ask at tourist offices in Alghero, Olbia, Palau and La Maddalena about companies offering these expeditions. Alternatively, individual outfits, such as Amfibie Treks (**T**020 3514 1037, **W**amfibietreks .co.uk), based on the east coast south of Olbia, offer sailing and windsurfing courses with accommodation in campsites.

Sardinia is one of the Mediterranean's best locations for **diving**. The best sites are around Alghero, Stintino, Santa Teresa Gallura, the Maddalena archipelago, Cala Gonone and Muravera; local outfits operate in all of these places, offering tuition and excursions with full equipment provided. Contact details are given in the Guide.

Shopping

Sardinia has no shortage of temptations for shoppers and souvenir-hunters. The island is renowned for its local craftwork, which includes basketware and ceramics in Castelsardo, cork objects in Gallura, carpets in the Barbágia and masks and shepherd's knives just about everywhere, though most famously in the mountains around Nuoro.

Every large village and town has at least one weekly **market**, and though these are usually geared towards household goods, they can be useful for picking up cheap clothing and items for the beach. These are the places where you can exercise your **haggling** skills – indeed, it's virtually *de rigueur* to negotiate when dealing with craft items and the like – ask for *uno sconto* ("a discount"). Bargaining is not practised for food, however, or in most shops, unless for quite costly items.(a rug or antique, for example).

Supermarkets are ubiquitous and good for food and day-to-day merchandise, including basic clothing. Sardinia's larger towns have branches of many of the well-known Italian **chains** for shoes, handbags and other fashion items, while smart **boutiques** proliferate in Cágliari, Sássari, Alghero, Olbia and Porto Cervo.

Tabacchi, or tobacco shops – recognizable by a sign displaying a white "T" on a black or blue background – also sell sweets, postcards, stationery, stamps and sometimes bus tickets and toiletries.

Note that shops, bars and restaurants are all legally obliged to provide you with a **receipt** (*una ricevuta* or *uno scontrino*). Don't be surprised when it's thrust upon you, as they – and indeed you – can be fined if you don't take it.

Travelling with children

Children are adored in Sardinia, and will be welcomed and catered for in bars and restaurants (all now smoke-free). Hotels normally charge around thirty percent extra to put a bed or cot in your room, though kids pay less on trains and enter museums and other tourist sites for free. Many coastal hotels and most campsites are well equipped for family holidays, and lay on a range of entertainments and activities for kids and parents.

Parents of **babies** and **toddlers** will find everything they need for their day-to-day requirements in pharmacies and supermarkets – nappies, baby food, medication, milk, etc. However, it's rare to find highchairs in cafés or restaurants, or changing facilities in public places, and breast-feeding in public is unusual.

Although there are few **attractions** designed specifically for kids, the island's beaches provide all the entertainment most kids would want, while the prehistoric *nuraghi*, the numerous castles and some archeological sites provide plenty of outdoor fun inland. Some attractions, such as the aquarium and "tourist train" in Alghero and Sardegna in Miniatura near Barúmini, have a universal appeal.

The main **hazards** when travelling with children in Sardinia are the heat and sun in summer. Sunblock can be bought at any pharmacy, and bonnets or straw hats in most markets. Other risks include the possibility of stepping on sea urchins or brushing against jellyfish (see p.47).

Take advantage of the less intense periods – mornings and evenings – for travelling, and use the quiet time of siesta time to recover flagging energy. The rhythms of the southern climate soon modify established patterns, and you'll find it more natural carrying on later into the night, past normal bedtimes. In summer, it's not unusual to see Sardinian children out at midnight, and not looking much the worse for it.

CONTACTS FOR TRAVELLERS WITH CHILDREN

Mark Warner Holidays UK ☏ 0844 273 1520, Ⓦ markwarner .co.uk. Holiday villages with children's entertainment, sports tuition and childcare available.

Rascals in Paradise US ☏ 415 273 2224, Ⓦ rascalsinparadise .com. Can arrange scheduled and customized itineraries built around activities for kids.

Thomson UK ☏ 0871 231 4691, Ⓦ thomson.co.uk. Family-friendly holidays with baby equipment, creches and activities for kids of all ages available.

Travel essentials

Costs

While Sardinia isn't particularly cheap compared with some other Mediterranean holiday spots, it's still noticeably less expensive than mainland Italy. You'll find that transport, food and accommodation are good value, but items such as fuel and car rental are quite pricey by southern European standards. Prices rise considerably July to September.

With a tight rein on your budget – camping or hostelling, buying some of your own food in the shops and markets – you could get by on £30–50/€37–62 per day; a more realistic **average daily budget** is around £50–90/€62–110 a day, including meals in restaurants, hotel accommodation and some travel costs; while on £90–150/€110–185 a day you could be living pretty comfortably. Most basic things are fairly inexpensive: a pizza and a beer cost around £8/€10 just about everywhere, a full meal with wine around €20–40/£16–33, less at lunchtime; buses and trains are relatively cheap, and distances between towns small; and hotel rooms in the cities start at around

£40/€50 a double. It's the snacks and drinks that add up: ice creams, soft drinks and coffee all cost around the same price as at home (if not more). And if you sit down for any of these, it'll usually cost around thirty percent more.

Of course, these prices are subject to where and when you go. Accommodation and food in the Costa Smeralda are downright expensive, and you might eat much better at a fraction of the price in an unpretentious trattoria in a small village. On the whole, the coastal resorts are more costly, while places in the interior are relatively cheap (though don't expect much choice of places to stay and eat). In holiday areas, you'll pay more in summer for accommodation, but you can find some fantastic bargains out of season, when nearly all establishments drop their prices. You'll often get a "special price" for rooms if you're staying a few days, but note that for single accommodation, which can be hard to come by, you may find yourself paying most of the price of a double room.

There are few benefits for **students** in Sardinia, though the various official and quasi-official youth/student ID cards may be useful for discounts for some performances and other entry tickets. Under-18s and over-65s, on the other hand, get into museums and archeological sites free. All full-time students are eligible for the **International Student ID Card** (ISIC, ⓦ isic.org), which costs £9.

You only have to be under 26 or younger to qualify for the **International Youth Travel Card**, while **teachers** qualify for the **International Teacher Card**, both carrying the same benefits, and costing the same as the ISIC card. All these cards are available in the Republic of Ireland from USIT, in the US and the UK from STA, and in North America from Travel Cuts (see p.26).

Several other travel organizations and accommodation groups also sell their own cards, good for various discounts. A university photo ID might open some doors, but is not as easily recognizable as ISIC cards.

Crime and personal safety

Mention **crime** in Sardinia to most people and they think of bandits in the hills. The abduction of rich industrialists or members of their families has been the most high-profile felony practised on the island since it was found to be more lucrative than sheep-rustling, though kidnapping is now a comparatively rare event, and should not affect tourists at all. In the interior, road signs peppered with gunshot are more an indication of bored youth than anything

---

EMERGENCIES

❶ **112** for the police (Polizia or Carabinieri)
❶ **113** for any emergency (emergenza) service
❶ **115** for the fire brigade (Vígili del Fuoco)
❶ **116** for road assistance (Soccorso Stradale)
❶ **118** for ambulance (Pronto Soccorso)

---

more menacing, and the feuds which occasionally erupt between families are always "domestic" affairs, and now rarely violent.

In fact, Sardinia is one of Italy's safest regions, with a remarkably low level of violence, drunkenness and delinquency. Most **petty juvenile crime** is connected with drug addiction in the cities of Cágliari and Sássari. You can minimize the risk of falling victim to muggings or pickpockets by being discreet: don't flash anything of value, keep a firm hand on your camera and carry shoulder-bags, as you'll see many Sardinian women do, slung across your body. You might consider entrusting money, credit cards and valuables to hotel managers, rather than leave them in your room, and it's wise to avoid badly lit or deserted areas at night. Confronted with a robber, your best bet is to submit meekly – panic can lead to violence, though very few tourists see anything of this.

If the worst happens, you'll be forced to have some dealings with the **police**. In Sardinia, as in the rest of Italy, they come in many forms. The most innocuous are the **Polizia Urbana** or **Polizia Municipale** (town police), mainly concerned with directing the traffic and punishing parking offences. The **Guardia di Finanza**, often heavily armed and racing ostentatiously through the cities in their cars, are responsible for investigating smuggling, tax evasion and other similar crimes. Most conspicuous are the **Carabinieri** and **Polizia Statale**; no one knows what distinguishes their roles, apart from the fact that the Carabinieri – usually in black uniforms – are organized along military lines and are a branch of the armed forces.

Hopefully, you won't need to get entangled with either, but in the event of theft you'll need to report it at the headquarters of the Polizia Statale, the **Questura**; you'll find their address in the local telephone directory. If you're staying for any length of time, the Questura is also where you obtain a *permesso di soggiorno* (residence permit) or visa extension.

In any brush with the authorities, your experience will depend on the individuals you're dealing with, though most Sard police officers – male and female – are unfailingly polite. Apart from **topless bathing** (tolerated in appropriate surroundings, but don't try anything more daring) and **camping rough**, don't expect a soft touch if you've been picked up for any offence, especially if it's drug-related. **Drugs** are generally frowned upon, and universal hysteria about *la droga* means that any distinction between the "hard" and "soft" variety has become blurred. The judicial process is notoriously slow and labyrinthine in Italy, and any possibility of getting caught up in it should be avoided. **Foreign consulates** (see below) are unlikely to be very sympathetic or do anything more than put you in touch with a lawyer.

EMBASSIES AND CONSULATES IN ITALY

There's a UK Honorary Consul in Cágliari, otherwise all the following consular agencies are located in Rome:

Australia ☎ 06 852 721, ⓦ italy.embassy.gov.au.
Canada ☎ 06 854 443 937, ⓦ international.gc.ca.
Ireland ☎ 06 585 2381, ⓦ ambasciata-irlanda.it.
New Zealand ☎ 06 853 7501, ⓦ nzembassy.com.
South Africa ☎ 06 852 541, ⓦ sudafrica.it.
UK consular agency in Cágliari: Viale Colombo 160, Quartu Sant'Elena ☎ 070 828 628; embassy in Rome: ☎ 06 4220 0001, ⓦ ukinitaly.fco.gov.uk.
USA ☎ 06 46 741, ⓦ italy.usembassy.gov.

Electricity

The supply is 220V, though anything requiring 240V will work. Most plugs have two round pins, but some have three: a travel plug is useful.

Entry requirements

British, Irish and other EU citizens can enter Sardinia and stay as long as they like on production of a valid **passport**. Citizens of the United States, Canada, Australia, New Zealand and South Africa also need only a valid **passport**, but are limited to stays of three months. All other nationals should consult the relevant embassies about **visa** requirements.

Legally, you're required to **register** with the police within three days of entering Italy, though if you're staying at a hotel this will be done for you. Although the police in some towns have become more punctilious about this, most would still be amazed at any attempts to register yourself down at the local police station while on holiday. If you're going to be living here for a while, you'd be advised

to obtain the necessary *permesso di soggiorno* (permit), usually available from the local Questura.

ITALIAN EMBASSIES AND CONSULATES ABROAD

Australia ☎ 02 6273 3333, ⓦ ambcanberra.esteri.it. Consulates in Melbourne (☎ 03 9867 5744), Sydney (☎ 02 9392 7900) and Perth (☎ 08 9322 4500).
Canada ☎ 613 232 2401, ⓦ ambottawa.esteri.it. Consulates in Montréal (☎ 514 849 8351) and Toronto (☎ 416 977 1566).
Ireland ☎ 01 660 1744, ⓦ ambdublino.esteri.it.
New Zealand ☎ 04 473 5339, ⓦ ambwellington.esteri.it.
South Africa ☎ 012 423 0000, ⓦ ambpretoria.esteri.it.
UK ☎ 020 7312 2200, ⓦ amblondra.esteri.it. Consulates in Edinburgh (☎ 0131 220 3695) and Manchester (☎ 0161 236 9024).
US ☎ 202 612 4400, ⓦ ambwashingtondc.esteri.it. Consulates in Chicago (☎ 312 467 1550), New York (☎ 212 737 9100) and Los Angeles (☎ 310 820 0622).

Gay and lesbian travellers

Sardinia has no open **gay** and **lesbian** scene outside a few scattered clubs, bars and beaches. While physical contact is fairly common – on the level of linking arms and kissing cheeks at greetings and farewells – any overt display of strong affection between members of the same sex may meet with disapproval. Gays and lesbians will find a more sympathetic atmosphere in the cities of Cágliari and Sássari, and in the clubs and beaches of the cosmopolitan Costa Smeralda. For general information on the gay and lesbian scene, contact Arcigay (☎ 051 095 7241, ⓦ arcigay.it) or Arcilesbica (☎ 051 649 2684, ⓦ arcilesbica.it). The website ⓦ gay.it also has a wealth of information for gays and lesbians in Italy.

Health

Citizens of all European Economic Area countries (EU plus Switzerland, Norway, Iceland and Lichtenstein) are entitled to **emergency medical care** under the same terms as the residents of the country, as well as reduced-cost or free medical treatment. For British citizens, this means presenting a **European Health Insurance Card** (EHIC), valid for up to five years. This can be applied for, free of charge, by calling ☎ 0845 606 2030 or online at ⓦ nhs.uk.

The Australian Medicare system also has a reciprocal healthcare arrangement with Italy. However, it's advisable for any non-EU citizen to take out ordinary travel insurance (see opposite).

On the whole, Sardinia doesn't present any more health worries than anywhere else in southern Europe – the worst that's likely to happen is suffering from the extreme heat in summer or from an upset stomach – shellfish or sunstroke are the usual culprits. Mosquitoes can also be a problem, especially wherever there is vegetation near the coast or a river. In the water, beware of sea urchins (*ricci*), black or brown spiky balls that lurk on rocks and can be extremely painful when stepped on – if this happens, ask advice on how to remove the spines. Jellyfish (*meduse*) are an occasional hazard at sea, according to the current. If stung, you should brush an ammonia stick (available from pharmacies) or your own pee on the affected area, and, if necessary, scrape off the sting (a credit card would do), being careful not to take off the skin.

Staff at an Italian **pharmacy** (*farmacia*) are well qualified to give you advice on minor ailments, and to dispense prescriptions. There's generally one open all night in the bigger towns; they work on a rota system, and you should find the address of the one currently open on any *farmacia* door or listed in the local paper. Condoms (*profilático*) are available over the counter from all pharmacists and some supermarkets; the contraceptive pill (*la pílola*) is available on prescription only.

If you need further treatment, your first port of call should be the local **doctor** (*médico*): ask at a pharmacy, or consult the local *Págine Gialle* (*Yellow Pages*) under *Azienda Unità Sanitaria Locale* or *Unità Sanitaria Locale*, or *Pronto Soccorso*. The *Págine Gialle* also list some specialist practitioners in fields such as acupuncture and homeopathy, the latter quite common in Italy. If you're eligible, take your EHIC with you to the doctor's: this should enable you to get free treatment and prescriptions for medicines at the local rate – about ten percent of the price of the medicine. For repeat medication, take any empty bottles or capsules with you to the doctor's – the brand names often differ.

The **Guardia Médica**, available in most towns, operates a service when doctors are not available (weekends, holidays and night-time). The local clinic is usually signposted and, though sometimes minimally equipped, is generally a useful first point of call. There may be a charge per visit of around €15 for anyone who is not a local resident.

If you get taken seriously ill, or are involved in an accident, head for the nearest **hospital** and go to the *Pronto Soccorso* (casualty) section, or phone ☎118 and ask for "*ospedale*" or "*ambulanza*". Small places without a fulll-blown hospital may still have a 118 emergency service with an ambulance and small drop-in clinic. Hospital standards don't differ significantly from other clinics in Western Europe. Don't expect medical and other hospital staff to speak fluent English, however. Throughout the Guide, you'll find listings for pharmacists, hospitals and emergency services in all the major cities.

Incidentally, try to avoid going to the **dentist** (*dentista*) while you're in Sardinia. These aren't covered by the health service, and for the smallest problem they'll make you pay through the teeth. Take local advice, or consult the local *Yellow Pages*.

If you don't have a spare pair of **glasses** or **contact lenses**, take a copy of your prescription with you; an optician (*óttico*) will be able to make you up a new pair should you lose or damage them.

Insurance

Even though EU healthcare privileges apply in Italy, you'd do well to take out an **insurance** policy before travelling to cover against theft, loss and illness or injury. Before paying for a new policy, however, it's worth checking whether you're already covered: some all-risks home insurance policies may cover your possessions when overseas, and many private medical schemes include cover when abroad. In Canada, provincial health plans usually provide partial cover for medical mishaps overseas,

---

ROUGH GUIDES TRAVEL INSURANCE

Rough Guides has teamed up with WorldNomads.com to offer great **travel insurance** deals. Policies are available to residents of over 150 countries, with cover for a wide range of **adventure sports**, 24hr emergency assistance, high levels of medical and evacuation cover and a stream of **travel safety information**. Roughguides.com users can take advantage of their policies online 24/7, from anywhere in the world – even if you're already travelling. And since plans often change when you're on the road, you can extend your policy and even claim online. Roughguides.com users who buy travel insurance with WorldNomads.com can also leave a positive footprint and donate to a community development project. For more information go to ⓦ**roughguides.com/shop**.

while holders of official student/teacher/youth cards in Canada and the US are entitled to meagre accident coverage and hospital in-patient benefits. Students will often find that their student health coverage extends during the vacations and for one term beyond the date of last enrolment.

If not already covered, you might want to contact a specialist travel insurance company, or consider the travel insurance deal we offer (see box, p.47). A typical travel insurance policy usually provides cover for the loss of baggage, tickets and – up to a certain limit – cash or cheques, as well as cancellation or curtailment of your journey. Most of them exclude so-called **dangerous sports** unless an extra premium is paid: in Sardinia this can mean scuba diving, windsurfing and trekking, though probably not kayaking or jeep safaris. Many policies can be chopped and changed to exclude coverage you don't need – for example, sickness and accident benefits can often be excluded or included at will. If you do take medical coverage, ascertain whether benefits will be paid as treatment proceeds or only after you return home, and whether there is a 24-hour **medical emergency number**. When securing baggage cover, make sure that the per-article limit – typically under £500 – will cover your most valuable possession. If you need to make a claim, you should keep receipts for medicines and medical treatment, and in the event you have anything stolen, you must obtain an official statement from the police (*polizia* or *carabinieri*).

Internet

Most towns in Sardinia have some kind of **internet point** (which we list in the Guide), and in smaller places someone can usually point out a bar or office that provides this service. The usual cost is around €1 for 20–30 minutes. Note that the law requires that personal ID – a passport or driving licence – must be presented when logging on at any public internet point.

Laundry

Coin-operated laundrettes are listed in the Guide for Oristano, Sássari, Alghero and Cala Gonone; the alternative is a **service wash** in a *lavanderia*, where items are individually charged – say €4 for a shirt, €5 for a skirt or trousers – to be collected a day or two later, immaculately ironed. Although you can usually get away with it, washing clothes in your hotel room is disapproved of, and the water supply itself may be limited in summer.

Mail

Post office opening hours are usually Monday-Friday 8.25am–7.10pm, Saturday 8.25am–12.35pm (smaller towns and villages won't have a service on weekday afternoons and/or on Sat morning). If you want stamps (*francobolli*), you can buy them in *tabacchi* too, as well as in some gift shops in the tourist resorts. The Italian postal service is one of the slowest in Europe – if your letter is urgent, consider spending extra for the express service.

Letters can be sent **poste restante** to any main post office in Sardinia, by addressing them "Fermo Posta", followed by the name of the town. When collecting something, take your passport, and if your name doesn't turn up make sure they check under middle names and initials.

Maps

The best large-scale **road maps** of Sardinia are published by the Touring Club Italiano, Marco Polo (both 1:200,000), Automobile Club d'Italia (1:275,000) and Michelin (1:350,000), all sold from bookshops and tourist outlets. Otherwise, State Tourist offices and local tourist offices in Sardinia may have maps of varying quality to give away.

For **hiking**, you'll need at least a scale 1:100,000 map (better 1:50,000), though there's not much around; those that are available can be from online specialists, or check with the Club Alpino Italiano ☎02 205 7231, ⓦcai.it. For specific towns, the maps in the Guide should be fine for most purposes, though local tourist offices also often hand out reasonable town plans.

Online, look up ⓦsardegnamappe.it, ⓦmappe .virgilio.it or ⓦviamichelin.com.

Money

In common with most other European Union countries, Italy's currency is the **euro** (€), which is split into 100 cents. **Notes** come in denominations of 500, 200, 100, 50, 20, 10, and 5 euros, and eight different **coin** denominations, including 2 and 1 euros, then 50, 20, 10, 5, 2, and 1 cents (*centésimi*). It's a good idea to have some cash in euros with you when you arrive in Sardinia, if only for the bus or taxi fare into town, though airports and ports will usually have banks with ATMs. In any case it's worth bringing enough euros with you to tide you over should your other financial arrangements for some reason fail to work immediately. The **exchange rate** at the time of writing is €1 = £0.81 or US$1.30; £1 = €1.23 and US$1 = €0.77.

Most small towns in Sardinia are supplied with at least one **bank**, usually with an ATM. Banking **hours** vary slightly from town to town, but generally banks are open Monday to Friday, 8.30am to 1.15pm and 3pm to 4.15pm. Outside these times you can change cash at most post offices and some large hotels, and at exchange shops in the resorts.

Credit cards are widely accepted everywhere, including most petrol stations, stores and supermarkets, but excluding the majority of B&Bs. MasterCard and Visa are most common, American Express less so. Cash withdrawals can be made from ATMs, though remember that these are treated as loans, with interest accruing daily from the date of withdrawal, and there's usually a transaction fee on top of this. Make sure you have a personal identification number (PIN) that's designed to work overseas, and always inform your bank or credit card supplier that you will be using your card abroad, to avoid it being blocked. You might also consider pre-paid debit cards, which work with a PIN for all transactions in places that take Visa cards, and in most ATMs.

Opening hours and public holidays

Basic **opening hours** for most shops and businesses in Sardinia are Monday to Saturday from 8 or 9am to around 1pm, and from around 4pm to 7 or 8pm, though some offices work to a more standard European 9am to 5pm day. Everything, except museums, bars and restaurants, closes on Sunday, though you might find *pasticcerie*, and fish shops in some coastal towns, open until Sunday lunchtime.

Occasionally you'll come across museums, churches and other monuments **closed for restoration** (*chiuso per restauro*). Some of these are long-term closures, though you might be able to persuade a workman or curator/priest to give you a peek, even if there's scaffolding everywhere.

Other disrupting factors are national holidays (see box above) – when you can expect shops and offices to be closed and a Sunday transport service – and strikes. Local religious holidays don't generally close down shops and businesses, but accommodation space may be tight.

Most **churches** open around 7 or 8am for Mass and close around 11am or noon, opening up again at 4 to 5pm, and closing at 7 or 8pm; smaller ones will only open for early morning and evening services; some only open on Sunday and on religious holidays.

PUBLIC HOLIDAYS

January 1 New Year's Day
January 6 Epiphany
Good Friday
Easter Monday
April 25 Liberation Day
May 1 Labour Day
August 15 Ferragosto; Assumption of the Blessed Virgin Mary
November 1 Ognissanti, or Tutti i Santi (All Saints)
December 8 Immaculate Conception of the Blessed Virgin Mary
December 25 Christmas Day
December 26 St Stephen's Day

Museums are generally open either all day or 9am to 1pm and 4pm to 8pm, 3pm to 7pm in winter. Those that aren't open daily are most likely to be closed on Monday. **Archeological sites** are usually open daily from 9am until an hour before sunset, in practice until around 5pm in winter, 8pm in summer. The most important *nuraghi* (Sardinia's famous prehistoric towers) share these hours, though most of the smaller ones are either open to anyone at all hours, or open only on request, or closed permanently. If you need to cross private land to reach them, it's best to ask first. In summer, some attractions stay open until midnight, though such decisions are usually made at the last minute, and late closing times have not been detailed in the Guide.

Phones

Public **telephones** come in various forms, usually with clear instructions in English. For the most common type, you'll need a **phone card** (*scheda telefónica*), available for €2.50, €5 or €10 from *tabacchi* or newsstands; the perforated corner must be torn off before the card can be used. Some kiosks still accept coins, though these are being phased out, and some take credit cards. Note that you need to insert your card or a coin (which will be refunded) even when dialling toll-free numbers. Alternatively you could find a call centre (see p.50) or phone from a hotel, where you'll normally be charged 25 percent more.

Mobile phones work on the GSM European standard. You'll hardly see an Italian without one; if you plan to join them, make sure you make the necessary arrangements with your mobile phone company before you leave. After arrival, your phone

---

INTERNATIONAL TELEPHONE CODES

Note that the initial zero is omitted from the area code when dialling the UK, Ireland, Australia, New Zealand and South Africa from abroad.

UK international access code + 44 + city code.
Republic of Ireland international access code + 353 + city code.
USA and Canada international access code + 1 + area code.
Australia international access code + 61 + city code.
New Zealand international access code + 64 + city code.
South Africa international access code + 27 + city code.

---

should lock onto one of the Italian frequencies – Vodafone, Wind or Tim, and you'll be texted the **tariffs** applicable; they're usually quite expensive, and you're also charged for part of the cost of incoming calls. Accessing your message centre can also be pricey, and you'll need to check with your company that this service will be available to you, and the relevant access number.

When **making calls** to Italian land lines, you must always dial the local area code with the number wherever you are (in Italy or abroad). All telephone numbers listed in the Guide include the entire number, including the relevant area code. Numbers beginning ☎800 are free, while those beginning ☎199 and ☎848 are charged at the national rate. ☎170 will get you through to an English-speaking operator. Dial ☎1254 for **directory enquiries** in Italy, or ☎176 for international directory enquiries.

For **calling Sardinia** from your home country, dial the international access code; then 39 (for Italy); then the area code including the first zero (mobile numbers do not start with zero); and then the subscriber number.

The cheapest way of **phoning home** from Sardinia (see box above for international codes) is to have a **Skype** account, enabling you to call for free from a laptop or an internet café. Alternatively, you might consider an **international phone card** (*carta telefónica internazionale*) available in various denominations from post offices, tobacconists and some other shops. All phones accept them, but before each call you need to dial the special access number and PIN number printed on the back of the card. The most reliable are those issued by Telecom Italia and **Edicard**, available from bars and tobacconists with a Sisal (lottery) terminal, in denominations of €5, €10 or €20.

A third option for making international calls is to seek out a **cheap-call centre,** an increasing number of which can be found in the island's main towns, often doubling as internet/fax points; you make your call in a sound-proof cabin and pay at the end.

To make a **collect/reversed charge** call (*cárico al destinatario*), dial ☎170 and follow the instructions.

Time

Sardinia (along with the rest of Italy) is one hour ahead of Britain. Italy is seven hours ahead of Eastern Standard Time and ten hours ahead of Pacific time.

Toilets

Public **toilets** are a rare thing in Sardinia. However, every bar has a toilet (*gabinetto, toeletta* or *bagno*) which you'll generally be allowed to use whether you're drinking or not – but ask first. Most places are fairly clean, though it's advisable to carry some toilet paper in your bag.

Tourist information

Outside Italy, the **Italian State Tourist Office** (Ⓦenit.it; see opposite for contact details) can usually provide maps, brochures, accommodation booklets and a list of pending cultural events – though much of this information can easily be picked up later in Sardinia.

Most Sardinian towns and the three principal airports have a **tourist office**: either one covering the province or one for the town, or both. Some places have a **Pro Loco** office, run by the town hall or by volunteers, which may have much the same kind of information, though these generally keep much shorter hours. All offices vary in usefulness, but you should at least be able to pick up a free town plan, accommodation list and information on local events. In the larger places, most of the staff will speak English, and some offices will reserve you a room and sell tickets for performances and seats at *feste*. You will also see unofficial **independent tourist offices** in some places, offering a host of other services such as car rental, apartment rental, excursions etc, as well as dispensing free information.

Summer **opening hours** are usually Monday to Friday 9am to 1pm and 4pm to 7pm, Saturday 9am to 1pm, but check the Guide for individual variations.

ITALIAN STATE TOURIST OFFICES

The website Ⓦ enit.it has information for all the following offices.
Australia Level 4, 46 Market St, Sydney NSW 2000,
Ⓣ 02 9262 1666.
Canada 110 Yonge St, Suite 503, Toronto ON M5C 1T4
Ⓣ 416 925 4882.
UK 1 Princes St, London W1B 2AY Ⓣ 020 7408 1254.
US 630 Fifth Ave, Suite 1965, New York NY 10111 Ⓣ 212 245 5618;
500 North Michigan Ave, Suite 506, Chicago, IL 60611 Ⓣ 312 644
0996; 10850 Wilshire Blvd, Suite 725, Los Angeles, CA 90024
Ⓣ 310 820 1898.

SARDINIAN WEBSITES

Ⓦ **marenostrum.it** Good general site with plenty of information, articles and links, plus lists of specialized operators for climbing, riding, diving and other watersports.

Ⓦ **paginegialle.it** Italian *Yellow Pages* online.

Ⓦ **paradisola.it** All-purpose Sardinian site, with articles on local dialects, fauna and flora, as well as recipes, festivals, activities, beaches and info on accommodation, museums and archeological sites. There are also discussion forums.

Ⓦ **sardegnacultura.it** Reams of infomration on Sardinian art, cinema, festivals, language and literature, all in Italian.

Ⓦ **sardegnaturismo.it** Official regional site, giving copious and wide-ranging background and specific information on the whole island, including what's on and examples of Sard music, with links to websites for all Sardinia's provinces.

Ⓦ **sardinia.net** Accommodation booking site, with information on hotels and campsites, plus itineraries and articles on culture, cuisine and history.

Ⓦ **sardiniapoint.it** Pages of useful information on the island, taking in everything from accommodation options and car rental to descriptions of local food, history and beaches. In Italian.

Ⓦ **sarnow.com** Good all-round introduction to Sardinia, in Italian and English, including features on food and wine, festivals, music and various localities, with photos.

Travellers with disabilities

Although most Sardinians are helpful enough if presented with a specific problem, the island is hardly geared towards accommodating **travellers with disabilities**. Things are (slowly) improving, but many sites and monuments may pose significant obstacles for anyone with restricted mobility, while few budget or mid-range hotels have lifts, let alone ones capable of taking a wheelchair (higher-grade hotels may have some rooms adapted for use by disabled visitors).

In the medieval city centres and old villages, narrow cobbled streets, steep inclines and chaotic driving and parking are hardly conducive to a stress-free holiday either, while crossing the street in Cágliari is a trial at the best of times. That said, Sardinia presents a much less frenetic level of bustle than other areas in Italy's south, while Alghero, the most popular resort, has a highly user-friendly grid of traffic-free streets.

However, there are measures you can take to make your visit to Sardinia easier. Contacting one of the organizations listed below puts you in touch with a wide range of facilities and information that may prove useful. **Organized tours** may be more expensive than planning your own trip, but accommodation is usually in higher-category hotels that should have experience of and facilities for disabled travellers; you'll also have someone on hand who speaks Italian to smooth the way. It's also worth consulting a specialist Sardinian tour operator (see pp.25–26) for an assessment of specific resorts and destinations.

CONTACTS FOR TRAVELLERS WITH DISABILITIES

In Italy

Accessible Italian Holiday Ⓣ 333 119 1809, Ⓦ accessibleitalianholiday.com. Accommodation, transport, tours and carers can be arranged, though currently only in Alghero.

Accessible Italy Ⓣ 378 941 111, Ⓦ accessibleitaly.com. Tour operator offering customized or set tours and a travel service – with limited coverage of Sardinia.

In the UK and Ireland

Irish Wheelchair Association Ⓣ 01 818 6400, Ⓦ iwa.ie. Information and listings for wheelchair-users travelling abroad.

Tourism for All Ⓣ 0845 124 9971, Ⓦ tourismforall.org.uk. Free lists of accessible accommodation abroad, and information on financial help for holidays.

In the US

Mobility International USA Ⓣ 541 343 1284, Ⓦ miusa.org. Information and referral services, access guides, tours and exchange programmes.

Society for Accessible Travel and Hospitality (SATH) Ⓣ 212 447 7284, Ⓦ sath.org. Non-profit educational organization that has actively represented travellers with disabilities since 1976. Articles and advice for travellers available online.

In Australia

National Disability Services Ⓣ 02 6283 3200, Ⓦ nds.org.au. Provides lists of travel agencies and tour operators for people with disabilities, mostly for members only.

Cágliari

58   Castello

64   Marina

66   Stampace

68   Anfiteatro Romano

68   Orto Botánico

69   Cave sites

69   Casa di Tigellio

69   Villanova

70   Poetto

CÁGLIARI

1

Cágliari

Situated at the centre of the broad curve of the Golfo di Cágliari, backed by lagoons and surmounted by an imposing ring of medieval walls, Cágliari is visually the most impressive of Sardinia's cities. Viewing it from the sea at the start of his Sardinian sojourn in 1921, D.H. Lawrence compared it to Jerusalem: "strange and rather wonderful, not a bit like Italy". Cágliari retains a very distinctive identity, offering both chic sophistication and medieval charm in the raggle-taggle of narrow lanes crammed into its high citadel and port area.

As the island's capital since Roman times at least, Cágliari is also littered with the relics of two thousand years of history, and has a splendid and diverse collection of museums, archeological remains and historic churches. The city's old core is small and compact enough to explore on foot, with almost all its attractions encompassed within the four oldest quarters of the city: Castello, Marina, Stampace and Villanova. You will probably do most of your sightseeing in the old citadel, **Castello**, location of the city's flamboyant cathedral and its finest museums, and the best place to take in the superb vistas. Beneath the citadel walls, the seafront **Marina** quarter holds most of the shops, restaurants, banks and hotels, as well as a couple of absorbing historical remains. Bounding the area to the north, pedestrianized **Via Manno** – home to some of the city's smartest boutiques as well as one of Sardinia's most elegant evening promenades – drops down to **Piazza Yenne**, one of the city's favourite venues for sitting with an ice cream or a beer, while arcaded **Via Roma** is another popular spot for a coffee and pastry, looking straight across to the port.

West of Largo Carlo Felice, the **Stampace** district contains some of the city's oldest churches, and lies within a short walk of a grand Roman amphitheatre and a residential complex from the imperial era. **Villanova**, the area extending east of Castello and Marina, is somewhat less picturesque, but it does contain two of Sardinia's most important religious monuments, the ancient church of **San Saturnino** and the **santuario di Bonaria**. And, if you succumb to sightseeing fatigue, you can unwind on the enormous expanse of sandy beach at nearby **Poetto**.

With Sardinia's best choice of hotels and some of its cheapest restaurants, Cágliari makes an ideal base for excursions farther afield, and is within easy reach of places in the southwest of the island (see p.80), and the south and southeast (see p.112).

HIGHLIGHTS
1. Sunset from the Bastione San Remy
2. Museo Archeologico
3. Mostra di Cere Anatomiche
4. Festa di Sant'Efisio
5. A day on the beach at Poetto
6. Bar-hopping in Castello

CÁGLIARI AREA

FESTA DI SANT'EFISIO

Highlights

❶ Sunset from the Bastione San Remy The majestic views over city, sea and mountain from this wide terrace in the old citadel are at their best at sunset. **See p.60**

❷ Museo Archeologico Set aside several hours for the island's most important archeological collection, whose treasures include nuraghic figurines, 6000-year-old female deities and Phoenician jewellery. **See p.62**

❸ Mostra di Cere Anatomiche A strangely beautiful waxworks collection, created in the nineteenth century for anatomy students, this is one of Cágliari's more offbeat attractions. **See p.63**

❹ Festa di Sant'Efisio Sardinia's biggest festival is a great opportunity to experience the island's traditional costumes, dances and songs. **See p.67**

❺ A day on the beach at Poetto Cágliari's seaside satellite has 6km of silky sand, with bars and parasols on hand for shelter and refreshment **See p.70**

❻ Bar-hopping in Castello The old citadel has some of the island's most congenial bars, best appreciated from the late evening on. **See p.75**

HIGHLIGHTS ARE MARKED ON THE MAP ON P.54

1

The Scuola di Stampace p.66
Festa di Sant'Efisio p.67

The Trenino Verde p.71
Cágliari's festivals p.76

Brief history

Probably founded by the **Phoenicians** in the seventh century BC, Cágliari went on to pass through many hands – from the Romans to the Catalans – before becoming part of modern Italy in the nineteenth century.

From the Roman era to the thirteenth century

Karalis – as it was then known – was a **Carthaginian** colony until its capture by the **Romans** in 238 BC. As an important and flourishing *municipium*, it became one of the major trading ports in the Mediterranean, but declined with the demise of Roman power, eventually falling to the Vandals and Goths in 455 AD. Following a brief period of Byzantine rule, Cágliari was repeatedly plundered by the **Saracens**, the threat becoming so great that, in the tenth century, during the era of the *giudicati* (see p.309) the site of Santa Igia, on a lagoon to the west of the city, was preferred as a more defensible base.

▲ 1 , 1 & SS125

Monte Urpinu

PIAZZA GARIBALDI

VIA PADRI

VIA TUVERI

VIA CARBONI

VIA DANTE

VIA ANTONIO SCANO

VIA VIDAL

VIALE EUROPA

PIAZZA REPUBBLICA

VIA CUGIA

VIA ALGHERO

VIA SONNINO

VIA BELLODA

VIA PESSINA

VIA DEGIOANNIS

Basílica di San Saturnino

VILLANOVA

VIALE DIAZ/ANDREA

VIA SAN LUCIFERO

PIAZZA SAN CÓSIMO

Exma

VIA LOGUDORO

VIA LANUSEI

VIA SONNINO

VIA CIMITERO

Cimitero di Bonaria

VIA XX SETTEMBRE

Santuario and Basílica di Bonaria

VIALE BONARIA

VIALE ARMANDO DIAZ

PIAZZA DEFFENU

VIA CRISTOFORO COLOMBO

Calamosca, Poetto & Villasimius

ACCOMMODATION	
AeR Bundes Jack	6
Arcobaleno	4
At Fourth	9
Calamosca	8
La Ghirlanda	5
La Terrazza sul Porto	2
Miramare	7
Sardinia Domus	3
T Hotel	1

RESTAURANTS	
Antica Hostaria	6
Buongustaio	11
Capítolo Due	1
Crackers	2
Da Fabio	9
Dal Corsaro	5
Da Lillicu	8
Da Serafino	12
Il Gatto	4
Quattro Mori	3
Su Cumbidu	10
Trattoria Gennargentu	7

SHOPS	
Feltrinelli	4
Iperpan	5
I Sapori dell'Isola	2
ISOLA	1
Rinascente	3

VENUES	
Fiera Internazionale	7
Teatro Lírico	1
Teatro Mássimo	2
Teatro delle Saline	8

BARS AND CAFÉS	
Antico Caffè	3
Caffè Svizzero	5
Caffè Torino	6
Il Merlo Parlante	4

0   300
metres

1

Cágliari's fortunes only revived in the middle of the thirteenth century after the local *giudichessa* granted the hill behind her capital to the **Pisans**. They walled and populated it, creating the citadel now known as Castello, which soon became the principal Pisan base in Sardinia, the fortifications later extended to encompass the city's lower quarters.

Rule by Spain and the House of Savoy

The formal cession of Sardinia to the **Aragonese** by Pope Boniface VIII in 1297 and a two-year siege of Cágliari by Alfonso d'Aragona led to the Pisans withdrawing from the city in 1326. Cágliari, however, retained its position under the Aragonese as Sardinia's capital, and Philip III opened the island's first university here in the early seventeenth century. Even so, absorption into the ramshackle Spanish empire proved a mixed blessing for Cágliari – in 1700, the city's population stood at a mere fifteen thousand, fewer than when the Spanish first arrived more than three centuries earlier.

In 1708, during the War of the Spanish Succession, the city was bombarded by an Anglo-Dutch fleet and occupied by an English regiment in the name of Austria; twelve years later, along with the rest of the island, it came under the rule of the Piedmontese **House of Savoy**. During the eighteenth century, the city first began to emerge from its protective walls, which were dismantled in the quarters of Stampace, Marina and Villanova, to be replaced by the broad boulevards along which the traffic rumbles today.

From independence to modern times

Although Cágliari repulsed an attack by French forces in 1793, the ideas of the French Revolution were infiltrating the island in other ways. The following year, the so-called "Sardinian Revolution" broke out in Cágliari against the centralizing tendencies of the Savoyard government, and was brutally suppressed. However, the city benefited over the following decades from the social and institutional reforms that filtered through under the Savoy dynasty, and, in common with the rest of the island, welcomed being integrated into the new kingdom of Italy in 1861.

During **World War II**, heavy aerial bombardment destroyed nearly half the city in February and May 1943. Much of the bomb damage has only recently been made good, but today Cágliari presents itself as a brisk, confident city, with a population of nearly a quarter of a million. True, the city may have the island's densest traffic, but Cágliari also has the most engaging museums and monuments, and the most progressive cultural scene.

Castello

Served by twice-hourly bus #7 from Piazza Matteotti, with a stop in Piazza Indipendenza; there are also lifts up from the lower town – from behind Santa Chiara (above Piazza Yenne) on Castello's western side, and from Via Fossario and Piazzetta Mundula on the eastern side

Secure on its hill, Cágliari's **Castello** district was traditionally the seat of Sardinia's administration, aristocracy and highest ecclesiastical offices. The intricate knot of alleys visible today, accessed from various points in its thick girdle of walls, has altered little in appearance since the Middle Ages, though most of the dwellings date from much later. Draped with washing strung across the balconies, many of the high blocks are run down and don't admit much light, though the lack of fuss or traffic makes for an agreeable stroll through the long alleys. During the day, there's a steady murmur of low-level activity in the antiques shops, restorers' studios and watch-repairers, while things get pretty ghostly at night, apart from on the western and southern sides where several chic bars cater to the local student population. The nucleus of the district is **Piazza Palazzo**, an elongated area lined with historic monuments, though not enhanced by its use as the area's main car park.

CASTELLO QUARTER

■ ACCOMMODATION
Antico Palazzo Crisaripa	**1**
Hostel Marina	**2**

■ BARS AND CAFÉS
Caffè degli Spiriti	**7**
Caffè dell'Elfo	**3**
Caffè Libarium	**1**
De Candia	**6**
Isola del Gelato	**4**
Old Coffee	**2**

■ VENUE
Teatro Civico	**5**

● RESTAURANTS
La Kasbah	**1**
Ritual Caffè	**2**

● SHOP
Birra & Dintorni	**1**

N

Museo Archeologico
Pinacoteca
Museo d'Arte Siamese
Cittadella dei Musei
VIALE BUON CAMMINO
Mostra di Cere Anatomiche
Entrance to Museums
PIAZZA ARSENALE
Torre San Pancrazio
PIAZZA INDIPENDENZA
VIA OSPEDALE
VIA PORCELL
VIA FIUME
Il Ghetto
Santa Croce
VIA SANTA RESTITUTA
VIA SANT'EFISIO
VIA SANTA MARGHERITA
VIA IARA
VIA CAMMINO NUOVO
VIA SANTA CROCE
VIA CORTE D'APPELLO
VIA LA MARMORA
VIA CANELLES
VIA MARTINI
PIAZZA MUNDULA
PIAZZA PALAZZO
Lift
Santa Chiara
Lift
VIA STRETTA
VIA DEI GENOVESI
PIAZZA CARLO ALBERTO
Palazzo Viceregio
VIALE REGINA ELENA
VIA SAN SATURNINO
PIAZZA YENNE
Torre dell'Elefante
Antico Palazzo di Città
Cattedrale
Museo del Duomo
VIA SAN GIOVANNI
VIA PICCIONI
VIA SAN GIACOMO
Università
Seminario Tridentino
VIA UNIVERSITÀ
VIA SAN GIUSEPPE
VIA CANELLES
VIA DUOMO
VIA FOSSARIO
Lift
VIA SPANO
VIA NAPOLI
VIA MANNO
VIA CIMA
VIA MAZZINI
San Sepolcro
PIAZZA MARGHINOTTI
PIAZZA COSTITUZIONE
Bastione San Remy
VIA SAN DOMENICO
VIA GARIBALDI
VIA BARCELLONA

0		100
	metres	

1

Bastione San Remy

The most evocative entry to the Castello district is from the monumental **Bastione San Remy** on Piazza Costituzione, the southern spur of the defensive walls, remodelled between 1899 and 1902. It's worth the haul up the grandiose flight of steps to the broad terrace above, which offers fabulous vistas over the port and the lagoons and mountains beyond. You can catch some of the best views at sunset, though it makes a good place for a pause at any time, with shady benches conducive to picnics or siestas, and a couple of bars (see p.75). A flea market sets up here most winter Sundays.

From the bastion, you can wander off in any direction to enter the tangled maze of Castello's alleys and steps. Leading off to the west, Via Università curves round the lower perimeter of the walls past the main **university** building and the old **Seminario Tridentino**, both built in the eighteenth century.

Torre dell'Elefante

Via Santa Croce • Tues–Sun: mid-June to Oct 10.30am–7pm; Nov to mid-June 10am–5pm • €4 • No under-7s • ☎ 320 052 2083

Hastily erected by Pisa as the main bulwarks of Cágliari's defences against the Aragonese threat, and tested in the siege of the city twelve years later, the **Torre dell'Elefante** – along with the Torre San Pancrazio farther up the hill (see p.62) – is considered a masterpiece of military engineering, designed by famed local architect Giovanni Capula. The Elephant Tower, named after a small carving of an elephant on a plinth to one side, dates from 1307, a little later than its sister tower, its sheer, unbattlemented walls constructed of great blocks of off-white granite. Like other Pisan towers, it has the inward-facing side completely open, giving it a half-finished look. If you want to climb only one of Cágliari's towers, this is the better choice, as it has access to the top terrace. At the bottom, notice the surviving gate mechanism and the spiked gate itself, menacingly poised over the entrance.

Il Ghetto

Via Santa Croce 18 • Tues–Sun: June–Sept 10am–9pm; Oct–May 9am–1pm & 4–8pm • €5 • ☎ 070 667 0190

Cágliari's old Jewish community – expelled in 1492 – was centred on Via Santa Croce, where the church of Santa Croce now occupies the site of the former synagogue. There are no traces of the old Jewish quarter left, though it is recalled in the name of a local exhibition centre, **Il Ghetto**, farther up the street in a well-restored building converted from eighteenth-century barracks. There is nothing relating to Cágliari's Jews within, but there are interesting temporary exhibitions, and views over the city from a small terrace. You can also enjoy the panorama from the bars on Via Santa Croce, with outdoor seating on the city walls.

The Cattedrale

Piazza Palazzo • Mon–Sat 7.30am–8pm, Sun 8am–1pm & 4.30–8.30pm • ☎ 070 663 837, ⓦ duomodicagliari.it

The buildings that line Piazza Palazzo are mostly eighteenth century, though the **Cattedrale di Santa Maria del Castello** has a longer history. Originally built in the thirteenth century, it later, as D.H. Lawrence put it, went through "the mincing machine of the ages, and oozed out Baroque and sausagey". Nothing of this is visible in the present frontage – Lawrence's sausages went back into the mincer in 1933, to be replaced by the present tidy pastiche of a typical Pisan Romanesque arcaded facade.

The interior

The cathedral's **interior** is a mixture of Gothic and Baroque, the ornate painted ceiling rising to a trim cupola. The nave is lined with shallow side chapels, the third on the right holding a vivid sculpture of devils being cast into hell by St Michael. The pair of massive stone **pulpits** which flank the main doors are adorned with carved reliefs showing scenes including the *Adoration of the Magi*, the *Baptism*, the *Sermon on the Mount* and the *Last Supper*. They were crafted around 1160 by Guglielmo da Innsbruck (also called Guglielmo da Pisa) as a single piece, which graced Pisa's cathedral for a century and a half before being presented to Cágliari, where it was divided in the seventeenth century. Four lions by the same sculptor adorn the steps leading up to the altar.

Of the numerous tombs crammed into the cathedral, the most important is the incredibly elaborate fifteenth-century sepulchre of Martin II of Aragon in the left transept, and those of the Savoyard royal family in the densely adorned subterranean **crypt** beneath the altar. Little of the walls and ceiling of this low, vaulted chamber hewn directly out of the rock has been left undecorated; the carvings include work by Sicilian artists of the Sardinian saints whose ashes were said to have been found under the basilica of San Saturnino (see p.69) in 1617.

Museo del Duomo

Via del Fossario 5 • Sat & Sun 10am–1pm & 4.30–7.30pm • €4 • ☎ 070 652 498, ⓦ museoduomodicagliari.it

Behind the cathedral, the **Museo del Duomo** is primarily worth seeing for two items. One, the fifteenth-century *Tríttico di Clemente VII*, is probably the work of more than one Flemish artist at various periods, and may itself be a copy of a lost painting by Rogier van der Weyden. The triptych shows the wan figure of the dead Christ with the Madonna in the central panel, flanked by Sts Anne and Margaret, the latter holding a dragon. The work once formed part of a collection of precious items stolen from the private apartments of Pope Clement VII during the sack of Rome in 1527, and brought to Cágliari by Catalan sailors, who, having been caught up in a fierce storm during the crossing from the mainland, confessed their guilt. The treasure was handed in to the archbishop of Cágliari, and the painting was subsequently presented to the cathedral by Pope Clement. The museum's second masterpiece is the powerful *Retablo della Crocefissione*, a six-panelled polyptych attributed to Michele Cavaro (1517–84) or, more probably, to his workshop.

Antico Palazzo di Città

Piazza Palazzo • Tues–Sun 10am–9pm, mid-Sept to June closes 6pm • €4 • ☎ 070 677 6482

Cágliari's old town hall, the **Antico Palazzo di Città**, has been restored to house an excellent gallery of local and regional art and crafts. You'll see lacework, embroidered fabrics, ceramics and paintings on the first floor, sacred art on the top floor and temporary exhibitions in the basement, which also reveals traces of the building's original fourteenth-century construction.

Palazzo Regio

Piazza Palazzo • July & Aug Mon–Fri 8am–8pm, Sat & Sun 9am–6pm; Sept–June daily 10am–1pm & 4–6pm • Free • ☎ 070 409 2000

Just up from the cathedral, the **Palazzo Regio** was built in the eighteenth century for Sardinia's governors and viceroys under the Piedmontese, and is now used for meetings of the provincial assembly. The porticoed Neoclassical facade sports a dedication to Carolus Emanuel III (Carlo Emanuele III), duke of Savoy and king of Sardinia. Inside, the stately staircase leads up to sumptuous reception rooms hung with the portraits of the be-wigged Piedmontese viceroys and adorned with low chandeliers, gilt mirrors and painted ceilings. Some rooms are used for temporary **exhibitions**, while the impressive **Sala Consiliare** (council chamber) hosts assembly meetings beneath huge paintings depicting heroic events in the island's history.

1

Torre San Pancrazio

Piazza Indipendenza • Tues–Sun: mid-June to Oct 10.30am–7pm; Nov to mid-June 10am–5pm • €4 • No under-7s • ☎ 320 052 2083

Via Martini leads up from Piazza Palazzo to the smaller Piazza Indipendenza, overlooked by the best-restored of Cágliari's fortified towers, the **Torre San Pancrazio**. Very similar in design to the Torre dell'Elefante (see p.60), and also open at one side, the tower repays the climb up four levels with magnificent views over the old town and port, extending south as far as the refinery at Sarroch and the sliver of land holding the remains of Nora. The tower, which rises to 36m, dates from 1305, and was the work of the renowned Giovanni Capula. It subsequently became a prison and later an observatory, when Alberto di Lamármora, Sardinia's greatest all-round scientist in the nineteenth century, installed star-gazing and cartographic instruments on its top in 1835.

The tower stands above the Porta di San Pancrazio gateway, usually busy with cars passing through Piazza dell'Arsenale, where a plaque records the brief visit made to Cágliari in 1573 by the Spanish author of *Don Quixote*, Miguel de Cervantes, shortly before his capture and imprisonment by Moorish pirates.

Cittadella dei Musei

A fortified arched gateway at the top of Piazza dell'Arsenale gives access to the **Cittadella dei Musei**, a museum and study complex erected on the site of the former royal arsenal. The modern concrete structure, softened by greenery, incorporates parts of the older building. The most essential collection here is the archeological museum, but the other, wildly contrasting displays are all worth exploring.

Museo Archeologico

Cittadella dei Musei • Tues–Sun 9am–8pm, last entry at 7.15pm • €3 • ☎ 070 605 181

The island's most important prehistoric, Phoenician, Carthaginian and Roman finds are gathered in the **Museo Archeologico**, including jewellery, coins, busts and statues of gods and muses, and funerary items from the sites of Nora, Tharros and Sant'Antíoco. Some of the museum's earliest exhibits are from the island's Bonu Ighinu culture (c. 4000–3500 BC), including, on the ground floor, striking sculptures of rotund **female deities**, with broad, inscrutable smiles. Elsewhere, a Phoenician bronze **statue of Hercules** highlights the strong trading links that stretched across the Mediterranean to Italy in the fourth century BC, and to Etruria and Greece before then.

Upstairs, look out for the **Stele di Nora**, a stone tablet showing, in Phoenician characters, what may be the first recorded occurrence of the name "Sardinia". The ninth- or eighth-century-BC stele, unearthed near Nora in 1773, is the most ancient Phoenician inscription to be found in the western Mediterranean, and appears to commemorate the building of a temple erected on the arrival of the first Phoenician settlers on the island.

The nuraghic *bronzetti*

The museum's most absorbing pieces come from Sardinia's nuraghic culture, notably a series of **bronze statuettes**, or *bronzetti*, ranging from about 30cm to 90cm in height, spindly and highly stylized but packed with invention and quirky humour. Representing warriors and hunters, athletes, shepherds, nursing mothers, bulls, stags and other wild animals, these figurines constitute the main source of information about this obscure phase of the island's history. Most were probably votive offerings, made to decorate the interiors of temples and later buried to protect them from the hands of invaders. You can recognize the chieftain by his cloak and raised right arm, and the warriors by their extravagantly horned helmets.

Other nuraghic items here have a more primitive look: fragments of pots, axe-heads, jewellery and various domestic implements. For more information on Sardinia's nuraghic culture, see Contexts (p.307).

Pinacoteca

Cittadella dei Musei • Tues–Sun 9am–8pm • €2, or €5 with Museo Archeologico • ☎ 070 662 496, ⓦ pinacoteca.cagliari.beniculturali.it

Adjacent to the archeological museum, the **Pinacoteca** art gallery holds an excellent collection of primarily Catalan and Italian religious art from the fifteenth and sixteenth centuries. The well-displayed paintings have mostly been brought here from local churches and include wooden altarpieces by the foremost Sard painters of the time, Pietro Cavaro and Antioco Mainas, as well as Flemish work and even a Sienese *Madonna* that ended up in Cágliari on account of a mistaken attribution. Other works to look out for include a *Giudizio Universale* (Last Judgement), showing distinct African elements, by the Sard Mastro di Olzai, and, next to each other on the top level, a trio of large, multi-panelled altarpieces: the *Retablo di San Bernardino* by Joan Figuera and Rafael Thomas, an *Annunciation* by Joan Mates and a *Visitation* by Joan Barcelo.

The lowest floor displays a collection of traditional **Sardinian jewellery** – amulets, necklaces, earrings and rosaries – worked in silver and gold, mostly dating from the nineteenth century. You can pick up a free catalogue with English translation on the way in.

Museo d'Arte Siamese

Cittadella dei Musei • Tues–Sun: June–Sept 9am–8pm; Oct–May 9am–6pm • €2 • ☎ 070 675 7624

Displaying items collected by a local engineer who spent twenty years in what is now Thailand, the **Museo d'Arte Siamese** is a cultural leap away from the Cittadella's other museums. Chinese bowls and boxes sit alongside Japanese statuettes and a fearsome array of weaponry, but most of the work is from Siam, including vases, silk paintings and ink drawings featuring vivid portrayals of Hindu and Buddhist legends.

Mostra di Cere Anatomiche

Cittadella dei Musei • Tues–Sun 9am–1.30pm & 4–7pm • €1.50 • ☎ 070 675 7627

The smallest and most surprising of the Cittadella's museums is the **Mostra di Cere Anatomiche**, displaying 23 somewhat gruesome wax models of anatomical sections made in the early nineteenth century by the Florentine Clemente Susini. Items include cutaways of a head and neck, showing the intricate network of nerves and blood vessels linking the brain and facial organs, and one of a pregnant woman displaying the foetus within the womb. Each display has explanatory diagrams in Italian and English.

Galleria Comunale d'Arte

Giardini Púbblici, Viale Regina Elena • Mon & Wed–Sun: late June to mid-Sept 10am–9pm; mid-Sept to late June 10am–6pm • €6 •
☎ 070 677 7598, ⓦ galleriacomunalecagliari.it

A short walk from the Porta di San Pancrazio – or take the lift on Piazzetta Mundula – a brief area of flat greenery below the walls of Castello constitute Cágliari's **Giardini Púbblici**. At the far end, Cágliari's **Galleria Comunale d'Arte** offers a more contemporary slant on Sardinia and its people than the city's Pinacoteca. Exhibitions of Sard artists take place alongside a permanent collection of some of the island's best modern artworks. Among the most notable of these is a moving sculpture by the Nuorese Francesco Ciusa (1883–1949), *Madre dell'Ucciso* ("Mother of the killed man"), depicting a barefooted crone swathed in a shawl, whose bony face is a poignant display of grief. Presented at the Biennale at Venice in 1907, the work helped to establish Ciusa's national reputation.

Other local artists are represented here by portraits of islanders and the local landscapes, illustrating aspects of the Sard experience and often focusing on Sardinia's interactions – and simmering tensions – with the outside world. The rest of the gallery is occupied by the **Ingrao collection**, a bequest of modern Italian art that includes drawings and pallid still lifes by the Bologna artist **Giorgio Morandi**.

Marina

Like Castello, the lanes of the **Marina** quarter are narrow and tightly packed, but unlike those in the upper town, these streets are always animated, busy with the coming and going from the city's main concentration of restaurants and hotels. Marina's proximity to the docks meant that it was heavily bombed during World War II, the damage still visible in places; elsewhere, the bombed-out buildings have been replaced by new constructions, sometimes startlingly at odds with the neighbourhood's predominantly medieval flavour.

Palazzo Comunale

Piazza Matteotti • Free • ☎ 070 6771

The neo-Gothic **Palazzo Comunale** or *Municipio* (town hall) – a white, pinnacled concoction from 1907, combining Catalan-Gothic with Art Nouveau motifs – was one of the victims of World War II bombing, but was rebuilt to match its prewar appearance, complete with bronze eagles and heraldic devices. Access is normally restricted, but you may be able to ask the custodian for entry, to view a notable Flemish tapestry from 1620 as well as paintings by the sixteenth-century Pietro Cavaro and the nineteenth-century Sard master Giovanni Marghinotti, among others.

Museo del Tesoro e Area Archeologica di Sant'Eulalia

Piazza Sant'Eulalia • Tues–Sun 10am–1pm & 4–7pm • €5 • ☎ 070 663 724

Attached to the church of **Sant'Eulalia** is the museum and archeological area together known as the **Museo del Tesoro e Area Archeologica di Sant'Eulalia**, or MUTSEU. In the subterranean complex lying directly beneath the church's altar, a fragment of the Roman city dating from the first century AD has been unearthed, which you can see from a raised walkway. The broad limestone slabs were unlikely to have been a main thoroughfare, judging by the absence of wheel-ruts, but more likely a pedestrian avenue giving access to a major temple. Another route leading down towards the port is visible, and there are also a couple of wells and even a public urinal. Most of the walls here belong to the medieval city built on the ruins of the Roman one, which was abandoned some time between the sixth and eighth centuries.

Upstairs, the **Treasury** displays priestly mantles and fine silverware, as well as a couple of interesting paintings: one, a fourteenth-century *Madonna and Child*, Tuscan in style, with additions by a Sard artist of the sixteenth century; the other, a Flemish *Ecce Homo* of the seventeenth century, painted on both sides, the rear of the canvas giving a close-up of Christ's gorily flayed back.

San Sepolcro

Piazza San Sepolcro • Daily 10am–noon & 4.30–7pm • ☎ 070 6771

One of Marina's most eye-catching churches is **San Sepolcro**, off Via Dettori, with a surprisingly spacious and painstakingly restored interior. Its treasures have also been cleaned up, most notably an eye-poppingly huge gilded altarpiece covering one entire wall, created in the seventeenth century to hold a Madonna revered by the wife of one of the Spanish viceroys after a supposed miracle. The viceroy had to drastically alter the church's fifteenth-century structure to hold the outsize wooden altarpiece, which he did by knocking through two chapels built into the rock, accounting for the church's unorthodox shape. At the same time, the **crypt** below it was hacked out of a natural

FROM TOP CASTELLO QUARTER (P.58); POETTO BEACH (P.70) >

1

hollow in the rock, comprising two large, bare rooms devoid of decoration except for some images of Death on the walls and ceilings, one of them bearing the words *Nemini parco* ("I spare nobody") scratched onto his scythe.

Back in the nave of the church, the sacristy to the right of the altar gives access to a much older relic of the building's long history: a large-scale paleo-Christian **baptismal font**, thought to date back to the fourth century. Set into the ground, the wide, circular basin in which converts were completely immersed was unearthed during routine maintenance work in 2000.

Stampace

Lying to the west of Largo Carlo Felice, the quarter of **Stampace** has given its name to Sardinia's most influential school of art (see box below), and five hundred years later it still retains an active – if low-key – working population of artists and craftsmen. To the north of the Corso, a scattering of **churches** are worth a brief visit, though you may find the crypts and caverns over which these were built of more immediate interest. Running off the top of Piazza Yenne, and parallel to Corso Vittorio Emanuele, Via Azuni gives access to four of Stampace's historic churches.

Piazza Yenne

At the top of Largo Carlo Felice, **Piazza Yenne** was the site of the old Porta Stampace gateway before the destruction of the quarter's walls. The cobbled square that now forms a pedestrianized enclave to one side of the bustling traffic marks the start of the Carlo Felice highway, Sardinia's main north–south artery (now the SS131). A pair of monuments recall the building of this: a bronze statue of its instigator, King Carlo Felice, dressed in Roman garb and for some reason gesturing away from the road, and, across the street, a pointed ball on top of a simple stone column. From here, the highway starts its journey up Corso Vittorio Emanuele, today a busy thoroughfare that begins grandly but soon narrows as it cuts through Stampace.

Sant'Anna

Via Azuni • Tues–Sun 7.30am–noon & 5–8pm

With its monumental white Neoclassical facade atop a grand flight of steps, and sporting a double tier of Corinthian columns and pilasters, the church of **Sant'Anna** was begun during the Savoy era in 1785 on the site of an earlier Pisan church, though not completely finished until the 1930s. Faithfully reconstructed after serious damage during the bombing raids of 1943, the late Baroque design is marked by strong Piedmontese features, notably its tall twin belltowers and octagonal cupola. The airy interior holds a fourteenth-century wooden crucifix and a painting by Giovanni Marghinotti, *Christ the Saviour*.

THE SCUOLA DI STAMPACE

Founded by Stampace resident Pietro Cavaro (died 1537), Cágliari's **Scuola di Stampace** influenced painting throughout Sardinia in the sixteenth century. It included artists such as Antioco Mainas and Pietro's son Michele Cavaro, and drew much of its inspiration from Spain, blending the influence of Raphael with late Gothic elements. Major works by members of the school can be seen in Cágliari's Pinacoteca (see p.63) and Oristano's Antiquarium Arborense (see p.143); few examples remain in Stampace itself, though the district's churches are still redolent of the tight-knit community that gave birth to the school.

Cripta di Santa Restituta

Via Sant'Efisio 14 • Tues–Sun 10am–1pm • Free • ☎ 070 640 2115

To the left of Sant'Anna, the narrow Via Sant'Efisio leads north past the mainly sixteenth-century church of **Santa Restituta** to a doorway that gives entry to the **Cripta di Santa Restituta**. Originally a place of pagan rites linked to the water collected here, this subterranean cavern was subsequently dedicated to Restituta, a victim of Diocletian's persecution, and provided a home for refugees from Africa during the fifth century, and later for a Greek Orthodox community. Later still it served as a prison, while the scribbled signatures faintly visible on the walls of the crypt belong to locals who sheltered here during air raids in 1943. The interior is mostly bare, but for an altar and a statue of the saint in the main chamber, which has niches and a maze of murky corridors running off it.

Sant'Efisio

Via Sant'Efisio • Daily 4.30–7pm

Dating from the eighteenth century, the small church of **Sant'Efisio** is intimately connected with the eponymous martyr and with the large-scale festa dedicated to him, which kicks off from here (see box below). Inside, the second chapel on the right holds the jaunty effigy of the saint that provides the focal point of the procession, with various offerings – medals, rosaries and the like – fastened to the wall alongside. A cross carried at Easter is in the third chapel on the right. At the back of the church, look out for the cannonballs embedded in the wall, originally fired by the French fleet during their attack on Cágliari in 1793 – the rout of the fleet was another miracle attributed to Sant'Efisio.

FESTA DI SANT'EFISIO

Popularly represented as a flamboyant knight with a plumed helmet, **Sant'Efisio** (St Efisins) was born in Elia, Asia Minor, and served as a soldier in the Roman army during the reign of the emperor Diocletian (283–310 AD). According to tradition, he was sent to Sardinia to combat the tribes of the Barbagia in the interior. Having refused to renounce his Christian faith, he was imprisoned in the hypogeum that is now the crypt of the Stampace church of Sant'Efisio, then taken to Nora where he was beheaded in 303. A cult soon grew up around the saint, increasing over the centuries with the attribution of various **miracles** to him – notably the rescue of the city from a plague in 1652 and the repulsion of the French attack on Cágliari in 1792–93.

Since saving the city from plague, the saint has been commemorated annually at the beginning of May in Sardinia's biggest religious festival, the **Festa di Sant'Efisio**. Setting forth from **Sant'Efisio church** on the morning of May 1, a solemn procession embarks on the long walk to **Nora**, 40km south along the coast (see p.84), bearing the holy statue of the saint, which at other times is kept in the church. As the procession makes its way through Cágliari, it is preceded by a long column of costumed participants from every part of the island, sometimes mounted, often accompanied by **traditional singing** and the playing of drums and instruments such as the *launeddas* (shepherd's pipes). The costumed part of the procession soon melts away, however, while the holy statue continues with a small retinue, joined for part of its way by villagers and bands in the places it passes through, before arriving at Nora on the evening of the following day. After religious services have taken place, the statue departs from the church at Nora on the evening of May 3, entering Cágliari the next evening to a much more muted reception.

The festa is a spectacular affair, and a great chance to view a panoply of traditional **costumes** from the villages, as well as to hear authentic Sard music. If you can't be present for the whole four-day event, the May 1 festivities are the highlight, for which you might consider a ticket for the stadium-like seats (*tribune*) around Piazza Matteotti and surrounding streets on the route, giving a high, unimpeded view of the proceedings. Contact the tourist office for information on where to buy tickets, which normally go on sale from mid-April, and quickly sell out.

1

Cripta di Sant'Efisio

Via Sant'Efisio • Irregular opening • Donations welcomed • ☎ 349 340 5509

Below the church of Sant'Efisio, one of the oldest of Cágliari's cavernous crypts, the **Cripta di Sant'Efisio**, once served as a hypogeum or cistern of the Punic-Roman city of Karalis. According to tradition, the Roman soldier, Efisius, was imprisoned here for his Christian beliefs before being taken to Nora to be decapitated. You can see the column to which he was supposedly bound, an object of veneration for local believers. There is evidence of a church in existence here as far back as the fifth century; more recently, the crypt served as an air-raid shelter and rubbish dump. If the entrance is closed (which is often), there may be someone to show you around in the church – otherwise call to arrange a view.

San Michele

Via Azuni • Mon–Sat 8–11am & 6–9pm, Sun 8.30am–noon & 7–9pm

Just up from Corso Vittorio Emanuele, the triple-arched facade of the church of **San Michele** beautifully frames the end of Via Azuni. Consecrated by the Jesuits in 1738, the highly ornamented building is one of Sardinia's most opulent examples of the Baroque. The striking porticoed facade gives a foretaste of the majestic interior, a densely stuccoed and painted octagonal space, sumptuously marbled and topped by a frescoed cupola. On the steps outside, a richly decorated **pulpit** – said to have been used by Charles V before setting off on his expedition against Tunis in 1535 – stands on four Corinthian columns.

Anfiteatro Romano

Viale Sant'Ignazio da Láconi • Currently closed for restoration • ☎ 338 277 4790, ⓦ anfiteatroromano.it

Though access to Cágliari's **Anfiteatro Romano** may be restricted, you can still appreciate its scale and structure from the outside. The amphitheatre was cut out of solid rock in the second century AD, when it could hold the city's entire population of about ten thousand. Despite its state of decay (much of the site was cannibalized to build churches in the Middle Ages) and the intrusion of scaffolding, you can make out the network of underground passages and chambers cut out of the rock, including cages and trenches for the animals. When it's open, the site is used for occasional concerts and dance performances in summer.

Orto Botánico

Viale Sant'Ignazio da Láconi • April–Oct Mon–Fri 8.30am–6pm, Sat & Sun 8.30am–1.30pm; Nov–March daily 8.30am–1.30pm • €3 • ☎ 070 675 3522

Downhill from the amphitheatre, the **Orto Botánico** is one of Italy's most famous botanical gardens, with around two thousand species of Mediterranean and tropical plants, including examples of local carob trees, lentisks and holm oaks, as well as exotic yuccas, palms, papyrus, cacti and some carnivorous species. The collection was initiated in the seventeenth century and transferred to this site in the second half of the nineteenth century (the mother of the writer Italo Calvino later became director of the gardens). You don't need to be a plant enthusiast to enjoy this quiet and shady retreat, especially on a sizzling afternoon. On the northwest side of the garden, you can also find Carthaginian and Roman remains, including four cisterns and a spring located at the base of a limestone cliff.

Cave sites

Various prices; call to book visit • ☏ 328 276 1164, ⓦ cagliaritour.com

History enthusiasts and keen cave-lovers may be drawn to explore three cave sites: the **Cavità di Via Vittorio Veneto** (Via Vittorio Veneto 40), a cavern used by Carthaginians and Romans and during World War II by city-dwellers as a bomb-shelter; the **Orto dei Cappuccini** (Vico I Merello), a garden, cistern and quarry for the Anfiteatro; and the **Galleria Rifugio Don Bosco** (Via San Giovanni Bosco), a long tunnel with lateral chambers. Guided visits to some or all of these can be booked with L'Isola Che Vorrei (see p.73), which offers tours in various languages to a number of city sites.

Casa di Tigellio

Via Tigellio • Tues–Sun: April–Oct 9am–1pm & 4–8pm; Nov–March 9am–5pm • €3 • ☏ 070 677 6470

Close to Corso Vittorio Emanuele, a fenced enclosure holds another remnant of Cágliari's Roman era, the **Casa di Tigellio**. The remains were supposedly the villa of Tigellius, a Sardinian poet whose singing and versifying were appreciated by the Roman emperor Augustus but loathed by perhaps better judges such as Horace and Cicero.

Excavations have also brought to light a later villa of the second and third centuries, quite a substantial complex arranged on either side of a narrow lane. On one side, a set of thermal baths is identifiable by the raised floor of the hypocaust, while three buildings from the imperial era with tetrastyle porticos stand opposite. The first, the atrium, where guests were received, has two Ionic columns and a *tablinum* (a room giving onto an atrium) with mosaic decorations, and is paved with black and white mosaics; the second – the "stuccoed house" – has remnants of patterned decoration on the walls; few traces remain of the third. Excavations continue, sometimes throwing up oddments like the lapidary monuments from nearby tombs currently displayed here.

Villanova

Much of the quarter of **Villanova** is modern and traffic-thronged, but the streets to the east of Viale Regina Margherita hold two important religious sites of great historical significance, the **basilica di San Saturnino** and the **santuario di Bonaria**.

Basilica di San Saturnino

Piazza San Cósimo • Daily 9am–1pm • ☏ 070 659 869

Just off the busy Via Dante, the fifth-century **basilica di San Saturnino** is an important surviving example of early Christian architecture in the western Mediterranean. The basilica was erected on the spot where the Christian martyr Saturninus met his fate during the reign of Diocletian (283–310), and is claimed to be one of Sardinia's two oldest churches, the other being San Giovanni di Sinis near Oristano (see p.151). The building sustained severe damage in World War II, and today the weathered stone of the tall, domed structure is offset by the modernistic darkened glass which makes up most of three sides. Despite this, the church retains an unmistakable Middle Eastern flavour, with its palm trees and cupola.

The monument is entered through an open atrium, within which a palm is surrounded by various remnants from the past: shattered pillars, fragments of Roman sarcophagi, slabs of stone carved with Latin inscriptions and seven cannonballs. The church's stark **interior**, of ponderous dimensions, is empty of any decoration or distraction, though the glass walls allow you to see an excavated **necropolis**, the tombs clearly visible on either side of the nave.

Exma

Via San Lucífero 71 • Tues–Sun: June–Sept 9am–1pm & 5–9pm; Oct–May 9am–1pm & 4–8pm • Free; charge for exhibitions • ☎ 070 666 399

A former *mattatoio* (slaughterhouse) has been rehabilitated and converted into one of the city's most intriguing cultural centres, **Exma**. The spacious courtyard is the occasional venue for jazz and classical concerts in summer (small-scale concerts are held indoors all year), and the surrounding galleries host regular **exhibitions**, mainly featuring the work of Sard artists.

Bonaria

Rising to the southeast of the city, the hill of **Bonaria** holds the **Cimitero Monumentale di Bonaria** – site of numerous grandiose tombs and mausoleums – and affords commanding views out to sea. Valued for its clean air ("*Buon'aria*") and for its distance from Cágliari's pestilential conditions, this was an important military base for the Aragonese during their efforts to prise the Pisans out of Cágliari. The fortifications quickly evolved into a significant city and port with a population of six thousand, and it was only when the Catalans were persuaded to transfer to Cágliari's castle in 1336, ten years after the Pisans were finally expelled from there, that Bonaria's fortifications were abandoned. A few decades later they were in ruins.

Santuario di Bonaria

Piazza Bonaria • Mon–Sat 6.30–11.45am & 4.30–8pm, or 4–7pm in winter, Sun 6.30–11.45am & 4.30–9pm, or 4–8pm in winter • Take any bus to Poetto or the frequent #5 (#5/11 on Sun), #30 or #31 from Via Roma

Built by the Aragonese in 1325, the **santuario di Bonaria** is said to be the first example of the Gothic-Catalan style in Sardinia. The church is now most famous for the legendary image of Our Lady of Bonaria housed within. When a Spanish trading vessel was caught in a storm on the way to Italy in 1370, its crew jettisoned everything on board in their efforts to save themselves, including one chest that refused to sink, and which allegedly had a miraculously becalming effect on the waters. The chest washed ashore, at a spot now marked by a column, and was found to contain an image of the Madonna holding the infant Jesus in one hand, a lit candle in the other. The church soon became a place of pilgrimage, of special significance to all sailors who have traditionally invoked the Madonna di Bonaria as protectress; viceroys, bishops and popes have all paid their respects.

Conserved on the high altar in the Gothic apse, the statue of the Madonna and Child, both crowned, is fashioned from a single piece of locust-tree wood, finely carved and painted. The first chapel on the right has an even more ancient and much venerated statue, the **Madonna del Mirácolo**, which has stood here since the church's construction. The sanctuary's original Aragonese belltower is visible from the park at the back of the church.

Basilica di Bonaria

Piazza Bonaria • Mon–Sat 6.30–11.45am & 4.30–8pm, or 4–7pm in winter, Sun 6.30–11.45am & 4.30–9pm, or 4–8pm in winter

Next door to the santuario di Bonaria, the imposing Neoclassical **basilica di Bonaria** almost overwhelms the plain lines of the older building. The basilica was constructed in 1704, but had all of its frescoes, stuccos and precious decoration devastated by a bomb in World War II. Its marbled interior has been carefully restored, and today it plays an integral role in the ceremonies next door.

Poetto

Bus PF or PQ from Piazza Matteotti (15min)

When you need a break from the city centre, head for the suburb of **Poetto**, where you'll find 6km of fine sandy beach (the Spiaggia di Quartu), with small bars and showers conveniently located nearby.

THE TRENINO VERDE

Cágliari is a starting point for expeditions into Sardinia's interior on the small-gauge trains of the ARST-run **Trenino Verde**. The ride is strictly for leisure, and only runs in the summer months. If you're in a hurry, take one of the more efficient train or bus services to reach your destination; otherwise sit back and enjoy the ride through some of Sardinia's most remote and scenic countryside.

From the Gottardo station in **Monserrato**, around 5km northeast of the centre (connected by Metropolitana trams every 10min from Cágliari's **Piazza Repubblica**, a 20min ride), eight trains daily run to Mandas (Mon–Sat; 1hr 30min). But the really interesting part is the separate service between Mandas and **Arbatax**, the port on Sardinia's eastern coast, operating between mid-June and mid-September twice daily (except Tues), currently leaving Mandas at 8.50am and 3.40pm, for which you'd need to leave Gottardo at 7.08am and 1.12pm (see ⓦarst.sardegna.it for full schedules). The Mandas–Arbatax stretch takes around five hours, a meandering, often tortuous journey through the beautiful highlands of the Sarcidano and Barbagia Seulo. Reckon on about seven hours for the whole one-way journey. For timetables, call ☎070 580 246 or see ⓦtreninoverde.com.

The liveliest of Poetto's beaches is at the westernmost end, where the tidy **Marina Píccola** provides an anchorage for boats and a lively promenading area in summer. Other spots along this beach strip can get fairly raucous throughout the summer. PQ buses run along the whole length of it, and PF buses cover most of it, allowing you to take your pick of the various stretches of sand, though there's little to distinguish between them, and all have similar facilities. The private **lidos** lining the beach charge around €5 for entry and use of showers and toilets, plus €10 for a parasol and €10 for sun-loungers per day, and it's usually also possible to rent pedalos, canoes and surf-bikes. **Windsurfing** courses are available too (see p.73).

ARRIVAL AND DEPARTURE   CÁGLIARI

BY PLANE

Cágliari airport (☎070 211 211, ⓦsogaer.it) sits beside the city's largest *stagno* (lagoon), 6km northwest of the centre. Facilities include banks with ATMs and an information desk (daily 8am–10pm in summer, 9am–9pm in winter). A bus service to Piazza Matteotti in the town centre runs at least every 30min from 7.25am until the last flight arrival – about 12.30pm – and takes 10min (tickets €4 from the ticket machine inside the airport); a taxi costs €15–20.

BY FERRY

Cágliari's port lies in the heart of the town, adjacent to Via Roma, the main thoroughfare; the Stazione Maríttima here has a left-luggage office (see p.77). The main ferry company operating from Cágliari is Tirrenia (☎892 123 or ☎02 2630 2803, ⓦtirrenia.it), whose ticket office is on Via Riva di Ponente opposite the Molo Sabaudo.
Destinations Civitavécchia (1 daily; 15–17hr); Naples (2 weekly; 16hr 15min); Palermo (1 weekly; 14hr 30min); Trápani (1 weekly; 10hr).

BY TRAIN

Cágliari's main station is centrally located on Piazza Matteotti, served by Trenitalia (FS) trains (☎892 021, ⓦferrovie dellostato.it). Gottardo station, for ARST trains (☎800 865 042 or ☎070 579 301, ⓦarst.sardegna.it) to Ísili, Mandas and

Arbatax (see above), is in Monserrato, north of the centre, reachable by tram from Piazza Repubblica (which you can get to on bus #30 or #31 from Piazza Matteotti). Services listed below are FS unless otherwise indicated.
Destinations Arbatax (mid-June to mid-Sept Wed–Mon 2 daily via Mandas; 6hr 45min–7hr 20min); Carbónia (Mon–Sat 13 daily, Sun 9 daily, with change at Decimomannu; 1hr 20min); Dolianova (ARST; Mon–Sat 11 daily; 25min); Iglésias (Mon–Sat hourly, Sun 9 daily, some with change at Decimomannu or Villamassargia; 55min–1hr 10min); Ísili (ARST; Mon–Sat 2 daily; 1hr 50min); Macomer (7–8 daily, some with change; 1hr 40min–3hr); Mandas (ARST; Mon–Sat 8 daily; 1hr 30min); Olbia (5 daily, some with change at Oristano or Ozieri-Chilivani; 3hr 30min–4hr 20min); Oristano (11–16 daily; 1hr–1hr 45 min); Sássari (4 daily, some with change at Ozieri-Chilivani; 3hr 25min–4hr 25min).

BY BUS

All buses, including the ARST airport bus, use the bus station on Piazza Matteotti. The main bus company is ARST (☎800 865 042 or ☎070 409 8324, ⓦarst.sardegna.it); Turmo also operates a limited service to and from Olbia and Santa Teresa di Gallura (☎0789 21 487, ⓦgruppoturmo travel.com). Services listed here are ARST unless otherwise indicated.

1

Destinations Barúmini (Mon–Sat 2 daily; 1hr 30min); Burcei (Mon–Sat 6 daily, Sun 3 daily; 1hr 25min); Calasetta (Mon–Sat 2 daily, Sun 1 daily; 2hr 15min); Capitana (mid-June to mid-Sept Mon–Sat 9 daily, Sun 6 daily; mid-Sept to mid-June Mon–Sat 6 daily, Sun 1–2 daily; 45min); Carbónia (Mon–Sat 4 daily, Sun 1 daily; 1hr 25min); Chia (Mon–Sat 1–3 daily, Sun mid-June to mid-Sept 3 daily; 1hr 15min); Costa Rei (mid-June to mid-Sept Mon–Sat 9 daily, Sun 1 daily; mid-Sept to mid-June Mon–Sat 3 daily, Sun 2 daily; 2hr 5min–2hr 35min); Dolianova (Mon–Sat 10 daily, Sun 3 daily; 45min); Iglésias (Mon–Sat 4 daily, Sun 1 daily; 1hr 15min); Ísili (Mon–Sat 6 daily, Sun 3 daily;

2hr); Mandas (Mon–Sat 6 daily, Sun 3 daily; 1hr 30min); Muravera (Mon–Sat 8 daily, Sun 2 daily; 1hr 45min); Nuoro (2 daily; 2hr 35min); Olbia (Turmo; 1–2 daily; 4hr 15min–5hr); Oristano (Mon–Sat 2 daily; 2hr); Portovesme (1 daily; 1hr 35min); Pula (Mon–Sat hourly, Sun 6–8 daily; 50min); Sanluri (Mon–Sat 1–2 hourly, Sun 5 daily; 50min–1hr 20min); Sant'Antíoco (Mon–Sat 3 daily, Sun 1 daily; 1hr 50min); Santa Teresa di Gallura (Turmo; 1 daily; 6hr 20min); Sássari (2–3 daily; 3hr 20min); Villasimius (mid-June to mid-Sept Mon–Sat 10 daily, Sun 6 daily; mid-Sept to mid-June Mon–Sat 6 daily, Sun 2 daily; 1hr 30min).

GETTING AROUND

You can easily **walk** between the main points of interest in Cágliari, though there are plenty of alternatives. For public transport-users and drivers alike, the bilingual website ⓦ muovetevi.it is a useful resource for getting round the city and environs.

BY CAR

Cágliari is not much fun to drive around, with heavy traffic, narrow or one-way streets and pedestrian areas. You'll need to pay for parking almost everywhere in the central area during peak hours (Mon–Sat 9am–1pm & 4–8pm; €0.50 for the first hr, €1 for every subsequent hr, or €2.50/day); if there are no meters within sight, there's usually a parking attendant hovering in the vicinity, or you can buy parking tickets from some newspaper kiosks or *tabacchi*.

Car rental Most agencies have offices at the airport, including Hertz (☎ 070 240 037, ⓦ hertz.it), who also have an office at Piazza Matteotti 8 (☎ 070 651 078), Ruvioli (☎ 070 240 323, ⓦ ruvioli.it) and Sixt (☎ 06 652 111, ⓦ sixt.it).

BY BUS

Piazza Matteotti is the terminus for most city buses.

Services and routes The most useful services are the circular #7 from Via Roma and Largo Carlo Felice to the Castello quarter and #58 (Sun #8N) from Piazza Matteotti to the Botanical Gardens and Roman amphitheatre. Bus #10 runs between Viale Trento to the west of the city and Bonaria to the east, taking in Corso Vittorio Emanuele, Piazza Yenne, Via Manno, Piazza Costituzione, Piazza Garibaldi and Piazza

Repúbblica. For all routes and schedules, call ☎ 800 078 870 or ☎ 070 20 911 (Mon–Thurs 8.20am–1.20pm & 3–6.30pm, Fri 8.20am–1.20pm) or see ⓦ ctmcagliari.it.

Tickets Tickets cost €1.30, valid for unlimited rides for 1hr 30min from when you punch the ticket on board for your first journey; €2, valid for 2hr, and €3, valid for one day (*biglietto giornaliero*). Buy them in advance from the kiosk in Piazza Matteotti and from some *tabacchi* and news kiosks, or on board (except for the *biglietto giornaliero*) for €0.50 supplement.

BY BIKE OR SCOOTER

Cágliari is too hilly and traffic-swamped to be traversed easily on two wheels, but rides to Poetto or destinations outside town are more feasible. Rentacar, behind the bus station at Via Molo Sant'Agostino 13 (☎ 070 656 503, ⓦ rentcagliari.com), has bikes for €18/day, €40 for three days. Scooters of 150cc or more are also available for around €50/day.

BY TAXI

There are taxi ranks at the airport and Piazza Matteotti; Coop Radio Taxi 4 Mori (☎ 070 400 101) and Rossoblu (☎ 070 6655) both operate 24hr.

INFORMATION

City tourist info Handy kiosks providing information about the city are located outside the Stazione Marittima; Piazza Ingrao (at the bottom of Viale Regina Margherita); Piazza Costituzione; Piazza Indipendenza; and Marina Píccola, Poetto (all daily 8am–8pm; ☎ 329 831 2033, ⓦ visit-cagliari.it).

Provincial tourist info For information on Cágliari province, there's an office inconveniently sited at Via Cadello 9B, fourth floor (Mon–Fri 8.30am–1pm, also Mon & Wed 3–5.30pm; ☎ 070 409 2965), reachable on bus #8. Some of Cágliari's information points should be able to provide an accommodation booklet covering the province.

TOURS AND ACTIVITIES

Cágliari Segway Tour ☎ 347 053 3196, ⓦ newway sardinia.it. Escorted rides around town on Segways

– upright, wheeled personal transporters – daily between mid-March and Nov. Tickets (€25 for 1hr 30min, €40 for

2hr 30min, including audioguide and refreshment) should be booked at the departure point at the Stazione Maríttima 10am–4.30pm.

City Tour ☎ 800 422 850, **⊛** citytourcagliari.com. Operates hour-long open-top bus tours of Cágliari, taking in Castello and extending as far as Poetto. Board at Piazza Yenne; tickets cost €10, including a multilingual audioguide.

L'Isola Che Vorrei Themed walking tours around the city and its environs with commentary in various languages and at various prices (**☎** 328 276 1164, **⊛** cagliaritour .com).

Windsurfing Club Marina Píccola, Poetto **☎** 070 372 694, **⊛** windsurfingclubcagliari.it. Tuition costs €100 for three 1hr lessons.

ACCOMMODATION

Most of Cágliari's **hotels and B&Bs** are in or around the **Marina** district, near the port and bus and train stations. Availability may be restricted in high season, and single rooms are at a premium at all times (though easiest to find at weekends). If you want to stay near a beach, head for the *Calamosca* hotel, or *At Fourth* B&B in Poetto. The nearest campsite is at Capitana, a 40min bus ride east along the coast (Easter to mid-Oct; **☎** 070 803 103, **⊛** piniemare.com), where you'll find pitches for €26.

★ **AeR Bundes Jack** Via Roma 75 **☎** 070 657 970, **⊛** hotelbjvittoria.it; map pp.56–57. Right across from the port, on the third floor (there's a lift), this *pensione* has spotless a/c rooms, mostly en suite, with solid wood furnishings and antique tiled floors. Larger rooms facing the front have great views and cost extra, but can be noisy. The host family is friendly, and there's a ten-percent discount on presentation of this book. €90

★ **Antico Palazzo Crisaripa** Via Canelles 104 **☎** 347 923 0287, **⊛** crisaripa.it; map p.59. Offering a rare opportunity to stay in Cágliari's Castello quarter, this B&B ticks all the boxes – a tasteful renovation of a seventeenth-century building (though parts date from much earlier), with three spacious en-suite rooms, a friendly owner and quirky details, such as the ancient cistern in the basement *cantina*. No credit cards. €80

★ **Arcobaleno** Via Sardegna 38 **☎** 070 684 8325, **⊛** affittacamerearcobalenocagliari.it; map pp.56–57. A great choice if you want to stay in the heart of Marina. The clean, spacious and modern en-suite rooms are in a renovated apartment with exposed brickwork, a/c and wi-fi. Try to get a room higher up, as street-facing ones can be noisy. Breakfast is at the nearby *Bar Roma*. €70

At Fourth Via Ísola Strómboli 3, Poetto **☎** 388 320 9394, **⊛** atfourthbb.com; map pp.56–57. A brief hop from the beach at Poetto, this B&B has two rooms with private (but separate) bathrooms and a back garden planted with citrus trees. Breakfast includes home-made cakes and jams. €90

★ **Calamosca** Viale Calamosca **☎** 070 371 628, **⊛** hotelcalamosca.eu; map pp.56–57. Right on the sea, this is an excellent choice for avoiding Cágliari's noisy centre, 2km away. The terrace overlooks a secluded cove near the lighthouse on Capo Sant'Elia, where there's a small beach, and you can also swim off rocks from the hotel garden. There's a restaurant and a good pizzeria next door. The far preferable sea-facing rooms cost slightly extra. The hotel's about 20min from the centre on bus PF or PQ from Piazza Matteotti, changing to #11 at Stadio Amsicora (summer only; on Sun, #5/11). €90

Hostel Marina Piazza San Sepolcro **☎** 070 450 9709 or **☎** 070 670 818, **⊛** hostelmarinacagliari.com; map p.59. Modern hostel in the heart of the Marina quarter, with dorms sleeping 3–6, family rooms and doubles. Non-members must pay for temporary membership (€3), but all prices include breakfast. Free wi-fi. Dorms €22, doubles €60

La Ghirlanda Via Baylle 7 **☎** 070 204 0610 or **☎** 339 889 2648, **⊛** laghirlandacagliari.it; map pp.56–57. Smart and central B&B *afittacámere* in a late nineteenth-century building with painted ceilings and five large rooms equipped with TV, a/c and bathrooms. Breakfast is at a bar on Via Roma. €80

La Terrazza sul Porto Largo Carlo Felice 36 **☎** 070 658 997 or **☎** 339 876 0155, **⊛** laterrazzasulporto.com; map pp.56–57. Funky, brightly painted rooms with TVs, wi-fi and CD players are available in this easygoing B&B, with shared or private bathrooms, self-service breakfasts and a communal roof terrace. A small apartment is also available. No credit cards. €50

Miramare Via Roma 59 **☎** 070 664 021, **⊛** hotel miramarecagliari.it; map pp.56–57. Chic boutique hotel, centrally located, with a range of boldly coloured rooms on two floors, each individually designed and equipped with a/c, TV and wi-fi. There's a comfortable lounge with sofas and books, and a mini-courtyard with ferns and orchids. Note that the cheaper rates don't include breakfast, which is a jaw-dropping €23 per person. €170

Sardinia Domus Largo Carlo Felice 26 **☎** 070 659 783, **⊛** sardiniadomus.it; map pp.56–57. Pleasant, professionally run B&B with smart, spacious rooms, all en suite and with internet connection. Rooms for three and four are also available. Breakfast is taken at a communal table. €100

T Hotel Via dei Giudicati **☎** 070 47 400, **⊛** thotel.it; map pp.56–57. Large, swish and contemporary hotel that's geared chiefly towards a well-heeled, business clientele, with fully equipped rooms, a fitness centre and a good courtyard restaurant. It's some distance from the old centre, but well-connected by bus #29 from Piazza Matteotti. €130

1

EATING

Cágliari has the best range of **restaurants** on the island, most clustered around Via Sardegna in the Marina quarter. Many don't start serving until 8.30–9pm and are full within thirty minutes, so pass by earlier or telephone ahead to make a booking if you want to be sure of a table. You'll find a similar choice of food everywhere, almost invariably Italian standards augmented by traditional Sard recipes, with a strong emphasis on seafood, though the local places have been joined in recent years by a handful of burger bars and Chinese, Indian and North African restaurants, which are generally cheap. For a top-notch restaurant a short drive outside Cágliari, seek out *Sa Cardiga e Su Schironi* (see p.84). For **takeaway food**, try one of two *salumerie* (delicatessens) on Via Baylle, Marina, which rank among Sardinia's oldest: Vaghi, here since 1902, and the slightly younger Pisu.

CASTELLO

Ritual Caffè Via Università 33 ☎ 070 652 071; map p.59. Gouged out of the rock, this cavernous place makes a memorable venue for dining on rather over-priced pastas (€12–14) and seafood dishes (€20). After the kitchen closes, the music is turned up and you can dance off the calories. Mon–Fri 7am–3am, Sat 7pm–3am.

MARINA

Antica Hostaria Via Cavour 60 ☎ 070 665 870; map pp.56–57. Upmarket though not over-formal restaurant, with antique trimmings. Meat and fish are given equal billing, and are usually good. You'll spend around €40 a head, excluding drinks. Mon–Sat 12.45–3pm & 8–11pm.

Buongustaio Via Concezione 7 ☎ 070 668 124; map pp.56–57. Close to the port, this casually smart restaurant is a notch up from the other cheapies in the neighbourhood, and popular with locals. Prices are comparatively low (around €7 for starters, €5–12 for mains) and there are occasional fixed-price menus. Mon & Tues 1–3.30pm, Wed–Sun 1–3.30pm & 7.30–11.30pm.

Da Fabio Via Sardegna 90 ☎ 070 682 140; map pp.56–57. Easygoing trattoria with the usual choice of meat and fish dishes and pizza in the evening, and an English-speaking boss. You'll share dining space with the artfully incorporated remains of a Roman wall and cistern, or sit outside in summer. Tourist menus are €18 and €20. Tues–Sun noon–3pm & 7.15–11pm; closed two weeks Nov.

★ **Dal Corsaro** Piazzale Regina Margherita 28 ☎ 070 664 318; map pp.56–57. The dominant tone is hushed elegance at this local institution run by four generations of the same family. The immaculate versions of classic fish and meat dishes are truly memorable, and there's a long wine list. It'll make a serious dent in your budget, with first courses around €16, mains €18–27, though the fixed-price lunches (€16–25) and dinners (€40) aren't bad value. Mon–Sat 12.30–2.30pm & 8–10.30pm.

★ **Da Lillicu** Via Sardegna 78 ☎ 070 652 970; map pp.56–57. This Cágliari institution with plain marble tables serves sensational *antipasti*, spaghetti and a limited menu of mainly fishy Sard specialities (mostly €12–25). Booking advised. Daily 1–3pm & 8.30–11pm, closed Sun lunch in winter.

Da Serafino Via Sardegna 109 & Via Lepanto 6; map pp.56–57. No-frills trattoria that's popular with locals, offering great value for its simple but well-prepared Sard staples (around €7 for firsts and mains). Daily except Thurs noon–2.30pm & 7.30–11pm.

★ **Su Cumbidu** Via Napoli 11 ☎ 070 660 017; map pp.56–57. This casual wood-beamed restaurant serves heaving plates of *antipasti*, combinations of pasta and mainly meaty Sardinian specialities. Service is friendly, and there are tables outside. Set-price menus range from €13 to €25. Daily noon–3pm & 7–11.30pm.

Trattoria Gennargentu Via Sardegna 60c; map pp.56–57. Straight-talking Sard trattoria with plain, narrow rooms, where good Sardinian staples are served at reasonable prices (€6–8 for pastas, €9–12 for main courses, plus tourist menus). Sample the tasty *Gnocchetti Sardi alla Gennargentu*, made with ham, bacon, olives and tomatoes. Daily except Wed 12.30–3pm & 8–11pm.

STAMPACE

★ **Capítolo Due** Corso Vittorio Emanuele 199 ☎ 070 451 0719; map pp.56–57. For a change from Sard cuisine, drop into this upmarket "multi-ethnic" restaurant with atmospheric brick vaulting and a range of sushi, sashimi, tempura and other Japanese dishes, as well as Thai, Indian and Mexican specialities. There's a €30 tasting menu. Mon 8.30–11pm, Tues–Sat 1–3pm & 8.30–11pm.

Crackers Corso Vittorio Emanuele 195 ☎ 070 653 912; map pp.56–57. Multi-awarded restaurant that specializes in Piedmontese cuisine, including a great choice of risottos cooked with asparagus, wild mushrooms or truffles for around €9; mains are about €15. Daily except Wed noon–3pm & 8.30–10.30pm.

Il Gatto Viale Trieste 15 ☎ 070 663 596; map pp.56–57. Spacious, vaulted restaurant and pizzeria near the main dining zone, off Piazza del Cármine. It's a little more innovative than most, offering expertly prepared seafood or meat dishes (€9–11 for pastas, €12–15 for mains, or a fixed-price menu at €18), plus a huge range of desserts and imported bottled beer. Mon–Fri 12.30–3pm & 7pm–midnight, Sat & Sun 7pm–midnight.

La Kasbah Via Santa Margherita 10 ☎ 070 654 267; map, p.59. North African fast-food restaurant off Piazza Yenne serving tasty couscous, tagines, kebabs, "Arab pizzas"

and panini, all €5–10; there are outdoor tables, and also a takeaway service. Mon–Sat 12.30–3pm & 7.30pm–1am, Sun 7.30pm–1am.
Quattro Mori Via Angioy 93 ☎070 650 269; map pp.56–57. This place off Corso Vittorio Emanuele is renowned for its Bacchanalian abundance of *antipasti*, whether you've ordered them or not. The accent is on seafood and traditional Sard dishes (€12–15 for starters and mains). It's a small space and booking is essential. Mon–Sat 1–2.30pm & 8.30–11pm.

DRINKING AND NIGHTLIFE

Cágliari is well endowed with places to drink, starting with the **cafés** under the arcades of Via Roma, most of which add fifty to eighty percent to the bill for table service. For a morning coffee or evening drink, **Piazza Yenne** is a pleasant spot to sit out, a safe distance from the traffic and quite lively at *passeggiata* time. The **Castello** quarter is worth exploring after dark for the new **bars** and **birrerias** that are opening up all the time. In summer, **Poetto** is gaudier, a blitz of bars, pizzerias, fairgrounds and ice-cream kiosks by the sea to provide an evening's entertainment. Note that the last bus from here leaves at around 11.30pm.

CASTELLO
Antico Caffè Piazza Costituzione ☎070 658 206; map pp.56–57. Dating from 1855, and the one-time haunt of illustrious artists and writers, this café next to the Bastione San Remy makes an agreeable spot for a midday pause, and serves good snack lunches and dinners too. There are outdoor tables, though the traffic can be oppressive. Daily 7am–2am.
Caffè degli Spiriti Bastione San Remy ☎339 882 2146; map p.59. This chic, loungey bar with great views over the city is a popular hangout on summer evenings, and there are DJs and live music until late at weekends. It's mostly outside, and food includes pizzas and steaks. April–Oct Mon–Thurs & Sun 9am–2am, Fri & Sat 9am–3am; March, Nov & Dec daily 9am–6pm.
Caffè Libarium Via Santa Croce 33 ☎346 522 0212; map p.59. With tables outside right on the old city walls, affording marvellous views, this is a peaceful spot for a snack and a drink from early morning to late at night. Daily 7.30am–2am, closed Mon Nov–May.
De Candia Via Marco de Candia 1–3, Bastione San Remy ☎070 684 8655; map p.59. Contemporary cocktail bar with tables out on the Bastione's wide terrace in summer, when there's live music or DJs from around 11pm and it's usually packed out. Good food, including steaks, available too. Daily 7am–2am, closes midnight in winter.
Old Coffee Via La Mármora 91 ☎320 648 6244; map p.59. Traditional-looking bar near the cathedral, but given added interest by its shelves of old gadgetry including antique radios and record players. Snacks served at small marble tables. Mon–Fri 7.30am–9pm, Sat 8am–1pm & 4–9pm.

MARINA
Caffè Svizzero Largo Carlo Felice 6–8 ☎070 653 784; map pp.56–57. Antique café with a vaulted ceiling, a genteel ambience and great coffee. There are a few tables inside, and smokers can sit in a gazebo on the busy Largo. Mon–Sat 7am–9pm.
Caffè Torino Via Roma 121 ☎070 664 765; map pp.56–57. A cut above the other bars lining Via Roma, because this one has its own bakery in the basement, producing wonderful pastries and cakes. Daily 4am–10.30pm.

STAMPACE
Caffè dell'Elfo Salita Santa Chiara 4–6 ☎070 682 399; map p.59. Intimate bar just up from Piazza Yenne, with exposed brick walls and a great evening atmosphere. It's open during the day for coffees, salads and panini, and there are tables outside. Mon–Sat 8am–1pm & 3pm–late.
Il Merlo Parlante Via Portascalas ☎333 977 4573; map pp.56–57. Tucked up an alley off Corso Vittorio Emanuele, this cramped, studenty *birreria* offers draught beers, music and panini, and a lively ambience. Daily 8pm–late.
★ **Isola del Gelato** Piazza Yenne 35 ☎070 659 824; map p.59. Cágliari's top gelateria offers a range of lip-smacking concoctions, including yoghurt with fresh fruit, making this a good breakfast stop. March–Oct daily 7am–midnight.

ENTERTAINMENT

In summer, music, dance and other entertainments are staged in the piazzas of Marina and Castello and on Poetto's beach – and occasionally at the Anfiteatro Romano (when it reopens following renovation work). Pick up details of all events from any of Cágliari's tourist points, or buy a local newspaper (*L'Unione Sarda* is best).

VENUES
Fiera Internazionale Viale Diaz 221 ⓦfieradella sardegna.it; map pp.56–57. Arena-style area east of the centre used for commercial fairs, exhibitions and concerts.
Teatro Cívico Via Marco de Candia, Castello ☎070 677 7660; map p.59. Partly open-air, this historic theatre stages rock and jazz concerts in summer as well as drama productions.

1

CÁGLIARI'S FESTIVALS

As well as the Festa di Sant'Efisio (see box, p.67), Cágliari has several other **festivals** and events that are worth catching. Usually in February or March, **Carnevale** is a rowdy affair, kicking off with a carousal through the streets of Castello on the first official day of the season – a long procession with dancing and extravagantly costumed celebrations, all accompanied by *sa ratantina*, a deafening drum tattoo. **Easter** is taken seriously in Cágliari, with a procession from the church of Sant'Efisio up to the Cattedrale taking place on the morning of Easter Monday, and cowled columns trailing through town on Good Friday and Easter Sunday. An international **jazz festival** takes place most years between September and December – dates and venues vary, but it has recently been held in Parco di Monte Claro, north of the centre (see ⓦjazzinsardegna.it for the latest information).

Teatro Lírico Via Sant'Alenixedda ☎070 408 2230, ⓦteatroliricodicagliari.it; map pp.56–57. Also known as the Teatro Comunale, this brutalist structure north of Castello is Cágliari's main venue for classical concerts, ballet and opera, in a season stretching between Sept and June. Tickets range in price from €10 to €70.

Teatro Mássimo Via De Magistris 12 ☎070 677 8120, ⓦteatrostabiledellasardegna.it; map pp.56–57. Off Viale Trento, this is one of the city's major theatre venues, with two stages. The season runs Oct–April.

Teatro delle Saline Viale La Palma ☎070 341 322, ⓦteatrodellesaline.it; map pp.56–57. On the eastern side of town towards Poetto, this theatre stages works by the Akròama company, from Shakespeare to contemporary drama.

SHOPPING

Via Manno, ascending to the Bastione di San Remy from Piazza Yenne, is the place to find **boutiques and fashion shops**. Running northeast from the Bastione, Via Garibaldi has more run-of-the-mill clothes outlets with cheaper prices. In Castello, Via La Mármora, below the cathedral, has a cluster of **galleries and antiques shops**. Sardinian **craftwork** is sold in numerous shops in the Castello and Marina districts. In the lower town, Via Sardegna has a few stores selling army surplus and equipment for campers and travellers, alongside Asian and African shops for clothes and **jewellery**. Largo Carlo Felice and Via Roma are popular spots for Asian and African traders hawking everything from leather **handbags** and Senegalese **masks** to lighters and nail-clippers. Via Roma's newspaper kiosks sell **foreign newspapers and magazines**, including same-day English titles.

SHOPS

Birra & Dintorni Via Santa Margherita 5a ☎070 668 679; map p.59. Part of a creeping beer renaissance in Sardinia, this place stocks some 450 different brews from all over the world, mainly in bottles but including draught beers. You can sample before buying; in the evening beers are served accompanied by *taglieri* – wooden trays of salamis and cheeses. Mon–Sat 10am–1pm & 5pm–midnight, or 4.30–11pm in winter.

Feltrinelli Via Roma 51 ☎070 650 256; map pp.56–57. This central bookshop has a good range of English-language publications and books on Sardinia. Mon–Sat 9am–8.30pm, Sun 10am–1.30pm & 5–8.30pm.

Iperpan Viale La Plaia ☎070 658 264; map pp.56–57. This huge supermarket has everything you'll ever need, located in the shopping centre on the road west out of town behind the train station. Daily 9am–9pm.

I Sapori dell'Isola Via Sardegna 50 ☎070 669 479; map pp.56–57. Sardinian specialities are sold here, from honey and cheese to *pane carasau* – the island's wafer bread. Mon–Sat 8am–1.30pm & 4.30–8.30pm.

ISOLA Via Bacaredda 176 ☎070 492 756; map pp.56–57. This government-sponsored store north of the centre is a great showcase for quality Sardinian handicrafts – bags, scarves, rugs, ceramics, jewellery (including coral) – though prices are steep. Mon–Fri 9.30am–1pm & 5–8.30pm, Sat 9.30am–1pm.

Rinascente Via Roma 143 ☎070 653 271; map pp.56–57. Well-stocked department store with a good range of quality items from bags to blouses. Mon–Sat 9am–9pm, Sun 10am–9pm.

MARKETS

Antiques and curios Piazza del Carmine becomes the scene of low-level haggling on the third Sunday of the month, as does Piazza Carlo Alberto (in front of the cathedral) on the second and fourth Sundays, and on the Bastione di San Remy on most Sundays in winter; all close down by lunchtime.

Food The vivacious covered Mercato di San Benedetto, a brief walk north of Castello at Via Francesco Cocco Ortu, is Cágliari's main market for foodstuffs and household goods of every description on two floors (Mon–Sat 7am–2pm). On Sunday mornings, a bigger outdoor food market sprawls around the Stadio Sant'Elia and Via Borgo, east of the centre.

DIRECTORY

Banks and exchange There's a cluster of banks on or around Largo Carlo Felice, all with ATMs and generally open Mon–Fri 8.20am–1.20pm & 3–4.30pm.

Consulates Denmark and Norway, Via Roma 121 ☎ 070 668 208; Germany, Via R. Garzia 9 ☎ 070 307 229; Netherlands and Sweden, Via Roma 101 ☎ 070 670 830; UK, Viale Colombo 160, Quartu Sant'Elena ☎ 070 828 628.

Hospital Ospedale San Giovanni di Dio, Via Ospedale 54 ☎ 070 6091.

Internet access Bips, Via Sicilia 23 (daily 9am–9pm) has internet access (€2/1hr) as well as phones with reasonable long-distance rates; Lamarì, Via Napoli 43, is a more relaxed internet café (Mon–Sat 8.30am–9pm; €3/1hr).

Left luggage Bags can be left at the newspaper kiosk at the bus station (€1 per bag per hr).

Pharmacy Farmacia Scanu, Largo Carlo Felice 46 (Mon–Sat 8.30am–1.30pm & 4.30–8.30pm). Night-opening pharmacies are listed on the door.

Post office Piazza del Cármine (Mon–Fri 8.25am–7.10pm, Sat 8.25am–12.35pm).

Travel agents CTS, Via Balbo 12 ☎ 070 488 260; Viaggi Orrù, Via Baylle 111 ☎ 070 659 858.

The southwest

84 Pula and around

87 Chia and around

88 The Costa del Sud

88 Teulada and around

89 Santadi

89 Montessu

89 Tratalias

90 Sant'Antíoco

97 San Pietro

100 Portovesme and Portoscuso

100 Carbónia

102 Monte Sirai

103 Iglésias

107 The Témpio di Antas

107 Grotta Su Mannau

107 The Iglesiente coast

109 The Costa Verde

TÉMPIO DI ANTAS

The southwest

Predominantly mountainous, Sardinia's southwest corner is a complex area of diverse identities, where you'll encounter superb beaches, thick forest, long swathes of undeveloped coast and a scattering of mountain villages, modern resorts and workaday towns. The region's eventful history is reflected in numerous remains of settlements, temples and fortifications, including towns that were founded by Phoenicians, colonized by Carthaginians and occupied by Rome. To the south and west of the region, Sulcis is the name given to the area most heavily settled by the Carthaginians, for whom the mountains provided valuable ores and minerals, as they have done for successive rulers almost until the present day. Traces of the mining industry are most evident in the Iglesiente region, to the north, a sparsely populated area whose cliff-hung coast punctuated by beaches benefits from the lack of development, though the tourist industry is beginning to wake up to its charms.

The most famous of the region's ancient settlements can be seen at **Nora**, 35km south of Cágliari on the SS195: a Carthaginian and Roman city whose ruins are picturesquely spread out over a promontory in the Golfo di Cágliari. Inland, the lively town of **Pula** is the main holiday centre for this area, though for swimming you'd do better to continue to **Chia** and beyond, where broad, dune-backed beaches stretch south as far as Capo Spartivento. The craggy, undeveloped **Costa del Sud** runs west from here, a spectacular string of tranquil creeks and coves studded with Pisan and Spanish watchtowers.

The western side of this region, **Sulcis**, was known as Solki to the Phoenicians and Carthaginians who established their main base on the island of **Sant'Antíoco**. The eponymous town here is packed with interest, not least its Punic remains and Christian catacombs. Sant'Antíoco and the neighbouring isle of **San Pietro** are among the area's most appealing destinations, bustling in summer, serene at any other time, and supplied with excellent restaurants.

Back on the mainland, just below another ancient Carthaginian settlement on **Monte Sirai**, the inland mining town of **Carbónia** was founded by Mussolini in his drive for Italian self-sufficiency, and today holds a trio of excellent museums. To the north, **Iglésias**, which retains an attractive old core, is the chief town of the **Iglesiente** territory, whose mountainous terrain shows ample evidence of the mineworkings that underpinned the region's economy, often in a poignant state of abandon. A short distance north of here, the Roman **Témpio di Antas** owes its fine state of preservation to its remote valley location, while some of Sardinia's choicest **beaches** lie to the west

Into the mountains p.84
La Notte dei Poeti p.85
Pula's summer entertainments p.87
Sant'Antíoco's festivities p.95
La Mattanza: San Pietro's tuna bloodbath p.97

San Pietro's festivals p.99
Ugolino della Gherardesca p.104
Iglésias festivals p.105
Mining the Iglesiente p.106

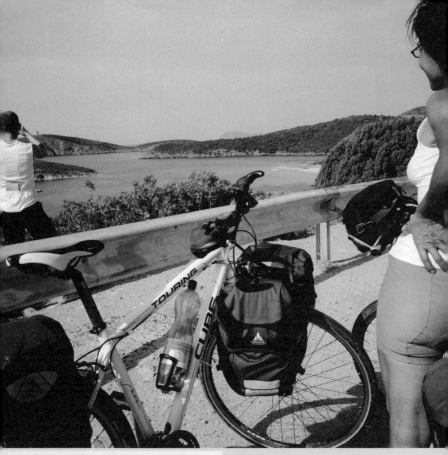

Highlights

❶ Drive or cycle the Costa del Sud This stunning coastline, rugged and undeveloped, offers photo opportunities at every turn – perfect for a leisurely drive or bike ride. **See p.88**

❷ Museo Archeologico, Sant'Antíoco Don't miss this outstanding display of finds from the island's rich history, packed with Carthaginian and Roman artefacts. **See p.92**

❸ Tuna on the island of San Pietro Feast on the fish for which San Pietro is famous, best between April and July; it's on every restaurant menu. **See p.97**

❹ Easter at Iglésias The town draws on its Spanish traditions to commemorate Easter, one of the island's most dramatic and atmospheric events. **See p.105**

❺ Témpio di Antas Occupying a lovely rural spot in the mountains, this temple mixes Carthaginian, Roman and Sard religious elements – and makes a great backdrop for a picnic. **See p.107**

❻ Swim off the Costa Verde Some of the island's most pristine beaches are located on this western coast of the Iglesiente, offering a real back-to-nature experience. **See p.109**

HIGHLIGHTS ARE MARKED ON THE MAP ON PP.82–83

THE SOUTH WEST

N

HIGHLIGHTS

1. Drive or cycle the Costa del Sud
2. Museo Archeologico, Sant'Antioco
3. Tuna on the island of San Pietro
4. Easter at Iglésias
5. Témpio di Antas
6. Swim off the Costa Verde

PROVINCIA DI CAGLIARI

PROVINCIA DI ORISTANO

Oristano, Nuoro, Sássari & Olbia

SS131

SS131

Barúmini

Sanluri

San Gavino
Monreale

Villacidro

SS126

Guspini

Arbus

Montevecchio

Ingurtosu

PROVINCIA
DI MEDIO
CAMPIDANO

Stagno di
Marceddì

Torre dei
Corsari

Funtanazza

Marina di Arbus

Piscinas

6 (Costa Verde)

Capo Pecora

Portixeddu

Buggerru

Fluminimaggiore

I G L E S I E N T E

Grotta su
Mannau

Témpio di Antas
5

SS126

Grotta di
San Giovanni

Domusnovas

Iglésias
4

Nébida

Masua

Cala Domestica

Pan di Zúcchero

2

INTO THE MOUNTAINS

Following the SS195 south of Cágliari, the first place you'll reach is the **Lido di Capoterra**, whose renowned seafood restaurant, *Sa Cardiga e Su Schironi* (☎070 71 652), is well worth a visit. Five kilometres inland from the Lido, the village of **Capoterra** is the starting point for a very minor road running some 40km through the mountains to Santadi (see p.89). It's a laborious drive, much of it on a stony surface, but it allows you to glimpse the wildest and remotest part of the **Sulcis mountains**, forested with holm oaks and thick with Mediterranean *macchia*. A lane branching off the Santadi road leads a few kilometres to the protected wildlife zone of **Monte Arcosu**, a rugged terrain sheltering *cervo sardo* (deer), martens, wildcats and boars, kestrels, buzzards, hawks and even golden eagles. There's a network of waymarked paths – contact Cooperativa Il Caprifoglio (☎347 346 3546, ⊛ilcaprifoglio.it) for walking advice and guided **excursions**.

---

on the highly scenic **Golfo di Gonnesa**, where the **Pan di Zúcchero** outcrop sprouts dramatically out of the sea. Apart from the occasional presence of old mines, the coast maintains an almost pristine feel, nowhere more so than on the **Costa Verde** – acres of untrammelled sand backed by an impressive system of dunes and lapped by uncontaminated waters.

GETTING AROUND   THE SOUTHWEST

By train FS trains (☎892 021, ⊛trenitalia.it) run to Carbónia and Iglésias; apart from the Iglésias–Cágliari line, almost all train journeys involve a change at Villamassárgia.
By bus ARST buses (☎800 865 042, ⊛arst.sardegna.it) cover Pula (for Nora) and the southern coast, and provide a regular service to Iglésias, Carbónia and Sant'Antíoco, running as far as Calasetta and Portovesme, both embarkation points for San Pietro.
By bike Cycling is an excellent way to explore the southern coast and its islands: you can rent bikes at Pula, Sant'Antíoco and Carloforte.

Pula and around

South of Cágliari, the large inland village of **PULA** has mushroomed as a holiday centre and a convenient bolthole for weekenders from Cágliari. Apart from its hotels and restaurants, the village is best known for its proximity to the seaside archeological site at Nora, and is home to a useful museum for visitors to the site.

Museo Archeologico

Corso Vittorio Emanuele 69 • Daily: April–Oct 9am–8pm; Nov–March 10am–1pm & 3–6.30pm • €5, or €7 including archeological site (see below) • ☎070 920 9610, ⊛coptur.net

Pula's Museo Archeologico consists of little more than one large room dedicated to Phoenician, Iberian, Greek, Gallic and Punic cups, glassware and pottery fragments fished out from the sea around Nora. Although the display is small – the most significant finds are in Cágliari's archeological museum – the background information, plans of the site and the model of its theatre as it would have appeared in the first century AD help put it all into context.

Nora

Thanks to its strategic position, dominating the Gulf of Cágliari, **Nora**, 4km south of Pula on the Capo di Pula promontory, flourished for over a thousand years under successive waves of invaders. These days it requires an imaginative leap to grasp the city's former scale, but its position on the tip of a peninsula gives it plenty of atmosphere, overlooked by a defensive tower built by the Spanish in the sixteenth century.

Brief history

The site of Nora was already a Sard settlement when the Phoenicians founded a colony here in the ninth century BC. It was ruled from Carthage from the sixth century BC and taken by the Romans in 238 BC, under whom it became the provincial capital for the whole island. However, the gradual incursion of the sea meant that the site became increasingly precarious, and it was abandoned after the third century AD.

The archeological site

Località Nora • Daily: June–Sept 9.30am–7.30pm; Oct –May 9.30am–dusk • €7 including museum • ☎ 070 920 9138, ⓦ coptur.net

2

Although a good part of the **site** is submerged beneath the sea, and little has survived intact above ground level, crashed arches and walls give some idea of the original size of Nora's buildings. Evidence of the long Carthaginian dominion is scant, despite the intense commercial activity suggested by the foundations of warehouses and the contents of tombs, though a slight elevation holds the ruins of a temple dedicated to Tanit, goddess of fertility. Other pre-Roman remnants, among them a Phoenician inscription featuring the first recorded use of the name "Sardinia", are displayed in Cágliari's archeological museum (see p.62). Most of the remainder belongs to the Roman period, including, near the Spanish watchtower, a temple, with a single column still standing, and a small theatre – much reconstructed, but splendidly sited, and still used for concerts and plays.

Farther on, four upright columns mark a patrician's villa, surrounded by one- and two-room dwellings. The villa's well-preserved black, white and ochre-coloured **mosaic floors** are among Nora's most arresting sights; the opulence of their simple but splendid designs – taken together with the town's four sets of baths and good network of roads with their drainage system still intact – suggests something of the importance of this Roman outpost. Free **tours** of the excavations (usually in Italian) take place whenever there are enough people to make a group and guides are available; otherwise you can get a pretty good picture by wandering about under your own steam, aided by diagrams and bilingual explanation boards.

Nora's beaches

Immediately north of the archeological site, the exquisite sandy bay of **Spiaggia di Nora** is lapped by crystal-clear water, though at peak season this can rapidly transform into day-tripper hell. Following the bay north for 500m or so, you'll come to another attractive beach, **Su Gunventeddu**, which is usually less congested.

Sant'Efisio

Località Nora • Sat 4.30–7.30pm, Sun 10am–noon & 4.30–7.30pm

Standing rather incongruously behind Nora's beach, the undistinguished-looking **church of Sant'Efisio** is actually one of Sardinia's most famous early Christian monuments. It was built by Vittorini monks in the eleventh century on the site of the martyrdom of

---

LA NOTTE DEI POETI

One memorable way to experience the site of Nora is to attend one of the **evening performances** in the Roman theatre. The season, entitled **La Notte dei Poeti** (ⓦ cedacsardegna.it), usually extends from early July to early August and features poetry readings, theatre, cinema, dance, jazz concerts and other musical events. The archeological site isn't the only venue: others include Nora's church of Sant'Efisio, Pula's Casa Frau, off Piazza del Pópolo, and the main piazza itself. Tickets cost €15–30, or €5 for film screenings, and can be bought at the gate, at Pula's information kiosk, and in Cágliari at the Box Office agency at Viale Regina Margherita 43 (☎ 070 657 428). A navetta **bus service** ferries festival-goers from Cágliari on performance evenings at 7.45pm, returning to Cágliari at the end of the evening (tickets €4 return). Most events start at 10pm.

St Efisius, a Roman soldier of the third century who converted to Christianity and was later credited with stemming an outbreak of plague in 1656. Since then the church has been the ultimate destination of Cágliari's May Day procession (see box, p.67). The rendered facade robs the front of the church of much of its character, but the interior is more pleasing: a dark, narrow nave lined with thick pillars and round arches.

Laguna di Nora

Località Nora • Daily: June & Sept 10am–7pm, tours at 10am, 11.30am & 5.30pm; July & Aug 10am–8pm, tours at 10am, 11.30am & 6.30pm • €8; canoe excursions €25/3hr, including entry ticket • ☎ 070 920 9544, ⊛ lagunadinora.it

South of the archeological site (to the right of the entrance), a placid circle of water, the **Laguna di Nora**, forms part of a small nature reserve. A learning centre with an **aquarium** stands on a rocky causeway built onto the lagoon, where school parties and other groups are guided on ninety-minute tours of exhibitions of the local ecology. The Laguna is also a monitoring centre for dolphins, whales and turtles out at sea; you can visit the Centro Recupero on the same ticket, where the injured and young are tended. Supervised snorkelling and canoe trips on the lagoon are also available, again with the primary aim of exploring the local ecosystems.

ARRIVAL AND DEPARTURE · PULA AND AROUND

By bus Hourly ARST buses connect Cágliari with Pula. If you want to go straight to the site of Nora, get off the bus at Pula's Via Corinaldi, from where there are services every 30min (fewer on Sun and in winter) on local buses (buy tickets on board). Coming by bus from the south, get off at Pula's Municipio, just up from the museum, for the same local bus service.

Destinations Cágliari (Mon–Sat hourly, Sun 6–8 daily; 50min); Chia (Mon–Sat 9–11 daily, Sun 5–8 daily; 25min); Santa Margherita di Pula (Mon–Sat 9–11 daily, Sun 5–8 daily; 10min); Teulada (5–7 daily; 1hr).

GETTING AROUND

By bus Follesa (☎ 070 920 9026, ⊛ follesa.com) operates a year-round bus service between Pula, Nora and Santa Margherita di Pula (up to 10 daily). In Pula there are stops at Piazza Municipio and Via Corinaldi. Tickets on board cost €0.70.

By bike ProBike, Corso Vittorio Emanuele 118 (☎ 070 920 8077, ⊛ probikeinresort.com) rents out bikes (€15/day) and organizes cycling excursions.

INFORMATION

Tourist office A kiosk on Piazza Municipio provides local information in summer (May–Sept Mon–Sat 9.30am– 12.30pm & 7–10pm, Sun 9.30am–12.30pm; ☎ 070 920 3333).

ACCOMMODATION

Pula has a couple of decent **hotels** for those who want to be close to a choice of bars and restaurants, otherwise there are good options nearer the sea at **Nora** or 4km down the coast in **Santa Margherita di Pula**, a dispersed area of luxury golf courses and pinewoods sheltering campsites and swanky hotels that cater largely to groups and families. Santa Margherita is accessible from the main SS195 coast road and on local buses (May–Sept).

Cala d'Ostia Santa Margherita di Pula ☎ 070 921 470, ⊛ campingcaladostia.com. The coast 2km south of Pula holds two campsites sheltered by pine woods and right by the sea. They're very similar, though this one has slightly better facilities and has access to a wilder beach. Caravans cost €55 for two in high season. Closed Nov–Easter. Pitches €32

Flumendosa Santa Margherita di Pula ☎ 070 920 8364, ⊛ campingflumendosa.it. Behind a popular stretch of beach, this site's a bit closer to Pula than *Cala d'Ostia*, and also has caravans (€43) and a minibus connection to Pula in summer. Closed Nov–March. Pitches €21

Quattro Mori Via Cágliari 10, Pula ☎ 070 920 9124. Flower-bedecked *pensione* near the centre of Pula offering good-value, very simple rooms with shared facilities (some singles have private bathrooms) – perfectly adequate for a night or two. No credit cards. €40

Su Gunventeddu Località Su Gunventeddu ☎ 070 920 9092, ⊛ sugunventeddu.com. At just 100m from the beach, surrounded by greenery, this modern *pensione* has spacious and quiet rooms and a good restaurant. It's 1km from Nora; local buses stop outside. €85

Villa Madau Via Nora 84, Pula ☎ 070 924 9033, ⊛ villamadau.it. This is the kind of place where you could

---

PULA'S SUMMER ENTERTAINMENTS

In summer, Pula's social hub, Piazza del Pópolo – the site of snack bars, cafés and pizzerias with tables outside – becomes the venue of **free concerts** and **dances** staged almost nightly. Entertainments are also organized at Nora's Roman theatre as part of the Notte dei Poeti festival (see box, p.85).

---

chill out for a few days, with colourful modern decor, a courtyard and a relaxed, indoor/outdoor café-restaurant.

There's wi-fi and a computer available for guests. Ask for a room away from the road to minimize noise intrusion. **€120**

2

EATING AND DRINKING

Madrigal Via XXIV Maggio 9 ☎ 070 800 3312. This "Irish" pub has bottled Danish and Belgian beers as well as Irish and Italian draught beers, and also serves *bruschette*, crêpes and grilled meat, all to a musical accompaniment. Daily 8pm–3am, closed Mon & Tues in winter.

Murales Via Caprera 6 ☎ 070 924 6029. This ristorante/pizzeria has excellent pizzas, *antipasti* and local dishes which you can eat in a courtyard. Prices are very reasonable – pizzas are €6–8, *primi* €7.50–9, *secondi* €5–7 for meat, €8.50–10 for fish (or €4/*etto*) – but service can be slow and offhand. Mon & Wed–Sat 7.30–11pm, Sun 1–3pm & 7.30–11pm.

★ **Su Furriadroxu** Via XXIV Maggio 11 ☎ 070 924 6148.

With tables in an arcaded courtyard, this place specializes in dishes with unpronounceable names from the Campidano area (the waiters will advise). Try the ravioli stuffed with ricotta and saffron, cooked in butter and orange, or a mixed meat grill. Pastas and soups are €7, mains €9–13. Booking essential. Daily except Wed 8–10.45pm.

Su Gunventeddu Località Su Gunventeddu ☎ 070 920 9092. The restaurant in this *pensione* serves tasty local dishes at moderate prices: recommended starters include *spaghetti con bottarga* (with fish roe) or *fregola con arselle* (semolina pasta with clams). Reckon on €25–35 for a full meal excluding drinks. Mon & Thurs–Sun 12.30–3pm & 8–11pm, Wed 8–11pm.

Chia and around

Eighteen kilometres south of Pula, **CHIA** is a scattered locality worth visiting mainly for its **beach**, a perfect sandy arc with a small lagoon behind, overlooked by a Pisan watchtower. Around the tower are the scant remains of the fourth-century-BC Phoenician and Carthaginian town of **Bythia**, and from the top of it are marvellous views south down the coast, taking in a range of inviting beaches.

Immediately south of Chia, the immense beach of **Sa Colonia** makes an irresistible spot for a dip. A series of sandy bays unfurls as you head south from Chia, right up to the point at **Capo Spartivento**. The road to the cape ends at another, much larger lagoon and the last good beaches on this stretch, backed by car parks which charge between May and September (about €5 for a half-day).

ARRIVAL AND INFORMATION

CHIA AND AROUND

By bus ARST buses running roughly hourly connect Chia with Cágliari, Pula and Teulada (less frequent in winter).

Tourist information A kiosk behind Chia's beach is open in summer (late June to mid-Sept daily 10.30am–12.30pm & 4–7.30pm).

ACCOMMODATION AND EATING

Al Nuraghe Chia Via Carducci, Chia ☎ 333 135 1415, ⦿ sacoloniachia.it. This luxurious, modern B&B with a lawned garden is in Chia village, a few minutes inland from the beach. The four rooms, including one with a balcony, have fridges, a/c and wi-fi, and there's a veranda. Breakfast is served on the terrace in summer, and guests have use of a separate kitchen for snacks. **€70**

Sa Colonia Località Chia ☎ 070 923 0001, ⦿ sacolonia chia.it. Signposted on a side road 150m away from the

beach, this *pensione* offers six traditionally styled rooms with en-suite bathrooms, a/c and wi-fi. There's a good but somewhat slow pizzeria/ristorante, serving fresh seafood and *fregola con arselle* (€12), with a fixed-price menu of €35. Half-board is obligatory for guests. May–Sept daily 12.30–3pm & 7.30–10.30pm. **€90** per person half-board

Su Giudeu Località Capo Spartivento ☎ 070 923 0260, ⦿ hotelsugiudeu.it. One of the few hotels around the southern cape, this peaceful spot is surrounded by gardens and lies 500m from a great beach. Half- or full board is required in summer; non-residents can eat in the restaurant here. Closed Nov–March. **€140**

Torre Chia Località Chia ☎ 070 923 0054, ⓦ campeggio

torrechia.it. Conveniently located just behind Chia's beach, this well-equipped campsite has shady pitches, small bungalows for up to four people and a tennis court. Closed Oct to mid-May. Bungalows **€115**; pitches **€24**

The Costa del Sud

West of Capo Spartivento, the road runs briefly inland, then climbs and swoops for some 20km along the largely deserted **Costa del Sud**, one of Sardinia's most scenic drives. To the north, groves of olive and eucalyptus give way to a backdrop of bare mountains, while the jagged coast of the **Golfo di Teulada** presents a procession of indented bays punctuated by lonely Spanish watchtowers. It can be a rewarding hike, though walkers will need to follow much of the route by road.

The sea is often difficult or unfeasible to reach, too, though swimming is possible from rocks or the few isolated **beaches** along the way. One popular bathing spot lies at **Tuerredda**, with silky white sand. To the west, the deep **Baia di Malfatano** provides shelter for boats and has a few scraps of beach, while at **Porto Teulada** you can go diving and rent dinghies, canoes or pedalos. Just beyond Porto Teulada, **Portu Tramatzu** has more alluring – and popular – beaches, with parasols and loungers to rent.

Teulada and around

From the main SS195, a turn-off leads to the small inland town of **TEULADA**, its drowsy air enlivened by odd pieces of **sculpture** dotted around its streets and squares. Sculptors come from all over the world to compete in the town's annual exhibition; they're given a block of local marble, granite or trachyte in June, when the theme – usually locally inspired – is announced. The pieces are finished by September, and then placed around the village. Other than sculpture, Teulada is distinguished for its **handicrafts**, available in various shops, in particular embroidery, tapestries, carpets, cork objects and terracotta pipes.

West of Teulada, the SS195 loops inland of the cliffy coast and Sardinia's southernmost tip, **Capo Teulada**, occasionally used for military exercises and effectively inaccessible. A right turn at the village of **Sant'Anna Arresi** (the last stop on the bus route from Cágliari) brings you to the pinewoods, dunes and lagoons of **Porto Pino**, a favourite place for day-trippers for its shady picnic spots and dazzling sand beaches.

Is Zuddas

Località Is Zuddas · April–Sept daily 9.30am–noon & 2.30–6pm; Oct–March Mon–Sat tours at noon & 4pm, Sun 9am–noon & 2.30–6pm · €10 · ☎ 0781 955 741, ⓦ grotteiszuddas.com

Twelve kilometres northwest of Teulada on the minor SP70, you can explore the dramatic **Is Zuddas** grottoes on hour-long guided tours. The five main chambers of the cave system reveal stalagmites resembling frozen cascades, organ pipes and Walt Disney characters, and marvellous formations of delicate white spiky aragonite. The cool temperatures here (16°C) make a welcome respite from a baking sun.

ARRIVAL AND ACCOMMODATION   TEULADA AND AROUND

By bus ARST buses run to Teulada from Cágliari (5–8 daily; 1hr 50min), and there's a summer service connecting Teulada with places on the coast, operating five times daily.

Portu Tramatzu Località Portu Tramatzu ☎ 070 928

3027, ⓦ campingportutramatzu.it. Popular campsite with direct access to the beach, a bar-restaurant and a shop. Self-catering caravans are available to rent (€60 for two). Closed Nov–March. Pitches **€26**

Santadi

Twenty-one kilometres north of Teulada on the SP70, the nondescript agricultural centre of **SANTADI** on the banks of the Rio Mannu is famous for its **Matrimonio Mauritano**, a re-enactment of a Mauretanian wedding on the first Sunday of August, said to derive from an African colony here during the Roman era. The village has a couple of small museums worth a glance.

Museo Etnográfico Sa Domu Antiga

Via Mazzini · Tues–Sat: March–May 9am–1pm & 3–5pm; June–Sept 9am–1pm & 4–8pm; Oct–Feb 9am–1pm & 4–6pm · €2.60 · ☎ 0781 954 203, ⓦ meditinera.it

Santadi has an engaging collection of rural and domestic bric-a-brac, on show at the **Museo Etnográfico Sa Domu Antiga** – a grand name for a typical peasant dwelling of the Sulcis region. The four rooms and garden are filled with an assortment of traditional items, including a loom, bread-making equipment and agricultural tools. The same ticket allows you into Santadi's **Museo Archeologico** on nearby Via Umberto, consisting of little more than one large room displaying fragments of pottery dug up in the area.

Montessu

Daily: mid-June to Aug 9am–1pm & 4–8pm; early June and early Sept 9am–1pm & 3–7pm; mid-Sept to May 9am–5pm · €5 · ☎ 0781 806 077, ⓦ montessu.it

West of Santadi and 3km north of the village of Villaperuccio (off the SP293 Giba–Siliqua road), the necropolis of **Montessu** is one of Sardinia's most important pre-nuraghic burial sites. Hewn out of a natural amphitheatre of trachyte rock by people of the Ozieri culture of the fourth and third millennia BC, the forty-odd tombs – popularly called *domus de janas*, or "fairy-houses" – have diverse forms. The square openings in either the top or sides were originally sealed with stone doors (one is still in place); four have wide canopies, behind which circular areas are marked out by stones, probably used for funerary rites. Niches and small annexes in several of the clean-cut chambers are pointed out on the hour-long guided tour: look out for the sacred symbols cut into the walls – graffiti, reliefs and incisions linked to earth cults, mostly representing the mother goddess and bull god. The best are visible in the **Tomba delle Spirali**, showing a cluster of alien-looking spirals, possibly the "eyes" of the goddess, and the **Tomba delle Corna**, with multiple horn shapes.

Linked to the same complex is a group of **menhirs** up to 5m tall situated in the open country about 1km south of Villaperuccio, in the **Terrazzu** district. Associated with obscure fertility rites, the stark monoliths are conspicuous landmarks amid the flat cultivated fields.

Tratalias

A short diversion from the SS195 heading west brings you to **TRATALIAS**, whose fine Romanesque church of **Santa Maria** was consecrated in 1213 as the cathedral for the entire Sulcis region, a status it retained for two hundred years. The transfer of the diocese from Sant'Antíoco was part of a general move inland from exposed coastal sites throughout this period. The original nucleus of Tratalias was the quarter now known as **Vecchio Borgo**, abandoned by its inhabitants when the creation of the nearby Lago di Monte Pranu in 1951 led to infiltration of water into the foundations of the houses, forcing the townsfolk to relocate to the modern town a little way north. Along with the church, one or two *palazzi* in Vecchio Borgo preserve their medieval lines, but most of the historic buildings have disappeared.

Santa Maria

Vecchio Borgo • Summer Tues 9am–1pm, Wed, Fri & Sat 9am–1pm & 5–8pm, Thurs & Sun 9am–1pm & 8pm–midnight; winter hours vary • €2.50, tickets from across the piazza • ☎ 0781 688 046, ⓦ meditinera.it

Excellently preserved, the Romanesque church of **Santa Maria** fuses Pisan and French styles, with a small rose window and a section of an external staircase at the top of its simple square facade – a Byzantine motif symbolizing the ascent to heaven. There's more of the staircase visible within, where the thick columns and plain bricks are topped by a wooden roof, though all the finery has long since disappeared. There are hourly **tours** around the church for groups of three or more.

EATING

Il Gallo Nero Vecchio Borgo ☎ 0781 697 003. Handy trattoria across from Santa Maria where local Sard dishes are served, such as *zuppa di cozze* and *culurgiones*, with fresh pecorino and beetroot. Starters are €7–12, mains €8–16. Easter–Sept Tues–Sun 12.30–2pm & 8–10.30pm, daily in Aug; Oct–Easter Tues–Thurs & Sun 12.30–2pm, Fri & Sat 12.30–2pm & 8–10.30pm.

TRATALIAS

★ **Locanda Monserrat** Vecchio Borgo ☎ 0781 688 376, ⓦ locandamonserrat.it. Perfectly positioned in front of the church, this swanky restaurant offers a gastronomic treat, with a menu strong on seafood and challenging on the wallet – expect to pay €40–50 excluding drinks. You can dine inside or in the romantic garden. Easter–Sept Tues–Sun 8–11.30pm, also Mon July & Aug.

Sant'Antíoco

The island of **Sant'Antíoco** is joined to the Sardinian mainland by a 3km-long isthmus that meets the coast 8km west of Tratalias. This causeway has existed since Carthaginian times, though the last section now runs over a modern bridge, dwarfing the remains of its Roman predecessor. The waters of the **Stagno di Santa Caterina** on the left are the occasional habitat of flamingos, cormorants and herons.

Some 16km in length, Sant'Antíoco has an agreeable, off-the-beaten-track appeal, with a cluster of historical **remains** (as well as the majority of the island's hotels and restaurants) concentrated in its main town, also called Sant'Antíoco. Elsewhere, the undeveloped rocky coast shelters some first-class **beaches**, most of them along the northwest and southeast littorals. The SS126 continues northwest from Sant'Antíoco town as far as Calasetta, embarkation point for the neighbouring isle of San Pietro. To reach the island's southern zone, turn left soon after the bridge (signposted *spiagge*). The road south follows the coast past bays and beaches before swinging over to the island's rocky western shore; only primitive tracks cross the hilly interior.

Brief history

Settled by Phoenicians as early as the ninth century BC, Sant'Antíoco was the main base of operations for the territory of **Sulcis** – or Solki as it was then known – forming an important link in their network of trade routes which extended to France and the Iberian peninsula. The area was also a valuable source of minerals, extracted with the help of the enslaved local population. Carthaginians and Romans followed in the wake of the Phoenicians, all keen to exploit the lucrative mines, though the importance of Sant'Antíoco itself declined, as Nora and Kalaris (Cágliari) became more dominant.

Sant'Antíoco town

Sant'Antíoco town centres on the long axis of Via Nazionale – a right turn after the bridge – which becomes Via Roma, Corso Vittorio Emanuele and Via Regina Margherita, interspersed by piazzas Repubblica, Italia and Umberto. Tree-lined Corso Vittorio Emanuele is pedestrianized in the evening, when it's filled with promenaders.

Basilica di Sant'Antíoco

Piazza Parrochia • Daily 9.30am–noon & 3.30–7.30pm (3–6pm in winter) • Tours of catacombs €2.50 • ☎ 0781 83 044

At the top of Via Regina Margherita, the **basilica di Sant'Antíoco** makes a good place to start a tour of the old town. Part-hidden behind the dilapidated facade of a bishop's palace, the Romanesque construction dates from the twelfth century, and is built over Christian catacombs. Near the entrance to the church, look out for a statue of the saint himself, who was interred in the **catacombs**, which can be accessed from the right transept. The catacombs were enlarged by early Christians in the sixth century from five existing Carthaginian hypogea (underground vaults). Guides are on hand to tour the dark and dingy corridors, pitted with numerous low-ceilinged mini-chambers and graves in which skeletons are displayed – the remains of Christians buried in the eighth century – along with reproductions of ceramic objects unearthed during excavation,

2

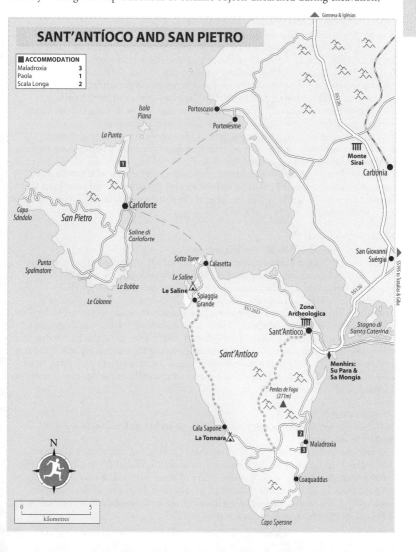

some of them of Byzantine origin. You'll also see the remains of a rare Byzantine tomb, and fragments of primitive frescoes.

The archeological zone and around

Various combinations of ticket are available; one that includes all the sites below costs €13, available from any of the sites • ☎ 0781 82 105, Ⓦ archeotur.it

The earliest traces of Solki, dating from the eighth century BC, are visible in and around the extensive **zona archeologica**, occupying a hillside at the top of the town. There are two entrances: one signposted up Via Castello from outside the basilica, the other towards the sea at the bottom of the hill, by the museum. Other sites are scattered around the residential streets to the west of the archeological zone.

Punic tofet

Zona Archeologica • Daily 9am–7pm • €4 • ☎ 0781 82 105, Ⓦ archeotur.it

Spread over a hilltop near the top entrance to the *zona archeologica*, Sant'Antíoco's extensive **Punic tofet**, or burial site, forms the most prominent part of the excavations, originally dedicated to the supreme Phoenician god, Baal-Hammon, and the fertility goddess Tanit. At the centre of the rocky, panoramic site are the ruined walls of the sanctuary surrounded by a scattering of funerary urns (mostly modern reproductions). The original urns were long held to contain the ashes of the sacrificed first-born children of Phoenician and Punic aristocrats, but this is now thought to have been Roman propaganda: the ashes, it seems, were the cremated remains of children stillborn or dead from natural causes, and of animals. At the summit of the site stand the massive square blocks of a Punic temple, commanding far-reaching views of the sea and Sardinian mainland.

Five hundred metres south stand the meagre remains of the **Punic acropolis**, little more than a few truncated columns and the surviving blocks of what once must have been massive walls. Audio-guides available at the entrance explain and identify different parts of the area.

Museo Archeologico

Zona Archeologica • Daily 9am–7pm • €6 • ☎ 0781 82 105, Ⓦ archeotur.it

At the bottom of the hill, you can view a thoughtfully presented sample of finds from the Punic acropolis in the modern **Museo Archeologico**. These include inscribed stelae and a plethora of amphoras, plates, ceramics and jewellery, including bracelets, earrings and necklaces made of bronze, amber, glass, gold and silver. The finds actually represent a tiny fraction of what is claimed to be one of the largest collections of Carthaginian ware outside the site of Carthage itself. There is also a model of how the port of Solki would have appeared in Carthaginian times, while the last room contains material from the Roman necropolis, including sculptures of human figures and bulls' heads, and some impressive mosaics, notably one in a North African style showing panthers apparently drinking from a plant pot (second to third century AD).

Villaggio ipogeo

Via Necrópoli • Daily: April–Sept 9am–8pm; early Oct 9am–1pm & 3.30–7pm; late Oct to March 9am–1pm & 3–6pm • €2.50 • ☎ 0781 82 105, Ⓦ archeotur.it

Outside the archeological zone, flights of steps carved out of the rock along Via Necrópoli lead between modern houses to the narrow chambers that make up the **villaggio ipogeo**, or Punic necropolis. Many of these were taken over and inhabited by townsfolk in later centuries but all lie empty now. Near one of the entrances, look out for the cannons dredged up from the sea and relocated here, belonging to a French man-of-war sunk in local waters in 1793.

Museo Etnográfico

Via Necrópoli • Daily: April–Sept 9am–8pm; early Oct 9am–1pm & 3.30–7pm; late Oct to March 9am–1pm & 3–6pm • €3 • ☎ 0781 82 105, ⓦ archeotur.it

There's quite a different tone in the last museum on the circuit, the small but engrossing **Museo Etnográfico** consisting of one capacious room crammed to the rafters with examples of rural culture – tools, agricultural implements, craftwork, bread- and pasta-making equipment, most of them only recently superseded by modern machinery. A few more pieces are displayed in a yard at the back.

Forte Su Pisu

Via Castello • Daily: April–Sept 9am–8pm; early Oct 9am–1pm & 3.30–7pm; late Oct to March 9am–1pm & 3–6pm • €2.50 • ☎ 0781 82 105, ⓦ archeotur.it

The **Forte Su Pisu** – also called the *Fortino Sabaudo*, or just *Castello* – is a Piedmontese stronghold built in 1812, incorporating parts of pre-existing nuraghic and Punic fortifications. Its garrison was massacred three years later by corsairs. There's little to see within, but there are good views to be enjoyed from the walls.

ARRIVAL AND DEPARTURE · SANT'ANTÍOCO TOWN

By bus ARST buses stop on Via Nazionale and Piazza Repubblica, in the lower town, before continuing on to Calasetta. For Cágliari, it's best to catch a bus to Carbónia or Iglésias and take a train from there.
Destinations Cágliari (Mon–Sat 1 daily; 2hr 20min); Carbónia (11–14 daily; 1hr); Iglésias (4–5 daily; 1hr 20min).

GETTING AROUND

By local bus Piazza Repubblica is a stop for the local minibuses operated by Senis (ⓦ autoservizisenis.it), connecting the centre of town with the *zona archeologica* (7–9 daily) and in summer with the beaches south of town at Maladroxia and Coaquaddus and with Cala Sapone on the west coast (mid-June to mid-Sept 5 daily); buy tickets on board (€1.50–2.50).
By bike, scooter or car Euromoto, Via Nazionale 57 (☎ 0781 840 907) has bikes to rent (€10–15/day), as well as scooters (€30–60/day) and cars (around €50/day).

INFORMATION

Tourist office Porticciolo, Lungomare Caduti di Nassirya (mid-June to mid-Sept daily 9am–1pm & 4–8pm; mid-Sept to mid-June Tues–Sun 9am–1pm & 3–7pm; ☎ 0781 828 205, ⓦ sulcisiglesiente.eu).
Pro Loco Piazza Repubblica (sporadically open; ☎ 0781 82 031, ⓦ comune.santantioco.it).
Internet Log on at the Porticciolo, Lungomare Caduti di Nassiriya (Mon–Sat 10am–1pm & 5–9pm).
Banks Banks with ATMs are on Piazza Umberto and Via Roma, just off Piazza Italia.

ACCOMMODATION

You won't find a particularly inspiring range of accommodation in **Sant'Antíoco town**, and prices tend to be high. Hotel choices **elsewhere on the island**, within a shortish drive or bus ride from the town, are covered later in this chapter (see p.96).

Eden Piazza Parrocchia ☎ 0781 840 768, ⓦ edenhotel .com. In the upper town, just behind the basilica and convenient for the museums and archeological site, this hotel is somewhat dowdy, but adequate for a night. Ask to see the hotel's own Punic hypogea, or necropolis, later transformed into Christian catacombs very similar to those at the nearby basilica. €80
Hotel del Corso Corso Vittorio Emanuele 32 ☎ 0781 800 265, ⓦ hoteldelcorso.it. On the town's main promenading route, this modern place above a bar has a panoramic roof terrace and fairly standard but spacious rooms with fridges (avoid front-facing rooms for more quiet). The staff are friendly, and breakfast features fresh pastries and fruit juice. €92

Il Nido Via Nazionale 110 ☎ 0781 841 046 or ☎ 349 730 1923, ⓦ ilnidobeb.it. Near Piazza Repubblica, this B&B run by a young couple has small but pretty attic rooms with wooden ceilings. They also offer a separate apartment nearby with a kitchen, or rural accommodation. No credit cards. €55
La Jacaranda Via Risorgimento 22 ☎ 0781 82 008, ⓦ lajacaranda.it. In a quiet lane a short walk from Piazza Garibaldi and the port, this B&B has spacious modern rooms with fridges, a/c and wi-fi. Breakfast and other meals are served in the garden in summer. €80
Moderno Via Nazionale 82 ☎ 0781 83 105, ⓦ hotel -moderno-sant-antioco.com. This renovated hotel a few

---

SANT'ANTÍOCO'S FESTIVITIES

The biggest date on Sant'Antíoco's calendar is the **Festa di Sant'Antíoco**, taking place around the second Sunday after Easter, with four days of traditional songs, poetry recitations and dancing, culminating in a procession to the sea and fireworks. Summer sees a full programme of evening entertainments, including free concerts and open-air films in the piazzas.

---

minutes' walk from the centre offers spacious, simply furnished rooms, friendly management and a highly rated restaurant (open April–Oct). €92

Solki Piazzale Pertini ☎ 0781 800 521, ⓦ hotelsolki.it.

Near the portside, but with only five rooms looking towards the sea, this modern hotel is spacious, quiet, well equipped and well run, but fairly dull. €120

EATING AND DRINKING

Sant'Antíoco's streets are a-buzz most evenings with amblers and scooters, the rich selection of **restaurants** here making up for their scarcity elsewhere on the island. **Snacks** and **ice creams** are available from bars on Piazza Italia and along Corso Vittorio Emanuele, the course of the evening promenade.

Del Passeggero Lungomare Vespucci 52 ☎ 0781 83 794. This traditional seafood restaurant across from the seafront offers such tasty dishes as *insalata di mare* (seafood salad) and *trofie alla cernia* (pasta with grouper fish). Good meat dishes and pizzas are also served. The fixed-price menu is €25. Daily 12.30–3.30pm & 8–11pm; closed Thurs in winter.

Il Brigantino Porticciolo, Lungomare Caduti di Nassiriya ☎ 0781 871 862. Modern ristorante-pizzeria with tables outside by the marina. The dishes are fine, if not particularly memorable, with generous portions and abundant pizzas. *Primi* are €7.50–10, *secondi* €9–13, and there are fixed-price menus for meat (€18) and fish (€20). Tues–Sun 8am–noon & 8pm–midnight, also Mon July & Aug.

La Compagnia del Moro Lungomare Colombo 85 ☎ 0781 876 317. This bar with outdoor tables facing the seafront makes an excellent place for a daytime pause or to wind up at the end of the evening. As well as beers

and cocktails, it serves panini, *pizzette*, salads and other light meals. Daily 7am–midnight; closed Wed in winter.

★ **La Fenicia** Viale Trieste 41 ☎ 329 355 0967. Intimate trattoria where you can sample grilled fish and local wines at reasonable prices – *antipasti* at €8–10, pastas €10–12 and mains €12–16. The *spaghetti con vóngole* (with clams) and steamed tuna are recommended, and there are some fine vegetarian dishes. Daily except Wed 12.30–2.30pm & 7.30–11.30pm; also Wed in Aug.

★ **Rubiu** Viale Trento 22 ☎ 0781 196 4107. An unusual find, a bit off the beaten track, this modern place specializes in *birre artigianali* – "artisan beers" – brewed here or elsewhere in Italy, and served with *taglieri* (wooden boards) of cold meats and seafood, salads, focaccia (€3–7) and its best pizzas (€6–10). Try Flavia, a fruity, full-bodied and much awarded light-coloured beer. Gets packed, so worth booking at weekends. Daily except Tues 7pm–1am.

South of Sant'Antíoco: the beaches and interior

Outside town, the island of Sant'Antíoco mainly consists of *macchia*-covered slopes, with a few white houses dotted among the vineyards and scrub. Most of the **beaches** lie on the southern and eastern shores, accessible from the road running south out of town. One of the best is at **Maladroxia**, a sheltered bay reached via a turn-off 5km down the road.

The main road south curls round towards the island's highest point, **Perdas de Fogu** (271m), from where hikers can enjoy distant views stretching out over the Sardinian mainland. Another left turn leads to another fine beach, **Coaquaddus**, equipped with deckchairs, parasols and a couple of bars. Much of the coastline around here is high and rocky, especially at the southern tip of the island at **Capo Sperone**, occupied by a solitary watchtower with a sandy beach below.

Bathing spots on the remoter **western side** of the island are harder to find: the best is probably **Cala Sapone**, a sheltered inlet with swimming mainly from rocks. Beyond here the going gets slow as the road loses its asphalt, and access is easiest from the north.

2

Hotel Maladroxia Località Maladroxia ☏0781 817 012, ⓦhotelmaladroxia.it. Tranquil, 1970s-style holiday hotel 100m from the beach, with spacious rooms, six of them facing the sea and three with a balcony. There's a veranda restaurant, also with good views. Closed mid-Sept to Easter. **€90**

Scala Longa Località Maladroxia ☏347 956 0034. *Affittacámere* with seven simple, en-suite rooms and

a panoramic terrace overlooking the sea. Breakfast is in a bar by the beach. No credit cards. Closed Oct–June. **€60**

Tonnara Cala Sapone ☏0781 189 6210, ⓦcamping tonnara.it. On the western side of the island, with a pool and direct access to the beach in a sheltered inlet. There's a restaurant and shop, and caravans and bungalows are available to rent. Closed late Oct to late April. Pitches **€32**

Calasetta

At the island's northern extremity, Sant'Antíoco's second town, **CALASETTA**, lies 10km from the main town. Most visitors come mainly for the ferry service from here to San Pietro, but some of the island's best **beaches** lie close by: a ten-minute walk west of the port will bring you to the **Sotto Torre** beach, small but perfect for a leisurely dip, while further southwest is the beautiful, dune-backed, fine-sand beach of **Le Saline**, its clean, shallow water ideal for families, and, a couple of kilometres farther down, there's **Spiaggia Grande**, soon after which the road becomes a dirt track. At Le Saline and Spiaggia Grande, umbrellas, deckchairs and boats are available to rent and bars serve refreshments.

Museo d'Arte Contemporanea

Via Savoia • July & Aug Tues–Sun 6–9pm; Sept Sat & Sun 6–7pm; Oct–June Sat 5–8pm, Sun 10am–1pm • €3 • ☏0781 887 813

Calasetta's right-angled grid of lanes holds one unexpected item of interest: the **Museo d'Arte Contemporanea**, an outpost of avant-garde art from the 1960s and 1970s. Occupying two large, white-walled rooms once used as an abbatoir, the collection displays works by around a hundred European artists, concentrating on abstract, concrete and constructivist genres.

By ferry Saremar (☏0781 854 005, ⓦsaremar.it) and Delcomar (☏0781 857 123, ⓦdelcomar.it) operate ferry services between Calasetta and Carloforte, on the island of San Pietro (every 1–2hr; 30min). Tickets cost around €6 per person, €11.50 for a medium-size car, depending on period and day (winter weekends are cheapest). At peak periods, drivers should arrive at the ferry port in good time, as queues develop. Keep an eye on times of last departures,

and book as early as possible; if you get stuck, however, note that Delcomar ferries make night-time crossings every 1hr 30min (tickets on board).

By bus ARST buses to and from Sant'Antíoco town and Cágliari pull up at the port.

Destinations Cágliari (Mon–Sat 1 daily; 2hr 20min); Carbónia (10–14 daily; 50min); Iglésias (4–5 daily; 1hr 50min); Sant'Antíoco (1–2 hourly; 25–30min).

ACCOMMODATION AND EATING

Most places in Calasetta require **half- or full board** in August.

Cala di Seta Via Regina Margherita 61 ☏0781 88 304, ⓦhotelcaladiseta.it. With friendly management, this centrally located hotel offers spacious and well-equipped rooms. Those at the top, costing extra, are wood-beamed and have great harbour views, and some have a balcony; the cheapest rooms look out into a courtyard. **€95**

FJBY Via Solferino 83 ☏0781 88 444, ⓦhotelfjby.it. Run by three brothers, this functional, rather old-fashioned two-star hotel with a panoramic terrace is the nearest accommodation to the port. Half-board in July is around €65/person. **€70**

Le Saline Località Le Saline ☏0781 88 615,

ⓦcampinglesaline.com. Well-managed campsite 2km southwest of town, with direct access to the beach of the same name. It's well organized, with modern facilities, a pizzeria and self-service restaurant, a tennis court and bungalows to rent (from €100). Pitches **€32**

Nord Oveste Lungomare C. Colombo ☏393 944 2798. You can dig into first-class and gigantic pizzas, tuna cutlets and seafood fry-ups at this casual place with pirate decor near the harbour – otherwise just drop in for a drink. You'll spend around €15 for a pizza, €25 for a fish dish (both including drinks). Daily 7am–midnight, closed Mon Oct–May.

San Pietro

The island of **San Pietro** has a more intimate and insular feel than neighbouring Sant'Antíoco, preserving a carefree, laidback air despite the boatloads of holidaymakers disembarking every summer. Most visitors confine themselves to the only town, **Carloforte** (named after the Savoy king, Carlo Emanuele), but the rest of the island is well worth exploring. Although the **eastern seaboard** is not exactly enhanced by the prospect of Portovesme's smoky industrial works on the Sardinian mainland, the few beaches on the **southern coast** are pleasantly secluded, while the high western shore vaunts some exquisite panoramas as well as one or two great places for swimming and snorkelling. The **west coast**'s cliffy terrain also provides sanctuary for a protected species of falcon. Dotted with white villas, most of the island's **interior** is covered with *macchia* that gives way to bare craggy or round peaks, the slopes rising to a height of about 200m. A car is not essential: an infrequent bus service covers most of the island (see p.98), though a bike would give you most independence (see p.98).

Almost all of San Pietro's facilities are located in Carloforte. Virtually all the island's restaurants feature **tuna** on their menus, a local speciality due to the rich harvest of tuna fished here every year. The annual slaughter of the tuna fish, **La Mattanza**, takes place in May and June (see box below).

Brief history

In former times San Pietro was known as Enosim by the Carthaginians and Accipitrum by the Romans, both names referring to the numbers of sparrowhawks that once dwelt here. Its present name derives from a legend according to which St Peter washed up on the island after being shipwrecked (a claim made by dozens of other Mediterranean islands), subsequently teaching the locals new fishing techniques. In fact the methods used in the tuna-fishing for which San Pietro is best known were probably bequeathed by a colony of Ligurians who were invited to settle here by Carlo Emanuele III in 1738. Originally from the town of Pegli, west of Genoa, the immigrants arrived from the island of Tabarka, near Tunisia, where they had scraped a precarious living as merchants and coral-gatherers since settling there in 1541. The newcomers were not left in peace for long, however: in 1793, San Pietro was occupied by French forces, and five years later it was the target of one of the last great corsair raids, when nearly a thousand of the Ligurians were abducted and taken back to Tunisia, enslaved. The islanders eventually returned to San Pietro in 1803 on payment of a hefty ransom by

---

LA MATTANZA: SAN PIETRO'S TUNA BLOODBATH

Though the annual tuna massacre is also enacted on Sant'Antíoco (at Punta Maggiore, southwest of Calasetta), San Pietro's age-old rite of **La Mattanza** is a much bigger, bloodier affair. Nets are laid down as early as March, but the killing mainly takes place in May and June, when the tuna pass through the northern straits on their way to their mating grounds in the eastern Mediterranean. Channelled through a series of nets culminating in the **camera della morte**, or death-chamber, the fish are bludgeoned to death as the net is slowly raised.

The *Mattanza* – the word is from Spanish roots ("the killing") – has mixed **origins**. The methods are identical to those used at other places where the Ligurians settled, such as the Égadi Islands off Sicily's western tip, but there's also a strong Arab influence evident in the use of titles such as *Raîs* (Arab for chief), referring to the coordinator of the operation. Although deplored by many for its brutality, the practice attracts crowds of spectators every season, and has given rise to a **festival** that highlights the tuna's central role in the island's economy, culture and cuisine: the **Girotonno**, taking place in late May/early June (see box, p.99). Even so, the gory details of the *Mattanza* are understandably played down in San Pietro's numerous restaurants that serve the fish, the island's top speciality. You can learn about the customs and methods of the *Mattanza* – and see graphic photos – in Carloforte's Museo Cívico (see p.98).

Vittorio Emanuele I. Still today, the local dialect is an antiquated version of Genoan, Ligurian elements remain in the local cuisine and dialect, and some of the buildings hark back to Genoan styles of architecture.

ARRIVAL AND DEPARTURE   SAN PIETRO

By ferry Carloforte is connected to Calasetta on Sant'Antíoco and Portovesme on the mainland by Saremar (☎0781 854 005, 🌐saremar.it) and Delcomar (Calasetta only; ☎0781 857 123, 🌐delcomar.it), with tickets around €6 per person, €12 for a car, depending on period and day. In Carloforte, the Saremar ticket office is on Piazza Carlo Emanuele; buy Delcomar tickets from a kiosk on the

quayside or on board the ferry. You should arrive at the embarkation point in good time in August and other peak periods, and be aware of last departure times to and from the island. There's a night-time service run by Delcomar on the Calasetta route only.
Destinations Calasetta (every 1–2hr; 40min); Portovesme (hourly; 30min).

GETTING AROUND

By bus A bus service links Carloforte with La Punta, Capo Sándalo and La Caletta, leaving from the stop on Piazza Carlo Emanuele every 1–2hr (tickets €2 return, available from *tabacchini* on Via Roma).
By bike or scooter Solg Mediazioni, Via Napoli 8 (☎0781

854 898 or ☎349 363 6739) rents bicycles (€10/day) and scooters (€35/day).
By taxi Capriata (☎0781 854 898 or ☎349 363 6739); Peloso Viaggi (☎0781 859 021 or ☎348 659 7137); Poma Tours (☎393 754 0126).

Carloforte

CARLOFORTE centres on broad and animated **Piazza Carlo Emanuele**. Planted with palms, the square opens onto the port, where water-polo matches take place in cordoned-off sections in summer. From here, **Corso Battellieri** runs south along the seafront to a placid lagoon, the occasional home of pink flamingos. An observatory sits between the lagoon and the sea, located on the exact line of the thirty-ninth parallel.

Museo Cívico

Via Cisterna del Re • Mid-June to mid-Sept Tues 10am–1pm & 4–8pm, Wed & Fri 9am–1pm, Thurs 4–8pm, Sat 5–8pm; mid-Sept to mid-June Tues & Thurs 10am–1pm, Wed & Fri–Sun 10am–1pm • €2 • ☎0781 855 880

A wander around Carloforte's *carruggi*, or alleys, should take in the small **Museo Cívico**, housed in an eighteenth-century guard-house at the entrance to the old citadel (follow signs from Piazza Repubblica). It's a tidy collection of items displayed in five small rooms, each dedicated to a specific aspect of the island's history and culture. The Sala dei Galanzieri evokes local life in the nineteenth century, while the Sala della Tonnara has photos and diagrams illustrating how tuna are caught in the island's annual *Mattanza*, with examples of nets and the hooks used. Other rooms hold fossils, molluscs and historical documents.

In front of the museum stands the **Cisterna del Re**, a curious domed archway marking the site of a cistern dating back to the town's construction in the eighteenth century.

INFORMATION   CARLOFORTE

Tourist office Piazza Carlo Emanuele (April–Sept Mon 10am–1pm, Tues–Sat 10am–1pm & 5–8pm; Oct–March Mon–Sat 10am–noon; ☎0781 854 009, 🌐prolocacarloforte .it). In summer, a kiosk on the quayside, mainly concerned with selling services, can also provide some information.
Websites As well as the tourist office's own website, it's

worth looking at 🌐carloforte.net, 🌐carloforte.com and 🌐carloforte.it, all packed with practical tips for walkers, wildlife enthusiasts and divers, as well as providing overviews of San Pietro's history, cuisine and culture.
Internet access Trycomp, Via Segni 68 (Mon, Tues & Thurs– Sat 9.30am–1pm & 5.30–8.30pm, Wed 9.30am–1pm).

TOURS AND ACTIVITIES

Boat tours Tickets for boat tours around San Pietro's coast are sold from kiosks on the quayside (€20–30/person). Most excursions depart from the port every morning and

afternoon between June and mid-Sept, visiting all the most important grottoes and some secluded beaches, taking around 3hr.

Diving Carloforte Tonnare Diving Center (☎ 349 690 4969, ⓦ carlofortediving.it) organizes dives and snorkelling expeditions from the Tonnare fishery, Località La Punta.

ACCOMMODATION

California Via Cavallera 15 ☎ 0781 854 470, ⓦ hotel californiacarloforte.it. About a 10min walk south of the port, near the lagoon, this friendly, family-run hotel has simple rooms with minibars, a/c, bathrooms and balconies. The same family has rooms and apartments to rent. **€80**

★ **Hieracon** Corso Cavour 62 ☎ 0781 854 028, ⓦ hotel hieracon.com. At the quiet end of the seafront, Carloforte's most stylish hotel is an ornate Art Nouveau concoction with period furnishings, a restaurant on two levels and an internal garden. Some rooms have harbour views, cheaper ones are loft conversions and viewless. **€100**

Il Carruggetto Via Spano 42 ☎ 347 179 1531, ⓦ carruggetto.it. Away from the port in the old town, this quirky B&B in an old grain deposit has exposed stone walls and quiet but boldly coloured rooms with private facilities. No credit cards. **€70**

★ **Il Ghiro** Piazza Repubblica 7 ☎ 338 205 0553, ⓦ carlofortebedandbreakfast.it. Eco-friendly B&B in a converted townhouse from the 1790s overlooking Carloforte's liveliest square (so not for light sleepers in summer). The two smallish, wood-beamed rooms have arty decor and organic breakfasts. No credit cards. **€55**

EATING AND DRINKING

A Galaia Via Segni 36 ☎ 0781 854 081. Relaxed back-street trattoria offering land- and sea-based dishes in attractive surroundings. First courses are €8–12, mains are €7–16, and there's a €20 fixed-price lunch menu. Tues–Sun noon–2.15pm & 7–11pm, open daily in July & Aug; closed Nov.

★ **Al Tonno di Corsa** Via Marconi 47 ☎ 0781 855 106. With two rooms adorned with paintings and old photos, and terraces with views over the town, this seafood restaurant is dedicated to the local *cucina tabarkina* in general, and tuna dishes in particular, though plenty of other fish are also present on the menu, not least among the excellent *antipasti*. You'll pay €40–50 for a full meal excluding drinks. The alley is most easily reached from the Lungomare via the steps at the top of Via Caprera. Tues–Sun 12.30–2.30pm & 8–10.30pm, open daily June–Aug.

Barone Rosso Via Venti Settembre 26. By day, this little bar with a few tables outside makes an ideal spot for a sit down, and provides such snacks as panini, toasties,

hamburgers and salads (€5–15). In the evening it's a modish hang-out with a funky charm and a good choice of bottled and draught beers and grappas, staying open till the small hours. Tues–Sun noon–4pm & 7pm–2am; closed mid-Nov to mid-Dec.

Da Nicolo Corso Cavour 32 ☎ 0781 854 048. One of Carloforte's finest restaurants, just up from Piazza Carlo Emanuele, with tables outside. The menu features local dishes such as *cuscus carlofortino*, *maccheroni con pesto* and, of course, tuna. There's a good-value two-course lunch menu for €20, otherwise starters are €15–18, mains around €20. Mid-May to mid-Sept Tues–Sun noon–3pm & 8–11pm, open daily in July & Aug.

Da Vittorio Corso Battellieri 16 ☎ 0781 855 200. Good but pricey fish restaurant with some pavement seating. The menu lists *zuppa di pesce* and *spaghetti all'aragosta* (with lobster sauce), among other items. Most starters are €10–15, mains €15–20, and there's a tourist menu for €30. Daily noon–3pm & 7–11pm; closed Tues Oct–May.

The western and southern shores

From Carloforte, a twisty road leads across to the island's western shore at **Capo Sándalo**, a rugged beauty spot on the western tip with memorable views along the coast. Most of

---

SAN PIETRO'S FESTIVALS

A full programme of festivities punctuates the summer in San Pietro. Over four days in late May/early June, in the wake of the *Mattanza* (see box, p.97) the **Girotonno** festival (ⓦ girotonno .org) celebrates the annual tuna catch, involving much eating and drinking from stalls, along with a buskers' festival and concerts and dance performances in Piazza Repubblica and on the seafront. The four-day **Creuza de Mà** (ⓦ festivalcarloforte.org) in mid-June celebrates film music, with free screenings, concerts and talks. The biggest religious festival of the year is the **Festa di San Pietro** on June 29, which features music, dancing, fireworks and a picturesque procession of boats. Lastly, **Posidonia** (ⓦ posidoniafestival.com), over three days in late July, is dedicated to art, the environment and sustainable development, with free workshops, concerts and debates. Book accommodation ahead if you're planning to stay during these times.

this coast is inaccessible without a boat, though you can reach **La Caletta**, the island's widest beach, in the Spalmatore district, along the road running south out of Carloforte and winding round the southern tip. Here, you'll find a cluster of houses and pristine sands amid trees and thick vegetation.

More rough strips of beach lie sheltered in a series of inlets on the island's southeastern edge, for example **La Bobba**, where the twin rock formations known as *Le Colonne* spring abruptly out of the sea.

North of Carloforte

North of Carloforte, a six-kilometre road ends up at **La Punta**, a bracing spot on San Pietro's exposed northern corner, looking towards the offshore **Isola Piana**. This is the venue for the annual tuna slaughter, but you can see the old *tonnare*, or tuna fisheries, at any time.

ACCOMMODATION — NORTH OF CARLOFORTE

Hotel Paola La Punta Tonnare ☎ 0781 850 098, ⓦ hotel paola.fotorossi.com. Signposted off the road to La Punta, 3km north of Carloforte and about a 10min walk from the sea, this three-star hotel enjoys fantastic views and an air of deep tranquillity. There's a good terrace restaurant, too. Closed Nov–March. **€80**

Portovesme and Portoscuso

On the mainland coast facing San Pietro, the smoking stacks of **PORTOVESME** are the biggest blot on the otherwise undeveloped west coast of Sulcis. Built as an aluminium extraction plant after coal exports dried up following World War II, it is the embarkation point for ferries to Carloforte, and connected to Cágliari by regular buses.

A couple of kilometres north, the low-key fishing port of **PORTOSCUSO** is usually overlooked by island-hoppers, but it still gets quite lively in summer. It has a few old tuna fisheries, a Spanish watchtower and a good beach close by (Portupaleddu), as well as banks, bars and hotels.

ARRIVAL AND DEPARTURE — PORTOVESME AND PORTOSCUSO

By bus ARST buses pull up in Via Palermo in Portoscuso, and at Portovesme's port. There are services from both places to Carbónia (Mon–Sat 9 daily, Sun 4 daily; 40min) and Iglésias (Mon–Sat 6 daily, Sun 4 daily; 50min), which both offer onward services to Cágliari.
By ferry Saremar (☎ 0781 854 005, ⓦ saremar.it) operates ferries between Portovesme and Carloforte (San Pietro) all year. The 30min crossing runs hourly from 6am, with last departures from Portovesme at midnight in summer, 10.20pm in winter, and from Carloforte at 11.10pm in summer, 9.10pm in winter.

ACCOMMODATION AND EATING

La Ghinghetta Via Cavour 26, Portoscuso ☎ 0781 508 143, ⓦ laghinghetta.com. Small, refined and romantic, this very fancy restaurant is renowned for its seafood, which is marvellous but steeply priced – first courses are €10–18, mains are €20–25, and there are set-price menus at €50 and €60. The *antipasti* alone are worth the visit, and reservations are essential. There are rooms, too, overlooking the sea. April–Oct daily 12.30–3pm & 8pm–midnight. **€145**
Panorama Via Giúlio Césare, Portoscuso ☎ 0781 508 077, ⓦ panoramahotel.cortehotels.it. Best budget choice in town is this smart, fairly modern hotel on the portside (rooms overlooking the port cost slightly extra). **€59**

Carbónia

Mussolini's push for self-sufficiency in the 1930s led to a series of initiatives to boost Sardinia's economy, the most ambitious of which was the founding of **CARBÓNIA** in 1938 as a coal-mining centre. With the dwindling of mining operations since the 1950s, mainly due to the costs of extraction and the poor quality of "Sulcis coal", the town has lost much of its *raison d'être*, but it's still worth a visit to sense the Duce's presence in the orderly streets of regimented workers' houses and to see a trio of first-rate museums.

Carbónia now has a high level of unemployment, which gives the place a somewhat somnolent air. At the centre of town, idiosyncratic **Piazza Roma** is dominated by the mud-brown tower of San Ponziano (a copy of the campanile of the cathedral of Aquileia) and the stout, four-square *Municipio*. Most of the town's activity, however, is concentrated on Viale Gramsci, a modern shopping street leading off from the top of the piazza – though any vitality that this might possess is soon dissipated as it gives way to anonymous, right-angled residential quarters.

Museo Archeologico

Villa Sulcis, Via Nápoli• April–Sept Tues–Sun 10am–2pm & 3–7pm, daily in Aug; Oct–March Wed–Sun 10am–3pm • €5, or €9 with Museo Paleoambienti Sulcitani and Monte Sirai • ☏ 0781 64 040, Ⓦ meditinera.it

Sited within Carbónia's Giardino Púbblico, the **Museo Archeologico** consists mainly of finds from Monte Sirai (see p.102). The most noteworthy exhibits are from the tombs found in the necropolis there: bone, silver and gold ornaments from the sixth century BC, an iron dagger and a necklace made of bone and shells. In one corner of the museum, a computer gives a good overview of the excavations, allowing you to view the site as it must have once appeared and home in on details, with full explanations. There are also objects from farther afield, including a smattering of pre-nuraghic items from the so-called Bonnanaro culture – necklaces and domestic implements – and Phoenician and Carthaginian amphorae from Sant'Antíoco.

Museo dei Paleoambienti Sulcitani

Località Serbariu • April–Sept Tues–Sun 10am–2pm & 3–7pm, daily in Aug; Oct–March Wed–Sun 10am–3pm • €4, or €9 with Museo Archeologico and Monte Sirai • ☏ 0781 662 199, Ⓦ meditinera.it

Across town, signposted off the SS126 to the west of Carbónia, the ex-mining centre of Serbariu hosts the **Museo Paleoambienti Sulcitani**, packed with a surprisingly engaging collection of rock specimens, fossils and caving bric-a-brac. The Sulcis area holds the oldest fossils anywhere in Italy, and the display is augmented by non-Italian material donated from around the world. The paleontological section progresses in chronological order, from trilobites from 590–225 million years ago, to ammonites from the Mesozoic era (225–65 million years ago), followed by corals, fish, fossilized wood and even four ants set in amber. From the Quaternary period (about a million years ago) a fossilized tree trunk, a skeletal reconstruction of the *Prolagus sardus* rodent unique to Sardinia (a sort of tailless rabbit extinct for the last thousand years) and the jaws and tusk of a dwarf elephant from the Palermo area take us up to the present era. The speleological collection consists mainly of photos and diagrams of local cave complexes, with glass cases displaying caving equipment.

Museo del Carbone

Località Serbariu • Late June to late Sept daily 10am–7pm; late Sept to late June Tues–Sun 10am–6pm • €6, or €10 with Museo Archeologico, Museo Paleoambienti Sulcitani and Monte Sirai • ☏ 0781 62 727, Ⓦ museodelcarbone.it

You can delve into the area's industrial history at the **Museo del Carbone**, or museum of coal, housed within the Serbariu mine itself, where various subterranean chambers and tunnels can be explored on a guided tour (English spoken). Modern installations illustrate the history of mining in the area, and photographs and films vividly bring to life the pitiful working conditions endured by the miners until the mine's closure in the 1960s.

2

By train The train station lies a couple of kilometres west of Piazza Roma, to which it's connected by buses (Mon–Sat every 30min).

Destinations Cágliari (every 1–2hr, some with change at Villamassargia-Domusnovas; 1hr 5min); Iglésias (every 1–2hr, with change at Villamassargia-Domusnovas; 35min).

By bus All out-of-town buses stop in Piazza Roma.

Destinations Cágliari (Mon–Sat 3 daily; 1hr 30min–3hr); Iglésias (Mon–Sat 14 daily, Sun 7 daily; 45min–1hr); Portovesme (Mon–Sat 8 daily, Sun 4 daily; 40min); Sant'Antíoco (7–9 daily; 30min).

ACCOMMODATION AND EATING

★ **Aquarius** Via Sardegna 3 ☎ 0781 662 143, ⊚ aquarius hotel.it. A sky-blue *pensione* with friendly management and well-equipped rooms. There's a decent restaurant, too, with idiosyncratic decor and moderate prices (the tourist menu is €17.50). €80

Fusionbar Via delle Poste ☎ 0781 673 495. For a sit down, a daytime snack or an evening aperitif, try this stylish but unpretentious modern bar off the top end of Viale Gramsci. Salads, panini and pastries are available, and

the staff are young and friendly. Mon–Sat 9am–2am.

Tanit Località Sirai ☎ 0781 673 793, ⊚ tanit.tv. Outside town on the Portovesme road, this hotel complex represents great value as well as offering interest in the form of an array of rural and agricultural tools and artefacts displayed within. There's wi-fi, a pool and two restaurants, including one outdoors for barbecues. Daily noon–4pm & 8pm–midnight; €70

Monte Sirai

Four kilometres northwest of Carbónia off the SS126 Iglésias road, a signposted turning leads up to the high, flat top of **Monte Sirai**. Phoenicians occupied the site around the eighth century BC, having ejected a pre-existent nuraghic settlement, and they were displaced in turn by Carthaginians at the end of the sixth century BC, who made this their principal military base on the island. The Romans then occupied the site, but abandoned it at the end of the second century AD for reasons that have never been identified.

The strategic advantages of the location are immediately obvious: from a height of nearly 200m, it dominates the surrounding tracts of sea and land for an immense distance, taking in the islands of Sant'Antíoco and San Pietro – come at sunset for the most exquisite panorama.

Archeological site

Località Sirai • April–Sept Tues–Sun 10am–7pm, daily in Aug; Oct–March Wed–Sun 10am–3pm • €5, €6 including tour, or €9 with Museo Archeologico and Museo Paleoambienti Sulcitani in Carbónia • ☎ 0781 64 040 or ☎ 320 571 8454, ⊚ meditinera.it

In a glorious location, with dwarf palms and olive trees bent almost double under the force of the *maestrale* wind, the **archeological site** of Monte Sirai was first excavated by a Tunisian team in 1966. Three streets of terraced houses were unearthed, of which only the foundations are now visible, everything else, made of mud and straw, having long since disappeared. More recently, the **tombs** of two substantial necropolises have come to light, many marked with the symbols of Tanit (or Tinit), the Phoenician goddess: a circle, horizontal line and triangle, looking something like a character from *Charlie Brown*. Some of the tombs can be entered, and you can see Tanit's symbol – for some reason upside down – in tomb number five. Apart from the red rubble of the crumbled walls, little else remains of the Phoenician/Carthaginian settlement, the major finds now on display in Carbónia's archeological museum. Guided **tours** in English or Italian lasting an hour or more are available, which will point out and explain some of the most interesting features of the site.

Iglésias

Surrounded by mine-shafts and quarries gouged out of the red rock, the principal city of the Iglesiente region, **IGLÉSIAS**, makes an appealing stop, its Spanish-tinged atmosphere especially evident during its flamboyant Easter festivities. Though it lacks much tourist infrastructure, the inland town is the biggest and liveliest in the area, with a handful of medieval churches worth visiting and the impressive ruins of a huge mine on the outskirts. The town is also a viable base for exploring the clutch of beach resorts a short drive away, as these have little in the way of accommodation.

The focus of the action in the modern town is the central **Piazza Sella**, lively by day and a noisy rendezvous every evening. At the top end of the square, what's left of the ruined Aragonese (originally Pisan) **Castello Salvaterra** crowns a knoll, its impact softened by landscaped flowerbeds. The castle is usually closed except for occasional performances and exhibitions.

The old town's labyrinth of traffic-free lanes and squares runs off Piazza Sella's western side. The main Corso Matteotti threads through the heart of the *città vecchia* almost as far as **Piazza Município**, site of the town hall and cathedral, and one of the few really classic Italian piazzas in this part of the island. It's a harmonious composition, with the town hall taking up one entire side, opposite the cathedral and bishop's palace, which are joined by an elegant enclosed bridge.

2

● RESTAURANTS	
Gazebo Il Medioevale	4
Sa Matracca	2
Villa di Chiesa	3
Volters & Murion	1

■ ACCOMMODATION	
Artu	2
Euro Hotel	3
Is Grifoneddus	1
Sa Lolla	4

UGOLINO DELLA GHERARDESCA

Iglésias enjoyed its greatest prosperity under the rule of the **Gherardesca family**, one of the foremost Tuscan dynasties, based in or around Pisa. At the beginning of the thirteenth century, they led the pro-imperial Ghibelline party of the Pisan republic against the pro-papal Guelf party led by the Visconti family of Milan, but **Ugolino della Gherardesca** (died 1289) became the most reviled member of the family by switching allegiance from the Ghibellines to the Guelfs. Having assumed control of Pisa, he soon alienated his allies and was eventually accused of treason in 1288 by the archbishop Ruggieri degli Ubaldini, who wanted to revive the republican order. Imprisoned in the tower of Gualandi along with two of his sons and two of his grandsons, Ugolino was said to have eaten his own children before himself dying of starvation, an event depicted in numerous works of art, most famously in Dante's *Divina Commedia*, in which the poet encounters the tyrant frozen in the ice of the ninth circle of hell (*Inferno*, canto 33); Archbishop Ruggieri is also there.

Ugolino is remembered with more affection in Iglésias, where, for the purposes of exploiting the area's mineral resources, he introduced Tuscan methods of planning and political organization. The resulting **statutory code** of local rights was enshrined in a *Breve*, or law book, a meticulously drafted volume which can be viewed on application in the town's Archivio Stórico, in Via delle Cárceri, near the church of Santa Maria delle Grázie (Mon–Fri 9am–1pm, also Mon, Wed & Fri 3.30–5.30pm; ☎0781 24 850). Ugolino's son, Guelfo, was imprisoned in the **Castello di Acquafredda**, a thirteenth-century fortress on a jagged elevation 4km south of Siliqua, off the SS130.

The more down-to-earth side of Iglésias is represented by its Art Nouveau-style mining institute on Via Roma, home to a mining museum, and by the Monteponi works outside town (see box, p.106). In summer, **outdoor concerts** take place in Piazza Municipio, Piazza Sella, the castle and other points of the old town – the tourist office has a full list of events.

Brief history

Iglésias owes both its present name and its former name of Villa di Chiesa to its numerous churches, of which a good number survive. Its livelihood has depended more on **mining** operations, however. The town was founded in the thirteenth century by the notorious Pisan Count Ugolino della Gherardesca (see box above), who reopened the old Roman mines. Gold, silver, iron, zinc and lead have all been extracted from the surrounding hills at different times, making Iglésias the chief mining centre of Sardinia, despite bearing little resemblance to the stereotyped image of a grimy mining town.

The Duomo

Piazza Município • Currently closed for restoration

Iglésias' **Duomo** shows a mixture of Pisan and Aragonese styles, reflecting the two dominant (and warring) powers in the region during the Middle Ages. The bell in the squat tower was cast by the great Tuscan sculptor Andrea Pisano in 1337. The main interest in the low-vaulted interior is the spectacular, gilded altarpiece in the left transept, carved in the seventeenth century to hold the relics of St Antiochus, which had been removed from the church at Sant'Antíoco during a spate of pirate raids and brought here for safekeeping. However, the bones – which were kept behind the curtain in the middle panel – were forcibly reclaimed in the nineteenth century after the clerics of Iglésias refused to return them. An image of the saint adorns the front of the sculpture, his hands blackened, according to legend, from the barrel of pitch in which he had been forced to hide to escape persecution; he appears again in the painting behind the altar in the bottom left corner, opposite St Clare.

San Francesco

Piazza San Francesco • Daily 8am–noon & 5–8pm

Across the piazza from the Duomo, take Via Pullo to reach the church of **San Francesco**, a predominantly Catalan-Gothic structure built between the fourteenth and sixteenth centuries. Behind a minimalist facade of pinkish trachyte stone, perforated by three circular windows, the nave has a wooden ceiling and seven chapels on either side, each framed by an ogival arch. The first chapel on the left shows a recently restored *Retablo della Vergine*, a lovely sixteenth-century triptych of the Madonna with saints by Antioco Mainas.

2

Santa Maria delle Grazie

Piazza Manzoni • Daily 7.30am–noon & 5.30–8pm

Squeezed between houses off Via Zecca, the tiny church of **Santa Maria delle Grazie** has a medieval stone facade incongruously topped by a pink Baroque upper portion. There's a good, antique-looking painted wooden panel inside depicting the Madonna enthroned with archangels, though this is in fact modern. To the right is a painting of San Saturnino of Cágliari, to whom the church was originally dedicated. Since 1925 the church has been run by Capuchin monks based in the annexed convent.

ARRIVAL AND DEPARTURE

IGLÉSIAS

By car Parking is not always easy to find, but should be available fairly centrally in blue-line spaces, for which tickets from parking attendants, meters and some *tabacchini* cost €0.50 for the first hour, then €1/hr subsequently.

By train The train station is on Via San Salvatore, a short walk southeast of the centre. You need to change at Villamassargia-Domusnovas for some trains to and from Cágliari, and for all trains to and from Carbónia.

Destinations Cágliari (every 1–2hr; 45min–1hr); Carbónia (Mon–Sat hourly, Sun 10 daily; 30min).

By bus Most out-of-town buses stop at the Giardini Púbblici,

on Via Oristano, a 5min walk from Piazza Sella; tickets and timetables are available from the bars fronting the square. Buses to and from Cágliari and some other places stop on nearby Piazza Mercato and at the train station instead.

Destinations Buggerru (4–5 daily; 1hr 10min); Cágliari (Mon–Sat 1 daily; 1hr 15min); Carbónia (Mon–Sat 11 daily, Sun 6 daily; 45min); Fontanamare (3–4 daily; 25min); Masua (2–3 daily; 40min); Nébida (2–3 daily; 35min); Portixeddu (4–5 daily; 1hr 5min); Portoscuso/Portovesme (Mon–Sat 10–11 daily, Sun 7 daily; 50min–1hr 5min); Sant'Antíoco (2–4 daily; 1hr 10min).

INFORMATION

Tourist office On Via Mazzini in the old quarter (April, May & Oct Thurs–Sat 10am–12.30pm & 4–8pm;

June–Sept daily 10am–12.30pm & 4–9pm; ☎0781 274 448, ⓦsulcisiglesiente.eu).

ACCOMMODATION

None of the lodgings in **central Iglésias** is ideal, but the town and its surroundings have a few options that are fine for a night or two. Alternatively, there are good options in and around **Gonnesa**, 7km south (see p.107).

IGLÉSIAS FESTIVALS

Iglésias comes into its own during its famous **Easter festivities**, when processions weave solemnly between the churches of the old town in a tradition dating back to the seventeenth century. Marching to the rhythm of traditional instruments, the white-robed, sometimes cowled, cortege (the dress is known as *baballotti*) performs this ritual during the whole of Easter week, though the highlight is the second procession, Christ's funeral, on Good Friday evening. Another traditional ceremony, **I Candelieri**, takes place on or around August 15. As in the better-known festa at Sássari that occurs on the same day (see box, p.207), seven (sometimes eight) huge candles, one for each section of the city, are borne through the streets in the evening, from the chiesa del Collegio to the cathedral, to be returned eight days later. If you're thinking of visiting Iglésias at either of these times, book your accommodation first.

Artu Piazza Sella 15 ☎ 0781 22 546, ⓦ hotelartuiglesias
.it. In a premium location in the centre of town, this family-
run hotel has small but clean and functional rooms, friendly
staff, a bar, a decent restaurant and a small garage (for a
small charge) – but it's desperately old-fashioned. **€90**
Euro Hotel Via Fratelli Bandiera 34 ☎ 0781 22 643,
ⓦ eurohoteliglesias.it. Completely over-the-top period
hotel, dripping with chandeliers, Rococo furniture and bad
art. It's certainly luxurious, though, with spacious rooms,
and prices drop in low season. Parking available. **€90**
Is Grifoneddus Via Ozieri 24 ☎ 349 383 9452,

ⓦ bebisgrifoneddus.it. In the heart of the *centro stórico*,
this B&B in a renovated townhouse has traditional Sard
touches to offset the modern decor. Rooms are clean and
airy, with en-suite bathrooms. **€60**
Sa Lolla Via Mameli 2–4 ☎ 0781 251 120, ⓦ hotel
salolla.it. Bland hotel south of the centre, with twelve
small but modern rooms, fully equipped with a/c, minibars
and free wi-fi. Excursions in the Iglesiente can be arranged,
and two bikes are available to guests. The same family runs
the *Le Due Anfore* B&B on the top floor, with more basic
accommodation (€50). **€60**

EATING AND DRINKING

Iglésias has no outstanding **restaurants**, but there are several places where you can eat reasonably well and cheaply. For
picnic ingredients, there's an indoor **market** open Monday to Saturday mornings just up from Piazza Sella on Via Gramsci.

Gazebo Il Medioevale Via Musio 21 ☎ 0781 30 871.
Full of atmosphere, this medieval-style, brick-vaulted hall
off Corso Matteotti offers a regular restaurant menu,
including *trofie alla Tabarkina* (pasta with prawns, tomato,
garlic, basil and white wine) and some innovative fish
dishes. The bill should be €25–35 each. Mon–Sat noon–
2.30pm & 8–11pm, open daily in Aug.
★ **Sa Matracca** Via Repubblica 46 ☎ 320 704 4741.
Intimate *osteria* with exposed stone walls (surviving from
the Roman, Pisan and Aragonese eras), wooden ceilings
and a well. You can eat outside in summer. Regional

specialities include tasty *fregola alla pescatora, gnocchetti
alla campidanese* and horsemeat, while the signature
pasta dish, *trofie Sa Matracca*, is superb. Mains are €10–15,
set-price menus €15–30. Daily noon–2pm & 7.30pm–
midnight; may close lunchtime.
Villa di Chiesa Piazza Municipio 2 ☎ 0781 31 641. This
restaurant enjoys the best location in town, especially
in summer when you can dine in the square. The menu
includes a short selection of fish and meat dishes – the
fresh pasta is recommended – and pizzas are also served
in the evening. Prices are reasonable: €8–12 for starters,

MINING THE IGLESIENTE

Travellers in the Iglesiente region can't fail to notice the numerous **mineworks** dramatically
pitting the landscape, though there's plenty more that's out of sight – all testament to the
mineral wealth excavated from the mountains since earliest times. If you're intrigued by the
industrial archeology of the area, you can view some excellent museums and visit many
of the old works on guided tours. We give details of some of the best museums below;
combined tickets are sometimes available for those planning to see more than one. The
website ⓦ parcogeominerario.eu provides **information** on mine sites throughout Sardinia.

Galleria Henry Buggerru. Dating from 1860, this site
provides insights into the life of the thriving community
that worked here until the mine's closure in 1991.
Cooperativa Igea (☎ 0781 491 300 or ☎ 348 154 9556,
ⓦ igeaspa.it) arranges guided tours (€8) that need to
be booked ahead.
Ingurtosu Ghostly remains of an old mining settlement
located off the SS126 southwest of Gúspini (see p.109).
Monteponi Iglésias Evocative site outside town, a
vast, desolate area of mineworkings abandoned in 1992.
Contact Cooperativa Igea (see above) for guided tours (€8).
Montevécchio ☎ 0781 973 173, ⓦ miniera
montevecchio.it. This venerable site, 8km west of
Gúspini, is one of Sardinia's oldest, and became Italy's
most important mine in the 1860s for its lead ore.
Easter–Sept daily 10am–1pm & 4–8pm; Oct–April

Sat & Sun 10am–noon & 3–5pm; last tour 1hr
before closing; €6.
Museo del Carbone Carbónia. Essential stop for an
all-round view of Sardinia's coal industry (see p.101).
Museo dell'Arte Mineraria Via Roma, Iglésias
☎ 328 809 4091 or ☎ 338 922 1392 ⓦ museoarte
mineraria.it. Displays mining machinery, models, photos
and reconstructions of the pit-face as well as a collection
of minerals dug out of the local rock. June–Sept Sat &
Sun 6.30–8.30pm; call to visit at other periods; €4.
Museo delle Macchine da Miniera Masua. Coastal
site, displaying extraction machinery and tools. Contact
Cooperativa Igea (see above) for visits (€3).
Porto Flavia Masua This mine on the coast dates from
1924. Contact Cooperativa Igea (see above) for guided
tours (€8).

€12–20 for mains. Tues–Sun 12.30–3pm & 7.30–11pm, open Mon eve July–Sept.
Volters & Murion Piazza Collegio ☎ 0781 33 788. Pub and restaurant with outdoor seating, offering simple snacks, including pizzas, pastas and meat dishes (fixed-price menus €10 and €15). Also a nice place to drop by for a late-night drink. Tues–Sun 10am–3pm & 6pm–1am, open Mon July & Aug; food served noon–2.30pm & 7pm–midnight.

The Témpio di Antas

2

Località Antas • April, May & Oct daily 9.30am–5.30pm; June daily 9.30am–6.30pm; July–Sept daily 9.30am–7.30pm; Nov–March Tues–Sun 9.30am–4.30pm • €4 • ☎ 0781 580 990 or ☎ 347 817 4989, ⓦ startuno.it • Take any bus running between Iglésias and Fluminimaggiore, then walk 2km from the main road

Fifteen kilometres north of Iglésias, a right turn off the twisty mountain road to Fluminimaggiore (the SS126) wanders down a valley to the remote **Témpio di Antas**, a heavily restored Roman temple built on the site of a nuraghic and later Carthaginian sanctuary. Its Punic origins are thought to date back to around 500 BC, but it probably assumed its final form in the third century AD. As an inscription records, the Romans dedicated the temple to Sardus Pater Babai, a local deity worshipped as the father of the Sards in the kind of synthesis of imperial and local cults that was practised throughout the Roman Empire. The Ionic-style columns are still standing, topped by a simple pediment, and you can see inside the remains of the sacred chambers, while rooms and houses used by the priests and other members of the ethnically mixed population are faintly visible behind. It's an idyllic spot, the air full of the aromas of the *macchia* and the jangle of distant goat bells, spoilt only by the pylons and cables strung across the valley.

Grotta Su Mannau

Località Mannau • Mid-April to Oct daily 9.30am–6.30pm • €10 • ☎ 0781 580 411 or ☎ 347 541 3624, ⓦ sumannau.it • Take any bus running between Iglésias and Fluminimaggiore, then walk 1km from the main road

A little way north of the Témpio di Antas, the **Grotta Su Mannau** is one of the most accessible of the many grottoes scattered throughout this area. A tourist trail penetrates for 800m, enough to see some spectacular rock formations, brilliantly illuminated, while cavers can go on for as far again inside the mountain. Hour-long tours leave every half-hour or so; in winter, groups can visit by booking ahead.

The Iglesiente coast

West of Iglésias, the remote villages and beaches on the coast have few transport links with the outside world, but are easily accessible under your own steam. The villages and resorts here are hardly the attraction: the real appeal is the refreshing emptiness of the coast, either cliff-hung tracts or wildernesses of bare dunes.

Gonnesa and around

GONNESA, 9km southwest of Iglésias, is a fairly unremarkable inland village in and around which are some good accommodation options for visitors to Iglésias and the nearby coast. From the SS126, a road branches 4km west to the long sandy beach at **Fontanamare**, a popular bathing spot with bars and a pizzeria open in summer, but quiet the rest of the time.

ACCOMMODATION AND EATING   **GONNESA AND AROUND**

Frau Via della Pace, Gonnesa ☎ 0781 45 104. In the village centre, this small B&B offers modest but clean accommodation at rock-bottom prices. It's run by a friendly signora who can rustle up a meal at short notice. Rooms are plain and share bathrooms, and breakfast is extra. No credit cards. **€36**

★ **Lo Sperone** Località S'Ortu de Coccu ☎0781 36 247. This relaxed *agriturismo* clearly signposted on the SS126 (opposite the Masua turn-off) is convenient for the Fontanamare beach (see p.107). Six rooms are available, all en suite; in July and Aug half- or full board (€50/person for half-board) or a three-night minimum stay is required. There are also two apartments for weekly rent, and riding is available from the stables. The food is authentic Sardinian country cuisine – non-guests can dine here with prior notice. No credit cards. **€50**

2 Nébida and around

The coastal route continues north along the mainly high and cliffy littoral of the **Golfo di Gonnesa**, one of Sardinia's most scenic stretches of sea and mountain. **NÉBIDA** is the first village you'll meet, perched above the water 3km north of Fontanamare. Next to a public garden and sports ground on the southern approach, a path rounding a cliffy promontory gives access to a **belvedere** offering the area's best views of the sheer coast on either side, as far as the Pan di Zúcchero *scoglio* to the north (see below). Below the path, at the bottom of a four-hundred-step descent, you'll see the ramshackle **Laveria La Mármora**, built in 1897 for the filtering and washing of mine products but now abandoned. At the north end of the village, a small lane dives steeply down to the tiny sandy cove of **Porto Banda**, where two large *faraglioni* – needle-shaped stacks of rock – poke up from the sea.

ACCOMMODATION AND EATING   NÉBIDA

Café del Operaio Belvedere di Nébida ☎338 916 5388. This bar built into a grotto on the cliff path makes a perfect venue for taking in the stirring sea views. Drinks are served until late, and there are snacks too, including *zuppa di cozze* (€9) and beefsteak (€12–14). Easter–Oct daily 7.30am–11.30pm.

Pan di Zúcchero Via Centrale 365 ☎0781 47 114, Ⓦhotelpandizucchero.it. Ideal for a stopover, this unprepossessing but good-value two-star hotel offers plain rooms, including some with great vistas, and self-catering apartments. There's a restaurant with meals for around €35 and excellent sunset views. March–Nov daily 1–2.30pm & 7.30–10.30pm; **€70**

Masua and around

North of Nébida, the mountain road winds 3–4km on to **MASUA**, where there are bars and a pizzeria, and a lovely but restricted **beach** backed by shade-giving rocks and ruined walls. The seascape is dominated by the colossal outcrop known as the **Pan di Zúcchero** (Sugarloaf), whose prodigious white hulk is depicted on countless postcards. Owing its name to its unique shape and colour, it's said to be the oldest such *scoglio*, or rock formation, in Italy.

More huge **mineworks** dominate the knot of houses at Masua, dedicated to extracting zinc and lead, the two main products of this region. One of the old mines and a mining museum can be visited on guided tours (see box, p.106).

Buggerru and around

From Masua, a tortuous road climbs 10km north to reach **BUGGERRU**, a fishing port and tourist resort superimposed on another old mining centre. Once accessible only by sea, Buggerru was largely self-sufficient during its mining days; it was the first place in Sardinia to have a regular electrical system, and the miners enjoyed health and recreational facilities long before such practices were introduced by other companies. As in Masua, you can tour one of the old mines here (see box, p.106).

Away from the regimented marina packed with small pleasure boats, there are some superb **beaches** in the vicinity, including the solitary **Cala Domestica**, a deep, sheltered and sandy inlet 4.5km south of Buggerru. There's a seasonal bar here for refreshments; parking costs €4 per day, and you can hire a parasol and deckchairs for €10 per half-day.

Alternatively, head north to the much wider **Portixeddu**, a sweeping swathe of sand with little or no construction nearby. The road ends a little farther north at **Capo Pécora**, a wild, deserted spot with a small stony beach.

ACCOMMODATION

BUGGERRU AND AROUND

Ortus de Mari Località Portixeddu ☏ 0781 54 964. Less than a kilometre inland of Portixeddu beach, this is the only campsite on this stretch of coast, offering very minimal facilities. There's a bar, hot water and shady trees. Closed Oct–May. Pitches €24

The Costa Verde

There is little that's "green" about the **Costa Verde**, stretching north from Capo Pécora, most of it consisting of arid rock, scrub and sand. Access is from the SS126, either from the village of Gúspini, from where a road twists for 25km to the desolate coast, or, 13km farther south, via the dirt road threading westwards from the deserted mining town of **Ingurtosu**. If your vehicle can stand it, this is the preferable route; it's shorter, and allows a stop at the ghostly ruins of this once vibrant community.

Piscinas

Seven kilometres below Ingurtosu, the road emerges on the coast at **Piscinas**, a barren spot, about as remote as it gets in Sardinia, with superb swimming. Apart from a few traces of nineteenth-century mineworks, there's nothing here but immense sand dunes and an upmarket hotel (see below), though in summer you'll find fast-food kiosks in the vicinity. If you don't want to pay to stay, camping rough is feasible in this out-of-the-way area.

ACCOMMODATION AND EATING

PISCINAS

★ **Hotel Le Dune** Piscinas di Ingurtosu ☏ 070 977 130, ⓦ leduneingurtosu.it. This chic, highly expensive retreat is a fabulous place to hole up for a few days if it's in your price range, or else to indulge in its restaurant (daily 1–2.30pm & 8–10pm), open to anyone and with tables outside – a memorable place to dine at sunset. Alternatively, you can use the bar, which serves panini. There's a minimum one-week stay in high season; rates plummet in low season. Closed mid-Oct to Easter. €290

Marina di Arbus and around

From Piscinas, a dirt road follows the coast north, passing more dune-backed sands and perfect seas, until it meets civilization among the shops, restaurants and holiday homes of **MARINA DI ARBUS**. There are more good beaches here and a couple of kilometres north at **Funtanazza**, lying below and out of sight of an eyesore of a ruined 1950s holiday complex, and reached along a private road that is barred at night but otherwise open to anyone.

From the junction beyond, a winding but scenic road threads inland towards the villages of Gúspini and Arbus, passing through what was once a productive mining area centred on **Montevécchio** (see box, p.106). Ten kilometres east of Montevécchio, **GÚSPINI** has a bank, fuel station and a couple of trattorias to meet all immediate requirements. Continuing east from here, the road crests the ridge of mountains to give long views over the plain of Campidano (see p.112).

Alternatively, heading about 10km north up the coast from Funtanazza, you'll reach a superb, broad sand beach backed by high dunes at **Torre dei Corsari**. The towering cliffs beyond, ending at **Capo Frasca**, are inaccessible by land. Curling eastwards, the road gives access to a causeway/bridge running across the Stagno di Marceddi and into Oristano province (see p.155).

Campidano, La Marmilla and Sarrabus

116 Uta

116 San Sperate

117 Sanluri

118 Sárdara and around

119 Villanovaforru and around

120 Las Plassas

122 Su Nuraxi

124 Tuili and around

125 La Giara di Gésturi

125 Dolianova

126 Gerrei

127 Villasimius and around

129 The Costa Rei

129 Castiadas and around

130 Monte dei Sette Fratelli

131 Muravera and around

CAPO CARBONARA

Campidano, La Marmilla and Sarrabus

The regions to the north and east of Cágliari are remarkably diverse in both tone and physical appearance, and include some essential stops as well as several worthwhile places well off the beaten track. To the northwest of Cágliari, Campidano is Sardinia's most extensive plain and its richest agricultural region, nourished by numerous rivers and benefiting from past drainage and anti-malaria schemes. North and east of here, the flat uniformity of Campidano gives way to the hill country of La Marmilla, location of some of the island's most important nuraghic remains. In Sarrabus, the region occupying Sardinia's southeastern corner, the farmlands give way to the inhospitable, jagged peaks of the Sette Fratelli mountains, much of the range too desolate even for shepherds, but with abundant birdlife and excellent hiking. The emptiness and desolation of this inland rugged wilderness are far removed from the holiday ambience of the coast, whose rocky indentations shelter some of Sardinia's finest beaches.

Much of this disparate territory could be explored on excursions from Cágliari, or on brief detours on your way farther afield. The main route north of the capital, for example, the SS131 – still known as the Carlo Felice highway after the king who commissioned it in the 1820s – brings you right past **Sanluri**, home to the well-preserved but rather diminutive medieval castle that houses what must be Sardinia's quirkiest museum collection. Farther up the SS131, you could pause at the villages of **Sárdara** and **Villanovaforru** for their diverse historical remnants. From here it's an easy ride through La Marmilla to the extensive complex of **Su Nuraxi**, the largest and most famous of all Sardinia's nuraghic sites. North of here, La Marmilla ends at the high plateau of **Giara di Gésturi**, a protected area of woods and scrubland that shelter a variety of birdlife and other fauna and flora, most famously a breed of miniature wild pony.

On the eastern edge of Campidano, due north of Cágliari, the agricultural centre of **Dolianova** is worth visiting chiefly for its Romanesque ex-cathedral. Again, this would make an easy stop on the road north into the mountainous **Gerrei** region, a magnificently rugged and empty stretch of country that holds the **Nuraghe Arrubiu**, another of the island's most impressive prehistoric monuments. The mountains dominating the interior of Sarrabus can be admired from the SS125, the twisty road linking Cágliari to the island's eastern seaboard, but they are best appreciated from close up, preferably on a hike. Development is sporadic along the Sarrabus coast, but gets more intense around the main resort here, **Villasimius**, as well as farther north on the popular **Costa Rei** and around the inland town of Muravera. In between the pockets of construction lies some of the island's most alluring coastline, and outside July and August you'll have the beaches pretty much to yourself.

A walk in the Monte dei Sette Fratelli
p.131

Muravera's festivals p.132

CASTELLO DI ELEONORA D'ARBOREA

Highlights

❶ Chiesa di Santa Maria, Uta Slightly off the beaten track, this perfectly preserved medieval church is southern Sardinia's Romanesque gem. **See p.116**

❷ Castello di Eleonora d'Arborea, Sanluri The delightfully eclectic collection of historical and military bric-a-brac in this well-preserved medieval castle provides a thoroughly entertaining couple of hours. **See p.117**

❸ Su Nuraxi The largest and most intriguing of Sardinia's ancient nuraghic complexes is an essential stop on any tour of the island. **See p.122**

❹ Giara di Gésturi This distinctive high basalt plateau rising above La Marmilla is teeming with wildlife, from rare orchids to miniature wild horses – perfect for a breather. **See p.125**

❺ Costa Rei beaches It's a modern, somewhat pricey holiday zone, but you'll enjoy some superlative swimming from flawless sandy beaches on this coast, as well as secluded coves. **See p.129**

❻ Sette Fratelli mountains Stretch your legs in one of Sardinia's great scenic wildernesses, easily accessible by road. **See p.130**

HIGHLIGHTS ARE MARKED ON THE MAP ON PP.114–115

HIGHLIGHTS
1. Chiesa di Santa Maria, Uta
2. Castello di Eleonora d'Arborea, Sanluri
3. Su Nuraxi
4. Giara di Gésturi
5. Costa Rei beaches
6. Sette Fratelli mountains

0 — 10 kilometres

Tortolì

PROVINCIA DI OGLIASTRA

del endasa

Perdasdefogu

Tertenia

Nuraghe rubiu

Escalaplano

Quirra

Ballao

SS387

San Nicolo Gerrei

Flumendosa

SS387

PROVINCIA CÁGLIARI

San Vito

Villaputzu

SS125

Muravera

Porto Corallo

Nuraghe Asoru

San Giovanni

Sa Picocca

Torre Salinas

Colostrai

Feraxi

ABUS

Burcei

6

MONTE DEI SETTE FRATELLI

Capo Ferrato

SS125

Castiadas

Costa Rei

5

Capitana

SP17

a Regina

FORESTA DI MINNIMINNI

Cala Sinzias

Torre delle Stelle

Villasimius

Solanas

Serpentara

Golfo di Carbonara

Stagno di Notteri

Simius

Spiaggia Del Riso

Capo Carbonara

Isola dei Cávoli

N

CAMPIDANO, LA MARMILLA & SARRABUS

GETTING AROUND	CAMPIDANO, LA MARMILLA AND SARRABUS

By car The dual-carriageway SS131, Sardinia's main north–south artery, is fast and convenient for Campidano and La Marmilla, while the SS125 is a slower link to Muravera and the eastern coast – though there is ongoing work to improve sections of this route. A car is best for Giara di Gésturi and to view the *nuraghi* of Genna Maria and Arrubiu.

By train From Cágliari's Gottardo (Monserrato) station,

there's a frequent service to Dolianova and twice-daily trains run to Ísili and Mandas (no trains on Sun). For more info, consult ARST on ☎ 800 865 042, ⑩ arst.sardegna.it.

By bus ARST (see above) runs frequent services from Cágliari to Uta, San Sperate, Sanluri, Dolianova, Villasimius and Muravera, plus a very sketchy service to Barúmini (for Su Nuraxi).

Uta

Campidano lacks scenic drama, but compensates with its range of cultural and historical sites, not least what is arguably the loveliest Romanesque church in southern Sardinia, located outside the agricultural centre of **UTA**, 15km northwest of Cágliari. Unless you're here during the last week of August, when the **Festa di Santa Lucia** is celebrated with a procession to the church of peasant carts, or *traccas*, there's little else to detain you here.

Chiesa di Santa Maria

Via Santa Maria • Occasionally open, call to arrange access • ☎ 347 876 1173

Built by Vittorini monks from Marseille around 1140, the **chiesa di Santa Maria** stands in the country outside the eastern end of the village, facing a landscaped area that was formerly a cemetery. Its light stonework is embellished with arcading running round under the roof, at the base of which human heads, rams, dogs, stags, calves and various abstract devices are chiselled. This florid Provençal style is fused with Pisan elements, apparent in the portals and the bare interior, where two columns of perfect round arches have well-restored capitals. The grey stone interior is in keeping with the outside – unadorned, with arches supported by columns from the Roman era.

ARRIVAL AND DEPARTURE	UTA

By bus ARST buses to and from Cágliari (Mon–Sat 6 daily, Sun 1 daily; 45min) stop in Piazza Santa Giusta, in Uta's centre.

San Sperate

Ten kilometres northeast of Uta, the village of **SAN SPERATE** is famous for its **murals** and **sculptures**. Dating from the late 1960s and executed by local artists in a variety of styles, including trompe l'oeil, the four hundred or so murals depict domestic and rural scenes that evoke an older, simpler and more parochial society. The tradition was probably initiated by **Pinuccio Sciola**, Sardinia's best-known contemporary sculptor, born in San Sperate in 1942. Several open-air sculptures by him are also on show, almost exclusively carved from the local trachyte – its mutating, seasoned textures particularly appropriate for Sciola's grand pieces, which resemble menhirs or even nuraghic Giants' Tombs burial stones.

ARRIVAL AND INFORMATION	SAN SPERATE

By bus There's a good ARST service to and from Cágliari (Mon–Sat 1–2 hourly, Sun 5–7 daily; 45min). Change at

Decimomannu for connections to or from Uta.

Tourist information See ⑩ turismo.sansperate.net.

EATING

Ada Via Cágliari 21 ☎ 070 960 0972. An excellent spot to sample traditional *campidanese* cooking, offering a rich

assortment of dishes using strictly seasonal local produce, for example ravioli stuffed with goat's meat and artichokes.

Pizzas and a huge range of "artisan" beers are also available. Opt for a fixed-price menu; otherwise count on around €30

for a full meal without drinks. Mon–Sat 12.30–2.30pm & 7.30–10.30pm; closed late Aug.

Sanluri

Occupying a commanding position in the hinterland between the *giudicati* of Arborea and Cágliari, Campidano's biggest town, **SANLURI**, 45km northwest of the capital, grew up around the thirteenth-century castle that is named after Eleonora, the warrior queen who spent a lifetime in arms against the Aragonese (see box, p.142) and who briefly resided here.

While you're here, call in at any Sanluri bakery for a loaf of the local **bread** – huge and flavoursome, it's renowned throughout Campidano.

Castello di Eleonora d'Arborea

3

Via Generale Villa Santa • Daily 9.30am–1pm & 4–8pm, 3–7pm in winter • €5 • ☎ 070 930 7184, ⓦ castellodisanluri.it

A high, square keep surrounded by fir trees off the main road slicing through the centre of Sanluri, the **Castello di Eleonora d'Arborea** was a linchpin of the Sard-Aragonese conflict that embroiled the island in the fourteenth and fifteenth centuries. The castle was the venue for a peace treaty signed by the Aragonese king, Pedro IV, and Mariano IV, father of Eleonora d'Arborea – though this turned out to be merely a breathing space. In 1409, following Eleonora's death, Pedro's son, Martino, won a definitive victory at Sanluri against forces commanded by the new *giudice*, a defeat that marked the end of Arborea's resistance and was followed by the swift occupation of almost the whole island by Aragonese forces. The castle later became home to the noble Villa Santa family, who amassed a motley collection of military and historical memorabilia as well as various works of art.

Museo Risorgimentale

Modern artillery pieces and copies of antique catapults arranged around the castle give some hint of what lies within. In fact, the so-called **Museo Risorgimentale** has little to do with the Risorgimento – Italy's struggle for independence in the nineteenth century – though much of it has a strong military flavour, most markedly in the Salone delle Milizie, once the stables of the castle, which now hold a fascinating collection of curios, portraits and trophies assembled by the local count, Generale Nino Villa Santa, and augmented by the donations of various enthusiasts in the 1920s. Museum guides will point out idiosyncratic mementos and relate details of the lives of the soldiers who fought in the Brigata Sássari, a renowned infantry brigade that suffered massive casualties in the long Alpine campaign of 1918. War-torn banners, yellowed photographs and newspapers and even a primitive bicycle are jumbled together, jostling for space with a veritable arsenal of weaponry. Other items are from the little-known Italian-Turkish war of 1911–12, from Mussolini's Ethiopian campaign of 1936 and from World War II, including, surprisingly, a batch of English postcards of the period.

The first floor and roof

Upstairs, the rest of the castle proves as absorbing as the military exhibits. Reached by a fine staircase, the succession of beamed rooms are richly furnished with rugs, tables, dressers and paintings, mainly from the eighteenth and nineteenth centuries, and including such items as an iron bed from the 1700s belonging to the Genoan Doria dynasty. In the study you can see fragments of writings by controversial Italian man of letters and swashbuckling patriot, Gabriele d'Annunzio, while an adjoining room displays a sabre belonging to Joachim Murat, Napoleon's brother-in-law, and drinking glasses used by Josephine (marked "J"). The next room has a collection of around

350 wax figurines, some dating as far back as the sixteenth century, and some by the master in the field Clemente Susini, whose ingenious creations can also be seen in Cágliari (see p.63). The most arresting waxwork, however, is by Gaetano Zumbo (1656–1701), "La Putrefazione" – a horrifically graphic study of a plague victim, half-consumed by rats and worms.

Before leaving, climb up to the castle's **roof** for a good view of the town and country (you may need to ask one of the museum staff).

ARRIVAL AND DEPARTURE
SANLURI

By bus Sanluri is easy to reach on any of the frequent buses that pass this way from just about everywhere.
Destinations Barúmini (Mon–Sat 4–5 daily; 30–55min); Cágliari (Mon–Sat hourly, Sun 5 daily; 50min–1hr 30min);

Oristano (Mon–Sat 2 daily; 1hr 10min); Sárdara (Mon–Sat 12–14 daily, Sun 3 daily; 15min); Tuili (Mon–Sat 4–5 daily; 35–55min).

ACCOMMODATION AND EATING

Mirage Via Carlo Felice ☎070 930 7100, ⊛hotel mirage.biz. At the northern entry into town, this modern, business-traveller's hotel is the area's best accommodation option, with spacious, well-equipped rooms, though breakfast is pretty functional. **€70**

Rosy Via Carlo Felice 510 ☎070 930 7957. For lunches

or evening meals, head for this ristorante/pizzeria just along from the *Mirage*, with outdoor seating in summer. It offers pizzas in three sizes and a good range of local food – all dishes are €7–12, and there's a €12 tourist menu. Daily except Tues 12.30–3.30pm & 7pm–midnight.

Sárdara and around

Nine kilometres northwest of Sanluri on the SS131, the otherwise unexceptional village of **SÁRDARA** and its environs hold a handful of relics from the nuraghic, Roman and medieval periods that are connected to the local therapeutic waters. The village also has the attractive fourteenth-century church of **San Gregorio**, its tall, narrow facade with a fine rose window a graceful blend of Romanesque and Gothic, while late-Gothic workmanship dominates in the fifteenth-century church of **Sant'Anastasia,** at Sárdara's highest point.

Two kilometres south, the squat ruins of the **Castello di Monreale** crown a hillock overlooking the surrounding plain – an evocative backdrop, though the sparse remains don't merit closer exploration.

Témpio Nurágico

Piazza Anastasia • Tues–Sun 9am–1pm & 5–8pm, 4–7pm in winter • €2.60, or €4.50 with Museo Cívico • ☎ 070 938 6011

Surrounding Sárdara's church of Sant'Anastasia is a much more ancient centre of worship, the **Témpio Nurágico**. Constructed in basalt and calcareous bricks, the site dates from around the eighth century BC and centres on a sacred well, known locally as Funtana de Is Dolus, or "Fountain of Pains", a reference to the various ailments its waters were supposed to cure. The remains of several nuraghic buildings clustered around the well have yielded some notable finds, including heavily ornate water jugs, some of them displayed in the town's museum.

Museo Cívico

Piazza Libertà • Tues–Sun 9am–1pm & 5–8pm, 4–7pm in winter • €2.60, or €4.50 with Témpio Nurágico • ☎ 070 938 7304

Eight rooms in Sárdara's ex-town hall hold various items unearthed in the town and at other local archeological sites. The cream of the crop has been transferred to Cágliari, but some of the more eye-catching finds have been copied for display here, including a handsome pair of nuraghic bronze archers.

Santa Maria Is Acquas

Località Santa Maria Is Acquas, 2km west of Sárdara • Open only for services

The late Gothic church of **Santa Maria Is Acquas**, a pretty, pale stone building surrounded by trees, is the venue for a **festival** deriving from the pagan water cult, taking place around the penultimate Monday of September when a holy image is carried here in procession from its normal home in Sárdara's church of L'Assunta, culminating in singing and dancing.

The Terme di Sárdara

Località Santa Maria Is Acquas, 2km west of Sárdara • ☎ 070 938 7200, Ⓦ termedisardara.it

Sardinia's prehistoric people weren't the only ones to value the waters around Sárdara: the Romans built the now-vanished Aquae Neapolitanae here, while today a modern spa hotel complex, the **Terme di Sárdara**, uses the sodium-rich waters issuing from the five hot springs to treat liver and digestive complaints. The complex has two outdoor **thermal pools** and a fitness centre that are open to all, and a range of therapies is available.

ARRIVAL AND ACCOMMODATION   SÁRDARA

By bus The village is served by buses from Cágliari (Mon–Sat hourly, Sun 4 daily; 1hr–1hr 45min) and Sanluri (Mon–Sat 12–14 daily, Sun 3 daily; 15min).

Terme di Sárdara Località Santa Maria Is Acquas ☎ 070 938 7200, Ⓦ termedisardara.it. The village has a couple of budget hotels, but the spa hotel 2km outside offers a much fancier experience, the price including access to all the facilities. Between mid-Nov and mid-May, it's open at weekends only. **€93**

Villanovaforru and around

Roads trail north and east from Sanluri and Sárdara into the hills of **La Marmilla**, on the confines of the provinces of Medio Campidano, Oristano and Nuoro. At its southern fringes, the quiet and tidy village of **VILLANOVAFORRU**, founded by the Spanish in the seventeenth century, was historically an important grain market for the surrounding area. Apart from its museum, however, the slow-moving village has little else to detain you.

Museo Archeologico

Piazza Costituzione • Tues–Sun 9.30am–1pm & 3.30–7pm, 3.30–6pm in winter • €3.50, or €5 with Genna Maria • ☎ 070 930 0050

In Villanovaforru's centre, a sympathetically restored grain store holds the **Museo Archeologico**, exhibiting some of the earliest evidence of local Bronze and Iron Age civilizations. The well-lit displays mostly consist of the contents of tombs: a procession of ritual vases, oil lamps (some boat-shaped), jewellery and assorted ceramics, sometimes painted with complex geometric patterns. Many of the metal items are distinctively polished, an effect attained using specially crafted bones. Finds from Su Nuraxi (see p.122) are well represented, while one section upstairs is entirely devoted to Carthaginian and Roman objects, including coins, the clay contents of a Punic tomb found at Villamar and part of a Roman millstone. The importance of water to the local communities is reflected in the abundance of containers found, often with elegantly curving designs.

Though stripped of its original furnishings, the grain store's interior retains its beamed ceilings, arched walls and a central well on the ground floor. A separate entrance beside the museum gives access to the small **Sala Mostre**, hosting occasional exhibitions.

Nuraghe di Genna Maria

Località Genna Maria • Tues–Sun: April–Sept 9.30am–1pm & 3.30–7pm; Feb, March & Oct 9.30am–1pm & 3.30–6pm; Nov–Jan 9.30am–1pm & 2.30–5pm • €2.50, or €5 including Museo Archeologico • ☎ 070 930 0050

A kilometre west of Villanovaforru, a left turn off the Collinas road leads to the **Nuraghe di Genna Maria**, occupying the summit of Marmilla's highest hill (408m) and commanding far-reaching views. From the car park it's a short but fairly steep climb to the site itself, which covers an extensive area dominated by a central ruined tower surrounded by the circular structures of a village. The remains are in worse condition than some of Sardinia's other nuraghic monuments, partly a result of the use of local sandstone as building material, but this still ranks among the island's most important sites, not least for the quantity of finds it has yielded. First excavated between 1951 and 1954 by the renowned Sardinian archeologist Giovanni Lilliu, but only fully revealed in 1977, the site is still the subject of digs. A raised walkway above the walls, in parts 3m high, allows you to look down on the chambers and passages of the main building and the lower walls encircling the small rooms pressed up against it.

3

The construction

The difficulties of building on this elevated site are shown in the many successive **stages of construction**. The central keep (*mastio*) was erected during the first phase, possibly as early as the fifteenth century BC, while the quadrilobate bastion and part of the curtain wall (*antemurale*) certainly go back to the thirteenth century BC. A new phase extended over the thirteenth and twelfth centuries BC, while the village dwellings were built between the twelfth and ninth centuries BC, the beginning of Sardinia's Iron Age. Finally, the curtain wall was completed during the ninth and eighth centuries BC. The village, some of whose buildings have a central courtyard, was also inhabited in Carthaginian and Roman periods until the third century AD.

To one side of the site, you can see diagrams illustrating how the complex might once have looked, while a map shows how densely the Marmilla is filled with other nuraghic settlements. From this high, windy vantage point, you can spot many of the hills and areas identified on the map, the most significant landmark being the high, flat Giara di Gésturi, to the north (see p.125).

ARRIVAL AND DEPARTURE

VILLANOVAFORRU AND AROUND

By bus ARST buses stop in Villanovaforru's centre. Note that there are no Sunday services.
Destinations Cágliari (Mon–Sat 3 daily; 1hr 25min–2hr);

Sanluri (Mon–Sat 3–4 daily; 15–35min); Sárdara (Mon–Sat 5–6 daily; 15min); Tuili (Mon–Sat 1 daily; 25min).

ACCOMMODATION AND EATING

Funtana Noa Via Vittorio Emanuele III ☎ 070 933 1020, ⊛ whotelfuntananoa.it. This large, convent-like hotel and restaurant in Villanovaforru has tiled floors, beamed ceilings, a/c rooms and a courtyard. The restaurant menu features such local dishes as *pasta fresca con sugo di cinghiale* (with boar sauce; €9). Main courses are €10–14.

Daily 1–3pm & 8–10.30pm. **€65**
I Lecci Località Genna Maria ☎ 070 933 1021, ⊛ hotel ilecci.com. A short lane opposite the turn-off to Genna Maria leads to this modern, good-value but somewhat characterless four-star, most of whose identikit rooms enjoy good views (ones on the first floor are best). **€75**

Las Plassas

East of Villanovaforru stretches a varied landscape of cultivated fields interspersed with some pasturage, overlooked by a horizon of knobbly brown peaks. The most prominent feature for miles around is the extraordinary conical hill of **Las Plassas** (274m), on whose round pinnacle fragments of the twelfth-century **Castello di Marmilla** stick up like broken teeth. The hill is a perfect example of the bosomy bumps characteristic of

the Marmilla region. To get closer, take a left turn off the straight SS197, just before the petrol station at the southern entrance to the nearby hamlet, also called Las Plassas; alternatively a brown signpost in the hamlet points you in the same direction. Five hundred metres along, opposite the majolica-tiled dome of the seventeenth-century church of **Santa Maria Maddalena**, a path weaves up the hillside to the scanty ruins: there is little to see of the castle itself, but the view makes it worth the brief climb. Traces of a previous nuraghic settlement have been unearthed below the castle.

Su Nuraxi

Sardinia's best-known nuraghic site, **Su Nuraxi**, lies 3km north of Las Plassas outside **BARÚMINI**. It's a draw for coachloads of visitors year round, spawning a cluster of other local attractions to capitalize on its fame, making this essentially run-of-the-mill village quite a hive of activity. Apart from the *nuraghe*-related sights, the only other item of interest in Barúmini itself is the bijou, seventeenth-century church of **Santa Tecla** (daily 8am–noon & 3–6pm), by the crossroads at the centre of the village, distinguished by its swirling rose window and battlements.

The site

Viale Su Nuraxi • Daily 9am–1hr before sunset • €8, or €10 with Casa Zapata and Centro Lilliu • ☎ 070 936 8128, ⓦ fondazionebarumini.it • 10min west of Barúmini on foot

The largest nuraghic complex on the island, as well as one of the oldest (dating from around 1500 BC), Su Nuraxi has been continuously excavated since 1949 and was listed a UNESCO World Heritage Site in 1997. There's plenty to take in, and all visits to the site are escorted by guides who provide a knowledgeable commentary (in various languages) – as well as warning you to keep off the walls, which would otherwise invite much clambering over.

Note that the dialect name of Su Nuraxi means simply "the *nuraghes*"; Sardinian x's are pronounced either with a "sh" sound, or like the French "j". "Su Nuraxi" is thus pronounced "Su Nurashi" or "Su Nuraji".

Brief history

Despite all the research, the origins of Su Nuraxi remain largely obscure, though it seems likely that it was a palace complex at the very least, possibly even a capital city. The first traces of human settlement on the site date from the middle Bronze Age (sixteenth to thirteenth centuries BC); the place was destroyed in the seventh century BC, then rebuilt and resettled until the Roman period. In between, the complex was constantly expanded, with towers added to the central bastion, which were joined by a stone wall. The whole area is thought to have been covered with earth by Sards and Carthaginians at the time of the Roman conquest, accounting for its good state of preservation.

You'll find more on Sardinia's nuraghic culture in Contexts (see p.307).

The central tower

The imposing **central tower**, built of dark grey basalt blocks, lies at the centre of a tight mesh of walled dwellings separated by a web of lanes. The tower originally reached 21m (now shrunk to about 14.5m), and contained three chambers, one above the other, of which two remain. At the end of a corridor, the tholos-type lower chamber has alcoves once lined with cork, and an opening halfway up the walls suggesting the existence of a wooden flight of stairs to reach the next storey. To reach this room now you have to backtrack along the elaborate network of passageways and rugged steps connecting the various inner chambers. Most of the topmost storey is missing, but still provides good views over the whole site.

Next to the tower on ground level, a deep crescent-shaped **courtyard** holds a well that still contains water.

The outer defences

The courtyard gives access to three of the four external towers that form the corners of the quadrilobate outer defences, part of a second phase of construction, probably dating from the thirteenth or twelfth centuries BC. The height of the enclosing walls was raised at a later period, an alteration clearly visible in the contrast between the more regular masonry of the later work and the rougher-hewn stones of the lower parts. The outer walls were strengthened between the twelfth and tenth centuries BC, and encompassed within a further line of defence: a polygonal **curtain wall** studded with (now roofless) round towers.

The nuraghic village

The same period saw the expansion of the settlement, though most of the **nuraghic village** dates from later, between the tenth and sixth centuries, when the nucleus of the settlement was already in a state of decay. Scattered around the curtain walls, it's a dense, untidy outgrowth of over two hundred circular and horseshoe-shaped buildings, all now roofless, but many reconstructed to a height of about 2m. In appearance, these huts must have resembled the small stone-roofed shepherds' *pinneddas* still used today in some parts of Sardinia (see p.157).

Centro Giovanni Lilliu

Viale Su Nuraxi • Daily: March & Nov 10am–1.30pm & 3–5.30pm; April, May & Sept 10am–7pm; June–Aug 10am–8pm; Oct 10am–6.30pm; Dec–Feb 10am–1.30pm & 3–5pm • €5, or €10 with Su Nuraxi and Casa Zapata; free when there is no exhibition • ☎ 070 936 1041, Ⓦ fondazionebarumini.it

A modern, bunker-like construction opposite Su Nuraxi holds the **Centro Giovanni Lilliu**, named after Sardinia's greatest archeologist, the first to excavate the site of Su Nuraxi. There are a few permanent displays here – primarily photographs of the excavations taken by Lilliu himself and items of local craftwork, including masks – but the space is normally used for temporary exhibitions. As entry to the exhibitions costs little more than the price of the Su Nuraxi/Casa Zapata ticket, it's usually worth a glance inside.

Casa Zapata

Via Roma, Barúmini • Daily: March & Nov 10am–1.30pm & 3–5.30pm; April, May & Sept 10am–7pm; June–Aug 10am–8pm; Oct 10am–6.30pm; Dec–Feb 10am–1.30pm & 3–5pm • €9, or €10 with Su Nuraxi and Centro Lilliu • ☎ 070 936 8476, Ⓦ fondazionebarumini.it

Finds from Su Nuraxi are displayed in Barúmini's **Casa Zapata**, the former residence of a Spanish family granted the fiefdom of La Marmilla in 1541. The palace was actually constructed over another nuraghic site, only discovered during renovations in 1990, and the remains are now revealed to form part of the museum, viewable from a walkway installed above. Among the displays, look out in particular for the diminutive bétilo, a 1.5cm-tall model of a nuraghic tower found in the *capanna delle riunioni*, or assembly chamber, in the nuraghic village – similar items, thought to have a totemic significance, have been found at several other nuraghic sites.

As well as the archeological material, the museum has an ethnographic section, including an impressive collection of *launeddas* (Sardinian pipes), and rooms devoted to the Zapata dynasty.

Sardegna in Miniatura

Località Lardi, 1.5km west of Barúmini • Daily: Easter–Sept 9am–8pm; Oct–Easter 10am–5pm • €10, plus €3 each for astronomy museum, planetarium and Charles Darwin exhibition, or €15 combined ticket • ☎ 070 936 1004, ⊕ sardegnainminiatura.it

Outside Barúmini, off the road to Tuili, **Sardegna in Miniatura** provides excellent family entertainment for whatever time you have left after visiting the area's main sights. The centrepiece is a (mainly) 1:25 scale version of Sardinia's most famous monuments and sights arranged on a miniature Sardinia-shaped island, from Cágliari's cathedral in the south to the beaches of the Costa Smeralda in the north, taking in Pisan churches and various archeological sites – including Su Nuraxi itself – en route. You can tour the model reconstructions by boat and get an overview of it from a wooden tower.

The park also holds a near life-size version of huts in a **nuraghic village**, complete with bearded mannequins and explanatory commentaries in Italian and English. Other attractions include a **museum of astronomy**, a **planetarium** and an exhibition devoted to **Charles Darwin** (separate tickets), and there's a restaurant and picnic area.

ARRIVAL AND DEPARTURE SU NURAXI

By bus Buses to Barúmini (none on Sun) stop in the centre of the village, from where it's a 10min walk to Su Nuraxi. Note that both departures to Cágliari are early-morning.

Destinations Cágliari (Mon–Sat 2 daily; 1hr 30min); Gésturi (Mon–Sat 2–4 daily; 7min); Láconi (Mon–Sat 2–3 daily; 35min); Tuili (4–7 daily; 5min).

ACCOMMODATION AND EATING

Casa Piras Traversa Seconda Principessa Maria 13, Barúmini ☎ 070 936 8372 or ☎ 349 883 7015. Simple, modern B&B with three rooms sleeping two, three or four guests, and two shared bathrooms. There's a *salone* with a fridge for guests' use, and a small garden. The house is tricky to find – look for signs off Corso Umberto and Via Roma. No credit cards. **€50**

★ **Sa Lolla** Via Cavour, Barúmini ☎ 070 936 8419, ⊕ salollarist@libero.it. This small, rustic-style *pensione* has only seven spacious and minimally decorated rooms, some overlooking the garden. The good restaurant – open to non-guests – has outdoor seating under a vine and concentrates on *campidanese* specialities; a full meal will cost around €30 (pizzas are also served). Daily 12.30–3pm & 6.30–10.30pm; closed Mon–Thurs in winter. **€70**

Tuili and around

Three kilometres west of Barúmini, **TUILI** is the most interesting of the villages circling the Giara di Gésturi. Its church of **San Pietro Apostolo** – marked out by its neat, round-topped belltower – contains a real treasure. Occupying the whole of a chapel at the back of the right-hand aisle, the vividly coloured polyptych, the **retablo di San Pietro**, was painted by the artist known only as the **Maestro di Castelsardo**, and is in fact the only one of his works that is datable – 1500, according to a legal document specifying his fee. Its style is predominantly Gothic, with few signs of the impact of the Renaissance. Against richly detailed landscapes, the central panels show Christ crucified and the Madonna with saints; on the left, St Michael (slaying the devil) and St Peter are depicted, on the right are St James and St Paul, respectively above and below. Considered by some to be Sardinia's finest work of medieval art, it's a solemn and absorbing study, the facial expressions and garments superbly rendered. To view it properly in the church's dim interior, make sure the lights are turned on (the switch is behind the painting on the left). The rest of the building is also richly painted – there's another *retablo* on the corresponding chapel across the nave, dated 1534, painted by another anonymous artist.

Five kilometres north of Barúmini, the village of **GÉSTURI** is dominated by the campanile of the church of **Santa Teresa d'Ávila**, reckoned to be Sardinia's very latest example of the Catalan-Gothic style, dating from 1674.

ARRIVAL AND DEPARTURE	TUILI

By bus ARST buses stop in Tuili's centre; note that there are no Sunday services.
Destinations Barúmini (Mon–Sat 4–5 daily; 5min);

Cágliari (Mon–Sat 1 daily; 2hr); Sanluri (Mon–Sat 5 daily; 50min); Sárdara (Mon–Sat 1 daily; 40min).

La Giara di Gésturi

North of Barúmini and Tuili, the high tableland of the **Giara di Gésturi**, or *Sa Jara*, dominates the landscape. Roughly 12km long, covering some 42 square kilometres at a maximum height of 560m, it is the largest of a series of basalt plateaux thrown up in ancient eruptions. Protected as a nature reserve, the area is controlled by rangers and has no roads. There are, however, surfaced tracks winding up from the villages at its base, leading to places where you can leave your vehicle. The Giara ("plateau") is fairly bare on its lower flanks, but as you climb you'll come across thicker brushwood and groves of ancient cork trees. On the flat summit, the impervious basalt rock has created *paulis*, or depressions, which fill up with rainwater to create swampy ponds; these, together with the thick vegetation, help to provide a perfect terrain for a variety of **wildfowl**, from buzzards to bee-eaters. Spring is the best season to visit, when the area is at its greenest and a magnet for migrating birds.

The plateau has also become home to goats and wild boars, though the most rarely seen beasts are those that appear most frequently on the tourist literature – packs of **wild ponies**, or *cavallini* (in dialect, is *quaddedus*). At the last count there were around five hundred of these diminutive creatures, which measure less than 130cm at shoulder height; a smaller number live in Le Prigionette protected zone at Porto Conte, near Alghero (see p.184). Their origins are unknown, but they are thought to have links with oriental breeds, possibly introduced by the Phoenicians three thousand years ago. Though free to roam at will, the ponies are either privately owned or the property of the local community. The best time to see them is after foaling at the end of March.

You're allowed to wander where you please over the rough terrain (you'll need stout shoes), though you might also consider using an experienced **guide**. Ask one of the forest rangers, normally stationed in shacks near the car parks, or contact Jara Escursioni (☎070 936 4277 or ☎348 292 4983, ⓦparcodellagiara.it), which conducts expeditions on foot (€40 for 2hr).

ARRIVAL AND DEPARTURE	LA GIARA DI GÉSTURI

By car The only way to reach the plateau is by car. The nearest villages are Génuri, Setzu, Tuili and Gésturi, which all have tracks leading to parking areas at the top

(unmissably signed "Altopiano della Giara"). Note that none of these villages has much in the way of tourist facilities.

Dolianova

Fifteen kilometres north of Cágliari, off the SS387, the market town of **DOLIANOVA** is the main centre of a region renowned for its olives and olive oil, and for its wines, which include Nuragus, Moscato and Malvasia. A workaday place with a few handsome nineteenth-century *palazzi*, Dolianova does have one outstanding relic in the form of its ex-cathedral, reached through an archway signposted off the town's main thoroughfare.

Chiesa di San Pantaleo

Via Vescovado • Daily 8am–noon & 3.30–7pm

Occupying one side of the large courtyard or small piazza, and topped by a short belltower, the **chiesa di San Pantaleo** – formerly the town's cathedral – sports blind arcading running right round the walls, adorned with eroded stone carvings of animals, plants, moons and some human forms. Started between 1150 and 1160 by a team which had previously worked on the church of Santa Giusta, outside Oristano (see p.154), the grey stone exterior was completed by Arab architects a century later, accounting for its *mudéjar* style, which mixes Romanesque, Gothic and Arab elements. Next to the entrance, a Roman sarcophagus protrudes incongruously from the main body of the church, suspended on slender columns. When the church is closed, call at the rector's house (with "parroco" on the bell) to the right of the church.

The interior

The church's **interior** is decorated with an impressive array of murals, one of them depicting Christ crucified on what looks like the tree of life; it is, in fact, an *álbero genealógico*, or family tree, a favourite theme in medieval art showing Abraham and the prophets (a quarter of it is missing). Next to this, an oriental-looking *ancona*, or six-panelled altarpiece, shows the martyrdom of San Pantaleo, probably the work of an unknown Spanish painter in the sixteenth century. There's a horribly immolated Christ on one wall of the church, and at the back, a stone *baldacchino* (canopy) which, like the wonky columns of the nave, is crudely carved with figures of animals, angels and a man and woman embracing.

ARRIVAL AND DEPARTURE   DOLIANOVA

By train Trains operated by ARST run to Dolianova's station at the west end of town, 15min walk from the centre.
Destinations Cágliari (Gottardo) (Mon–Sat 14 daily; 25min); Ísili (Mon–Sat 2 daily; 1hr 10min); Mandas (Mon–

Sat 8 daily; 50min–1hr 10min).
By bus ARST buses connect Dolianova with Cágliari (1–2 daily; 45min) and San Nicolò Gerrei (Mon–Sat 3 daily, Sun 1daily; 1hr).

Gerrei

The main reason for heading north from Dolianova into the bleak, sparsely inhabited highlands of the **Gerrei** region is to visit one of Sardinia's most important nuraghic sites, standing alone on a high, wind-blown plain. There's no easy way to reach it, but the tortuous mountain road from Dolianova to **San Nicolò Gerrei**, without a building to be seen along its whole 33km length, will allow you to savour this little-visited area. At **Ballao**, 11km north of San Nicolò Gerrei, the minor SP10 continues north to the *nuraghe*, midway between the nondescript villages of **Escalaplano** and **Orroli**.

Nuraghe Arrubiu

SP10 • Daily 9.30am to 1hr before sunset • €4 • ☎ 0782 847 269

Thought to have been built between 1400 and 900 BC, **Nuraghe Arrubiu** – sometimes called Orrubiu – is the only five-towered nuraghic complex in existence, and one of the biggest, with a central tower which may once have reached a height of 27m, reduced now to 16m. Seven towers remain on the outer walls, and there are the remnants of five more, survivors of the 21 towers that, according to archeologists, originally stood here. The formidable ruin, which takes its name ("red") from the reddish basalt stone and the orange lichen covering it, was opened in 1996. Curiously, no nuraghic finds have so far been unearthed, only Punic, Roman and even Mycenaean artefacts, though future excavations are expected to throw up more valuable material. The Roman finds, which include mills, basins and stone tools used for pressing olives and grapes, are displayed in a separate walled area near the site's entrance.

Visitors are guided round the murky chambers and corridors on hour-long tours, usually in Italian (no tours 1–3pm). If you're in the area on a summer night, you can sign up for one of the atmospheric illuminated **night tours** (€3/person, with a minimum of 25 people). **Refreshments** are available from a bar at the entrance.

Villasimius and around

South and east of Gerrei, the equally wild and sparsely populated **Sarrabus** region is dominated by the Sette Fratelli ("seven brothers") mountains but fringed by pockets of development along the beach-studded coast. The biggest of the holiday centres, **VILLASIMIUS**, was little more than a small and unassuming village not so long ago, but has assumed the typical dual identity of a resort town – a hotbed of bars, boutiques, pizzerias and revving scooters in summer, practically deserted the rest of the time, with most facilities closed between October and May.

Although it's located a kilometre or two inland, Villasimius is within easy reach of some enticing coastline and a choice of fantastic beaches. Past the central Piazza Gramsci and the smaller, adjacent Piazza Generale Incani, the main Via Umberto forks left to the nearest stretch of sand at **Simius**, 1.5km east of town, and right to **Marina di Villasimius** (or the Porto Turistico), from where you can take **boat tours** in summer. The tourist port lies in the **Golfo di Carbonara**, named after the charcoal produced in the nearby forests, a by-product of which was the black powder added to gunpowder for damp-proofing (favoured by Nelson among others). Just south of the port is the **Fortezza Vecchia**, a square fortification probably dating from the fourteenth century, now used for exhibitions.

Museo Archeologico

Via Frau • Tues–Sun 10am–1pm & 4–7pm • €3 • ☎ 070 793 0271

The only sight of any interest in Villasimius is the town's **Museo Archeologico**, off the main Via Umberto. Exhibits in four rooms range from local Phoenician, Carthaginian and Roman finds, including amphoras, statues and coins to weaponry and other items recovered from a sixteenth-century Spanish shipwreck.

The beaches

To reach the town's nearest beach, **Simius**, you only have to follow the main drag east to where an arc of pale gold sands backed by luxury hotels face the offshore isles of **Serpentara**, a long strip of bare rock, and the more southerly **Isola dei Cávoli**. You'll find less developed bathing spots heading south towards **Capo Carbonara**, where the eastern shore of the thin peninsula is backed by the calm **Stagno di Notteri** lagoon, a stopover for flamingos in winter.

East of Capo Carbonara and north of Marina di Villasimius lies another prize beach, **Spiaggia del Riso**, adjacent to a campsite (see p.128), beyond which are the smaller beaches of **Campulongu** and **Campus**, with turquoise and aquamarine waters. There are more scraps of sandy beaches west of Capo Boi, in the **Golfo di Cágliari**, sometimes visible from the tortuous coast road that winds west towards Cágliari, as at **Cala Regina**, **Torre delle Stelle** and – the prettiest village on this stretch – **Solanas**, next to one of the numerous sentinel towers dotting the Gulf's coast. Less picturesque are the uniform rows of peach-coloured villas that intrude upon the scene.

ARRIVAL AND DEPARTURE	VILLASIMIUS AND AROUND
By bus The frequent buses that connect Cágliari and Villasimius can drop you at any of the beaches en route between the two. In Villasimius, ARST buses stop on Via	Umberto and Via del Mare; buy tickets from Easymius, Via Umberto 122. Destinations Cágliari (Mon–Sat 6–12 daily, Sun 2–8 daily;

1hr 30min); Castiadas (Mon–Sat 2–3 daily; 40min); Costa Rei (Mon–Sat 3–10 daily, Sun 2–7 daily; 40min–1hr 10min); Muravera (Mon–Sat 4–6 daily; 1hr 20min–1hr 50min).

GETTING AROUND

By bus Easymius runs a shuttle bus service connecting Villasimius with Marina di Villasimius, Simius and all neighbouring beaches eight times daily between mid-June and mid-Sept. Buy tickets (€2.50, or €5 on board) from various kiosks and bars in the centre displaying the Easymius sticker, or from La Via del Mare agency at Via Umberto 122.

By car, bike or scooter Car, bike and scooter rental is available at La Via del Mare, Via Umberto 122 (☏070 791 009, ⊛laviadelmare.com). A small car costs €70–85 a day, scooters are around €35 and bikes €10.

INFORMATION

Tourist office Piazza Giovanni XXIII, next to the church off Piazza Gramsci (May, Sept & Oct Mon–Sat 10am–1pm, also Mon & Thurs 3–6pm; June–Aug Mon–Sat 10am–2pm & 3–6pm; Nov & Dec Mon–Fri 10am–1pm; ☏070 793 0271, ⊛villasimiusweb.com). Winter hours are flexible; when the office is closed, the staff at the Museo Archeologico can supply information.

ACCOMMODATION

Prices rise steeply if you want to stay near the sea, though low-season rates are more reasonable. The La Via del Mare agency, Via Umberto 122 (☏070 791 009, ⊛laviadelmare.com), deals with weekly **apartment rentals** in the area.

Acquarius Hotel Via Umberto 41 ☏070 790 276, ⊛acquariushotel.it. Central choice, with smart and spacious rooms, two of them giving onto a sunny roof terrace, and there's a good pizzeria/restaurant. Prices plummet in low season. Closed Dec & Jan. **€110**

Fiore di Maggio Località Campulongu ☏070 797 382, ⊛fioredimaggio.it. Smaller and more personal than most of the hotels hereabouts, this family-friendly place lies 2km from town and 80m from the beach of Campulongu. Overlooking a citrus grove, the rooms have Sardinian decor, and there's a pool and restaurant. At least half-board is usually required in the summer months. Closed mid-Oct to April. Half-board per person **€100**

Spiaggia del Riso ☏070 791 052, ⊛villaggio spiaggiadelriso.it. If you want to stay near the sea without paying high hotel prices, try this clean and well-equipped campsite with access to two beaches; non-campers can rent four-bed bungalows or stay in (rather pricey) B&B rooms. There's a 20-day minimum stay in peak season. Closed Nov–April. Rooms and bungalows **€130**; pitches from **€26**

Stella d'Oro Via Vittorio Emanuele 25 ☏070 791 255. The cheapest option in town is this family-run hotel centrally located off Piazza Incani. Rooms have a/c and en-suite bathrooms, but are fairly spartan, most of them looking onto an interior courtyard. There's parking (a big plus in Villasimius) and a good restaurant (see below) – at least half-board may be required in August, at €85 per person. Closed Nov–April. **€85**

EATING AND DRINKING

Carbonara Via Umberto 60 ☏070 791 270. Sober seafood restaurant with local art on the walls and a traditional feel. Among the *primi* (mostly €8–12) are *linguine alla spada* (pasta with swordfish), while mains (mostly €13–18) include *pesce alla griglia* (grilled) and *alla vernaccia* (cooked in wine). Feb–Dec daily except Wed 12.30–2.45pm & 7.30–11pm; open daily in Aug.

La Mora Bianca Via Roma 14 ☏345 846 3642. If you can stomach the lounge-style background music, this elegant place makes an excellent venue for dinner, both for its tranquil courtyard setting and its adventurous cuisine. Alongside the original range of pizzas (€7–10) are some choice meat and seafood dishes, including shrimps on skewers and grills. Most starters are €10, mains are €15,

and there's a €28 tourist menu. May–Oct daily 7–11pm.

Stella d'Oro Via Vittorio Emanuele 25 ☏070 791 255. The courtyard of this hotel (see above) gets packed with diners in the evening, tucking into excellent local dishes and a good selection of Sardinian wines. A house speciality is *malfatti* – literally "badly made" spinach and ricotta balls in tomato sauce – and the *seppie alla griglia* (grilled cuttlefish) are also worth sampling. Starters are €8–12, most mains around €15. May–Oct daily 7–11pm.

Tartana Piazza Incani ☏345 883 2725. This central bar with outdoor tables makes a cheerful daytime or evening stop for its pastries, rolls and salads, not to mention aperitifs, beers and cocktails. Daily 7am–midnight; closed Mon Sept–April.

DIRECTORY

Internet Log on at Internet Point, Via Umberto 62 (Mon–Sat 9.30am–1pm & 5.30–8pm, also June–Sept 9.15pm–midnight; €5/10min).

Market A food market takes place on Saturday

mornings in Via Donatello, next to the Carabinieri barracks.

Post office Via del Mare 72 (Mon–Fri 8.25am–1.35pm, Sat 8.25am–1.35pm).

The Costa Rei

The long ribbon of beaches that makes up the **Costa Rei**, famous for its shimmering expanses of fine white sand lapped by crystal waters, begins 18km north of Villasimius, reached via a circuitous coastal road. Here, **Cala Sinzias** is a broad swathe of sand cupped within a beautiful small bay, though the area's hinterland is rapidly being developed. Most of the new construction is concentrated in the central section of the bay, where the seafront is backed by villas, promenades and bars, and a range of watersports is available in summer. Even if you're here between June and September, you can always avoid the crowds by moving on to the top end of this bay, towards the pine-clad **Capo Ferrato**, where dirt tracks running off the road lead to remoter scraps of sandy beach. Around the cape, the asphalt degenerates into a dusty track that winds behind Capo Ferrato to the next bay, and more dazzling beaches.

3

ARRIVAL AND DEPARTURE

THE COSTA REI

By bus ARST buses provide services to and from Costa Rei, though much reduced in winter.
Destinations Cágliari (Mon–Sat 4–10 daily, Sun 2–6 daily; 1hr 30min–2hr 10min); Muravera (Mon–Sat 4–5 daily; 40min–1hr); Villasimius (Mon–Sat 4–12 daily, Sun 2–6 daily; 40–55min).

ACCOMMODATION AND EATING

Albaruja Via C. Colombo ☎070 991 557, ⓦalbaruja.it. Almost all the accommodation on the Costa Rei is in villas rented out by the week, though there are a couple of expensive hotels, including this well-maintained place 100m from the beach, with two-storey suites grouped around a garden, a pool and access to a tennis court. Closed Oct–April. €178

Capo Ferrato Monte Nai ☎070 991 012, ⓦcamping capoferrato.it. This central campsite is shaded by mimosa and eucalyptus and has bungalows available; it's right by a broad sweep of sand, though perhaps too close to the

ranks of holiday villas for comfort. There are shops and windsurfing and canoeing facilities nearby. Closed Nov–March. Bungalows €79; pitches €28

L'Escargot Via Marco Polo 4 ☎070 991 6111. Romantic if fairly pricey spot above the beach, with a terrace and an upper balcony with enchanting sea views. Try the swordfish carpaccio, *quadrotti Costa Rey* (seafood ravioli) and grilled fish, but don't bother with the pizzas. A two-course dinner with wine will cost around €40 per person. June–Sept daily 12.30–3pm & 7.30–11pm.

Castiadas and around

Inland of the Costa Rei, the land is largely flat and verdant. The main settlement here, up a slight ascent 7km west, is **CASTIADAS**, centred on a straggle of buildings around the pink walls of an ex-penal colony set up in the nineteenth century, now part-occupied by a museum. There's not much else here, but Castiadas makes a convenient starting point for exploring the Monte dei Sette Fratelli to the north (see p.130), and the Foresta di Minniminni, a couple of kilometres south.

Museo Storico Comunale

Via Centrale · Daily: June–Sept 9.30am–12.30pm & 5–11.30pm; early Oct 9.30am–12.30pm & 5–8.30pm; last entry 1hr 15min before closing · €3 · ☎070 9945 0307

The offices of Castiadas' former penal colony have been smartly restored to house the **Museo Storico Comunale**, dedicated to the inmates of the prison during its existence from 1875 to 1956. The men – mostly from the mainland – were kept busy clearing the surrounding forest and cultivating the land at a time when malaria was rife, claiming the lives of many of the workers. The hour-long guided tours take in holding cells, photographs of the colony and background information on the history and geography of the area, as well as two fifteen-minute documentary films (one from 1954). It's all in Italian but you get the gist. Some rooms also hold examples of local art and handicrafts.

Foresta di Minniminni

A protected area of holm oak and thick *macchia*, the **Foresta di Minniminni** is only passable on foot, donkey or, to an extent, in 4WD vehicles. As well as the ubiquitous arbutus, juniper and cyclamen of the *macchia*, the area holds two plantations of pine trees left by the inmates of the Castiadas penal colony, one from 1875, when they arrived, the second from when the colony was closed down in 1956. Waymarked trails wind through the forest to the summit of Monte Minniminni, only 723m high but affording wonderful views over the surrounding coast.

ARRIVAL AND DEPARTURE   CASTIADAS

By bus ARST buses connect Castiadas with Cágliari (Mon–Sat 3 daily; 2hr 10min) and Villasimius (Mon–Sat 3–4 daily; 40min). The stop is right outside the old prison.

INFORMATION AND ACTIVITIES

Tourist information The website ⓦ castiadasonline.it is packed with information on the whole district, including local accommodation possibilities.
Excursions Cooperativa Monte dei Sette Fratelli, Via Centrale (☎ 070 994 7200 or ☎ 328 462 9860, ⓦ monte settefratelli.com) offers guided excursions in the Foresta di Minniminni and the Sette Fratelli range, either on foot or in an off-roader.

EATING AND DRINKING

Le Vecchie Carceri Via Centrale ☎ 070 994 7171. Grab a snack or a meal at this bar/trattoria, with local specialities including *salsiccia alla griglia* (sausages), horse and donkey, as well as pizzas. Most dishes are €7–13. June–Sept Mon–Fri 7–11.30pm, Sat & Sun noon–2pm & 7–11.30pm; Oct–May Sat & Sun noon–2pm & 7–10pm.

Monte dei Sette Fratelli

Linking Cágliari with Muravera, the tortuous and highly scenic SS125 cuts through the heart of Sarrabus, where the dramatic **Monte dei Sette Fratelli** ("Seven Brothers") range reaches a height of about 1020m. If you want to strike out on foot, there are plenty of opportunities to stop along the way (see box opposite). For more ambitious climbs, however, you'll need expert guidance, such as the excursion group based in Castiadas (see above). The steep, granite slopes are either *macchia*-covered or forested with cork oak and holm oak, and provide a habitat for the rare *cervo sardo*, the short Sardinian stag for which this is a protected zone; about 750 are estimated to exist in the region.

The only significant settlement in these parts is **BURCEI**, a small village at a height of 648m, famed for its cherry trees which come to full, flamboyant blossom in May.

Nuraghe Asoru

At the eastern end of the Sette Fratelli range, at the bottom of the desolate gorge of the River Picocca, littered with monolithic boulders, you'll pass the **Nuraghe Asoru** (also called Nuraghe S'Oro), unmissable by the side of road. It was constructed between the tenth and eighth centuries BC in a dominating position over the surrounding plain and the inland approaches and is the only *nuraghe* worthy of note in these parts, which evidently proved too barren even for the hardy locals. There's a small internal courtyard, and a hole in the coarse masonry of the wall reveals a bench running all around its interior.

A WALK IN THE MONTE DEI SETTE FRATELLI

This moderately easy **hike** in the Sette Fratelli takes you into the heart of the range, along paths strewn with wild clematis and fennel. Climbing skills are not required, but bring stout shoes, at least one litre of water per person and some sun protection; also, let other people know where you're bound (there's a Forestry Corps station near the beginning of the walk). The entire walk should take less than four hours, not counting breaks.

You can reach the **start of the route** on public transport along the SS125 from Cágliari or Muravera. Coming from Cágliari, soon after the junction for Burcei on the left, look out for a bridge over a small river (signposted Rio Campuomo), on the far side of which there is a clearing on the right where drivers can park, immediately before a Corpo Forestale station. The path begins here, signposted "Sentiero Italia, Campuomo, Castiadas". The route is waymarked with the symbol of a white diamond with a red stripe across.

Follow the level track for about ten minutes until you reach a fork, where you should bear left (uphill); there's no symbol here, but you'll see them again soon. It gets a little steeper up the rough path before it emerges onto a good unasphalted road, where there's a signpost: follow "Conventu" to the left. A few minutes later, there's an unsignposted second fork – take the right-hand path, slightly descending before levelling out and climbing again. About 45 minutes after setting out, you'll reach the ruins of a former monastery, the **Conventu de Sette Fradi** (also called Convento dei Sette Fratelli), in a shady clearing (600m). The name of the range might derive from the erstwhile inhabitants of this establishment, or it may refer to the peaks themselves. Travellers on the route between Burcei and Castiadas would lodge here for the night.

Proceed past the monastery; after five minutes or so, take a right-hand fork onto a rough mule-track, which descends through woods to a river, the **Riu Guventu**. If there's water here, you can cross on stepping stones, before climbing steeply up the far side (following the symbols) along a smaller riverbed. The trail soon diverges to the left, continuing up through dense woods, where the symbols are fairly sparse. The path continues uphill in a similar vein, with occasional clearings affording good views on the way, until, less than an hour after leaving the convent, you'll reach the bare summits of the Sette Fratelli. The path dives in and out of the woods as far as the highest peak, **Punta Sa Ceraxa** (1015m). From here, the trail continues towards Castiadas. From Sa Ceraxa, your return journey should take another ninety minutes or so.

3

ARRIVAL AND DEPARTURE

MONTE DEI SETTE FRATELLI

By bus Buses between Cágliari and Muravera stop along the SS125 running through the range (Mon–Sat hourly, Sun 3 daily).

Muravera and around

The River Picocca flows into a flat, fertile area, with thick groves of citrus and lesser growths of almonds and other fruit and nut trees. Having accompanied the river as far as its outlet on the coast, the SS125 swings north, passing close to some choice beaches before heading inland again to enter **MURAVERA**. The only centre between Villasimius and Tortolì, it's a thriving agricultural town, known as the island's **citrus** capital, and with the neighbouring villages of Villaputzu and San Vito renowned for the authenticity of such local produce as honey, wine and *dolci*. Muravera doesn't invite much lingering, however, its main Via Roma a constant stream of traffic with pedestrians squeezed onto minuscule pavements. Among the first-class **beaches** in the vicinity, the nearest is **San Giovanni**, 2km south, beyond which the fine sands of **Torre Salinas**, **Colostrai** and **Feraxi** are backed by lagoons where you can see a range of aquatic birdlife.

From San Vito, the SS387 curls inland along the course of the River Flumendosa and into the hilly Gerrei region (see p.126), a panoramic route into the interior. North of Muravera, the SS125 follows the course of the **River Quirra**, separated from the coast by a wall of mountains. It's a fertile area, with scattered nut trees that burst into blossom

> ### MURAVERA'S FESTIVALS
> Muravera's biggest **festival** is the **Sagra degli Agrumi** (Citrus Fair), held on the first or second Sunday before Easter to celebrate the end of winter, marked by parades of peasant wagons laden with fruit. Other significant dates are around August 28, featuring music and costumed festivities for the four-day **Festa di Sant'Agostino**, and December 6, for two days of poetry competitions, singing and dancing in the **Festa di San Nicola**.

in early spring. After about 20km, the road crosses the Cágliari–Ogliastra provincial boundary, continuing north to the villages of Tertenia and Lanusei (see p.304).

Porto Corallo

East of Villaputzu, the river joins the sea near **Porto Corallo** where, on the approximate site of a long-disappeared Phoenician port, a small harbour has been re-created, this time for pleasure craft. Overlooked by a Spanish watchtower, Porto Corallo was the scene of one of the last battles against North African pirates, when the locals succeeded in driving back their attackers in 1812. South of the river mouth, the broad beach is backed by eucalyptus woods, and there are picnic tables and a bar/pizzeria and gelateria close at hand.

ARRIVAL AND DEPARTURE
MURAVERA AND AROUND

By bus ARST buses to and from Muravera stop at various points along Via Roma, including the central Piazza Europa. If you're leaving town, buy tickets at any of the bars showing the ARST sticker.
Destinations Cágliari (Mon–Sat hourly, Sun 3 daily; 1hr 45min–3hr 30min); Castiadas (Mon–Sat 3–4 daily; 40min–1hr 15min); Costa Rei (Mon–Sat 4–5 daily; 35min–1hr); Porto Corallo (July & Aug 3–4 daily; 20min) Villasimius (Mon–Sat 4–6 daily; 1hr 15min–2hr).

INFORMATION AND ACTIVITIES

Tourist information Muravera has a summer-only tourist office on Via Roma (June–Sept daily 9am–2pm & 3–7pm; ☎ 070 993 0760).
Diving Ocean Dreams (☎ 346 850 5273, ⓦ divesardinia .com), run by an Irish-German couple in Porto Corallo, offers trips snorkelling (€50–70 for a half-day) and diving (€90 for two dives), tuition at all levels and equipment to rent. They also arrange other activities including biking, riding and hiking excursions.

ACCOMMODATION

Corallo Via Roma 31 ☎ 070 993 3392, ⓦ albergocorallo .it. In the centre of town, this modern hotel can't boast much character but is fine for a night or two, with spacious, wi-fi-enabled rooms with balconies, parking, and an outdoor pizzeria. **€85**
Ostello San Priamo Via Rio Cannas 16, San Priamo ☎ 070 999 720, ⓦ ostellosanpriamo.it. 10km south of Muravera and 4km south of Torre Salinas, this hostel is set in a verdant part of the coast, 4km from the beach and 200m from the ARST bus stop. Accommodation is in dormitories for 3–4 people and doubles – all with en-suite bathrooms – or in rooms with cooking facilities and a/c (€75 in July). Prices include breakfast, and there's free wi-fi. Closed mid-Sept to May. Dorms **€25**, doubles **€59**
★ **Su Pasiu** Via Speranza 8 ☎ 070 993 0589 or ☎ 348 474 5706, ⓦ locandasupasiu.it. Signposted off Via Roma, this relaxed B&B managed by a young couple is set around a traditional courtyard. Rooms are cool, spacious and beautifully decorated, with a/c and large showers. There's wi-fi, an honesty bar, abundant breakfasts and bikes to rent. **€80**

CAMPING
Quattro Mori Località Is Perdigonis ☎ 070 999 110, ⓦ 4mori.it. The nearest campsite to town (5km south), this provides everything for a self-contained holiday right by the beach, with four-star, family-friendly facilities including a pool and self-catering four-bed mini-apartments to rent (from €79 /night). Closed mid-Oct to late April. Pitches **€30.50**
Torre Salinas Località Torre Salinas ☎ 070 999 032, ⓦ camping-torre-salinas.de. Very close to a good beach 8km south of Muravera, this eucalyptus-shaded, German-run campsite has bungalows and caravans available (from €45 a night), and you can also rent tents (from €41 for two). There's a pizzeria and a tennis court. Closed Nov–March. Pitches **€25.50**

EATING AND NIGHTLIFE

Restaurants are easy to find in the summer season, less so in winter. Piazza Europa, off Via Roma, is the venue for nightly **concerts** and other entertainments in summer. Head to **Porto Corallo** for the lively summer bar scene until the small hours.

Green Gallery Via Roma 128 ☎347 179 1903. This pub has German draught beers and an outdoor eating area for its panini, fresh pasta and grilled fish; mains are around €10, and it offers a fixed-price lunch menu for €12.50. Mon–Sat 11am–3pm & 7pm–2am, Sun 7pm–2am.

★ **Su Nuraxi** Via Roma 257 ☎070 993 0991. At the northern end of the main drag, this is the best choice in town for pizzas and such dishes as *pesce spada agli agrumi* (swordfish with citrus dressing). Mains are €10–15 and there's a €20 tourist menu. Feb–Dec daily 12.30–3pm & 7.30–11pm.

DIRECTORY

Market Muravera's fresh produce is sold at the fruit and veg market off Via Roma on Monday mornings.
Post office Piazza Europa (Mon–Sat 8am–1.15pm).

Internet Log on at Micro Service, Via Roma 144 (Mon–Sat 9am–12.45pm & 5–7.45pm; €3 for 30min, then €5/hr).

3

Oristano and around

140 Oristano

148 The Sinis peninsula

153 Santa Giusta

154 Arborea and around

155 Fordongianus

156 Samugheo and around

157 The Vernaccia triangle

157 Santa Cristina and around

158 Ghilarza and around

159 Sédilo

159 Nuraghe Losa

160 Santu Lussurgiu and around

162 Cúglieri

162 Santa Caterina and around

S'ARDIA HORSE RACE

Oristano and around

The province of Oristano roughly corresponds to the much older entity of Arborea, the medieval *giudicato* which championed the Sardinian cause in the struggle against the Spaniards. Then as now, the city of Oristano was the region's main town, and today it retains more than a hint of medieval atmosphere, mixed with equal measures of burgeoning youth culture and prim parochialism. The small-town, pedestrian-friendly tone makes this an undemanding stop whose top attraction is one of Sardinia's best museums, the Antiquarium Arborense.

West of Oristano, the **Sinis Peninsula** is a flat, largely empty wedge of land, with good beaches and some important historical sites. You can still spot the traditional rush-constructed boats, or *fassonis*, on the peninsula's **lagoons**, used for fishing, hunting and racing. There's a museum dedicated to the lagoons' past inhabitants in **Cabras**, the only town hereabouts, with the best choice of accommodation locally. There's a lot more zip in the nearby summer resort of **Marina di Torre Grande**, though this too reverts to a more lethargic pace out of season.

Farther west along the peninsula, the church of **San Salvatore**, destination of an annual barefoot race from Cabras, is built over an ancient pagan sanctuary. Almost Middle Eastern in appearance, the much older church of **San Giovanni di Sinis** stands on the southern tip of the peninsula, very close to **Tharros** – one of the best-preserved classical sites on the island. Comparable to Nora (see p.84) in scale and location, the extensive remains of this venerable Punic-Roman town lie on a prong of land jutting from the coast. Elsewhere on Sinis, the watery terrain is a magnet for all kinds of birdlife, while the dune systems backing the coast are a protected zone – helping to preserve the choice **beaches** around here from excessive development.

On the southern outskirts of Oristano, don't miss the basilica of **Santa Giusta**, one of the earliest of Sardinia's Pisan-Romanesque churches. In the 1920s the fertile land south of here was drained and farmed by settlers from the mainland, who recreated a little corner of their native northern Italy in the town of **Arborea**, which still exudes the orderly virtues of Fascist town planning. There are traces of Roman occupation a short way inland at **Fordongianus**, where a system of baths occupies a scenic spot on the banks of the River Tirso. Just off the main route north of Oristano lie a couple of important nuraghic sites: **Santa Cristina**, where a pleasantly ramshackle *nuraghe* and an impressive sacred well are nestled within an ancient olive grove, and the monumental complex of **Losa**. Just east of Losa, **Ghilarza** has a museum devoted to the great political theorist Antonio Gramsci, who grew up here. Near the coast, **Cornus** was the scene of a historic Roman victory and provides a few archeological remnants in a remote-feeling but easily accessible spot. The prize beaches flanking the resort of **Santa Caterina di Pittinuri** are just a brief hop away.

Accommodation is scattered rather thinly throughout the region, with the best selection in Oristano itself. Apart from hotels and a few campsites (which are all on the coast), there are also several B&Bs both here and in the smaller centres.

Local festivals p.139
Eleonora d'Arborea p.142
Sa Sartiglia p.146
La Corsa degli Scalzi p.151

Antonio Gramsci p.159
Horsing around – Santu Lussurgiu's festivals p.161

ANTIQUARIUM ARBORENSE, ORISTANO

Highlights

❶ Antiquarium Arborense Oristano's superb collection of art and archeology is a richly rewarding introduction to the region, from Roman glassware to Renaissance canvases, with copious material on nearby Tharros. See p.143

❷ Festa di Sa Sartiglia Costumed pageantry and thrilling equestrian prowess make this one of Sardinia's most flamboyant festivals. See p.146

❸ Cycling around Sinis The flat landscape of this compact peninsula west of Oristano is ideal for touring by bike, with a choice of inviting beaches for cooling off. See pp.148–153

❹ Tharros The ruins of this Carthaginian and Roman city occupy a magnificent spot on the very tip of the Sinis peninsula. See p.151

❺ Santa Cristina In the midst of an olive grove, the sacred well and other monuments from the nuraghic era exude a powerfully pagan atmosphere. See p.157

❻ Casa Gramsci, Ghilarza Dedicated to one of the architects of Communism in Europe, this small museum staffed by enthusiastic volunteers draws devotees from far and wide, but will also appeal to anyone interested in twentieth-century history. See p.158

HIGHLIGHTS ARE MARKED ON THE MAP ON P.138

Brief history

In prehistoric times, the area that subsequently became Oristano province was the cradle of a flourishing **nuraghic culture**, of which the complexes of Nuraghe Losa and Santa Cristina are only the most visible remnants – in fact the area around Paulilátino has the highest concentration of *nuraghi* anywhere on the island. The arrival of the **Phoenicians** in the second half of the eighth century halted the growth of the nuraghic culture, though the two peoples lived mainly in harmony. The Phoenicians' chief base was at Tharros, which was to remain the centre of commercial and political activity for the best part of the next two millennia.

Carthage and Rome

Phoenicians and Sards joined forces against **Carthaginian incursions** during the sixth century BC, and both suffered as a result of the Punic triumph. As the island passed under the direct control of Carthage following the treaty with Rome of 509 BC, North African colonies were established at Neapolis, on the southern coast of the Golfo di Oristano, and at Cornus, near present-day Cúglieri. It was at Cornus that a combined

HIGHLIGHTS
1. Antiquarium Arborense
2. Festa di Sa Sartiglia
3. Cycling around Sinis
4. Tharros
5. Santa Cristina
6. Casa Gramsci, Ghilarza

ORISTANO PROVINCE

LOCAL FESTIVALS

The province has some of the island's most compelling **annual festivals**, mostly with a horsey theme: Oristano's medieval **Sa Sartiglia** at Carnival time is the most famous, and well worth going out of your way for, but there are smaller, less trumpeted affairs at **Sédilo**, northeast of Abbasanta, and **Santu Lussurgiu**, in the wooded folds of Monte Ferru.

force of Sards and Carthaginians suffered a decisive defeat by the **Romans** in 216 BC, an event which helped to bring about the total occupation of Sardinia by Rome. The Oristano region was thoroughly penetrated by the new rulers, as witnessed by the thermal baths of Forum Traiani, now Fordongianus. Tharros was revitalized, and it remained the local capital until its decline and eventual evacuation in the face of Arab assaults during the second half of the first millennium.

The Middle Ages

Most of the inhabitants of Tharros resettled inland at Oristano, which became the principal power base during the **Middle Ages**, and the capital of one of Sardinia's four *giudicati* (autonomous territories) in the tenth century. In common with the other three, the **Giudicato of Arborea** depended for its authority on the endless power shifts and temporary alliances between Pisa, Genoa and Aragon. Arborea reached its zenith during the thirteenth and fourteenth centuries, first under **Mariano II** (d.1298), and later at the forefront of the island's resistance to the Aragonese. **Eleonora d'Arborea** (see box, p.142) emerged as the champion of independence in the few areas of the island that remained free of Aragonese domination. Her fortitude and success ensured that she would become one of the greatest figures in Sardinia's history, though her near-legendary fame is also due to the **Carta de Logu**, a body of laws she introduced in 1392, which formed the basis of Sardinia's legislative structure until 1817.

The Spanish and modern periods

After Eleonora's death in 1404, anti-Aragonese resistance collapsed, and her realms joined the rest of the island under Aragonese – and subsequently Spanish – colonial rule. Arborea itself disappeared, while Oristano sank into provincial oblivion, languishing in neglect until Sardinia was taken on by the **Piedmontese** in the eighteenth century. The linking of Oristano to the Carlo Felice highway (now the SS131) in the 1820s gave the town a much-needed boost, and programmes of social reform were attempted, but other problems – principally the increasingly encroaching malarial marshland – were not addressed until **Mussolini**'s initiatives got under way after 1924. His land-reclamation scheme south of Oristano was sustained by colonies of settlers from northern Italy, centred on the new town he originally called "Mussolinia" – later renamed Arborea. The whole territory became a **province** in 1974.

GETTING AROUND

ORISTANO PROVINCE

By car A car provides the best means for exploring the region, and is particularly useful for the Sinis peninsula. Neither of the area's main nuraghic sites is much more than a 20min drive northeast from Oristano on the SS131; Santa Caterina is about the same distance up the SP292, running inland of Sinis, while the Roman baths at Fordongianus are slightly farther on the smaller SP388 eastbound.

By train Oristano itself is on the main north–south rail line; for train info consult ☎ 892 021, ⓦ trenitalia.com.

By bus Public transport isn't much use to reach some of the remoter historic sites, but you can rely on buses from Oristano to Sinis in summer, and there are regular year-round services to Cabras, Santa Giusta, Fordongianus and Santa Caterina di Pittinuri. The main operator is ARST (☎ 800 865 042, ⓦ arst.sardegna.it).

By taxi For destinations that aren't served by buses, non-drivers should be able to negotiate a reasonable taxi fare from Oristano, especially if there are three or four of you.

Oristano

The city of **ORISTANO**, 100km northwest of Cágliari, is a flat, unprepossessing place, its old walls mostly replaced by busy traffic arteries. The quiet centre has a relaxed yet purposeful ambience, however, with quiet nooks and unexpected pleasures. Though it lies just 4km from the sea and is surrounded by lagoons, irrigation systems and the River Tirso, the city has an inland air, the prosperous centre of a richly productive agricultural zone.

At its heart, Oristano's **Duomo** is as old as anything in town, dating from the early thirteenth century, though a seventeenth-century refashioning has given it an overlay of Baroque opulence. The medieval stamp is more evident in the central Piazza Roma, where the **Torre di Mariano II** has been a sturdy survivor of the city's chequered fortunes since its erection in the thirteenth century; another, much smaller remnant of the old defences, the **Portixedda**, lies a short walk away. But the old town's most essential attraction is the marvellous repository of prehistoric and classical finds and medieval works of art at the local museum, the **Antiquarium Arborense**.

The best time to be in Oristano is for the colourful medieval **Sa Sartiglia**, a vivid, highly ritualized horseback competition at Carnival (see box, p.146). Advance bookings are essential for **accommodation** during that time; indeed, they're a good idea at any period, as hotel space is scarce. There are, however, plenty of **restaurants** and **bars**, and local cuisine makes good use of the area's agricultural produce and seafood.

Piazza Eleonora d'Arborea

The heart of Oristano, pedestrianized **Piazza Eleonora d'Arborea** holds the Neoclassical town hall and one of the town's most important churches, and is the main arena for Oristano's annual Sa Sartiglia festivities (see box, p.146). Presiding over all is the marble **statue of Eleonora**, sculpted in 1881, showing the *giudichessa* with the scroll bearing the famous *Carta de Logu* with which she is associated, while inset panels depict her various victories (see box, p.142).

San Francesco

Piazza Eleonora d'Arborea • Daily 7.30–11.30am & 5–8pm, 4–7pm in winter

At the western end of the elongated piazza, four stout Ionic columns front the nineteenth-century church of **San Francesco**. Designed by the eminent Cágliari architect Gaetano Cima, the building incorporates the remains of a much older construction, traces of which – Gothic arches and Corinthian columns – are visible on the right-hand side. The most compelling item within the church's octagonal domed interior is the so-called *Crocifisso di Nicodemo*, housed in a Neoclassical marble altar on the left side. Carved in the fourteenth century by an unknown Catalan, the crucifix is considered one of the most precious and influential wooden sculptures on the whole island; the emaciated, sunken-eyed Christ, his skin scored by cuts and raw abrasions, is drenched with emotion.

If there's someone around, ask them to admit you to the **sacristy** to see the central panel of Pietro Cavaro's polyptych of St Francis receiving the stigmata, the rest of which is now in the Antiquarium Arborense (see p.143). Opposite is a small sculpture of St Basil by Nino Pisano.

Torre di Mariano II

Piazza Roma

Narrow, pedestrianized Corso Umberto links Piazza Eleonora with Piazza Roma, where pavement bars cluster around the base of the crenellated **Torre di Mariano II**.

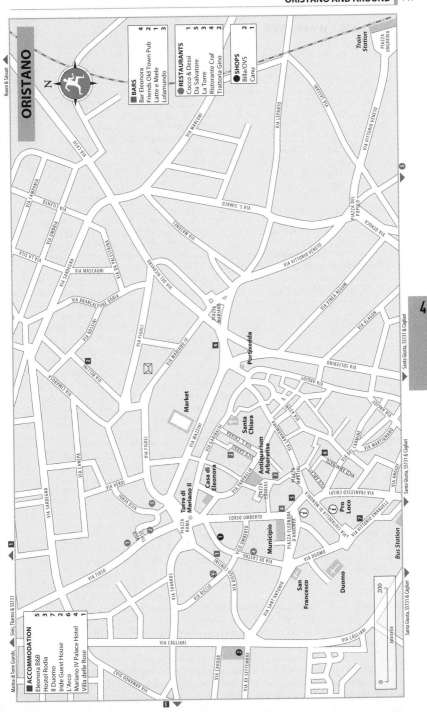

ORISTANO

BARS
Bar Eleonora	4
Friends Old Town Pub	2
Latte e Miele	1
Lolamundo	3

RESTAURANTS
Cocco & Dessi	1
Da Salvatore	5
La Torre	3
Ristorante Craf	4
Trattoria Gino	2

SHOPS
Billa/OVS	2
Canu	1

ACCOMMODATION
Eleonora B&B	5
Hostel Rodia	3
Il Duomo	7
Iride Guest House	2
L'Arco	6
Mariano IV Palace Hotel	4
Villa delle Rose	1

4

ELEONORA D'ARBOREA

As the last of Sardinia's medieval rulers to enjoy any significant success against the island's aggressors, **Eleonora of Arborea** (c.1340–1404) is venerated throughout the island. Occupying a sort of Joan of Arc role in the popular imagination, she also made a significant contribution to the evolution of **civil rights** in Sardinia with her promulgation of a book of law that eventually became the benchmark of local freedoms for the whole island.

When Eleonora's father, the *giudice* Mariano IV (reigned 1346–76) – himself a Catalan – was required by the Aragonese King Pedro IV to have his two daughters betrothed to Spanish princes, he matched one, Beatrice, with Amerigo VI of Narbonne, but allowed Eleonora to be wedded instead, in 1366 or 1367, to the Genoan **Brancaleone Doria**, scion of Spain's main rivals in Sardinia at that time (though they were nominally Aragon's vassals). Eleonora spent most of the following fifteen years in Castelsardo (then called Castelgenovese) and Genoa, where she ingratiated herself with the doge and laid the foundations of a future anti-Aragonese alliance.

Following the assassination of her brother, Eleonora became **regent of Arborea** in 1383. As the wife of a vassal of Aragon, she managed to maintain a delicate balance of power and negotiate a degree of independence, enabling her to concentrate on the concerns of her subjects. In a short time she had acquainted herself with the entire *giudicato*, her tours round the territory greeted with enthusiastic acclaim. Her popular appeal was no doubt enhanced by the ten years of **tax exemptions** she granted to the downtrodden population, exhausted by the economic hardship induced by the long period of war.

The struggle against Aragon simmered on, however. Even when her husband Brancaleone was imprisoned (an event interpreted by some as his desertion to the enemy), Eleonora refused to submit. Her intransigence finally paid off in 1388, with the signing of a **treaty** that guaranteed Arborean independence in return for restoring to Aragon the cities occupied by the *giudicato*, and even returned Brancaleone to the fold. From her new position of strength, Eleonora forged a tactical alliance with the Genoans and launched a new offensive against Spain, as a result of which Brancaleone, with Genoan help, even managed to occupy Sássari on her behalf.

Of more lasting benefit was Eleonora's formulation around 1392 of a legal code, or **Carta de Logu**, for Arborea. Although her statue in the centre of Oristano represents this as a brief scroll, in fact the document comprised 198 chapters, addressing rural, civil and penal issues and attempting to define the legal status and rights of people at every level of society – including children, slaves and (in particular detail) women. First mooted by her father, Mariano IV, the code was far ahead of its time in its scope and application, and it remains the most enduring legacy of Eleonora's rule. It was adopted by the Aragonese in 1421, and later extended throughout the island, remaining in force until the enactment of the Carlo Felice code by the Piedmontese in 1817. As the eighteenth-century English lawyer and traveller John Tyndale put it: "The framing of a body of laws so far in advance of those of other countries, where greater civilization existed, must ever be the brightest ornament in the diadem of the Giudichessa."

Eleonora's military achievements, however, did not long survive her death from plague in 1404, following which the Aragonese were quickly able to occupy Arborea and its territories. Her rule marked the final glorious chapter of Sardinian independence, and her brief triumph was all the more poignant in light of the obstacles she faced on every side – not just her severely circumscribed role as regent for infant male heirs, but above all her status as a woman in a feudal, male-dominated society.

Also known as the Torre di San Cristóforo, the tower was erected by one of Oristano's greatest rulers, the *giudice* Mariano II, in 1290. The bastion originally formed the centrepiece of Oristano's medieval fortifications. The walls to which it was joined were demolished at the end of the nineteenth century; the gateway through it, the Porta Mariano or Porta Manna, was the city's northern gate. The tower is occasionally open for exhibitions in summer and during festivals, when you can climb the three levels to view the huge bell at the top and, on a clear day, vistas of the sea.

Portixedda

Via Mazzini • Ask at Antiquarium Arborense for access • Free

Besides the more imposing Torre di Mariano II, the only survivor of the city's defences is the squat **Portixedda** ("little gate"), off Via Garibaldi – one of two towers protecting the eastern approaches into town. These days it holds small temporary exhibitions and you can climb to the top for rather limited views around town.

Casa di Eleonora

Via Parpaglia 6–12

Just off Piazza Roma on Via Parpaglia, the so-called **Casa di Eleonora** can only ever have had a tenuous connection with Eleonora d'Arborea – if any – since it was built over a century after the *giudichessa*'s death. Nonetheless, with its preserved medieval window, it remains a good example of sixteenth-century architecture. It's now partly abandoned, and partly occupied by a bar.

Santa Chiara

Via Garibaldi • Open only for services, currently Mon–Sat 7.15am, Sun 8.30am • ☎ 0783 78 093

The fourteenth-century church of **Santa Chiara** was long thought to hold the burial place of Eleonora d'Arborea, but the tomb here is in fact that of her aunt, Costanza di Saluzzo. The church is part of a convent, making access difficult unless you drop in during the daily Mass or make a request to the resident Clarisse sisters.

4

The Duomo

Piazza Duomo • Daily 8.30am–6.30pm

With its detached octagonal, onion-roofed fourteenth-century belltower, Oristano's **Duomo** forms an atmospheric ensemble with the next-door seminary dating from 1712. The present building is mostly the result of a Baroque-era renovation, with only sections of the apses surviving from the original thirteenth-century construction.

The Duomo's spacious but fussy **interior** has three ornate chapels on either side of the nave. The first on the right has a painted wooden statue of the *Annunziata*, thought to be by **Nino Pisano** (c.1315–68). Full of expression, the statue is surrounded by a majolica and gilt altar busy with *putti* (cherubim). The two **marble panels** in front were carved by an anonymous Catalan in the fourteenth or fifteenth century. Far more interesting, however, are the other sides of the slabs, carved three hundred years earlier: eleventh- and twelfth-century Byzantine work, illustrating biblical scenes, including a portrayal of Daniel in the lions' den.

Antiquarium Arborense

Piazzetta Corrias • Mon–Fri 9am–8pm, Sat & Sun 9am–2pm & 3–8pm • €5 • ☎ 0783 791 262

A handsome sixteenth-century merchant's house holds one of Sardinia's most absorbing museums – Oristano's **Antiquarium Arborense**. As well as rotating exhibitions of nuraghic, Phoenician, Roman and Greek artefacts, the museum gives permanent space to Tharros and its occupants, and includes a good gallery of late medieval art.

Ground floor

The Antiquarium's **ground floor** displays pre-nuraghic and nuraghic finds, including Neolithic blades, axeheads and spearheads – many of obsidian or flint – from the Sinis peninsula, and a small collection of jewellery, bone hairpins and other personal items recovered from tombs. More gripping are the finds from Carthaginian Tharros, much of it from burial sites, including masks to ward off the evil eye, elegantly shaped *askoi* (curved vessels) and terracotta figurines, mostly from the fifth century BC and often Ionic Greek in inspiration. There are equally numerous exhibits from the Roman period in Tharros: pins, plates, ceramic objects, bottles and myriad other glass containers including first-century AD cinerary urns from northern Italy and Gaul. One display case is devoted to items of foreign manufacture found in Tharros tombs, including Cretan, Etruscan and mainland Greek ceramics.

First floor

Up on the **first floor** you'll find an imaginative reconstruction of Roman Tharros as it might have appeared at the height of its power in the fourth century AD. Around it, texts in Italian explain the various buildings and monuments: the port, baths, amphitheatre, the tetrastyle Doric temple, the houses, roads, aqueduct and excavated tombs. Display cases on the balcony above hold funerary items from a Phoenician necropolis excavated at San Giovanni di Sinis (see p.151), and Roman and Byzantine objects from Tharros and Cabras.

The Pinacoteca

The air-conditioned **Pinacoteca** houses a small but rich collection of medieval and Renaissance art. The chief exhibits come from the studio of Renaissance Cágliari artist Pietro Cavaro. His most outstanding work, the nine-panelled *Retablo del Santo Cristo* (1533), from Oristano's church of San Francesco, depicts Franciscan saints, portrayed with great subtlety and sensitivity. The central panel, showing St Francis receiving the stigmata, remains in the sacristy of San Francesco (see p.140).

There are two other famous *retabli* (paintings on wood) here: the *Madonna dei Consiglieri* by sixteenth-century artist Antioco Mainas (also from Cágliari), showing five bearded town councillors kneeling around the Madonna and baby Jesus, with Sts Andrew and John the Baptist, and the much earlier *Retablo di San Martino*, two parts of a triptych by an anonymous early fifteenth-century Catalan. The central panel shows the Madonna surrounded by angels playing medieval instruments; the right panel has St Martin cutting off part of his cloak to give to a beggar.

ARRIVAL AND DEPARTURE

ORISTANO

By train Oristano's train station is in Piazza Ungheria at the eastern end of town, a 20min walk from the centre. Local buses connect it with the centre every 20–35min; buy tickets (€1, or €1.50 on board) from authorized bars – there's one outside the station (the bus stop is across the road). Train information can be accessed at ☎892 021, ⓦtrenitalia.com.

Destinations Abbasanta (7–9 daily; 30min); Cágliari (10–15 daily; 1hr–1hr 30min); Macomer (7–9 daily; 45min–1hr); Olbia (5 daily, some with change at Ozieri-Chilivani; 2hr 30min–3hr); Sássari (4 daily, some with change at Ozieri-Chilivani; 2hr–2hr 40min).

By bus All ARST buses pull in at Oristano's bus station, centrally located off Via Cágliari, with pedestrian access also from Via Episcopio, off Via Vittorio Emanuele; some buses also make a stop at the train station. For information,

call ☎0783 355 808 or toll-free ☎800 865 042, ⓦarst.sardegna.it.

Destinations Abbasanta (Mon–Sat 10 daily; 1–2hr); Arborea (Mon–Sat 1–2 hourly; 25min); Bosa (Mon–Sat 4 daily; 2hr); Cabras (Mon–Sat 1–2 hourly, Sun 4–9 daily; 15min); Cágliari (Mon–Sat 2 daily; 2hr); Cúglieri (Mon–Sat 5 daily, plus July–Aug Sun 2; 1hr); Is Aruttas (July–Aug 5 daily; 50min); Marina di Torre Grande (Mon–Sat 12 daily, Sun 5 daily; 25min); Putzu Idu (Mon–Sat 2–6 daily, July–Aug also Sun 4 daily; 45min); Samugheo (Mon–Sat 5–6 daily, July–Aug also Sun 1 daily; 1hr 10min); San Giovanni di Sinis (July–Aug 5 daily; 35min); Santa Caterina di Pittinuri (Mon–Sat 5 daily, July–Aug also Sun 2 daily; 45min); Santa Giusta (Mon–Sat 1–2 hourly; 10min); Santu Lussurgiu (Mon–Sat 6 daily; 50min–1hr 10min); Sássari (1–3 daily; 1hr 45min); Tharros (July–Aug 5 daily; 35min).

GETTING AROUND

By car Much of Oristano's centre is pedestrianized or barred to non-resident drivers. Parking restrictions are in force (for parking between the blue lines) Mon–Fri 9am–1pm and 4–8pm, Sat 9am–1pm; tickets from machines cost

€0.60 for first hour, then €1/hr. Car rental is available at Avis, Via Liguria 17 (☎0783 310 638, ⓦavis.com); Europcar, 4km south of town in Zona Industriale Nord (☎0783 359 814, ⓦeuropcar.it); and Sardinya, Via Cágliari 436 (☎0783 779

106, ⓦautonoleggiosardinya.it).

By bus Linea Rossa ("Red Line") and Linea Verde ("Green Line") buses terminate at Piazza Mariano, and Linea Verde buses also stop at the central Piazza Roma; Linea Azzurra buses head out to Marina di Torre Grande. It's worth telling the driver your intended destination, as there may be a more convenient stop. Buy tickets at authorized outlets (€1) or on board (€1.50). For detailed information, call ☎0783 355 808 or toll-free ☎800 865 042, ⓦarst .sardegna.it.

By taxi You'll find taxi stands outside the train station in Piazza Ungheria (☎0783 74 328) and in Piazza Roma (☎0783 70 280); the fare should be around €5 for most destinations in town.

By bike or scooter Bikes can be rented at Dore, Via Tirso 138 (☎0783 212 172, ⓦfrancescodore.net); rates are €7/5hr, €12/day. There's another rental outfit on the Sinis peninsula (see p.149). Alternatively, rent scooters from Marco Moto, Via Cágliari 99 (☎0783.310 040); 125cc scooters cost €40 for one day, €180 for five days.

INFORMATION

Tourist office Information on the whole province is dispensed at Piazza Eleonora 19 (Mon–Fri 8.30am–1pm & 3–6pm, Sat 9.30am–1.30pm & 4–8pm, Sun 9.30am– 1.30pm; ☎0783 368 3210, ⓦgooristano.com).
Pro Loco The volunteer-run office at Via Ciutadella de

Menorca 14 has information on the city but keeps erratic hours (officially June–Oct Mon–Fri 8.30am–1.30pm & 3.30–8.30pm, Sat 8.30am–1.30pm; Nov–May Mon–Fri 9am–1pm & 3.30–7.30pm; ☎0783 70 621).

ACCOMMODATION

Oristano has a small selection of **hotels** and **B&Bs** scattered around town. During the Sa Sartiglia festivities in particular, you'll need to book way ahead. The nearest **campsite** is 6km away at Marina di Torre Grande (see p.150).

Eleonora B&B Piazza Eleonora d'Arborea 12 ☎0783 70 435 or ☎347 481 7976, ⓦeleonora-bed-and-breakfast .com. On the old town's central piazza, this B&B is in a medieval palazzo and has five large rooms, including four-bed suites, with wi-fi access. Rooms overlooking the garden are quietest. €70

Hostel Rodia Viale Repubblica ☎0783 251 881, ⓦhostelrodia.it. Around a 15min walk from the old centre, this modern complex houses both a hostel and a hotel, though as hostel accommodation is in en-suite doubles, twins and family suites, there's little to distinguish these from the hotel rooms, except the latter have minibars and TVs. Breakfast costs €2–7, meals are €15, and there's internet access and bikes to rent (book ahead). Beds in shared rooms €25, doubles €80

★ **Il Duomo** Via Vittorio Emanuele 34 ☎0783 778 061, ⓦjostoalduomo.net. Just across from the Duomo, this hotel is a modern refurbishment of a seventeenth-century building. The bright, plush en-suite rooms set around a central court-yard have satellite TV and internet connections. There's a bar, restaurant and private parking. €108

Iride Guest House Via Bellini 29 ☎0783 70 435,

ⓔirideguesthouse@gmail.it. Six modern apartments outside the old centre provide stylish accommodation with use of kitchen facilities for stays of three days or more. Modern art by local artists adorns the walls. Breakfast is at a nearby bar. €80

★ **L'Arco** Vico Ammirato 12 ☎0783 72 849 or ☎335 690 4240, ⓦarcobedandbreakfast.it. Centrally located off Piazza Martiri, this spotless, wood-beamed and relaxed B&B with friendly hosts has two good-size rooms, simply but elegantly furnished, with a/c and a shared modern bathroom. There's a small terrace, too. No credit cards. €65

Mariano IV Palace Hotel Piazza Mariano 50 ☎0783 360 101, ⓦm4ph.eu. Modern, capacious hotel with polish but no great charm close to the centre. Breakfast is nothing special, and it could all do with a revamp, but it's fine for a night. €90

Villa delle Rose Piazza Italia ☎0783 310 101, ⓦhotel villadellerose.com. A good hotel choice on a quiet piazza off Via Lombardia, a 10min walk from Piazza Roma. Rooms are solidly furnished, each with a spacious bathroom. There's a bus stop right outside on the Linea Verde for connections with Piazza Mariano and the train station. €80

EATING

★ **Cocco & Dessi** Via Tirso 31 ☎0783 252 648. In former hotel premises, this idiosyncratic but elegant place retains a retro feel, and has five eating areas, including a gazebo and a balcony. The menu is strong on seafood (mains are €11–15), and there are pizzas in the evening. You might finish your meal with a glass of Oristano's celebrated Vernaccia dessert wine. Daily 12.30–2.30pm & 7.30–11.30pm.

Da Salvatore Via Carbónia 1 ☎0783 357 134. The relatively remote location means that this place is often empty, which is a shame, considering the great seafood dishes and low prices (a couple of courses for €20–25). It's on the southern outskirts of town, signposted to the right of the main road into town from Santa Giusta; the Linea Rossa bus route passes nearby. Mon–Sat 12.30–3pm & 8–10.30pm.

La Torre Piazza Roma ☎0783 301 494. For down-to-earth and authentic pizzas, head for *La Torre*; their speciality is *pizza ai funghi porcini* (with mushrooms). Pizzas are around €7, other dishes cost €6–8 for pastas, €10–17 for meat and fish mains. Tues–Sun noon–3pm & 7–11pm, open daily in Aug.

Ristorante Craf Via De Castro ☎0783 70 669. This intimate, brick-vaulted restaurant specializes in local dishes (all €10–15), especially meat, including horse and donkey. The *antipasti* are worth dipping into, and vegetarian dishes include the delicious *risotto alla bonarcadese*, with mushrooms. There's a great range of Sardinian wines, and the atmosphere is smart but not over-formal. Mon–Sat 12.30–3pm & 7.30–10pm, Sun 7.30–10pm.

★ **Trattoria Gino** Via Tirso 13 ☎0783 71 428. This straightforward, reliable little eatery features traditional Sardinian dishes such as *gnocchi sardi* and *sebadas* (warm, cheese-filled pastry-cases topped with honey). Everything is well prepared, and service is polite and friendly. Pastas are €8–10, mains €9–13. Arrive early or book – there are only ten tables. Mon–Sat 12.30–3pm & 8–11pm.

SA SARTIGLIA

Oristano's flamboyant **Sa Sartiglia** festival is the biggest date in the town's calendar – indeed some complain it's the only thing that moves this insular, provincial town. The three-day event, which features jousting and various horseback stunts, along with traditional costumes, music and dancing, takes place between the last Sunday of Carnival period and Shrove Tuesday.

The **arcane rituals** of the festival perhaps originated with knights on the Second Crusade, who may have brought the trappings of Saracen tournaments to Sardinia in the twelfth century. On the other hand, it could be a Spanish import – a similar annual festival, *La Sortilla*, is held on the island of Menorca in June. Whatever the case, under Spanish rule, similarly lavish feasts were held for Oristano's knights at regular intervals throughout the year; in time, these celebrations took on a more theatrical aspect, finally merging with the annual Carnival revelries. With all participants masked and costumed, the whole affair exudes a theatrical spirit unrivalled by Sardinia's other festivals.

The main events take place on the first and third days, staged by the guilds of San Giovanni (representing the farmers) and San Giuseppe (the carpenters) respectively. Each event is presided over by a white-masked arbiter known as **Su Componidori**, chosen for his riding prowess. The *Componidori* represents the continuation of the *giudice's* role, and is decked out in a bizarre pastiche of medieval garb, complete with mask, ribbons and top hat. The *Componidori* initiates the proceedings, riding up and down the sanded track on Via Duomo, blessing the track, contenders and audience alike with a bouquet of violets. The **joust** itself consists of mounted charges with an extended rapier, with the aim of lancing a star-shaped ring – *stella* or *sartiglia* – suspended 3m above the ground. Each charge is heralded by a fanfare of drums and trumpets, and followed by groans of disappointment or wild cheering according to whether the ring is speared or missed; traditionally, more hits represent a better chance of a good harvest and thus good luck for the townspeople.

After the *corse alla stella*, the afternoon is given over to **Le Pariglie** – hair-raising **horseback stunts** (for example several riders balancing on steeds tied together at full gallop), usually taking place on a sanded track along Via Mazzini, with prizes given to the greatest equestrian feats. The whole rigmarole is repeated two days later for the *gremio* (guild) of San Giuseppe, while on the second day, a relatively recent addition, the **Sartigliedda**, is dedicated to younger riders mounted on the miniature horses of the Giara di Gésturi (see p.125).

Other highlights of the festa include the *vestizione*, or formal dressing of the *componidori*, which generally takes place in Via Aristana for the San Giovanni *sartiglia*, and in the church of Sant'Efisio for San Giuseppe's, and the equally elaborate *svestizione*, or disrobing, at the end of each day; the proclamation to announce the opening of each day's proceedings, read out by a mounted herald accompanied by a phalanx of drummers and trumpeters (normally around 10am in Piazza Roma and Piazza Eleonora); and the **songs** and traditional **dances** in Piazza Eleonora on the eve of the festivities and at the end of them.

Although the festival draws big **crowds** of both locals and tourists, it's usually possible to get a view of the events. The best vantage, however, is from the **grandstand seats** on Via Duomo and Via Mazzini, for which **tickets** cost €15–25, available a few days before the event from the **Fondazione Sa Sartiglia** office on Piazza Eleonora or online at ⓦ sartiglia.info. If you don't want to attend the whole three-day event, Tuesday is the best day to be here, when the crowds are smaller.

DRINKING AND NIGHTLIFE

Oristano has plenty of congenial **bars** to while away an afternoon or evening, many of them staying open late. On summer nights, locals converge on the bars and clubs in Marina di Torre Grande (see p.150).

Bar Eleonora Piazza Eleonora d'Arborea ☎0783 301 71 454. A great breakfast bar or coffee stop at any time, with *cornetti*, pastries and *pizzette*, and some outdoor seating on the piazza. Mon–Fri 7.15am–8.30pm, Sat 7.15am–2pm & 4–8.30pm.

Friends Old Town Pub Vico Antonio Garau ☎328 288 5758. Lively *birreria* with music (karaoke on Thurs, live on Fri, DJs Sat) and food (grills, panini, salads). You can sit in booths inside or in the small garden on hot evenings (though the pub may close in Aug). Tues–Sun 8pm–late.

Latte e Miele Via De Castro 15 ☎0783 71 209. Traditional and civilized but buzzing café with *cornetti*, pastries and good coffee; table service adds 25 percent to the bill. Mon–Sat 7am–1am, Sun 7am–1.30pm & 5–1am.

★ **Lolamundo** Piazzetta Corrias ☎0783 301 284. For daytime snacks or an evening drink, this contemporary café in a quiet piazza next to the Antiquarium has a cool vibe and tables outside in summer. It's also good for snack lunches. Mon–Sat 7am–midnight.

SHOPPING

Billa/OVS Via Diaz 53 ☎0783 78 191. Useful store for a range of food, drink and reasonably priced clothes and accessories. Mon–Sat 8.30am–9pm, Sun 8.30am–1.30pm & 4.30–9pm.

Canu Via De Castro 20 ☎0783 78 723. Stocks a good range of guides as well as some English-language books. Mon–Fri 8am–1pm & 4–8pm, Sat 8am–1pm & 5–8pm.

MARKETS

Food, clothes and household goods The main food market is between Via Mazzini and Via Mariano IV (accessible from either), Mon–Sat mornings. Clothes, household goods, fruit and vegetables are traded on Via Aristana, near the train station, Tues–Sat mornings.

Antiques and curios An antiques and curiosity market sets up in Piazza Eleonora on the first Sat of the month.

DIRECTORY

Hospital Ospedale San Martino, Via Rockefeller ☎0783 3171.

Internet access Genius Point, Via Pietro Riccio 4, off Via De Castro (Mon–Sat 8.30am–1pm & 4.15–8.15pm; €4/hr).

Laundry Coin-operated machines at Lava Più, Via Campanelli 13, west of Via Cágliari (daily 8.30am–10pm; €4 for 7kg, €1.50 for a dryer).

Pharmacy Farmacia Sanna, Piazza Roma (Mon–Sat 8.30am–1.30pm & 4–8pm). See rota posted on pharmacy doors for current late-night opening.

Post office Via Mariano IV (Mon–Fri 8.25am–1pm, Sat 8.25am–1pm). You can change cash and travellers' cheques here.

Travel agencies Alerica Viaggi, Via De Castro 59 ☎0783 300 203, can arrange tickets for air and sea journeys.

The Sinis peninsula

For many visitors, Oristano is just a stop en route to the **Sinis peninsula**, the low-lying promontory at the northern end of the Golfo di Oristano. Fringed with beaches and dotted with lagoons where reserves protect the birds that nest here for part of the year, Sinis is unlike anywhere else in Sardinia, and merits unhurried exploration, ideally by bike. The **peninsula** also holds one of Sardinia's most important archeological sites, the ruined Punic and Roman city of **Tharros**, superbly situated by the sea, 20km west of Oristano.

The marshes and lagoons of Sinis teem with fish, providing a livelihood for locals, who have perfected the art of negotiating the watery terrain on reed-built craft, or **fassonis** – coracle-like, flat-bottomed boats for which the peninsula is famous. There is evidence of these in use since prehistoric times, and though they are now mainly taken out for ceremonial occasions, you may still see the flimsy-looking vessels on remote backwaters, usually being punted along from a standing position. Resembling truncated canoes, they can be assembled by experts in a matter of minutes.

A museum in the peninsula's main town of **Cabras** gives a good overview of the history and geography of the area, though there is little other reason to hang about here unless for the banks, hotels and restaurants. Accommodation is otherwise pretty sparse in Sinis, though there's a campsite at **Marina di Torre Grande**, by Oristano's nearest beach.

GETTING AROUND AND INFORMATION	THE SINIS PENINSULA

By car Drivers will be able to access the whole peninsula relatively easily, though you'll need robust suspension to reach some of the beaches, such as Is Arenas. The better-known beaches have staffed car parks where you pay between mid-June and mid-Sept (around €2.60 for 1–4hr).

By bus Tharros, Is Aruttas, Putzu Idu, Mandriola and Su Pallosu are connected to Oristano by 4–5 ARST buses daily in July and Aug, and there are good year-round services to Cabras and Marina di Torre Grande.

By bike The cooperative running the tourist office listed below rents out bikes (€2.50/hr or €5.50 for 8hr) and offers bike tours (€20–25 for 1–2hr). There's also a luggage deposit here and they plan to include canoe rental and diving trips.

Tourist information The independent tourist office in Pratza de Is Ballus, near Tharros and San Giovanni di Sinis church (see p.151), covers the whole Sinis peninsula (April–Oct daily 10am–6pm; ☎ 349 530 3029, ⓦ cultour .sardegna.it).

Cabras

Spread along the eastern shore of the **Stagno di Cabras** lagoon, the site of **CABRAS** has been settled since Sardinia's earliest prehistory, as shown by the abundance of archeological finds in the area. Today Cabras is a low-key, low-built town, probably best known for its **Corsa degli Scalzi**, a race to the church of San Salvatore during the first weekend of September (see p.151). You won't find much in the way of commotion or excitement at other times, and lacking a central piazza or other focal point the town has rather an aimless air, though it does boast a good museum and has a couple of excellent eating and accommodation options. With the lagoon mostly out of view, the bulky, domed profile of the seventeenth-century parish church of **Santa Maria** is the town's only distinctive feature, behind which you might pick out the scanty traces of a castle belonging to the *giudici* of Arborea that once stood here.

The local lagoons or *stagni* are abundant sources of fish, especially eels and mullet, the basis of one of Sardinia's oldest-known dishes: *sa merca*, salted mullet cooked in herbs (the dialect name suggests a Phoenician ancestry). Excavation work around the southern mouth of the Stagno di Cabras lagoon – at **Kukkuru S'Arriu** (or Cúccuru is Arrius), three or four kilometres south of Cabras – has revealed a huge shrine and necropolis with finds going back to the Bonu Ighinu culture of the fourth millennium BC.

Museo Cívico

Via Tharros 121 • Daily 9am–1pm & 4–8pm, 3–7pm in winter • €4, or €7 including Tharros • ☎ 0783 290 636

On the banks of the lagoon near the southwest entrance to town, the **Museo Cívico** is well worth a look for its archeological exhibits, imaginatively displayed in a modern purpose-built block. As well as the nuraghic and pre-nuraghic items from throughout the Sinis peninsula, there are shelves full of objects from Tharros – including a Roman milestone, stelae, needles, amphorae and vases – and space is given to often illuminating temporary exhibitions. The museum explains plenty about the ecology and flora of the peninsula, too, and gives a close-up look at the wonderful *fassonis*. When you've had your fill, take a breather along the eucalyptus-fringed lagoonside park behind the museum.

ARRIVAL AND DEPARTURE	CABRAS

By bus ARST buses stop in the centre and near the museum.

Destinations Is Aruttas (July–Aug 5 daily; 35min);

Oristano (Mon–Sat 1–2 hourly, Sun 5–10 daily; 15min); San Giovanni di Sinis (July–Aug 5 daily; 20min).

ACCOMMODATION AND EATING

Il Caminetto Via Cesare Battisti 8 ☎ 0783 391 139. Under the same ownership as the *Villa Canu* hotel, this is

the best place in town for sampling local dishes sourced from the lagoons or the open sea. Such specialities as pasta with *bottarga di muggine* (mullet roe) and grilled eels are always on the menu. Most mains are €12–16. Tues–Sun 12.30–2.45pm & 8–10.30pm; open daily in Aug.

Sa Cottilla Via Quattro Mori ❶ 333 229 5405, ⓦ sacottilla .it. Colourful B&B in a quiet street run by a young couple. All rooms have private bathrooms and wi-fi, breakfast is served

on the veranda, and there's a garden. No credit cards. **€70**

Villa Canu Via Firenze 9 ❶ 0783 290 155, ⓦ hotel villacanu.com. A restored country house in the centre of town, this is the most appealing among the hotels in Cabras. Most rooms have access to an internal patio, and there's a small pool and wi-fi access. Closed Nov–Feb. **€98**

Marina di Torre Grande

The main lido for both Oristano and Cabras, **Marina di Torre Grande**, 8km west of the provincial capital, is centred on the solid cylindrical Aragonese watchtower for which it is named. From here, Lungomare Eleonora d'Arborea runs for about a kilometre along the seafront, lined with ranks of holiday homes and dwarf palms, and with twinkling views across the gulf to Tharros. With its broad beach and a bay ideal for **windsurfing**, Torre Grande makes a lively place to visit in summer, a-buzz with the bikes and blaring radios of Oristano's youth and offering a choice of animated bars and pizzerias. The nightlife kicks off with a vivacious evening *passeggiata* up and down the Lungomare.

ARRIVAL AND DEPARTURE   MARINA DI TORRE GRANDE

By bus Apart from the regular ARST bus service from Oristano and Cabras, local buses of Oristano's seasonal

Linea Azzurra connect Oristano's train station and centre with the resort once or twice hourly in July and Aug.

ACCOMMODATION AND EATING

Il Pescatore Lungomare Torregrande ❶ 347 619 5014. A kilometre or so west along the beach, this isolated white shack right on the sand specializes in grilled fish at reasonable prices. There are set-price menus for €25 and €30. No credit cards. Daily except Wed 12.30–3pm & 8–11pm, open daily in summer.

Spinnaker Strada Torre Grande ❶ 0783 22 074,

ⓦ spinnakervacanze.com. Less than 1km east of Torre Grande and the nearest campsite to Oristano, this well-equipped complex set in pinewoods has its own private beach, a pool and bungalows (€79). In summer, frequent buses on Oristano's Linea Azzurra stop right outside. Closed Oct–March. Pitches **€25**

ACTIVITIES

Windsurfing Eolo, which operates from the beach in summer, offers windsurfing courses and equipment rental (❶ 329 613 6461 or ❶ 327 560 9844, ⓦ eolowindsurf.com).

They also organize various beach sports, rent out loungers and parasols and run a beach bar.

San Salvatore

Six kilometres west of Marina di Torre Grande (signposted off the Tharros road), **San Salvatore** is one of Sardinia's *chiese novenari* – churches open for just nine days a year, when devotees live in nearby *cumbessias*, or pilgrims' lodgings. The *novena* of San Salvatore takes place between August and September, culminating in the **Corsa degli Scalzi** (see box opposite). The rest of the time the place is eerily deserted, the sixteenth-century church surrounded on all sides by the shuttered pilgrims' shacks. Indeed, the scene recalls nothing so much as an adobe-built ghost town, and if it all looks vaguely familiar, it may be because the place was used as a set for various spaghetti Westerns in the 1960s and 1970s.

The pagan sanctuary

Ipogeo di San Salvatore • Mon–Sat 9.30am–1pm & 3.30–6pm, Sun 9.30am–12.30pm, Nov–March mornings only (call first) • Free, but donation appreciated • ❶ 347 818 4069

Belying its unexceptional appearance, the church of San Salvatore reveals a fascinating past, since it was erected on top of an ancient **pagan sanctuary**, connected in nuraghic times with a water cult and later dedicated to Mars and Venus. When the building is open,

---

LA CORSA DEGLI SCALZI

Run between Cabras and San Salvatore on the first weekend of September, the **Corsa degli Scalzi** is a re-enactment of a frantic rescue mission undertaken four centuries ago to save the statue of San Salvatore from Moorish attackers. Departing from Cabras, 8km away, the first part of the race is run on Saturday at dawn by the town's boys, all barefoot and clad only in white shirts and shorts. The following day, the boys return, bearing aloft the holy statue from its sanctuary to safe custody in Cabras. It's a spirited caper, infused with rowdy enthusiasm.

---

a guide will accompany you down into the fourth-century subterranean chambers, where you can just make out some faded frescoes of Venus, Cupid and Hercules.

In addition to these, there are black-inked drawings and graffiti from a number of sources, most intriguingly a repeated "RF". This may be a Carthaginian prayer for healing (*Rufu* in their Semitic language), but the use of the Latin alphabet suggests that a degree of Punic culture survived later into the Roman era than was previously thought. Greek and Arabic writing adds to the cultural mix, which can be explained by the fact that the holy site lay close to Tharros, then an important port. The pictures of boats – including a Sard *fassoni* and a Spanish galleon – were possibly votive drawings, while an image of a person in a cage could well be a prisoner's doodle from when the chambers were used as a gaol during the Spanish period.

ACCOMMODATION AND EATING   SAN SALVATORE

Abraxas Località San Salvatore di Sinis ☎ 347 132 5254. This bar at the entrance to the huddle of *cumbessias* is decked out in the style of a Western saloon – appropriately, given the spaghetti Westerns that were filmed here. It has pastas (€6–9), salads (€7), grilled meat (€12–15) and beers. Daily 9am–9pm, closed Mon in winter.

Sa Pedrera Strada per Cabras ☎ 0783 370 018, ⓦ sapedrera.it. 2km outside San Salvatore, this friendly hotel has large, clean rooms arranged around a garden, two tennis courts and an excellent restaurant. Wonderful beaches are just a short distance away, but you need a vehicle. Rates plummet out of season. Closed Jan to mid-Feb. **€118**

San Giovanni di Sinis

Località San Giovanni di Sinis • Daily 9am–1hr before sunset

The sixth-century church of **San Giovanni di Sinis**, 4km south of San Salvatore, vies with Cágliari's San Saturnino (see p.69) for the title of Sardinia's oldest church. Standing on the roadside at the base of the limb of land on which Tharros sits, the paleo-Christian church presents a rather oriental – or Byzantine – appearance, with its red dome, irregular stonework and roof slung low over an asymmetrical facade. That it should still be standing at all after its long years of exposure to pirate raids is largely thanks to the French Vittorini monks who took it over in the eleventh century. Thoroughly and sympathetically renovated, the interior is pleasingly dim and bare, stripped clean of all decoration.

Near the seashore behind the church, look out for the thatched huts, or *domus di cruccuri*, once used by local fishermen, now converted into unobtrusive holiday homes. Opposite the church, bars, pizzerias and restaurants cater to the stream of coach parties visiting Tharros. The comings and goings of these, combined with the bustle of people attracted to the arc of beach a few hundred metres further up the road, make for a fair amount of activity around here in high summer.

Tharros

Località San Giovanni di Sinis • Daily 9am to 1hr before sunset • €7, including museum at Cabras • ☎ 0783 370 019 • Tharros is linked to Oristano by a summer bus service operated by ARST (July–Aug 5 daily; 35min)

The spit of land ending at **Capo San Marco** protrudes like a knobbly finger into the Golfo di Oristano, with a sturdy Spanish watchtower dominating its highest point.

The peninsula also holds the atmospheric ruins of the Punic-Roman town of **Tharros**, one of Sardinia's most significant sites from this era.

Brief history

Providing safe anchorage on either side according to the direction of the wind, the peninsula has been settled since earliest times. Inevitably, given its strategic advantages, Phoenicians established a base here as early as 800 BC, and Tharros subsequently flourished under the Carthaginians and Romans – the latter built the baths and streets seen today. The town was already in decline by the imperial era, however; with the demise of the *Pax Romana*, it fell prey to Moorish raids, and was finally abandoned in 1070 in favour of the more secure Oristano.

The site

You can tour the **site** alone, but it makes more sense to use a guide for at least part of the way. There is usually one available who speaks English, though you may have to wait for a sizeable group to form (note that guides are usually not available 1–4pm).

For the most part, the site consists of Punic and Roman houses arranged on a grid of streets, of which the broad-slabbed **Decumanus Maximus** and **Cardo Maximus** are the most impressive, the latter with a deep open sewer visible down the centre, now partly covered over. This was probably the main shopping street – a large number of coins have been found along it, along with other clues such as a slab of stone with a groove for a sliding door. At the top of the Cardo Maximus, a basalt Roman wall stands near the remains of a **tophet** (burial ground) from the earlier Punic settlement, and the hill is crowned by the former Carthaginian acropolis, with a wide ditch alongside which was used for defence by the Carthaginians and as a burial site by the Romans, as evident from the tubular-shaped tombs dug up here.

The site's most prominent remains are the two strikingly white **Corinthian columns** on the site of a first-century BC Roman temple, though these are in fact largely composite reconstructions, incorporating much modern concrete. Alongside lies the site's best-preserved Carthaginian structure, a **cistern** walled with large rectangular blocks. Towards the sea, east of here, are the remains of a bath house from the end of the second century AD, though these are not as large or impressive as the **thermal complex** on the southern edge of the site, which dates from a century later. The sheltered site to the north of the earlier baths, overlooking the sea, was probably used as a theatre by the Romans; seating has been provided for the performances that take place in summer. The Romans also built a minuscule amphitheatre; its remains are still visible on the hill near the Punic tophet. Tharros has much more waiting to be revealed, submerged underwater as a result of subsidence, and marine archeologists periodically return to fish out more valuable traces.

The Sinis coast

Outside the peak holiday season, an air of profound calm lies over the peninsula's western coast. Straight roads branch westwards over the Sinis peninsula to a string of undeveloped **beaches** (there is no coast road). Though certain parts get crowded in summer, you can always find unoccupied stretches of sand if you're prepared to walk a little.

Is Aruttas

One of the best beaches, **Is Aruttas** consists of a long white strand of fine quartz, lent interest by rocky outcrops to the north and south, beyond which more beaches extend in both directions. Occasional rollers attract surf enthusiasts, and can also bring pungent heaps of seaweed ashore. There's a bar open in season, and pedalos and windsurf boards are available for rent. The beach is easily reached in summer by bus (see p.149).

Mari Ermi and around

Three kilometres north of Is Aruttas (drivers have to backtrack inland, then head north and west again), the beach at **Mari Ermi** presents a similar picture, with bar and beach facilities, but here the sands back onto a small lagoon, and there's a high headland a brief distance north, **Capo Sa Sturaggia**.

North again, there's a much larger lagoon, the elongated **Stagno di Sale Porcus**, which often hosts a swarm of flamingos in winter, and may dry out completely in summer. The area is managed by LIPU, the Italian bird protection society (🖝 lipu.it).

Putzu Idu and around

There are signs of civilization – bars and ugly holiday homes – around **Putzu Idu**, where there's a sheltered beach, and adjoining **Mandriola**. The bulbous promontory to the north, **Capo Mannu**, attracts surf enthusiasts in search of what are reputed to be the biggest breakers in the Mediterranean – however, the sea can be very flat too. In summer, you'll find various outfits with equipment to rent as well as surfing, kitesurfing and windsurfing courses.

You'll also find excellent bathing spots beyond Capo Mannu – **Sa Mesa Lunga** is idyllic – and on the north side of the peninsula, at **Cala Su Pallosu** and the endless, dune-backed **Is Arenas**. You can reach Sa Mesa Lunga and Cala Su Pallosu with your own transport, but for Is Arenas you need a four-wheel drive or you can walk from Cala Su Pallosu or Santa Caterina di Pittinuri (see p.162).

Mal di Ventre

Apart from passing ships, the only feature punctuating the horizon from the Sinis coast is a small island 10km out, the oddly named **Mal di Ventre** ("stomach ache"). The origin of the name is uncertain, but, in view of the fast winds that can make for rocky sailing conditions hereabouts, it may either refer to seasickness or be a corruption of *Malu Entu*, dialect for bad wind (of the gusty sort). The island is uninhabited and is now a marine reserve, though boats call here daily in summer. The remains of a double-towered *nuraghe* testify to the island's occupation in prehistoric times.

4

ACCOMMODATION   **THE SINIS COAST**

Baiablu Via S'Arrodelli 30, Mandriola 🕿 0783 52 046. Relaxed but pretty basic *pensione* of six rooms – three with views over to the sea – with meals available. The beach is a few minutes' walk away. **€84**

Is Aruttas Località Marina Is Aruttas 🕿 0783 192 5461,

🖝 campingisaruttas.it. Near the beach of the same name, this campsite has caravans (€90; 3–7 nights minimum) and tents to rent (€54), plus a pizzeria and shop. Bike rental and internet access also available. Closed Oct–March. Pitches **€24**

ACTIVITIES

Boat tours Excursions to Mal di Ventre leave daily in summer from Mandriola and Putzu Idu (around €25). Among the operators, try Capo Mannu at Mandriola (🕿 0783 52 197 or 🕿 329 612 0372, 🖝 capomannu.it), who

also offer trekking on the island and snorkelling stops. **Windsurfing** Capo Mannu Windsurf School, Lungomare Putzu Idu (🕿 347 688 1793, 🖝 capomannuwindsurf.it) offers courses (€35 for 1hr) and board rental (€15–20 for 1hr).

Santa Giusta

Once the Punic town of Othoca, **SANTA GIUSTA** is now little more than a suburb of Oristano, 3km north. As such, it only merits a stop for its celebrated basilica, though the lagoon immediately west of town, the **Stagno di Santa Giusta**, makes a pleasant venue for picnics shaded by the encircling eucalyptus woods. Birdwatchers are also attracted by the itinerant population of aquatic wildfowl that continues to feed on the lagoon, despite the passing traffic and the industry along its western shore. On the first Sunday of August a **regatta** is held here, using the *fassonis* (see p.148).

Basilica di Santa Giusta

Via Manzoni • Daily 8.30am–12.30pm & 4.30–6.30pm • ARST buses leaving Oristano for Arborea and Cágliari stop by the basilica (Mon–Sat 1–2 hourly; 10min)

The austere Romanesque **basilica di Santa Giusta** was one of the earliest of the string of Tuscan-style churches built in the eleventh to fourteenth centuries across central and northern Sardinia. This one, whose severe lines suggest Lombard influence, dates from around 1135 and was elevated to cathedral status in the sixteenth century. Prominently sited in the centre of town at the top of a flight of steps behind a public garden, the church's facade displays a black basalt cross and a triple-mullioned window, topped by a typically Pisan recessed rhomboid motif in the tympanum. Below the cross, the tall portal is flanked by two truncated columns and a pair of stone lions. Three rusting cannons lie within a railed area to the right, while the main entrance is on the left side of the building.

Inside, a wooden-beamed ceiling covers the **nave**, which is illuminated by slit windows cut into the walls and apses, and lined with a motley array of marble and granite columns, some of them scavenged from the ruined city of Tharros, though the first two columns on the left and the second on the right show evidence of Arab workmanship. Round arches give access to brick-vaulted aisles and a series of lateral chapels, the first of which on the right has a painted altar and ceiling and a wooden crucifix. Otherwise, there is little concession to ornament. Round the back of the church, the square, rather graceless belltower is less than a hundred years old, a poor replacement for the original. The basilica is the venue for four days of celebration around its saint's day on May 14, featuring a large bonfire in the piazza.

Arborea and around

Five kilometres south of the Stagno di Santa Giusta, a smaller lagoon, the **Stagno di S'Ena Arrubia**, has a greater variety of birdlife, including sandpipers, herons and the rare whiteheaded ducks. Although this area has been left a protected site, the land south of here, the **Bonifica di Arborea** was the subject of a large-scale land-reclamation scheme in 1919. What was formerly a malarial swamp was transformed by drainage, canalization and irrigation into a richly fertile zone, and the area is still famous for its fruit and vegetables, tobacco and beetroot. The land also supports herds of cows that account for most of the island's milk production, while the country surrounding **Terralba** to the south is famous for its wine.

The area's main town is **ARBOREA**, a quiet, rural, twentieth-century settlement whose name is a conscious throwback to the old *giudicato*. Founded in 1928 during the campaign to maximize Sardinia's domestic production, the town was originally called "Mussolinia", and was intended to house the rural colonies introduced into the area from the Veneto, Friuli and Emilia-Romagna regions, to which the town owes its incongruous northern Italian appearance. This is most noticeable in the main square, **Piazza Maria Ausiliatrice**, where a formal garden with neat flowerbeds and palm trees is overlooked by a red-brick parish church and town hall, all surrounded by right-angled, tree-lined streets.

The whole place exudes the cardinal Fascist values of planning and orderliness, and the neo-Gothic church, **Cristo Redentore**, even sports a tidy grotto carved into the left side, with a Madonna presiding. On nearby Corso Italia, a renovated mill houses a museum dedicated to the *bonifica* (reclaimed land), but it's been closed for years with no sign of reopening.

The Arborea coast

Much of the **coast** hereabouts is fringed by a dense pine forest, with sandy beaches looking across the Golfo di Oristano to Tharros. The main settlement is **MARINA DI**

ARBOREA, little more than a handful of houses behind the shore, but there's more interest 11km south of Arborea off the SP69, where the placid **Stagno di Marceddì** lagoon, with picnic tables and benches under the pines, forms a natural frontier between Oristano's cultivated plains and the rugged hills of Medio Campidano province. Near the mouth of the lagoon, the sleepy village of **MARCEDDÌ** has a low-key port, or *porticciolo*, with a small selection of bars and restaurants. A narrow causeway runs south across the lagoon to Sant'Antonio di Santadi and the Costa Verde (see p.109).

ARRIVAL AND DEPARTURE
ARBOREA AND AROUND

By bus ARST buses running almost hourly connect Arborea with Santa Giusta (15min) and Oristano (25min).

ACCOMMODATION AND EATING

★ **Da Lucio** Via Lungomare 40, Marceddì ☎ 0783 867 130. Steps from the seafront, this is an excellent end-of-the-road spot to sample the local seafood accompanied by a glass of Terralba wine. The menu features the freshest fish grilled, poached or roasted, *anguille* (eels) and sea urchins; main courses are around €14 and there's a €31 tourist menu. The upstairs terrace is open at weekends for pizzas. Daily except Thurs June–Oct 12.30–2.45pm & 8.30–10.45pm.

Gallo Bianco Piazza Ausiliatrice, Arborea ☎ 0783 800 241, ⓦ locandadelgallobianco.it. Endearingly old-fashioned hotel on Arborea's central square, whose boxy Mussolini-era rooms cannot be modernized due to their historic character. The restaurant (open to all) offers Sard and Italian dishes (including polenta), mostly €8–12. Daily except Thurs 12.45–3.30pm & 8–11pm. **€55**

Horse Country Strada a Mare 24 ☎ 0783 80 500, ⓦ horsecountry.it. This grand hotel complex on the coast (signposted from the main road north of Arborea) is great for families, with a pool and fitness centre, and the beach just a few steps away beyond the curtain of pinewoods. The main attraction, though, is the riding facilities, among the best in Sardinia. All ages and levels are catered for, and excursions are organized along the coast, through the woods and inland. Look out for good online deals and discounts for families and for longer stays. Half-board may be required in summer. **€112**

Il Canneto Marina di Arborea ☎ 0783 800 027, ⓦ ilcannetoarborea.it.gg. Right on the sandy beach, this *pensione* has ten simple, en-suite rooms that fill quickly in summer. The ristorante-pizzeria below specializes in grilled fish – a couple of courses will cost €20–25. Daily noon–2.30pm & 7–10.30pm. **€50**

Fordongianus

East of Oristano, 28km up the River Tirso from Oristano, **FORDONGIANUS** was a Roman spa town founded at the end of the first century AD under the emperor Trajan; the present name is a corruption of Forum Traiani. A Roman bridge still spans the river, on whose banks the old **baths** are still in fairly good condition and visitable.

The town has several examples of public **sculpture** carved out of the local red trachyte. Some are entries for – or past winners of – an international competition held annually in Fordongianus; if you're here in July and August, you'll see the sculptors chiselling away in the streets.

Casa Aragonese

Via Traiano • Tues–Sun: April, May & Oct 9.30am–1pm & 3.30–6.30pm; June & Sept 9.30am–1pm & 3.30–7.30pm; July & Aug 9.30am–1pm & 3.30–8pm; Nov–March 9.30am–1pm & 3–5pm • €4, including Terme Romane • ☎ 0783 60 157, ⓦ forumtraiani.it

Signposted left near the western entrance to Fordongianus, **Casa Aragonese** is constructed from the distinctive red stone typical of the locality, and marked out by its pillared portico. The dwelling is thought to have been built for a noble Catalan family at the end of the sixteenth or beginning of the seventeenth century. The mostly bare rooms show few signs of life, but you'll see Gothic decorated windows and doors, and the window seats where the ladies of the household would sit and sew. The building hosts regular exhibitions, and there are more of the town's trachyte sculptures outside and in the back garden.

Terme Romane

Località Cadda • Daily: April, May & Oct 9.30am–1pm & 3.30–6.30pm; June & Sept 9.30am–1pm & 3.30–7.30pm; July & Aug 9.30am– 1pm & 3.30–8pm; Nov–March 9.30am–1pm & 3–5pm • €4, including Casa Aragonese • ☎ 0783 60 157, ⓦ forumtraiani.it

The **Terme Romane** (Roman baths) stand on the banks of the River Tirso at the lower end of town. The baths retain much of their original structure, the oldest sections including the main pool, while the frigidarium, tepidarium and calidarium date from a third-century expansion. Behind the main building, part of a **forum** still stands, from which a stairway leads to what is thought to be either an ancient hotel or butcher's shop, partly frescoed. Half the pleasure here, though, is the evocative riverside site, the sulphurous water steaming as it gushes into the river at a temperature of 54° centigrade. Local women still occasionally use the hot spring water to scrub their laundry, as they have done for millennia.

Is Bangius

Località Cadda • Daily: April, May & Oct 9.30am–12.30pm & 3.30–6.30pm; June & Sept 9.30am–12.30pm & 3.30–7.30pm; July & Aug 9.30am–12.30pm & 3.30–8pm; Nov–March 9.30am–12.30pm & 3–5pm • €4, or €5 on Sun • ☎ 0783 60 157, ⓦ forumtraiani.it

If you fancy a wash-down in the healthy mineral waters, seek out **Is Bangius** (Bagni Termali), the dank nineteenth-century bath-houses tucked away below the road by the river, 200m from the Roman baths. Take a swimming costume and sandals, and you can rent a towel and bathing cap at the ticket office. Sessions last half an hour.

Chiesa di San Lussório

SS388 • Daily: April, May & Oct 9.30am–1pm & 3.30–6.30pm; June & Sept 9.30am–1pm & 3.30–7.30pm; July & Aug 9.30am–1pm & 3.30–8pm; Nov–March 9.30am–1pm & 3–5pm • €2.50 • ☎ 0783 800 60 157, ⓦ forumtraiani.it

A kilometre or so west of Fordongianus on the Oristano road, the church of **San Lussório** stands within a walled enclosure, its wonky red trachyte facade looking rough and unadorned at first glance. Closer inspection in fact reveals a very eroded relief around the base of the doorway, and another on one of the columns around the apse, where excavations of a paleo-Christian necropolis are currently under way. The interior is bare but atmospheric.

ARRIVAL AND DEPARTURE   FORDONGIANUS

By bus ARST buses connect Fordongianus with Oristano (Mon–Sat 7–8 daily; Sun in July & Aug 1 daily; 40min).

ACCOMMODATION AND EATING

Grand Hotel Terme SP23 ☎ 0783 605 016, ⓦ terme sardegna.it. You can sample the therapeutic effects of the local water in the rather institutional surroundings of this modern thermal complex on the north bank of the river. Accommodation is in balconied a/c rooms, with free use of the two naturally heated pools, and you can choose from among a range of treatments from massage to mud-packs

(book ahead to ensure availability). Closed July. **€160**

Su Montigu Via Carlo Alberto Dalla Chiesa ☎ 0783 60 018. Traditional country restaurant which offers tasty and moderately priced dishes (€20–30 for a full meal including drinks). Lamb, boar and the local mushrooms are among the top choices. No credit cards. Tues–Sun 11.45am– 2.30pm, Aug also 7.45–10.30pm.

Samugheo and around

A right turn off the SP388 east of Fordongianus leads south to Allai (this is a much shorter route than the zigzagging SP33 going directly there from Fordongianus) and **SAMUGHEO**, a large village of the Mandrolisai region, famous for its textiles (*tessile*). Throughout August, a craft fair, the **Mostra dell'Artigianato del Mandrolisai**, takes place, with huge piles of rugs, blankets, tapestries and furniture for sale in the shops and stalls.

San Sebastiano

Piazza Sedda • Daily 8.30am–12.30pm & 4.30–6.30pm

Opposite Samugheo's *Municipio*, the sixteenth-century church of **San Sebastiano**, built of pink trachyte blocks, is worth a whirl, sporting an Aragonese-Gothic facade and an eighteenth-century campanile. Its unusual interior has a low-vaulted altar and a lovely old wooden pulpit carved with faces and resting on a single stone column.

Castello di Medusa

Three or four kilometres south of Samugheo on the SP38 Asuni road, a dirt track – indicated by a yellow signpost on the left – leads off towards the **Castello di Medusa**, a ruined redoubt in the Araxisi gorge, which makes a rewarding trip either on foot or with your own transport. On the way you'll pass several *pinneddas*, igloo-type constructions used by the local shepherds; they resemble miniature *nuraghi* at first glance, but are made of much lighter, smaller stones. As you follow the high ridge with steep drops below, look out for glimpses of the distant peaks of the Gennargentu mountains to the east. The castle itself is about 5km along the track: for orientation, aim for the orange church visible on the horizon. The ruins appear suddenly below the track on the left, utterly isolated above a gorge.

Little is known of the origins of the castle, though it's thought that it was an outpost of Fordongianus during the Roman occupation and rebuilt under the Byzantines. The fortified site was later used by Arborea's *giudicati*. The straggling ruins give little idea of how it might have appeared when intact, but it's a grand spot nonetheless, overlooking high pastoral country crossed by dry-stone walls and dotted with herds of goats and sheep, and with sudden rocky outcrops.

ARRIVAL AND DEPARTURE   SAMUGHEO

By bus Samugheo has bus connections with Fordongianus (Mon–Sat 4–5 daily, Sun in July & Aug 1 daily; 30min) and | Oristano (Mon–Sat 4–5 daily, Sun in July & Aug 1 daily; 1hr 5min).

The Vernaccia triangle

Travelling up the main SS131 from Oristano, you'll soon pass through the so-called "**Vernaccia triangle**", an area bounded by the villages of Zeddiani, Barátili San Pietro and Solarussa that forms the core of the Vernaccia wine-producing region. The villagers of Barátili San Pietro are also famous for their skills in making and navigating the reed-built *fassonis*. Farther on, you might stop to buy a kilo or two of what are reputed to be Sardinia's best oranges, grown around **Milis**; the season extends over ten months of the year.

Santa Cristina and around

SS131 • Daily 8.30am–1hr before sunset • €5 with Museo Etnográfico • ☏ 0785 55 438 or ☏ 347 774 6747, ⊚ archeotour.net

Twenty-five kilometres north of Oristano, look out for the signposted exit from the superstrada to the nuraghic complex of **Santa Cristina**, dispersed within a shady grove of olive trees, and comprising a *nuraghe*, a sacred well and other nuraghic buildings, some of them dating back to 1800 BC. The *nuraghe*'s main tower, about 15m high, has an egg-shaped "tholos"-type interior, hewn with niches and alcoves. From the top, the views over the green, wooded surroundings take in other fragments of this extensive site, including a **capanna lunga** – a long, stone-built, open-topped structure of unknown function, which has yielded Roman finds from the third century BC.

But the most impressive part of the complex is a short walk away, a **sacred well** and underground shrine reached down a narrow-walled flight of perfectly smooth steps. Back on the surface, a round meeting room stands nearby, among several more nuraghic remains in varying states of preservation.

It's an impressive grouping, the overall effect enhanced by the mossy green ambience and ancient olive trees, one of which is said to be over a thousand years old. The entry ticket includes a guided tour of the site in Italian (no tours 1–3pm), and also includes entry into the **Museo Archeologico-Etnográfico** in the centre of **Paulilátino**, 5km northwest.

Museo Archeologico-Etnográfico

Via Nazionale 127, Paulilátino • Tues–Sun 9.30am–1pm & 4.30–7pm, 4–6.30pm Oct–April • €5 with Santa Cristina • ☎ 0785 55 438, ⓦ archeotour.net

Housed in a handsomely restored building from the seventeenth century in the centre of **Paulilátino**, 5km northwest of Santa Cristina, the **Museo Archeologico-Etnográfico** includes finds from Santa Cristina alongside items of social history – local photographs, traditional furnishings, tools and other exhibits of folkloric interest. In summer, temporary exhibitions are laid out on the roof and in the courtyard.

Ghilarza and around

4

Merging into the sister town of Abbasanta, 8km northeast of Paulilátino, small, run-of-the-mill **GHILARZA** has achieved worldwide fame as the hometown of the great political theorist **Antonio Gramsci**. Although born near Oristano, Gramsci spent most of his youth in this unassuming place, in a house that is now devoted to his life and works.

East of Ghilarza, **Lago Omodeo** is Italy's largest artificial lake, covering an area of 22 square kilometres, and supplying electricity as well as drinking water and irrigation to the area. It's extremely scenic, but access is difficult – try the eastern shores around the village of Bidoni.

Casa di Antonio Gramsci

Corso Umberto 57 • May–Sept daily except Tues 10am–1pm & 4–7pm, daily in Aug; Oct–April Fri–Sun 10am–1pm & 3.30–6.30pm • Donations appreciated • ☎ 0785 54 164, ⓦ casagramscighilarza.org

The modest house where Gramsci and his family lived, near the church on the town's narrow main street, has been converted into the **Casa di Antonio Gramsci**, a study centre and museum dedicated to Gramsci's life and writings. Much of the small building is taken up by a meeting hall and library, where taped reminiscences by people who knew him are stored alongside shelves of books and documents. Items on display are a mix of the personal – letters to his mother, boyhood photographs, toys – and writings relating to his academic and political development. Photos of and objects from the prison cell outside Bari where he spent five years for anti-Fascist activities can be seen upstairs, and there's a 35-minute film narrating his life and achievements. T-shirts and posters are available for sale.

ARRIVAL AND DEPARTURE
GHILARZA

By train There's a mainline train station at neighbouring Abbasanta, with frequent connections to Oristano and Ozieri-Chilivani (for trains to Sássari and Olbia). From Abbasanta station, it's a 30min walk to Ghilarza, or you could take a taxi or catch a bus (Mon–Sat roughly hourly).

By bus ARST services stop close to the main Corso Umberto.
Destinations Fordongianus (Mon–Sat 3–4 daily; 25min–1hr 15min); Oristano (Mon–Sat 2 daily; 1hr 10min–1hr 50min); Sédilo (Mon–Sat 5 daily; 15–50min).

ANTONIO GRAMSCI

Italy's most influential political theorist of the Left, **Antonio Gramsci** (1891–1937), was born in the village of Ales, southeast of Oristano, but grew up in Ghilarza, where his father worked with the land registry. Never physically strong, Antonio suffered from rickets as a child, a condition aggravated by poverty after his father was jailed for "administrative irregularities". Despite such obstacles, the young Gramsci doggedly pursued his education, leaving Ghilarza before he was 18 to attend the lyceum in Cágliari, where his brother Gennaro was already involved in socialist politics.

By the time he was 20, Antonio had enrolled to study letters at the University of Turin. Here, he was drawn into working-class politics, and in 1921 became one of the founders of the **Italian Communist Party**. The following year, he took part in an Italian delegation to Moscow, and in 1924 he was elected to the Chamber of Deputies, where he became one of the most effective and articulate **opponents of Fascism**. Inexorably, the regime closed in. Gramsci was arrested in November 1926; he was 35, and would spend the rest of his life in jail, dying of tuberculosis in 1937.

As it turned out, Gramsci's imprisonment allowed him to develop his ideas untainted by Stalinism, and his **Prison Notebooks**, when they were published immediately after World War II, helped to revitalize the discredited Left during the 1950s and 1960s. The alternative theoretical framework that he provided was a decisive factor not just in the evolution of the Italian Communist Party but in the development of the "Eurocommunism" that underlay the electoral successes of Sard Enrico Berlinguer in the 1970s.

Sédilo

4

Just north of Lago Omodeo, the town of **SÉDILO** hosts the annual **S'Ardia** horse race, held in honour of the Roman emperor Constantine in his saintly guise of San Costantino. The race takes place at dawn on July 6 and 7 at breakneck speed and over a danger-strewn course, around the church of **Sant'Antine di Sédilo**. It's an attractive, woody spot outside the village and within sight of the lake, though tranquillity is notably absent during the S'Ardia itself. The risks to participants and spectators alike are increased by people whose sole job is to harass the horses and their riders, to the extent of shooting dud bullets at them. It's a thrilling spectacle, full of hot tempers, commotion and displays of virility. Folk concerts take place in the evenings, and there's a race on foot on the following weekend.

The church of **Sant'Antine** – a *novena* church, open for nine days a year – deserves a look for the copious ex-votive graffiti scribbled on its walls.

ARRIVAL AND DEPARTURE

SÉDILO

By bus ARST buses run to Sédilo from Ghilarza (Mon–Sat 5 daily; 15–50min). There are no direct connections with Oristano.

Nuraghe Losa

Località Nuraghe Losa, SS131 (3km from Abbasanta train station) • Daily 9am–1hr before sunset • €3.50 • ☎ 0785 52 302, ⓦ nuraghelosa.net

Standing alone in bare, flat country just west of the SS131, the **Nuraghe Losa** makes an easy stop for anyone following Sardinia's main north–south highway in either direction (look out for the exit signs). Dating from the Middle Bronze Age (the second millennium BC), the flat, grassy site is encompassed within a prodigious perimeter wall, giving a better idea of the extent of a nuraghic settlement than other similar structures in Sardinia.

What most commands attention, however, is the massive sheer-walled trilobate (three-cornered) *nuraghe* – the compact, fortified structure growing in impact as you approach. Composed of regular basalt stones half-covered with striking orange lichen, the tapering walls of the truncated **central tower** are smoother than those of most other *nuraghi*, and reach a height of nearly 13m. The design and arrangement of the various parts of the complex are, as ever, baffling. Directly in front of the *nuraghe*'s main entrance, a circular meeting chamber leaves little room for coming and going, and there are equally cramped spaces on the *nuraghe*'s western side, where an inner rampart forms an additional protective belt, enclosing a small courtyard accessible through a lintelled door. Two minor **defensive towers** – now topless – are incorporated into the rampart, furnished with narrow slits for viewing the surrounding area and for archers to fire through. Cradled within the rampart at the northern end are more remains of stone buildings, and an entrance – again tiny – for access to the northern tower of the trilobate.

The central tower

The **central tower** – the oldest part of the structure – is entered through a narrow corridor with a large recess hacked out of the right-hand wall, possibly for a sentry. To the left, a flight of stone steps curls up to a second-floor chamber, continuing on to the open terrace from which, on a clear day, you can see the peaks of the Gennargentu mountains to the east. Back on ground level, the main corridor also has lateral passages leading to the bare windowless chambers within the bastion's two southern towers. The main central tower has a tall conical interior, dimly lit by electric lighting, with alcoves and niches gouged out of the walls. The overall complex shows continuous occupation from around 1500 BC to the seventh century AD, while most of the village to the northeast and southwest of the bastion has yet to be uncovered.

The perimeter wall

Either before or after visiting the *nuraghe* itself, take a bit of time to follow the **perimeter wall** round for new angles on the central structure, and to explore the three shattered **external towers**, which provided secondary entrances to the complex. The wall encloses the scanty remains of a **prehistoric village** and, just inside the site's main entrance, the remains of a first- to second-century AD cemetery from the settlement's post-nuraghic phase, showing exposed cinerary urns.

The museum

The site holds a small **museum** of very fragmentary local finds. Needles and vases from the nuraghic period, pottery with zigzag designs from the fifth and sixth centuries AD, and photos of other *nuraghi* in the area from which some of the finds originate. The best stuff, however, is on view or in store in Cágliari's museum (see p.62). You can read more on Sardinia's nuraghic culture in Contexts (see p.307).

Santu Lussurgiu and around

The large village of **SANTU LUSSURGIU** sits in the crater of an extinct volcano some 35km north of Oristano and 15km west of Abbasanta on the SP15. The surrounding landscape of bare craggy hills and woods of olives and chestnut was once a highly volatile seismic zone, though nowadays the atmosphere is one of utter serenity. In the village itself, not even cars can enter the tight web of steep cobbled lanes that make up the old centre, which harbours several handsome churches. One of the finest is the heavily buttressed, late fifteenth-century **Santa Maria degli Ángeli** above the public gardens, containing a wooden altar from the eighteenth century.

Museo della Tecnologia Contadina

Via Deodato Meloni • No fixed opening hours – call at least a day in advance to make an appointment • €3 • ☎ 0785 550 617 or ☎ 347 835 8308, 🔇 museotecnologiacontadina.it

Below the public gardens, the **Museo della Tecnologia Contadina** gathers together everyday items from different eras and areas of Sardinia. The eleven rooms are dedicated to various aspects of rural culture, starting with agricultural tools and taking in weaving, bread-making, wine-making, children's toys, craftwork and archeology. Rat-traps, coffee-grinders and flax-combs are among some of the more unexpected items here.

ARRIVAL AND DEPARTURE
SANTU LUSSURGIU

By bus Santu Lussurgiu is served by buses to and from Abbasanta/Ghilarza (Mon–Sat 2 daily; 25min) and Oristano (Mon–Sat 7 daily; 50min–1hr 25min).

ACCOMMODATION AND EATING

⭐ **Antica Dimora del Gruccione** Via Michele Obinu 31 ☎ 0783 552 035, 🔇 anticadimora.com. Based in a renovated eighteenth-century villa, this *albergo diffuso* has rooms in various locations in the village – all different, with modern or period furnishings. The gourmet restaurant concentrates on local meat products, with an endless selection of *antipasti*, and charges €35 for a full meal (reservation required if you're not staying). In summer you can eat in the courtyard garden.

Feb–Dec daily 8.30pm–late. **€90**

⭐ **Sas Benas** Via Cambosu 4 ☎ 0783 550 870, 🔇 sasbenas.it. One of three *alberghi diffusi* in Santu Lussurgiu (with rooms in various buildings) – this one has exposed stone walls, arches and richly atmospheric rooms, not to mention a superb restaurant offering local and seasonal specialities, with set menus at €30. Tues–Sun 1–2.15pm & 8–9.30pm. **€80**

San Leonardo de Siete Fuentes

North of Santu Lussurgiu, weekend picnickers head up the minor road towards Macomer (see p.194) for the wooded area around the hamlet of **SAN LEONARDO DE SIETE FUENTES**. The village's Spanish name ("Seven Fountains") is a reference to its highly prized mineral waters, which attract droves of connoisseurs. The crumbly old Romanesque church is the burial place of Guelfo, son of Count Ugolino della Gherardesca, who died in 1292 (see box, p.104). San Leonardo is also the scene of a **horse fair** held every June 2 – one of Sardinia's most important markets of this kind. A much smaller-scale market of everyday items also sets up here on Sundays in summer.

Monte Ferru

West of Santu Lussurgiu looms the mainly forested **Monte Ferru** – or Montiferru, the name a reminder of the iron once mined here – which reaches a height of over 1000m. This former volcanic zone is now endowed with an abundance of rivers and springs which nourish its thick forests of oak, elm and chestnut. Mouflons and deer inhabit certain parts, such as the **Sa Pabarile** area.

HORSING AROUND – SANTU LUSSURGIU'S FESTIVALS

Rearing and riding horses is in the blood in Santu Lussurgiu, and at no time is this more apparent than in the village's annual party, a horse race spread over three days during **Carnival** (usually Sunday, Monday and Shrove Tuesday). As in Oristano, riders gallop hard through the narrow streets of the old town, though there are few or no costumed theatrics here – this is serious bareback riding, and highly exciting to watch. The village's saint's day, around **August 21**, is also an excuse to saddle up for horseback competitions during four days of festivities. The horses take a break at **Easter**, however, which Santu Lussurgiu marks with choral singing, but the equine theme is always present in the local craftwork for sale in the village shops.

If you're tempted to get a closer look, the twisty and highly scenic SP19 heading north and west of Santu Lussurgiu offers opportunities to explore on foot – Sa Pabarile can be reached from the lane on the left leading up to the RAI TV transmitter, 8km from the village. A further 10km or so along the SP19, you'll spot the ruined **Castello di Monte Ferru** (in Sard: "Casteddu Etzu"), a formidable twelfth-century hilltop fortification subjected to over-zealous restoration, reachable via a side road.

Cúglieri

The silver dome of the basilica at the top of the village of **CÚGLIERI** makes a prominent landmark for miles around. There are superb panoramic views over the coast from here, but the church itself is a disappointment, its broad brown exterior only feebly enlivened by two marble carvings on either side of the portal and with a run-of-the-mill interior. The rest of Cúglieri doesn't inspire much interest either, though there are a couple of excellent restaurants.

ARRIVAL AND DEPARTURE   CÚGLIERI

By bus Cúglieri is a stop on the ARST bus route between Bosa and Oristano.
Destinations Bosa (Mon–Sat 5–6 daily; 1hr); Oristano

(Mon–Sat 5–6 daily, Sun in July & Aug 2 daily; 1hr); Santa Caterina (Mon–Sat 5–6 daily, Sun in July & Aug 2 daily; 20min).

EATING

Desogos Vico Cugia, off Via Cugia ☎0785 39 660. The four women who run this authentic back-street trattoria are carrying on a 65-year family tradition. The fixed-price menus (€20 and €30 including drinks) are geared to carnivores – lamb, boar cooked with olives, and hare or donkey stew. Daily 12.30–2.30pm & 7.30–10.30pm.

★ **Meridiana** Via Angioy 11 ☎0785 39 400. Signposted off the main road that descends through the old town, this smart but cosy restaurant has won numerous plaudits for its seafood dishes, which you can sample on a five-course tasting menu (€45). Booking advisable. Wed–Sun 1–2.30pm & 8.30–10pm.

Santa Caterina and around

From Cúglieri, the SP292 heads rapidly downhill and south along the western flank of Monte Ferru to the main resort on this stretch of coast, **SANTA CATERINA DI PITTINURI**, a busy summer holiday centre. In winter, the local economy relies on olive production – the area is famed for its olive groves and is one of the island's major sources of olives and olive oil. The **beaches** hereabouts are also renowned, a mixture of sand and rocks sheltered within pretty inlets. The most photogenic are at **Su Archittu**, a couple of kilometres south of town, where a ruined watchtower stands on a point above the natural rock arch it is named after, which you can swim through and climb above. South of here, the long, dune-backed strand **Is Arenas** extends for 6km (see p.153). Santa Caterina itself, however, almost overwhelmed by holiday homes, has little of interest.

Cornus

Località Cornus, off SP292 · Always open · Free

A kilometre or so south and inland of Su Archittu, a signposted dirt road leads 2–3km to the site of **Cornus**, an ancient settlement that was the focus for an alliance of Carthaginian and Sard forces, led by a local chieftain, **Ampsicora**, opposed to the growing power of Rome. The rebellion was swiftly crushed by Roman forces in 216 BC, Ampsicora took his own life, and with the Carthaginian threat banished for ever, the way was clear for Rome's domination of the island.

The battlefield itself is a little farther inland on a hill, though there's nothing to mark the exact spot. The main site of Cornus, however, reveals the interesting remains of an early Christian centre of worship established here in the third and fourth centuries AD. The outlines of a double-apsed **basilica** are clearly visible, with tombs jammed into every available space, even the apses. A **baptistery** is marked out by a well-preserved cruciform font. It's a serene, deserted spot, within sight of the sea, ideal for a quiet picnic.

ARRIVAL AND DEPARTURE   SANTA CATERINA

By bus Services between Bosa, Cúglieri and Oristano stop on Santa Caterina's main street.
Destinations Bosa (Mon–Sat 4 daily; 1hr 20min); Cúglieri (Mon–Sat 5–6 daily, Sun in July & Aug 2 daily; 20min); Oristano (Mon–Sat 5–6 daily, Sun in July & Aug 2 daily; 40min).

ACCOMMODATION AND EATING

Is Arenas Località Is Arenas ☎ 0783 52 103, ⍟ villaggio isarenas.com. The smaller of two adjacent campsites shaded by thick pinewoods with direct access to the beach at Is Arenas, this has a shop, restaurant and bungalows for rent (€70). Closed Oct–March. Pitches €23

La Baja SP292 ☎ 0785 389 149, ⍟ hotellabaja.it. Upmarket lodgings are available at this tidy four-star signposted off the SP292 north of Santa Caterina. Its clifftop location affords marvellous sea views, and there are steps down to the beach (there's a pool too). €126

La Scogliera Corso Alagon ☎ 0785 38 231. The best thing about this trattoria near the beach is its veranda with spectacular views. Seafood dishes (mostly €12–14) include *seppiette alla griglia* (grilled cuttlefish), and pizzas are available. Jan & April–Dec daily 1–2.20pm & 8–11pm, closed Wed Oct–May.

4

Alghero and the northwest coast

169 Alghero

180 Around Alghero

187 Bosa

194 Macomer and around

195 Stintino and around

GROTTA DI NETTUNO

5

Alghero and the northwest coast

Sardinia's northwest coast shelters a trio of the most attractive seaside resorts on the island, separated by some of its most spectacular coastline. The biggest and busiest of the towns, Alghero, has long been a tourist hotspot, its old centre a tight web of narrow lanes packed with boutiques, bars and restaurants. It is the most "Italian" of Sardinia's holiday towns, and though it may lack the glamorous sheen of mainland resorts like Sorrento or San Remo, it's also refreshingly free of their cynical hard sell. At the same time, Alghero retains a distinctive Catalan character – the result of intense Spanish colonization in the fourteenth century – that sets it apart from anywhere else in Italy. Nearby, you'll find enticing beaches and fascinating archeological sites, not to mention the famous Grotta di Nettuno (Neptune's Grotto) on the point at Capo Caccia.

North of Alghero, the ghost town of **Argentiera** and Sardinia's only natural lake, **Lago di Baratz**, make diverting half-day trips, while the resort of **Stintino**, at Sardinia's northwestern tip, merits a more prolonged exploration, not least for the largely undeveloped coastline on either side. The pick of the beaches here are the once-seen, never-forgotten sands around the point at **La Pelosa**, where calm, turquoise waters extend to rocky offshore isles. Boat excursions from Stintino call at the biggest of these islands, **Asinara**, a nature reserve with yet more exquisite beaches.

The unspoiled rocky coast south of Alghero has a wild grandeur, and is one of the last habitats in Sardinia of the griffon vulture. The stretch of coast ends at the River Temo, where a ruined castle presides over the medieval port of **Bosa** and its compact warren of streets. Despite being a stop for coach parties, Bosa preserves a quiet, low-key charm that is perfectly in tune with the slow rhythms of the local community. Its seaside satellite, **Bosa Marina**, keeps beach aficionados happy, while inland, **Macomer** has some intriguing nuraghic sites, but should otherwise detain you only as a transport junction.

Accommodation options are rather limited in Stintino and Bosa, but plentiful in Alghero, which also has most of the **campsites**. There are **hostels** at Fertilia (near Alghero), Argentiera and Bosa. However, availability can be very scarce throughout the region in summer, and many places are closed altogether between October and April.

GETTING AROUND
THE NORTHWEST COAST

Although **public transport** services are adequate for travelling between the main towns and villages, a **bike** or **car** offers more freedom to roam the sparsely populated terrain. There's plenty of scope for **walkers** too, with few overly strenuous tracts and mostly traffic-free roads.

The Catalan Dialect p.169
Apartment rentals p.176
Festivals and entertainment p.179
Alghero's coral trade p.179
Getting to the Grotta di Nettuno p.182

Inland explorations from Bosa p.191
Bosa's festivals p.193
Stintino's festivals p.195
Diving around Stintino p.196
Tours to Piana and Asinara p.197

Highlights

❶ Walk along Alghero's sea walls The formidable old walls of the port offer great views across to Capo Caccia by day, and a cooling breeze on summer nights. See p.174

❷ Seafood in Alghero Feast on lobster and other seafood treats in one of the town's renowned fish restaurants. See p.177

❸ Cycle along the Alghero–Bosa coast This wild stretch of coast warrants a leisurely ride, with stops at secluded beaches. See p.186

❹ Castello Malaspina, Bosa Once you've recovered your breath, take in the wonderful views from this lofty vantage point, and admire the medieval frescoes in the small church. See p.190

❺ La Pelosa This is one of Sardinia's premier beaches – sandy, shallow, and surrounded by alluring waters and magnificent scenery. See p.197

❻ Boat trip to Asinara Off-limits for centuries, the island's wildlife and pristine beaches can be visited on boat tours from Stintino. See p.197

HIGHLIGHTS ARE MARKED ON THE MAP ON P.168

Cala Arena
Cala d'Oliva
6 Asinara

Golfo dell'Asinara

Fornelli
Piana
La Pelosa
Capo Falcone
5 Stintino

Castelsardo

Le Saline

Porto Torres

Sorso

Palmádula
Sássari

Argentiera

Lago di Baratz
NURRA

Porto Ferro
Santa Maria La Palma
Torre del Porticciolo
Anghelu Ruju
Olmedo

Le Prigionette
Nuraghe di Palmavera
Nurra!

Baja di Conte
Porto Conte

Capo Caccia
Grotta di Nettuno
Fertilia

1 Alghero
2

PROVINCIA DI SASSARI

La Speranza

Villanova Monteleone

Lago del Temo
Monteleone Rocca-Doria

3

Pozzomaggiore

Bonorva

Olbia (70km)

SS131

Capo Marargiu

PLANARGIA

Temo

PROVINCIA DI ORISTANO

PROVINCIA DI NUORO

Bosa Marina
Bosa
4

Nuraghe di Santa Barbara
Silanus

Tresnuraghes

Macomer

Santa Sabina

N

0   10
kilometres

HIGHLIGHTS
1 Walk along Alghero's sea walls
2 Seafood in Alghero
3 Cycle along the Alghero–Bosa coast
4 Castello Malaspina, Bosa
5 La Pelosa
6 Boat trip to Asinara

Oristano (35km)

ALGHERO & THE NORTHWEST COAST

Alghero

The predominant flavour in **ALGHERO** is Catalan, owing to the wholesale Hispanicization that followed the overthrow of the Doria family by Pedro IV of Aragon in 1353 – a process so thorough that the town (*Alguer* in Catalan) became known as "Barcelonetta". A walk around the intricate mesh of car-free lanes that make up the atmospheric **old town** reveals Catalan street names (*carrer*, *plaça*, *iglesia* and *palau* for "via", "piazza", "chiesa" and "palazzo"), handsome sixteenth-century architecture in a congenial Catalan-Gothic style, and Catalan dishes such as *paella* on restaurant menus. It's this mixed heritage that sets Alghero apart from other Sardinian towns, and has helped make it one of Sardinia's most favoured tourist destinations. Thankfully, however, the resort has escaped the fate of many other Mediterranean hotspots and stood firm against both tweeness and commercial hype. Instead, it remains a sophisticated and easygoing place with a sharp but good-humoured population, who themselves like nothing better than a good night out in a trattoria.

Brief history

While archeological finds in the area around Alghero suggest a degree of social organization as early as 6000 BC, the history of the modern town really begins in the first half of the twelfth century with the fortification of an obscure fishing port by the Doria family of **Genoa**. The town successfully defended itself from assaults by the Pisans and Aragonese until 1353, when, after the conquest of Cágliari and Sássari, a large **Spanish fleet**, supported by the Venetians, routed the Genoans at the nearby bay of Porto Conte and took possession of Alghero. Following an uprising in which the Spanish garrison was massacred, the town was subjected to a thorough "ethnic cleansing", in which waves of **Catalan settlers** displaced the locals, forcing them to settle at Villanova, a mountain village 25km to the south. Laws were passed limiting the number of native Sards who could enter, and compelling them to leave town at the sound of a trumpet signal.

A Catalan colony

Because of its geographic and strategic importance on Sardinia's northwestern coast, Alghero quickly became the foremost **port** for traffic between Sardinia and Catalonia. From the fourteenth to the sixteenth century, its defences were massively strengthened; most of the ramparts and towers still standing today date from this period, when they sheltered a substantial garrison and fleet, providing a powerful bulwark against seaborne raids on Sássari and the whole western interior.

The town suffered a downturn in its economic fortunes following the expulsion in 1492 of its substantial **Jewish community**, or *Aljama*. This forced the Aragonese to reopen Alghero to foreign and Sard traders – though the core of the town remained stoutly Catalan in character and culture. Links with Spain were bolstered in 1541, when the emperor **Charles V** made a historic visit to the town, accompanied by his admiral Andrea Doria – the most eminent member of the Genoan dynasty, formerly in the vanguard of the emperor's enemies before becoming his staunch ally. The two were en route to flush out the corsair **Hassan Aga** from his lair in Algiers, for which they had assembled one of the biggest fleets ever seen. (The pirate chief was himself a Sard: born of shepherds,

---

THE CATALAN DIALECT

The most obvious index of Alghero's distinctive culture, the *catalano* or *algherese* **dialect**, has largely lost the battle against uniformity. While older townsfolk – many of whom still regard themselves as primarily Catalan – are attached to it, few of the post-1960s generations are at all adept, and the existence of evening classes for locals to learn or perfect their knowledge of *catalano* is a gauge of its present precarious state. The best way to hear the *algherese/catalano* dialect today is to drop in on one of the church services conducted in the local vernacular at the church of San Francesco (see p.173).

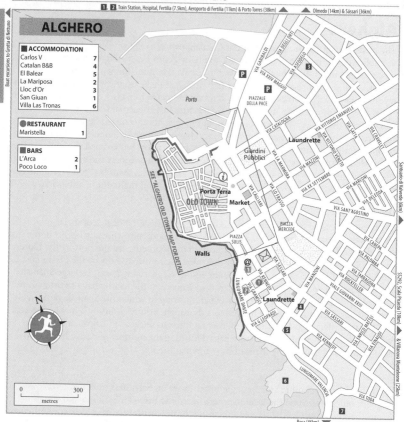

he was abducted as a slave, forcibly converted and castrated for harem service, and swiftly rose to become right-hand man to the feared Khair al-Din, or Barbarossa.)

Modern times

After Sardinia was taken over by the **House of Savoy** in 1720, Alghero became increasingly marginalized. The destruction of its landward-facing walls in the nineteenth century was unable to arrest its steady decline, a process that was only halted in the 1960s, with the flow of new money into the town in the wake of its discovery and development as a package **tourist resort**. The last fifty years have seen the establishment of Sardinia's greatest concentration of hotels and restaurants in Alghero, with a string of new developments along the coast north of the centre. However, the town's remoteness from the mainland has enabled it to escape total mass-market annihilation, while its well-established port has ensured the continuation of the key role of fishing in the local economy.

Giardini Púbblici

Via Catalogna

Near the port, Alghero's **Giardini Púbblici** (Public Gardens) are the location of the tourist office and main bus stop, and are an obvious starting place for any exploration of the *centro stórico*. The shady and well-tended gardens are always busy with families, off-duty taxi-drivers and chatting pensioners. A remnant of the old town's defensive structure lies at the bottom of the gardens, towards the port, where the huge hollow shell of the **Bastione della Maddalena** holds a tower embedded within the crumbling ruins, and is now a venue for open-air entertainment in summer.

Torre di Porta Terra

Piazza Porta Terra • Mon–Sat 10.30am–1pm & 5.30–8pm • €3 • ☎ 079 989 7502, ⓦ smuovi.com

Any walkabout around the old town should take in the series of seven towers dominating Alghero's centre. One of the towers, the **Torre di Porta Terra**, stands at the top of the public gardens, originally intended to guard one of the two gates into the walled town. Also known as the Torre del Portal, it has been identified by some as the medieval *Torre dels Ebreus*, erected by Alghero's Jewish community. Today, the tower has an incongruous Art Deco-style war memorial, and a tourist bookshop has been installed inside, from which you can gain access to the roof for a good view over Alghero's rooftops.

Piazza Cívica

The main square of the old town, **Piazza Cívica**, is a traffic-free but bustling arena of locals and tourists, lined with bars and boutiques. The elongated piazza provides access to the port through the **Porta a Mare**, one of the two main gateways of the old city. The opposite side of the square holds the Gothic **Palazzo d'Albis** (*Palau Albis*), the former governor's palace with mullioned Gothic and Renaissance windows, from which the emperor Charles V addressed the crowds in 1541 before embarking for Algiers on his campaign against the Turks. He is said to have uttered the words, long cherished in local lore as granting instant nobility to the assembled throng, *Estade todos caballeros* ("You are all knights"). The palazzo now contains private apartments.

The Cattedrale

Piazza Duomo • **Interior** Daily 7am–noon & 5–7.30pm • Guided tours (free) Feb–Oct Mon–Fri 10am–noon & 4–6pm • **Campanile**
Via Príncipe Umberto • April, May, Sept & Oct Mon, Tues & Thurs 10.30am–1pm, Fri 10.30am–1pm & 4–8pm; June–Aug Mon & Thurs
10.30am–1pm, Tues & Fri 10.30am–1pm & 7.30–9pm; may close in bad weather • €2.50, €4.50 with Museo Diocesano • ☎ 079 973 3041

From Piazza Cívico, Via Manno leads to the four tall, fluted columns that dominate the white Neoclassical facade of Alghero's **Cattedrale**, a grandiose entry somewhat out of keeping with the sixteenth-century edifice. Founded in 1510, seven years after Alghero was promoted to city status, the cathedral was not fully completed or consecrated until 1730, though it had long since been established as the customary place for Spanish viceroys to take a preliminary oath before assuming office in Cágliari.

The interior

The **interior** is a bit of a hotchpotch: the alternating pillars and columns on either side of the lofty nave survive from the original construction, the impressive dome and creamy marble central altar date from the eighteenth century, and the lateral chapels are predominantly Neoclassical or Baroque. Behind the altar, an ambulatory said to derive architecturally from the Islamic mosque of the old Moorish city gives onto five radiating chapels, also part of the original building. The left transept holds the well-executed marble funerary monument of the Savoy duke of Monferrato, brother of King Carlo Felice, dated 1799. Elsewhere, the flaking walls show the need of a long overdue restoration.

The exterior and bell-tower

To see an original part of the cathedral's **Gothic exterior**, walk round to the back of the building, where there's a lovely carved portal. The doorway sits at the base of the octagonal, sixteenth-century **campanile**, which can be climbed for stunning views. Near the top you might just make out two eroded carvings representing Ferdinand and Isabella of Castile.

5

Museo Diocesano

Piazza Duomo • Early Jan to late March Fri–Sun 10am–1pm & 4.30–7.30pm by arrangement; late March to June, Sept & Oct daily except Wed 10.30am–1pm & 5–8pm; July & Aug Mon–Sat 10.30am–1pm & 6–9pm; Nov to early Dec by arrangement; early Dec to early Jan daily except Wed 11am–1pm & 4.30–7.30pm • €3.50, €4.50 with cathedral campanile • ☎ 079 973 3041

Close to the cathedral, the former church of the Rosario holds the **Museo Diocesano**, a collection of sacred treasures connected to the cathedral and other churches in town,

■ ACCOMMODATION		● RESTAURANTS						■ CAFÉS & BARS	
Aigua	4	Al Tuguri	10	Casablanca	9	Mabrouk	4	Café Latino	1
La Margherita	5	Al Vecchio Mulino	6	Da Pietro	7	Nettuno	1	Diva Café	3
La Rocca	2	Andreini	8	Il Ghiotto	2			Jamaica Inn	4
La Terrazza sul Porto	1	Angedras	5	Il Pavone	12			La Bajada	2
San Francesco	3	Bella Napoli	3	La Lépanto	11				

including paintings, Catalan silverware, wooden statues and crucifixes. The old stone walls and Baroque ornament of the church make a fitting setting for the crosses and cups, whose wide-ranging provenance – from Barcelona, Palermo and even Palestine – testifies to Alghero's one-time importance at the heart of the Mediterranean world. Exhibitions are also held here.

Palazzo Carcassona

Via Sant'Erasmo

North of Piazza Duomo along Via Sant'Erasmo, or accessible from the bastions, the elegantly austere **Palazzo Carcassona** is worth a swift detour to admire its well-restored exterior enlivened by brown-and-white patterns around the windows. The palace was probably owned by the Jewish Carcassona family before their eviction in 1492; the ground floor is now a restaurant, the rest apartments.

Via Príncipe Umberto

Of the long lanes running the length of the old town, **Via Príncipe Umberto** is one of the quietest and most attractive. Notable buildings include, on the right, the decrepit seventeenth-century **Palazzo Machin** at no. 9–11, still retaining its Catalan-Gothic windows and Renaissance portal. Farther up, Piazza Teatro holds the eighteenth-century **Teatro Cívico**, the venue for dramatic performances in winter.

Via Carlo Alberto

Stretching between Piazza Cívica and Piazza Sulis, **Via Carlo Alberto** is the busiest of old Alghero's lanes, crowded with amblers browsing among the succession of tourist shops and bars. Many of the shops are jewellery stores, specializing in the coral for which Sardinia's northwestern coast in general and Alghero in particular are famous. The street also holds a couple of the town's most important **churches**.

San Francesco

Piazza San Francesco • Daily 7.30am–noon & 5–8.30pm

Halfway along Via Carlo Alberto, the fifteenth-century church of **San Francesco** is architecturally the finest of Alghero's churches. The building encompasses several different styles, its Gothic campanile and some of the lateral chapels – survivals from the original construction – blending successfully with the Renaissance ceiling, round arches and swirling carved windows. The centrepiece of the dim interior is a polychrome marble altar, though this vies for attention with a horribly emaciated (*grattugiato*) figure of Christ bound to a column to the left; it looks modern, but is in fact seventeenth-century. Behind the statue, prayers and personal items – even jewellery – are pinned up as votive offerings.

To the left of the altar, the **presbytery**, with its happily irregular cross-vaulted Gothic ceiling, gives onto a simple **cloister** with round, rough-hewn arches originating from the beginning of the fourteenth century. In summer, the cloister is an occasional venue for alfresco classical concerts. **Services in Catalan** are held in the church on Sundays at 8pm (6pm or 7pm Sept–June).

San Michele

Via Carlo Alberto • Open daily 30min before Mass, currently Mon–Sat 7pm, Sun 9am & 7pm

The majolica-tiled cupola of **San Michele** is a sparkling feature of Alghero's skyline, though the haughty interior remains true to its seventeenth-century Jesuit origins. One of the elaborately stuccoed and decorated chapels contains a sculpture of St Michael slaying the dragon; look out also for the gilt wooden choir box over the main entrance.

5

Piazza Sulis and around

At the southern end of Via Carlo Alberto, **Piazza Sulis** marks the end of the old town and the start of the traffic. Nonetheless, it makes an airy, pleasant space by the seashore, a meeting point for the town's youth – and their bikes. The square's main feature is the sturdy **Torre Sulis**, also called Torre dello Sperone (*Torre de l'Esperò Reial* in Catalan), which once served as a place of detention and is named after its most celebrated prisoner, Vincenzo Sulis, incarcerated here for thirty years for his part in the Cágliari uprising of 1794–5.

Running northwards off Piazza Sulis, Via Kennedy extends a few metres to Largo San Francesco, site of another of Alghero's defensive towers, **Torre di San Giovanni**, the venue for occasional exhibitions.

Mare Nostrum Aquarium

Via XX Settembre • April–July, Sept & Oct daily 10am–1pm, plus 3–8pm in April & May, 4–9pm in June & Oct, 5–11pm in July & Sept; Aug daily 10am–1.30pm & 5pm–12.30am; Nov–March Sat 3–8pm, Sun 10am–1pm & 3–8pm • €8 • ☎ 079 978 333

Alghero's **Mare Nostrum Aquarium** holds more than a hundred species of marine life, including turtles, piranha and "nurse" sharks. However, the cramped underground complex is badly maintained and in need of a facelift, while many of the tanks appear too small for the moray eels and other creatures. It's also over-priced – far better to glimpse the real fish in the sea just a few metres away, if you can.

The bastioni

On its sea-facing side, the old town is encompassed by a stout girdle of protective walls, or **bastioni**, that make a serene place to escape Alghero's bustle and savour the views out to Capo Caccia – especially memorable at sunset. You'll pass three more of the town's defensive towers along the way: **Torre di San Giácomo**, **Torre della Polveriera** and **Torre di Sant'Erasmo**. There's a lot more coming and going here on summer evenings, with streams of people drifting between the bars and restaurants.

The port and seafront

Spread out below the lofty walls on the north side of Alghero's old quarter, the wide, usually thronged quays of the **port** are nudged by tourist excursion craft, fishing boats and ranks of sleek yachts. Farther north, an easy walk or bike ride from town, the sandy beaches around **Lido di San Giovanni** aren't the best in the vicinity, but they're clean and convenient; some are private lidos, where you'll pay around €10 per day for an umbrella and two sun-loungers.

Otherwise, it's worth carrying on to the pinewoods and dunes of **Maria Pia**, about 2km north of Alghero, where the beach gently slopes into the shallow and sheltered bay – good for families, with shade provided by the trees and a couple of bars open in summer. A drive or a bike- or bus-ride further up the coast brings you to the area's best swimming spots (see p.183). Don't expect much elbow-room in any of these places in peak season, however.

ARRIVAL AND DEPARTURE

BY PLANE

Alghero's Aeroporto di Fertilia (☎ 079 935 282, ⊚ aeroporto dialghero.it) lies 10km north of town, outside Fertilia, and is served by Air One (☎ 892 444, ⊚ flyairone.it), easyJet (☎ 199 201 840, ⊚ easyjet.com) and Ryanair (☎ 899 552 589, ⊚ ryanair.com), among other companies. The terminal has a tourist office (see opposite) and banks with ATMs; the post office here can also change cash.

Transport from/to the airport Local Al.F.A buses to and

from town leave hourly until 10.30pm (Alghero) or 11pm (airport), stopping in both Fertilia and at Alghero's train and bus stations. At the airport, you can buy tickets from one of the machines in the terminal (€1), for which coins are required, or on board (€1.50). In the other direction, the buses run from Alghero's Piazza Mercede, with a stop on Via Cágliari at the Giardini Púbblici. Buy tickets from a *tabacchino* or from the office on Via Catalogna. The journey takes around 25min. Taxis into Alghero cost €20–25.

Long-distance services There are also departures (some of them summer-only) from the airport to other major towns and resorts operated by different companies, including ARST (see below), Logudoro Tours (☎079 281 728, ⓦ logudorotours.it), Digitur (☎079 262 039, ⓦ digitur.it), Redentours (☎0784 30 325, ⓦ redentours .com) and Sardabus (☎079 510 554, ⓦ sardabus.it).

Destinations (from airport) Alghero (Al.F.A; 5.20am–11pm hourly; 25min); Bosa (ARST; Mon–Sat 3–4 daily, Sun 1–4 daily; 1hr 15min); Cágliari (Logudoro Tours; April–Oct 2 daily; 3hr 30min); Castelsardo (Digitur; June–Sept: 1–2 daily; 1hr 15min); Nuoro (Redentours; 2 daily; 2hr 30min); Oristano (Logudoro Tours; April–Oct 2 daily; 2hr 15min); Santa Teresa di Gallura (Digitur; June–Sept: 1–2 daily; 2hr 30min); Sássari (ARST; 9 daily; 30min); Stintino (Sardabus; June–Sept: 5 daily; 55min).

BY CAR

If you're driving into town, try to park before reaching the old centre as spaces here are extremely limited; your best bet is the portside car park off Via Garibaldi, just north of the centre, or across the road in Piazzale della Pace. Alternatively, park anywhere you see a space, avoiding yellow (reserved) lines; between blue lines, you pay €0.30 for 30min, €0.90 for the first hr, €1.20 for the second hr, and €1.70 for the third (June–Sept daily 9am–2pm & 5–10pm; Oct–March Mon–Fri 9am–2pm & 4–8pm, Sat 9am–2pm & 4–9pm); tickets can be purchased at the meters.

BY TRAIN

The small station for ARST services to and from Sássari (9–12 daily; 35min) lies some way north of the centre on Via Don Minzoni. It's served by frequent local buses (buy tickets from the bar inside the station): Buses AP (Mon–Sat every 20min, Sun every 40min) and Al.F.A. (hourly) run into town from the bus stop across the road; in the opposite direction, the AF runs to Fertilia, for those heading straight to the hostel or campsite there. To get to the station from the centre of town, catch a bus at the Giardini Púbblici or on the seafront.

Train information For information on ARST trains to Sássari, call ☎079 950 785 or visit ⓦ arst.sardegna .it; for FS services from Sássari, call ☎892 021 or visit ⓦ trenitalia.it.

BY BUS

Local and regional buses arrive at and depart from Via Catalogna, by the Giardini Púbblici. All buses are operated by ARST; tickets must be bought beforehand from the ticket office next to the bus stop at the Giardini Púbblici.

Destinations Bosa (2–5 daily; 55min); Capo Caccia (Mon–Sat 1–3 daily, Sun April–Sept 1–3; 50min); Porto Conte (Mon–Sat 6–10 daily, Sun 3–10 daily; 30min); Porto Ferro (3–5 daily; 20–40min); Porto Torres (5–7 daily; 1hr); Sássari (Mon–Sat 10 daily, Sun 4 daily; 1hr); Villanova Monteleone (Mon–Sat 7–8 daily, June–Sept Sun 3 daily; 45min).

GETTING AROUND

By bus Alghero is easily explored on foot, though you may use local buses for journeys to the train station, the local campsite, Fertilia and the local beaches – service AF (every 20min) is useful for the beaches north of the centre off Via Lido. Tickets from *tabacchi* and some bars cost €1, otherwise pay €1.50 on board. Call ☎079 950 458 for bus information.

By bike A bike is good for short trips around the town and its environs. You can rent bikes at MTB, near the public gardens at Via Catalogna 28 (☎079 952 992; €8–18/day) and Raggi di Sardegna, Via Maiorca 119 (☎334 305 2480; €7–12/day).

By car You don't need a car to get around town, but Alghero is a useful place to pick up a rental vehicle for exploring further

afield. Most of the rental agencies have offices out at Fertilia airport, such as Avis (☎079 935 064, ⓦ avis.com), Europcar (☎079 935 032, ⓦ europcar.it) and Maggiore (☎079 935 045, ⓦ maggiore.it). Avis also has an office at Piazza Sulis 9 (☎079 979 577), Europcar has one at Via Vittorio Emanuele 57 (☎079 981 630), and the local firm Rent-a-Car Express – which can deliver and collect – is at Via Satta 52 (☎079 985 937, ⓦ rentacarexpress.it). Rates may be around €70 for one day, €115 for two, with unlimited mileage – though you'll find much better deals online.

By taxi The main rank is on Via Vittorio Emanuele, Giardini Púbblici (☎079 975 396 or ☎348 038 7687); for 24hr service, call ☎079 989 2028.

INFORMATION

Tourist office Alghero's main information office (April–Oct Mon–Sat 9am–8pm, Sun 9am–noon; Nov–March Mon–Sat 9am–7pm; ☎079 979 054, ⓦ alghero-turismo .it), at the top end of the Giardini Púbblici, is probably the

most efficient on the island, with helpful, multilingual staff equipped with reams of maps, accommodation lists and sight details. There's also a desk at the airport (closed at time of writing; ☎079 935 150).

TOURS AND ACTIVITIES

Boat tours The main company, Navisarda, explores the coast and various grottoes in trips lasting 2hr 30min (€13); ask about this and other excursions at their booth at the

port (☎079 978 961, ⓦ navisarda.it).

Diving Adventure Diving, Via Aggius 14 (☎079 973 9039, ⓦ adventurediving.it); Blue Service Alghero, La Mariposa

5

campsite, Via Lido 18 (☎ 342 757 1434, ⓦ blueservice alghero.com); Nautisub, Via Garibaldi 45 (☎ 079 952 433 or ☎ 330 935 350, ⓦ nautisub.com). One dive costs €40–65, two or three dives work out cheaper. There's another dive centre at Porto Conte (see p.184).

Il Cocchio This "horse-drawn" – actually electrically-operated – coach performs a circuit of the old centre in around 25min, leaving from the port every 30min or so and with a taped commentary (March–Oct); €5, €3 for 2–10-year-olds; ☎ 079 976 927).

Il Tróttolo To view or reach the coast in comfort, board this open-top double-decker that follows the coast as far as Capo Caccia 3–4 times daily, stopping at beaches en route (March–Oct daily, Nov Sat & Sun; €18, €12 for under-16s, €56 family ticket; ☎ 079 399 110, ⓦ trottolo.it); tickets are valid all day, enabling you to hop on or off wherever you like.

Trenino Catalano If you've got kids, or you're just tired, you might want to tour the old town on this miniature "train" leaving from the port (April–Oct; €5, €3 for 8–14-year-olds; ☎ 336 691 836).

Walking tours Cooperativa Smuovi, Torre di Porta Terra (☎ 079 989 7502 or ☎ 329 438 5947, ⓦ smuovi.com), leads guided tours of Old Alghero (in Italian, English or other major languages), lasting 2–3hr and including free entry to a couple of the sights plus audio-guides (€6 for 1hr 30min, €7.50 for 2hr 30min).

Sailing excursions You can embark on sea trips from the port on 8hr cruises aboard the *Andrea Jensen*, a traditional 80ft sailing ketch, with swimming and snorkelling stops (May to mid-Oct; €99, or €49 for children aged 6–12; ☎ 338 970 8139, ⓦ ajsailing.com). Prices include food, drink and snorkelling equipment, groups are small, and Italian, Spanish and English are spoken.

ACCOMMODATION

Alghero's choice of accommodation is extensive, though booking is essential at any time; availability can be especially scarce and **hotel** prices rocket in high summer, while most places close altogether in winter. However, the resort also has a profusion of more affordable **B&Bs**, which tend to remain open all year. Most places lie outside the historic core, either spread out along the seafront to either side or in the grid of parallel streets that make up the new town. The few places in the old centre don't have parking facilities. The local **campsite** is an easy bus ride north from the centre, and there are two other sites 7–12km along the coast around Fertilia (see p.182); a fourth, more secluded site is located out at Torre del Porticciolo (p.184). Fertilia also has a **hostel**.

Aigua Via Machin 22 ☎ 340 077 7688, ⓦ aigua.it; map p.172. Six mini-apartments in two centrally located buildings, most with vaulted wood ceilings, exposed brick-work and tiled floors. Rooms come equipped with basic kitchen facilities for self-service breakfasts. Closed Jan & Feb. €75

Carlos V (Carlos Quinto) Lungomare Valencia 24 ☎ 079 972 0600, ⓦ hotelcarlosv.it; map p.170. One of the plushest hotels in town, this five-star pampers with spacious, balconied rooms, most overlooking a good-sized pool surrounded by palm trees. Official rates are high, but you can find bargains online and in low season. It's worth paying the supplement for sea-facing rooms. €268

Catalan B&B Via Manzoni 41 ☎ 079 981 909 or ☎ 347 833 5230, ⓦ bed-and-breakfast-alghero.com; map p.170. Modern apartment in the new town, a 10min walk from the old centre. There are three rooms – one with its own bathroom (the others have wash-basins), one with

a balcony, all with a/c – and a buffet breakfast. A separate apartment with a roof terrace is also available to rent. €80

El Balear Lungomare Dante 32 ☎ 079 975 229, ⓦ hotel elbalearcom; map p.170. This three-star hotel, a pleasant 15min walk south of the old centre, has an enviable position facing the sea near two (rocky) beaches, but it could do with a facelift and some rooms are small. Lunch and dinner are each €15. Closed Nov–March. €95

La Margherita Via Sássari 70 ☎ 079 979 006, ⓦ hotel lamargherita.it; map p.172. Close to the old town, this family-run hotel is old-fashioned in the best sense, while boasting a spa bath and indoor pool in the basement and a grand roof terrace where breakfast is served in summer. Rooms have fridges and front-facing ones have a small balcony, with the best views on the fourth floor. €90

La Rocca Via Roma 75 ☎ 328 481 5988, ⓦ bblarocca .com; map p.172. In a restored sixteenth-century *palazzo* in the heart of the old town, this B&B has just one room, but

---

APARTMENT RENTALS

If you're staying in Alghero for a week or more, consider renting a **private apartment**; off-season rates are particularly favourable, but don't expect to find many bargains or availability in August unless you've booked far ahead. Agencies include Casa Vacanze Cau, Via Gaudi 8 (☎ 079 952 478, ⓦ appartamenticau.it); Marisal, Viale Europa 35 (☎ 333 572 9797, ⓦ marisal-alghero.com); and Gli Eucalipti, Via Lido 127 (☎ 079 951 187, ⓦ residenceucalipti.it) – the tourist office has a full list. Prices in summer range from €400 to more than €1000 per week for a one-room apartment for two.

it's spacious and charmingly dated. An apartment is also available. No credit cards. **€85**

La Terrazza sul Porto Piazza Cívica 19 ☎079 973 1054, ⓦbblaterrazzasulportoalghero.it; map p.172. Located on the old town's central piazza, this modern fourth-floor B&B (there's a lift) has four rooms with their own balconies, and there's a communal terrace where breakfast is taken in summer, with fantastic harbour views. **€110**

Lloc d'Or Via Logudoro 26 ☎334 289 7130, ⓦllocdor .com; map p.170. Within a short walk of the old town, this friendly B&B has just two rooms, both big and airy, with a shared bathroom, and a self-contained apartment. There's a patio and a small kitchen and washing machine for guests' use, and breakfasts include fresh fruit and yoghurt. No credit cards. **€60**

★ **San Francesco** Via Machin 2 ☎079 980 330, ⓦsan francescohotel.com; map p.172. The only hotel in the old town was formerly a convent attached to San Francesco church, and preserves a reclusive air. The 21 rooms are small but clean and quiet, with telephones, a/c and private bathrooms. Breakfast is eaten in the cloisters. Drivers must find their own parking space. Closed Nov–Feb. **€100**

San Giuan Via Angioy 2 ☎079 951 222, ⓦhotelsan giuan.it; map p.170. A 15min walk north of the centre, this modern three-star hotel doesn't have a great deal of character and some of the plain rooms suffer from traffic noise, but it has a roof terrace, is near the beaches and has comparatively reasonable rates. Some rooms have balconies. There's no restaurant. Closed Nov–March. **€120**

Villa Las Tronas Lungomare Valencia 1 ☎079 981 818, ⓦhotelvillalastronas.it; map p.170. Grandly sited on a promontory a 10min walk south of the centre, this castellated former royal residence from 1884 is full of character, still retaining a baronial air with its elegant old furnishings. There's also an excellent restaurant, a spa, a gym and a saltwater pool carved out of the rock. **€330**

CAMPING

La Mariposa Via Lido 22 ☎079 950 480, ⓦlamariposa .it; map p.170. A couple of kilometres north of the centre, this usually busy and crowded campsite has direct access to the beach, part of which is sectioned off for campers. Eucalyptus and pine provide shade and soft ground, and there's a bar, restaurant and shop, as well as a diving centre, windsurfing, sailing, bikes and scooters to rent, plus internet access. Bungalows, caravans and simple cabins with bunks are also available (from €32). Local bus AF runs here from the train station and the public gardens; alternatively, walk 10min from the train station. Closed mid-Oct to March. Pitches **€30**

EATING

The quality of Alghero's restaurants is highly impressive – the presence of the fishing port ensures a regular supply of fresh **seafood** (spring and winter are the best seasons), including lobster (*aragosta*), a local speciality. The local cuisine also makes good use of Catalan culinary traditions – you might find *paella*, and for dessert, *crema catalana*, a sort of caramelized custard. The town is additionally blessed by its proximity to some of Sardinia's most famous vineyards. For the freshest fruit and vegetables, drop in at the **market** (Mon–Sat 8am–1pm) off Via Sássari between Via Génova and Via Mazzini.

Al Tuguri Via Maiorca 115 ☎079 976 772, ⓦaltuguri .it; map p.172. Minuscule restaurant – two rooms on two floors – specializing in authentic Catalan cuisine. The name is dialect meaning "old abandoned house", helping to explain the faintly rustic ambience. It's select and chic, but makes a memorable splurge. Pastas are €13–16, mains €20–25; alternatively, go for the five-course sampling menu (€40), which comes with a vegetarian option (€36). March–Nov Mon–Sat 12.30–2pm & 8–10pm.

★ **Al Vecchio Mulino** Via Don Deroma 3 ☎079 977 254; map p.172. The locals' choice: low-vaulted cellars in the old town, with friendly staff and a good selection of white wines. For a change from seafood, try the *spaghetti al Vecchio Mulino*, made with mushrooms, ham and cream; pizzas are also available. Fish and meat dishes cost around €15. Daily 7pm–midnight; closed Tues in winter, all Nov & two weeks in Jan.

Andreini Via Ardoino 45 ☎079 982 098, ⓦristoranteandreini.it; map p.172. This elegant and upmarket restaurant in an atmospheric, grotto-like dining room specializes in land-based dishes such as kid and boar, not to mention the Sard classic *porcetto sardo* (young pig spit-roasted). Seafood dishes are also available, and the *antipasti* are excellent. You can eat outside in summer. Mains are €20–25, and there are tasting menus for €60–70. Daily 12.30–2.30pm & 7.30–11pm; closed Mon Nov–March.

Angedras Via Cavour 31 and Bastioni Marco Polo 41 ☎079 973 5078, ⓦangedrasrestaurant.it; map p.172. Part of a smart, modern hotel, this restaurant has a large, sleek, contemporary-looking dining room as well as space on the *bastioni*, for lunching alfresco or soaking up the memorable sunsets. The menu is seafood-based, including lobster and swordfish. There's a €16 lunchtime menu, otherwise starters are €10–16, mains €14–18. April–Oct daily noon–2.45pm & 7–10.30pm.

Bella Napoli Piazza Cívica 29 ☎079 983 014; map p.172. Popular Neapolitan-run ristorante/pizzeria, with generous portions, good salads and tables in the square; traces of an ancient *frantoio*, or olive-mill, are visible inside. Pizzas (€7–13) are also available at lunchtime; mains are around €16. Daily noon–midnight; closed Wed Nov–March.

5

★ **Casablanca** Via Príncipe Umberto 72 ☎ 079 983 353; map p.172. With vaulted rooms, this is the best place in town for a straightforward pizza or pasta dish in a convivial atmosphere with good service; mains are €10–15. Daily 12.30–2.30pm & 7.30–11.30pm; closed Mon & Thurs lunchtime June–Sept, all Wed Oct–May.

Da Pietro Via Machin 20 ☎ 079 979 645; map p.172. Popular with tourists, this vaulted fish restaurant is highly variable – dishes range from very good to very mediocre – but you might strike lucky, and prices are relatively low, with set-price menus for €15–25. The ambience is authentically old-school, with the TV usually on. Daily 12.15–2.30pm & 7.30–10.30pm; closed Wed Oct–June.

Il Ghiotto Piazza Cívica 23 ☎ 079 974 820; map p.172. This place sells great takeaway items and has a *távola calda* inside where pastas, meats and seafood are served (mostly under €10) – a good option if you don't want to pay restaurant prices at lunchtime. There's a fine selection of local Sardinian wines, served with free canapés in the evening. Daily 12.30–2.30pm & 7–11.30pm; closed Mon Nov–Feb.

Il Pavone Piazza Sulis 3 ☎ 079 979 584; map p.172. An exclusive enclave to sample some of the best of *cucina algherese*, including *antipasti*, paella and vegetarian dishes, and the black chocolate *gelato* is a show-stopper. First courses weigh in at around €15, mains at €17–22, and there are fixed-price menus for €50 and €60. Dine on the patio or in the two small, mirrored rooms, which are filled with antiques. Daily noon–3pm & 7.30pm–midnight; closed Mon Oct–March.

La Lépanto Via Carlo Alberto 135 ☎ 079 979 116, 🌐 lalepanto.com; map p.172. With large windows looking across Piazza Sulis and out to sea, this long-established, rather formal seafood restaurant is renowned for its lobster – though it's pricey. The fresh fish is enticingly displayed, meat dishes are also excellent, and there's a delectable range of Sardinian sweets. Count on €50–60 per head. Daily except Tues noon–3pm & 7.30pm–midnight; closed Wed lunchtime mid-Sept to June.

★ **Mabrouk** Via Santa Barbara 4 ☎ 079 970 000; map p.172. This is about as near as Alghero comes to a cosy neighbourhood trattoria, where there's no written menu but a democratic €40 fixed-price dinner for everyone – including unlimited house wine and limoncello. It's mainly seafood: a typical meal might start with five *antipasti*, followed by three types of pasta, the catch of the day, prawns, calamari and delicious desserts. Mid-March to Oct Tues–Sun 8–11pm; July & Aug open daily.

Maristella Via Kennedy 9 ☎ 079 978 172; map p.170. Reasonable prices, tasty fare and terrific desserts at this place near Piazza Sulis. Popular with locals, so it's worth booking, especially if you want pavement seating. Pastas are €9–12, mains mostly €10–15. Daily 12.15–2.30pm & 7.30–10.30pm; closed Sun eve Oct–Feb.

Nettuno Via Maddalenetta 4 ☎ 079 979 774; map p.172. This pizzeria/ristorante overlooking the port is touristy, but worth a try, if only for the rooftop terrace open in summer, for which there's a ten-percent supplement, and balcony seating, for which booking is essential. Most pizzas are €7–10, pastas €10–14 and main courses €14–22. Daily 1–11pm; closed Wed Oct–April.

DRINKING AND NIGHTLIFE

CAFÉS, BARS AND BIRRERIAS

Alghero's rich selection of bars and cafés keep going into the small hours in summer, though things get pretty quiet out of season. For sunset views, opt for one of the places lining the town's ramparts. The following are some of the best choices staying open all year.

L'Arca Lungomare Dante 6 ☎ 079 982 662; map p.170. Seafront hangout with table football and regular live music at weekends throughout the year and daily in Aug. April–Sept daily 8am–2am; Oct–March Tues–Sun 8am–10pm.

Café Latino Piazza Duomo 6 ☎ 079 976 541; map p.172. Stylish place for an evening aperitif, with outside tables beneath parasols on the walls overlooking the port. Snacks and ice creams are also served, though prices are high. Daily 9am–2am; closed Tues Oct–May.

★ **Diva Café** Piazza Municipio 1 ☎ 079 982 306; map p.172. Tucked up a side street off Piazza Cívica, this long-established, locals' bar has tables outside and serves toasties and other snacks (including pizzas in summer). Daily 8.30am–2am, closed Sun Nov–May.

Jamaica Inn Via Príncipe Umberto 57 ☎ 079 973 3050; map p.172. This pub – right in the thick of things – is a lively spot for cocktails to an endless Bob Marley soundtrack. There's an open-air terrace across the road where (mediocre and fairly pricey) meals are served. Daily 1–3pm & 7.30pm–2am; closed Mon Oct–June.

La Bajada Via Roma 22 ☎ 348 275 5038; map p.172. A quiet nook just a few steps away from the bustle, this is a cool place for a quiet drink, best at night. Snacks and meals are available, from panini to salads and tasty ravioli. Daily 10.30am–12.30am.

Poco Loco Via Gramsci 8 ☎ 079 983 604; map p.170. Beers, pizzas, live jazz (usually Fri & Sat) and general carousing in this spacious hall off Piazza Sulis, with bowling upstairs (not Wed) and internet access. Daily 7pm–late.

CLUBS

Clubs and discos proliferate in Alghero and the surrounding area in summer, and often disappear altogether in winter (but may reopen for New Year's Eve). Many of the latest spots come and go, and some are attached to hotels. The music is predominantly commercial and house. Count on about €15 **entry**, usually including the first drink; subsequent drinks cost €5–10.

5

FESTIVALS AND ENTERTAINMENT

Alghero's Spanish inheritance is particularly manifest during its **Easter** festivities, when the rituals of the *Misteri* (representing the Passion of Christ) and *Incontru* (the symbolic meeting of the Virgin with Christ) are enacted, with statues carried through town amid solemn processions. In contrast, **Carnival** is a feisty affair, involving plenty of masked antics and the burning of the *pupazzo* (a "guy" representing a French soldier), ceremonially put on trial and burnt on the bonfire on Shrove Tuesday. May sees a steady procession of pilgrims to the sanctuary of Valverde, 6km east of town, in thanksgiving for the Madonna's intervention at times of disaster. A major milestone in the Italian year is **Ferragosto** (August 15), in which the Feast of the Assumption is celebrated with a range of musical and folkloric events, fireworks and boating competitions.

Religion and secular games are mixed at the **Festa di Sant'Agostino** day on August 28, and there are waterborne events and feasting organized as part of the **Sagra dei Pescatori**, or Fisherman's Fair, on a Saturday or Sunday in September, the precise date varying from year to year. Towards the end of September, Alghero's patron saint, St Michael, is commemorated in the four-day **Nit de Sant Miquel**, with open-air concerts and dance performances, culminating in a spectacular fireworks display over the harbour.

Less specifically, a wide-ranging programme of cultural **events** takes place throughout July–September in various parts of the town, including concerts, cabaret and folk dances, often free. In particular, look out for **open-air classical concerts** and other performances held at the Bastione della Maddalena and at the church of San Francesco in July and August; the tourist office has details.

Il Ruscello 2km northeast of Alghero on the Olmedo road ☎328 958 8788. Among the permanent fixtures, this is frequented mainly by the 18–25 age group. There are open-air dancefloors and occasional live bands. From 11.30pm: June & Sept Fri & Sat; July & Aug nightly; Oct–May Sat.

La Siesta Località Scala Piccada, 10km southeast of town on the SS292 Villanova road ☎079 980 137. With a pedigree dating back to the 1960s, this club is famous for its magnificent views over the coast. It caters for a mixed audience, with four dancefloors playing different sounds. An ARST bus service for getting there and back operates from Via Catalogna three times nightly between June and August (15min); otherwise you'll have to depend on taxis, which may cost upwards of €30 each way. June–Aug most Fri & Sat from midnight.

SHOPPING

Il Ghiotto Piazza Cívica 23 ☎079 974 820. Apart from meals, this place has local specialities and Sardinian wines to take away. Daily 12.30–2.30pm & 7–11.30pm; closed Mon Nov–Feb.

Libreria Mondadori Via Carlo Alberto 119 ☎079 980 496. A range of English books, guides and maps is sold. Daily 9am–1pm & 4–9pm.

Oviesse Piazza Sulis ☎079 973 2096. Useful general store for clothes and accessories. Mon–Sat 9.30am–9pm, Sun 10am–9pm.

Porta Terra tower Piazza Porta Terra ☎079 989 7502. Tourist guides and maps are available here. Mon–Sat 10.30am–1pm & 5.30–8pm.

Salumerie Tipico Via Sássari 27 ☎079 973 8801. Quality cold meats, cheeses, wines and artisan breads. Mon–Sat 7am–2pm & 5–9pm, Sun 7am–2pm.

Sisa Via Sássari 49 ☎079 973 1067. Supermarket with a good food hall. Mon–Sat 8am–9pm, Sun 8.30–1.30pm & 5–9pm.

MARKETS

A daily food market occupies the block between Via Cágliari and Via Sássari, and Via Genova and Via Mazzini. Wed mornings see a large and lively general market along

ALGHERO'S CORAL TRADE

Not for nothing is this stretch of coast known as the **Costa del Corallo** – the two promontories at the southern end of Porto Conte are walled with **coral** colonies, mainly in grottoes deep underwater. The coral extraction industry is heavily controlled, but there seems to be no shortage of outlets for the precious stuff, fashioned into jewellery and trinkets of every description. Prices are high, but if you're interested, it's worth browsing in different stores in town (there are plenty in and around Alghero's old centre) to compare prices – and don't hesitate to bargain.

5

Viale Europa, near the Lido di San Giovanni. There's also a Sat morning general market on Via Fiume, Fertilia (see p.183). In summer, stalls selling local sweet delicacies – biscuits and pastries – among crafts and other knick-knacks set up along Alghero's Via Garibaldi and at the port every night until late.

DIRECTORY

Hospital Ospedale Civile, Via Don Minzoni ☏ 079 996 200. In an emergency, call ☏ 079 996 233 or ☏ 118.

Internet access Fotoclub, Piazza Cívica 7 (daily: summer 9.30am–9pm; winter 9.30am–1.30pm & 4.30–8.30pm; €1.50 for 15min); *Poco Loco*, Via Gramsci 8 (see p.178).

Laundry Coin-operated laundrettes can be found at Via Sássari 113 (daily until 10.30pm) and Via Vittorio Veneto 3 (daily until 9.30pm). Both charge around €4 for 7kg.

Left luggage Valige Italia, Via Cágliari 31 (Mon 5–9pm, Tues–Sat 9am–1pm & 5–9pm; €3/half-day or €5/day per article).

Pharmacy Farmacia Cabras, at Piazza Sulis 20, is the most central pharmacy (Mon–Sat 9am–1pm & 4–8.30pm, or 5–9pm in summer). Late-closing pharmacies are detailed on this and other pharmacy doors, with a telephone number for out-of-hours emergencies.

Post office Via Carducci, off Via Sássari (Mon–Fri 8.25am–7.10pm, Sat 8.25am–12.35pm). You can also change cash here.

Travel agency Agenzie Marittime Sarde, Via Vittorio Emanuele 27 ☏ 079 979 005.

Around Alghero

It's almost *de rigueur* for visitors to Alghero to make the trip out to the **Grotta di Nettuno**, one of Italy's most awesome cave complexes, at Capo Caccia, 15km due west of town. Most people visit on one of the frequent boats that leave from the port throughout the year. It's a thrilling ride along the coast, though it's cheaper to go the slow way by bus, and in some ways more rewarding, as you get to experience a dizzy descent down cliffs.

If you visit the grotto by boat, you'll pass the deep bay of **Porto Conte**, a beauty spot favoured by sailors, divers and windsurfers, part of which is set aside as a wildlife reserve. The land journey will take you through the low-key resort of **Fertilia**, 7km west of Alghero. Originally one of Mussolini's settlements linked to his land-reclamation programme, the town is remarkably quiet after the vivacity of Alghero, but it has some good eating and sleeping options, and is close to the region's best **beaches**.

Fertilia also lies near the area's most important nuraghic complex, **Nuraghe di Palmavera**, one of a pair of archeological sites that make a stimulating contrast to the sun-and-sea attractions of the rest of the region. The other site is **Anghelu Ruju**, set amid the endless vineyards that produce some of Sardinia's most renowned wines.

Farther afield, the undeveloped coast **south of Alghero** is a jagged and dramatic interplay of rock and sea, with a few select beaches tucked out of sight. There are no signs of habitation until you climb to the village of **Villanova Monteleone**, situated inland amid a bare mountainous terrain. In the opposite direction, the country **north of Alghero** is much flatter, but there are a couple of places worth exploring: **Lago di Baratz**, harbouring protected wildlife, and the abandoned mining centre of **Argentiera**, dominated by the eighteenth-century workings of a once flourishing industry.

Grotta di Nettuno

Capo Caccia • Daily: April & Oct 9am–7pm; May–Sept 9am–8pm; Nov–March 10am–4pm; tours (45min) depart hourly, on the hour; last tour 1hr before closing • €13 • ☏ 079 946 540

The most touted of the excursions from Alghero's port is west along the coast to the **Grotta di Nettuno**, or Neptune's Grotto, tucked below Capo Caccia, the sheer promontory visible from the town. The spectacular cliffs here are riddled by deep marine caves, including the Grotta Verde and Grotta dei Ricami – visited on some boat tours – but the most impressive is the Grotta di Nettuno itself, just west of the cape.

From the grotto's entrance, tours are led single-file by guides who provide commentaries in various languages. The long, snaking passage delves far into the rock, past fantastical,

BOSA (P.187) >

5

> ## GETTING TO THE GROTTA DI NETTUNO
>
> **Boats** operated by Navisarda (☎079 950 603, ⓦnavisarda.it) depart from Alghero hourly June–September 9am–5pm, March–May and October 10am–3pm (call to check departure times); return tickets cost €15, excluding entry to the grotto. The boat ride takes thirty minutes, the entire visit and return trip taking about two and a half hours. Navisarda also operates hourly boat departures from Porto Conte (see p.184). Note that sailings are cancelled in bad weather. A cheaper alternative to the boat trip from Alghero is to drive, cycle or take the ARST **bus** to Capo Caccia from Via Catalogna, a fifty-minute ride (June–Sept 3 daily; Oct–May 1 daily; €2.50 one-way, €4.50 return).

dramatically lit **stalagmites** and **stalactites** and along walls shimmering with phosphorescence. The guides relate the discovery of the cave complex by fishermen, pointing out imagined resemblances to helmeted warriors, toothy witches and popes. Less fanciful are the likenesses of organ pipes and columned cathedral interiors, after which two of the chambers are named. Signs point out that touching the rock and photography are both forbidden, though neither injunction is strictly observed. The green colouring visible on some of the rock is mould, mostly caused by the lighting system.

Arriving via the land route, you'll have to negotiate a steep and spectacular 654-step descent down the **Escala del Cabirol** (the Catalan name means "goat's steps", presumably a reference to the only animal that could negotiate the perilous path before the construction of the stairway in 1954). The sheer cliff-face and dark-blue water below are almost as impressive as the grotto interior itself. Try to time your arrival at the cave so that you don't have to wait up to an hour for the next tour: the descent takes ten to fifteen minutes. On the ascent back, you can reward yourself with a well-earned ice cream or thirst-quencher at the bar opposite the top of the steps.

Note that the grotto is closed in **rough weather** – worth checking beforehand as conditions on the cape may be dramatically different from those in town.

Fertilia

Providing a quiet contrast to bustling Alghero, **FERTILIA** appeals mostly for its curiosity value – the settlement was a creation of Mussolini in the 1930s, named to evoke the agricultural abundance that local land drainage would bring about (indeed, the rich agricultural land has produced some excellent wines, notably Torbato, a fairly sweet white). The arcaded **Via Pola** is the main avenue, connecting Piazza Venezia Giulia with the broad Piazzale San Marco next to the sea, marked by a memorial to the migrants who settled the area from the Friuli-Venezia region of northeast Italy. There's little else in the town, and, out of season, little movement more frenetic than the slow padding of stray dogs.

Immediately east of town lies the long lagoon, **Stagno di Cálich**, collecting the outflow of two rivers. Its mouth is crossed by a medieval bridge sinking picturesquely into the water, known locally as the **Ponte Romano**, or "Roman" bridge; it has been superseded by a modern road bridge, and the old structure is now mainly used as a perch for fishermen.

ARRIVAL AND DEPARTURE   FERTILIA

On foot or by bike From Alghero, you can walk or cycle the seven flat kilometres along the seafront and past pine-fringed beaches, and there's even a protected bicycle lane running part of the way.

By bus Local AF and Al.F.A. buses leave for Fertilia from Alghero's Giardini Púbblici, seafront and train station.

ACCOMMODATION

Calik Blu SS127bis ☎079 930 111, ⓦcampingcalikblu.it. Just outside Fertilia, right across the road from the beach on the Alghero road, this is the larger of the area's two campsites, with pitches by the lagoon and equipped with a good restaurant, self-service laundry and evening entertainment. Spacious bungalows (€56) are also available – choose one (or a pitch) away from the noisy bar/restaurant area. Closed Oct–May. Pitches **€32.50**

Hostal de l'Alguer Via Parenzo, off Via Zara ☎079 930 478, ⓦalgherohostel.com. At the western end of town, this secluded hostel is modern and clean, if rather institutional. Dorms have four to ten beds and there are some private rooms with en-suite bathrooms. There are no cooking facilities, but evening meals are prepared (€10), and there's a laundry and internet access. Non-HI members can buy temporary membership for €2. Call first to check availability, as it's popular with groups even in low season. Dorms €18, doubles €52

Nurral SS291 ☎079 930 485, ⓦcampnurral.it. Much smaller than *Calik Blu*, this site in pinewoods lies 100m along the SS291 running north to Santa Maria La Palma. It isn't that close to the sea (300m), but it has friendly service, good facilities and basic but clean caravans and self-catering bungalows to rent at €45–70 per night in high season. Bike hire and free wi-fi are also available. Closed mid-Oct to April. Pitches €16

EATING

Acquario Via Pola 34 ☎079 930 239. This traditional trattoria close to Piazzale San Marco offers well-prepared meat and fish dishes (try *scampi alla gianni*) at reasonable prices, with tourist menus at €20 and €22. Pizzas are available in the evenings. March–Oct Tues–Sun 12.30–2.30pm & 7.30–10.30pm, open daily in Aug.

Il Paguro Via Zara 13 ☎079 930 260. Near the hostel, this place has a covered terrace and does a good trade in grilled fish and pizzas. *Primi* include *spaghetti al cartoccio* – pasta with crab, squid and prawns cooked in the oven. There's a good-value fixed-price menu for €16. Daily except Wed 12.30–2.30pm & 7.30pm–midnight, open daily in Aug.

Nuraghe di Palmavera

SP127bis Porto Conte road • Daily: April & Oct 9am–6pm; May–Sept 9am–7pm; Nov–March 10am–2pm • €3, or €5 with guided tour; €5 with Anghelu Ruju (see p.184), or €9 with guided tour at each site • Served by Capo Caccia bus (not Sun in winter), leaving at 9.15am from the Giardini Púbblici, returning at about 12.30pm • ☎329 438 5947

One of the largest nuraghic sites in this region, the **Nuraghe di Palmavera** lies just off the Fertilia–Porto Conte road, 10km west of Alghero. The site comprises a ruined palace dating from the fourteenth and thirteenth centuries BC, surrounded by fifty or so circular huts. It's well worth a visit, relatively well preserved and clearly laid out. The central tower is entered through a corridor with niches on either side, probably for sentries, and a trap door in the roof for extra security. The interior is of the rounded "tholos" type, with more shallow niches. An elliptical bastion and a minor tower were added to the main building in the second phase of construction, around the ninth century BC, when some of the round huts scattered outside the ramparts were also erected. Most of these were probably dwellings, but one, the **Capanna delle Riunioni**, distinguished by a low stone bench running round the circular walls, is believed to have been used for meetings and religious gatherings. The stool at the centre is a plaster copy of the original, now on display in Sássari's Museo Sanna (see p.203), along with numerous other finds from the site.

A third building phase took place a hundred or so years later, when more buildings were added, this time in limestone, as opposed to the softer sandstone of previous stages. The complex is thought to have been abandoned in the eighth or seventh century BC, possibly on account of fire. See Contexts for more on Sardinia's nuraghic culture (p.307).

Le Bombarde and Lazzaretto beaches

Buses running to Porto Conte and Capo Caccia stop at the junctions for Le Bombarde and Lazzaretto, from where it's roughly a 10min walk down to the beaches

Side roads off the Fertilia–Porto Conte road lead to two of the area's best **beaches**, set in beautiful sandy coves facing Alghero across the bay. Both of these swimming spots can get quite busy in summer, with bars, toilets and beach equipment for hire between June and September (around €6/day for a parasol and sun-lounger). Parking is charged in summer (€4/half day).

Two kilometres west of Fertilia, a straight, narrow track leads to the lovely crescent of **Le Bombarde**, a thin, white sandy strip with clear, clean water and a shallow seabed. **Windsurfing** courses are held here, and boards are available to rent, as well as pedalos and canoes (€10/hr each). The rocky seabed full of marine life makes it ideal for

5

snorkelling, but beware of sharp rocks in places. The beach of **Lazzaretto**, guarded by a Spanish watchtower, lies about 700m farther west, at the end of another signposted turn-off close to Nuraghe di Palmavera (see p.183). Again, pedalos and canoes are available, and the water is crystal-clear. A string of smaller beaches lie beyond, which you can count on having pretty much to yourself on weekdays out of season.

Porto Conte and around

The lovely inlet of **Porto Conte** lies a couple of kilometres beyond Lazzaretto, about 10km west of Alghero. Romantically named Portus Nimpharum ("Port of the Nymphs") by the Romans, the intensely blue bay is a favourite anchorage for luxury yachts, which can be admired from the terraces of the clutch of top-notch hotels nestled among the trees. The road tracing the bay's eastern shore ends at a lighthouse; if you're looking for good bathing spots, follow the main road to Capo Caccia, turning left for the beach of **Baja di Conte** near the hotel of the same name. There are some scant **Roman ruins** here and **windsurfing** facilities on the beach.

Le Prigionette

Porto Conte • Mon–Sat 8am–4pm, Sun 9am–5pm • Free • ☎ 079 949 060, ⓦ parcodiportoconte.it

To the west of Porto Conte, the slopes of Monte Timidone (361m) hold **Le Prigionette**, a protected wildlife zone, roughly 12 square kilometres in size, clothed in a rich abundance of Mediterranean *macchia* (scrub). The park is home to miniature horses and asses from Asinara (see p.197), as well as assorted wild boar, deer, Barbary partridge and, around the coastal cliffs, griffon vultures and peregrine falcons. Forest trails wind through the area.

ARRIVAL AND ACCOMMODATION

PORTO CONTE AND AROUND

By bus From Alghero's Giardini Púbblici, 3–10 buses daily depart for Porto Conte (30min).

Torre del Porticciolo Santa Maria La Palma road ☎ 079 919 007, ⓦ torredelporticciolo.com. The largest campsite in the region (and the priciest), this is signposted on the west coast about 5km north of Porto Conte. It's a

self-contained holiday complex, equipped with children's activities, two pools and a private beach in the round bay below, and organizes diving and riding holidays. Bungalows are available (€110), with a minimum week-long stay in high season (though this could be relaxed). You'll need your own transport, though. Closed mid-Oct to April. Pitches **€35**

ACTIVITIES

Diving Diving Center, Porto Conte (☎ 338 325 3695, ⓦ divingportoconte.it) provide equipment and tuition at various levels. Alghero's tourist office has a list of diving outfits in the area (see p.175).

Boat excursions Navisarda (☎ 079 946 642, ⓦ navisarda .it) runs hourly trips to Neptune's Grotto from Cala

Dragunara, an inlet on the western arm of Porto Conte, between June and Sept 9.30am–5.30pm (also March–May and Oct by arrangement); return tickets cost €11, excluding entry to the grotto. The boat ride takes about 10min, the entire visit and return trip taking 1hr 30min. Sailings may be cancelled in bad weather.

Anghelu Ruju

SS292 Porto Torres road • Daily: April & Oct 9am–6pm; May–Sept 9am–7pm; Nov–March 10am–2pm • €3, or €5 with guided tour; €5 with Nuraghe di Palmavera (see p.183), or €9 with guided tour at each site • By bus, take the service for San Marco (not Sun), leaving at 2.30pm from the Giardini Púbblici, returning at about 5.15pm (inform driver of destination) • ☎ 329 438 5947

The necropolis of **Anghelu Ruju**, a pre-nuraghic cave complex of some forty hypogea 10km north of Alghero, was discovered by chance in 1903, shortly after the land was purchased by the Sella e Mosca winery – now one of Sardinia's most celebrated wine producers (see opposite). The necropolis – which now stands in the midst of the vineyards of Cannonau grapes beneath the planes roaring to and from nearby Fertilia airport – is a creation of the late Neolithic Ozieri culture dating back to about 2900 BC, though it was reused throughout the Copper Age (2900–1500 BC). Gouged out of the ground and accessed by low-lintelled doorways, the tombs constitute Sardinia's best examples of the so-called *domus de janas* (fairies' or witches' houses), of which there are scores on the island, for the most part murky chambers, or groups of them, some connected by sloping passages. The dead were embalmed within, occasionally in mass burials, sometimes half-cremated and in some cases skinned before burial.

Visitors are free to scramble around the tombs, though there is little specific to see: the rich contents have been removed to the archeological museums of Cágliari and Sássari. In some cases, however, you can just make out, carved on the lintels or in the depths of the darkness, symbolic shapes including bulls' horns in tombs A, XXb, XXVIII and XXX, the last of these – carved on the left wall of the "atrium" – a simple line which could also be a boat. Bring a torch, and be prepared for some serious stooping.

Museo e Tenuta Vitivinícola

Località I Piani • June–Sept Mon–Sat tours (90min) at 5.30pm, other times by appointment • Free • ☎ 079 997 700, ⓦ sellaemosca.it •
Wine shop June–Sept Mon–Sat 8.30am–8pm, also Sun 9am–1pm & 4–8pm in Aug; Oct–May Mon–Sat 8.30am–6.30pm • By bus, take
the service for San Marco (not Sun), leaving at 2.30pm from the Giardini Púbblici, returning at about 5.15pm (inform driver of destination)

Vermentino, Cannonau and Torbato wines are produced at the vast Sella e Mosca estate, Sardinia's largest winery, which cultivates more than 1,200 acres of vines in Alghero's hinterland and is open to tours in summer. The entrance lies less than 1km north of Anghelu Ruju on the Alghero–Porto Torres road. The guided tours – in Italian and English – explain the various stages of winemaking, and take in the cellars and the **Museo e Tenuta Vitivinícola**. There's a short film which, with Vittorio Sella's black-and-white photographs, bring the history of the vineyard to life, and part of the museum is dedicated to Anghelu Ruju, displaying copies of some of the finds together with diagrams of the site. Needless to say, the tour includes a tasting accompanied by *pane carasau*, and the full range of the estate's wines are represented in the on-site **wine shop**.

Lago di Baratz

North from Alghero, Fertilia and Porto Conte, good roads lead across the territory of Nurra to **Lago di Baratz**, Sardinia's only natural lake. A path curves round the reeds and marshes of the perimeter, allowing a close-up view of some of the protected plants and – if you're lucky – animals gathered here. Among these is a species of turtle (*Emys orbicularis*), while wildfowl include the little- and great-crested grebes as well as a multitude of mallards and coots. The *macchia* which partially encroaches on the shores is a pungent mêlée of rosemary, myrtle, wild lavender and various species of wild orchid.

Just over 1km west from the lake, easily walkable (there's also a road for drivers), the bay of **Porto Ferro** is guarded by three watchtowers and framed by a luscious long **beach**.

Argentiera

A drive or ride of 40km from Alghero, 5km west of the nondescript settlement of Palmádula, the old abandoned mining town of **ARGENTIERA** was once the greatest producer of silver on the island. Worked since Roman times, the seams were exhausted and extraction halted in 1963, and now the little town sits by itself at the end of a road on one of the most deserted expanses of the western coast. Its forlorn, haunted air is full of the echoes of its former industry: shafts lie abandoned, miners' quarters stare blindly out, and there is little movement at all outside July and August. However, things are changing, holiday homes are increasingly evident, and a museum of mining is promised. There are some good shingle and sand **beaches** in the vicinity, one of which you pass on the way into town – an unasphalted track leads to five more much smaller ones. You might also stretch your legs by heading out to **Capo dell'Argentiera**, a headland with terrific coastal views, about 3km southwest of the old mining centre.

5

By bus There's a bus connection with Sássari (Mon–Sat 5 daily; 1hr), where travellers to/from Alghero will need to change.

ACCOMMODATION AND EATING

Hostel Argentiera Via Argentiera ☏079 530 343, ⓦhostelargentiera.it. An impersonal block on the left as you enter Argentiera, this is a cross between an independent hostel and a hotel, with an institutional ambience but clean, spacious rooms sleeping 2–4 people, with en-suite bathrooms, wi-fi and a/c. There's a decent restaurant, a wide terrace with excellent views and breakfasts for €7. Closed mid-Sept to May. Dorms €̲3̲5̲, doubles €̲7̲0̲

Il Veliero Via Carbónia 1 ☏079 530 251. This bar-trattoria serves panini, mixed salads and some meat and fish dishes – a *frittura mista* (fish fry-up) is €18. Tues–Sun 7.30am–11pm, open daily in Aug.

Villanova Monteleone and around

There are two routes running **south of Alghero**, both strongly recommended, but very different from each other. As one route runs inland and the other along the coast, and each ends at Bosa (see opposite), you could cover both in a round-trip. The SS292 inland route southeast from Alghero climbs above the coast, affording magnificent views and leading, after 25km of twisting road, to **VILLANOVA MONTELEONE**, the mountain settlement to which the original *algherese* population was banished in 1354 after their town had been taken over by the Spanish. There's precious little to see or do here, except at the end of August, when the local **Festival of St John the Baptist** is celebrated with traditional processions and horseback races. The local craft speciality is linen embroidered with angular animals and other geometric designs.

A right turn out of Villanova takes you along the minor, little-used road which eventually winds up in Bosa, a 40km trawl through an empty but often inspiring wilderness of *macchia* and mountain. Alternatively, continue east another 9km on the SS292 to the dammed **Lago del Temo**, from which the eponymous river flows down to Bosa on the coast. It's a good place to mosey around, with grassy banks ideal for picnics.

By bus Villanova Monteleone is served by buses to Alghero (Mon–Sat 7–12 daily, Sun mid-June to mid-Sept 5 daily; 45min) and Bosa (Mon–Sat 2–3 daily; 1hr).

Monteleone Rocca Doria

Thirteen kilometres southeast from Villanova Monteleone, rising on a hill above the Lago del Temo, the village of **MONTELEONE ROCCA DORIA** was a Dorian foundation which endured a three-year siege by the combined forces of Aragon, Sássari, Bosa and Alghero, ending with its complete destruction in 1436. Monteleone's refugees joined Alghero's deportees in Villanova (hence that village's composite name), though the ruined Monteleone was later resettled and rebuilt. These days, with a population of 125, it's a bit of a backwater, but you'll find the traditional atmosphere a nice contrast to the holiday-orientated coast, and there's a pretty Romanesque basilica and a couple of bars on hand to supply refreshment while you watch the antics of the local dogs.

The coast road to Bosa

The SP105/SP49 **coast road** south of Alghero travels through a rugged, rocky landscape, the vistas encompassing an ever-changing succession of coves and inlets. Some of these shelter first-class **beaches** where, in the summer months, you're charged a few euros to park and there are umbrellas and drinks available. **La Speranza**, for example, lies 8km south of town, a stop on the Alghero–Bosa coastal bus route; there's an excellent bar and restaurant here, too (see opposite).

5

You could also experience this undeveloped tract of coast at a leisurely pace on foot or by bike – though the only viable route is along the road. The rocky terrain holds Sardinia's only significant colony of **griffon vultures** (a few others nest around Capo Caccia, west of Alghero). Many of these are being wiped out by the poisons left out by local farmers for foxes and stray dogs, and despite strictly enforced measures fewer than fifteen breeding pairs are thought to exist here today. Visitors to the area should not approach nesting sites in July and August.

Capo Marargiu

The best chances of spotting a griffon vulture is around **Capo Marargiu**, 12km north of Bosa, one of the remotest sections of the coast. The area achieved a brief notoriety in the 1980s when it was revealed that a secret right-wing commando group, Gladio, used the headland as a training ground. There are good swimming spots from the rocks hereabouts.

ARRIVAL AND DEPARTURE THE COAST ROAD TO BOSA

By bus The road is served by buses between Alghero and Bosa (2–5 daily); be sure to take the coastal bus route, not the inland one via Villanova Monteleone.

EATING

★ **La Speranza** La Speranza, 8km south of Alghero ☎ 079 957 6107. You could combine a lunch or dinner at this beachside restaurant with a swim. Fresh seafood, cooked in a variety of ways, is the main item on the menu, costing €5 or €6 per 100g (pasta dishes are €10–12), and it's as good as anything in Alghero. The main draw, however, is the fabulous location, with tables just steps from the sea. April–Oct: bar daily 9.30am–7pm; restaurant daily 12.30–2.30pm & 7.30–10.30pm; closed Wed May & Oct.

Bosa

Surrounded by mountains, huddled around the base of a hill capped by a ruined castle, **BOSA** (40km south of Alghero) has a self-contained air, cocooned from the main currents of Sardinian life in the middle of one of the island's last remaining stretches of undeveloped coast. The town makes a soothing spot to hole up for a few days, located on the banks of the placid River Temo, Sardinia's only navigable river of any length, and within easy reach of some fine beaches. It's a refreshingly uncommercial place, though increasingly aware of its tourist potential, and development is beginning to make a significant impact, particularly around **Bosa Marina**, the town's coastal offshoot 3km west, where hotels, bars and restaurants cluster around a sandy arc of beach.

Brief history

Phoenicians and Romans are known to have settled the banks of the River Temo, with the **Roman** town located near the site of the church of San Pietro, a couple of kilometres upstream from the present town. After the Romans left, Bosa fared badly and was repeatedly battered by barbarian and Moorish raids. In the twelfth century, the settlement was refounded by the Ligurian **Malaspina** family around their fortress on the Serravalle hill. Many who had been living on the coast, near present-day Bosa Marina, willingly migrated to this more defensible spot, establishing the Sa Costa quarter on the slopes of Serravalle.

Bosa changed hands several times during the ensuing vicissitudes of war, at one time allying itself with the anti-Aragonese coalition headed by Eleonora d'Arborea, but eventually forging a happy working relationship with the **Spanish**, under whom it prospered. After an interlude of decay, the town achieved wealth and security in the **eighteenth and nineteenth centuries**, when it was briefly a provincial capital renowned for the working of precious metals, coral-gathering and leather-tanning. Much of Sa Piana, the lower town, dates from this era. Since 2005, Bosa has been part of the province of Oristano, though culturally it has little in common with the rest of the province.

5

The Cattedrale

Corso Vittorio Emanuele • Daily 8am–noon & 4–7pm

Surmounted by its colourful dome, Bosa's **Cattedrale** lies on the northern side of the old town bridge, its fifteenth-century origins largely obscured under an overlay of Baroque. The Rococo facade gives access to a lavish interior, a riot of grand arches and polychrome marble. A few individual items here are worth picking out: carved lions subduing dragons on the altar steps, frescoes in the apse painted by Emilio Scherer at the end of the nineteenth century and, behind the seventeenth-century altar, another fresco from the same period showing a town plan of Bosa – the town's appearance is scarcely different today.

Corso Vittorio Emanuele

From the cathedral, the main **Corso Vittorio Emanuele** extends west through the **Sa Piana** neighbourhood, its tone set by well-preserved *palazzi* on either side. At the Corso's western end, the grand **Palazzo Don Carlos**, dating from the eighteenth century, overlooks the outdoor bars on **Piazza Costituzione**, beyond which lie the newer outskirts of town.

Casa Deriu

Corso Vittorio Emanuele 59 • June to mid-July Tues–Sun 10am–1pm & 6–8.30pm; mid-July to mid-Sept Tues–Sun 10am–1pm, 4–8.30pm & 10pm–midnight; mid-Sept to May Mon–Fri 10am–1pm & 3–5pm, Sat & Sun 10am–1pm & 3–6pm • €4.50 • ☎ 0785 377 043

Halfway along the Corso on the right, the nineteenth-century **Casa Deriu** has been restored as a museum and gallery, where you can tour a suite of rooms furnished in period style, including frescoes, ceramic floors, Art Nouveau paintings and even an Art Nouveau chandelier. Everything is a bit faded and there's a slightly dingy air about the place, but it gives a good impression of how the upper classes once lived. The third floor is devoted to local painter and ceramicist **Melkiorre Melia** (1889–1982), including local scenes and works completed when he was director of a ceramics school in Libya.

Your entry ticket also admits you to another permanent exhibition across the road, where rather more arresting paintings by another local artist, **Antonio Atza** (1925–2009), are displayed, including surrealist and abstract works. A few pictures by other Sard artists are also displayed here.

Sa Costa

Take any of the lanes off the Corso to the north to penetrate the web of alleys that make up Bosa's **Sa Costa** quarter. Full of medieval gloom, corridor-like streets follow the steep contours of Serravalle, a fairly strenuous clamber of fifteen minutes or so to the brow of the hill and the castle. On the way up or down, take a look at the **Chiesa del Cármine**, on Via del Cármine, a richly decorated Baroque edifice with an elegant facade from 1779.

5

Castello Malaspina

Via Castello • April–June daily 10am–1pm & 3.30–6.30pm; July daily 10am–1pm & 4–7.30pm; Aug daily 10am–8pm; Sept to mid-Oct daily 10am–1pm & 3.30–6pm; mid to late Oct 10am–1pm & 3–5pm; Nov–March Sat & Sun 10am–1pm • €4 • ☎ 348 154 4724, ⓦ castellodibosa.it

Only the shell of Bosa's medieval **Castello Malaspina** survives, but its commanding position imbues it with plenty of atmosphere. Erected by the powerful Malaspina family in 1112, the walls incorporate a series of towers, notably the **torre nord**, open-sided in the fashion of other towers in Oristano and Cágliari, and the **torre maggiore**, taller and more refined than the others, and thought to have been the work of Cágliari's celebrated military architect Giovanni Capula, responsible for the Torre dell'Elefante and Torre di San Pancrazio in his home city (see p.60 & p.62); the pentagonal **torre ovest** is Aragonese. The bird's-eye views from the castle's red trachyte ramparts are worth savouring, giving you the chance to get to grips with the area's geography.

Within the walls, the only older construction still intact is the church of **Nostra Signora di Regnos Altos**, which contains a rare cycle of vibrant, Catalan-style frescoes from about 1300 and a couple of statues of the Madonna. Brief **guided tours** of the castle (in Italian or English) will help you to get the most of your visit, and there are leaflets indicating the main points of interest.

If you're driving, you can reach the entrance by following signs along the road skirting the back of town, leading round to the castle gate from Piazza Cármine or Piazza Dante.

Along the river

Meandering through the landscape, with brightly painted fishing boats tethered to the quays, the broad **River Temo** invites closer inspection. On the south bank, near the old bridge, you can wander around the **Sas Conzas** quarter, site of the former leather tanneries that were central to the local economy from the eighteenth century to World War II.

Museo delle Conce

Via delle Conce • Daily 9.30am–1.30pm, also July & Aug Sat & Sun 3–5pm; visits by guided tour (also in English) • €5 • ☎ 0785 376 224

The last of Bosa's tanneries closed in the 1960s, but one of them has been renovated to house the **Museo delle Conce** devoted to the local tanning industry. The ground floor displays the original *vasche*, or basins where the leather was soaked and washed – each had a different function in the process, most containing lime, tannin and other vegetable substances, but some including dog excrement for "purging". As one might expect, it was a smelly business, for which Bosa became known as *Bosa puzzolente* ("stinky Bosa"). Upstairs you can view more equipment and old photos. The end product was put to a variety of uses, including shoes, saddles and bookbinding.

San Pietro

Via San Pietro • April–June Tues–Fri 9.30am–12.30pm, Sat 9.30am–12.30pm & 3.30–6.30pm, Sun 3.30–6.30pm; July & Aug Tues–Fri 9.30am–12.30pm, Sat 9.30am–12.30pm & 4–7pm, Sun 4–7pm; Sept & Oct Tues–Fri 9.30am–12.30pm, Sat 9.30am–12.30pm & 3–5pm, Sun 3–5pm; call for winter visits • €2 • ☎ 333 544 5675

From Bosa's old bridge, a rural road runs eastward parallel to the river's south bank, fetching up after a couple of kilometres at the former cathedral of **San Pietro**. Built over an early Christian necropolis (see the upside-down Latin inscription on one of the recycled stones at the base of the apse, at the back of the building), the main body of the church is pure Lombard Romanesque in inspiration, dating from 1073, though it later underwent modifications. The square belltower and the apse were constructed in the twelfth century, while the Gothic facade was added by Cistercian monks at the end of the thirteenth century. Here, beneath a trio of small rose windows, the architrave of the west door is embellished with naively carved vignettes taken from a tomb, representing the Madonna and Child with Sts Paul, Peter and Constantinus de Castra, the church's founder (or it may represent St Constantine).

> **INLAND EXPLORATIONS FROM BOSA** 5
>
> From the castle or the river, you can strike out **inland** on foot, heading northeast and picking up tracks that lead up into the mountainous hinterland for fabulous views of the Temo valley. With the castle in view, it's difficult to get lost, and you can make a circular walk by returning along a different track. Don't forget to take a supply of water.

The sombre **interior** has two rows of solid, broad-stoned, rectangular columns; on the first on the right, you might just be able to make out an inscribed dedication by Bishop Constantinus de Castra. There's little else in the way of decoration, making it a silent, moody place.

Bosa Marina and around

During Bosa's long history, its inhabitants have settled on various sites along the banks of the River Temo. One of these is now **BOSA MARINA**, at the mouth of the river – a conventional minor resort with a small choice of hotels and trattorias. Here, on the main Via Cristóforo Colombo, the small FdS station is the terminus for the **Trenino Verde**, a restored old train running seasonally on a narrow-gauge line from Macomer.

Bosa Marina's broad sandy **beach** is surveyed by a stark Spanish watchtower, while yachts and fishing boats lie at anchor in the lee of the islet of **Isola Rossa**, now linked to the mainland by a bridge. The sheltered beach is a favourite place for windsurfers, with equipment usually available to rent in summer, when the place gets thronged. The tower, or **Torre Aragonese**, is sometimes open in summer for temporary exhibitions, but is worth visiting even without these for its examples of Catalan decorative masonry work and its views encompassing two more Spanish towers along the coast.

Remoter patches of sand lie 2km south in the **Turas** district, and about the same distance north, though if you're looking for true isolation, you're best off visiting the rugged littoral north of Bosa, where you'll find rocks to swim off interspersed with patches of sandy beach.

ARRIVAL AND DEPARTURE   BOSA

By car All roads in and out of town are twisty, and the centre is not conducive to driving. Parking by the river or at the free car park on Via Cugia are the easiest options for avoiding tight lanes and one-way systems.

By train Bosa Marina is a terminal for the narrow-track Trenino Verde to Macomer, 30km inland (mid-June to mid-Sept Fri & Sun at 4.30pm; 2hr; ☎070 580 246, ⓦ treninoverde.com). Info on FS services from Macomer can be had at ☎892 021, ⓦ trenitalia.com.

By bus ARST buses pull up at various points of the town – on Viale Alghero, Piazza Zanetti (Bosa's main bus terminal) and Via Nazionale – and some also make stops at Bosa Marina. Tickets are sold at *Gold Bar*, Via Azuni, near Piazza Zanetti, and at the bus depot on Via Nazionale.

Destinations Alghero (Mon–Sat 4–6 daily, Sun 2–4 daily; 55min); Cúglieri (Mon–Sat 7–9 daily, Sun 2–3 daily; 45min–1hr 10min); Macomer (Mon–Sat 4–7 daily, Sun 2–3 daily; 45min); Oristano (Mon–Sat 4–5 daily; 2hr); Sássari (Mon–Sat 3 daily; 2hr 15min); Villanova Monteleone (Mon–Sat 1 daily; 1hr).

GETTING AROUND

On foot Bosa's few specific sights are all easily reached on foot. A modern road bridge crosses the river farther downstream, near Bosa Marina, and between the two there's a small foot-bridge.

By bus or tourist train For travelling between Bosa and Bosa Marina, you can make use of either the year-round ARST buses or, in summer, the *trenino turistico* – a tourist "train" on wheels that shuttles between the two (daily 11am–noon & 4–6pm; €5), departing from Corso Vittorio Emanuele II.

By taxi Taxi services are sparse; call ☎335 659 0568.

INFORMATION AND ACTIVITIES

Tourist information There's no information office in Bosa, though you'll find general – but often out-of-date – information on the town at ⓦ bosaonline.com.

Diving Excursions, supervision, instruction and equipment rental are offered at Bosa Diving Center, Via Colombo 2, Bosa Marina (☎335 818 9748, ⓦ bosadiving.it).

5

ACCOMMODATION

Most of Bosa's **hotels** stay open all year. If you want to stay near the sea, head for Bosa Marina, though none of the hotels there has much character. The modern resort also has one of Sardinia's rare youth hostels. For a longer stay, consider booking an **apartment**, either a traditional, renovated place in the old centre or a more modern property in Bosa's newer districts or at Bosa Marina.

Àghinas Piazza Cármine 17 ☎0785 605 827, ⓦaghinas .com. An *albergo diffuso* – with rooms in two separate buildings – this hotel in the old town has most of its rooms in a beautifully restored nineteenth-century *palazzo*, two others in a more modest townhouse dug out of the rock nearby in Sa Costa. All have modern fixtures and facilities, fridges and wi-fi. Breakfast is taken in *La Taverna* (see opposite). **€85**

★ **Bainas** Via San Pietro ☎339 209 0967 or ☎333 396 7819, ⓦagriturismobainasbosa.com. A 10min walk from Bosa, this peaceful *agriturismo* is surrounded by fields and orchards which supply its excellent restaurant (see below), where guests can dine for €20. The ranch-style house has rooms giving onto a veranda. No credit cards. **€70**

Corte Fiorita Lungo Temo De Gásperi 45 ☎0785 377 058, ⓦalbergo-diffuso.it. With rooms distributed among three buildings, this hotel has its main base in a *palazzo* overlooking the river, combining a rustic feel – rafters, tiled floors, exposed stonework – with opulent trimmings. Check the rooms first, as each one is different; those with a balcony and river view cost extra, but ones on the side are quieter. All have internet connections and satellite TV. **€89**

Mannu Viale Alghero ☎0785 375 307, ⓦmannuhotel .it. This three-star hotel less than 1km from both Bosa and Bosa Marina offers fairly good value for its comfortable facilities, though the location on a main road opposite a supermarket is hardly inspiring. Half- or full board may be required in summer, worth considering anyway as there's a plaudit-winning restaurant (see opposite). Bikes are available for €15/day. **€75**

Ostello Malaspina Via Sardegna 1, Bosa Marina ☎0785 850 681, ⓦvalevacanze.com. This quiet, modern youth hostel near the beach has a relaxed atmosphere, with a veranda, meals and four-bed family rooms available. It should remain open all year, but check in winter. No credit cards. Dorms **€16**, doubles **€40**

S'Ammentu Via del Cármine 55 ☎348 721 8492, ⓦsammentu.com. Old-town lodging on four floors (there's a lift), with small but comfortable en-suite rooms, full of

character, with a/c, wi-fi and TVs. The abundant breakfasts are usually served in a separate building nearby. **€70**

★ **Sa Balza** Corso Vittorio Emanuele II 45 ☎0785 374391 or ☎349 542 6676, ⓦsabalza.it. Right on the main street, the three rooms here are located around a courtyard with their own entrances. They don't have views but are clean, spacious and quiet, each with its own modern bathroom, a/c and fridge. There's no breakfast. The friendly and helpful owner works in the next-door SWS travel agency. **€65**

Sa Pischedda Via Roma 8 ☎0785 373 065, ⓦhotel sapischedda.it. Just across the river from the centre, this fine old *palazzo* has a grand staircase and flashy glass lift leading up to attractive, a/c rooms with wi-fi, some with balcony and good river views – some are quite cramped, however. There's a classy restaurant and pizzeria, too. **€90**

Stella Maris Via Colombo 11–13, Bosa Marina ☎0785 375 162, ⓦstellamarisbosa.com. Friendly three-star hotel near the river and beach, adorned with garish modern art and offering a dozen fairly ordinary en-suite rooms, some pretty small. There's a decent restaurant, bikes are available to rent and various activities from diving to boat excursions can be arranged. Half- or full board may be required in season. Closed Nov–Feb. **€90**

Vecchia Bosa Via Bonaria 23 ☎0785 377 035 or ☎320 172 5966, ⓦvecchiabosa.com. In the heart of the old town, this friendly B&B has four quiet, tastefully decorated rooms in two separate buildings, all with a/c, satellite TV and private bathrooms. There's a good choice at breakfast. No credit cards. **€60**

APARTMENT RENTALS

Lemon Tree House, run by an English couple (☎0785 374 236, ⓦhouseinbosa.it), has two apartments in Sa Costa neighbourhood, one with spectacular views, the other with a garden (from €525 per week in July). Otherwise, agencies include San Marco Immobiliare (☎0785 375 521, ⓦsmimmobiliare.com) and Bosa Holiday Rentals (☎0785 374 236, ⓦbosa-holiday-rentals.eu).

EATING

Bosa has a good spread of **restaurants**, all getting quite busy in summer. Most of the places listed below are in the main town; Bosa Marina has a few more choices, mainly attached to hotels. If you want to buy your own food, there's a handy **supermarket**, Sigma, by the old bridge on the southern bank (Mon–Sat 8am–8pm, Sun 8am–1pm).

Bainas Via San Pietro ☎339 209 0967 or ☎333 396 7819. This *agriturismo* outside town (see above) serves delicious and wholesome organic dishes using its own home-grown produce, but you need to call ahead. Meals cost €27–35 including drinks. No credit cards. Daily 8.30pm–late.

Barracuda Viale Repubblica 17 ☎0785 373 719. With tangerine and yellow walls and terrace seating, this modern trattoria off the tourist track offers good-quality but no-frills local cuisine (mostly seafood) and great pizzas. Pastas are around €10, mains €10–15. Daily noon–2.30pm & 7.30–

10.30pm; closed Mon mid-Sept to May.

Borgo Sant'Ignazio Via Sant'Ignazio 33 ☎0785 374 129. Rustic restaurant in an alley above the Corso offering the freshest seafood and local specialities such as *brasato di cinghiale* (wild boar cooked in white wine). Main courses cost €12–16. Daily 12.30–3pm & 7.30–11pm; closed Mon & eves in winter.

★ **Da Giancarlo e Rita** Viale Alghero ☎0785 375 306. Part of the *Mannu* hotel (see opposite), a kilometre or so from the centre, this sober, semi-formal place has won awards for its culinary excellence, and such local dishes as spaghetti with lobster and fried mussels won't disappoint. Reckon on €30–40 for a three-course meal, though tourist menus are sometimes available. There's a good selection of island wines, too. Daily 1–2.30pm & 8–10.30pm; Oct–April closed Sun eve.

Mangiambuto Piazza Modoleddu ☎0785 373 736. Well hidden on a traffic-free square, this wine bar and restaurant has a cheerful, easygoing air and a select menu

of fresh seafood. Try the *risotto con crema di gámberi* (with prawn sauce) or couscous with tuna, and leave room for such desserts as *pannacotta al whiskey*. Mains are €10–18. The staff are friendly but service can be slow. March–Oct daily 1–2.30pm & 8–11pm.

Ponte Vecchio Via delle Conce ☎0785 376 140. Operated by the same family that runs the *Sa Pischedda* hotel (see opposite), this informal seafood restaurant has a perfect riverside location. The food is fine – think *fregola allo scoglio* (semolina pasta with shellfish; €12) or *spigola alla malvasia* (sea-bass in wine; €16) – but its main appeal is the site. March–Oct daily 12.30–2.30pm & 7.15–10.30pm.

Verde Fiume Via Lungotemo De Gasperi 51 ☎0785 373 482. This small riverfront trattoria – with some tables by the riverside in summer – specializes in fresh, local and seasonal produce. You can also bring your own fish which they'll cook for you and serve with an *antipasto* and coffee for €15. Otherwise starters are around €10, mains €10–15. Daily 12.30–3pm & 7.30pm–midnight; closed Mon in winter.

DRINKING

The bars in Piazza Costituzione are good for a leisurely drink, but the service charge is high. Make sure you sample the renowned **Malvasia** wine while in Bosa; the amber-coloured, Vermouth-like drink is served at most bars and restaurants, usually as an apéritif or with dessert.

Alla Corte del Malaspina Corso Vittorio Emanuele 39. Friendly *birreria* with a good selection of draught and bottled beers. Panini and chips are also available. Opening is erratic, and it gets very quiet in winter. Daily 8pm–late.

Bar Mouse Piazza Zanetti ☎339 117 4216. Cool, secluded café and wine bar with a terrace, also serving snacks – a mellow retreat on summer evenings. Mon–Sat 6am–2pm & 4–10pm, Sun 6am–2pm.

★ **La Taverna** Piazza Cármine ☎331 850 4785. This backstreet café-bar makes a quiet spot for a pause over a beer and/or an ample and delicious *panino* (around €5), inside or on the terrace. Daily 7am–11pm; closes midnight

in summer, closed Thurs Oct–June.

Su Camasinu Via del Cármine 104 ☎339 573 1677. This cave-like cantina is the place to sample the best local Malvasia, run by the Columbu family who produce some of the region's finest. Snacks are provided to accompany it. It's often closed – if so, call or ask at the *Ághinas* hotel. Daily 10.30am–2pm & 5.30pm–late.

Zio Tora Lungo Temo De Gásperi ☎347 660 9003. Neighbourhood bar opposite the old bridge, with outdoor tables and late closing, good for people-watching. It's best in the evening – by day the passing traffic can be a turn-off. Daily 7.30am–late.

DIRECTORY

Internet access Web Copy Internet Point, Via Gioberti 12 (Mon–Sat 9am–1pm & 4.30–8pm, closes later in summer).

Markets Tuesday is market day, with hundreds of stalls on Corso Garibaldi selling everything from hats and

---

BOSA'S FESTIVALS

The best **festivals** are centred on the river: the **Festa dei Santi Pietro e Paolo** on June 29 involves a regatta as far as the church of San Pietro, with local foods, while in the **Sagra di Santa Maria del Mare**, on the first Sunday of August, an image of the Madonna is transported by boat from Bosa Marina to the cathedral, returning in the afternoon for an open-air Mass and fireworks display. The **Sagra di Nostra Signora di Regnos Altos** on the second Sunday of September is a great chance to attend an open-air Mass at the castle, watch local groups perform traditional songs and dances and enjoy local food and drink. In addition, **Carnival** in Bosa has a riotous, pagan flavour around Shrove Tuesday, and **Easter** is also enthusiastically celebrated. There's a country festival, the **Festa dei Santi Cosma e Damiano**, on September 26, accompanied by traditional singing and dancing.

5

handkerchiefs to cactus plants (mornings only). Antiques and curios are sold on Piazza Gioberti on Fridays.

Pharmacy Farmacia Sardu, Corso Vittorio Emanuele 51 (Mon–Sat 9am–1pm & 4.30–8pm; closed alternate Thurs & Sat). Night rotas are posted on pharmacy doors.

Post office Via Pischedda, off Viale Giovanni XXIII (Mon–Fri 8.25am–7.10pm, Sat 8.25am–12.35pm).

Travel agency SWS Viaggi, Corso Vittorio Emanuele 41 ☎ 0785 374 391.

Macomer and around

Thirty kilometres inland of Bosa on the SS129, **MACOMER** is not a particularly alluring destination, though you may be tempted to make a swift stop here for its *nuraghi* and Byzantine church. Called Macopissa in Roman times, when it was a major military base, the town was the site of the last serious revolt against the Aragonese by the Sards in 1478. More recently, it has become a centre of livestock, dairy farming and wool. On Sant'Antonio Abate's day, January 17, a mighty bonfire is lit outside Macomer's church of Santa Chiara for the **Festa di Su Tuva**.

Nuraghe di Santa Barbara

1km north of town • Free

Macomer's surviving *nuraghi* are the most noteworthy of an intense concentration of nuraghic sites in the area, though both lie out of the centre. The **Nuraghe di Santa Barbara**, situated outside town beside the Carlo Felice highway (SS131) and tricky to find, has a mossy central tower that reaches 15m, with primitive cupolas, minor towers and bastions tacked onto the main structure. Little more is known about the building's origins other than that it was abandoned in the ninth century BC, but used again in the Carthaginian and Roman eras as a centre of worship.

Nearby, on the other side of the highway, the ruined state of **Nuraghe Ruju** (or Ruggiu) reveals a cross-section of how a nuraghic cupola was constructed. *Domus de janas* tombs are scattered about below it, their contents on view at Sássari's Museo Sanna (see p.203).

Santa Sabina

10km east of Macomer on the SS129 Nuoro road • Daily 9am–1.30pm & 4–8pm or dusk • €3.50 • ☎ 338 833 4859 • Take any bus to Silanus or Nuoro

In the middle of a plain outside the village of **Silanus**, look out for the charming little Romanesque chapel of **Santa Sabina** on the right (travelling eastwards), harmoniously juxtaposed with a well-preserved *nuraghe* close by. The church, possibly eleventh-century, is unlike any other of Sardinia's churches, with its Byzantine-style tiled cupolas and simple domed and arched interior. Even more bare is the basalt-built *nuraghe*, which is thought to date from around 1600BC; rough-hewn steps lead to the top for a good perspective on the church.

Try to be here for the **Festa di Santa Sabina** on the second weekend of September, a typical country festival with eating, drinking and making merry.

ARRIVAL AND DEPARTURE

MACOMER

By bus Right on the SS131 highway, Macomer is a stop on most bus routes between Oristano, Sássari and Nuoro.
Destinations Alghero (1 daily; 1hr 55min); Bosa (Mon–Sat 4–5 daily, Sun 2–4 daily; 50min); Oristano (Mon–Sat 4 daily, Sun 1 daily; 50min); Sássari (Mon–Sat 9 daily, Sun 4 daily; 1hr–1hr 15min).

By train Macomer lies on the main FS north–south train line, and is the terminal for the rattling old narrow-gauge

ARST trains for Nuoro. The train station is at the western end of town. For FS train services, call ☎ 892 021 or consult ⓦ trenitalia.com; ARST info is available at ☎ 800 865 042 or ⓦ arst.sardegna.it.
Destinations Cágliari (8 daily; 1hr 40min–2hr 10min); Nuoro (Mon–Sat 6 daily; 1hr 10min); Sássari (4 daily, some with change at Ozieri-Chilivani; 1hr 10min–1hr 45min).

Stintino and around

The thin peninsula that forms the western arm of the **Golfo dell'Asinara** is an inhospitable, sparsely populated landscape of rock and *macchia*. The only town here is **STINTINO**, until a few decades ago nothing more than a remote jumble of fishermen's cottages jammed between two narrow harbours. Its discovery by the tourist industry has added conspicuous layers of concrete, new roads and miles of street-lighting, but the tone of the place is essentially the same – small and laidback, though now furnished with a few bars, tourist facilities and a bank. The big hotels have established themselves farther up the coast, where most of the sunning and swimming take place around the ravishing beach of **La Pelosa**. At the end of the peninsula, **Capo Falcone** overlooks the isles of **Piana** and **Asinara**, one a tiny blip, the other an ex-prison colony also known as a habitat of the miniature white ass from which gulf and island both take their name. It's one of Sardinia's more spectacular corners, though increasingly threatened by encroaching tourist developments.

Stintino itself – 50km north of Alghero and 30km west of Porto Torres – is mostly modern, if somewhat lacking in charm, and ebullient in summer, but pretty dead in winter. The compact layout is a right-angled grid of mainly residential streets spreading out from the main Via Sássari. Two harbours lie on either side of the promontory: to the north, **Portu Mannu**, also known as Porto Nuovo, caters mainly to pleasure craft, while the southern **Portu Minori**, or Porto Vecchio, is crowded with small fishing vessels. As there is no central piazza, these two inlets provide the town's main reference points. **Lungomare Colombo**, the one-way street running round the promontory, is good for an easy promenade about town, taking in a selection of good bars and restaurants.

Brief history

Stintino was founded little more than a century ago, when the Italian state appropriated the island of Asinara for use as a penal colony. The 45 families of the resident fishing community – specializing in the trapping and killing of tuna, once a major activity in these parts – were transferred to this sheltered spot between two natural inlets. The town today holds a population of a little over one thousand, to which must be added the tens of thousands who flock here every year.

ARRIVAL AND DEPARTURE STINTINO

By bus In addition to the regular ARST service to Sássari (Mon–Sat 5–6 daily, Sun 1–4 daily; 50min–1hr 10min), Sardabus (☎079 510 554, ⊛sardabus.it) operates a summer link to Alghero and Fertilia airport (June–Sept 5 daily; 55min–1hr 10min). All buses stop outside the town hall at the start of the main Via Sássari.

GETTING AROUND

By shuttle bus Between mid-June and mid-Sept, a local bus (*navetta*) operated by Sardabus connects Stintino with all the beaches (buy tickets on board, €1), a good option to avoid expensive car parking charges. ARST also operates a less frequent service between Sássari and La Pelosa in summer. **By car** Car rental is available at La Nassa, Via Tonnara 35 (☎079 520 060, ⊛stintours.com) for €50–80/day. **By taxi** Call ☎079 523 382 or ☎333 266 4463.

INFORMATION

Tourist office Via Sássari 123 (June, July & Sept daily 9.30am–12.30pm & 3–8pm; Aug daily 9.30am–12.30pm, 3–8pm & 10pm–midnight; Oct Mon–Sat 9.30am–12.30pm; Nov–May Mon–Sat 11am–12.30pm; ☎079 520 081,

STINTINO'S FESTIVALS

Try to be in Stintino at the end of August for the **Regatta della Vela Latina**, when the waters are filled with yachts, some of them restored vintage vessels. The other major **festival** is on September 8, when a procession re-enacts the exodus of Asinara's inhabitants to their new home in Stintino.

5

ⓦ infostintino.it).
Internet access Log on at La Nassa, Via Tonnara 35

(June–Sept daily 8.30am–1pm & 5–8pm; Oct–May Mon–Sat 9am–12.30pm & 4–7pm; €3.50 for 30min).

ACCOMMODATION

Al Martin Pescatore Via Tonnara 30 ⓣ079 520 062, ⓦalmartinpescatore.it. A central B&B run by the owners of La Nassa agency, offering fairly basic en-suite rooms, though all have TVs and minibars; rooms with a view of the port cost extra. There's free internet access, and breakfast is optional – if taken, it's at *Lu Fanali* (see below). **€67**

Geranio Rosso Via XXI Aprile 8 ⓣ079 523 292, ⓦhotel geraniorosso.it. Small, central hotel with friendly staff and tastefully decorated rooms (including family rooms) with a/c and modern bathrooms. Some rooms are cramped, though – check first. Buffet breakfasts are good, with proper coffee. **€92**

Il Porto Vecchio Via Tonnara 69 ⓣ339 435 3582, ⓦbbstintino.com. This simple B&B has mostly spacious rooms, some facing the port, with Sardinian decoration.

There's free wi-fi, and the abundant buffet breakfasts are served on the veranda in summer. Closed Jan & Feb. No credit cards. **€70**

Lina Via Lepanto 30 ⓣ079 523 071, ⓦlinahotel.it. Overlooking the Porto Minori, this is the cheapest of the town's three hotels. There's no restaurant and therefore no half-board requirement. Half the rooms (all with a/c and private bathrooms) have balconies facing the boats; others have no view but go for the same rates. Closed Oct–March. **€80**

★ **Silvestrino** Via Sássari 14 ⓣ079 523 007, ⓦsilvestrino.it. On the town's main street, this hotel has a touch of luxury in its rooms, some of which have their own terrace and terrific views. The restaurant is one of Stintino's best (see below). Closed Dec & Jan. **€100**

EATING AND DRINKING

La Darsena Lungomare Colombo 6 ⓣ079 520 072. Atmospheric bar and restaurant with tables on decking by the water, offering fishy feasts at moderate prices (€7–12 for pastas, €14–18 for mains); try the squid salad or mussel soup. It makes a nice venue for a drink by day or in the evening too. Bar daily (except Mon in winter) 8.30am–late; restaurant Easter–Sept daily noon–3pm & 7–11pm.

Lina Via Lépanto 30 ⓣ079 523 505. The best thing about this trattoria (next to a hotel of the same name) is its location, with a terrace overlooking the fishing boats moored in Portu Minori. Dishes are well prepared but expensive, though there are set-price menus at lunchtime for €14 and €17. Easter–Oct daily 10am–3pm & 7.30–11pm.

L'Ormeggio Via Asinara 41 ⓣ349 226 4794. Just up from Portu Mannu, this modern *birreria* and *spaghetteria* has various pasta dishes, panini and salads for under €7. For a full meal, there are tourist menus for €13 and €16.

Service can be slow, however. It's a cool spot for a late drink, too. Easter–Sept daily except Mon 9am–11.30pm, open daily in July & Aug.

Lu Fanali Lungomare Colombo 89 ⓣ079 523 054. Popular spot comprising a snack bar, pizzeria, restaurant and gelateria, with some alfresco seating for the best harbour views. The thin and crispy pizzas are the best choice here, and there's a kids' menu. Pastas are €7–11, mains around €14. March–Oct daily except Wed 7am–midnight, food served noon–3pm & 7–11pm; open daily June–Sept.

★ **Silvestrino** Via Sassari 14 ⓣ079 523 007. Attached to the eponymous hotel (see above), this place offers first-class seafood, including delicious lobster soup and a tangy seafood risotto. First courses will set you back €10–15, mains are €14–20, and tourist menus are occasionally available for around €25. There's a deck for outdoor seating in summer. March to mid-Oct daily 12.30–2.30pm & 7.30–10.30pm.

Le Saline

With most of the shore around Stintino rough and rocky, you'll have to go north or south of town to find decent beaches. About 1km to the south, near an old watchtower, a narrow road leads to the fine, *macchia*-backed beach of **Le Saline**, once site of a salt-works owned by the monks of Santa Maria di Tergu (see p.220).

DIVING AROUND STINTINO

The exceptionally clear waters around Stintino, La Pelosa and the islands offer superb opportunities for **diving**. There are several outfits based in the area in summer: try Asinara Diving Center (ⓣ079 527 000 or ⓣ328 425 5073, ⓦasinaradivingcenter.it), which has a base on the beach at Porto dell'Ancora, or Roccaruja Diving Center (ⓣ339 398 4451 or ⓣ347 512 7472, ⓦroccarujasub.com), on the beach in front of the *Roccaruja Hotel*. Both offer equipment rental and courses – one dive costs €35–40, equipment costs €5–10 per day per article; snorkellers pay around €25 for an excursion including equipment.

There are bars and facilities for renting deckchairs and parasols. A Spanish bastion stands nearby, and you might see the occasional flock of flamingos attracted to the salt-pan/lagoon here.

La Pelosa

North of Stintino, tourist villages clutter the hills backing the coast almost as far as the northern tip of **Capo Falcone**, site of Torre Falcone, a Spanish watchtower. Leading up to the cape, the beach of **La Pelosa** is one of Sardinia's premier swimming spots, lapped by a shallow, turquoise sea of crystalline clarity. You won't be alone here, though – it can get horribly congested. The tiers of holiday homes spreading over the slopes are a blot on the landscape, but the perfect views over the outlying islands of Piana and the much larger Asinara are enchanting.

Asinara

In summer, regular boat tours depart from Stintino, Porto Torres and (occasionally) La Pelosa to sail round the islands' coasts and make a landing. On **Piana**, what you see is what you get: a tiny flat patch of land with a solitary watchtower standing guard. There is more on **Asinara**, 16km long, though visitors are only permitted within certain areas on organized boat tours. A prison colony from 1885 until the late 1990s, it is now a national park. The wildlife that you probably won't see – it's out of bounds – includes breeding turtles.

Called Sinuaria by the Romans on account of its indented form – making it appear from a distance like a whole archipelago of separate islands – Asinara has been sporadically inhabited in the last two millennia, even serving in 1638 as a base for French pirates. The Savoyard king sold it to the duke of Vallombrosa in 1775, but it never yielded a significant income, and was used both as a quarantine hospital for victims of cholera and a place of incarceration. At its northern end, the island's highest point (408m) is poignantly named **Punta della Scomúnica** ("Excommunication Point").

Asinara's protected status has allowed a range of **wildlife** to thrive, including the white wild donkeys for which the island is named, falcons, mouflons, pigs and goats. Both islands are still used to pasture cattle, which are walked across the shallow straits between Capo Falcone and Piana twice a year, in November and May.

TOURS TO PIANA AND ASINARA

Access to the islands of Piana and Asinara is only possible on authorized **boat excursions** from Stintino or – less frequently – Porto Torres (see p.216), normally departing between Easter and September. Once on **Asinara** (most boats sail past Piana without stopping), you can join an organized tour or set forth under your own steam to explore the various features of the coast and some of the prison buildings, or simply laze on the pristine sandy beaches of Fornelli, Cala Sabina, Cala d'Oliva and others in the north of the island. Alternatively, you can rent a bike (or bring your own), which can only be ridden on the surfaced roads. In summer a **bus service** operates, connecting Cala Reale, Cala d'Oliva and Fornelli several times daily (tickets €5, valid all day; pay on board). Bring your own food and drink, or use the bar at Cala Reale.

Excursions currently leave from Stintino's Portu Mannu at 9–10am, returning at 5–6pm, or later in summer. When there's sufficient demand, there may be additional departures and returns during the day. There are various options, ranging from a simple day return ticket (€18) to a range of packages including catamaran trips to get there and tours in a bus or off-road vehicle (€40–70).

Further information can be obtained and tickets purchased at ☎079 503 388 or from Asinara's website, ⓦparcoasinara.org. In Stintino, the agency La Nassa, Via Tonnara 35 (☎079 520 060, ⓦescursioniasinara.it), among others, deals with ticket sales.

Sássari and around

200 Sássari

213 The Sássari Riviera

213 Porto Torres and around

216 Castelsardo and around

220 Inland from Castelsardo

222 South of Sássari:
Logudoro

CASTELSARDO

Sássari and around

Sardinia's second city, Sássari, is for many the island's most interesting centre, with its crowded medieval quarter and Spanish associations. Around it, the land of the ancient territories of Logudoro and Anglona ranges from high tableland riven by sudden gullies to craggy peaks and valleys, with a long sandy arc edging the Golfo dell'Asinara on the northern coast. Inland and inward-looking, Sássari is less cosmopolitan than Cágliari, though there's also a high level of culture, and plenty of interest in its churches and excellent archeological museum.

A short ride northwest of Sássari lies an ancient monument unique not just in Sardinia but in the whole Mediterranean basin – the "ziggurat" of **Monte d'Accoddi**, a sanctuary dating from around the third millennium BC. If you come to Sardinia by sea, you could well arrive at **Porto Torres**, to the north of Sássari, the original capital of the *giudicato* of Torres. It still holds some impressive Roman remains along with the **Basilica di San Gavino**, perhaps the island's finest example of Pisan-Romanesque architecture.

Some fine **beaches** line the Golfo dell'Asinara coast, dotted with small summer resorts and the larger town of **Castelsardo**. Capped by a fortified citadel, the town's scenic location and the local skill with handicrafts have made it a magnet for tourists, and it makes a good base for some inspiring scenic drives inland into the mountains of the **Anglona** region.

To the south and east of Sássari, the old territory of **Logudoro** is richly endowed with **medieval churches**, most of them splendidly positioned in improbably remote corners of the countryside. The medieval refinement of these buildings forms a sharp contrast to the ramshackle grandeur of the equally striking *nuraghi*. The densest concentration of them is at **Torralba**, with an outstanding museum of nuraghic culture and, a short distance outside, the majestic **Nuraghe Santu Antine**.

GETTING AROUND
SÁSSARI AND AROUND

Sássari is the region's major transport hub.

By train Apart from the 15min train connection between Sássari and Porto Torres, the only other rail service in the area is the occasionally useful line from Sássari to Ozieri-Chilivani, operated by FS (☎ 892 021, ⊚ trenitalia.it).

By bus For the most part, non-drivers wanting to explore the area around Sássari will have to rely on bus services operated by ARST (☎ 800 865 042, ⊚ arst.sardegna.it). The coast is well served, though most inland places have very limited connections, sometimes with just one or two buses on weekdays.

Sássari

First impressions of Sardinia's second city, **SÁSSARI**, do little to encourage anything more than a cursory visit; its inland location and sparse tourist facilities might seem a poor substitute for the holiday diversions of the nearby coast. But it is this very lack of glamour that gives Sássari its special interest as an unpretentious – and not unattractive

| Sássari's festivals p.207 | Castelsardo's festivals p.216 |
| Fainè p.210 | Artigianato in Castelsardo p.218 |

DUOMO DI SAN NICOLA, SÁSSARI'S OLD QUARTER

Highlights

❶ Sássari's old quarter The maze-like old town retains its medieval air, with a glorious Baroque cathedral at its heart. **See p.205**

❷ La Cavalcata, Sássari One of the island's most flamboyant festivals, with feats of horsemanship, traditional costumes and performances of music and dance in the main piazza. **See p.207**

❸ San Gavino, Porto Torres Beautifully preserved, this atmospheric monument dates from the Pisan programme of church-building in the eleventh century. **See p.214**

❹ Museo dell'Intreccio Mediterraneo, Castelsardo The old citadel's castle, boasting far-reaching views, is an extraordinary location for this collection of the local, highly distinctive basketware. **See p.217**

❺ Santíssima Trinità di Saccargia With its rocket-like belltower rising abruptly above the bare countryside, this striking Romanesque church has been a landmark for nine hundred years. **See p.222**

❻ Nuraghe Santu Antine A fascinating relic of Sardinia's ancient culture, this venerable prehistoric palace is the most imposing of the many *nuraghi* strewn about the area. **See p.224**

HIGHLIGHTS ARE MARKED ON THE MAP ON P.202

– working town, steeped in tradition. Sássari's historic character is most palpable in the vibrant **old quarter**'s dense network of medieval streets, old churches and *palazzi*, among them some of Sardinia's few Renaissance buildings. This atmospheric labyrinth is connected to the modern city by a sequence of squares, culminating in the stately and impressive **Piazza Italia**. Close by, **Museo Sanna** houses one of the island's top archeological collections.

As a regional transport hub, Sássari makes an invigorating alternative to a base by the sea, with an excellent range of **bars and restaurants**, a small but decent choice of **accommodation** and lower prices all round.

SÁSSARI AND AROUND

Corsica, Barcelona, Vado Ligure, Genoa, Marseille & Civitavecchia · Santa Teresa di Gallura

HIGHLIGHTS
1. Sássari's old quarter
2. La Cavalcata, Sássari
3. San Gavino, Porto Torres
4. Museo dell'Intreccio Mediterraneo, Castelsardo
5. Santíssima Trinità di Saccargia
6. Nuraghe Santu Antine

Brief history

Built on an ancient site known as **Tatari**, or Tathari, the modern city of Sássari has roots going back to settlers from the Roman colony at what is now Porto Torres. As the port declined, so the inland town expanded; by the fourteenth century it possessed its own statute of laws and a ring of walls. Sássari was inevitably sucked into the conflict between Pisa and Genoa; then, in 1323, **James II of Aragon** established a power base here and, after a brief interlude under the control of the *giudicato* of Arborea, the city spent the next four centuries as an integral part of the Catalan-Aragonese hegemony, though that did not prevent it from being plundered several times by Moorish raiders. Ten years under Austrian rule preceded the coming of the House of Savoy in 1720. In the course of the nineteenth century, the Aragonese castle and walls were demolished, allowing the city to expand gradually.

The Spanish stamp is still evident in Sássari, not least in its churches. The city also has a strong tradition of intellectual independence; in the sixteenth century the Jesuits founded Sardinia's first **university** here, and in recent years Sássari has produced two national presidents, Antonio Segni and Francesco Cossiga, as well as long-time head of the Italian Communist Party, Enrico Berlinguer (1922–84).

Today, with just 120,000 inhabitants, Sássari presents something of a split personality – the well-to-do urbanity of Via Roma's café society contrasting with the medieval vitality of the old town, lately reinvigorated with a conspicuous immigrant population.

Piazza Italia and around

Sássari has no obvious centre, though the largest piazza and the venue for most of the city's *feste* is grand, monumental **Piazza Italia**. The imposing **Palazzo della Provincia** that occupies one side and the neo-Gothic **Palazzo Giordano** facing it (now bank offices) both date from around 1880 – surprisingly, given their very different styles. Between them, framed by palm trees in the middle of the square, a statue of King Vittorio Emanuele II lends an almost colonial flavour. The statue's inauguration in 1899 was the occasion for the revival of Sássari's main festival, La Cavalcata (see box, p.207).

The stately mood of Piazza Italia is continued for a short distance up **Via Roma**, where the succession of smart cafés is abruptly terminated by the stern Fascist hulk of the **Palazzo della Giustizia**. Its ponderous presence is slyly undermined by the semi-restored Rococo villa opposite, at no. 46, sporting a cream-coloured facade adorned with whimsical *putti*. South of Piazza Italia, Via Carlo Alberto leads down to the **Giardini Púbblici**, a shady oasis of calm amid rushing traffic.

Museo Sanna

Via Roma 64 • Tues–Sun 9am–8pm • €4 • ☎ 079 272 203, ⓦ museosannasassari.it

The modern city's principal attraction, **Museo Sanna** is Sardinia's second-most important archeological museum (after Cágliari's), housed in a modern, well-planned block within its own garden.

Ground floor

On the ground floor, most of the museum's **prehistoric** items date from around 2700 BC, including pottery fragments and necklaces belonging to Sardinia's Ozieri culture, and numerous slivers of smooth obsidian (used to make arrow heads and cutting tools), which was the island's major export in Neolithic times. One room dedicated to the unique Copper Age *ziggurat* of Monte d'Accoddi (see p.215) holds a hologram of the temple, while objects from the Bonnanaro culture include sacred skulls, each one – for reasons that remain obscure – trepanned.

6

The Carthaginian, Roman and classical sections display a miscellany of coins, ceramics, busts and mosaic floors. From the **Phoenician and Carthaginian period** (sixth to fourth centuries BC), there are beautifully preserved articles of jewellery, terracotta masks, Greek-inspired amphorae painted with battles and sex scenes and inscribed stelae. **Roman** remains include material from Nora and Tharros: statuettes, gold rings, pendants, knives and a decree carved in stone from 69 AD commanding a group of mountain-dwellers to leave the low-lying region of the Campidano. Relating to a later period is a model of medieval Sássari, with its girdle of walls intact.

Elsewhere on the ground floor, there's a small but fascinating **pinacoteca**, or art gallery, whose chronological arrangement kicks off with a fine fourteenth-century triptych, probably by a Pisan or Florentine artist, and ends with modern Sardinian works. Space has also been set aside for temporary art exhibitions.

First floor

The museum's prime attraction is its **nuraghic** collection, displayed on the upper floor. Here, fragments of pottery, jewellery and household implements are interspersed with plans and models of *nuraghi*, sacred wells and "giants' tombs", with explanations (in English and Italian) of their structure and use. Most engrossing is the display of **bronze statuettes**, including warriors with boldly stylized ox-head helmets, boats with equally extravagant prows and a shepherd holding either a dog or goat on the end of a lead. The material was unearthed at various sites throughout the province, notably the Valle dei Nuraghi (see p.224). Some of the finds – a statuette of a bearded man from the Levant, Phoenician ceramics, a necklace of Baltic amber – illustrate the strikingly far-flung trading contacts of the nuraghic civilization. One of the oldest of these items is a Mycenaean vase from around 1400 BC, excavated at Nuraghe Arrubiu (see p.126). For a sketch of Sardinia's nuraghic culture, see Contexts (p.307).

Museo della Brigata Sássari

Piazza Castello • Mon–Thurs 8am–noon & 12.30–4.30pm, Fri & Sat 8am–noon • Free • ☎ 079 208 5111

Off the northwestern side of Piazza Roma, the arcades of Portici Bargone e Crispo lead onto long, sloping **Piazza Castello**, site of an Aragonese castle until the nineteenth century. One side of the square is still lined by an army barracks, within which the **Museo della Brigata Sássari** is dedicated to the renowned Sardinian regiment whose bravery and heavy losses during World War I are taught in every Italian school. Fighting mainly against Austrians in the Alps, the troops were involved in a horrific campaign of trench warfare which resulted in nearly four thousand missing or dead and more than nine thousand wounded. The story is recalled via an absorbing collection of old photos, posters and mementos, alongside a more predictable array of military uniforms, maps and documents.

Corso Vittorio Emanuele

Sássari's compact **old quarter** is a quirky counterpoint to the grid of the modern city. Although it is surrounded by noisy main roads, little traffic can penetrate the interior network of alleys and piazzas, making it a great place to stroll around. Effectively bisecting the old town, **Corso Vittorio Emanuele** is a long, partly cobbled ascent from Piazza Sant'Antonio, just along from the train station, to Piazza Azuni. Given its rather run-down appearance, it's easy to miss the medieval doorways, flaking *palazzi* and fragments of Gothic windows jammed in among the shops and alleys, but you should look out in particular for the fifteenth-century **Casa Farris** at no. 23, and the Catalan-Gothic **Casa di Re Enzo** from a century earlier at no. 42, distinguished by its elegantly carved mullioned windows.

Teatro Cívico

Corso Vittorio Emanuele 35 • Tours Tues–Sat 10am–1pm & 5–9pm • Performances Nov–Feb; call ☎ 079 997 8956

Transformed into a theatre after 1880, the **Teatro Cívico** was built by a Piedmontese architect in 1830 as the seat of the municipality, and is still the place where Sássari's mayor traditionally meets representatives of the local guilds during the Candelieri festival (see box, p.207). The facade has been elegantly restored, and you can view the grand interior at a performance or on a free **guided tour**, usually in Italian – book at the tourist office, behind the theatre (see p.209).

The Duomo

Piazza Duomo • Mon–Sat 8.30am–noon & 4–6.45pm, Sun 8.30–11.30am & 5–6.45pm

At the core of the old town, the **Duomo di San Nicola** is an unexpected eruption of flamboyance amid the cramped jumble of streets. Rearing above the semicircular Piazza del Duomo, its florid seventeenth-century facade is Sardinia's most dazzling example of Baroque architecture, in which statues of the *Turritani* saints Gavino, Proto and Gianuario (see p.214) are surmounted by St Nicholas. The **campanile** alongside is a survival from the original thirteenth-century building, with gargoyles and other Gothic details. Enter the church and you'll find a simpler Aragonese-Gothic structure from the fifteenth and sixteenth centuries. The eighteenth-century choir stalls, carved in walnut and much copied in other local churches, are worth seeking out.

Palazzo Ducale and Via Turritana

Squeezed behind the cathedral on Via Santa Caterina, the **Palazzo Ducale** was designed by a Piedmontese architect at the end of the eighteenth century for the duke of Asinara;

6

SÁSSARI: OLD QUARTER

Piazza Italia

Porto Torres

Alghero

Frumentaria

City Walls

VIA CAGLIARI

VIA BRIGATA SÁSSARI

Museo della Brigata Sássari

PIAZZA CASTELLO

Teatro Verdi

VIALE UMBERTO

VIA SEDDIO

VIA SCANO

VIA USAI

LARGO CAVALLOTTI

VIA AL CARMINE

PIAZZA AZUNI

VITTORIO EMANUELE

Palazzo d'Usini

VIA LAMARMORA

VIA MERCATO

VIA BATTISTI

PIAZZA TOLA

Casa Fabris

Teatro Civico

VIA SATTA

Casa di Re Enzo

VIA ROSELLO

VIA RAMAI

CORSO VITTORIO EMANUELE

PIAZZA MAZZOTTI

Supermarket

VIA SAN SISTO

VIA SAN SISTO

VIA SAN DONATO

VIA S. CRISTOFORO

VIA MOSCATELLO

VIA LAMARMORA

CORSO TRINITA

VIA MURAGLIA

VIA ROSELLO

PORTA ROSELLO

VIA SAN SISTO

PIAZZA SANT'ANTONIO

VIA SANT'APPOLLINARE

VIA ROSE

VIA CAPRA

VIA TEMPIO

VIA SAN CONDOTTO

VIA GAZOMETRO

CORSO VICO

Sant'Antonio Abate

VIA SAFFI

Teatro Il Ferroviario

Train Station

PIAZZA STAZIONE

VIA XXV APRILE

VIA BRIGAGLIA

VIA STRISAIOLA

VIA DEI CORSI

VIA TRISAILI VECCHIA

VIA MADDALENEDA

VIA MADDALENA

Duomo

PIAZZA DUOMO

Laundrette

Palazzo Ducale

LARGO PAZZOLA

VIA TURRITANA

VIA UNIVERSITÀ

Università

PIAZZA UNIVERSITÀ

VIA MONSIGNORE

VIA TURRITANA

VIA CAPO D'ORO

VIA ARBOREA

LARGO USSINI

City Walls

VIA TORRE TONDA

Local Bus Terminus

Giardini Pubblici

CORSO MARGHERITA DI SAVOIA

CORSO ANGIOI

Bus Station

N

RESTAURANTS
Bella Bè	4
Dido	7
Faine Sassu	2
L'Assassino	1
La Vela Latina	8
Le Antiche Mure	6
Oasi	5
Pizzalmetro	3

ACCOMMODATION
Capo di Sopra	2
Casachiara	4
La Serra sui Tetti	1
Vittorio Emanuele	3

BARS & CAFÉS
Caffè Accademia	3
Coffee Break	1
Micro Café	2

0   100
metres

today, it houses the *Comune* and hosts occasional exhibitions and concerts. Behind it, the long **Via Turritana** was once a hive of gold- and silver-workers, a tradition maintained today by a few watchmakers and jewellers.

Piazza Tola and around

Sássari's old commercial centre was located on the northern side of Corso Vittorio Emanuele, at **Piazza Tola**, where a small daily market is a faint reminder of its former role. The piazza, known until the last century as *Carra Manna* (Sard for public weighing device), takes its present name from the judge and historian whose statue stands at its centre, Pasquale Tola (1800–74). Various architectural styles can be seen in the buildings facing the square – most eye-catching is the Renaissance Palazzo d'Usini, dating from 1577, once the home of the duke of Asinara and now the municipal library.

A short distance from Piazza Tola, **Via Rosello**, lined with jewellers, leads to the northeastern edge of the old city and the Porta Rosello gate. Opposite this, a grain store dating from around 1600 has been converted into a gallery for temporary exhibitions: **La Frumentaria** (Mon–Sat: June–Sept 10am–1pm & 4–8pm; Oct–May 10am–6pm; free).

Fonte Rosello

Corso Trinità • Tues–Sun: March–Sept 10am–8pm; Oct–Feb 10am–5pm • Free

Cross Corso Trinità from Porta Rosello to reach the city's most exquisite Renaissance relic, the graceful **Fonte Rosello**, hidden away at the bottom of a grassy

---

SÁSSARI'S FESTIVALS

Originally staged for the benefit of visiting Spanish kings and other dignitaries, **La Cavalcata** takes place in Sássari on the penultimate weekend of May, the highlight of a month of cultural activities. As one of Sardinia's showiest festivals, it attracts hundreds of richly costumed participants from villages throughout the province and beyond.

The festival is divided into three stages, the morning featuring a **horseback parade** and a slow **procession**, in which the embroidered and decorated costumes unique to each participating village are displayed. In the afternoon, the scene shifts to the **Ippodromo** (race track) on the southern outskirts of town, where hectic **horse races** and ever more daring equestrian feats are performed before a large crowd. Saturday and Sunday evenings are devoted to traditional songs and dances in Piazza Italia, showcasing groups from all over the island – the close-harmony singing is especially impressive. A large fair takes over the centre of town during the week leading up to the Cavalcata, so expect lengthy traffic hold-ups.

A much more local affair held on the afternoon of August 14 is **I Candelieri** (or *Li Candareri*), linked to the Pisan devotion to the Madonna of the Assumption. It became a regular event when an outbreak of plague in Sássari mysteriously abated – though there is some dispute as to which particular plague this was, those of 1528, 1580 and 1652 being the main contenders – since when the ritual has been repeated annually on the eve of the feast of the Assumption. For all its religious intent, I Candelieri is a crowded, rumbustious occasion, involving bands of **gremi**, or medieval guilds of merchants, artisans and labourers, decked out in Spanish-style costumes, staggering through the old town under the weight of nine gigantic wooden "candlesticks", 8m tall, weighing 200–300kg and laden with colourful ribbons and other symbols of the guilds they represent. **La Faradda** (the descent through the town) usually begins at Piazza Castello around 6pm, ending at the church of Santa Maria di Betlem, with a stop en route at the Teatro Cívico, where the representative of the farmers hails Sássari's mayor with a hearty *A zent'anni!* ("May you live a hundred years!"), a traditional salute to all the *sassaresi*. If you're in town on the previous afternoon, you should drop in on the **palio**, or bareback horse race, that takes place in the Ippodromo.

flight of cobbled steps from Corso Trinità, below a flyover. The small, square monument, sculpted by Genoan stonemasons in 1606, is delicately carved with four statues representing the seasons, one on each corner, with dolphins curled around their feet.

Fed by a spring that was once one of Sássari's main sources of drinking water, the fountain was traditionally one of the busiest hubs of local life, where throngs of women would converge to scrub clothes and chat. The reconstructed wash-house alongside helps to recall its one-time role, though there's no echo of its former animation. Nonetheless, the *sassaresi* continue to regard the fountain as their greatest treasure.

The medieval walls

Corso Trinità holds a substantial surviving section of the **medieval walls** that ringed Sássari until they were pulled down in the nineteenth century. Just by the fuel station, you can make out three heraldic devices bearing symbols of the alliance on which the old city depended: a tower representing Sássari, a cross for the Church and a lily for Pisa. More fragments of the old walls are scattered around the historic centre, notably along Via Torre Tonda.

Sant'Antonio Abate

Piazza Sant'Antonio • Daily 8.30am–noon & 4–6pm

At the bottom of Corso Vittorio Emanuele, the church of **Sant'Antonio Abate** is a noble Baroque structure of clean lines and elegantly proportioned arches. Inside, the star attraction is a gigantic gilded wooden **altarpiece** executed by local craftsmen to a design by Bartolomeo Augusto, a Genoan master of the seventeenth century.

Santa Maria di Betlem

Piazza Santa Maria • Daily 9am–noon & 4–7pm; not Sun during Mass

South of the train and bus stations on the edge of the old quarter, the most striking landmark is the silver-grey dome of **Santa Maria di Betlem**, one of the city's oldest churches and the one dearest to the local people. The building has accumulated a range of different styles during its long lifetime, much of it overlaid with heavy Baroque. Its best and oldest feature is the Romanesque facade, with its sprinkling of Gothic and even Arab styles in the zigzag cornice, rose window and French Gothic columns. The lowest part dates back to the thirteenth century, while the upper part containing the rose window was added in 1465.

The interior

Apart from its fifteenth-century Gothic vaults, the **interior** is overwhelmingly Baroque, the result of a going-over in the nineteenth century when the elliptical cupola was added. The lateral chapels are still there, though, each one dedicated to one of the local guilds which became attached to the church and convent in the thirteenth century, when this was the city's chief Franciscan centre. The best preserved is the first on the left, the Catalan-style stonemasons' chapel; others belong to builders, carpenters, tailors and so on.

Also on show here are the *candelieri*, massive wooden candles associated with the guilds, each one heavily festooned with ribbons and decoration. The items are stored in the church in readiness for their annual outings at the festival of I Candelieri (see box, p.207) – if they're not displayed here, you'll usually find them in the adjoining cloisters.

ARRIVAL AND DEPARTURE

By plane Fertilia airport near Alghero (see p.174) lies 30km southwest of Sássari, connected by ARST buses with Sássari's bus station (see below).

By car If you're driving, make sure you park legally: seek out a parking attendant or parking meter, and display a ticket (€1/hr) to avoid a fine during the times when restrictions are in force (Mon–Sat 9am–1pm & 4–8pm). Free spaces can be hard to find: try around the station area or Viale Umberto.

By train Sássari is on the main FS train network (☎ 892 021, ⓦ trenitalia.it), with frequent departures to Porto Torres and Ozieri-Chilivani, the main junction for Cágliari, Olbia and Oristano. ARST (☎ 800 865 042, ⓦ arst.sardegna .it) also operates regular services to Alghero and Sorso on branch lines, and a summer-only, once-weekly Trenino Verde service (☎ 079 245 740, ⓦ treninoverde.com) to Tempio-Pausanias, Arzachena and Palau.

Destinations Alghero (9–12 daily; 35min); Arzachena (1 weekly, currently Fri; 4hr); Cágliari (5 daily, some with change; 2hr 50min–3hr 45min); Macomer (6 daily, some with change; 1hr 10min–1hr 45min); Olbia (6 daily, some with change; 1hr 45min); Oristano (5 daily, some with change; 2hr–2hr 40min); Ozieri-Chilivani (7 daily; 40min); Porto Torres (3–7 daily; 20min); Palau (1 weekly, currently Fri; 4hr 25min); Sorso (Mon–Sat 15 daily; 15min); Tempio-Pausanias (1 weekly, currently Fri; 2hr 40min).

By bus The bus station is on Via XXV Aprile, a right turn out of the train station; however, at the time of writing,

long-distance buses are using a stop nearby on Via Padre Zirano while works are under way at the bus station – with no definite date for completion. ARST (see above) operates most routes, but Digitur (☎ 079 262 039, ⓦ digitur.it) also runs a limited service to Bosa and Porto Torres (tickets on board); Turmo (☎ 0789 21 487, ⓦ gruppoturmotravel .com) operates a once-daily service to Olbia's airport and ferry port (currently leaving at 8pm; tickets on board), and Logudoro Tours (☎ 079 281 728, ⓦ logudorotours.it) runs to Árdara (currently at 9am; tickets on board).

Destinations Alghero (4–10 daily; 45min–1hr); Árdara (1 daily; 25min); Argentiera (Mon–Sat 5 daily; 1hr); Bosa (Mon–Sat 3 daily; 2hr 10min); Cágliari (2–3 daily; 1hr 45min–2hr); Castelsardo (Mon–Sat 10–11 daily, Sun 4–5 daily; 1hr); Chiaramonti (Mon–Sat 5–6 daily, Sun 2 daily; 1hr); Fertilia airport (9 daily; 30min); Monte d'Accoddi (1–2 hourly; 20min); Nuoro (4–6 daily; 1hr 50min–2hr 25min); Olbia (1–2 daily; 1hr 25min–1hr 45min); Oristano (1–3 daily; 1hr 45min–2hr); Ozieri (Mon–Sat 7–8 daily, Sun 2–3 daily; 1hr–1hr 30min); Porto Torres (1–2 hourly; 30min); Santa Teresa Gallura (2–5 daily; 2hr 15min–2hr 40min); Santíssima Trinità di Saccargia (Mon–Sat 5–6 daily; 30min); Sédini (Mon–Sat 4 daily, Sun 1 daily; 1hr 30min); Sorso (Mon–Sat 1–2 hourly, Sun 8–11 daily; 35min); Stintino (Mon–Sat 5–6 daily, Sun 1 daily; 45min–1hr 15min); Torralba (Mon–Sat 1–2 hourly, Sun 3 daily; 40min–1hr).

GETTING AROUND

By bus Everything of interest in Sássari is easily reached on foot, though bus route #8 is useful, plying a circular route every 12min between the bus and train stations, Corso Trinità, Piazza Italia and Via Roma. Buy tickets (€1.20, valid 90min) before boarding at *tabacchi* or from the kiosk on Via Tavolara in the Giardini Púbblici (public gardens), the main city bus terminus. For more info on city buses see ⓦ atpsassari.it.

By taxi There are taxi ranks on Emiciclo Garibaldi, Piazza

Castello and the train station, or call ☎ 079 253 939, ☎ 079 260 060 or ☎ 079 251 515 (24hr).

By car For excursions beyond town, car rental is available at Avis, Via Predda Niedda 23a (☎ 079 263 9011, ⓦ avis .com); Maggiore, Via Predda Niedda 38 (☎ 079 260 409, ⓦ maggiore.it); and Sardinya, Viale Caprera 8a (☎ 079 299 931, ⓦ autonoleggiosardinya.it). Most companies also have agencies at Fertilia airport (see p.174).

INFORMATION

Tourist office Via Sebastiano Satta 13 (Tues–Fri 9am–1.30pm & 3–6pm, Sat 9am–1.30pm; ☎ 079 200 8072,

ⓦ comune.sassari.it).

ACCOMMODATION

Most of Sássari's **hotels** are geared to business travellers, though there are a few reasonably priced **B&Bs** in the centre, for which you should book ahead. Campers should head to Alghero (see p.177) or to the north coast east of Platamona (p.213).

Capo di Sopra Corso Vittorio Emanuele 24 ☎ 079 202 8095 or ☎ 339 119 2757, ⓦ capodisopra.com; map p.206. Central B&B preserving some of its antique style, run by an ex-DJ. The three spacious rooms have high ceilings, private bathrooms and small balconies overlooking the Corso. **€65**

Casachiara Vicolo Bertolinis 7 ☎ 079 200 5052 or ☎ 333 695 7118, ⓦ casachiara.net; map p.206. This

relaxed B&B on the second floor of an eighteenth-century *palazzo* in the old quarter has rather dark but colourfully painted rooms with private bathrooms, TVs and a/c. Guests have use of the kitchen and washing machine (€10 each) and free wi-fi. No credit cards. **€65**

La Serra sui Tetti Via al Cármine 18 ☎ 334 121 7623, ⓦ laserrasuitetti.it; map p.206. This B&B in the old centre has an elegantly Bohemian appeal and loads of character, but its greatest assets are its airy top-floor lounge and its roof terrace with 360-degree views – a perfect perch for a glass of wine in the evening. No credit cards. **€60**

★ **Quattrogatti** Via Sant'Eligio 5 📞 079 237 819 or 📞 349 406 0481, 🖥 quattrogattibnb.it; map p.204. Just outside the old quarter, this B&B offers lively, individually decorated rooms with DVD players, TVs, wi-fi and private bathrooms. There's a small courtyard and delicious

breakfasts, and the chatty, bilingual owner offers use of the kitchen, washing machine and wi-fi. **€70**

Vittorio Emanuele Corso Vittorio Emanuele 100 📞 079 235 538, 🖥 hotelvesassari.it; map p.206. An old-town *palazzo* with original architectural features and antiques and artworks scattered around, but flashily renovated to appeal to business folk. It's comfortable, reasonably priced and equipped with a good restaurant, though bedrooms (with satellite TV and internet access) are a bit bland, and there's no car park. **€80**

EATING

Sássari's scattered range of **restaurants** are generally superb and prices are among the lowest in Sardinia. In the old town, there are still a few places left that serve **fainè** (see box below), and you'll often find horsemeat (*cavallo*) on the menu, along with donkey (*asinello*) and roast snails (*lumache* or *monzette*). In autumn, it's worth sampling the local mushrooms (*porcini* or *antunna*). If you're **self-catering**, pick up items from the supermarkets on Piazza Matteotti or Via Cavour.

THE OLD QUARTER

Bella Bè Via Usai 8 📞 079 481 6373; map p.206. Italian "tapas" are offered at this chic restaurant in a large, vaulted and white-walled room, with some seating in a courtyard. Choices include *involtini di melanzane* (rolled aubergine), fried ricotta with herbs, grilled squid and cold meats (all around €3). Alternatively, tuck into the home-made pasta (€9–10) and such traditional mains as horsemeat steaks (€14–16). Lunchtime set menus are €7 and €10. Mon–Sat 12.30–3pm & 7.30–11.30pm.

Didò Largo Pazzola 8 📞 079 200 6089; map p.206. Simple but honest local food is served at this old town restaurant, for example seafood *risotto* and *spaghetti Didò*, with horsemeat, mushrooms and fresh tomatoes. You'll spend €15–20 for a starter and main, and good-value fixed-price menus are available on weekdays at lunchtime (€7.50–11.50). Desserts include chocolate *sebadas*, and delicious pizzas are available in the evening. Daily noon–3pm & 8pm–midnight; July & Aug closed lunchtime Sat & Sun.

★ **Fainè Sassu** Via Usai 17 📞 079 236 402; map p.206. An unpretentious but renowned central spot for *fainè* fans (see box below). The menu is confined to this Ligurian and *sassarese* speciality, ideal for a snack, costing €5–8, and also available to take away. Service is brisk. Oct–May

Mon, Tues & Thurs–Sun 7–11pm.

L'Assassino Vicolo Pettenadu, off Via Satta 19 📞 079 233 463; map p.206. With tables in a lovely courtyard or in a vaulted room inside, this place offers local dishes such as *salsiccia con i fagioli* (sausage with green beans). Food quality and service are variable, however. Fixed-price menus are €24 and €28. Daily 12.30–3pm & 7.30pm–late; closed Sun in summer, Mon in winter.

La Vela Latina Largo Sisini 3 📞 079 233 737; map p.206. Smart, modern trattoria hidden away in the old town, specializing in traditional *sassarese* dishes and island wines. The *antipasti* and *fregola in brodo di pesce* (soupy seafood pasta) are terrific. You can eat out in the piazzetta in summer. Mains cost €10–15; fixed-price menus are €25 and €35. Mon–Sat 1–2.30pm & 8–10.30pm.

Le Antiche Mure Piazza Sant'Antonio 📞 079 236 725; map p.206. Close to the train station with some tables outside, this place is pretty spartan, but the pizzas (€6–10) are consistently good and the service is friendly. No credit cards. Mon–Sat 8–11pm.

Oasi Via Usai 9 📞 079 237 499; map p.206. This smart neighbourhood trattoria offers a fantastic range of *antipasti* and pasta dishes, including tasty *penne alla carnacina* (with mushrooms, ham and cheese) and justly renowned *spaghetti ai ricci* (with sea-urchins). Starters cost

---

FAINÈ

No exploration of Sássari's cuisine would be complete without sampling **fainè** (*farinata* in Italian, meaning "floured") – a popular local dish originating in Genoa, and a legacy of that city's former close association with Sássari. This winter speciality (most *fainè* places are closed in summer) consists of *ceci* (chickpea) flour fried into a sort of thick pancake, served either plain (*normale*), or cooked up with onions (*cipolle*), sausage (*salsicce*), anchovy (*acciughe*) or some combination. Best eaten with your hands, they're normally dispatched more quickly than pizza, with second and third helpings as appetite demands; beer is the usual accompaniment. They make a great fast-food snack, costing around €6 per helping.

SANTÍSSIMA TRINITÀ DI SACCARGIA (P.222) >

around €10, mains about €15, and local crêpes are available in summer. Mon–Sat 12.30–3pm & 7.30–10pm.

Pizzalmetro Via Usai 10 ☎079 492 0837; map p.206. In this boisterous place, sizzling pizza is ordered to eat in or take away by the square metre – just point out how much you want (half a metre costs €6.50–11). The *Antunna*, made with local mushrooms, is luscious. You can eat alfresco in summer. Daily 7–11pm; closed Sun in summer, Mon in winter.

THE NEW TOWN

Il Posto Via E. Costa 16 ☎079 233 528; map p.204. A casually smart trattoria in the new town, with a salmon-hued, vaulted interior hung with tasteful artworks. A good range of pizza (€5–9) and pasta (€7–10) is available, including *pennette ai quattro formaggi* (with four cheeses). Mon–Sat 7.45–11.30pm.

L'Antica Hostaria Via Cavour 55 ☎079 200 066, ⓦlanticahostaria.it; map p.204. In traditionally decorated rooms with pale orange walls, this refined and long-established eatery has earned a gourmet reputation for its creative versions of traditional Sard and Sicilian dishes. It's worth the relatively high prices: expect to pay €35–45 per head for a complete meal (excluding drinks). Mon–Sat 1–3pm & 8–11pm; closed 2 weeks Aug–Sept.

DRINKING

There's no lack of good **bars** and **cafés** in Sássari, most of them packed out and open late during summer. The ones in Piazza Castello and along Via Roma are most animated, sometimes with live music.

THE OLD QUARTER

Caffè Accademia Via Torre Tonda 11 ☎079 230 241; map p.206. Congenial spot in the university district with an enclosed veranda for sitting with an ice cream, snack or *marocchino* (espresso mixed with chocolate). Mon–Sat 7.30am–midnight.

Coffee Break Piazza Azuni 19 ☎079 200 9061; map p.206. Quiet bar for a daytime pause or a late drink with a huge range of frappés and free wi-fi. It also makes an excellent lunchtime stop on weekdays for its good-value, all-you-can-eat buffets (€8). Mon–Sat 8am–11pm.

Micro Café Largo Sisini 3 ☎328 739 4747; map p.206. As the name implies, this bar is tiny, but it's got tables in the piazzetta and a great atmosphere, making this a cool, secluded retreat for an aperitif or late-night cocktail. Mon–Sat 7am–2am.

THE NEW TOWN

Caffè Giordano Piazza Italia 27 ☎079 230 635; map p.204. Ices, yoghurts and other snacks are served at this smart place, which has tables inside, under the arcades and, in summer, on the square. Daily 7.30am–midnight; closed Sun eve June–Sept.

Caffè Italiano Via Roma 38 ☎335 667 0718; map p.204. Chic bar near the archeological museum, with tables outside, stylish decor within and occasional live music. Mon–Sat 7.30am–midnight, Sun 6pm–midnight; closed Sun in summer.

Il Giardino degli Aranci Via Coppino 2/A–4 ☎347 323 3358; map p.204. Popular with students, this relaxed bar has a garden and serves meals in the next-door restaurant. On Thurs evenings there's live music, accompanied by couscous, pasta and good wines. Mon–Sat 7am–midnight.

SHOPPING

MARKETS

Food, clothes and household goods There are a few stalls every morning (not Sun) in Piazza Tola, mainly household items and clothes, but also some fruit and veg. The city's main food market is nearby, off Porta Rosello (mornings only). There's an extensive open-air market of food, clothes, toys and tools on Monday mornings at Piazzale Segni, near the stadium (up Via Adua from Piazza Conte di Mariano at the southeast end of Viale Umberto), and a much smaller market of local produce in the centre at Emiciclo Garibaldi on Saturday mornings.

Antiques and curios An antiques fair is held in Piazza Santa Caterina on the last Sunday of each month (Sept–June 8am–1pm).

DIRECTORY

Hospital Ospedale Civile Santíssima Annunziata, Viale Italia ☎079 206 1000.

Internet access Internet Point, Piazza Matteotti 4 (Mon–Sat 9am–11pm, Sun 11am–11pm); €1 for 15min; also long-distance calls and fax service.

Laundrette Lavalandia, Corso Vittorio Emanuele 150 (daily 9am–9pm); €4 per 6kg, dryer €1 per 10min.

Pharmacy V. Simon on Piazza Castello, open all day and night except 1–4.30pm.

Post office Central Ufficio Postale is on Via Brigata Sássari. An exchange facility for cash is in the room on the left; Poste Restante (*Fermo Posta*) and stamps are in a separate room on the right. Mon, Tues, Thurs & Fri 8.25am–7.10pm, Wed 8.25am–1.35pm, Sat 8.25am–12.35pm.

Travel agencies Ajo Viaggi, Piazza Fiume 1, ☎079 200 222, for internal and international tickets.

The Sássari Riviera

When the *sassaresi* need a break, they head 15km north to the long stretch of pine-backed beaches that make up the **Sássari Riviera**. The main resort is **PLATAMONA**, where a row of bars and pizzerias stand a stone's throw from the sea and lidos charge a few euros a day for a parasol and sun-lounger, plus the use of showers and a car park. You'll find fewer crowds farther east, however, where the fine sand beaches are sheltered from the SP81 coast road by a curtain of pines, eucalyptus and juniper trees, offering numerous hideaways for a private swim or even camping rough (be extra careful not to start fires).

There's another concentration of beachside activity at **Marina di Sorso**. Five kilometres inland, the village of **SORSO** lies at the centre of the fertile **Romangia** region, whose fruit and vegetables liberally fill the shops and markets hereabouts. The local grapes go into some of Sardinia's best Cannonau, Moscato, Vermentino and Monica wines, and the place is also famed for its baskets woven with dwarf-palm leaves.

ARRIVAL AND DEPARTURE   THE SÁSSARI RIVIERA

By bus City buses BB ("Buddi-Buddi") and MP leave for Platamona from Via Tavolara in Sássari's Giardini Púbblici every 40min (every 1hr 20min in winter), taking about half an hour. Buy tickets before boarding from the kiosk (€1.20 valid 1hr 30min, or €3 valid all day).

ACCOMMODATION

Li Nibari Località Marina di Sorso ☎079 310 303, ⓦcampinglinibari.com. Signposted off the coast road 5km or so east of Platamona, this three-star campsite offers a bar, restaurants and a supermarket, as well as various sports facilities in summer, including two pools (one for children), while the private beach is just metres away. Two- and four-bed caravans and bungalows are available for €40–80 for two in the off-peak season, plus extras. Pitches €24

Porto Torres and around

Sixteen kilometres northwest of Sássari, the Carlo Felice highway ends its long run from Cágliari at **PORTO TORRES**, once the main Roman base on this coast and, thanks to its port, still one of the main gateways into Sardinia today. It's an unprepossessing place, with a smoky industrial zone dominating the western side of town, but it's worth pressing on to view its magnificent Romanesque **Basilica di San Gavino** and a cluster of **Roman remains** to the west of the centre.

Most of the action in Porto Torres takes place on the main **Corso Vittorio Emanuele**, where you'll find most of the town's banks, travel agents and bars. In summer, the **port** gets pretty lively too, overlooked by an Aragonese tower. The best local **swimming** spots lie east of here – secluded rocky coves followed by sandy beaches leading to Platamona (see above), 7km east.

Brief history

There have always been settlements on this site, drawn to its natural harbour and position at the mouth of the River Mannu, one of the island's longest rivers. Most traces of the town's pre-Roman past have long been effaced, though there is considerable evidence of the Roman colony, **Turris Libyssonis**, supposedly founded by Julius Caesar in the first century BC.

Porto Torres quickly developed as an important shipping stop between the Italian mainland and the Iberian peninsula, and subsequently became the centre of a cult devoted to the *Mártiri Turritani* – three local martyrs (see p.214). By the tenth century the town had become the capital of one of Sardinia's four *giudicati*, and continued to wield commercial influence under the Pisans, though Saracen raids and Genoan assaults eventually led to its decline and a transfer of power inland to Sássari.

Today, Porto Torres is thriving once more, its economic role buoyed by the petrochemical works to the west of town as well as constant shipping traffic.

Basilica di San Gavino

Corso Vittorio Emanuele • Daily: April & Oct 9am–1pm & 3–6pm; May–Sept 9am–1pm & 3–7pm; Nov–March call for tours • €2, €3 with guided tour • ☎ 348 899 6823, ⓦ turrisbisleonis.it

From the port, follow the main Corso Vittorio Emanuele to find the **Basilica di San Gavino**. Originally standing in open country, its present backstreet location diminishes the monument's grandeur, though, as Sardinia's largest and – according to some – finest Romanesque structure, it still makes quite an impact. The slits of windows and blind arcading around the fine yellowy stonework contribute to its austere, fortified appearance, a reminder that it survived innumerable Saracen attacks during the Middle Ages.

Occupying the site of a Roman necropolis, there has been a church here since the sixth century, dedicated to the *Mártiri Turritani* – San Gavino, San Proto and San Gianuario, three Roman soldiers beheaded in 304. The present basilica was begun by Pisans in around 1030 and probably finished by 1090, though in the twelfth century the church was enlarged and given an unusual second apse, lending it a slightly confused, directionless look. Of the three lateral doors, the one on the north is oldest, decorated with human and animal figures; the other two are later additions, one of them, the main entrance, Catalan-Gothic from 1492.

The interior

Gloomily lit by the narrow windows, the naves and aisles of **the interior** are separated by 28 marble columns, dug up from the old Roman town. At the back of the nave, with its harmonious wooden roof, a prominent catafalque carries wooden images of the three *Mártiri Turritani*, near a dashing seventeenth-century statue of San Gavino on a horse. Across the nave, stairs lead down to the first of the basilica's two **crypts** (€1.50), a long room dating from the seventeenth century and lined with statues of saints and several Roman sarcophagi, one of them elaborately carved with figures of a seated man and woman – whose tomb this was – surrounded by Apollo and the nine Muses.

At the far end, a door gives access to the foundations of the original paleo-Christian church. From the ante-crypt, more steps lead down to a lower **crypt**, where the bones of the martyrs – placed here in the nineteenth century – are displayed in arched niches, together with more sarcophagi.

The Antiquarium

Via Ponte Romano • Mon–Sat 9am–7.30pm, Sun in summer 9am–2pm • €2, guided tour (9.30am–1pm & 3.30–7pm) €2.50; archeological site €4 • ☎ 079 514 433, ⓦ turrisbisleonis.it

The major archeological remains in Porto Torres lie on the seafront on the western edge of town (less than a 10min walk from the Corso, beyond Maríttima train station). Here, the poorly marked **Antiquarium Turritano** displays finds from various digs in the area of Turris Libyssonis, chiefly from the archeological site adjacent. Among the highlights here is the **Maschera Maetske**, a ferocious-looking marble satyr's head, originally the mouth of a fountain, that was unearthed here in 2003. Other exhibits include ceramics and votive ornaments, a lead sarcophagus, fragments of mosaic floors and some well-preserved busts and statuettes. Labelling is practically nonexistent, however, and you'd do well to hire an **audio-guide** (€3) in various languages; alternatively you can join a **guided tour**, though groups are preferred – ask for details at the museum desk.

The archeological site

The **archeological site** holding remains of the Roman city is only accessible as part of a guided tour from the museum. Reached along flagstoned roads bordered by stumps of columns, the centrepiece is the so-called **Palazzo di Re Bárbaro** ("Palace of King Barbarus"), named after the semi-mythical Roman governor who presided over the martyrdom of the town's saints. In fact, the remains are primarily those of the shattered baths complexes, or *terme*, dating from the third or fourth century BC, including the frigidarium and richly mosaicked floors. A custom-built bunker shelters the most vivid mosaics of all, including the voluptuous **mosaico di Orfeo**, showing Orpheus strumming his lyre surrounded by birds and beasts.

6

The Roman bridge

Another 200m west of the Antiquarium, almost hidden between newer bridges and thick growths of bamboo, you can see the seven arches of a **Roman bridge** crossing the River Mannu. This well-preserved monument was used by traffic until the 1980s, but now looks sadly redundant on the outskirts of the town and modern industrial complex. You can visit the bridge on the same guided tours that go round the museum and archeological site.

Monte d'Accoddi

Tues–Sun: March–June, Sept & Oct 10am–6pm; July & Aug 10am–8pm; Nov–Feb 10am–2pm • €3 • ☏ 334 807 4449

Six kilometres southeast of Porto Torres, a right turn off the Carlo Felice highway (SS131) brings you to **Monte d'Accoddi** where, surrounded by cereal fields, a sanctuary dating back to the Copper Age (2450–1850 BC) has been excavated. There's little visible construction remaining, but the long tapering mound, measuring 30m by 38m, and the earthen ramp ascending to a platform at its top are clearly defined. This alone sets the site apart from anything else found in Sardinia, or in the entire Mediterranean. The flat-topped pyramid seems to have more in common with Mesopotamian or Aztec temples, hence its popular name of "ziggurat" or "ziqqurat".

The outlines of various structures – including stonewalled dwellings and even a menhir – can be seen on either side of the ramp, and there's evidence that there may have been some kind of sacred spot here from as early as 3000 BC. The sanctuary was probably used for sacrifices and other ceremonial functions, though you need to make an imaginative leap to picture it as it might have once appeared – it helps to have seen the laser image in Sássari's Museo Sanna (see p.203). It's an impressive site, nonetheless, with views back to Sássari and north to the Golfo dell'Asinara.

ARRIVAL AND DEPARTURE
PORTO TORRES

BY FERRY

Ferries use either the old harbour in the centre of Porto Torres or the Porto Industriale 2km west of town, connected to the centre by a shuttle bus (*navetta*). Usually, Tirrenia (☏ 892 123 or ☏ 02 2630 2803, ⓦ tirrenia.it), Moby (☏ 199 303 040, ⓦ moby.it), SNCM (ⓦ sncm.fr) and La Meridionale (ⓦ lameridionale.fr) use the central harbour, while Saremar (☏ 079 523 688, ⓦ saremar.com) and Grimaldi (☏ 081 496 444, ⓦ grimaldi-lines.it) dock at the Porto Industriale. The *navetta* to the Porto Industriale leaves from the Aragonese tower at the port two hours before sailings, making a stop at the Maríttima train station.

Reservations If you're leaving Sardinia from Porto Torres, make sure you book as early as possible, especially in peak season, and particularly if you're shipping a vehicle. Buy tickets directly from the ticket offices, by phone, online, or from one of the authorized travel agents in town, such as

Paglietti, Corso Vittorio Emanuele 19 (☏ 079 514 477), the official outlet for tickets for SNCM and La Meridionale.

Destinations Barcelona, Spain (Grimaldi; April to early Oct 2–5 weekly; 11hr 45min); Civitavécchia (Grimaldi; April to early Oct 2–5 weekly; 7hr 15min); Genoa (Tirrenia & Moby 1–3 daily; 9–13hr); Marseille, France (SNCM & La Meridionale; 2–5 weekly; 11–17hr); Propriano, Corsica (SNCM & La Meridionale; 2–3 weekly; 3hr 30min); Vado Ligure, Savona (Saremar; June to mid-Sept 3–4 weekly; 10hr–11hr 15min).

BY TRAIN

Porto Torres has two train stations: Porto Torres, a 10min walk south of the harbour, near the basilica, and Porto Torres Maríttima, nearer the museum and port. Services to and from Sássari (3–7 daily; 20min) and Cágliari (may involve change at Sássari and Ozieri-Chilivani; 2–4 daily; 3hr 50min–4hr 30min) stop at both.

BY BUS

ARST (see p.200), Sardabus (for Castelsardo; ⓦsardabus .it), and Digitur (for limited services to Sássari, Bosa, Castelsardo and Santa Teresa Gallura; ⓦdigitur.it) buses stop at Via Mare, by the harbour.

Destinations Alghero (5–6 daily; 1hr); Bosa (1 daily; 2hr 30min); Castelsardo (1–2 daily; 40min); Monte d'Accoddi (1–2 hourly; 10min); Santa Teresa Gallura (June–Sept; 1 daily; 2hr); Sássari (1–2 hourly; 35min); Stintino (Mon–Sat 5–6 daily, Sun 2–5 daily; 40min).

INFORMATION AND ACTIVITIES

Tourist office Piazza Garibaldi 17, off the main Corso Vittorio Emanuele (June–Sept daily 9am–1pm & 4–7pm; ☎079 500 8711).
Tours to Asinara Boat tours to the island of Asinara (see p.197) leave in summer from the port, taking around 1hr

30min. Delcomar (ⓦdelcomar.it) has operated the service in the past – ask at the tourist office for the company currently operating. Note that services are more frequent, shorter and cheaper from Stintino (see box, p.197).

ACCOMMODATION

Al Faro Via Paglietti 14a ☎079 502 799 or ☎320 457 1113, ⓦbb-alfaro.it. Near the lighthouse after which it's named (a short walk west of the Corso along Via Petronia), this B&B offers simple, sparkling clean rooms with great views over the sea and archeological site. The owners are helpful and friendly, and early breakfasts are provided for

ferry-catchers. No credit cards. **€65**
Elisa Via Mare 2 ☎079 513 260, ⓦhotelelisaportotorres .com. The most central hotel in town, right on the port, this old-fashioned three-star is low on atmosphere but has most rooms overlooking the boats, and some have balconies. Front-facing rooms can be noisy, though. **€80**

EATING AND DRINKING

★ **Gelateria Capriccio** Corso Vittorio Emanuele 114 ☎079 515 178. Before or after a visit to San Gavino, take time to sample one of the fifty-odd flavours of luscious ice cream on offer here, in cones, cups and frappés, up to five flavours at a time. Daily 9am–midnight.
La Bottega Piazza Venti Settembre 1 ☎079 514 834. This *alimentari* at the bottom of the Corso is the perfect stop for a do-it-yourself lunch or food for the ferry; apart from panini they sell a range of local cheese, salami, wine, yoghurt

and bread. Mon–Sat 8am–1.30pm & 4.30–8pm.
Piazza Garibaldi Piazza Garibaldi ☎079 501 570. Occupying a prime position among the cluster of bars and restaurants in this busy piazza, this ristorante-pizzeria has won awards for its pizzas (€4–8), and the meat and fish dishes aren't bad either (around €10), including delicious *cozze alla marinara* (mussels) and *pennette allo scoglio* (seafood pasta). The outside tables fill up quickly in summer. Daily 1–3pm & 8pm–midnight.

Castelsardo and around

Northeast of Sássari, the compact region of **Anglona** is a hilly landscape bound by Logudoro and Gallura to the south and east, and scattered with the remains of a prehistoric "petrified forest". The rocky northern littoral is the perfect setting for Anglona's main town, **CASTELSARDO**, picturesquely draped over a promontory overlooking the Golfo dell'Asinara, with reddish-grey houses huddled below the stout castle. The fortified citadel here was the Doria power base in Sardinia for nearly 250 years, and the historic centre preserves a pungent medieval flavour. However, while it retains a small fishing fleet, Castelsardo is first and foremost a fully fledged **holiday resort**, thanks to its photogenic setting and its pre-eminence as a centre of Sard **handicrafts**, prominently displayed in the narrow lanes of the old quarter (see box, p.218).

CASTELSARDO'S FESTIVALS

Castelsardo's **Easter festivities** are known for the dramatic torchlit procession, **Lunissanti**, a tradition predating the Spanish conquest of the town, in which a cortege of cowled figures threads through the old town on Easter Monday to the accompaniment of medieval chants in Latin and Sard. The town's other major festival is on August 2, when the **Madonna degli Ángeli** is celebrated with games and traditional dancing.

Outside the historic centre, there's little of specific interest in the newer neighbourhoods, though the rocky cove immediately below and west of the citadel is undeniably pretty, sheltering an attractive sandy beach. Farther west, the **Porto di Frigianu** fishing anchorage and yachting marina is watched over by an old defensive tower, and there are a couple of bars if you want to sit and watch the low-key activity. Eastwards, there's another small beach squeezed up among the rocks on the far side of town, easily reached on foot and good for a dip.

Brief history

Genoa's powerful Doria dynasty established a stronghold at Castelsardo at the start of the twelfth century, giving it the name of "Castel-genovese". Embroiled in the power clashes between Genoa, Pisa and Spain, the strategically crucial town was one of the last Genoan centres in the Torres *giudicato* to hold out against the Spaniards. When he finally took possession of the town in 1448, Alfonso V immediately changed its name to Castel Aragonese, though the locals were mollified when, in 1511, Charles V accorded the port the same rights and privileges as the rival Spanish sea-base at Alghero. Supported by four thousand French troops, the Doria made a last, futile effort to recapture their home base in 1527, then virtually disappeared from the Sardinian scene altogether. The town's present, safely neutral name was given by the Savoyard kings in 1769.

The old centre

It's a steep but rewarding ascent up the steps and alleys of Castelsardo's old quarter. Home-made baskets and other artefacts are displayed in doorways, brightly coloured plants are draped over walls, and time-weathered arches and crumbling doorways adorn the minute lanes. Glimpses of the rocky shore and sea below bring relief from the closed, insular air of the place, though the best views, of course, are from the top, crowned by the battlements of the heavily restored **castello**. From here, it's an uninterrupted prospect across the gulf to the isle of Asinara, off Sardinia's northwestern point; to the northeast, it's sometimes possible to sight the coast of Corsica – though for this the conditions need to be particularly good. The sunsets here are especially memorable.

The castello

Via Marconi • July to mid-Sept daily 9am–midnight; late Sept daily 9.30am–1pm & 3–6.30pm; Oct–June Tues–Sun 9.30am–1pm & 3pm–1hr before sunset • €2 • ☎ 079 471 380

The abode of the powerful Doria dynasty for two centuries, and for ten years home to Eleonora d'Arborea and Brancaleone Doria after their marriage in 1376 (see box, p.142), the Castelsardo's **castle** now houses a basketwork and weaving museum, the **Museo dell'Intreccio Mediterraneo** (same hours as castle), artfully incorporated into the small chambers. There's much to admire in this assortment of bowls, plates, bottles and lobster traps, often skilfully patterned, some of the most prized items woven from the leaves of the local dwarf-palm. For the most part, these are the traditional tools of everyday life, utilized by bakers, farmers and fishermen; there's even a grass-woven boat here – the truncated-looking *fassoni* used around Oristano (see p.148). Somewhat incongruously, there's a quotation from Joyce's *Ulysses* daubed onto a door – translated into the Sard dialect, it refers to local people's attachment to the land. Elsewhere in the castle you'll come across replicas of medieval **weaponry** – a battering ram, a crossbow, a catapult and the like.

Santa Maria delle Grazie

Piazza Santa Maria • Daily: summer 9am–7pm; winter 9am–5.30pm

From the castle, it's a short walk to the **church of Santa Maria delle Grazie**, a misshapen building squeezed into the available space. The richly decorated church holds a special

6

ARTIGIANATO IN CASTELSARDO

Many people come to Castelsardo purely to shop, and the lower town has plenty of outlets. The famed local **artigianato**, or handicrafts, has grown in the last twenty years from a small cottage industry to a major year-round money-spinner. Cork, coral and ceramic goods are here in abundance, as well as shelves full of the African-looking Sard wooden masks, though the main craft for which Castelsardo is known is l'intreccio, or **basketwork**. Straw, wicker, reeds, raffia and asphodel leaves are all used to create an incredible variety of containers, trays and furniture, though the material most associated with Castelsardo is dwarf-palm leaves, locally picked.

A good place to visit before shopping is the **museum of basket-weaving** in Castelsardo's castle (see p.217), to get an idea of what the best examples of the genre should look like. As for the emporia, don't spend too much time shopping around – you'll see the same products everywhere, with very similar price tags, and much of it is made elsewhere using synthetic materials. More satisfying is to buy directly from the weavers themselves in the old quarter – mostly women working the stuff on their doorsteps amid displays of their wares – for which you'll need to sharpen up your bargaining techniques. You can also find some good work in nearby villages such as Tergu (see p.220), where the quality is at least as good as that in town.

---

role among the townspeople, as the repository of the sacred *Critu Nieddu*, or Black Christ, a fourteenth-century crucifix kept in the sacristy. The church marks the start and end of Castelsardo's Easter Monday procession.

Sant'Antonio Ábate

Piazza Sant'Antonio • **Church** Daily: summer 9am–7pm; winter 9am–5.30pm • **Crypt** Daily: summer 9am–1pm & 3.30–7pm; winter 9am–1pm & 3.30–5.30pm • €3

After the cramped lanes of most of the old centre, it's a surprise to come across the relatively large terrace that accommodates Castelsardo's cathedral, **Sant'Antonio Ábate**. Overlooking reddish boulders washed by the sea, it's an evocative spot, the octagonal campanile with its majolica-tiled cupola adding a splash of colour. The church itself retains some evidence of the original Gothic structure, and its sixteenth-century rebuilding and Baroque accretions are not unsympathetic.

Inside, the centre of the fussy marble altarpiece holds the building's main treasure, the **Madonna with Angels**, a fragment of a work by a local fifteenth-century painter known simply as the **Maestro di Castelsardo**, whose synthesis of Italian and Flemish Gothic elements was hugely influential in Sardinia. Other items worth looking out for are the painted wooden pulpit hanging off one of the piers in front of the altar, the sculpted figures of musicians and animals on the capitals of the pillars on either side of the altar, and, behind this, some finely carved choir stalls.

To the left of the altar, a flight of steps leads down to the **crypt**, where, in four sombre stone chambers connected by narrow steps, there are more works of religious art, notably further sections of the Maestro di Castelsardo's *retablo*, one depicting four apostles, another – with liberal use of Byzantinesque gold – showing the Holy Trinity.

The Roccia dell'Elefante

SP134, 5km southwest of Castelsardo

Exiting eastwards from Castelsardo, you can't miss the **Roccia dell'Elefante**, whose elephant-shaped profile is featured on hundreds of postcards, its drooping "trunk" practically swishing the passing vehicles. Clearly the wind-eroded trachyte monolith has long held an emblematic power, for there are some pre-nuraghic *domus de janas* tombs hewn beneath it; look carefully on the wall of the right-hand chamber to make out a carving of the curling bull-horns which are such a pronounced motif on nuraghic figurines.

Nuraghe Paddaggiu

Valledoria road, 6km southwest of Castelsardo

On a grassy knoll by the roadside a kilometre or so east of the Roccia dell'Elefante, the well-preserved **Nuraghe Paddaggiu** was built during the last phase of *nuraghe* culture. Also (erroneously) called Nuraghe Su Tesoru, its correct name – "haystack" – probably refers to the use to which most farmers assigned these ancient structures. The *nuraghe* consists of a niched central chamber, with the remains of stairs leading up to a second storey that no longer survives. Traces of two lateral towers can also be seen.

Lu Bagnu

Five kilometres west of Castelsardo, the blandly functional holiday resort of **LU BAGNU** has good swimming in limpid waters off the rocks at the bottom of cliffs, an excellent hostel (see below) and some lively bar-life in summer that might entice you on a night out from Castelsardo.

ARRIVAL AND DEPARTURE

CASTELSARDO

By bus All buses stop at the central Piazza Pianedda, at the bottom of the old town, and there's another bus stop by the beach in the lower town. ARST runs most of the routes; Digitur (☎ 079 262 039, ⓦ digitur.it) operates a fast but infrequent summer service connecting Castelsardo with Valledoria, Santa Teresa Gallura, Porto Torres and Fertilia airport, while Sardabus (☎ 079 684 087, ⓦ sardabus.it) runs between Castelsardo, Valledoria, Lu Bagnu and Tergu, and to Tempio Pausania in summer. Logudoro Tours (☎ 079 281 728, ⓦ logudorotours.it) also operates a seasonal service to the airport.

Destinations Bulzi (Mon–Sat 4–5 daily, Sun 1 daily; 30–40min); Porto Torres (June–Sept 2 daily; 40min); Santa Teresa Gallura (3–7 daily; 1hr 15min–2hr 40min); Sássari

(Mon–Sat 11–13 daily, Sun 5–7 daily; 1hr); Sédini (Mon–Sat 4–5 daily, Sun 1 daily; 25min); Sorso (Mon–Sat 9–11 daily, Sun 2–3 daily; 30min); Tempio Pausania (mid-June to mid-Sept 3 daily; 1hr 30min); Tergu (Mon–Sat 2–5 daily; 10–20min); Valledoria (2–9 daily; 25min).

By car If you're driving, leave your vehicle around the piazza, or in the car park reached from the piazza's top-right corner. You could drive up the main Via Nazionale and take your chances parking on the road leading up to the castle, but spaces are usually limited (tickets €0.50 for first hr, then €1/hr); don't get tangled up in the tight web of alleys that make up the old centre, usually resulting in frantic reversing and scraped bodywork.

GETTING AROUND AND INFORMATION

By bus A local circular bus operates in summer linking Castelsardo with the beaches at Lu Bagnu (every 60–90min; €1). There are stops at Piazza Pianedda and Lungomare Anglona.

Tourist information The tourist office is on Via Bastione, near the castle (April–Oct Mon–Fri 9am–1pm & 3–7pm; ☎ 079 470 220; ⓦ castelsardoturismo.it). There's also a Pro Loco next door, keeping erratic hours (☎ 079 471 506).

ACCOMMODATION

The seafront **Lungomare Anglona** is where most of Castelsardo's accommodation can be found, about a 1km walk from the citadel. Drivers staying in the **old town** won't be able to park nearby. In August, most of the hotels will demand a minimum stay of three to seven nights at half- or full board. If everywhere in town is booked up, try the beach resort of Lu Bagnu, the site of a good hostel (see below).

★**Casa Doria** Via Garibaldi 10 ☎ 349 355 7882, ⓦ casadoria.it. Old-town B&B with wooden ceilings, antique Sardinian furnishings and a lovely breakfast room at the top with breathtaking views. One room (costing €85) is en suite, two share facilities, and all have a/c. No credit cards. **€75**

Janus Via Roma 85 ☎ 079 479 422, ⓦ janushotel.it. Just off the seafront, this "design hotel" is about as contemporary as they come in Castelsardo, with plush, wi-fi-enabled rooms and cool colours. Front-facing rooms will have great views and some have balconies, but the road can be noisy in summer. Closed Oct–March. **€90**

Nadir Via Colle di Frigiano 1 ☎ 079 470 297, ⓦ hotelnadir.it. The unfortunately named *Nadir* is actually one of the smarter hotels on the Lungomare. Rooms are fully equipped – sea-facing ones with balconies cost more – and there's a good, fifth-floor restaurant with an open terrace. Look out for discounted on-line deals. Wi-fi access. **€106**

Ostello Golfo dell'Asinara Via Sardegna, Lu Bagnu ☎ 079 474 031, ⓦ ostellodicastelsardo.com. On the outskirts of the resort of Lu Bagnu, 5km west of Castelsardo, this spacious hostel lies amid greenery off the Tergu road, with great views from its wide terrace. Prices include

6

breakfast, and you can eat dinner here for €11. No credit cards. Closed Oct–May. Dorms €14, doubles €40

Pinna Lungomare Anglona 7 ☎ 079 470 168. This family-run *pensione* is Castelsardo's cosiest option, above a popular trattoria overlooking the beach. The ten rooms are clean and simply furnished. At least half-board (€65 per person, excluding breakfast) may be required during August. €70

Sa Domo de Minnanna Via Mezzu Teppa 5 ☎ 079 471 049 or ☎ 349 367 6105, ✉ sadomodeminnanna@yahoo.it. Directly below the *centro stórico*, this simple B&B offers excellent value, with three clean and quiet rooms with private bathrooms. No credit cards. €50

CAMPING

La Foce Valledoria, 15km east of Castelsardo ☎ 079 582 109, ⓦ foce.it. On the banks of the Coghinas river and close to acres of sandy beach, this campsite is the biggest and best equipped of the sites in the area, with a range of family-orientated facilities including two pools and a lagoon across which campers are ferried to a good beach. Kayaking, sailing and windsurfing are on hand, and bungalows and caravans are available (from €100 for two in high season). Closed Oct to late April. Pitches €40

EATING AND DRINKING

Castelsardo has a good selection of places to **eat** and **drink**, some (in the old town) quite expensive, but many offering good-value tourist menus. There's a better choice of bars and trattorias lower down; it's worth remembering that the *Pinna pensione* (see above) has a cheerful trattoria with a terrace facing the sea, and the *Nadir* (see p.219) has a posher fifth-floor restaurant, strong on seafood.

Aragona Via Manganella ☎ 079 470 081. On a terrace above the sea, just along from the cathedral, this bar/restaurant run by two brothers serves drinks and light meals until late, and makes a good choice if you're looking for a view. The brothers' speciality is *pasta al mirto* (flavoured with myrtle), and there are set-price menus for €18 and €20. March–Oct daily 9am–2am, meals served noon–3.30pm & 7–11.30pm; closed Mon in winter.

Bounty Via Lamarmora 12 ☎ 079 479 043. Among the stand-out dishes at this place near the castle are excellent *zuppa di pesce* (fish soup), *risotto agli scampi*, roast pork and some of the best *seadas* you'll find anywhere. Each of the two floors has its own character, the traditional, brick-vaulted lower floor connected by spiral staircase to the more modern part upstairs. Pasta dishes are €10–15, mains €15–20 and tourist menus €20 and €25. Daily noon–3.30pm & 7pm–midnight; Oct–April closed Wed.

Il Cormorano Via Colombo 5 ☎ 079 470 628, ⓦ ristorante ilcormorano.net. This smart, traditional-looking place in an unprepossessing location near Piazza Pianedda has some of

the best food in town, with the freshest seafood dishes, a strong list of island wines and a veranda, but high prices: €12–15 for first courses, €23–25 for mains. April–Oct Tues–Sun 12.30–2.30pm & 7.30–10.30pm; Nov–March Fri & Sat same times, Sun lunchtime only.

La Guardiola Piazza Bastione 4 ☎ 079 470 755. Just below Castelsardo's castle, this posh eatery has a terrace with romantic views over the sea and a menu offering such dishes as *gamberoni al mirto* (king prawns with myrtle). Given its location, it's predictably pricey, with starters costing around €15, mains €18–22, but there's an affordable fixed-price lunch for €16. Daily noon–3.30pm & 7.30–10.30pm; Oct–Easter closed Mon.

★ **La Trattoria** Via Colombo 6 ☎ 079 470 661. An excellent mid-range choice round the corner from Piazza Pianedda, focusing on *cucina casalinga* – local dishes such as *zuppa gallurese* and roast pork or lamb. Starters cost €8–13, mains are €10–16 and pizzas €6–9. Arrive early for tables with sea views. Tues–Sun 12.30–2.30pm & 7.30–11.30pm; closed Nov.

Inland from Castelsardo

With your own vehicle, you'll be able to explore the hill country **inland of Castelsardo**, stamped with the traces of Sardinia's ancient and medieval civilizations. A foray of only a few kilometres will bring you into the very heart of Anglona.

Tergu

From Lu Bagnu (see p.219), a road winds 7km inland to **TERGU**, a small village best known for its square-faced Pisan-Romanesque church of **Nostra Signora di Tergu** (also called Santa Maria; open daily 9am–7.30pm), from the early thirteenth century. The facade is the most interesting feature, with blind arcading and red trachyte stone alternating with paler limestone, and there are the ruins of a once-powerful Benedictine monastery alongside. The church is unmissable at the southern end of the village.

A visit to Tergu is a good opportunity to seek out examples of local craftwork, often similar to the items on sale in Castelsardo, but cheaper.

Sédini

Fifteen kilometeres southeast of Castlesardo on the SP134, **SÉDINI** preserves a number of Aragonese-Gothic buildings, and, right on the main road in the centre of the village, a group of ancient tombs – or *domus de janas* – gouged out of a massive calcareous rock known as **La Rocca**. Used as a prison in the Middle Ages, and incorporated into a dwelling in the nineteenth century, the tombs now exhibit a collection of fossils, agricultural tools and other ethnographic items (May–Sept daily 10am–1pm & 3–7pm; Oct–April call ☏349 844 0436; €2).

San Pietro delle Immágini

SP134, 3km south of Bulzi

Arguably the prettiest of the churches scattered around Sássari's hinterland is **San Pietro delle Immágini** (also called San Pietro di Simbranos). Marooned in a flowery meadow in a valley 3km south of **Bulzi**, a village 7km east of Sédini on the SP134, the church was founded by monks from Monte Cassino in 1112, and became an important Benedictine centre during the twelfth and thirteenth centuries. It owes its excellent state of preservation today to its safe distance from coastal raiders.

The **facade** blends Romanesque and Gothic, with a brown-and-white striped pattern similar to that of the church in Tergu, and pointed blind arches surmounted by a pediment. Above the door, a lunette holds a crude relief of an abbot and two monks – the "images" from which the church takes its name. Within is a stoup formed from trunks of petrified – or, more accurately, silicified – trees, of which the surrounding area holds a considerable quantity. You'll be lucky to find the church open, though: weekends are the best bet, or be here for the Festa di San Pietro, forty days after Easter.

Laerru and Chiaramonti

If you're taking the slow but scenic route towards Sássari on the SS127, you'll pass through the village of **Laerru**, 7km south of Bulzi, internationally reputed for the carving of tobacco pipes from briar, olivewood and juniper. Shortly before reaching the faster SS672 Sássari–Tempio road, **Chiaramonti** is worth a stop for its intricate network of narrow streets grouped around the base of a twelfth-century Doria fortification. Though not particularly high (440m), there are fantastic views from the ruins over the mountains on all sides, most strikingly Monte Limbara (1359m) to the east and Monte Sassu (640m) – a famed haunt of bandits and kidnappers – to the southeast.

Castel Doria

Inland of Valledoria, follow the course of the River Coghinas for 8km up the Perfugas road to reach the poetic ruins of **Castel Doria**. Poised over the Lago di Castel Doria, the castle (now inaccessible) was built in this craggy spot in the twelfth century to guard Anglona's eastern approaches. Marking the boundary with Gallura, the river feeds the artificially created lake, which has allowed the drainage of Anglona's only plain of any size, around Valledoria.

South of Sássari: Logudoro

The sparsely populated country south of Sássari is the heartland of the territory historically known as **Logudoro**, whose present-day inhabitants retain the distinction of speaking the purest form of Sard, softer and more rolling than the island's other dialects. The former wealth and importance of the region is attested today by the presence of some outstanding **Pisan churches**, magnificently stranded in open countryside, while it also holds one of Sardinia's most important nuraghic complexes, the **Nuraghe Santu Antine**. The area's only town of any size, **Ozieri**, holds remnants of the Neolithic culture to which it has lent its name.

ARRIVAL AND GETTING AROUND   **LOGUDORO**

A **car** is needed to reach most places, though the villages of Torralba and Ozieri have good **bus** connections with Sássari.

Santíssima Trinità di Saccargia

SS597 • April to mid-Oct daily 9am–2hr before sunset • €2.50 • ☎ 347 000 7882

Sixteen kilometres southeast of Sássari, the church of **Santíssima Trinità di Saccargia** makes a striking apparition to anyone travelling on the main Sássari–Olbia road. Standing tall and solitary amid the surrounding flat country, its zebra-striped facade and belltower conspicuously mark its Pisan origins.

The church, built in 1116, supposedly owes its remote location to a divine visitation that took place while the *giudice* of Torres and his wife stopped here on the way to Porto Torres, where they intended to pray for a child at San Gavino's shrine. During the night, a celestial messenger informed the *giudice*'s wife that the pilgrimage was unnecessary since she was already pregnant, whereupon the grateful *giudice* built an abbey on this spot. The basalt and limestone facade was added some sixty years later and has survived remarkably well, although some of the carved dogs, cows and other beasts on the lovely Gothic **capitals** at the top of the entrance porch, are reconstructions.

Showing elements of Lombard architecture, the stark, tall-naved **interior** is mostly unadorned but for a gilded wooden pulpit embedded in one wall and some vivid eleventh- or twelfth-century **frescoes** covering the central apse. These, illustrating scenes from the life of Christ, are attributed to a Pisan artist and are a rare example in Italy of this type of Romanesque mural. Look out, too, for the stone image at the front of the nave on the left, possibly representing Costantino I, the *giudice* supposed to have founded the church and thought to be buried here.

Santa Maria del Regno

Árdara • Daily 9am–1pm & 3–7pm

The nondescript village of **ÁRDARA**, 15km east of Santíssima Trinità di Saccargia along the SS597, shows few traces of its one-time role as Logudoro's capital, though the restored basilica of **Santa Maria del Regno** hints at its former glory. Built by Pisans around 1100, using black and brown basalt, the Romanesque church provided the model for a series of lesser churches in the region. The church was the venue for the marriage in 1239 of Enzo, son of Frederick II of Hohenstaufen, by which he came into possession of the *giudicati* of Torres and Gallura, enabling him to claim the title of king of Sardinia. Though Enzo abandoned wife and island soon afterwards, he clung onto the title, even during the last 23 years of his life in prison in Bologna.

The **interior**, which has frescoed columns, is dominated by a highly ornate sixteenth-century tableau of thirty gilded panels behind the altar, the work of various artists, depicting scenes from the lives of the Virgin Mary, Jesus and various prophets, saints and martyrs. Some of the scenes are colourfully reproduced on the frescoed columns. The church is the focus of an annual costumed **carnival** with horses on July 29.

Sant'Antíoco di Bisarcio

SS597 • Tues–Sun: April–Oct 9.30am–7pm, Nov–March 9am–5pm • €2.50 • ☎ 079 780 257

There's yet another isolated Pisan relic visible about 10km east of Árdara along the SS597: the church of **Sant'Antíoco di Bisarcio**. Built in 1090 and reconstructed in 1170, it was the venue for the coronations of many of Logudoro's *giudici*. Even when closed, the building is worth a circuit to admire the French-style portico, apse, blind arcading and campanile, and for the views over the hills.

Ozieri and around

A signposted turn-off from the SS597 brings you to **OZIERI**, the main centre for this area. Arrayed along a slope that creates a natural amphitheatre, it's a wealthy-looking place, with stuccoed, sometimes faded, Neoclassical houses, though you'll also come across vividly coloured contemporary murals depicting scenes of rural life and the horrors of war. The town's best-known local products are the little almond biscuits known as **suspirus** ("sighs", also called *sospiri*, or *guelfos*), for sale in any of the town's bakeries and most bars.

The town has given its name to a whole era of Sard prehistory, the **Ozieri culture**, which prevailed mainly in the northwest of Sardinia in the fourth and third millennia BC. It is also known as the San Michele culture, after the local grotto where most of the finds identified with it were discovered.

The last Sunday of September sees Ozieri's biggest **festa**, La Sagra della Madonna del Rimédio, during which groups from all over the island participate in medieval chanting and costumed processions.

Museo Archeologico

Piazza P. Micca • Tues–Sat 9am–1pm & 4–7pm, Sun 9.30am–12.30pm • €5, or €6 with grotto • ☎ 079 785 1052

A good selection of finds relating to the Ozieri culture can be seen in the town's **Museo Archeologico**, annexed to the Convento Clarisse, signposted at the top of the town, a few minutes' walk from the main Piazza Garibaldi. Exhibits include the bone jewellery and ceramics painted with a spiral pattern that are characteristic of the culture, as well as nuraghic ornaments, Punic and Roman coins and domestic items from the Middle Ages.

Grotta di San Michele

Piazzale Ospedale • Tues–Sun 10am–1pm & 2–5pm • €3, or €6 with museum • ☎ 079 785 1052

The **Grotta di San Michele**, where many of the finds displayed in Ozieri's archeological museum were unearthed in 1914, lies a walk or brief drive from the museum along the panoramic Viale Vittorio Veneto, on the northern edge of town. The complex of caves consists of little more than a deep hole in the limestone, with connecting tunnels and passages, but guides on hand will fill out the picture with background information.

Cattedrale dell'Immacolata

Via Grixoni • Daily 8am–noon & 4–6pm

In the lower part of town, Ozieri's **Cattedrale dell'Immacolata**, an Aragonese-Gothic structure overladen with Neoclassical and Baroque, merits a brief stop. Inside there's a noteworthy polyptych, the *Madonna di Loreto*, its seven panels painted by the so-called **Maestro di Ozieri**, the foremost Sard painter of the sixteenth century.

ARRIVAL AND DEPARTURE   OZIERI AND AROUND

By bus ARST buses stopping at Piazza Garibaldi provide frequent connections to Sássari (Mon–Sat 8–9 daily, Sun 3 daily; 1hr–1hr 30min) and to the train station of Ozieri-Chilivani, 10km west towards Chilivani, a main junction for passengers between Sássari, Olbia and Cágliari.

ACCOMMODATION

Janas Country Resort Località Baddingusti, SP63 10 ☏ 079 707 9916, ⓦ janashotel.it. There's nowhere special to stay in Ozieri itself, but this hotel-resort a 15min drive west (towards Mores) offers clean and contemporary accommodation surrounded by lawned grounds. Rooms have terraces and wi-fi, and a pool, tennis and horseriding are available. Free pick-up is offered from Ozieri-Chilivani train station. **€85**

Torralba and around

Thirty kilometres south of Sássari, an easy detour from the SS131 takes you to the village of **TORRALBA**, whose only point of interest is a remarkable nuraghic museum, a short distance from one of Sardinia's greatest prehistoric monuments, the Nuraghe Santu Antine.

Museo di Torralba

Via Carlo Felice 153 • Daily: 9am–sunset • €5 • ☏ 079 847 298, ⓦ nuraghesantuantine.it

Easy to find in the centre of the village, the **Museo di Torralba** focuses on the nearby nuraghic complex, with a model on the ground floor, and upstairs some of the seventeen thousand shards of pottery found on the site, testifying to the continuous use of the monument and surrounding area from the twelfth century BC until the Roman era. Other items include ceramic combs, smith's tools and projectiles, while bits and pieces of Phoenician and Greek ware are evidence of extensive trading links. Also on the first floor are Roman columns and capitals, coins and pottery fragments, and there are more Roman finds in the garden, including a collection of inscribed milestones found alongside the Cágliari–Olbia road, the first one built by the Romans on the island.

Nuraghe Santu Antine

Valle dei Nuraghi • Daily 9am–sunset • €5 • ☏ 079 847 410, ⓦ nuraghesantuantine.it

The **Nuraghe Santu Antine** lies just over 4km south of Torralba, in the heart of the so-called Valle dei Nuraghi, an area copiously dotted with the ancient structures. This royal palace is the biggest and most impressive of them – hence its common name *Nuraghe Majore* – and is considered to be technically the finest nuraghic structure on the island. The oldest sections date back to the fifteenth century BC, though the site was continuously worked on and augmented, not least by the Romans.

Note that guided **tours** – though not always in English – and audio-guides in English are available. A bar at the entrance to the site serves snacks, and there's a shop with guides to the *nuraghe* in English. The site lies about a kilometre north of an exit from the SS131.

The central complex

Built of square basalt blocks, the central complex consists of three external bastions, mostly crumbled, connected by a defensive wall and grouped around the original massive three-storey circular tower, with walls up to 5m thick and 17.5m high. The tower is thought to have once reached 21m, before the uppermost of its three circular rooms was demolished in the nineteenth century. Corridors and staircases link the different parts of the tower, and the grounds include a well in an internal courtyard. With its intricate network of steps, ramps, chambers and curving passages, it's a fascinating place to scramble around.

Outlying nuraghi

From the railed area on top, other *nuraghi* are visible among the cultivated fields – though the closest and most perfect specimen is a recent reconstruction. A scattering of circular huts lies around the walls of the main complex, the ruins of the nuraghic village onto which Carthaginian and Roman structures were added.

San Pietro di Sorres

Località Borutta • Daily 9.30am–noon & 3.30–7.30pm

The hilly area north of Torralba holds one of the best preserved of Sardinia's Romanesque churches, the twelfth-century basilica of **San Pietro di Sorres**. Surmounting a bluff with sweeping views over the villages of Bonnanaro and Borutta, and still attached to a Benedictine convent, the former cathedral displays more Tuscan precision than Sardinia's other Pisan churches, while its grand dimensions and ornate style also suggest French influence. The partly striped facade of white and dark grey stone has three levels of blind arcading, each embellished with coloured geometrical motifs and delicate stonework.

The slightly forbidding **interior** is a more emphatic restatement of the two-tone scheme, containing a decorated Gothic pulpit supported by four arches, and an open sarcophagus from the twelfth century, belonging to a local bishop. A wander round to the rear of the building, past the monks' plantations in pinewoods, affords extensive views over the high, cultivated country on every side.

6

Gallura

232 Olbia and around

237 South of Olbia

239 Golfo Aranci

240 Porto Rotondo and around

241 San Pantaleo

241 The Costa Smeralda

244 Baia Sardinia

244 Arzachena and its prehistoric sites

247 Cannigione and around

248 Palau

250 Porto Pollo

250 The Maddalena Islands

255 Santa Teresa Gallura and around

260 Inland Gallura

LA MADDALENA

Gallura

Sardinia's northernmost region, Gallura, is a land of raw granite mountains and startling wind-sculpted rocks, which combine with its extraordinary coastline to imbue the area with a unique edge-of-the-wilderness appeal. The largest town in this mountainous wedge, Olbia, owes its phenomenal growth in the last half-century or so to the annual influx of tourists bound for the numerous holiday spots up and down the coast. With its wide selection of hotels, bars and restaurants, it makes a good temporary base for the region, and has a couple of first-rate sights.

7

South of Olbia, the islands of **Tavolara** and **Molara** are a constant presence off the coast, and can be visited by boat from the modern resort of **Porto San Paolo**. This and **San Teodoro**, farther south, typify the holiday developments hereabouts – deserted for most of the year, and buzzing in summer.

North of Olbia, the port of **Golfo Aranci** has more beaches within a short radius, but glamour-seekers should follow the tide to one of the Mediterranean's loveliest stretches of coast and premier holiday zones, the **Costa Smeralda**. The five-star development of the "Emerald Coast" in the 1960s not only transformed the local economy but also kick-started the tourist industry in the entire island, setting new standards of planned, environment-friendly tourism. On the whole, the devotion to luxury has not compromised the extraordinary natural beauty of the indented rocky coast, but you'll need a full wallet to get the most out of it.

Fortunately, the Costa Smeralda is only a tiny part of Sardinia's northeastern littoral; elsewhere on the coast, it's still possible to have fun without spending stacks of money. Near the inland centre of **Arzachena** – itself worth a visit for the prehistoric sites lying within a short distance – there are miles of shoreline still undeveloped, while offshore the **Maddalena archipelago** consists of over sixty minor islands, which you can explore on boat tours from points along the coast. From the resort of **Palau**, a daily ferry service runs to the archipelago's biggest island and eponymous main town, **La Maddalena**. Linked to this island by a road causeway, **Caprera** has an absorbing museum devoted to Giuseppe Garibaldi, the hero of Italy's independence movement, located in his former home.

West of Palau, the SS125 passes a scintillating succession of bays before reaching **Santa Teresa Gallura**, Sardinia's northernmost point. This port for ferries to Corsica is also one of the island's liveliest holiday centres, within easy reach of some of the most splendid **beaches** anywhere in Italy, cradled in coves and inlets on either side. Sailors and windsurfers have long appreciated the brisk wind conditions in the Straits of Bonifacio, and there are numerous watersports outfits around.

Olbia's festivals p.237
Tavolara and Molara p.238
The making of the Costa Smeralda p.241
Watersports in Porto Pollo p.250
Getting to La Maddalena p.252
Nelson in the Maddalena Islands p.252

Garibaldi on Caprera p.254
Boat tours from Santa Teresa p.258
Summer events in Santa Teresa p.259
Tempio's Carnival p.262
Berchidda's jazz festival p.263
The Bachelors' Feast p.264
A Sardinian vendetta p.265

WINDSURFING AT PORTO POLLO

Highlights

❶ Arzachena's prehistoric remains
Scattered in fields and woods way off the tourist track, nuraghic and pre-nuraghic sites around Arzachena – including a pair of "giants' tombs" – make a refreshing contrast to the more sensory pleasures of the coast. **See pp.244–246**

❷ Wind- or kitesurfing at Porto Pollo Take advantage of the excellent conditions around this resort, which attracts windsurfers and watersports fans of all abilities. **See p.250**

❸ Boating around the Maddalena archipelago Swimming stops feature prominently on any boat tour of these islands off the northern coast, and the views are breathtaking. **See p.253**

❹ Capo Testa's beaches The dramatic granite rockscape west of Santa Teresa Gallura makes a fantastic backdrop for unforgettable swims. **See p.257**

❺ Aggius This traditional Gallura village is home to the region's two best museums: an ethnographic collection, full of unexpected curiosities, and an exhibition focusing on the banditry that flourished hereabouts in the nineteenth century. **See p.264**

HIGHLIGHTS ARE MARKED ON THE MAP ON PP.230–231

GALLURA

HIGHLIGHTS
❶ Arzachena's prehistoric remains
❷ Wind- or kitesurfing at Porto Pollo
❸ Boating around the
   Maddalena archipelago
❹ Capo Testa's beaches
❺ Aggius

N

Bonifacio (Corsica)

Santa Teresa
Gallura

Capo Testa ❹

Rena Maiore

SS 200

Portobello di
Gallura   Vignola

Aglientu   Luogosanto

Costa Paradiso   GALLURA

Ísola Rossa

Trinità
d'Agultu

Badesi Mare

Badesi   Nuraghe
                                Izzana

Castelsardo   Aggius   Nuraghe
                        ❺   Maiori   Luras

                                                Calangia

                        Tempio
                        Pausánia

PROVINCIA DI   *Monte Limbara*
SÁSSARI
                                *Punta Balístr
                                (1359m)*

                        SS127

Sássari

                                        Berchidda

Sássari

                        *Lago
                        Coghinas*

                        Óschiri

Oristano & Cágliari

The ever-present backdrop to this indented shore is the jagged line of granite **mountains**. Hidden within them is a world that most tourists never discover, thickly forested with the **cork oaks** which, after tourism, provide most of Gallura's revenue. Now somewhat isolated from the main currents of life in the region, the grey, granite town of **Tempio Pausania** lies within sight of the pine-clad slopes of the region's highest mountain, **Monte Limbara**, and within easy reach of some of the interior's best walking routes. Excursions can also be made in the bizarre landscape of granite rubble around **Aggius**, northwest of Tempio, and in the cork forests surrounding **Calangianus** to the east.

GETTING AROUND
GALLURA

The **traffic** on Gallura's coastal roads can be unbearably slow, especially in summer when motor-homes add to the congestion already created by trucks bearing massive loads of quarried granite. **Public transport** is adequate for all the towns mentioned here, with a fuller service in summer, but is less useful for the beaches.

By train Olbia is linked to Golfo Aranci by FS trains (☎ 892 021, ⓦ trenitalia.com), while the summer-only Trenino Verde (☎ 070 580 246 or ⓦ treninoverde.com) is operated by ARST to a limited timetable through the mountainous heart of Gallura from Palau to Tempio Pausania – an appealing if somewhat laborious way to see parts of the region you might otherwise miss.

By bus Frequent bus connections link Olbia, Arzachena, Santa Teresa Gallura and Tempio Pausania with the region's other towns and villages. Most services are provided by ARST (☎ 800 865 042, ⓦ arst.sardegna.it), supplemented by Turmo buses (☎ 0789 21 487, ⓦ gruppoturmotravel.com) and, in summer, Sun Lines buses (☎ 348 260 9881).

Olbia and around

When the English barrister John Tyndale visited **OLBIA** in the 1840s, he compared its Greek name, meaning "happy", with the state he found it in: "A more perfect misnomer, in the present condition of the town, could not be found…The whole district suffers severely from *intemperie* [malaria]. The wretched approach across these marshes is worthy of the town itself. The houses, none of which have an elegant or neat appearance, are built mostly of granite, and are whitewashed, as if to give a greater contrast to the filth and dirt within and around them."

Malaria has long vanished, together with the marshes and the filth, as a result of land-drainage schemes and DDT-saturation in the 1950s and the income that tourism has been bringing since the 1960s. Olbia today is once more a happy place, enjoying its new-found prosperity both as the nearest Sardinian port to the mainland and the main gateway to the Costa Smeralda.

Nonetheless, few of the tourists pouring through the docks and airport stay long in town, for Olbia – the least Sardinian of all the island's centres – holds no more character than most transit towns. Past the unsightly ring of apartment blocks, however, is an attractive seafront and a largely traffic-free old centre, whose narrow lanes are lined with bars and restaurants busy with tourists. Partly pedestrianized **Corso Umberto** cuts through the centre of town from the seafront, at the bottom of which is the Art Nouveau **Municipio** (town hall). Apart from an impressive **archeology museum** and the Pisan-Romanesque church of **San Símplicio** – the focus in May for the town's biggest festival – there's little in the way of sights, but it is at least a manageable place, with the bus terminal and train station conveniently located in the centre of town and the airport and ferry port just short bus rides away.

Brief history

Olbia was the first Sardinian town to be taken by the **Romans**, who in 259 BC expelled the Carthaginians who had been established here since the fourth century BC. The great Carthaginian general Hanno was killed in the fighting, and was buried with full military honours by the victorious Lucius Cornelius Scipio. Under Rome, the city expanded and flourished as the only natural port on Sardinia's eastern seaboard, though malaria was almost always prevalent due to the surrounding marshy lagoons.

Having survived numerous Vandal and Saracen raids in the Dark Ages, the town was completely rebuilt by Pisa after 1198. It went on to become one of the principal strongholds of the *giudicato* of Gallura, preserving its independence from Spain until the fifteenth century. Now called **Terranova Pausania** (a name which it retained until 1939), the city suffered complete destruction in 1553 at the hands of the Turkish admiral Dragut, in alliance with France, and half its population was carried away as slaves.

Spain's shift of focus towards its Atlantic empire deprived the port of its prominent role, and Olbia languished. In 1711 the English admiral Norris briefly occupied the city, and six years later an **Austrian army** landed and took possession, intending to march on Alghero. According to the story, however, the priest they commandeered as a guide led them into a trap, and the Austrians were captured and led back to Olbia by a Sardinian force – a triumph of cunning that is still the subject of mirth among the local population.

The last century has seen the arrival of the railway, a good road connecting the port with the SS131 and the eradication of malaria, all of which have helped to restore the fortunes of the city, which today has a population of around 55,000.

Museo Archeologico

Molo Brin • Mon, Tues & Fri–Sun: mid-June to mid-Sept 10am–1pm & 8–11pm; mid-Sept to mid-June 10am–1pm & 5–8pm • Free • ☎ 0789 28 290

Seated on a miniature island by the portside, Olbia's **Museo Archeologico** is housed in a modernist, fortress-like construction surrounded by its own tiny moat. The museum, arranged around an atrium, is well planned and presented, and is destined to hold the area's main archeological treasures, though currently has only scanty items on view. Displays range from Proto-Sard prehistory through to the Carthaginian, Greek and Roman eras, and include a magnificent terracotta head of Hercules wearing a lion's mane – a Roman copy of a Greek original, with a full-size modern replica alongside, garishly painted to approximate to its original appearance. Many of the exhibits were dredged out of the old Roman port of Olbia, located on this very spot. The collection is currently free, but charges will probably be levied once there's a bit more to see. Evening musical performances are occasionally held in the atrium.

Basilica di San Símplicio

Via S. Símplicio • Daily 7am–1pm & 4–8pm

The **basilica di San Símplicio**, set in a piazza apart from Olbia's bustle, formed part of the great Pisan reconstruction programme of the eleventh and twelfth centuries. The best feature of the simple granite structure, the **facade**, was added in the twelfth century, capped by a mullioned window. The nave's narrow windows permit little light to penetrate the murky **interior**, whose two aisles are separated by recycled Roman columns, and even the stoup for the holy water was formerly an urn that held cremated ashes. The church is bare but for two thirteenth-century frescoes in the apse, showing San Simplicio on the left and, on the right, a figure possibly representing Vittore Vescovo, a bishop ordained by Pope Gregory the Great in the sixth century. There are also two carved capitals, Lombard in inspiration, one carved with a human head, the other with that of a ram.

San Paolo

Piazza Civitas • Daily 8am–noon & 4–7pm

Just off Corso Umberto, the church of **San Paolo** is easily recognizable by its tall campanile and multicoloured cupola. The church, built in 1747 on the site of a Punic temple, is typical of its time. Within the unadorned granite-faced exterior, a lovely wooden pulpit of the eighteenth-century Venetian school has inlaid panels and a canopy from which a wooden hand grasping a crucifix is thrust out. The date 1421, engraved on one of the arches of the nave, suggests San Paolo was raised on a site where there was already a church, or else that its builders utilized some material from another church. Otherwise, the interior has quite a modern appearance, its white walls splashed with murals of saints.

Sa Testa

SP82, about 5km west of Olbia towards Golfo Aranci • Daily: March–Oct 11am–7pm; Nov–Feb 11am–3pm • ☎ 348 882 2278 • Take any bus bound for Golfo Aranci or city bus #4 from Via S. Símplicio; drivers should turn right at the Dettori Market shopping complex before the Q8 fuel station

Set in a dry, grassy site below a modern shopping centre outside Olbia, the sacred well of **Sa Testa** dates from the late nuraghic era (eighth–sixth century BC). The well is approached through a circular area bounded by rough-hewn stones – probably a sort of waiting room for devotees who had come to perform their rites. The vestiges of a bench run round the circumference, and there's also rudimentary seating in the small paved recess at the far end, from where seventeen steps lead down to a tholos-shaped chamber holding the spring. It's one of Sardinia's cruder examples of a sacred well – you can see more sophisticated ones at Santa Cristina, near Oristano (see p.157) and Su Tempiesu, near Nuoro (see p.279) – but it makes a pleasant excursion, and a viable destination by bike from Olbia.

Pittulongu

Served by bus #4 from Via San Símplicio, Olbia

A kilometre or two beyond Sa Testa on the Golfo Aranci road, you can cool down with a swim at one of Olbia's favourite bathing spots, **Pittulongu**. The three beaches that make up the resort, La Playa, Lo Squalo and Pellicano, look across the bay to the island of Tavolara, and are lined with bars, with facilities for renting sun-loungers and parasols in summer – they can get very crowded, though.

ARRIVAL AND DEPARTURE

OLBIA

7

BY PLANE

Olbia's Aeroporto di Costa Smeralda (ⓦ olbiairport.it), 3km southeast of town, has frequent flights to and from the Italian mainland, Germany, France and the UK, operated by Air One (☎ 892 444, ⓦ flyairone.com), easyJet (☎ 199 201 840, ⓦ easyjet.com) and Meridiana (☎ 892 928, ⓦ meridiana.it), among other airlines. The airport has a tourist office (see p.236) and banks with ATMs.

Getting into town Buses #2 and #10 leave the airport every 20–30 min until 11.40pm, taking just 10min to reach Via Mameli, at the bottom of Corso Umberto (tickets €1 from the ticket machine in the terminal, €1.50 on board). Taxis into town cost about €20.

Long-distance services There are summer-only bus services from the airport to the resorts of Porto Cervo and Cannigione (4 daily) and to Cala Gonone (4 daily), and a year-round service to Nuoro (3–6 daily); other destinations can be reached from Olbia's centre. If you want to arrive at your coastal destination directly by taxi from the airport, expect to pay around €60 to Arzachena, €80 to Palau.

BY FERRY

Stazione Maríttima Ferries dock at the Stazione Maríttima in Isola Bianca, 2km from the centre; it has ATMs, a left-luggage office (daily 6am–10pm; €2/bag until 10pm) and a bar-restaurant. From here, city bus #9 runs into town twice hourly (€1 from the information office, or €1.50 on board), or you can take one of the infrequent trains to Olbia's main train station in the centre. Buses also run from the Stazione Maríttima to Porto Cervo, Arzachena, Palau, Santa Teresa Gallura, Nuoro and Sássari.

Ferry companies and tickets The Stazione Maríttima holds the ticket offices for Tirrenia (☎ 892 123 or ☎ 02 2630 2803, ⓦ tirrenia.it), Saremar (☎ 0789 23 291, ⓦ saremar .com) and Moby Lines (☎ 199 303 040, ⓦ moby.it) – Sardinia Ferries to Livorno leave from Golfo Aranci, 15km up the coast. You can also pick up tickets (including for Sardinia Ferries from Golfo Aranci) at travel agencies in Olbia, for example Unimare, Corso Umberto 1 (☎ 0789 23

524). Book early for all departures.

Destinations Civitavécchia (Tirrenia, Saremar & Moby; 1–6 daily; 4hr 45min–8hr); Genoa (Tirrenia & Moby; 3–12 weekly; 10hr–15hr 30min); Livorno (Moby; 1–2 daily; 5hr 45min–8hr 30min); Piombino (Moby; June to early Sept 3–6 weekly; 4hr 30min).

BY CAR

Drivers may have to park some distance away from their lodgings; try the large car park by the museum on the seafront, or the small car park off Via Milano near the train station, both free.

BY TRAIN

FS trains from Sássari and Cágliari arrive at the station just off Corso Umberto, with some continuing to the Isola Bianca station for the ferry port. Most journeys to and from Cágliari, Oristano and Sássari involve a change at Ozieri-Chilivani. There are also infrequent departures to the same destinations from the Isola Bianca station. For information, call ☎ 892 021 or visit ⓦ trenitalia.it.

Destinations Cágliari (5–6 daily; 3hr 30min–5hr 30min); Golfo Aranci (5–7 daily; 30min); Oristano (4–5 daily; 2hr 35min); Sássari (5–6 daily; 1hr 50min).

BY BUS

ARST buses (☎ 800 865 042, ⓦ arst.sardegna.it) use the stops on Corso Vittorio Veneto, just past the level crossing at the bottom of Corso Umberto, and most also stop at the airport and at Isola Bianca for the ferry port. Tickets are sold at *Adela Café* on Corso Vittorio Veneto, from inside the Stazione Maríttima at the port and on board the buses at the airport. Summer-only Sun Lines buses for Porto Cervo and Cannigione leave from Piazza Crispi, on the seafront, while Turmo buses, which run year-round services to and from Cágliari and Santa Teresa Gallura, stop outside the Municipio at the bottom of Corso Umberto; buses belonging to both companies also stop at the port and airport.

Destinations Arzachena (11–19 daily; 30–50min); Cágliari (Mon–Sat 1 daily; 4hr 20min); Golfo Aranci (mid-June to mid-Sept 5–8 daily; 25min); Nuoro (4–9 daily; 2hr 35min); Palau (6–17 daily; 1hr 10min); Porto Cervo (June–Sept 4–5 daily; Oct–May Mon–Sat 1 daily; 1hr 35min); Porto San Paolo (3–5 daily; 40min); Posada (Mon–Sat 7–8 daily, Sun 3–7 daily; 1hr 15min–1hr 35min); Santa Teresa Gallura (4–14 daily; 1hr 30min–2hr 15min); San Teodoro (Mon–Sat 7–8 daily, Sun 3–7 daily; 45min–1hr); Sássari (1–2 daily; 1hr 20min–1hr 45min); Tempio Pausania (Mon–Sat 6 daily, Sun 3; 1hr 20min).

GETTING AROUND

By car There are several car rental companies at the airport, including Europcar (☎0789 69 548; also at Via Catello Piro 18 ☎0789 206 074; ⊛europcar.it); Hertz (☎0789 66 024; also at Via Regina Elena 34 ☎0789 28 114; ⊛hertz.com); Maggiore (☎0789 69 457, ⊛maggiore.it); and Pinna (☎0789 69 440, ⊛autonoleggiopinna.it). Expect to pay from around €70/day, which can rise in July and Aug.

By bike or scooter Palarent, at Via Regina Elena 119 (☎0789 24 310, ⊛palarent.it) rents out bikes (€15/day), scooters (€30–40/day) and 700cc motorbikes (€90/day).

By bus For information on Olbia's city buses, consult ASPO at ☎0789 553 800, ⊛aspo.it.

By taxi There are ranks on Corso Umberto, outside the train station (☎0789 22 718), at the port (☎0789 24 999) and at the airport (☎0789 69 150); otherwise call ☎340 580 0416 or ☎320 696 7030.

INFORMATION

Tourist office Information on the city is dispensed at the Municipio at the bottom of Corso Umberto (Mon–Sat 9am–2pm, Aug also Thurs–Sat 5–8pm; ☎0789 52 206, ⊛olbiaturismo.it). The office covering the whole province is at Via Nanni 39 (July & Aug Mon–Fri 9am–1pm & 3–6pm, Sat 9am–1pm; Sept–June Mon–Fri 8am–2pm; ☎0789 557 732, ⊛olbiatempioturismo.it), and there's an information desk at the airport (daily 8am–11.30pm; ☎0789 563 444).

ACCOMMODATION

There's no shortage of **accommodation** in Olbia, though most places are quite pricey. The nearest **campsites** are north of town near the Golfo di Cugnana (see p.240) or south at Porto San Paolo (p.238), both about a 20min drive or bus ride away.

Cavour Via Cavour 22 ☎0789 204 033, ⊛cavourhotel.it. This tasteful modern renovation of a traditional building on a central alley has smart, simply furnished rooms, free parking and wi-fi. The ambience is cool, clean and white. Triples and quadruples also available. **€90**

⭐ **Gallura** Corso Umberto 145 ☎0789 24 648, ☎0789 24 629. Close to the train station, this smart, family-run three-star has an unashamed old-fashioned quality, but the rooms are clean and fully equipped, albeit with smallish bathrooms. The building is full of rustic trimmings, there's a renowned ground-floor restaurant (see opposite), and breakfasts are scrummy. **€80**

⭐ **Janas** Via Lamármora 61 ☎339 109 2836 or ☎349 872 8140, ⊛janasaffittacamere.com. This B&B in a renovated old house has three spacious ground-floor rooms, all with private bathrooms, and one giving on to the shady garden where breakfast is taken. **€70**

⭐ **Panorama** Via Mazzini 7 ☎0789 26 656, ⊛hotel panoramaolbia.it. Classy four-star in the heart of the old town, boasting a roof terrace with sun-loungers and fantastic views, plus spa facilities (€22 per 1hr 30min session) and a gym (free). Rooms are clean and spacious, staff are multilingual and friendly, there's a garage (a bonus in Olbia, and included in the price), and breakfasts are abundant and fresh. **€129**

Porto Romano Via Nanni 2 ☎349 192 7996, ⊛bedand breakfastportoromano.it. Central but quiet B&B, offering two doubles with private or en-suite bathrooms and a self-contained "bedsitter" (costing more) with cooking facilities. There's a patio with a barbecue. No credit cards. **€70**

Terranova Via Garibaldi 3 ☎0789 22 395, ⊛hotel terranova.it. Central hotel, OK for a night or two, but you can do better elsewhere for longer stays. It has comfortable and quiet but otherwise unremarkable rooms with a/c (some with balconies), impersonal service and a restaurant. The car park costs €7 a day. **€85**

EATING AND DRINKING

Self-caterers and picnickers will find everything they need at the Superpan **supermarket** on the seafront, Via Genova (Mon–Sat 8.30am–8.30pm, Sun 8.30am–1.30pm).

Antica Trattoria Via delle Terme 1 ☎0789 24 053. Popular place with a buzzing atmosphere, a tasty array of *antipasti* and sizzling pizzas. There are good-value tourist menus (€15–25) and a small garden for eating alfresco.

Mon–Sat 12.30–2.45pm & 7.15–11.15pm; open daily in Aug.

Caffè Cosimino Piazza Margherita ☎0789 21 001. Good for coffees, fresh *cornetti* and a good selection of

> **OLBIA'S FESTIVALS**
>
> The basilica di San Símplicio is the venue for Olbia's biggest **festa**, three days of processions, costumed dancing, poetry recitals, traditional games and fireworks around May 15, commemorating San Símplicio's martyrdom in the fourth century. The other big local festivals are Sant'Agostino on June 24 and Santa Lucia on the first Sunday of September, both lasting three days. Nightly free **concerts** and other events take place by the water on Molo Brin throughout the summer from late July, as well as performances on Piazza Margherita.

Sardinian wines. Choose a seat on the square or inside, where the walls have faded photos of old Olbia. Daily 7am–midnight.

★**Gallura** Corso Umberto 145 ☎0789 24 648. Attached to the eponymous hotel (see opposite), this is one of the top spots in the region to sample delicious, authentic *gallurese* dishes, with an endless and mostly incomprehensible menu – though the helpful staff will sort you out. You'll have to exercise restraint, though, unless you're aiming for a blow-out; most meat dishes cost around €18, fish (by weight) usually more, and a full meal with wine might set you back at least €80 each. Despite the high prices, the atmosphere is cheerfully informal. Booking essential. Tues–Sun 1–2.30pm & 8–10.30pm.

Il Gámbero Via Lamármora 6 ☎0789 23 874. Brass pots, ceramics and hangings adorn the walls of this centrally located restaurant with a huge fireplace. The fare is mainly seafood, with good *antipasti* including *affumicati di mare* (smoked tuna and swordfish). Count on €50–60 for a full meal for two including drinks. In summer, there are tables outside in the alley. Tues–Sun 12.30–2.30pm & 7.30–10pm, July & Aug open daily.

La Fonte del Gelato Via Regina Elena 12 ☎0789 23 874. Choose from among the thirty-odd flavours of lip-smacking home-made ice cream here, or try the refreshing iced yoghurt. April–Oct daily 9am–12.40pm & 3.30pm–late, Nov & Dec same times, closed Tues.

La Lanterna Via Olbia 13 ☎0789 23 082. Tucked away in an alley off the Corso, this cellar restaurant offers superb pizzas (€8–10) alongside an impressive menu that includes grilled mussels, *fregola sarda* (semolina pasta) and outstanding *antipasti*, all artistically presented. There's a good list of Sard wines, and the home-baked bread is delicious. Try the four-course menu for €30. Daily except Wed 6.30–10.30pm; open daily in Aug.

La Tasca Via Cavour 3 ☎347 853 6185. Handy spot for a daytime sit-down and snack, or to down a cocktail in the evening, when there are DJs and live music. Salads and pizzas are €6–8. June–Sept daily 10am–2am; Oct–May Mon–Sat 10am–midnight.

DIRECTORY

Hospital Via Leonardo da Vinci, Località Tannaule, on the Tempio road ☎0789 552 200. Call ☎118 for an ambulance.

Internet Log on at Intersmeraldo, Via Porto Romano 6b (Mon–Sat 9.45am–8.30pm, closes 1.15–4pm Oct–May; €5/hr). ID required.

Markets General markets take place outside the central area on Via Imperia (Tues morning) and Via Aldo Moro (Sat morning).

Pharmacy Most pharmacies are open 9am–1pm & 4.15–7.35pm, closed on Sat afternoon & Sun, though Lupacciolu on Piazza Margherita stays open weekdays until 8.20pm in summer. Night rotas are posted on pharmacy doors or in the local newspaper.

Post office Main office at Piazza Mercato (Mon–Fri 8.25am–7.10pm, Sat 8.25am–12.35pm).

Travel agent Avitur, Corso Umberto 142b ☎0789 24 327; Unimare, Corso Umberto 1 ☎0789 23 524.

South of Olbia

The coastal stretch **south of Olbia** has rapidly grown from a wilderness of rock and scrub to become a favourite with Olbians and other holidaymakers who throng the area's beaches every summer. The cubic pink and coral-coloured constructions that have sprouted haphazardly in the last couple of decades have blighted much of the landscape, though the seaward view remains unaltered, dominated by the dramatically looming profiles of the islands of **Tavolara** and **Molara**. You can visit them from **Porto San Paolo**, a resort village 14km south of Olbia, catering like other holiday centres along this coast mainly to families. Farther south, **San Teodoro** is more of the same, a bland colony of bungalows interspersed with hotels and campsites near a wonderful beach.

Porto San Paolo and around

The biggest centre on the coast south of Olbia, **PORTO SAN PAOLO** is a modern settlement that's pretty dull for most of the year but attracts a lively crowd of Olbians and Italian holidaymakers in summer. There's a sandy **beach** here but the best ones are a short distance to either side. A couple of kilometres north, **Porto Istana** is a sandy bay with calm waters sheltered by the hulking form of Tavolara, with sun-loungers to rent and a bar open in summer. From here, it's an easy excursion to **Capo Ceraso**, the southern tip of the Golfo di Olbia, where you'll find more good beaches among the thick growth of *macchia* and pink rocks. A stairway once used to reach a World War II gun emplacement leads from here to the top of **Monte Mandriolo** (126m), affording outstanding views across to Tavolara and north to Capo Figari.

Three kilometres south of Porto San Paolo, there's good swimming at **Porto Taverna**, but more seclusion another kilometre or so farther down on the curly cape known as **Capo Coda Cavallo** – "horse's tail" – which enjoys spectacular views across to Molara.

7

ARRIVAL AND INFORMATION

PORTO SAN PAOLO AND AROUND

By car Drivers should note that they have to head inland on the Nuoro road, then turn off at signs for Murta Maria, to reach Porto San Paolo and other points along this coast (the old SS125 south of the airport is closed to traffic).
By bus Porto San Paolo can be reached on a good ARST

service from Olbia (3–5 daily; 40min), while Porto Istana is the last stop on the #5 local bus route from Olbia's centre (4–6 daily; 1hr 10min).
Tourist office Via Pietro Nenni (June–Sept daily 9am–1pm & 5–10pm; ☎ 0789 40 012).

ACCOMMODATION

Cala Cavallo Località Cala Cavallo ☎ 0784 834 156, ⓦ calacavallo.it. On the cape, this shady and well-equipped

campsite has its own pool and tennis courts, and four-bed caravans (€55) and bungalows (€88) to rent. Closed mid-Sept

TAVOLARA AND MOLARA

Rising sheer above the flat coast east of Olbia, the islands of **Tavolara** and **Molara** make rewarding destinations for a day-trip from Porto San Paolo. Boat excursions combine close-up views of these tall eruptions of rock with opportunities to swim in crystal-clear waters from one of the beaches around their sides.

Tavolara is the more impressive of the two islands: a giant wedge 4km long and 1km wide, its precipitous walls towering to a height of 564m. Peregrine falcons and storm petrels are among the rare birds to look out for here. Its eastern flank is a military zone and off-limits, but the western side, which is inhabited and even has a cemetery, is freely accessible, and there's a good beach at Spalmatore di Terra on the southern tip. In summer, there are bars and a couple of restaurants, *La Corona* (☎ 0789 36 695 or ☎ 347 378 8432) and *Da Tonino* (☎ 0789 58 570), for which advance booking is required. The island hosts an open-air **film festival** of non-mainstream Italian movies, screened on the beach during five nights in mid-July. Special boat excursions ferry ticket-holders to and from the alfresco arena. For dates and times, contact the tourist office at Olbia or Porto San Paolo, or visit ⓦ cinematavolara.it.

In contrast to calcareous Tavolara, the smaller, circular isle of **Molara** is composed of granite, and covered with wild olive trees. On its eastern shore, at Cala di Chiesa, are the remains of a medieval village, **Gurguray**, with the shell of a church, San Ponziano. Molara is a protected area with limited landings; there are no refreshments so if you do visit, bring food and drink along.

At Easter and between May and September, **boats** to Tavolara set off from Porto San Paolo's Pontile della Marina every half-hour or hour from 9am until 1.30pm, with returns from 1pm to 6.30pm (you can choose to come back at any time throughout the afternoon); return **tickets** are around €15. There's a less frequent service to Molara, and some operators also make a stop at **Piana**, a tiny rock just big enough to hold a lovely sandy beach. There are also **longer cruises** around all the isles, with swimming stops, costing around €30. These currently depart daily from Porto San Paolo (May–Sept) at 9.30am and 3pm, with returns from Tavolara at 12.15pm, then 3–6pm, as you choose. For more information on all excursions, ask at the kiosk by the port or call ☎ 349 446 5993.

to May. Pitches €35

★ **Camping Tavolara** Località Porta Taverna ☎ 0789 40 166, ⓦ camping-tavolara.it. Three kilometres south of Porto San Paolo lies this excellent campsite close to the beach of Porto Taverna. It's friendly and well maintained, and offers caravans to rent, use of a tennis court and a diving centre; the site is around 500m from the beach, linked in summer by a shuttle service. Closed Nov–March. Pitches €28

Castello di Tavolara Via Tavolara 2 ☎ 0789 480 012, ⓦ hotelcastelloditavolara.com. Most of the vacationing on this coast takes place in holiday apartments, but there's one good-quality, central hotel in Porto San Paolo that stays open all year (with prices falling sharply outside the peak months), though there's a minimum three-night stay in summer. Rooms are swish, breakfasts are abundant and it's a stone's throw from the beach. €140

EATING

★ **La Conchiglia** Viale Don Sturzo 29 ☎ 0784 40 158. With plastic chairs and a bustling atmosphere, this place at the southern end of the resort on the SS125 lacks airs, but delivers huge helpings of home-made pastas (one portion is enough for two) and such tasty dishes as *cozze ala marinara*. You'll pay €25–35 each for two courses, and pizzas are also available. March–Sept daily

12.30–2.30pm & 7.30–11pm; closed Tues lunch except June–Sept.

S'Anticu Griglieria Via Raffaelle Sanzio 23 ☎ 347 668 8999. Superb grilled meats and local wine are served here, outside the village off the SS125. It's got a smart rustic feel and friendly service. *Primi* are €9–12, *secondi* €10–18. Daily noon–2.30pm & 7–11pm; closed Wed Oct–Easter.

San Teodoro

Fourteen kilometres south of Porto San Paolo, past the long **Stagno di San Teodoro** lagoon, used by wading flamingos and cranes, **SAN TEODORO** is another popular beach resort, its modern villas, bars and restaurants thickly planted behind the **Cala d'Ambra** beach. There's another great beach north of town on **La Cinta**, a long bar of sand separating the lagoon from the sea. **Diving** is possible at various points along this coast, and **windsurfing** is also much in evidence in summer, especially from La Cinta.

ACCOMMODATION   SAN TEODORO

San Teodoro Via del Tirreno ☎ 0784 865 777, ⓦ camping santeodoro.com. One of San Teodoro's two campsites, this lies north of the centre with direct access to La Cinta beach,

with plenty of shade, and bungalows sleeping four (€105) for weekly rental, but no pool or restaurant (there's one 80m distant). Closed mid-Oct to April. Pitches €30

Golfo Aranci

The Golfo di Olbia reaches its northern extent at **GOLFO ARANCI**, a major port whose picturesque name – "Gulf of Oranges" – belies the down-to-earth reality. If you've crossed over from Livorno, this may well be your first landing in Sardinia, but otherwise there's no strong reason to venture here – it's not a particularly inspiring town, nor a great foretaste of what Sardinia has in store. Much of the long peninsula on which the town stands has been invaded by the uniform holiday villas that have become increasingly dominant along this stretch of coast, though the blandness of the architecture is compensated by the ever exuberant vegetation, with bougainvillea, tiger lily and hibiscus injecting a tropical brilliance to the granite rock. It's also a cheaper and calmer alternative to the glittery bustle of Olbia, and has a couple of good beaches and even, in the hills behind, a nature reserve that is overlooked by most visitors.

The town and beaches

If Golfo Aranci has any centre, it's the port and train station, next to each other at its eastern end. Just a few metres from here is the town's only item of historical interest, the **Pozzo Sacro Milis**, a rough-hewn nuraghic sacred well with steps, whose location close to the railway tracks strips it of much atmosphere. There's a fine, sandy **beach** near the centre off Via Colombo, though the best bathing spots lie to the south, round the curve of the **Golfo degli Aranci**, where Cala Sássari includes several small sandy coves, one of which, **Sos Aranzos**, lent its name to both the gulf and the port and has beautifully limpid water. Other beaches worth seeking out include the aptly named **Cala Banana**, signposted off the Olbia road, and dune-backed **Cala Sabina**, on the northern side of the peninsula.

A *sagra di pesce*, or **fish festival**, takes place on August 14, when seafood and wine are doled out to all and sundry.

Capo Figari

Behind the town rears the immense mass of rock occupying **Capo Figari**, a protected area where thick *macchia* is interlaced with holm oaks and junipers. A few of Sardinia's long-horned **mouflons** (wild sheep) have been reintroduced here and on the offshore islet of Figarolo, whose steep slopes are visible, similarly clad in *macchia* and twisted olives.

7

ARRIVAL AND DEPARTURE   GOLFO ARANCI

By ferry Sardinia Ferries (☎ 199 400 500 or ☎ 0789 46 780, ⓦ sardiniaferries.com) operates crossings to and from Livorno all year (4–9 weekly; 6hr 30min–10hr 30min). For approximate costs, see Basics (p.25); it's worth asking about any possible reductions on return crossings, such as last-minute or advance bookings. Book early for sailings in high season.

By train Golfo Aranci is connected with Olbia by infrequent trains (3–5 daily; 25min); the station is right by the port.

By bus A summer bus service links Golfo Aranci to Olbia (mid-June to mid-Sept 5–8 daily; 25min).

ACCOMMODATION AND EATING

La Lámpara Via Magellano 3 ☎0789 615 140, restaurant ☎346 418 5086, ⓦlalamparahotel.com. Small, bright hotel, 500m from the port and just steps from the town beach, with clean, simple rooms and friendly staff. The good restaurant here is open to all, with a relaxed atmosphere and tasty seafood dishes (mains €10–14), including wonderful spaghetti with crab sauce. Easter–Sept noon–3pm & 7–11pm. €120

La Spígola Via Colombo 19 ☎0789 46 286. Right on the town beach, this is probably the best choice in town for home-made pasta, the freshest fish, good pizzas and unrivalled sea views. First courses cost €8–12, mains €15–18. Snack lunches are available too, and the owner speaks perfect English. April–Sept daily noon–3pm & 7–11pm.

Porto Rotondo and around

Built in 1963 in the wake of the Costa Smeralda's development, **PORTO ROTONDO**'s rows of orange villas snake remorselessly over the *macchia*-covered hills, grouped more thickly around the round marina. Chic boutiques and fashion shops set the tone in central Piazzetta San Marco, from which a wide stairway leads up to the modern granite church of **San Lorenzo**. A few metres away, there's a modern open-air theatre, also granite, where entertainments are staged in summer.

But the best feature of the place is the proximity of a number of fabulous **beaches**, though these can get overwhelmed in high season. On **Punta della Volpe**, the thin headland north of Porto Rotondo, try **Spiaggia Sassi**, which has a bar, parking and sunbeds to rent, or **Cugnana**, with less in the way of facilities but more seclusion. In summer the beaches are connected by a minibus service.

ACCOMMODATION   PORTO ROTONDO AND AROUND

Camping Cugnana Località Cugnana ☎0789 33 184, ⓦcampingcugnana.it. Although this three-star campsite gets very crowded, it offers excellent facilities, including a generous pool. Bungalows are available (€500/week), and there's a pizzeria/restaurant and minimarket. It lies 2km from the beach at Marina di Cugnana, and a minibus shuttles campers to this and some of the Costa Smeralda's best beaches. ARST and Sun Lines buses between Olbia and Porto Cervo stop right outside. To reach it by car, backtrack some 10km from Porto Rotondo towards the SS125 and turn right onto the Porto Cervo road before reaching the highway. Closed mid-Oct to March. Pitches €23.60

San Pantaleo

With its backdrop of granite peaks, the village of **SAN PANTALEO**, 5km inland of the Costa Smeralda, has caught some of the airs of that fabled jetsetters' haunt but still provides a refreshing antidote to its brasher excesses. It's prettiest around its spacious, pedestrianized central piazza, where a few bars and craft shops look across to a simple granite church. The square makes a great venue for concerts and festivals throughout the summer – the village's **saint's day** is celebrated around July 26, while Thursday sees a busy **market** of crafts, clothes and trinkets.

ACCOMMODATION AND EATING   SAN PANTALEO

Café Nina Piazza Vittorio Emanuele ☎ 338 368 7288. Chic little wine-bar on San Pantaleo's piazza, perfect for a beer or apéritif. Snacks are also served – a cold meat and cheese platter costs €10. March–Oct daily 7am–late.

Locanda Sant'Andrea Via Zara 36 ☎ 0789 65 205, ⚲ locandasantandrea.com. Upmarket lodging that has all the sophistication of the Costa Smeralda without its pretensions. Artistically designed, it's small – just twelve pastel-hued rooms – with a high-ceilinged, quality restaurant and a courtyard pool surrounded by bougainvillea. **€150**

The Costa Smeralda

The **Costa Smeralda** is a strictly defined 10km strip on the western shore of the Golfo di Cugnana, beginning some 12km north of Olbia. Protected by rigorous building regulations, the natural beauty of the granite littoral and the cleanliness and transparency of the sea are striking, though the coastline can hardly be described as pristine, with ribbons of red-tiled holiday chalets spreading over some areas, interspersed with a luxury golf course or two. The few centres flaunt an air of exclusivity, notably **Porto Cervo**, the only "town" on this stretch of coast, and the place to be if you want to mingle with the in-crowd. Other parts have a bland, almost suburban feel about them, however – don't

> ## THE MAKING OF THE COSTA SMERALDA
>
> Occupying an iconic, almost mythic role in Sardinia's international profile, the Costa Smeralda has even evolved its own legendary back-story, according to which the **Aga Khan** Prince Karim IV, Imam and spiritual leader of the Ismaili Muslims, first stumbled upon the charms of this idyllic coast in 1958, when his yacht took shelter from a storm in one of its narrow creeks. Whatever the truth of the legend, four years later the fabulously wealthy tycoon was leading a consortium of businessmen with the aim of developing this wild coastal strip. The first step was acquiring the land, and local farmers were easily persuaded to part with their largely uncultivable properties – though stories have circulated ever since of the stratagems used to dupe the locals into selling their land for a fraction of its value.
>
> The consortium's plans were on a massive scale, limited only by the conditions imposed by the regional government. These included proper sewage treatment and disposal, restrictions on building and the insistence that the appearance of the landscape should not be unduly changed. Multistorey hotels, advertising hoardings, fast-food restaurants and even garish filling stations were banned, only local building materials could be used for new constructions, and only indigenous vegetation planted – so that pines, eucalyptus and poplars, for example, were banished in favour of oleander, mimosa, arbutus and myrtle.
>
> By the end of the 1960s, the development included VIP-class hotels, a prestigious golf course and the yacht marina at Porto Cervo, and had become a by-word for wealth and luxury, in turn putting Sardinia on the tourist map. The original consortium sold their stake in the Costa Smeralda in 1994 – the majority holding is currently with the **emir of Qatar** – but the coast's cachet among the rich and famous has if anything increased, and various royals, Hollywood stars, Russian oligarchs and super-models continue to spend leisure time here, though usually in guarded seclusion – as is the case of playboy and ex-prime minister **Silvio Berlusconi**, whose Villa Certosa here was the scene of notorious "bunga-bunga" parties, and hosted Tony and Cherie Blair, among others.

expect to find anything like a genuine fishing community surviving hereabouts, nor even the lively local markets you'll see in other parts of Sardinia.

Shorn of the disorderly and spontaneous, the Costa Smeralda might lack the local touch, but this does not discourage the waves of holidaymakers who flood the **beaches** dotted along the indented coast every summer. Even with the crowds, these beaches rank among Sardinia's finest, though they sometimes require a little perseverance and a good set of car springs to reach. The best advice is to follow any dirt track – the rougher it is, the more promising – down to the sea. The most popular places are signposted, and these are the ones with bars, toilets, sun-loungers and other facilities.

Porto Cervo and around

To soak up the full flavour of the Costa Smeralda, you could start at its northern end with a wander around **PORTO CERVO**, the "capital", with most of the shops and facilities. Here, the scale of the tidy, pastel-coloured architecture characteristic of the region becomes almost surreal – more virtual "Mediterranean village" than authentic resort. The main activities consist of window-shopping in the likes of Gucci, Versace, Prada and Cartier, eyeballing the incredibly grand yachts at the marina and sipping the obligatory apéritif in the **Piazzetta** – a panoramic terrace at the heart of this warren of paths and passages and the place to lounge in style. A small beer at one of the bars here starts from €12, though the price includes a front-row seat for people-watching.

Steps lead down from the Piazzetta to the **Sottopiazza**, an area of posh boutiques and classy craft shops. Elsewhere, you'll find banks, phones, pharmacies, travel agents, estate agents and a supermarket

The marina

Nearly a kilometre west of the Piazzetta, Porto Cervo's huge yacht **marina** merits a look, awash with the ostentatious baubles of the ultra-rich. The marine facilities are the most expensive in Sardinia, and reputedly the best, with berths for seven hundred vessels, each with electricity and fresh water supplies. In odd-numbered years, antique sailing boats gather here during the first days of September, usually followed by a race in the Straits of Bonifacio.

Stella Maris
Via Stella Maris • Daily 9am–dusk

The marina's gleaming ranks of yachts are overlooked from a height by the **Stella Maris** church, a rough-textured, whitewashed building which houses a seventeenth-century organ and – surprisingly – a *Mater Dolorosa* by El Greco, the bequest of a Dutch aristocrat. The church was designed in 1968 by Roman architect Michele Busiri Vici, who was also responsible for the grotto-like shopping arcade in Porto Cervo's centre.

Liscia di Vacca

You'll need your own transport to get to the sequestered **beaches** around Porto Cervo, only a few of which are clearly marked. A couple of kilometres northwest of the resort, one of the best is at **Liscia di Vacca**, an exquisite bay at the end of a long, bumpy dirt road, with deck chairs to hire and bars for refreshments in season.

Cala di Volpe and around

The bay of **Cala di Volpe**, 6km south of Porto Cervo, holds a concentration of some of Italy's most select hotels as well as the eighteen-hole, 72-par **Pévero golf course**, spread out across a rolling expanse of green. It's one of Europe's most prestigious, the creation of architect Robert Trent Jones. Some of the area's most popular beaches lie within a short distance: to the northeast, **Cappriccioli** and **Romazzino**, facing the offshore islands of Soffi and Mortorio, and, off Via degli Asfodeli on the road to Romazzino, the smaller **Spiaggia del Príncipe**, said to be named after the Aga Khan; south of Cala di Volpe, **Liscia Ruja** is the biggest beach on the Costa Smeralda, with white sand and the full range of facilities but not too many people. In season, parking costs around €2 per hour.

ARRIVAL AND DEPARTURE

By bus Porto Cervo is served by ARST and, in summer, Sun Lines buses.
Destinations Arzachena (Mon–Sat 4–7 daily; 25–40min);

THE COSTA SMERALDA

Baia Sardinia (June–Sept 4 daily; 10min); Olbia (Mon–Sat 5–11 daily, Sun June–Sept 4 daily; 25min–1hr 10min); Porto Rotondo (June–Sept 4 daily; 35min).

GETTING AROUND

By car You're best off having your own wheels to reach the beaches and other spots along the Costa Smeralda. You can rent a small car for around €60–75 a day from Europcar, Via della Marina 104, Porto Cervo (📞0789 957 085, 🖥europcar.it).
By bike or scooter Bikes and scooters can be rented from

Treforsail, Località Abbiadori (📞0789 971 057, 🖥treforsail.it). Bikes are €12/day, scooters €35–50/day, and quadbikes and dinghies are also available.
By taxi Porto Cervo always has taxis available outside the *Cervo Hotel* (📞0789 92 250). For other places call 📞0789 96 023 or 📞368 351 9386.

INFORMATION

Tourist information The Costa Smeralda has no tourist office, but you'll find limited – and often outdated – information on the websites 🖥portocervo.net and

🖥consorziocostasmeralda.com. Otherwise consult the tourist office at Arzachena (see p.247).

ACCOMMODATION

Even three-star hotels have five-star prices on the Costa Smeralda. Cheaper alternatives lie close by, in Arzachena (see p.247), Baia Sardinia (see p.244) and San Pantaleo (see p.241), and there's a fully-equipped campsite at Cugnana (see p.240).

Cala di Volpe Cala di Volpe 📞0789 976 111, 🖥caladivolpe.com. One of the Costa Smeralda's most stylish hotels, designed by celebrated architect Jacques Couelle in the 1960s and looking from the outside something like an adobe Moorish fortress. The interior is all swooping lines and grand vistas over the lawns and magnificent pool framed by the idyllic bay (there's another pool on the roof). From the hotel's marina, a boat whisks guests to a private beach. The food is gourmet-class, and

though the prices are daunting you'll often find big discounts on the internet. Closed late Sept to mid-May. **€545**
Dolce Vita Località Liscia di Vacca 📞0789 91 855, 🖥hotel-dolcevita.it. This small four-star hotel lies a kilometre or so from Porto Cervo's marina and a 20min walk from Pitrizza beach. Rooms have hints of *gallurese* decor, there's a diminutive pool area, and restaurants are also within walking distance. Closed Oct–May. **€179**

EATING, DRINKING AND NIGHTLIFE

Billionaire Località Sottovento 📞0789 94 192, 🖥billionairelife.com. If you want to mix with the glitterati, head to the cluster of classy nightclubs a couple of kilometres south of Porto Cervo, none more ostentatious than this haunt of models, TV presenters and footballers' wives, owned by Flavio Briatore of Benetton and Formula 1 racing fame. Dress up, and expect a steep entrance fee. There are also two swanky restaurants here. July & Aug daily 10pm–late.
Il Peperone Via Cerbiatta, Porto Cervo 📞0789 907 049. Near the Piazzetta on the corner of Via Sa Conca, this pizzeria/ristorante has live music and a veranda. The *porcetto allo spiedo* (roast sucking pig) is especially good, and the pizzas are authentic. Set-price menus are €20 and €30; cover charge is high at €4 per person. Easter–Oct daily noon–4pm & 8pm–midnight.
Lord Nelson Piazza della Marina, Porto Cervo Marina

📞392 695 4921. Beneath a black-and-white, Pisan-style tower on the harbourfront, this pub makes a pleasant place to spend an evening, with live music Thurs–Sun (mainly rock and Latino) and a menu of sandwiches, burgers and a €10 "English breakfast" every morning. May–Oct daily 7am–3am.
Yachting Piazza della Marina, Porto Cervo Marina 📞0789 94 206. Given that this place decked out all in white calls itself a fashion café and occupies a fabulous location overlooking the yachts, it's somewhat surprising to find that it serves decent food at non-extortionate prices. The *pasta all'astice* (with lobster sauce) is a dream. Also good for breakfast, salads, pizzas (at lunchtime too) and a great choice of ices. *Primi* are mostly €15–20, *secondi* around €25, and there's a €20 tourist menu. June to mid-Sept daily noon–11pm.

7

Baia Sardinia

West of Porto Cervo, just outside the controlled zone of the Costa Smeralda though sharing its elite ethos, the headland and modern resort of **BAIA SARDINIA** has a scattering of high-class hotels discreetly hidden among the granite boulders. On the Cannigione road, the Aquadream amusement park is a hit with kids (mid-June to early Sept daily 10am–7pm; €18, children €12; ⊚aquadream.it), though the main attraction is the **beach** below the headland.

ACCOMMODATION   BAIA SARDINIA

Costa Smeralda Località Lu Comitoni ☎ 0789 99 811, ⓦ bbcostasmeralda.com. A kilometre outside the centre on the Porto Cervo road (ask for directions beforehand), this dainty B&B offers reasonable rates for its three spacious rooms, with the owner's art on the walls and stunning views of sea and mountain from the terrace. Breakfast is a cornucopia of home-made treats, and there's free wi-fi. Closed Nov–Feb. **€110**

Arzachena and its prehistoric sites

Outside the luxury zone but enjoying many of the Costa Smeralda's natural advantages, the **Golfo di Arzachena** is a deep, narrow bay whose western shore holds most of the tourist facilities. **ARZACHENA** itself is inland and lacks the glamour of the nearby upscale resorts, though it has some excellent eating and sleeping options; its old centre has character and it's close to two of the biggest and best-preserved nuraghic "giants' tombs" on the whole island.

At the centre of town, **Piazza Risorgimento** is the venue for nightly entertainments in summer and the centre of a **market** on Wednesday mornings. Nearby, take a look at the **Roccia Il Fungo**, or "mushroom rock" (also called *Monti Incappidatu*), one of Gallura's weathered natural sculptures, conspicuous on a rise at the end of Via Limbara, a short walk from the piazza. Fragments found here suggest that it provided shelter to Neolithic and nuraghic folk; there's no doubting its choice location, commanding extensive views up and down the coast.

Nuraghe Albucciu

Località Albucciu · Easter–Oct daily 9am–sunset; Nov–Easter book visits · €3, €5 for any two of the sites or €7.50 for three · ☎ 340 820 9749, ⓦ anemos-arzachena

From Arzachena, follow the SS125 2km southeast to **Nuraghe Albucciu**, nestled in an olive grove by the side of the road. It's one of Gallura's best-preserved nuraghic monuments, with one chamber, on the right of the main corridor, still roofed and intact. Near the entrance to the *nuraghe*, you can just make out a groove that was probably made by a device for sealing the door. Linked by sight to other *nuraghi* in the area, the structure is built on an almost rectangular plan, and still displays the jutting supports for the vanished wooden roof.

Tempietto Malchittu

Località Malchittu · Easter–Oct daily 9am–sunset; Nov–Easter book visits · €3, €5 for any two of the sites or €7.50 for three · ☎ 340 820 9749, ⓦ anemos-arzachena

Behind the ticket and tourist office outside Nuraghe Albucciu, a pleasant track (not for cars) winds north for less than 2km through fields and around hills to **Tempietto Malchittu**, dating from the first nuraghic phase (between 1500 and 1200 BC) and now overgrown with trees and scrub. The roofless ruin was probably a place of worship and possibly a sacrificial site, its granite walls enclosing two rooms connected by a low doorway. If you want to carry on walking, tracks continue into the *macchia*.

Coddu Vecchiu

Località Capichera • Easter–Oct daily 9am–sunset; Nov–Easter book visits • €3, €5 for any two of the sites or €7.50 for three • ☎ 335 127 6849 or ☎ 335 127 6851

Four and a half kilometres south of Arzachena, on the road to Sant'Antonio di Gallura, branch right onto the Luogosanto road and turn left after another 2km to reach the site of **Coddu Vecchiu** (or *Coddu Echju*), one of the most complete of Sardinia's so-called *tombe dei giganti* ("giants' tombs") consisting of carved granite slabs laid end-up in a semi-circular, or bull-horn-shaped, formation. Their popular name was given by people who were clearly mystified by the enigmatic objects but they are now known to be collective burial chambers and places of worship.

The central stele, over 4m tall, resembles an immense doorway, probably symbolizing the entry into another world. The low opening at the base, which would presumably have been sealed after burial, leads into two long chambers. Excavations here have thrown up evidence that members of the older Bonnanaro culture also used this site, and that it was later adapted by the nuraghic people.

La Prisgiona

Località Capichera • Easter–Oct daily 9am–sunset; Nov–Easter book visits • €3, €5 for any two of the sites or €7.50 for three • ☎ 393 914 7992

A kilometre along the minor road past Coddu Vecchiu brings you to a monument that was possibly associated with that *tomba dei giganti*, **La Prisgiona** (also known as *Nuraghe Capichera*). Built at any time between 2000 and 1000 BC on a height overlooking the whole Arzachena plain, this trilobate (three-sided) construction has a central tower 6.5m tall, surrounded by three smaller towers and the very sparse remains of an external wall. Three niches survive in the main chamber (which is not central in respect of the tower itself), there's a well in the space between the rampart and the wall, and huts have been excavated in the vicinity, with work ongoing.

Li Lolghi

Località Li Muri • Easter–Oct daily 9am–sunset; Nov–Easter book visits • €3, €5 for any two of the sites or €7.50 for three • ☎ 335 127 6849 or ☎ 335 127 6851

You can reach two more of Arzachena's prehistoric sites by continuing west along the Luogosanto road for nearly 3km, making a right turn and keeping right for another couple of kilometres. Just off this track on the left, the giants' tomb **Li Lolghi** has a lower central stele than Coddu Vecchiu, but its inner chamber is nearly twice as long, and is considered to be the finest example of its type in Gallura. Again, the small arched doorway leads into a passage containing the two chambers where bodies were laid.

Li Muri

Località Li Muri • Easter–Oct daily 9am–sunset; Nov–Easter book visits • €3, €5 for any two of the sites or €7.50 for three • ☎ 335 127 6849 or ☎ 335 127 6851

From Li Lolghi it's a short distance to the oldest of Arzachena's sites, **Li Muri**, a site of wild grandeur, reached by backtracking for a couple of hundred metres to take the left-hand (west) fork off the track leading from the Luogosanto road. The track gets pretty rough, so drivers should leave their vehicles at the first suitable spot and proceed on foot, unless they have a 4WD.

The **stone circles** that make up the site constituted a third-millennium BC necropolis once thought to belong to a so-called "Arzachena culture" – probably a variation of the Ozieri culture (3400–2700 BC). Each of the five central circles (5–8m in diameter) contained a body interred in a crouching position together with votive offerings, while smaller circles dating from a subsequent period are distinguished by a double row of stones with better-worked sides. These were probably used in funerary rites, possibly for the skinning of the corpse before burial.

ARRIVAL AND GETTING AROUND

By car Driving, you can reach Arzachena from Olbia in about 30min on the SS125.

By train Arzachena's train station is about 1km west of town, served by diesel trains operated by ARST between late June and mid-Sept (currently Wed–Sat) on the scenic Tempio Pausania–Palau line.

Destinations Calangianus (Wed–Sat 1 daily; 1hr 10min); Palau (Wed–Fri 1–2 daily; 20min); Sássari (Fri 1 daily; 3hr 30min); Tempio Pausania (Wed–Sat 1–2 daily; 1hr 20min).

By bus ARST services run to most places along the coast,

ARZACHENA AND ITS PREHISTORIC SITES

and there are daily Turmo connections to Olbia, Palau and Santa Teresa. In Arzachena, buses pull up on Via San Pietro, off Via Dettori (the road signposted for Luogosanto). Buy tickets at *Bar Castello*, Via Dettori 43.

Destinations Cannigione (3–13 daily; 10min); Olbia (8–19 daily; 45min); Palau (5–14 daily; 20min); Porto Cervo (Mon–Sat 4–7; 25–40min); Santa Teresa Gallura (6–12 daily; 1hr).

By taxi If you want to take a taxi from Arzachena to any of the nuraghic sites, you'll find ranks on Via Dettori (☎ 0789 96 023) and off the central Piazza Risorgimento (☎ 0789 82 900).

INFORMATION

Tourist office The main information office is at Piazza Risorgimento 8 (Mon–Thurs 9am–2pm & 4–7pm or 3–6pm in winter, Fri & Sat 9am–2pm; ☎ 0789 844 055, ⍟ arzachena -costasmeralda.it); there's also an office outside town at Malchittu, between Arzachena and Cannigione (Mon–Sat

9am–2pm & 3–6pm; ☎ 0789 83 306).

Post office Viale Costa Smeralda 159 (Mon–Fri 8.25am–7.10pm, Sat 8.25am–12.35pm); you can change cash here or at any of the banks on Viale Costa Smeralda, all with ATMs.

ACCOMMODATION

Il Vecchio Ginepro Sotgiu Pietruccia ☎ 347 388 3557, ⍟ ilvecchioginepro.it. About 1km west of the centre, reached from Via Mameli or the bypass, this traditional B&B on a farm has five independent suites giving onto gardens, each with a fridge, and three with kitchenettes. Breakfast includes home-produced salamis and jams, goat's milk and cheese. No credit cards. **€100**

★ **L'Abba Maistra** Località Nicola Calta ☎ 0789 844 092 or ☎ 338 212 9548, ⍟ labbamaistra.com. Utterly tranquil *agriturismo* in a stone-walled *stazzo* (traditional *gallurese* rural dwelling), 8km west of town off the Bassacutena road. The five spacious, en-suite rooms are furnished with antiques, and there's a small pool amid the rocks. It's a little hard to find, best reached in daylight. No credit cards. Closed Oct–March. **€80**

Lu Pastruccialeddu Località Lu Pastruccialeddu

☎ 0789 81 777 or ☎ 340 814 6330, ⍟ pastruccialeddu .com. In granite-walled converted farm buildings, this B&B lies in open country 2km north of Arzachena (turn right at the Despar supermarket heading west out of town). The rooms, including junior suites and a family apartment, have a rustic Sardinian feel. Generous breakfasts are alfresco and include home-made yoghurt and home-baked cakes and pies, and there's a small pool. Closed Jan & Feb. **€100**

★ **Santa Lucia** Via Cágliari 11 ☎ 0789 83 012 or ☎ 338 269 3640, ⍟ bbslucia.it. This B&B in a beautifully renovated old townhouse lies in a quiet backstreet in the centre of town, with a minimalist walled garden where breakfast is taken. There are five spacious rooms with fridges, a/c and wi-fi, and freshly baked cakes for breakfast. No credit cards. **€80**

EATING

Il Fungo Vicolo d'Annunzio ☎ 0789 83 340. In a quiet lane off Via Ruzzitto, near the central piazza, this traditional trattoria with some outside seating serves a range of Sardinian specialities and pizzas. Service is friendly, and there's occasional live music. First courses are €6–12, seconds around €14. Daily noon–3pm & 7.30pm–midnight.

La Terrazza Viale Costa Smeralda 51 ☎ 0789 82 575. Handy *spaghetteria* and pizzeria on the main drag with very reasonable prices; try the *Spaghetti La Terrazza*, with sausage, or *vegetariana*, or the *Petra Niedda* pizza, with gorgonzola. Pastas are €5–7, mains €10–15. Daily 12.10–2.30pm & 7.10–11pm; closed Mon except July & Aug, when closed Sun lunch.

Cannigione and around

Most tourists gravitate towards the coast, with a concentration of facilities around the small resort and yacht-stop of **CANNIGIONE**, on the western shore of the Golfo di

Arzachena. It's an inviting spot to dispatch a *gelato* on a stroll by the portside and there are some decent beaches to the north, though its expensive air is borne out by the high prices. Coastal boat excursions, taking in La Maddalena archipelago (see p.250), leave from the marina in summer.

Continuing north, beyond the satellite resort of **La Conia**, the narrow coast road winds west to the **Golfo di Saline**, a bay sheltering an exquisite, relatively undeveloped, sandy **beach**. At its far end, the headland, **Capo d'Orso**, takes its name ("Cape Bear") from a huge, strange bear-shaped rock known since ancient times and claimed to be the dwelling-place of the Laestrygonians, the mythical cannibal tribe which destroyed the fleet of Ulysses when it legendarily docked here. To reach it, you have to pass a gate and climb. At 122m high, its views are sensational, embracing the Maddalena Islands, Santa Teresa Gallura and Corsica.

ARRIVAL AND DEPARTURE

By bus ARST and, in summer, Sun Lines buses serve Cannigione.

Destinations Arzachena (3–13 daily; 10min); Olbia (June–Sept 4 daily; 1hr 40min); Porto Cervo (June–Sept 4 daily; 30min).

CANNIGIONE AND AROUND

INFORMATION

Tourist office Via Orecchioni, Cannigione (Mon & Tues 9am–2pm & 4–7pm, Wed–Sun 9am–2pm & 3–8pm or 4.30–7.30pm in winter; ☎0789 88 229). There's also a private office at Via Nazionale 47 (April–Oct Mon–Sat 9am–12.30pm & 6–8pm, Sun 9–11am; ☎0789 88 510).

ACCOMMODATION AND EATING

Capo d'Orso Località Le Saline ☎0789 702 007, ⓦcapodorso.it. Enjoying a good location close to the eponymous headland and to the beach of Le Saline, this campsite is equipped with a diving centre, boat rentals, windsurfing facilities, caravans (€52) and bungalows (€107). Closed Oct to mid-May. Pitches €27

Centro Vacanze Isuledda La Conia ☎0789 86 003, ⓦisuledda.it. A couple of kilometres north of Cannigione, this family-friendly campsite is right on the shore, with excellent bathing spots, and has caravans and bungalows to rent. It gets a bit overwhelmed in August, and there's not much shade. Sun Lines buses stop outside in summer. Closed Nov–March. Pitches €37

Hotel del Porto Via Nazionale 94 ☎0789 88 011, ⓦhoteldelporto.com. The best value of Cannigione's hotels, this place has compact rooms, some (costing extra) with balconies overlooking the marina. Rates plummet in winter. The hotel has a good café and restaurant open to all, offering a set-price lunch menu for €14; otherwise pastas cost €10–14. Daily 12.30–2pm & 7.30–10pm. €140

★ **Tavola Azzurra** Via Vasco da Gama 12 ☎347 121 5328. Below the church, this simple *rosticceria* has a brisk, authentic feel, offering delicious portions of fresh seafood and other hot snacks for €3.50–6 each (pastas are around €10). April–Sept daily 9am–3pm & 5–11pm.

Palau

For years a minor port best known as the embarkation point for the Maddalena archipelago, **PALAU** has raised its profile in recent years thanks to the growth of the local holiday industry, and is now quite a lively local centre and a useful base for exploring the excellent beaches in the vicinity. It has enough bars, restaurants and all-star summer entertainments to keep you amused for an evening or two, while by day there's a choice of boat excursions for touring the coast and islands.

Fortezza di Monte Altura

Monte Altura • Tours (45min) daily: April & May 10.15am, 11.15am, 12.15pm, 3.15pm 4.15pm & 5.15pm; June–Aug 10.15am, 11.15am, 12.15pm, 5.15pm, 6.15pm & 7.15pm; Sept to mid-Oct 10.15am, 11.15am, 5.15pm, 6.15pm & 7.15pm • €3 • ☎329 604 1373

Lying 3km north of town, the **Fortezza di Monte Altura** is a defensive bastion built in the nineteenth century on a rocky height above Palau. To get here, take the signposted turn-off on the right as you head towards the SS125. The winding road leads up to a set of impregnable-looking granite walls, and the tall gates from which guided tours leave. A surreal-looking flight of stone steps gives access to towers and the empty emplacements for guns installed during World War II, from where you can enjoy magnificent views over the Maddalena Islands. The fortress is the occasional venue for concerts and other performances in summer.

ARRIVAL AND DEPARTURE   PALAU

By train In summer, an infrequent Trenino Verde service operated by ARST connects Palau to Arzachena and Tempio Pausania; the service currently runs from late June to mid-Sept Wed–Sat 1 daily at 9.30am. The train station is by the port at the end of the main Via Nazionale.
Destinations Arzachena (20min); Calangianus (1hr 30min); Tempio Pausania (1hr 50min).
By bus ARST and Turmo buses stop in Palau.

Destinations Arzachena (Mon–Sat 13–19 daily, Sun 8–15 daily; 20min); Olbia (Mon–Sat 13–19 daily, Sun 9–14 daily; 1hr 10min); Santa Teresa Gallura (6–13 daily; 35–45min); Tempio Pausania (2–4 daily; 1hr 30min).
By ferry Next to train station, the Stazione Maríttima holds ticket offices for the various companies operating ferries to the Maddalena Islands (see box, p.252).

GETTING AROUND

By car Sardinya, Via Nazionale 97 (April–Oct; ☎ 0789 709 083, ✆ autonoleggiosardinya.it) rents out cars for around

€60 for one day, and scooters for around €40.
By taxi Call ☎ 0789 709 218 or ☎ 348 798 8281.

INFORMATION AND ACTIVITIES

Tourist office Piazza Fresi, signposted off Via Nazionale (Mon–Sat 9am–1pm & 3.30–7.30pm, limited hours in winter; ☎ 0789 707 025, ✆ palauturismo.com).
Diving Courses and packages are available at Nautilus Diving Center, Piazza Fresi 8 (☎ 0789 709 058, ✆ divesardegna.com).
Boat tours Excursions around the Maddalena archipelago

leave from the port daily between June and Sept at around 10am or 10.45am, returning at 5–6pm. Most tours cost €30–40 and include several swimming stops as well as lunch on board. Contact Lady Luna (☎ 339 387 7196, ✆ giteinbarca.it) or Delfino Bianco (☎ 338 962 1717, ✆ delfinobiancopalau .com), or just turn up at the port.

ACCOMMODATION

Baia Saraceno Località Baia Saraceno ☎ 0789 709 403, ✆ baiasaraceno.com. The nearest campsite to Palau, this is a good option if you want to stay near the beach, located in a pinewood close to Punta Nera, less than a kilometre east (10min on foot). It's clean and quiet, with access to rocky inlets and sandy coves. Cabins (€44) and bungalows (€84) are available. Closed Nov–Feb. Pitches **€30**
La Roccia Via dei Mille 15 ☎ 0789 709 528, ✆ hotel laroccia.com. Named after the granite boulder that intrudes into the garden and lobby, this smart three-star hotel has friendly staff and smallish, simply decorated rooms with balconies, satellite TV and free wi-fi. There's

free parking too. Closed Oct–Easter. **€95**
L'Orso e il Mare Vícolo Diaz 1 ☎ 331 222 2000, ✆ orso eilmare.com. Well-managed B&B close to the port, with three airy rooms, one (costing more) with a balcony. All have private bathrooms, a/c, a fridge, TV and free wi-fi. Breakfast includes fresh bread and fruit salad. Closed Dec–Feb. No credit cards. **€70**
Palau Vecchio Via dei Mille 16 ☎ 0789 709 333 or ☎ 339 214 2232. Of the three rooms in this B&B near the port, try to get the one at street level with its own front door and kitchen. The other two are in a modern apartment upstairs. Closed Oct–April. No credit cards. **€60**

EATING

Da Robertino Via Nazionale 20 ☎ 0789 709 610. On the main road, this *ristorante* has an intimate interior decorated with ceramics and mementos. Portions are big and tasty, but not cheap: pastas cost €10–15, mains around €20, much more if you order the speciality *aragosta alla catalana* (lobster), priced by weight. There's a great array of *antipasti* too. Mid-Feb to mid-Nov daily 1–2.30pm & 8–10.30pm; closed Mon in winter.
Samore Via Demartis 24 ☎ 392 673 8767. Small, elegant restaurant that does not have a propitious location – in a side

street near the seafront – but compensates with its local cuisine that includes *zuppa gallurese* (baked bread and cheese soaked in meat broth) and grilled meats. There's an €18 tourist menu. June–Sept daily 12.30–3pm & 8–10.30pm.
San Giorgio Largo La Maddalena 4 ☎ 0789 708 007. Cheerful and unpretentious eatery with a veranda, offering a good range of pizzas (eves only) as well as pastas and seafood. First courses are around €12, mains €12–18. It's a left turn off the main street going towards the port. March–Oct daily 12.30–2pm & 7.30–11.30pm; closed Wed in winter.

WATERSPORTS IN PORTO POLLO

Among Porto Pollo's windsurfing and kitesurfing outfits, try Sporting Club Sardinia (☎0789 704 016, ⓦportopollo.it) or North Kite School (☎333 403 6522, ⓦnorthkiteschoolsardinia.com). For windsurfing, you'll pay €18–30 for the first hour for board rental, less for consecutive hours, and for tuition around €100 for four hours for group lessons, €60 per person for one hour's private lesson. For kitesurfing, it's about €40 for one hour's equipment rental, €60 for one hour's tuition. Operators have stalls on the beach near Isola dei Gabbiani, and they also rent dinghies and can arrange **sailing** and **diving** excursions.

Porto Pollo

Between Palau and the port of Santa Teresa Gallura, the dramatic rocky coastline is indented by a succession of lovely creeks and bays. The few small resorts get very busy in summer, but are generally deserted the rest of the time, when most hotels and campsites close.

Two or three kilometres out of Palau, **Porto Pollo** (also called Porto Puddu) is a scattered locality which has become established as Sardinia's busiest watersports centre. A slender isthmus of beach ending in a bulbous promontory, **Isola dei Gabbiani**, divides the two bays of Porto Pollo and Porto Liscia, creating a breakwater and thus ideal conditions for **windsurfing** and **kitesurfing**: downwind of the sandbank, the sea is flat; upwind, it's choppy, fast and more suited to experts. There's a whole network of surf schools and rental operations, but even if you're not a surfer, the dune-backed beaches are worth going out of your way for, not least at night when there are regular beach parties.

GETTING AROUND   **PORTO POLLO**

By bike or scooter Dodo's Rental (☎334 148 4950, ⓦdodosrental.com) has mountain bikes for €15/day, scooters for €45–65/day.

ACCOMMODATION AND EATING

Isola dei Gabbiani Isola dei Gabbiani ☎0789 704 019, ⓦisoladeigabbiani.it. This campsite sprawls across the "island" from which it takes its name, with splendid swimming spots along the shores, though it all gets very crowded in summer. Bungalows (€80) are available too. Closed mid-Oct to early April. Pitches €30

Le Dune ☎0789 704 013, ⓦhotelledune.it. This fortress-like three-star is the only hotel hereabouts, in a wonderful position around 200m from the sea on a height, with views across to the Maddalena Islands. Half- or full board is required in the functional rooms. The restaurant (open to all) is run-of-the-mill, with a menu ranging from pizzas to seafood, but enjoys the same stunning panorama. April–Oct daily 12.30–2.30pm & 7.30–10.30pm. €80 per person half-board

The Maddalena Islands

From Palau, it's a short hop across to the **Maddalena archipelago**, a cluster of seven larger islands and a sprinkling of smaller ones. The archipelago is a favourite with yachters, and hosts a number of regattas, but most people come for its glorious beaches, which are mainly small and pristine. Boats dock at the largest of the group, **La Maddalena**, holding almost all the hotels and restaurants and a small museum of naval archeology. From the main island, you can drive, bike or hike across to neighbouring **Caprera**, where Garibaldi spent the last 25 years of his life. The hero of the struggle for Italian unification is remembered in a museum – his former home – which gives a fascinating insight into his long career on the world stage and his reclusive existence on the island.

La Maddalena is also the departure point for a range of boat tours to the other isles: **Santo Stéfano**, **Spargi**, **Budelli**, **Razzoli** and **Santa Maria**. Set amid myriad jutting rocks, they have some perfect scraps of beach to swim from, but little else besides rock and scrub.

The islands form part of Sardinia's first **national park** (ⓦlamaddalenapark.it), whose boundaries extend south to the islands of Mortorio and Soffi off the Costa Smeralda. Accordingly, there are restrictions on sailing activities, fishing and building, and some of the smaller islands are completely off-limits. The most conspicuous **wildlife** in evidence are the gulls, cormorants and herons that perch on the innumerable granite rocks poking out of the sea; it's unlikely you'll catch sight of the extremely rare Mediterranean monk seal.

La Maddalena

Just 2km from the Sardinian mainland, and measuring roughly 6km by 4km, the island of **La Maddalena** has the only town on the archipelago and some of its finest

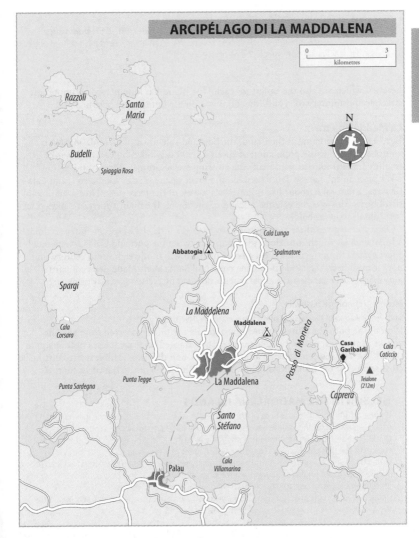

ARCIPÉLAGO DI LA MADDALENA

0 ———— 3
kilometres

7

Razzoli
Santa Maria
Budelli
Spiaggia Rosa
Cala Lunga
Abbatogia
Spalmatore
Spargi
La Maddaléna
Cala Corsara
Maddalena
Passo di Moneta
Casa Garibaldi
Cala Coticcio
Punta Sardegna
Punta Tegge
Lá Maddalena
Teialone (212m)
Caprera
Santo Stéfano
Palau
Cala Villamarina
N

7

GETTING TO LA MADDALENA

From Palau, the main port of embarkation for the Maddalena archipelago, **ferries** for the island and port of La Maddalena leave every 15–30min (less frequently in winter), run by Enermar (☎0789 708 484, ⓦenermar.it), Saremar (☎0789 709 270, ⓦsaremar.it), NGI (☎0789 708 484, ⓦngi-spa.it) and Delcomar (☎0781 857 123, ⓦdelcomar.it). Last departures from Palau on the regular service are at around 9.30pm, after which there's a night-time **service** run by Delcomar roughly hourly (tickets on board). Crossing time is around 20min.

Tickets for daytime crossings are sold at Palau's Stazione Maríttima and cost around €9 return per person, €40 return for two in a medium-sized car, with significant discounts for tickets bought on the preceding day. It can be a hectic bustle for tickets in high season, so it's worth arriving half an hour early. Don't bother arguing with queue-jumpers: island residents get priority.

It's much faster for pedestrians; you could park your vehicle in the **car park** behind the ticket office at Palau (a hefty €2/hr); cars parked in front get fined. Alternatively, you can sometimes find a space in a nearby street where you can park for free.

If you don't want to stay on the archipelago, you might consider one of the **boat tours** from Palau (see p.249) or Santa Teresa Gallura (see box, p.258). Alternatively, **rent a boat** from one of the kiosks near Palau's port, which charge from €80 for a day.

---

beaches, which are also the easiest to reach. The island has long played an important strategic and military role, and Mussolini was briefly imprisoned here in 1943.

La Maddalena town

Bearing the same name as the island, the port and sole town of **LA MADDALENA** is an upbeat place whose population of about 11,500 is swollen by vast numbers of (mainly Italian) tourists who make the crossing every summer. Most of the action takes place in the narrow lanes between the main square, Piazza Umberto I, and **Cala Gavetta**, a natural harbour five minutes' walk west of the ferry port. Now a marina for small boats, this was the original nucleus of the town. The main *passeggiata* takes place here, along Via Garibaldi.

Once you've given these areas the once-over, there's little else of specific interest, though Via Améndola, which runs along the seafront between the port and Cala Gavetta, holds a few *palazzi* from the period of the port's main growth in the eighteenth century, and, not far from here, the modern-looking church of **Santa Maria Maddalena** contains a couple of silver candlesticks and a crucifix donated by Nelson (see box below).

Museo Archeologico Navale

Strada Panorámica, Località Mongiardino • Closed at time of writing • ☎ 0789 790 663

West of the port, the **Museo Archeologico Navale** has finds recovered from ancient wrecks in the area, notably a Roman cargo ship dragged up from the sea near Spargi in the 1950s. The vessel foundered around 120 BC, and the prize exhibit is a reconstructed cross-section of the hull, showing how some two hundred of the hundreds more

---

NELSON IN THE MADDALENA ISLANDS

Between 1803 and 1805, the fleet of Admiral Nelson was a constant presence in what he called "Agincourt Sound", or the Straits of Bonifacio. It lurked in the waters around the Maddalena archipelago for fifteen months while Nelson stalked the French fleet during the run-up to the Battle of Trafalgar. Nelson never once set foot on shore throughout this long wait, but he sent a stream of letters to the Admiralty in London urging that steps be taken to secure Sardinia for England – it was then the only neutral shore in this part of the Mediterranean: "And I venture to predict, that if we do not…the French will." The French, docked at Toulon (nicknamed "Too-Long" by Nelson's impatient sailors), eventually fled to the West Indies before returning to meet Nelson at Trafalgar.

amphorae recovered – mostly containing wine from Campania – would have been stored for the sea passage. A second room has lead anchors and photos showing the excavation operations. Call or check with the tourist office to find out if the museum has reopened after restoration work.

Around the island

The rest of the island invites aimless wandering and offers a variety of sandy and rocky beaches in mostly undeveloped coves. The **beaches** on the northern and western coasts are most attractive, particularly those around the tiny port of **Madonnetta**, 5km west of La Maddalena, and at **Cala Lunga**, 5km north of town. At **Spalmatore**, there's a small, sheltered sand beach with a jetty, bar and disco. One of the nearest swimming places to town is just 2km southwest at **Punta Tegge**, where the low, flat rocks make access to the sea easy; there's a summer-opening bar here, too.

ARRIVAL AND GETTING AROUND LA MADDALENA

By ferry Ferries from Palau (see box opposite) and excursion boats dock close to the central Piazza Umberto I in La Maddalena town.

By bus Local buses run on two routes, one ("Panoramica") taking in the beaches, the other ("Nido d'Aquila-Caprera") going to Caprera, leaving roughly every hour from the Colonna Garibaldi near Via Améndola and the port (reduced service in winter). Tickets are €1 from tobacconists or €1.50 on board.

By bike or scooter Rent bikes or scooters from Megamotors, Via Améndola 2 (☎0789 737 606), or Nicol Sport, Via Améndola 18 (☎0789 735 266, ⓦnoleggilamaddalena.it), both on the seafront towards Cala Gavetta. Prices start at around €10 a day for a bike, €40 for a scooter (less in low season); you'll need ID and/or a deposit.

By taxi You'll find a rank at the port, or call ☎340 361 6466, ☎347 370 6074 or ☎347 791 2610.

INFORMATION AND TOURS

Tourist office The office on Piazza Barone des Geneys, Cala Gavetta, covers information for the whole archipelago (Mon & Wed 8am–2pm & 3–6pm, Aug 3–7pm, Tues, Thurs & Fri 8am–2pm, Aug & Sept also Sat & Sun 8am–2pm; ☎0789 736 321, ⓦcomune.lamaddalena.ot.it).

Boat tours Various excursions around the archipelago leave daily from the port at 9.30–10.45am, most costing €25–35. The tours include several swimming stops as well as lunch on board. The Flotta del Parco is a consortium of the main operators (☎0789 735 319 or ☎339 232 6737).

ACCOMMODATION

Il Gabbiano Via Giulio Césare 20 ☎0789 722 507, ⓦhotel-ilgabbiano.it. West of the centre beyond Cala Gavetta, this refurbished 1960s hotel enjoys a fantastic location on a point looking across to Santo Stéfano and Palau. Rooms are pretty standard and without a/c, but all face the sea and some have balconies. **€85**

★ **La Petit Maison** Via Livenza ☎0789 738 432 or ☎340 646 3722, ⓦlapetitmaison.net. Quirky and welcoming B&B 5min from the centre, decorated with works of art, including some by the owner. The ochre- and pastel-hued rooms have private bathrooms and there's a lovely courtyard garden where breakfast is taken. No credit cards. **€95**

La Piccola Parigi Via Italia 8 ☎347 058 8615, ⓦlapiccolaparigibedandbreakfast.it. B&B on two floors of a renovated palazzo in the old centre, with airy, modern rooms, separate private bathrooms and internet access. Breakfasts are meagre, but guests have use of a kitchen. No credit cards. **€80**

Residenza Mordini Via Príncipe Amedeo 3 ☎0789 737 325, ⓦresidenzamordini.it. In a renovated 1930s

building close to the ferry port, this swish hotel offers well-equipped rooms with a blend of antique and modern furnishings, spa facilities and free parking. **€150**

CAMPING

Abbatoggia Località Abbatoggia ☎0789 739 173, ⓦcampingabbatoggia.it. This campsite in the north of the island has a superb location close to four of the island's best beaches, but shade is minimal and facilities are spartan. However, the shop has the essentials, there's a basic *távola calda*/pizzeria on-site, and improvements are ongoing. Book early to rent a caravan (€60) or mobile home (€115). Closed mid-Sept to May. Pitches **€18**

Maddalena Località Moneta ☎0789 728 051, ⓦcampingmaddalena.it. The best-equipped of the island's campsites lies close to town and Caprera, and is sheltered and clean with friendly staff. It's got a great restaurant, too, but choose a pitch away from it for more peace. Caravans and bungalows are available (from €60). Closed Oct–May. Pitches **€22**

7

EATING

Osteria da Liò Via Vittorio Emanuele 4 ☎ 0789 737 507. Simple and authentic backstreet *osteria*, with some outdoor tables and good seafood – the *spaghetti bottarga e vongole* (with fish roe and clams) is exceptional. Fixed-price menus are €15 and €18; alternatively you'll pay around €40 each without drinks. April–Oct daily noon–3pm & 7.30–11pm.

Perla Blu Piazza Barone des Geneys ☎ 320 938 8860. It's somewhat over-priced, but this place is worth a visit for its terrace overlooking the boats on Cala Gavetta. Fresh pastas are €12–13 and such dishes as *fritto di calamari,*

gambarie e verdure (squid and prawn fry-up) are mainly €15–18. They serve pizzas too. April–Oct daily noon–3.30pm & 7pm–midnight.

Ristorante Pizzeria 48 Corso Garibaldi 48 ☎ 320 938 8860. This central place is ideal for pizzas (€6–13) and straightforward island dishes, including *trofie casarecce mari e monti* (home-made pasta with meat and seafood) and *tagliatelle con cozze e menta* (with mussels and mint). The tourist menu is €20; otherwise mains are €12–20. April–Oct daily noon–3pm & 7pm–midnight.

Caprera

A simple bridge built in 1891 stretches for 600m across the **Passo di Moneta** that separates La Maddalena from **Caprera**. Measuring around 7km from top to bottom, the island has been protected from development and, apart from Garibaldi's house and a couple of self-contained tourist complexes, consists primarily of woods and rocky scrub. Strike out in any direction along a network of trails to reach tranquil spots that are a welcome relief after the tourist bustle around Garibaldi's museum. Caprera's flora and fauna are among the most interesting of the islands, especially during spring when the heather, hawthorn and juniper present a multicoloured mosaic amid the pines, holm oaks and myrtles, and the birdlife includes royal seagulls, shearwaters, sparrowhawks and buzzards.

Among the small beaches around the shore, the most popular is **Cala Coticcio**, on the island's east coast (about a 40min walk from the bridge, less from the museum). A handful of fortifications lie dotted around, some built by the Savoy regime in the eighteenth century, and some from around the time of World War I. You can also climb a long stairway leading to the lookout tower on **Teialone**, at 212m the highest point of the Maddalena archipelago.

Compendio Garibaldino

Tues–Sun 9am–1.30pm & 2–7.15pm • €5 • ☎ 0789 727 162, ⓦ compendiogaribaldino.it

At the end of a tamarisk-lined road, the **Museo Garibaldino** is in Garibaldi's old house, the elegant South American-style Casa Bianca, which has been preserved pretty much

---

GARIBALDI ON CAPRERA

The most swashbuckling and erratic of all Italian patriots, **Giuseppe Garibaldi** (1807–82) came to live on Caprera in 1855, after a glorious and highly eventful career in arms, much of it spent in exile from Italy. It was from here that he embarked on his spectacular conquest of Sicily and Naples in 1861, accompanied by his thousand Redshirts, and it was here that he returned at the end of his campaigns, to resume a simple farming life. Having first seen the island on his flight from Rome in 1849, he subsequently bought the northern part of it for £360, no doubt attracted by its proximity to the Piedmontese naval base. Increasingly marginalized by the new king of Italy, Vittorio Emanuele, and the government in Piedmont, Garibaldi eventually became something of a recluse on Caprera – while still keeping abreast of affairs, receiving numerous deputations and making regular pronouncements on issues of the day. He devoted the rest of his time to writing his memoirs and a handful of bad novels, and tending his property. His neighbour was an Englishman named Collins, with whom he had some celebrated disagreements concerning wandering herds of goats, as a result of which Garibaldi built a wall dividing their properties, which can still be seen. After Collins's death in 1864, a group of English admirers provided the money for Garibaldi to buy the rest of Caprera from his ex-neighbour's family.

as he left it. Visitors are escorted past a collection of memorabilia which include an iconic *camicia rossa* (red shirt), the bed where he slept, a smaller one where he died, various scrolls, manifestos and pronouncements, a pair of ivory and gold binoculars given to him by the future King Edward VII and a letter from London, dated 1867, conferring on him honorary presidency of the National Reform League. A stopped clock and a wall calendar indicate the precise time and date of his death. The tour ends with Garibaldi's grave in the garden, its rough granite contrasting with the more pompous tombs of his last wife and five of his children. Garibaldi had requested to be cremated, but his corpse was embalmed on the wishes of his son Menotti. In 1932, fifty years after his death, his tomb was opened to reveal the body perfectly intact.

Santo Stéfano

Halfway between La Maddalena and the coast, the island of **Santo Stéfano** was briefly captured by French forces in 1793 in an abortive attempt to take possession of Sardinia. From here, the young **Napoleon Bonaparte**, then a lieutenant-colonel in the Corsican National Guard, commanded a bombardment of La Maddalena. Part of the island is occupied by the Italian navy, and most trippers disembark on the more interesting eastern side at the **Spiaggia del Pesce** beach, where there are a couple of holiday enclaves, and at the southern end, **Cala Villamarina**, where traces of Neolithic life have been found.

Spargi

West of La Maddalena, **Spargi** is renowned for its sparkling beaches, the best of which – and one of the finest on the archipelago – lies on the southern littoral at **Cala Corsara**, with transparent water, though it's a regular stop for boat tours. Nearby, the wreck of a Roman vessel from the second century BC was hauled out of the sea in 1958; it's now preserved in La Maddalena's naval museum (see p.252).

Budelli

On **Budelli** the famous **Spiaggia Rosa** ("pink beach"), immortalized by the director Michelangelo Antonioni in his film *Il Deserto Rosso* (*Red Desert*, 1965), is now protected and out of bounds, but other beautiful beaches elsewhere around the island compensate. For physical beauty and exquisite, crystal-clear sea, try **Cavaliere** and the lagoon-like **Le Piscine Naturali**. The limpid waters also attract **scuba divers** – contact the tourist offices at Palau and La Maddalena for local dive operators.

Santa Teresa Gallura and around

On Sardinia's northern tip, the small town of **SANTA TERESA GALLURA** is the main port for ships to Corsica, whose cliffs are clearly visible just 11km away. This is no mere transit town, however. If **beaches** are your thing, Santa Teresa must rank as one of the island's most attractive holiday destinations, surrounded by scintillating stretches of sand, with exhilarating views across the Straits of Bonifacio. To cope with the demand, the town has Gallura's widest selection of hotels, restaurants and bars, and has recently spawned the region's liveliest bar-culture – though life grinds to a much slower and calmer pace outside the summer months. In winter, especially, it can get very windy.

Like most of Gallura's coastal towns, Santa Teresa Gallura has a prosaic, modern look. It's arranged on a regular grid of modern streets that centre on the main **Piazza Vittorio Emanuele**, a brief walk up from Santa Teresa's beach, **Rena Bianca** – a beautiful stretch of sand, though some prefer the less congested beaches to either side of town. Jammed with yachts and blue and white fishing vessels, the **marina** and **port** area lie out of sight in the deep inlet of Longone (or Longosardo), reached from Via del Porto. Here you'll find kiosks selling tickets for Corsica and various boat tours (see box, p.258).

Brief history

Though there was a Roman settlement in the region, and garrisons were stationed here at different times by the Genoans and Aragonese, the present town was only founded in 1808 by order of the Savoyard king Vittorio Emanuele I, who named it after his wife Maria Teresa of Austria. Apart from a Spanish watchtower, however, few buildings date even as far back as the nineteenth century, and it owes its prevailing tone to the holiday development of the late 1950s. More recently, the growth of its yachting marina and the swelling pockets of holiday homes on the eastern side of the Longone creek have helped to make Santa Teresa one of Sardinia's most full-on holiday resorts.

Torre Spagnola

June–Sept daily 10am–1pm & 4–8pm, closes midnight in Aug • €2

North of Piazza Vittorio Emanuele, Via del Mare ends after a couple of hundred metres at a high bluff dominated by the **Torre Spagnola**, a well-preserved Spanish watchtower from the sixteenth century, sometimes called Torre Aragonese and officially known as Torre di Longosardo. The tower is open in summer for far-reaching views and to take in the regular exhibitions of photography, ceramics and other local craftwork. A panoramic path leads beyond the tower and down to the waterside, and there are also steps leading west of the tower to Rena Bianca.

The beaches east of Santa Teresa

Some of Sardinia's most alluring **beaches** lie only a short ride east out of Santa Teresa, all with views over to Corsica. To reach them from town, turn off at the signposts on the main Via Nazionale or turn off the SS133bis Palau road, or use the summer bus service (see p.258). Swimmers, sailors and windsurfers should all beware of the **strong currents** coursing through the Straits of Bonifacio, particularly around the northernmost cape of Punta Falcone.

There's safe swimming three kilometres or so east along the coast, in the deep inlet of **Porto Quadro**. Another couple of kilometres farther east, **Punta Falcone** is the Sardinian mainland's most northerly point, sheltering to its east the biggest sandy beach along here at **La Marmorata**, an exquisite spot marred by the proximity of intrusive villa complexes. The swimming, though, is superb, with the serrated profile of the Isola di Marmorata out to sea. The next beach down, **Marazzino**, is reached from the same turn-off from the SS133bis (and there are capacious parking areas here and at La Marmorata). **La Licciola** also has a scattering of holiday houses, though not enough to overwhelm this small beach.

Some twelve kilometres east of Santa Teresa, **Porto Pozzo** is a small beach and fishing settlement at the edge of the deepest of the inlets hereabouts, also called Porto Pozzo. In the season, **boat trips** depart for the islands of Spargi and Santa Maria from the quay, and you can eat at the beachside bar/pizzeria.

Capo Testa and around

Three kilometres west of Santa Teresa, **Capo Testa** is one of Sardinia's finest bathing localities, a rocky promontory at the end of a narrow isthmus, surrounded by turquoise sea. The headland has some scraps of sandy beach and even some meagre remains of the Roman settlement of **Tibula** – truncated granite columns and some fragments of stone by the waterside. Material from the nearby quarries was used both for the columns of the Pantheon in Rome and for Pisa's cathedral. Beyond, standing amid a clutter of surreal, wind-chiselled rock formations, a lighthouse casts its beam from the point.

The beaches

Among Capo Testa's **beaches**, take your pick between those facing Corsica on one side, and those with views towards the northern Sardinian coast sloping away westward on the other. The most popular ones are the **Spiaggia dei Due Mari** – situated on either side of the isthmus, facing north and south – and those actually on Capo Testa, such as **Spiaggia Rosa**. The **Spiaggia Levante** (also called Baia Santa Reparata) on the north side, and **Spiaggia Ponente** (or Cala La Colba) on the south, are the places to rent surfboards and other craft or to enrol on a diving or sailing course.

If you want to go farther afield, there are more beaches and plenty of privacy behind the thick pinewoods flanking the SS200 coastal road headed southwest. First and best of these is the extensive **Rena Maiore**, 8km due south of Santa Teresa and Capo Testa. Smaller beaches follow in quick succession farther west, all worth investigating, including a cluster around **Vignola**, about 10km west of Rena Maiore, popular with the kitesurfing crowd. The area is named after the vineyards which produce the region's best wine, **Vermentino di Gallura**.

ARRIVAL AND DEPARTURE

By ferry From the port on the eastern side of town, Saremar (☎ 0789 754 156, ⓦ saremar.it) and Moby Lines (April–Sept; ☎ 0789 751 449, ⓦ moby.it) operate sailings to Bonifacio in Corsica (2–7 daily; 50min; €16.50–23 one way, plus €26–35/car). Look out for special discounts for booking specified return dates and for car/passenger packages. Ticket offices normally open an hour prior to departure.

By bus Buses stop at Via Eleonora d'Arborea off Via Nazionale, the main road into town. Timetables and tickets

SANTA TERESA GALLURA AND AROUND

for ARST buses are available from Tabacchi Fanari, Piazza Vittorio Emanuele 26. For Turmo buses (☎ 0789 21 487, ⓦ gruppoturmotravel.com) to Cágliari, Digitur (☎ 079 262 039, ⓦ digitur.it) to Castelsardo, and Sardabus (ⓦ sardabus .it) to Tempio Pausania, buy tickets on board.

Destinations Arzachena (6–12 daily; 1hr); Cágliari (1 daily; 6hr); Castelsardo (4–5 daily; 1hr 35min); Olbia (6–12 daily; 1hr 20min–1hr 50min); Palau (6–12 daily; 40min); Sássari (3–5 daily; 2hr 35min); Tempio Pausania (Mon–Sat 2–4 daily, Sun mid-June to mid-Sept 2 daily; 1hr 10min).

GETTING AROUND

By bike, scooter or car Global Rent, Piazza San Vittorio 7 (☎ 0789 755 080); Gulp (see self-catering, opposite); Just Sardinia, Zona Artigianale (☎ 0789 754 343, ⓦ justsardinia .it), and Sardinya, Via Maria Teresa 29 (☎ 0789 759 090, ⓦ autonoleggiosardinya.it) have bikes (€25/day), scooters (from €30/day) and cars (from €65/day) to rent.

By bus From mid-June to mid-Sept, Sardabus operates eight local buses daily between Santa Teresa and the

beaches of Marmorata and Capo Testa (tickets on board; €1.50). Other buses towards Castelsardo can drop you at or near the beaches at Rena Maiore and Vignola.

By taxi Taxi rank near the bus station on Via Eleonora d'Arborea; call ☎ 339 248 1265, ☎ 347 632 1592 or ☎ 333 838 7487. Just Sardinia (see above) also operates a taxi service. The run to Olbia airport costs around €100.

INFORMATION AND ACTIVITIES

Tourist office Piazza Vittorio Emanuele 24 (mid-July to mid-Sept Mon–Fri 9am–1pm & 5–10pm, Sat & Sun 9am–1pm & 5–9pm; mid-Sept to mid-July Mon–Fri 9am–1pm; ☎ 0789 754 127, ⓦ comunestg.it). There's also a seasonal office at the port (June–Sept daily 10am–noon & 5–7pm; ☎ 0789 755 113).

Diving Local diving operators include Centro Sub, Via Tibula 11 (☎ 338 627 0054, ⓦ marinadilongone.it), and No Limits, Via del Porto 16 (☎ 0789 759 026, ⓦ diving mediterraneo.it). Dives cost €30–40 per dive, €35–50 for night dives, plus €10–15 for equipment rental.

ACCOMMODATION

Bocche di Bonifacio Località Capo Testa ☎ 0789 754 202, ⓦ xoomer.virgilio.it/bocchebonifacio. The best-value hotel in the Capo Testa area doesn't exactly ooze charm, but you can stay comfortably here in simple, clean rooms just a few metres above the sands, and there's a restaurant that serves the freshest seafood. Closed mid-Oct to Easter. **€59**

Comfort Scano Inn Via Lazio 4 ☎ 0789 754 447, ⓦ albergoscano.it. Small and functional, family-run hotel off the Capo Testa road, offering standard rooms with a/c and a decent restaurant. Slightly smarter and pricier rooms in another nearby hotel owned by the same family are available in summer. **€80**

★ **Da Cecco** Via Po 3 ☎ 0789 754 220, ⓦ hoteldacecco .com. Great-value small hotel situated in a pink and green palazzo above the port, with friendly owners, private parking and a roof terrace. Rooms are small and don't have a/c, but some have balconies with stunning views. Closed Nov–Easter. **€80**

Domus de Janas Via Carlo Felice 20 ☎ 338 499 0221, ⓦ bbdomusdejanas.it. You can't get nearer the action than this B&B right next to the main piazza, which you can observe from the roof terraces – look in the other direction and you'll see Corsica. "Rainforest" showers, delicious breakfasts and use of a kitchen are further attractions. Closed Nov–March. **€100**

BOAT TOURS FROM SANTA TERESA

Between Easter and September, **boat tours** from Santa Teresa around the coast and to the islands can be booked at Consorzio delle Bocche, Piazza Vittorio Emanuele 16 (☎ 0789 755 112, ⓦ consorziobocche.com), the Marco Polo agency, Via XX Settembre 16 (☎ 0789 754 942, ⓦ marcopolo2.net) or directly from booths at the port. The most popular excursions take in the western isles of the **Maddalena archipelago** (9.15am–5.15pm), including stops at the beaches of Santa Maria and Spargi and a stroll around the town of La Maddalena, or else follow the coast down to the **Costa Smeralda** (9am–5.30pm), with stops at Baia Sardinia and Porto Cervo; both cost around €40–50 per person, including lunch on board.

★ **La Chicca di Francesca** Via Basilicata 4 ☎347 335 0779, ⊛lachiccadifrancesca.com. Set in a shady garden a 5–10min walk from the centre, this B&B has three rooms with balconies, parquet floors, private bathrooms, wi-fi and a/c. Breakfasts are a joy, with home-made cakes. The owner is very sociable and also offers apartments. No credit cards. **€70**

Marinaro Via Angioy 48 ☎0789 754 112, ⊛hotel marinaro.it. Occupying a quiet spot near the town centre, this solid old building houses a bright, clean-cut hotel, with a cheerfully striped interior. Rooms on two floors are a decent size and fully equipped, with wi-fi available in the reception rooms. **€85**

★ **Moderno** Via Umberto 39 ☎0789 754 233, ⊛modernohotel.eu. This friendly, centrally located hotel has airy rooms – including family rooms – in pale blues and greens with Sardinian motifs and spacious bathrooms. Wi-fi and a/c are available. Closed Nov–March. **€90**

Sandalion Via Valle d'Aosta 12 ☎0789 754 541, ⊛hotelsandalion.it. Uninspiring but perfectly adequate hotel offering reasonable rates for its plain and clean rooms with fridges and balconies. Billiards, table tennis and internet access are all available; breakfasts are self-service and there's a restaurant. Closed Nov–March. **€85**

CAMPING

La Liccia SP90, Km59 ☎0789 755 190, ⊛camping laliccia.com. The nearest campsite to Santa Teresa lies 6km south, signposted off the Castelsardo road and a 10min walk from a good beach. Pitches are large, terraced and shady, and there are caravans and bungalows (from €42). Boat excursions and bike hire are available, and ARST buses stop outside. Closed Sept to mid-May. Pitches **€21**

SELF-CATERING

The weekly tariff for a two-bed apartment in town ranges from €300 to €800 in July, more at one of the bathing localities. There's normally a minimum stay of one or two weeks. The main rental agencies are Gulp, Via Nazionale 58 (☎0789 755 689, ⊛gulpimmobiliare.it), Sardinia Holiday, Via Capo Testa 30 (☎0789 754 411 or ☎06 450 5688 in winter, ⊛sardiniaholiday.net) and Randa Tour, Via Eleonora d'Arborea (☎0789 754 544, ⊛randatour.it), for apartments in town and at Capo Testa, Porto Quadro, Marmorata and Rena Maiore.

EATING

Da Thomas Via Valle d'Aosta 22 ☎0789 755 133. This lively *ristorante* has an unusually large menu with an emphasis on fresh fish. Dishes such as *pasta allo scoglio* (with seafood) are huge, but leave room for the excellent *seadas* (cheese-filled pastries with honey). Gluten-free dishes are also available. Starters are €10–15, meat and seafood dishes €12–18. Book ahead in summer, as it gets very busy. Daily noon–3pm & 7–11pm.

Gallura Grill Via Carlo Felice 51 ☎347 571 4281. Grilled meats are the speciality here, from Sardinian sausages and steaks to spit-roast pork, and there are fish dishes too. Most mains are around €15, tourist menus are €15 and €20. There are a few tables outside, though without much to look at. Easter–Sept daily noon–2.30pm & 7–11pm.

Marlin Via Garibaldi 4 ☎0789 754 557. Seafood is the main event here – the mixed grill is a massive feast – but they also serve delicious fresh pastas and meat dishes as well as pizzas in the evening. First courses are €11–14, mains are €12–18. March–Dec daily noon–2.30pm & 7–10.30pm; closed Wed Oct–Dec.

Papè Satan Via Lamármora 20 ☎0789 755 048. This *ristorante*/pizzeria with a courtyard and garden specializes in Neapolitan-style pizzas (served all day; €7–12), and other Neapolitan specialities such as spaghetti with octopus (€14). April–Oct daily noon–3pm & 7–11.30pm.

DRINKING AND ENTERTAINMENT

Bar Caffè Conti Via Regina Margherita 2 ☎0789 755 133. This comfortable bar off Piazza Vittorio Emanuele makes a cool vantage point for the comings and goings. There's a Santana soundtrack, snacks to nibble and late-night cocktails. Daily 8am–midnight.

Éstasi Località Buoncammino ☎392 054 1900. Seek

SUMMER EVENTS IN SANTA TERESA

There are few evenings between July and September when there isn't some organized entertainment in Santa Teresa. The main festivals include the **Sagra del Pesce**, or fish festival, with samplings, usually on a Saturday in the first or second week of July; a **sailing regatta** between Corsica and Sardinia at the end of July; a procession of fishing boats between the port and Rena Bianca beach for the Assumption at **Ferragosto** (Aug 15), and **Musica sulle Bocche**, an international jazz festival with outdoor concerts over four days in late August/early September (⊛musicasullebocche.it). **Windsurfing** championships are also held in the straits most years. For more sedate entertainment, head for the **open-air Cinearena Odeon** on Via Capo Testa (nightly screenings mid-June to Aug at 9.45pm).

out this secluded club when you feel like a dance under the stars, reached from a signposted turn from the SS125 3km south of town, near the church of Buoncammino. The music is mainly house and summer chart hits, with entry costing €20–30 including a drink. The adjacent *Free Jazz Café* is an open-air piano-bar for more sedate entertainment. Easter to mid-Sept Fri, Sat & other selected dates 11.30pm–late.

Groove Café Via XX Settembre. A "risto-disco-pub" on the corner of the main piazza, with *pizzette* and other snacks, nightly DJs and occasional live music. Daily 8am–2am; closed Sun in winter.

DIRECTORY

Internet access Log on for free at the Mediateca Comunale, next to the tourist office on Piazza Vittorio Emanuele (Mon–Fri 9.30am–1.30pm & 5–8pm or 3.30–6.30pm in winter).

Laundry There are coin-op machines at Jefferson's, Via del Porto (daily 8.30am–10.30pm; €5–7 for a wash, €2–5 for drying).

Pharmacy Piazza Vittoria (Mon–Sat 9am–1pm & 4–8pm or 4.30–7.30pm in winter).

Post office Via Eleonora d'Arborea, by the bus station (Mon–Fri 8.25am–1.35pm, Sat 8.25am–12.35pm. Cash can be changed here.

Travel agent Viaggi Sardorama, Via Tíbula 11 (☎0789 754 464) can arrange air and sea tickets, as well as excursions in the area and beyond.

Inland Gallura

Although most people are content to admire from afar the dramatic mountainscape backing onto Gallura's coast, you can't fail to be intrigued by the spiky pinnacles lying just a short way inland, where the small towns and villages retain far more of Gallura's essential character than any of the coastal resorts. Where the country is not bare and arid, it's covered with a thick mantle of holm oak and **cork oak** forest, the latter providing the area's main industry. In September and October you are sure to notice lorry-loads of the silver and red bark being transported to processing plants in Olbia and Arbatax, and you can see at all times the lower trunks stripped to their rust-red stems.

Come in winter and you'll find the peaks snow-clad, while spring is the best time to appreciate the *macchia*-covered lower slopes, woven with cistus, gorse, juniper, heather, myrtle and a hundred other wild and pungent species, some of whose flavours find their way into the famous bitter **honey** produced in these parts and for sale in the local shops: you'll probably already have sampled it poured over *seadas*.

Gallura is one of the few areas in Sardinia where you'll see isolated farmsteads, or *stazzi*, originally founded by settlers from Corsica fleeing the strife on that island in the eighteenth century – and the *galluresi* still have a reputation for the touchy sense of honour and ancient grievances for which Corsicans are famous.

Inland Gallura's main centre, **Tempio Pausania**, has most of the region's accommodation and restaurants, making it a convenient base for excursions. The obvious destination for local outings is nearby **Monte Limbara**, Gallura's highest mountain, with stirring views in all directions. Northwest of Tempio, **Aggius** provides an opportunity to dig into *gallurese* culture with its pair of fascinating museums, while to the east, Gallura's cork-processing centre of **Calangianus** is a good place to purchase cork products to take home, and lies near to the village of **Luras**, site of some intriguing prehistoric dolmens. South of Monte Limbara, the museum in the village of **Berchidda** reveals insights into the world of Vermentino and other wines, while one of Sardinia's many artificial lakes, **Lago Coghinas**, makes a great area to hike around.

GETTING AROUND   INLAND GALLURA

Though **public transport** will get you to the towns and larger villages easily enough, you'll need your **own vehicle** to get the most out of the region.

Tempio Pausania and around

The chief town of Gallura since the Romans established camps here to control the region's inland tracts, and now joint capital of the province of Olbia-Tempio, **TEMPIO PAUSANIA** has all the slow-moving solidity of a typical mountain settlement. As you might expect at a height of 566m, it makes a cool retreat in summer, and has long views stretching out on every side – most dramatically towards the region's highest mountain, Monte Limbara (see p.263).

Tempio had a greater profile in the eighteenth and nineteenth centuries, when, as well as being the administrative centre of the Gallura region, it benefited from the presence of therapeutic mineral waters. Though the springs remain, the town has been left behind as commercial activity has shifted to the coast and to Olbia. This at least has saved Tempio from the unplanned construction that has blighted much of Olbia since the 1960s, and the present-day town has a homogeneous appearance, its granite-grey centre a pleasant place for a wander. At its centre, Piazza Gallura is a good place to start, dominated by the **Municipio** and close to a harmonious ensemble of churches.

The Cattedrale

Piazza San Pietro • Daily 7.30am–noon & 3.30–7.30pm

Behind Piazza Gallura, Via Roma leads to the **Cattedrale**, originally a fifteenth-century Romanesque construction, though its present appearance owes much to a drastic nineteenth-century restoration. Only the belltower is original, and even this was modified in 1822, while the interior is mostly Baroque and devoid of much interest, though the third and fourth chapels on the left have good wooden altars.

Oratorio del Rosario

Piazza San Pietro • Daily 7.30am–noon & 3.30–6.30pm

Opposite the cathedral, with an arched Aragonese entrance, the **Oratorio del Rosario** dates from the fourteenth century but has undergone much modification since then, its austere front mixing late-Romanesque and Baroque motifs. The bare interior has a wooden altarpiece decorated with pure gold. It's thought that the church stands on the site of the Roman temple that gave its name to the town.

Oratorio di Santa Croce

Piazza San Pietro • Daily 7am–noon & 3.30–6.30pm

The trio of granite churches is completed by the **Oratorio di Santa Croce**, located behind the cathedral and joined to it at its restoration in the nineteenth century. Like the other two churches, Santa Croce is a hotch-potch of different periods, preserving a wooden altar from the early eighteenth century, originally from a Franciscan monastery in Alghero, and wood bas-reliefs on the right from the seventeenth century.

Fonti Rinaggiu

Via San Lorenzo

An easy stroll out of town will bring you to the **Fonti Rinaggiu**, a wooded spot that would make a nice venue for a picnic. The waters are prized for their diuretic qualities, and the spring is often crowded with locals filling up flagons with the stuff. It's a couple of kilometres southwest of the centre – follow signs, *Alle Terme*, up Via San Lorenzo from Largo de Gásperi.

Nuraghe Maiori

Località Conca Marina • April–Oct 9.30am–7pm; Nov–March call ahead • €2.50, or €3 guided visit (in Italian) • ☎ 347 299 5933

Tempio's most compelling sight, **Nuraghe Maiori**, lies 2km north of the centre on the Palau road (SS133), signposted off to the right amid a thick cork forest. Constructed entirely of huge granite slabs, the 3000-year-old *nuraghe* has round, tholos-style

7

TEMPIO'S CARNIVAL

Tempio's week-long **Carnevale** celebrations have grown hugely in recent years to become one of Sardinia's principal festivities. The pagan element is strong, featuring parades of outlandish allegorical floats, and the high points include the symbolic marriage of two puppets, Re Giorgo (King George, a sort of Carnival King) and the peasant girl Mennena, on Carnival Sunday, followed by a distribution of corn fritters (*frittelle*); on Shrove Tuesday, King George is burned in a ceremonial bonfire.

chambers to right and left as you enter, and a corridor that gives access to the courtyard. A colony of Lesser Horseshoe **bats** has taken up residence inside one of the chambers, which you can glimpse above with the aid of a torch provided at the ticket office (don't train the light on them, though). Usually arriving in early April, the bats give birth here in June and July, and leave in October.

From the courtyard, steps wind up to the parapet, affording glorious views of Gallura's jagged peaks, also taking in Tempio and Aggius as well as miles of fields and vineyards. A quirky bar-restaurant near the entrance provides refreshments.

ARRIVAL AND DEPARTURE
TEMPIO PAUSANIA

By train Tempio's train station for the Trenino Verde summer service (late June to mid-Sept) is a few minutes south of the centre.
Destinations Arzachena (Wed–Fri 1–2 daily; 1hr 10min–1hr 25min); Calangianus (Wed–Fri 1–2 daily; 20min); Palau (Wed–Fri 1–2 daily; 1hr 30min–1hr 45min).

By bus ARST buses stop at the train station and in the centre.
Destinations Aggius (Mon–Sat 1–2 hourly, Sun 4–6 daily; 5min); Arzachena (Mon–Sat 4 daily, Sun 2 daily; 1hr 10min); Calangianus (Mon–Sat 9–11 daily, Sun 3–5 daily; 25min); Olbia (Mon–Sat 6–7 daily, Sun 3–4 daily; 1hr 20min); Sássari (3–5 daily; 1hr 20min).

INFORMATION

Tourist office Piazza Gallura (Mon–Sat 10am–1pm & 4–7pm; ☏ 079 631 273, ⍟ prolocotempio.it). There's a second office in the old market building (now used for

exhibitions) on nearby Piazza Mercato, but it keeps more erratic hours (☏ 079 639 0080, ⍟ comune.tempiopausania .ot.it).

ACCOMMODATION

★ **Il Gallo di Gallura** Corso Matteotti 28 ☏ 079 671 035, ⍟ ilgallodigallura.com. This B&B in the heart of the old centre has fully renovated rooms embellished with elegant, modern furnishings and good bathrooms. No credit cards. **€70**
Pausania Inn SS133, Km1 ☏ 079 634 037, ⍟ hotel pausaniainn.com. In tranquil rural surroundings a kilometre north of town (on the Palau road), this large,

modern hotel has a tennis court and good-size outdoor pool, and there's a top-quality but moderately priced restaurant. **€80**
Petit Largo De Gásperi ☏ 079 631 134, ⍟ petit-hotel.it. The most central of the town's hotels, this is a functional business-folks' lodge with a restaurant. Rooms are blandly modern, though they're well equipped and some enjoy fine valley views. **€89**

EATING AND DRINKING

Friends Viale Valentino 17. For a snack or drink, head for this relaxed, modern bar off Largo De Gásperi, with comfortable seating, a good view from the back and terminals for internet access. Lunchtime menus are €9. Mon–Sat 8am–9pm.
Il Giardino Via Cavour 1 ☏ 079 671 247. Homely pizzeria/ristorante off Piazza Gallura dating from 1926, with a pleasant ambience and outdoor seating. Choices include *scottadito di agnello* (grilled lamb chops), and there's a €15 tourist menu. Daily except Wed noon–2.30pm & 7–11.30pm.
★ **Il Purgatorio** Via Garibaldi 9 ☏ 079 634 394.

Opposite the eponymous church, this proudly old-fashioned, semi-formal restaurant excels in such local specialities as hare (*lepre*), boar (*cinghiale*) and snails (*lumache*), at around €15 a dish. Sample the mushrooms in autumn and the authentic *zuppa gallurese* at any time. Daily except Tues 12.30–2.30pm & 8–10.30pm.
La Gallurese Via Novara 2 ☏ 079 639 3012. This trattoria off Corso Matteotti serves typical local items such as *zuppa gallurese* (€7.50) and *cinghiale a Cannonau* (boar in red wine and olives; €12.50). There's a set-price menu for €15. Tues–Sun noon–3.30pm & 7–10.30pm; open Mon lunch in summer.

DIRECTORY

Internet Free access at Mediateca, in the library on Piazza del Cármine (Mon–Fri 8.30am–1.45pm & 4.45–7.15pm, or 3.45–7.15pm in winter). You can also log on at *Friends* (see opposite).

Pharmacy Piazza Gallura (Mon–Wed, Fri & Sat 9am–1pm & 4–8pm).

Post office Largo De Gásperi (Mon–Fri 8.25am–1.35pm, Sat 8.25am–12.35pm).

Monte Limbara and around

Though not huge by Italian standards, the **Monte Limbara** massif – beloved of hikers and free climbers – towers above the rest of Gallura. To reach the thickly wooded peak, take the signposted left turn about 8km along the main road south to Óschiri; you could park your vehicle here and walk, or else drive up along a narrow road that twists up the pine-clad flanks of the mountain. The road climbs for a long way, affording fantastic views all around, then follows a ridge before reaching a forest of TV antennas and satellite dishes. Near here is a *punto panorámico* where a statue of the Madonna and Child stands festooned with an odd miscellany of personal mementos – charms, bracelets, lighters, hair-grips, even strips of gum – donated by the faithful. Nearby, the plain **church of Santa Madonna della Neve** stands at the site of a spring.

The road passes numerous examples of the manically contorted rocks that are such a feature of the area, and within a few hundred metres of the highest summit, **Punta Balistreri** (1359m), with bracing views as far as Tavolara island to the east. The tourist office in Tempio Pausania can supply a very rough map of the myriad paths and tracks and a list of local operators for **guided excursions**.

Lago di Coghinas

The Tempio–Óschiri road continues south, descending from **Passo della Limbara** (640m); it's a scenic ride through cork forests and *macchia*, the road usually empty but for flocks of sheep. At the bottom of the valley, **Lago di Coghinas** swings into view. Dammed in 1926 to provide a reservoir and hydroelectric power, the artificial lake has a lovely shore, alternately rocky and sandy, that makes a good venue for a picnic. The scanty ruins of a medieval castle and church, a Roman fort and a *nuraghe* all lie close to each other between the lake and the village of Óschiri, three or four kilometres east (and a stop for FS **trains** between Olbia and Ozieri-Chilivani).

Berchidda

East of the Lago di Coghinas, just off the main SS199, **Berchidda** is an important producer of Vermentino wine – one of Sardinia's most renowned whites – as well as of pecorino cheese and an intriguing goat's-milk liqueur. Surprisingly, given its remoteness, the village is the venue for a distinguished jazz festival (see box below).

Museo del Vino

Via Grangiorgio Casu 5 • April–Sept Tues–Sun 10am–2pm & 4–7pm; Oct–March Tues–Sat 9am–1pm & 3–6pm, Sun 10am–1pm & 5–7pm • €3 • ☏ 0789 705 268, ⓦ muvisardegna.it

If you've spent any time in Gallura, chances are you'll have sampled a glass of the local Vermentino with your meal, a light, dry white wine usually drunk as an *aperitivo* or to

---

> **BERCHIDDA'S JAZZ FESTIVAL**
>
> Over a week in mid-August, Berchidda hosts the **Time in Jazz festival**, attracting musicians from around the world. It's staged mainly in the central Piazza del Pópolo, but also in such venues as the wine museum and local fields. The respected, Berchidda-born trumpeter **Paolo Fresu** is the artistic director and a regular guest. Tickets for the concerts in Piazza del Pópolo cost around €20, while events elsewhere are normally free. For details call ☏ 079 703 007 or see ⓦ timeinjazz.it.

> ## THE BACHELORS' FEAST
>
> On the first Sunday of October, the **Festa di li 'Agghiani** ("Bachelors' Feast") takes over the village of Aggius. Traditionally an opportunity for the young folk to meet and make merry, it's now mainly an excuse for the locals to consume a lot of *suppa cuata*, the favourite *gallurese* soup recipe.

accompany seafood. At Berchidda's **Museo del Vino**, the secrets of producing this and other Sardinian wines are explained in an airy modern building, which also displays ancient presses and agricultural equipment, and allows you to sample (and buy) the end product.

Aggius

Six kilometres northwest of Tempio, **Aggius** is a popular highland retreat, enlivened by its colour-washed granite houses with wrought-iron balconies. The village occupies a superb panoramic position in the midst of massive boulders and corkwoods – cork and granite are the two mainstays of the local economy, helping to account for the well-to-do appearance of the solid-looking houses.

Museo Etnográfico

Via Monti di Lizu • May to mid-Oct daily 10am–1pm & 3–7pm; mid-Oct to Dec & Feb–April Tues–Sun 10am–1pm & 3.30–5.30pm • €4 • ☎ 349 453 3208, ⓦ museomeoc.com

As well as cork and granite, Aggius is known for its woven carpets, produced using traditional methods. You can see examples among numerous other artefacts in the imaginatively presented **Museo Etnográfico** on a backstreet signposted off the main Via Roma. Within the restored old building, each of the rooms is dedicated to an aspect of the culture and traditions of the locality, embracing everything from cork trees and cork-fashioned objects to nuptial garments, olive-pressing and cheese-making, as well as the gorgeously coloured rugs and carpets. Fascinating old photos and jars of aromatic spices from the *macchia* add to the overall experience.

Museo del Banditismo

Via Pretura • April to mid-Oct daily 10am–1pm & 4–6pm; mid-Oct to Dec, Feb & March Tues–Sun 10am–1pm • €4 • ☎ 349 453 3208

Aggius holds Sardinia's only museum dedicated to criminality, or more specifically the banditry that was endemic in this corner of the island in the eighteenth and nineteenth centuries. The **Museo del Banditismo** tells the fascinating story of the individuals driven (usually by desperation) to this outlaw life, of the arms they used and the forces ranged against them. Rows of mug-shots of prisoners who were often tortured before being executed cover one wall, and there's an arsenal of weaponry, as well as material on the feuds (*faide* or *nimistai*) that tore local communities apart.

La Valle della Luna

Leaving Aggius northward, a left turn towards Trinità d'Agultu and Ísola Rossa soon brings you to a wilderness of rocky debris, dubbed **La Valle della Luna**. In this "lunar valley", boulders are strewn across an arena-like hillside as if flung around by a petulant giant. Many have been carted away by illegal quarriers, though plenty remain, including some said to resemble human figures – one on the left of the road is said to recall Plato's head. There's also a *nuraghe* here, **Nuraghe Izzana**, reached along a rough track on the right after the road curves to the left. The road leading northwest of here as far as the coast at Isola Rossa makes a highly scenic drive or cycle, with numerous possibilities for walks and roadside picnics. Alternatively, take the **Strada Panorámica di Aggius** signposted to the left, an even more striking and slightly shorter route to the coast.

A SARDINIAN VENDETTA

In the annals of Aggius's past, the area was the hiding place of a sinister character known as **Il Muto di Gallura** – the mute of Gallura, the last scion of a family locked in a long and deadly vendetta in the nineteenth century that claimed 72 lives and left only six survivors. Il Muto – who was born deaf and dumb – carried on the feud from his lonely eyrie, from which he descended only to dispatch his enemies. He ended his terror with the murder of the 12-year-old son of his principal antagonist, the head of the opposing family. The boy was of an unsurpassed beauty, so the story goes, and was cut down while walking through the cork forests lost in song.

ACCOMMODATION AND EATING   **AGGIUS**

★ **Il Muto di Gallura** Località Fraiga ☎ 079 620 559, ⓦ mutodigallura.com. There's an outstanding *agriturismo* just outside Aggius, signposted up a dirt track to the right on the Tempio road. The old *stazzo* occupies a splendid position with mountain views from the bedroom windows; the farm includes goats, pigs and horses, and offers horseriding expeditions (€20/hr) and tuition at all levels. Even if you don't stay, the place has the best restaurant for miles around – good country cooking in an endless stream of courses; set-price meals cost €20–40 including wine (booking essential). Half-board comes to €84 per person, and there are discounts for stays of two days or more. Summer daily 1–2.30pm & 8–10.30pm, closed lunchtime July & Aug; winter Sat & Sun same times. **€96**

Calangianus

Seven kilometres east of Tempio, the road skirts Monte Limbara to **CALANGIANUS**, a small town surrounded by a jagged ring of peaks and, closer to hand, cork factories. This is the centre of Sardinia's biggest cork-producing area, and it's no surprise to see the local shops overflowing with the stuff, fashioned into an endless variety of unusual forms. In September, the village stages an **exhibition of cork** and its various uses.

Luras

Notable for its *logudorese* dialect – as opposed to the *gallurese* spoken elsewhere – the village of **LURAS**, 3km north of Calangianus, has a cluster of pre-nuraghic dolmens, or funerary stones, which date back to the second or third millennium BC. To reach the nearest and most impressive of these, **Dolmen Ladas**, follow the road north through the village, turn right into the last asphalted street and follow the minor road for about 350m, following the brown signs – a couple of kilometres in all. Standing on a low hill, the tall rectangular dolmen measures 6m in height and over 2m in width.

Sant'Antonio di Gallura and around

The tiny village of **SANT'ANTONIO DI GALLURA** lies 18km northeast of Calangianus on the SP427 (and the same distance south of Arzachena), close to the **Lago di Liscia**, the artificial lake which supplies irrigation and drinking water to much of the coastal region. The neighbourhood also holds an ancient forest of wild olive trees, some reaching 14m high and 11m broad, among which is thought to be the oldest wild olive tree in Sardinia, estimated to be 2000 years old. You'll need local advice to find it, however: it's out of sight in a secluded little valley near the banks of the lake. The area is renowned for its **Nebbiolo** wines.

ACCOMMODATION AND EATING   **SANT'ANTONIO AND AROUND**

★ **Li Licci** Località Valentino ☎ 079 665 114, ⓦ lilicci .com. This great *agriturismo* is located 9km south of Sant'Antonio and 3km west of Priatu, on the minor SP38 Olbia road. The delicious rustic fare – *antipasti, zuppa gallurese* and *porcheddu arrosto*, washed down with Vermentino wine – is all home-produced, and there's a €44 set menu (non-guests should always call ahead). Half-board in rooms with private bathrooms comes to €75/person; there's a supplement of €7.50/person for one-night stays. Early April to Oct daily noon–2pm & 7.30–10.30pm. **€110**

7

Nuoro and Ogliastra

271 Nuoro

278 North and west of Nuoro

280 Oliena and around

282 The Barbagia Ollolai

287 The Barbagia Belvì and the Gennargentu massif

291 Láconi

293 Ísili and around

295 The eastern coast

ORGÓSOLO MURAL

Nuoro and Ogliastra

For the most part, the provinces of Nuoro and Ogliastra have little in common with Sardinia's modern sun-and-sand image. While many of the resorts and beaches of the east coast are as inviting as any on the island, inhospitable cliffs and mountains predominate, dotted with introverted villages and endless flocks of sheep. For many people, however, these once inaccessible tracts are the most interesting parts of the island, which have never known the heel of foreign conquerors, and whose scattered and isolated communities have retained a fierce sense of independence and loyalty to centuries-old practices.

Travelling around these provinces, don't be surprised to find a few elderly folk still unselfconsciously wearing their local costumes. However, the most practical place to view the region's huge range of costumes is the ethnographic museum in the city of **Nuoro**. Although unprepossessing, this high inland town has plenty more to discover, thanks mostly to the remarkable roster of artists and writers who lived and worked around here before achieving national fame.

Nuoro is a good starting point for trips into the surrounding mountains. North of town, the first obvious stop would be **Su Tempiesu**, a sacred well of the nuraghic era, splendidly sited on the side of a valley east of the village of **Orune**. West of **Bitti**, where there's a small ethnographic museum, the castle of **Burgos** occupies a lofty perch with stunning views over the Tirso valley.

South of Nuoro stretches Sardinia's **Barbagia** region, the mountainous heart of the island that encompasses its highest peaks. The name is a dialect version of *Barbaria*, the term given to this central core by the Romans who, like Sardinia's other conquerors, never managed to subdue it completely, foiled by the guerrilla warfare for which the mountains proved ideal. Amid forested slopes, Barbagia's population is concentrated in small, self-contained villages, interconnected by twisting mountain roads and little changed since the novelist Salvatore Satta described them as "minuscule settlements as remote from one another as are the stars". Although material conditions have improved in recent years, Barbagia is a world apart from the whitewashed luxury of the Costa Smeralda just a couple of hours' drive away.

The region is divided into different districts, of which the **Barbagia Ollolai** is the nearest to Nuoro. En route to this area, **Oliena** is the best departure point for expeditions to **Supramonte**, the dramatic massif visible from Nuoro, and, with its wide range of accommodation, is a useful base for the whole region. South of here, the village of **Orgósolo** once had one of the island's worst reputations for banditry and violence, though it is now best known for its striking murals. Westwards,

Mountain festivals p.271	**Banditry and kidnapping in the**
Artigianato in Nuoro p.272	**Barbagia** p.287
Literary Nuoro p.274	**Fonni's festivals** p.288
The Sagra del Redentore p.278	**Aritzo's festivals** p.290
Oliena's festivals p.280	**D.H. Lawrence in Sardinia** p.291
The walk to Valle Lanaittu and Monte	**Sant'Ignazio da Láconi** p.292
Tíscali p.281	**The tale of the bean** p.295
Orgósolo's Scarlet Rose p.282	**A hike in the Gola di Gorroppu** p.299
Mamoiada's Mamuthones p.284	**Boat trips from Cala Gonone** p.301

Highlights

❶ Museo della Vita e delle Tradizioni Sarde, Nuoro The island's most comprehensive collection of costumes, masks and handicrafts provides a fascinating overview of the rural culture of the interior. **See p.275**

❷ Easter at Oliena Grief, joy, drama and exuberant local costumes all feature in the Easter rituals of this mountain village – and the accompanying gunfire makes ear-plugs essential. **See p.280**

❸ The murals of Orgósolo Sardinia has several places daubed with vibrant murals, but those at Orgósolo win hands down for their sheer inventiveness and humorous spirit. **See p.283**

❹ Hiking in the Gorroppu gorge A thrilling scramble through this precipitous gorge south of Dorgali is the highlight of one of Sardinia's most satisfying walks. **See p.299**

❺ The beaches around Cala Gonone Accessible by boat, these bare patches of sand, backed by soaring cliffs, rank among the island's most memorable beaches. **See p.300**

HIGHLIGHTS ARE MARKED ON THE MAP ON P.270

NUORO & OGLIASTRA

Ala dei Sardi

PROVINCIA DI OLBIA-TEMPIO

Ozieri

Lago di Pattada

PROVINCIA DI SÁSSARI

Pattada

Buddusò

Bultei

Bitti

Bono

Bottida

Orune

Su Tempiesu

Lollove

Nuoro

❶

Monte Ortobene

Su Gologone

Oliena

❷

Punta Corrasi (1463m)

Orani

Mamoiada

Orgósolo

❸

MONTES

Monte San Giovanni (1316m)

Fonni

Funtana Bona (1052m)

PROVINCIA DI NUORO

Monte Spada (1595m)

Sórgono

Monte Bruncu Spina (1829m)

Tonara

Desulo

Belvì

Punta La Mármora (1834m)

Aritzo

GENNARGENTU

BARBAGIA BELVÌ

Láconi

Lago del Flumendosa

Ísili

Orroli

Mandas

Lago Mulargia

PROVINCIA DI CÁGLIARI

Cágliari

Posada

La Caletta

Santa Lucia

Siniscola

Capo Comino

BARONIA

Cala Liberotto

Cedrino

Orosei

Spiaggia Osalla

Spiaggia Cartoe

Grotta di Ispinigoli

Dorgali

❺

Cala Gonone

Grotta del Bue Marino

Cala Luna

Golfo di Orosei

Cala Sisine

Capo di Monte Santo

Civitavecchia & Genoa

Serra Orrios

Lago del Cedrino

Valle Lanaittu

Monte Tiscali (515m)

Monte Tiscali

Golà di Gorroppu

❹

Genna Sílana

Urzulei

Baunei

Santa Maria Navarrese

Arbatax

Tortolì

Porto Frailis

Lido Orri

Lánusei

PROVINCIA DI OGLIASTRA

Perdasdefogu

Tertenia

Muravera

BARBAGIA OLLOLAI

PROVINCIA DI NUORO

SARCIDANO

N

HIGHLIGHTS

❶ Museo della Vita e delle Tradizioni Sarde, Nuoro
❷ Easter at Oliena
❸ The murals of Orgósolo
❹ Hiking in the Gorroppu gorge
❺ The beaches around Cala Gonone

0   10
kilometres

MOUNTAIN FESTIVALS

The mountain villages of Nuoro and Ogliastra host some of Sardinia's most atmospheric **festivals**, usually smaller and less lavish than those organized in the cities, but possessed of a fiery exuberance – and occasionally a distinctly dark mood. Every place has at least one festa, for which preparations are made months in advance, though the Carnival period, Easter and the festival of the Assumption in mid-August are usually the most spectacular. All provide a good opportunity to view traditional costumes – the tourist office at Nuoro can supply you with an illustrated booklet with dates and details.

Mamoiada presents one of Sardinia's most spectacular Carnival displays, while **Orani** has an absorbing museum featuring the graceful sculptures of Costantino Nivola, an eminent local artist.

Farther south, the small town of **Fonni** is one of the main gateways to the once impenetrable **Gennargentu** massif, the island's highest range, from which all of Sardinia's major rivers flow – most of them dammed to create mountain lakes. The loftiest peak, **Punta La Mármora** (1834m), can be reached on foot without too much difficulty, one of scores of treks that can be made in the area. The forested slopes of the **Barbagia Belvì**, which borders this range, shelter more close-knit communities, of which **Belvì** and **Aritzo** are the most attractive. South of here in the **Sarcidano** region, the gradients are milder, though the village of **Láconi**, surrounded by woods, still retains a fresh, mountainous feel, while **Ísili** has a superb single-towered *nuraghe* worth a photo-stop.

The **eastern coast** preserves the rugged character of the interior, though the sheer walls rearing above the sea also leave space for some fantastic beaches. These are more popular in the northern parts, where the town of **Posada** provides a lofty vantage point from its ruined castle. South of the inland centre of **Orosei**, the swimming spots are much more inaccessible apart from those at the holiday enclave of **Cala Gonone** and around **Arbatax**, one of the few ports along this littoral, connected to the Italian mainland by ferry.

8

GETTING AROUND   NUORO AND OGLIASTRA

The provinces are best explored using your **own vehicle**, but it's not impossible to get around by public transport.

By train ARST-run trains (☎ 800 865 042, �𝕨 arst.sardegna .it) connect Nuoro with Macomer, a stop on the main rail network, and in summer ARST also operates two infrequent but highly scenic Trenino Verde services from Mandas (which has good transport connections with Cágliari), one line passing through Ísili, Láconi, Belvì/Aritzo and Sórgono, the other to Lanusei and Arbatax – however, it's a slow chug, best treated as a travelling experience rather than as a means of crossing the island. Check timetables at ☎ 070 580 246 or ☎ 800 460 220, ⟨w⟩ treninoverde.com.

By bus ARST buses from Nuoro pass through most of the villages in the area at least once a day (but usually no services on Sun). For more info, consult ☎ 800 865 042, ⟨w⟩ arst.sardegna.it.

Nuoro

"There is nothing to see in Nuoro: which to tell the truth, is always a relief. Sights are an irritating bore," wrote D.H. Lawrence, after stopping here during his Sardinian excursion of 1921. The town appeared to him "as if at the end of the world, mountains rising sombre behind". Since Lawrence's visit, an overlay of ugly apartment blocks, administrative buildings and banks has been added, but **NUORO** still preserves its end-of-the-world feel, with faded Fascist graffiti from the 1930s visible on its walls and an old-fashioned air hanging over the place. However, while it shares some of the insular and parochial qualities of Sardinia's inland villages, Nuoro occupies a unique place in the island's **cultural life**, both for its extraordinary literary fame and the artists

8

ARTIGIANATO IN NUORO

Sardinia's interior is known for its **handicrafts** and other rustic artefacts – knives, carpets, musical instruments, masks and the like – and Nuoro has numerous outlets where these are sold. Try Il Carro, Via Tola 21 (near the Duomo), or Fancello, Via Trieste 64, which have shelves full of *artigianato* (folk arts and crafts). The quality is generally good, though if you're travelling through Barbagia, you can often find the same items cheaper in the villages where they're made.

who lived and worked here. The town's specific sights afford fascinating glimpses into the local arts scene as well as the region's rural culture, while there is no denying Nuoro's superb position, beneath the soaring peak of Monte Ortobene and opposite the sheer heights of Supramonte – a rather more inspiring panorama than Lawrence's brusque assessment might suggest.

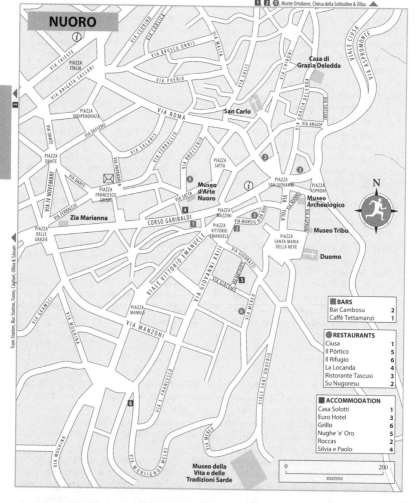

NUORO

1 2 1 Monte Ortobene, Chiesa della Solitudine & Olbia

Train Station, Bus Station, Fonni, Cagliari, Olbia & Sássari

■ BARS
Bar Cambosu	2
Caffè Tettamanzi	1

● RESTAURANTS
Ciusa	1
Il Pórtico	5
Il Rifugio	6
La Locanda	4
Ristorante Tascusi	3
Su Nugoresu	2

■ ACCOMMODATION
Casa Solotti	1
Euro Hotel	3
Grillo	6
Nughe 'e' Oro	5
Roccas	2
Silvia e Paolo	4

0   200
metres

Nuoro's **old quarter** is the most compelling part of town, spread around the pedestrianized axis of **Corso Garibaldi**, at its best during the buzzing *passeggiata*. Within walking distance of here, each of Nuoro's main attractions focuses on aspects of Sardinia's core identity, contrasting and complementing each other: the **Museo della Vita e delle Tradizioni Sarde**, an engrossing overview of the island's rural culture including a colourful exhibition of local costumes; the **Museo d'Arte Nuoro** and **Museo Tribu**, which showcase modern art, chiefly by local artists; and the **Museo Archeologico**, delving into the area's and the island's history. Other attractions include the **Casa di Grazia Deledda**, the restored birthplace of one of the city's literary stars, offering an insight into the city's domestic life of a hundred years ago, and, outside town, **Monte Ortobene**, whose summit marks the end-point of the procession in the annual **Sagra del Redentore** festival (see box, p.278).

Museo d'Arte Nuoro

Via Satta 27 • Tues–Sun 10am–1pm & 4–8pm • €3 • ☎ 0784 252 110, ⓦ museoman.it

In a renovated nineteenth-century palazzo just off Corso Garibaldi, the **Museo d'Arte Nuoro** is filled with the works of Sardinia's best-known modern artists. The ground and top floors are devoted to temporary exhibitions, while the middle two floors have a permanent display of artists from the nineteenth, twentieth and twenty-first centuries, including moody abstracts by Mauro Manca (1913–69), and sculptures by two outstanding locals, Costantino Nivola (1911–88) and Francesco Ciusa (1883–1949). The gallery also hosts occasional poetry readings and classical and jazz concerts.

Piazza Satta

Works by Costantino Nivola – one of the local sculptors represented in the Museo d'Arte Nuoro – can be seen in the usually deserted **Piazza Satta**, at the top of Via Satta. Here, the poet Sebastiano Satta, who was born nearby (see box, p.274), has been honoured with a cluster of menhir-like granite blocks in which small bronze figures evoking nuraghic *bronzetti* have been placed – the work of Nivola in the 1960s. The bronze statuettes depict the poet at different stages of his life.

San Carlo

Piazza San Carlo • Daily 8am–1pm & 4–7pm

Off Via Chironi, a plaque on a renovated townhouse shows it to be the birthplace of **Francesco Ciusa**. The sculptor's tomb lies opposite in the pink, rustic-looking church of **San Carlo**, which also contains a copy of Ciusa's best-known sculpture, *Madre dell'Ucciso* ("Mother of the killed man") – the original can be seen in Cágliari's Galleria Comunale d'Arte (see p.63). When the church is closed, you can obtain a key from Via Deledda 53, opposite the Casa di Grazia Deledda (see below).

Casa di Grazia Deledda

Via Deledda 44 • Mid-March to mid-June Tues–Sun 9am–1pm & 3–6pm; mid-June to Sept daily 9am–7pm; Oct to mid-March Tues–Sun 10am–1pm & 3–5pm • Free • ☎ 0784 258 088

Corso Garibaldi ends at Piazza San Giovanni, from where a left turn up Via Deledda brings you to the **Casa di Grazia Deledda**, once the home of the Nobel Prize-winning author (see box, p.274), now restored and partly furnished to present an authentic example of a typical Nuorese house at the turn of the twentieth century. Much of the restoration has followed Deledda's own description of the house in her posthumous autobiographical novel *Cosima*, notably the **kitchen** with its hanging cheeses and array of brass pans. Elsewhere you'll see manuscripts, first editions, photos, letters and

---

LITERARY NUORO

In Sardinia, Nuoro can boast what is almost a monopoly where **literature** is concerned, a standing discreetly advertised by the scraps of poetry and prose inscribed on the walls of the old town. The best-known Sard poet, **Sebastiano Satta** (1867–1914), was Nuorese, and his name has been given to innumerable streets and piazzas throughout the island – though he's hardly known outside Italy. In his home town, the street where he lived is named after him, as is the square at one end of it, Piazza Satta (see p.273).

In 1926, the author **Grazia Deledda** (1871–1936) became one of the six Italians to have won the Nobel Prize for Literature. It was a tribute to a steady writing career and a corpus of work based on the day-to-day trials and passions of simple folk in Nuoro and the villages around. Praised by D.H. Lawrence, she has been compared with Thomas Hardy in her style and subject matter. The house where Deledda grew up, described in her autobiographical work *Cosima*, can be seen on Via Deledda and is now a museum (see p.273); her tomb is at the bottom of Monte Ortobene, in the church of Santa Maria della Solitúdine, which also recurs in her writing. For Grazia Deledda's works in English, see Contexts (p.320).

For the town's greatest modern writer, **Salvatore Satta** (1902–75), "Nuoro was nothing but a perch for the crows", as he wrote in his semi-autobiographical masterpiece, *The Day of Judgement*. No relation to his poetic namesake Sebastiano, Satta earned his living as a jurist, which placed him at the heart of the tangled intrigues of this provincial town. His posthumously published book chronicles life in Nuoro at the turn of the twentieth century, yet much of it still rings true today, written in a dry but readable style that treads a fine line between soap opera and existential angst. A plaque at Via Angioy 1, just up from Piazza Mazzini, indicates the house where Satta wrote parts of his novel (see p.320).

---

clippings, and upstairs the author's **bedroom** and a film of her life. There's also a shady garden with a selection of her works to browse through (some in English).

The Duomo

Piazza Santa Maria della Neve • Daily 8am–1pm & 4–7pm

Framed by two belltowers, the orangey Neoclassical exterior of Nuoro's nineteenth-century **Duomo** often crops up on local postcards, but it lacks much presence from close up. The cool, spacious interior holds various items of religious art, including panels showing the Stations of the Cross by local twentieth-century artists Carmelo Floris and Giovanni Ciusa Romagna. Try to persuade someone to let you into the **belvedere** to one side of the cathedral, from which there is a superb view of the town and the precipitous valley below.

Museo Tribu (Museo Ciusa)

Piazza Santa Maria della Neve • Tues–Sun 10am–1pm & 4.30–8.30pm • €3 • ☎ 0784 253 052, ⓦ tribunuoro.it

Next to the Duomo, the **Museo Tribu** is mainly devoted to the work of Nuoro's most celebrated artist, **Francesco Ciusa**, whose early twentieth-century sculptures invest lowly peasant figures with a heroic stature. Some of his most poignant works can be seen here, such as the powerful *L'Anfora Sarda*, showing a mother drinking from a jug while her baby breastfeeds, and *La Filatrice*, depicting a woman threading a needle. The rest of the gallery holds temporary exhibitions of pieces by other local figures in the fields of graphic art, ceramics, embroidery and jewellery.

Museo Archeologico

Piazza Asproni • Tues & Thurs 9am–1pm & 3–5pm; Wed, Fri & Sat 9am–1pm • €2 • ☎ 0784 31 688

In Nuoro's **Museo Archeologico**, which can be accessed from Via Mannu or Via Asproni, the simple chronological arrangement takes in everything from rocks, bones and skulls to carved vases, cooking pots and bronze spearheads. The examples of Neolithic jewellery are worth lingering over, including necklaces made from boars' teeth and amber. However, the items of nuraghic art are the most impressive: statuettes and bronze figurines of cloaked chiefs and archers, and mouflons and bulls with majestic curved horns, all probably offered as votive gifts by pilgrims to a nuraghic sanctuary, dating from the eleventh to ninth centuries BC. The well-presented museum also has stone inscriptions and amphorae from the Roman era.

Museo della Vita e delle Tradizioni Sarde

Via Mereu • Tues–Sun 10am–1pm & 4.30–8.30pm • €1 • ☏ 0784 257 035

Beyond the crude carts and wine presses that greet you at the entrance, the **Museo della Vita e delle Tradizioni Sarde** – more simply known as the Museo del Costume or Museo Etnográfico – has Sardinia's most comprehensive range of local costumes, jewellery, masks, carpets and other handicrafts, arranged in a modern purpose-built complex whose sequence of rooms, steps and courtyards is intended to evoke a Sardinian village. The most striking items on show are the **costumes**, showing an incredible diversity of pattern, design and colour, according to both their place of origin and the circumstances in which they were worn: scarves, skirts and bodices for unmarried women or widows; blouses and shawls for mourning or feasting; shirts, tunics and pantaloons for the menfolk.

Rooms 4–5

Room 4 is devoted to costumes from the Barbagia villages of Bitti, Fonni, Gavoi, Ollolai and Désulo – black hats and boots for the men, lace shawls for the women – while **room 5** has rugs, carpets and a horizontal-type oak loom from Bono from the nineteenth century. **Funerary carpets** on which the deceased were placed during wakes are draped on the walls.

Rooms 6–8

Room 6 focuses on Sardinia's **musical instruments**, including various drums (*tamburi*), flutes made from canes from Barbagia and La Marmilla and rudimentary clarinets (*benas*) made from oat stems. Some of these were tied together to make *launeddas*, or shepherd's pipes, said to be the island's oldest and most original instrument, made of three tubes of cane of differing lengths and diameters, and individually spaced finger-holes. Another display shows sheep- and goat-bells, the various sizes used to identify different flocks – one of the characteristic accoutrements in Barbagia's masked processions.

The next room has examples of the various *dolci* and **breads** you may have encountered in restaurants and pastry shops throughout Sardinia, but particularly common in the Nuoro region, elaborately fashioned as birds, hearts and bows. The famous *pane carasau* – a crispy disc of bread – is also here; traditionally made once a month, it was originally the preserve of the better-off classes, but is now in general use.

Rooms 9–13

Guns and **swords** share space in **room 9** with **lacework** and **basketwork**, while **room 10** – downstairs and across a yard – has solemn photos from the late nineteenth century, costumes from Atzara and Samugheo and more carpets on the walls. **Rooms 11–13** display costumes from Oristano and Cabras, lace from Cágliari and an impressive collection of **jewellery** used by both men and women, crafted out of silver plate, polychrome glass, precious stones and silver filigree-work, and sometimes incorporating fragments of shell, sharks' teeth, boars' tusks and crystals to ward off evil.

Rooms 14–15

Rooms 14 and **15** have sober dark-brown and black garments from Macomer and Íttiri, more flamboyant women's dresses from Ósilo and brocaded wedding and feast gowns from Sénnori, Ploaghe and Bono. The costumes in the last rooms are much more dramatic, including the very sinister-looking black gowns tied with ropes and bells belonging to **Sos Thurpos** of Orotelli – a chain of twenty or thirty hooded and stick-wielding men swathed in thick black cloth with only their soot-blackened faces exposed, who leap upon their victims during the village's Carnival procession and truss them up, as seen in the photos displayed here. You can also see the hairy goatskin costumes of Mamoiada's Carnival, the masks at once menacing and tragic (see box, p.284), and those of **Sos Merdules** of Ottana.

Santa Maria della Solitúdine

Via della Solitúdine • Daily 8am–noon & 4–7pm

At the base of Monte Ortobene at the northeastern end of town, the church of **Santa Maria della Solitúdine** (known locally as the chiesa di Grazia Deledda) merits a pause. The church, an austere granite structure at the top of a flight of shallow steps, was designed in the 1950s by local artist Giovanni Ciusa Romagna on the site of an earlier church that was often mentioned in the books of Grazia Deledda (see box, p.274), and contains the author's simple granite tomb.

Monte Ortobene

Bus #8 (not Sun) runs from Nuoro's Via Manzoni and the Duomo up to the summit of Monte Ortobene hourly between mid-June and mid-September (last bus down at around 8.15pm), twice daily in winter (last bus down at around 3.30pm)

On Nuoro's eastern flank, 8km outside town, the summit of **Monte Ortobene** affords awe-inspiring views over the deep valley separating Nuoro from Monte Corrasi (1463m) and the Supramonte massif. The heavily wooded slopes are a favourite destination for the townsfolk at weekends, and the **Farcana** locality (signposted off the only road leading up the mountain) has a sports complex open in summer that includes an Olympic-size open-air pool, tennis courts and stables for riding. However, there are still plenty of areas that feel remote enough to get lost in, and the woods are perfect for picnics and walks, with paths trailing off.

Near the top of the mountain (955m), a huge bronze **statue** of the Redeemer (*Redentore*) stands poised in an attitude of swirling motion over the immense void. The figure attracts pilgrims at all times – as shown by the trinkets and other devotional gifts left here, and by Christ's polished right toe (the only part of the statue within reach) – and is the destination for the procession that weaves up from the town during Nuoro's annual Sagra del Redentore (see box, p.278). Others come for the stupendous panorama, with its dizzying views down to the valley floor.

ARRIVAL AND DEPARTURE NUORO

By train ARST (☎800 865 042, ⚲arst.sardegna.it) runs services from Nuoro to Macomer (Mon–Sat 6 daily; 1hr 10min), a stop on the main north–south line (for information on FS services, call ☎892 021 or visit ⚲trenitalia.it). From Nuoro's train station it's a 15min walk to the centre of town along Via Lamármora – not much less on any of the city buses that stop on the opposite side of the road (tickets €1 from the station bar, on the right as you exit the station).

By bus The bus station is on Viale Sardegna (a 10min walk south of the train station); for the centre, take bus #1 or #3 from the stop to the right as you exit (tickets from the newspaper kiosk across the road). Most bus routes within Nuoro province are operated by ARST (see above). The other main companies are Turmo (☎0789 21 487,

⚲gruppoturmotravel.com) connecting Nuoro with Cágliari, Olbia and Santa Teresa Gallura; Deplano for Olbia airport (☎0784 295 030, ⚲deplanobus.it), and Redentours for Alghero's Fertilia airport (☎0784 30 325, ⚲redentours.com). Destinations Arbatax (Mon–Sat 1 daily; 3hr); Aritzo (1 daily; 2hr); Belvì (1 daily; 1hr 45min); Bitti (Mon–Sat 6 daily, Sun 2 daily; 1hr 5min); Cágliari (4 daily; 2hr 40min–3hr); Cala Gonone (Mon–Sat 6–7 daily, Sun 4–5; 1hr 10min); Dorgali (Mon–Sat 6–8 daily, Sun 4–5; 50min); Fertilia airport, Alghero (2 daily; 2hr 30min); Fonni (Mon–Sat 11–12 daily, Sun 3 daily; 40min–1hr 30min); Ísili (1–2 daily; 3hr 10min); Láconi (1 daily; 2hr 35min); Macomer (5–6 daily; 1hr–1hr 40min); Mamoiada (Mon–Sat 9 daily, Sun 4 daily; 20min); Monte Ortobene (local buses; Mon–Sat summer hourly, winter 2 daily; 20min); Olbia (3–5 daily; 1hr 50min–3hr 30min); Olbia airport (7–10 daily; 1hr 40min–3hr 30min); Oliena (Mon–Sat 14 daily, Sun 5 daily; 20min); Orani (Mon–Sat 6–7 daily, Sun 1 daily; 25min); Orgósolo (Mon–Sat 9 daily, Sun 3 daily; 35min); Oristano (1 daily; 1hr 35min); Orosei (Mon–Sat 9–10 daily, Sun 3 daily; 50min); Orune (Mon–Sat 6 daily, Sun 2 daily; 40min); Posada (6–5 daily; 1hr 20min–2hr 20min); Santa Maria Navarrese (Mon–Sat 4 daily, Sun 1 daily; 2hr 25min); Sássari (4–5 daily; 1hr 40min–2hr 10min); Sórgono (Mon–Sat 5 daily; 1hr 40min); Tonara (1 daily; 1hr 30min).

GETTING AROUND

By car Drivers should avoid the old centre as much as possible; park your vehicle in between the blue lines, for which tickets are available from meters. For car rental, try Europcar, Piazza Véneto 19 (☎0784 399 104, ⓦeuropcar.it) or Maggiore, Via Convento 32 (☎0784 30 461, ⓦmaggiore.it).

By bus ATP (☎0784 35 195, ⓦatpnuoro.it) operates Nuoro's local network. Apart from the brief ride between the stations and the centre, local buses are mainly useful for reaching Monte Ortobene (see opposite); buy tickets (€1 valid for any journeys within 1hr 30min, or €2.50 for the day) from newsagents or *tabacchini* before boarding.

By taxi There are ranks on Viale Sardegna and by the train station. Call ☎0784 31 411 or ☎335 399 174.

INFORMATION

Tourist office Piazza Italia 19 (Mon & Wed–Fri 8.30am–2pm, Tues 8.30am–2pm & 3.30–7pm; ☎0784 238 878), for information on the town and province. The independent Punto Informa at Via Garibaldi 36 (☎0784 208 016, ⓦpuntoinforma.com) keeps erratic hours but can advise on tourist services in and around Nuoro.

ACCOMMODATION

★ **Casa Solotti** Monte Ortobene ☎0784 33 954 or ☎328 602 8975, ⓦcasasolotti.it. Nuoro's neighbouring mountain has an excellent, friendly B&B, with a spacious garden, assorted pets and a helpful owner who can arrange (and sometimes leads) tours to local sights, including Tíscali. There are fantastic views from most of its quiet, comfortable rooms, four of which have private bathrooms and three of which have access to a roof terrace. Some rooms also have cooking facilities, and there's wi-fi and a terminal for guests' use. Breakfast may include home-made yoghurt and jams. Located 5km from the Grazia Deledda church, just after the Farcana turn-off, it has a bus stop right outside, and the owner will also collect guests. No credit cards. €60

Euro Hotel Via Trieste 62 ☎0784 34 071, ⓦeurohotel nuoro.it. Combining 1930s-style furnishings with a corporate feel, the *Euro* doesn't invite a lengthy stay, though it has a kind of quirky charm that might appeal to retro fans. It's close to the train station and a 15min walk from the old centre. Rooms have fridges and free wi-fi, and there's parking. €90

Grillo Via Monsignor Melas 14 ☎0784 38 678, ⓦgrillo hotel.it. Modern and characterless, this three-star is a convenient, fairly central choice, whose functional rooms have a/c. There's a restaurant, but breakfasts are modest affairs, and there's no garage. €78

Nughe 'e' Oro Via Matteotti 14 ☎0784 182 3255 or ☎340 805 2769, ⓦnugheoro.it. On the sixth floor of a modern block near the Duomo, this B&B has bright, airy, wi-fi-enabled rooms with or without private facilities. Arty photos by the friendly host adorn the walls, and there are views over the roofs from the small terrace. No credit cards. €50

Roccas Parco Sedda Ortai, Monte Ortobene ☎0784 36 565 or ☎349 233 7211, ⓦroccas.eu. Set amid woods a short drive or bus ride from Nuoro, this *agriturismo* offers no-frills camping or accommodation in *pinnettus* (basic shepherd's huts). There's a six-night minimum stay in Aug, and also a good restaurant (open to all). Closed mid-Oct to mid-March. Pitches €20, huts €30

Silvia e Paolo Corso Garibaldi 58 ☎0784 31 280 or ☎328 921 2199, ⓦsilviaepaolo.it. In the heart of the old centre, this B&B has three modern, spotless rooms with shared or en-suite bathrooms, all overlooking the Corso and with wi-fi. There's a pleasant terrace. €50

EATING AND DRINKING

Nuoro is surprisingly well off for **restaurants**, generally with very reasonable prices. On some menus, or in bars, you might find traditional **pastries**, such as *s'arantzada*, a sticky local sweet made with honey and fresh oranges. This and other local specialities are also available from places on the Corso, for example Zia Marianna at no. 174. For fruit, veg and other takeaway items, there's a Saturday morning **market** on Piazza Italia, and a **supermarket** on Via Lamármora.

Ciusa Viale Ciusa 55 ☎0784 257 052. At the western end of town, this traditional restaurant with elegant, dark brown walls pulls in a well-heeled crowd for its tasty, seasonal dishes such as risotto with wine and melted sheep's cheese, meat grills and even prawn curry. Most main courses come to €16–20, and pizzas are available. Tues–Sun 1–2.30pm & 8–11pm.

★ **Il Pórtico** Via Monsignor Bua 13 ☎0784 217 641.

8

> ### THE SAGRA DEL REDENTORE
>
> Many costumes similar to those displayed in Nuoro's ethnographic museum are aired in the town's biggest annual festival, the **Sagra del Redentore**. Held during the last ten days of August, it involves participants from all over the island, but especially the villages of the Barbagia. The festival combines solemn religious rites with a flamboyant celebration of Sardinia's cultural heritage. The evenings are dedicated to traditional dancing and singing, enthusiastically performed in the old town's squares, while costumed parades take place during the day, culminating on the last day in a long procession out of Nuoro to the statue of the Redeemer on Monte Ortobene and the nearby church of Nostra Signora di Montenero. Together, these events constitute one of the most vibrant *feste* on the island's calendar, and accommodation at this time is at a premium.

You'll find an innovative approach to the traditional Sard dishes on offer in this smart place with modern art on the walls – such as *lados con tonno fresco* (fresh pasta with tuna), *laganelle con cozze e zucchine* (fresh pasta with mussels and courgettes) and *spigola con crosta di patate* (sea bass in a potato crust). Leave space for the lip-smacking desserts, and there's a good wine list. Starters are about €12, mains around €14. Daily except Wed 12.30–2.30pm & 8–10.45pm.

★ **Il Rifugio** Via Mereu 28 ☎0784 232 355. There's usually a full house for this consistently good ristorante/ pizzeria specializing in such regional specialities as *filindeu nel brodo di pecora* (stringy pasta in a mutton broth). Main courses cost €8–18, and service is brisk but friendly. Daily except Wed 12.45–3pm & 7.45–11.30pm.

★ **La Locanda** Via Brofferio 31 ☎0784 31 032. There are no airs or graces in this traditional *osteria* in a large, plain room, which offers fresh pasta and authentic *nuorese* dishes at rock-bottom prices. You won't spend more than €20 including drinks, and the €9.20 fixed-price menu scores highly among local workers at lunchtime. Mon–Sat 12.30–3pm & 8.30–10.30pm; closed 2 weeks Aug.

Ristorante Tascusi Via Aspromonte 13 ☎0784 37 287. Local dishes are served in simple white rooms decorated with Sard art. The meaty menu might include *culurgiones al sugo di cinghiale* (ravioli with boar's meat sauce) and *pane frattau* (bread soaked in tomato sauce and pecorino), and pizzas are also served. All dishes are €8–11, and set-price menus are sometimes available. Mon–Sat 12.30–3.30pm & 7.30–11pm; open daily in Aug.

Su Nugoresu Piazza San Giovanni 9 ☎0784 258 017. One of the rare places in Nuoro where you can dine alfresco, this trattoria has tables on a pretty piazza, and a wide-ranging menu that includes such concoctions as *bavette alle vóngole* (pasta with clams and a creamy pistachio sauce) as well as pizzas. Most dishes are €10–15. June–Sept Mon–Fri 12.30–3pm & 8–11pm, Sat & Sun 8–11pm.

BARS

Bar Cambosu Via Monsignor Bua 4 ☎0784 31 731. On the corner of Piazza Vittorio Emanuele, this old-fashioned place has comfy chairs and lots of chat, and there's a separate smoking room. A good breakfast stop. Daily 6am–9pm; closed Mon eve in winter, Sun eve in summer.

Caffè Tettamanzi Corso Garibaldi 71. Nuoro's oldest bar (from 1875) has the usual tables outside, but the mirrored interior has more character, with a painted ceiling and cherubs flitting about. Mon–Sat 6am–2am; open Sun in summer.

DIRECTORY

Hospital Ospedale San Francesco, Via Mannironi, northwest of the train station ☎0784 240 237.
Pharmacy Gali, Corso Garibaldi 65 ☎0784 30 143 (8.30am–1pm & 4.30–8.30pm or 4–8pm in winter).

Late-closing pharmacies operate on a rota – check on any pharmacy door to see the address of the current one.
Post office Piazza Francesco Crispi (Mon–Fri 8.25am–7.10pm, Sat 8.25am–12.35pm).

North and west of Nuoro

The country **north and west of Nuoro** has a less dramatic appeal than that of the more famous Barbagia, but its scattered hamlets and high plains merit a slow exploration, preferably with your own transport. Bus connections are sporadic, and accommodation is virtually nonexistent, but much of the region can be visited on trips out of Nuoro.

Su Tempiesu

Daily 9am–sunset • €3 • 328 756 5148, sutempiesu.it

The nondescript hill settlement of **Orune**, 13km north of Nuoro, has little intrinsic interest, but you'll need to pass this way to visit the remote site of **Su Tempiesu**, a sacred well and temple dating from nuraghic times. At the entrance to the village, take the signposted (and mostly unsurfaced) road that dips 5km east to the entrance to the site, where there's a bar selling drinks and snacks. The temple itself is hidden in the valley below the road, reached along a steeply descending path. Knowledgeable guides will explain (usually in Italian) the significance of the site, which, discovered by a farmer in 1953, constitutes Sardinia's best-preserved example of a **sacred well** from this period, and remains a good illustration of the importance of water at a time when it was often (surprisingly) in chronically short supply. Health-giving and prophetic properties were attributed to springs by the numerous cults that grew up around them, and temples were built over the outlets.

The structure

Many of Sardinia's sacred wells conform to the general design of Su Tempiesu, which has sturdy, slab-built walls with a triangular entrance, and is topped by a steeply pitched roof. Benches run along the tapering walls of the "atrium", from where shallow, cleanly hewn steps descend to the spring, and a conduit channels any excess water when the level rises. The surrounding walls have niches built into them to hold the bronze statuettes and other votive objects that were found during the excavations, some of them dating from between the twelfth and ninth centuries BC.

The visible remains don't take very long to absorb, but the peaceful, bucolic setting and the enthusiasm of the guides, who will point out the various plants and sculptures they have installed along the path, add to the appeal of the place. Similar examples of sacred wells, albeit in very different settings, can be seen at Santa Cristina, near Oristano (see p.157), and Sa Testa, outside Olbia (see p.234).

Bitti

Twelve kilometres of mountain road north of Orune, the village of **BITTI** is famed for its singing tradition; the local male group, **Tenores di Bitti**, has established an international reputation for its four-part harmonies. Other than the museums, Bitti has a couple of bars and *alimentaris*, and a bank at Via Deffenu 2.

Museo del Canto a Tenores

Via Mameli • Tues & Thurs 9.30am–12.30pm, Wed & Fri–Sun 9.30am–12.30pm & 3.30–6.30pm, or 2.30–5.30pm in winter • €3 • 0784 414 314

You can find out about the famous **Tenores di Bitti** and Sardinia's polyphonic singing tradition in general at the small **Museo del Canto a Tenores**, signposted up an alley off the main Corso Vittorio Veneto (where you should park). Tapes and videos give a broad overview of the different singing styles, and allow you to pinpoint the contributions of each of the components of the foursomes.

Museo della Civiltà Contadina e Pastorale

Via Mameli • Tues & Thurs 9.30am–12.30pm, Wed & Fri–Sun 9.30am–12.30pm & 3.30–6.30pm, or 2.30–5.30pm in winter • €3 • 0784 414 314

Ethnographic collections are not exactly rare in Sardinia, but there's always something of interest to view. Sharing a building with the Canto a Tenores museum, Bitti's **Museo della Civiltà Contadina e Pastorale** is spread out over ten rooms and devoted to the local farming and peasant culture. It's a fairly low-key collection, with sections devoted to bread-making, shoe-making and weaving.

Burgos

In Sássari province, some 40km west of Bitti, the village of **BURGOS** is visible from miles around, mainly on account of its castle, **La Reggia**, dramatically poised on a granite pinnacle high above. Although founded in the fourteenth century by Mariano IV of Arborea, the village has a predominantly modern aspect, containing not much more than a bank (in Via Marconi) and a couple of bars. However, the scenic road running 35km northwest towards Torralba (see p.224) passes through the **Foresta di Burgos**, a wooded area that's home to miniature horses, and across an evocative landscape of high, empty plains, before descending to the SS131.

La Reggia

Vícolo Castello • Tues–Sun 9am–12.30pm & 3–7pm, or 2.30–6pm in winter • €3 • ☎ 349 448 7275

Completed in 1133, the formidably walled redoubt was strategically vital for its commanding position over the Tirso valley, at a point where the three *giudicati* (territories) of Torres, Arborea and Gallura met. It was briefly occupied by Eleonora d'Arborea (see box, p.142), and was used as a prison for various unwanted family members – guides will point out the remains of cells as well as of stables and barracks, and of an extensive space that may have been a church or central dining-hall. At one end, the square tower looming over the ruins is a rather incongruous renovation from the 1950s. The same ticket admits you to the **Museo dei Castelli** (same times), below the castle entrance, where you can see temporary exhibitions and a permanent display on castles throughout Sardinia.

8

Oliena and around

The nearest village of any size to Nuoro, **OLIENA** is easily visible from the provincial capital, sprawled along the side of **Monte Corrasi** to the south. Rising to 1463m, this rugged limestone elevation forms part of the **Supramonte massif**, famed as the haunt of **bandits** until relatively recently. Oliena itself prefers its reputation as the producer of one of the island's finest wines: **Nepente**, a variety of the prized Cannonau – a dry, almost black concoction that turns lighter and stronger over the years. Oliena is also the best base for hiking excursions in the surrounding mountainous terrain. You can gain access to Monte Corrasi from Località Maccione, a wooded area 3km south of town off the very squiggly old road to Orgósolo (see p.282).

Su Gologone

Off the Dorgali road, 6km east of Oliena, **SU GOLOGONE** makes an attractive starting point for mountain expeditions (see box opposite). The area is named after a fast-flowing spring emerging from underground close to the church of **San Giovanni**, and there are usually a few locals here filling jerrycans with the therapeutic springwater. It's a good spot to picnic under the eucalyptus trees, and you can follow the course of the stream or

---

OLIENA'S FESTIVALS

The best time to visit Oliena would be during one of its annual **feast days**. The most striking are around **Easter**: on Good Friday, when a mournful procession shuffles through the streets, at the end of which the whole village pours into a pitch-black church to watch an intensely dramatic re-enactment of Christ's Deposition, and on Easter Sunday, a much more boisterous affair, when hundreds gather to witness the *Incontru*, or meeting, between the figures of the Virgin Mary and the resurrected Jesus. On this latter occasion, there's much gunfire, villagers don traditional dress (an elegant black and white or red and white costume, complete with jewellery), and there's dancing, music and free tastings in the main square. The costumes and dancing can also be viewed during the four days of revelry around **San Lussorio's day** on August 21.

a choice of tracks leading into the mountains. There's a hotel with a renowned restaurant here too (see p.282). ARST buses stop at the turn-off for Su Gologone.

ARRIVAL AND DEPARTURE

OLIENA AND AROUND

By bus Oliena is connected by almost hourly buses (fewer on Sun) with Nuoro (Mon–Sat 14 daily, Sun 5; 20min) and Dorgali (Mon–Sat 8–9 daily, Sun 4–5; 25min); the last bus to Nuoro leaves at 8.15pm (9.10pm on Sun). Dorgali-bound buses can drop you at the turn-off to Su Gologone, from where it's a brief walk to the spring.

INFORMATION AND ACTIVITIES

Tourist office Corso Deledda 32, Oliena (Mon–Sat 9am–1pm & 4–7pm, closed Sat Nov–Easter; ☎ 0784 286 078, ⓦ olienaturismo.com).
Guided expeditions For exploring Supramonte's caves and crags, Oliena's main operators are Barbagia Insólita, Corso Vittorio Emanuele 48 (☎ 0784 286 005, ⓦ barbagia insolita.it), and Sardegna Nascosta (☎ 0784 288 550 or ☎ 349 443 4665, ⓦ sardegnanascosta.it).

ACCOMMODATION

CiKappa Corso M. Luther King 2, Oliena ☎ 0784 288 024, ⓦ cikappa.it. Functional hotel much favoured by outdoors enthusiasts, offering seven fairly standard modern rooms and a popular restaurant (see p.282). The staff here can also arrange expeditions of various sorts. **€70**
★ **Cooperativa Turistica Enis** Località Maccione ☎ 0784 288 363, ⓦ coopenis.it. Off a steep, rough-surfaced road that corkscrews up the mountain 3km south of Oliena (signposted off the old road for Orgósolo), this hotel, campsite and restaurant complex – also known as *Monte Maccione* – is perfectly situated for mountain walks. The clean rooms, basic pitches in the woods and the restaurant (see p.282) all have lofty views. **€80**, pitches **€17**
Santa Maria Corso Deledda 76, Oliena ☎ 0784 287 278

8

THE WALK TO VALLE LANAITTU AND MONTE TÍSCALI

One of the most rewarding expeditions you can make on Supramonte is to **Valle Lanaittu**, a grand, secluded valley overlooked by **Monte Tíscali** (518m), which holds the remains of a nuraghic village. The best advice is to take a guide, which the tourist office in Oliena (see above) can arrange; expect to pay around €40 including lunch, sometimes with a minimum of four people. Although it's possible to reach the site unaccompanied – it's a relatively short and straightforward **hike** of four or five hours, depending on your starting point – there are some tricky sections where there's a risk of straying off the route, not least in locating the start of the ascent, and indications are few and far between. Moreover, some of the approaches are too rough for any but off-road vehicles to negotiate, meaning that you'll have a long way to walk to reach the interesting section. If you do attempt it on your own, make sure you let someone know where you're headed before leaving. Either way, you should have adequate equipment: robust walking shoes or boots, protection against the sun and at least a litre of water per person.

There are two **routes** into the Valle Lanaittu, one signposted from the **Sorgente Su Gologone**, a natural spring just by the *Su Gologone* hotel complex (see p.282) on the Oliena–Dorgali road, and the milder but longer and not so dramatic ascent that starts from the same point as the walk to the Gorroppu canyon (see box, p.299), near Dorgali. The signposting is better on the latter option, more advisable for unaccompanied walks.

As it's well concealed behind trees, it's a bit of a shock to find the **nuraghic village of Tíscali** (daily: April–Sept 9am–7pm; Oct–March 9am–5pm; €5) in such an isolated spot, dramatically sited within a vast hollow space inside the mountain itself. Once providing a last refuge from foreign incursions during the first millennium BC, the site was inhabited well into Roman and medieval times, but was only rediscovered about a century ago, and is still under excavation. Few of the buildings have survived in a recognizable form, but it's a fascinating place nonetheless, the yellow limestone walls and stalactites giving it a weird, ghostly atmosphere. A huge hole punched through the rock where part of the roof collapsed creates a soft twilight within, and once enabled the villagers to keep an eye on any comings and goings in the valley below. There's vegetation and even trees growing inside, but the lack of ready water must have been a constant problem, probably preventing the community from ever growing very large.

From here, you can either retrace your steps back down, or – preferably with an experienced guide – you might continue along the path past Tíscali, descending into the **Flumineddu valley** to the east.

or ☏ 328 117 8551, 🌐 bbsantamaria.it. Modern, central B&B with spacious rooms including a traditionally styled suite with its own balcony. All rooms have private bathrooms, a/c and wi-fi, and there's a large, panoramic roof terrace. No credit cards. **€50**

Su Gologone Località Su Gologone ☏ 0784 287 512, 🌐 sugologone.it. Armed with your own transport and a comfortable budget, you can't do better than this luxurious complex in a rustic setting next to the spring of the same name, equipped with a swimming pool, tennis court and fitness centre. The hotel offers a full programme of walking, horseriding and 4x4 expeditions, including "lunch with the shepherds" – a hike or jeep ride which culminates in an open-air feast. The hotel lies 7km east of Oliena on the Dorgali road. Closed Nov to late March. Rates are per person per night half-board. **€150**

EATING

CiKappa Via M. Luther King, Oliena ☏ 0784 288 024. In this lively ristorante/pizzeria, you can have a full meal of traditional rural cuisine for around €25. The menu specializes in land-based dishes, often incorporating wild mushrooms and boar. Daily 12.30–3pm & 7.30pm–midnight.

★ **Cooperativa Turistica Enis** Località Maccione ☏ 0784 288 363. The terrace restaurant at this hotel complex up a steep hill 3km south of Oliena beats all the competition for its fabulous views over the valley. Pizzas are available alongside such dishes as rabbit stew and roast sucking pig on fixed-price menus costing €18.50–35. Daily 12.30–3pm & 8–10.30pm; call ahead Nov–Feb.

Masiloghi Via Galiani 68, Oliena ☏ 0784 285 696. A 5min walk from the centre on the Dorgali road, this place is the most highly rated of Oliena's restaurants, with a semi-formal but self-consciously "rustic" ambience and delicious meat and seafood platters. Tasting menus are €30. You can eat on the veranda in summer. Daily 12.30– 3pm & 7.30–11pm; closed Tues Nov–March.

Su Gologone Località Su Gologone ☏ 0784 287 512, 🌐 sugologone.it. The restaurant attached to this luxury hotel 7km east of Oliena is reasonably priced but pampers diners with a succulent succession of such local dishes as ravioli with fennel, *gnocchetti* with boar-meat sauce, meat on the spit (vegetarians have a limited choice). First courses come to around €10, mains about €15. Late March to Oct daily 12.30–2.30pm & 8–10.30pm.

The Barbagia Ollolai

To the south and east of Oliena, the villages of the **Barbagia Ollolai** region offer contrasting glimpses into local culture and folklore: **Orgósolo** is famous for its ancient banditry and its vivid, politicized murals; the otherwise unremarkable village of **Mamoiada**, 11km west and 16km south of Nuoro, is the venue of a highly pagan Carnival, while farther west, **Orani** has a museum devoted to artist Costantino Nivola. Lacking the dramatic landscape of other parts of the Barbagia, the area is less conducive for walking, though the **Montes** region south of Orgósolo has an appealing empty grandeur that's worth experiencing.

Orgósolo and around

At the end of a straggly 18km road from Oliena, **ORGÓSOLO** is stuck with its label of **bandit capital** of Sardinia. The clans of Orgósolo, whose menfolk used to spend the greater part of the year away from home with their flocks, have always nursed

---

ORGÓSOLO'S SCARLET ROSE

Orgósolo's most notorious son is **Graziano Mesina**, the so-called "Scarlet Rose", who won local hearts in the 1960s by supposedly robbing only from the rich to give to the poor and only killing for revenge against those who had betrayed him. Roaming at will through the mountains, even granting interviews to reporters and television journalists, he was eventually captured and incarcerated in Sássari prison. Escaping in 1968, he was recaptured near Nuoro and flown by helicopter the same day to appear on television in Cágliari. In July 1992 he was dispatched to Sardinia from a mainland prison to help negotiate the release of Farouk Kassam, an 8-year-old boy held hostage for seven months in the Barbagia (see box, p.287). Mesina was finally freed in 2004, having served forty years behind bars, and returned to live with his sisters in Orgósolo.

an animosity towards the settled crop-farmers on the Barbagia's fringes, a tension that occasionally broke out into open warfare. On top of this, there was conflict between rival clans, which found expression in large-scale sheep-rustling and bloody **vendettas**, such as the *disamistade* (enmity) that engulfed Orgósolo at the beginning of the twentieth century. The feud arose from a dispute over the inheritance of the village's richest chieftain, Diego Moro, who died in 1903, and lasted for fourteen years, virtually exterminating the two families involved. Between 1901 and 1954, Orgósolo (with a population of four thousand) clocked up an average of one murder every two months. In 1953 the first of the postwar **kidnappings**, which would soon become endemic in this region of Sardinia, took place near Orgósolo, and the connection was crystallized with the screening of Vittorio de Seta's film *Banditi a Orgosolo* in 1961.

Orgósolo's murals

Saddled with its semi-legendary background, Orgósolo plays host to a constant trickle of visitors hoping to find traces of its violent past amid the shabby collection of grey breeze-block houses, and the locals have obliged by peppering various of the village's name-plates and signs with bullet holes, and by painting a sinister scarlet and white face on a rock by the side of the main road into town.

But this is just a harbinger of things to come, for Orgósolo's narrow alleys have been daubed with a vivid array of **murals** covering whole houses and shopfronts. Most have a political element, the suppression of the many by the few or Sardinian independence, for example, while others comically depict the collision of traditional culture with the modern world. One of the most heavily painted buildings is the Municipio at the eastern end of the main Corso Repubblica, whose garish collection of cartoon figures and slogans are poignantly shot through with more bullet holes – the work of local hotheads.

Montes

Within easy reach of Orgósolo lies a tract of high country well worth exploring. Following the road through the village, a left turn takes you south out of town and steeply uphill, leading after about 5km to the high plateau of **Montes**, an empty, desolate expanse, green but rugged, suitable for hiking or riding, and site of a good hotel and restaurant (see below). A small road continues as far as **Funtana Bona**, at a height of 1052m, only a kilometre or two's walk from the peak of **Monte San Giovanni** (1316m), near the source of the Cedrino river.

ARRIVAL AND DEPARTURE	ORGÓSOLO AND AROUND

By bus A regular ARST service plies the route between Orgósolo and Nuoro (Mon–Sat 9 daily, Sun 3 daily; 35min).

ACCOMMODATION AND EATING

★ **Ai Monti del Gennargentu** Località Settiles, Montes ☎0784 402 374 or ☎0784 194 5152, ❻mes .org@tiscali.it. Drivers will be able to reach this remote but wonderful restaurant serving healthy mountain fare, including the local *filindeu* (stringy pasta) and *porcetto arrosto* (roast pork). There are eight plain, en-suite rooms if you want to stay, and the staff can help if you want to do any walking or riding in the area. Half-board costs €65/ person, and the meals come to around €25 for two courses. It's about 3km from the SS389 Nuoro–Arbatax road, from the junction at Pratobello. Easter–Oct daily 12.30– 2.30pm & 7.30–10.30pm; €60
Il Pórtico Via Giovanni XXIII ☎0784 402 929. Orgósolo doesn't have much in the way of culinary hotspots, but this

simple and friendly trattoria off the main Corso Repubblica should see you right. The menu has meaty Sardinian specialities such as *lados al ragù di pecora* (pasta with mutton sauce) and *bistecca di manzo* (beefsteak), and pizzas are available. Fixed-price menus are €15–18, and there's a discount on presentation of this book. Daily noon–3pm & 7–11pm.
Sa 'e Jana Via Lussu ☎0784 402 437, ⓦalbergosaejana .com. The best feature of this hotel, restaurant and pizzeria is the far-reaching vistas it enjoys over the valley. Half the rooms have balconies – though you have to put up with kitsch murals on some of the walls. It's at the entrance to the village on the Mamoiada road, signposted past the graffiti-daubed school. €60

8

Mamoiada

Like Orgósolo, the deeply traditional the village of **MAMOIADA**, 11km west, has achieved its own particular fame, but in this case for its twice-yearly, highly theatrical **Carnival rituals** rather than for its murals or banditry (see box below). Surprisingly, the family of Juan Perón originated in Mamoiada, and according to some the Argentine president was himself born here.

Museo delle Máschere Mediterranee

Piazza Europa • Tues–Sun 9am–1pm & 3–7pm, June–Sept also Mon same times; guided tours on the hour (free) • €4 • ☎ 0784 569 018, ⓦ museodellemaschere.it

If you're not in Mamoiada for the masked festivities, the next best thing is to visit the **Museo delle Máschere Mediterranee**, housed in the *biblioteca* (library), at the bottom of the main Corso. The local masks, costumed mannequins and photos on show are augmented by examples from the Veneto and Fruili regions of Italy as well as places farther afield, from Greece to Korea. The guided commentaries (also in English) are informative, and you'll glean something of the appearance of the Carnival shenanigans from the ten-minute video, if not its spirit.

Fonte Romana

Off Via Tola

Signposted opposite the library, the **Fonte Romana** (*Su 'Antaru Vetzu*) merits a brief glance, though it amounts to little more than a couple of simple spouts over granite basins in a small piazza. Only the lower part is thought to be authentically Roman, supplying a garrison stationed nearby.

8

MAMOIADA'S MAMUTHONES

The **Mamuthones of Mamoiada** are among the best known of Sardinia's traditional costumed figures, associated with the festivities around Carnival time, but with obscure roots going back several centuries. Despite their spooky, rather disturbing appearance – decked out in dark, shaggy sheepskins on which rows of jangling goat-bells are strung, and with heavy, black, oversized masks – the *Mamuthones* are symbols of abundance and good times, as manifested by the food and drink liberally dispensed during the proceedings.

The **main events** take place on Shrove Tuesday and the preceding Sunday, usually kicking off at 3pm and 3.30pm respectively. Two columns of masked *Mamuthones* stalk the main street, Corso Vittorio Emanuele, accompanied by red-jacketed **Issohadores** – or *Issokadores* – each wielding a lasso (*sa soca*). As the *Mamuthones* advance solemnly, they perform curious synchronized leaps, causing the hundreds of goat-bells tied across their backs to clang simultaneously, while the *Issohadores* twirl their lassos and ensnare victims, often from a distance of several metres, sometimes targeting spectators watching from balconies along the route. At the end of Shrove Tuesday's procession, a masked puppet known as **Juvanne Martis** is hauled on a cart through the village by participants supposedly weeping to lament the end of Carnival, though the evening sees a general carousal in Piazza Santa Croce anyway, with plates of pork and beans, traditional sweets and glasses of the local wine handed around, and dancing. There's also plenty of similarly rustic fare to eat and drink throughout the ceremonies, offered at stalls and shops around the village.

There's an alternative opportunity to view these celebrations at the **Festa di Sant'Antonio Abate**, the traditional beginning of the Carnival period, usually January 16 and 17. Then, bonfires are lit around the village and kept burning through the night, attracting groups of half-drunk revellers shuttling between them. Locals contend this is the best time to view the *Mamuthones*, when there are fewer distractions from the other costumed Carnival celebrations on the island, and fewer tourists.

At other times, you can view the *Mamuthones* and other local costumes at Mamoiada's Museo delle Máschere Mediterranee (see above).

By bus Daily ARST buses connect Mamoiada with Nuoro and the villages of Barbagia.
Destinations Aritzo (1 daily; 1hr 35min); Belvì (1 daily; 1hr 30min); Cágliari (1 daily; 4hr 30min); Fonni (Mon–Sat 6 daily, Sun 1 daily; 20min); Nuoro (Mon–Sat 9 daily, Sun 4 daily; 20min).

Tourist information General information is available online at ⓦ mamuthonesmamoiada.it.

ACCOMMODATION AND EATING

Sa Perda Pinta Via Nuoro 33, Località Boeli ☎ 0784 56 689 or ☎ 320 352 0920, ✉ perdapinta@tiscali.it. Friendly B&B just outside the centre, occupying a pink villa on a slight elevation (opposite *Maps Pub*) with three doubles, one with its own bathroom, and a single room. The main point of interest, however, is a standing stone, or stele, displayed in the garden, thought to be 5000 years old; unearthed by chance by the owners, it's incised with odd circular symbols that may be linked to a fertility cult.

No credit cards. **€60**

Sa Rosada Piazza Europa ☎ 0784 56 713, ⓦ sarosada.it. The rooms of this B&B and restaurant have been preserved to an almost fanatical degree according to how they would have appeared when the house was built in the nineteenth century (the bathroom is shared). The restaurant has a limited choice of authentic local dishes, often including *porceddu* (roast pork), but it's a bit pricey at around €30 a head. Daily except Wed noon–2.30pm & 8.30–11pm; **€60**

Gavoi

Twenty twisty kilometres southwest of Mamoiada, **GAVOI** has gained kudos in recent years as the venue for Sardinia's main **literary festival**, held over four days in late June/early July. As well as readings and debates – some in English – there are films and alfresco music and theatre: see ⓦ isoladellestorie.it for details.

Orani

Sixteen kilometres north of Gavoi, the unassuming village of **ORANI** is worth a stop for the museum dedicated to its most famous son, the sculptor **Costantino Nivola** (1911–88). In fact, Nivola only spent a short part of his life here, working with his stonemason father until the age of 15 before studying in Sássari and then fleeing Fascist persecution in 1938. After spending some time in Paris, he emigrated to the US, where he forged a long association with the architect Le Corbusier and taught at Berkeley and Harvard.

Museo Nivola

Via Gonare 2 • Mon 4–9pm, Tues–Sun 9am–1pm & 4–9pm, closes 8pm Oct–May • €2.50 • ☎ 0784 730 063, ⓦ museonivola.it

Most of the works in the **Museo Nivola**, located in a former public wash-house near the bottom of the village, are from the last period of Nivola's life, and reflect the artist's attitudes towards his homeland upon revisiting it after his long American exile. The small-scale and low-key bronze sculptures are beautifully displayed in simple, well-lit surroundings, both indoors and outside in the small courtyard. Many of the objects, whose sleek, minimalist lines are reminiscent of Brancusi, are clearly inspired by ancient menhirs and nuraghic *bronzetti*; other works use cement and marble, and the technique of sandcasting pioneered by Nivola.

Sant'Andrea Apostolo

Su Campusantu Vezzu

Just up from the Museo Nivola, take a glance at the square, pinnacled tower of the ruined church of **Sant'Andrea Apostolo**, from the Pisan era – somehow the tower and facade escaped the ravages of time suffered by the rest of the building. You can just make out a cross of St Andrew carved above the main doorway.

By bus ARST buses stopping in Piazza Italia link Orani with Fonni (Mon–Sat 5 daily, Sun 1 daily; 1hr) and Nuoro (Mon– Sat 7–8 daily, Sun 1 daily; 25min).

The Barbagia Belvì and the Gennargentu massif

The **Barbagia Belvì** holds a significant chunk of the **Gennargentu** chain of mountains – the name means "silver gate", referring to the snow that covers them every winter – including the island's highest peaks, **Punta La Mármora** and **Monte Bruncu Spina**. The villages hereabouts were traditionally shepherds' communities, but nowadays local people send their children to university or they go to seek work in mainland Italy and don't come back, leaving behind slowly atrophying communities whose salvation is deemed to lie in a greater awareness of their tourism potential.

Many villages have in fact succeeded in adapting to the new economic reality, serving the expanding leisure industry, even if the season is short and has only a partial impact on the local economy. Though the villages themselves are often unprepossessing and fairly uniform in appearance – **Fonni**, for example, one of the main centres on the northern outskirts of the Gennargentu range, or **Sórgono**, loathed by D.H. Lawrence during his visit to Sardinia – some, such as **Aritzo** and **Belvì**, respectively Sardinia's chestnut and cherry capitals, are beautifully sited and also have good museums. But the real pleasures here are the bits between the villages: the distant views over thickly wooded slopes, where you may come across wild pigs and deer and, in the air, goshawks, sparrow hawks, peregrine falcons, griffon vultures and eagles.

The villages certainly make good bases for **walking**, best undertaken in spring and summer, and there are good, reasonably priced hotels in Aritzo, Belvì, Fonni and **Tonara**.

8

GETTING AROUND   THE BARBAGIA BELVÌ AND THE GENNARGENTU MASSIF

By train The infrequent narrow-gauge train service – the Trenino Verde – running south from Sórgono is a ponderous way to reach Tonara and Belvì-Aritzo, only to be used by those with time and patience to spare.

By bus The mountain roads can be convoluted and slow, and public transport is usually infrequent, but every village is connected to large centres by at least one bus route. Be prepared, however, for complicated short hops to travel *between* the villages, and also for some very early morning departures.

Fonni and around

Sixteen kilometres due south of Mamoiada, in a hilly area thick with vineyards, corks and oak forests, **FONNI** is, at 1000m, Sardinia's highest village. As a popular destination for skiers and walkers in the Gennargentu mountains – whose loftiest peaks, Bruncu Spina and La Mármora, are visible from the village – Fonni is also one of the Barbagia's biggest centres, a role it has occupied since the seventeenth century, when a community of Franciscans helped to make this the focus of the whole region.

BANDITRY AND KIDNAPPING IN THE BARBAGIA

Until a short time ago, the villages of the Barbagia were primarily communities of shepherds, whose isolated circumstances and economic difficulties in the postwar years led to widescale emigration and, among those who stayed behind, a crime wave. Sheep-rustling and internecine feuding came to be replaced by the infinitely more lucrative practice of **kidnapping** and ransoming of wealthy industrialists or their families. This phenomenon reached epidemic proportions during 1966–68, when scores of Carabinieri were drafted into the area to comb the mountains for the hideouts, rarely with any success. The most high-profile case in recent years was that of Farouk Kassam, an 8-year-old abducted from the Costa Smeralda in 1992 and held for seven months on Monte Albo, near Siniscola; part of his ear was severed by his kidnappers to accelerate the ransom payment. Since then, however, there has been a lull in the kidnappings, partly due to improvements in police intelligence.

FONNI'S FESTIVALS

The image of Madonna dei Mártiri (see below) is escorted through Fonni's streets during the village's two principal **festivals**, both in June: on the Monday following the first Sunday in June and again for St John's day on June 24. Both occasions are costumed extravaganzas, with columns of immaculately turned-out women and men on horseback, also in traditional dress, filing through the village.

Madonna dei Mártiri
Piazza dei Mártiri • Daily 7.30am–noon & 3.30–7.30pm

The church of **Madonna dei Mártiri** annexed to Fonni's Franciscan convent is still the most significant of the Barbagia's churches, both for its wealth and for its image of the Madonna, said to have been made from the crushed bones of martyrs. You can see the domed church at the highest point of the village, in the centre of a large open space off Piazza Europa, surrounded by *cumbessias*, or pilgrims' houses. Originally dating from the seventeenth century, but remodelled a hundred years later, the church is a substantial building with a peeling, salmon-coloured facade and tall, granite-grey spire. The interior is richly frescoed and painted with wooden altarpieces and pulpit; an elaborate shrine on the right as you enter holds the artless but much-venerated Madonna.

Around Fonni: the Gennargentu mountains
Fonni is well placed for exploring the heights of the Gennargentu mountains. Eight kilometres south of the village, on a signposted left turn off the Désulo road, you can follow paths that wind up to **Monte Spada** (1595m) and, to the south, **Bruncu Spina** (1829m), both of which can also be approached on a tarmacked road. It's a magnificent landscape, with bracken and other hardy shrubs taking over above the tree line, covered in snow for a good part of the year. The views from the top extend as far as Gallura and even Corsica to the north.

From Bruncu Spina, properly equipped hikers can reach the top of the island's highest peak, **Punta La Mármora** (1834m), a little way to the south, in less than three hours. You don't need to be an experienced climber to tackle either of these summits, though a guide is advisable; excursions between May and September can be organized at Fonni's hotels or from the various villages on the flanks of the mountains.

ARRIVAL AND DEPARTURE | **FONNI AND AROUND**

By bus Fonni is well connected to the most important Barbagia villages.

Destinations Aritzo (1–2 daily; 1hr 15min); Belvì (1–2 daily; 55min–1hr 10min); Cágliari (1 daily; 4hr 10min); Mamoiada (Mon–Sat 7 daily, Sun 2 daily; 20min); Nuoro (Mon–Sat 7 daily, Sun 2 daily; 40min); Orani (Mon–Sat 4–5 daily, Sun 1 daily; 1hr); Sórgono (Mon–Sat 2 daily; 1hr–1hr 25min); Tonara (Mon–Sat 2 daily; 1hr 5min).

ACCOMMODATION AND EATING

Barbagia Via Umberto 106 ☎ 0784 58 329. Unpretentious bar/ristorante/pizzeria at the southern end of town, where you can tuck into *penne al gorgonzola* or more local dishes such as *malloreddus* or *maccarrones* (both pasta dishes). Starters are €4–8, mains around €8. Tues–Sun noon–3pm & 7–10pm.

Cualbu Viale del Lavoro ☎ 0784 57 054, ⓦ hotelcualbu .com. This large and fairly modern hotel has a pool, gym, garden and (occasional) disco, with standard, smallish rooms. The restaurant is fine but breakfast is a meagre affair. **€90**

⭐ **Sa Orte** Via Roma 14 ☎ 0784 58 020, ⓦ hotelsaorte .it. An elegantly restored granite building with period trappings in the cobbled heart of the old town, this has spacious, modern rooms with wi-fi, professional staff, a good restaurant and abundant breakfasts. Family rooms and suites are also available. **€80**

Belvì

As the crow flies, it's 18km south of Fonni to **BELVÌ**, a compact cluster of dwellings crowded along the side of a valley, but it's nearly twice that distance on the twisty mountain roads. The village is famed for its cherries, and once wielded a certain amount of influence locally – as reflected in the fact that it has given its name to this whole sector of the Barbagia – but it's a very low-key place now, providing useful accommodation and refreshment, and diversion in the form of its volunteer-run museum.

Museo di Scienze Naturali
Via San Sebastiano • Daily 9am–1pm & 4–7pm, 3–5pm in winter • €3 • ☎ 339 792 0232 or ☎ 339 753 1025

An eclectic pot-pourri of fossils, minerals, mammals, butterflies and nearly four hundred stuffed birds, this private collection is crammed into a modern apartment just off Belvì's main street. The items aren't confined to the Barbagia, but include marine shells and a giant Caretta Caretta turtle. The collection was begun in the 1970s by the entomologist Friedrich Reichsgraf Von Hartig. If you're keen, call first to make sure it's open.

ARRIVAL AND DEPARTURE **BELVÌ**

By bus ARST buses stop on the main Via Roma. Destinations Aritzo (Mon–Sat 6–8 daily, Sun 1 daily; 5min); Cágliari (1–2 daily; 2hr 40min–3hr); Fonni (1–2 daily; 1hr); Láconi (1–3 daily; 45min–1hr 10min); Mamoiada (1–3 daily; 1hr 25min); Nuoro (1–3 daily; 1hr 45min); Sórgono (Mon–Sat 5 daily; 40min); Tonara (Mon–Sat 6 daily, Sun 1 daily; 20min).

ACCOMMODATION AND EATING

Edera Via Roma ☎ 0784 629 825. This basic hotel with a bar-restaurant attached offers twelve very simple but comfortable en-suite rooms. Breakfast costs extra (€3 or €10). The excellent basement restaurant serves typical local cooking, including lamb stew and wild boar, with main courses around €15. If you don't want a full meal, the bar upstairs has delicious sausage sandwiches (€8). Daily 1–3pm & 7.30–10pm; €60

Aritzo

Just 3km west of Belvì, **ARITZO** is a similar huddle of grey buildings around a long main street, though it's larger and has a livelier aspect than many of the Barbagia's other villages. Corso Umberto holds everything of interest, including craft shops, a bank, the parish church and a first-class museum. The imposing crenellated structure on the left as you ascend is the neo-Gothic **Castello Arangino**, its tower and loggia lending it an old Tuscan character, though it was only built at the beginning of the twentieth century. Gaps in the buildings will allow you to appreciate the views across the valley, where the solitary **Monte Téxile** (975m) punctuates the horizon with its oddly square profile.

Museo della Montagna
Via Marconi • Tues–Sun 10am–1pm & 4–7pm, 3–6pm in winter • €3 including Sa Bovida (Prigioni Spagnoli) • ☎ 0784 629 801

Housed in the basement of a school, Aritzo's absorbing **Museo della Montagna** (signposted Museo Etnografico) is a fascinating jumble of artefacts connected with rural culture in the Gennargentu region. Between walls hung with agricultural implements and sepia photos are displayed articles for cheese- and wax-making, artisans' tools, local costumes and looms, all in fine condition. Aritzo once earned a good living selling snow for chilling drinks and preserving foodstuffs, and you can see here the containers in which it was transported.

Sa Bovida
Via Scala Cárceri 6 • Tues–Sun 10am–1pm & 4–7pm, 3–6pm in winter • €3 including museum • ☎ 0784 629 801

With your museum ticket, you can take a peek in the **Sa Bovida** (also known as Prigioni Spagnoli, or Spanish prison), on an alley below the Corso. Dating back to the sixteenth century, the well-restored, schist-built structure was used as a jail until the 1940s, and manacles and other items relating to its former function are displayed. The rooms here were also used by the Inquisition in former times, and there's an exhibition of various objects used in local "**witchcraft**" practices, for which some women were

8

ARITZO'S FESTIVALS

If you're in Aritzo in late October, you can participate in local celebrations for the **chestnut harvest**, the **Sagra delle Castagne**, taking place on the last Sunday of the month. For days before and after, the village is permeated with the aroma of roasting chestnuts, which are distributed free, along with hazelnuts, walnuts and the various confectionaries made from them. Local arts and crafts are also much in evidence. Aritzo's renowned **lemon sorbets** are consumed in the festival of **Sa Carapigna**, around August 15. The crushed-ice drink was originally made from mountain snow.

---

charged and one was burned at the stake. Providing a cultural contrast, there's a cabinet of Nigerian effigies used in occult African rituals, too.

ARRIVAL AND INFORMATION
ARITZO

By bus ARST buses stop on the main Corso Umberto. **Destinations** Belvì (Mon–Sat 6–8 daily, Sun 1 daily; 5min); Cágliari (1–2 daily; 2hr 35min–3hr); Fonni (1–2 daily; 1hr 15min); Láconi (1–3 daily; 35min–1hr 5min); Nuoro (1 daily; 2hr); Sórgono (Mon–Sat 5 daily; 45min);

Tonara (Mon–Sat 6 daily, Sun 1 daily; 25min).
Tourist office Corso Umberto 55 (Mon 9.30am–12.30pm, Tues–Sun 9.30am–12.30pm & 5.30–7pm, 4.30–6pm in winter; ☎ 0784 628 205).

ACCOMMODATION AND EATING

La Capannina Via Maxia 36 ☎ 0784 629 121, ⊛ hotel capannina.net. Old-fashioned, chalet-style hotel with a garden and restaurant. En-suite rooms are on the small side but clean and tidy, and some have balconies with valley views. **€75**
Moderno Viale Kennedy 6 ☎ 0784 629 229, ⊛ hotel modernoaritzo.it. At the top of the Corso, this hotel run by a young couple has seen better days, but it's adequate for a night or two, with a good restaurant open to all and a shady garden. April–Nov daily 12.30–2.30pm & 7.30–

10pm. **€60**
★ **Sa Muvara** Via Funtana Rubia ☎ 0784 629 336, ⊛ samuvarahotel.com. The smartest of the local hotels – and one of the best in Barbagia – lies just outside the south entrance to the village. Sheltered behind trees and abundant parkland, the four-star has rooms with balconies and a good-size pool, fitness centre and sauna; bikes are available. The restaurant is well worth sampling even if you're not staying. April–Oct daily 1–2.30pm & 7.30–10.30pm. **€130**

Tonara

Fifteen kilometres north of Aritzo, **TONARA** shares the same forested environment. Chestnuts are one of the foundations of the local economy, and the village is also famed for the manufacture of cattle bells and for its *torrone* nougat – a rich sticky feast of honey, nuts and egg whites, usually for sale in local shops and at village *feste*.

ARRIVAL AND DEPARTURE
TONARA

By bus ARST buses pull up on the main drag. **Destinations** Aritzo (Mon–Sat 6 daily, Sun 1 daily; 25min); Belvì (Mon–Sat 6 daily, Sun 1 daily; 20min); Cágliari (1–2 daily; 3hr–3hr 20min); Fonni (Mon–Sat 2 daily; 1hr 5min);

Láconi (1–2 daily; 1hr 5min); Mamoiada (1 daily; 1hr 10min); Nuoro (1–2 daily; 1hr–1hr 30min); Sórgono (Mon–Sat 6 daily; 20min).

ACCOMMODATION AND EATING

Il Castagneto Via Muggianeddu 2 ☎ 0784 610 005. On a height at the northern end of the village, this pizzeria enjoys wonderful views over the wooded slopes from its tables outside. Apart from pizzas, dishes include *cinghiale* (boar) and local mushrooms, with pastas costing around €5, mains €10–12. Easter–Oct Mon & Wed–Sun 5–11pm.
★ **Locanda del Muggianeddu** Via Monsignor Tore 10 ☎ 0784 63 885. Seven spacious en-suite rooms are available

here, with wooden ceilings and schist walls. Adorned with local masks, the intimate restaurant has hearty mountain dishes including *zuppa di patate e formaggio* (potato and cheese soup) and *fettuccine ai funghi porcini* (pasta with local mushrooms). Tues–Sun noon–2.30pm & 8–9.30pm; closed Feb. **€55**
Sa Colonia Via Muggianeddu 4 ☎ 0784 194 6170 or ☎ 392 128 2340, ⊛ campingsacolonia.it. It's unusual to

D.H. LAWRENCE IN SARDINIA

"Comes over one an absolute necessity to move," begins *Sea and Sardinia*, the travelogue by **D.H. Lawrence**, written in response to a restless desire to take a break from Sicily, where he was then living with his wife Frieda. Disembarking in Sardinia in January 1921, the couple made the briefest tour of the island, just six days, for most of which they were in trains and buses, having decided to travel the hardest route – straight up through the interior from Cágliari on the painfully slow narrow-gauge railway. At Sórgono, the Lawrences changed onto a bus to Nuoro and proceeded to Olbia, whence they returned by ferry to the mainland.

It was Sardinia's inland villages that left the deepest impression, however. **Sórgono** – which at first appeared like "some little town in the English West Country" – possessed just one hotel, the *Risveglio*, where the only bedroom available contained "a large bed, thin and flat with a grey-white counterpane, like a large, poor, marble-slabbed tomb in the room's sordid emptiness; one dilapidated chair on which stood the miserablest weed of a candle I have ever seen: a broken wash-saucer in a wire ring: and for the rest, an expanse of wooden floor as dirty-grey-black as it could be, and an expanse of wall charted with the bloody deaths of mosquitoes." A stroll through the village did not improve his mood: "A dreary hole! A cold, hopeless, lifeless, Saturday-afternoon-weary village, rather sordid, with nothing to say for itself."

Despite the ill humour that characterizes much of the book, it's a good read: a close-up description of travelling on the cheap interspersed with observations on the state of the world in the wake of World War I. For more on the book, see Contexts, p.319.

find a campsite this far inland. This simple site, signposted from the northern end of the village, is shady and clean, and has a ristorante-pizzeria and barbecue grills. Pitches €20
Tia Zicca Via Galusè 2 ☎ 0784 610.007 or ☎ 346 012

3114, ☷ tiazicca.it. In the older part of the villlage, this simple B&B has two en-suite rooms, a garden and a panoramic terrace where breakfast can be served. No credit cards. Closed Nov & Jan. €55

8

Sórgono

West of Tonara, the road careers through forests of chestnut and oak for 10km before reaching the small town of **SÓRGONO**, the northernmost point of the narrow-gauge railway from Cágliari. As the centre of the Mandrolisai wine region, the town enjoys a certain fame, but it's a long, dull sprawl, devoid of any great interest and useful only as a transport junction. D.H. Lawrence and his wife Frieda stopped here en route to Nuoro in 1921, and hated it (see box above).

ARRIVAL AND DEPARTURE

SÓRGONO

By train The station serving the ARST-run narrow-gauge trains from Mandas is at the eastern end of the village, off the main street. All services run Tues only from mid-June to mid-Sept, currently departing from Sórgono at 4.30pm. Destinations Belvì-Aritzo (45min); Désulo-Tonara (35min); Ísili (3hr); Láconi (2hr 10min); Mandas (3hr 20min).
By bus Sórgono is well connected by ARST buses to the other villages of the Barbagia.

Destinations Aritzo (Mon–Sat 4 daily; 45min); Belvì (Mon–Sat 5 daily; 40min); Cágliari (1–2 daily; 3hr 15min); Fonni (Mon–Sat 1 daily; 1hr 25min); Ísili (1 daily; 1hr 20min); Láconi (1–3 daily; 50min–1hr 25min); Mandas (1 daily; 1hr 50min); Nuoro (Mon–Sat 4 daily; 1hr 35min–2hr 20min); Oristano (Mon–Sat 5–6 daily, July & Aug Sun 1 daily; 1hr 40min–2hr 30min); Tonara (Mon–Sat 7 daily; 20min).

Láconi

On the southern fringes of the Barbagia, the **Sarcidano** region is a quickly changing landscape of verdant hills and desolate basalt plains. There's ample evidence here of Sardinia's prehistory, starting with a fascinating collection of menhirs in the museum at **LÁCONI**. The village is a pleasurable place to explore, with a surprising number of attractions and a fresh, wooded feel.

Menhir Museum

Piazza Marconi • Tues–Sun: April–Sept 10am–1pm & 3.30–7pm; Oct–March 10am–1pm & 3–6pm • €5 including guided tour •
☎ 0782 693 238, ⓦ menhirmuseum.it

Not the least of Láconi's attractions is the elegant Neoclassical **Palazzo Aymerich** across from the town hall off the main Corso Garibaldi. Designed in 1846 by Sardinia's most eminent architect, Gaetano Cima (1805–78), it was the last home of the local *marchese*, and now holds the fascinating **Menhir Museum**, primarily dedicated to Sardinia's extraordinary prehistoric menhirs, an unusual concentration of which has been found in this area. Most of the bigger examples of these megaliths, which are mainly of trachyte stone and reach up to 7m in height, have been left in their original sites, as seen in photographs displayed here, but the museum has a fine selection of smaller pieces, grouped according to the genre they represent. The majority date back to the **Neolithic cultures** of Ozieri and Arzachena in the second half of the fourth millennium BC, and are a principal source of information for this obscure era, particularly regarding its divinities. The museum also displays Neolithic ceramics and obsidian arrowheads.

Male and female menhirs

The earliest menhirs have few, if any, characteristic marks, though later ones bear primitive facial characteristics, mainly nose and eyes. These more interesting "anthropomorphic" menhirs may be male or female in form, and are especially common around Láconi; the "males" are distinguished by the horn-shaped tridents embossed on one side, perhaps indicating membership of a warrior class, while "feminine" menhirs have a smaller and less defined form, with disc-shaped breasts. One, in Sala 2, shows a grooved circle below the "neck", perhaps representing a hair arrangement. Others are "asexual", though still retaining the facial features.

Casa Natale di Sant'Ignazio

Via Sant'Ignazio • Always open • Free • ☎ 0782 869 027

From Corso Garibaldi, the cobbled Via Sant'Ignazio leads to the **Casa Natale di Sant'Ignazio**, family home of one of Sardinia's most revered saints (see box below). You need to go round to the back to appreciate how the dwelling must have originally appeared in the eighteenth century – the rough stonework here is quite unlike the spruced-up exterior of the front. The house itself is little more than a bare room with a typical wood-beamed and bamboo-covered ceiling, and there are benches for prayer and meditation facing a shrine festooned with rosaries.

Sant'Ignazio

Via Sant'Ambrogio • Daily 9.30am–9pm

Behind the Casa Natale, walk up Via Don Minzoni and turn left at the little remembrance park to reach the church dedicated to **Sant'Ignazio**, conspicuous by

---

SANT'IGNAZIO DA LÁCONI

Born Vincenzo Peis, and apparently called "Il Santarello" even in his youth because of his extreme piety, Sardinia's most popular "modern" saint, **Sant'Ignazio da Láconi**, became a lay Capuchin monk in 1721. He spent the next sixty years practising penitence, humility and charity; as an inscription in his birthplace relates, *"Conobbe le cose occulte, penetrò il segreto dei cuori, ed ebbe il dono dei miracoli"* ("he knew occult things, he penetrated the secrets of the heart, and he had the gift of miracles"). Though born in Láconi, he lived for most of his life in Cágliari, where he is said to have performed various miracles, dying there in 1781 and spawning an enthusiastic cult. Beatified in 1940, he was canonized in 1951.

its metal dome and square, pointy campanile. The bronze sculpted doors, carved in the 1980s, depict miracles and scenes from the saint's life, the first chapel on the left was where he received his baptism and the second one, richly mosaicked, holds his reliquaries.

Parco Aymerich di Láconi

Via del Parco • Daily 8am–1hr before sunset • Free

Below the church of Sant'Ignazio, the terraced **Parco Aymerich di Láconi** makes an ideal place to take a breather or have a picnic. Once over a bridge that crosses a pretty stream, you'll find a marvellous shady retreat full of surprises: springs, grottoes, waterfalls, a pond with goldfish and much bigger, darker fish lurking, great overhanging rocks and beautifully crafted rustic benches. Everything is verdant, damp and mossy. All around are trees from Europe, Asia and the Americas (they're labelled, and a list at the entrance gives their scientific nomenclature, their names in Italian and in the Láconi dialect), and rare orchids also grow here.

Castello Aymerich

Buried within the park's thick groves is the **Castello Aymerich**, a ruined redoubt, parts of which go back to 1051. The building sports some engaging details, such as the small carving of a castle above the arched gateway, and windows with an ace of spades motif. In front of the roofless hall there's a terrace with fine views over the valleys and countless paths curving round the hill.

8

ARRIVAL AND DEPARTURE

LÁCONI

By train Láconi is a stop on the narrow-gauge Trenino Verde, with services running from mid-June to mid-Sept on Tues only. The station is a 10min walk west of town. Destinations Belvì-Aritzo (1hr 20min); Désulo-Tonara (1hr 35min); Ísili (50min); Mandas (1hr 15min); Sórgono (2hr 10min).

By bus ARST buses stop right by the museum on Corso Garibaldi.

Destinations Aritzo (1–3 daily; 40min–1hr 5min); Belvì (1–3 daily; 45min–1hr 10min); Cágliari (2–3 daily; 2hr–2hr 15min); Ísili (Mon–Sat 5–8 daily, Sun 2 daily; 20–35min); Mandas (2 daily; 50min); Nuoro (1 daily; 2hr 35min); Oristano (Mon–Sat 5 daily; 1hr 30min–2hr); Sórgono (1–3 daily; 55min–1hr 25min); Tonara (1–2 daily; 1hr 5min).

ACCOMMODATION AND EATING

Antico Borgo Via Sant'Ambrogio 5 ☎0782 869 047, Ⓦanticoborgoweb.it. Láconi has a first-rate place to stay in the form of this B&B, in an old house situated below the church. Each of the attic rooms has its own bathroom, and the hosts are genial. No credit cards. **€70**

Le Magnolie Corso Garibaldi ☎0782 869 821, Ⓦlemagnoliehotel.com. This place has a fantastic terrace to enjoy the mountain views – an inspiring accompaniment to such local dishes as *spaghetti alla laconese* (with pork sauce) and *salsiccia* (sausage). You'll pay under €20 for two courses. Plain rooms are available, some with stunning vistas. Daily noon–2pm & 8–9pm. **€60**

Ísili and around

Heading southward from Láconi, the SS128 winds 8km across a calcareous landscape studded with outcrops to **ÍSILI**. Like so many of Sardinia's inland villages, it makes little visual impact, though it has a handful of attractions and some striking country worth exploring in the vicinity. In recent years it has been a popular base for free climbers, attracted to the sheer rock faces of the surroundings, though the village has a longer-established fame as a centre of *artigianato*, particularly copperware, which is readily available in the shops in and around the central Corso Vittorio Emanuele III.

It's the area around Ísili that commands most interest, however, studded as it is with prehistoric remains. Least compelling but nearest to hand are two **domus de janas**

– so-called "fairy houses", actually pre-nuraghic tombs – which are easily visited on foot from the western end of the Corso. A sign points the way along a cul-de-sac on the edge of town, from where a path leads to square-cut openings giving onto low-roofed chambers.

Farther afield, you can explore the **Lago di San Sebastiano**, a dammed lake visible from the village's western side and overlooked by the ruins of a church. Three or four kilometres west of town, the canyon of **Is Borroccus**, carved out by the Mannu river, is one of the rare nesting sites in Sardinia of Bonelli's eagle.

Museo per l'Arte del Rame e del Tessuto

Piazza San Giuseppe • Tues–Sun 10am–1pm & 4.30–7.30pm, or 4–7pm in winter • €3.50, or €6 with Is Paras • ☎ 0782 802 641

You can see the best examples of the local craftsmanship in the **Museo per l'Arte del Rame e del Tessuto**, housed in a seventeenth-century convent. The copperware here consists mainly of an array of domestic items, while the art of weaving – another field in which the locals traditionally excelled, and to which the museum is also dedicated – is illustrated by rugs and tapestries.

Is Paras

Località Is Paras • April–Oct Tues–Sun 10am–1pm & 2.30–dusk; Nov–March call to visit • €3, or €6 with museum • ☎ 0782 802 641 or ☎ 380 455 3856

Splendidly sited on a bare hillock on Ísili's northern outskirts (unmissable from the SS128 from Láconi or from the train), the **nuraghe of Is Paras** constitutes one of Sardinia's most impressive single-towered nuraghic monuments. Its smooth-walled "tholos" interior is also, at 12m, the highest on the island. Inside you'll find a small chamber in front of the main entrance and a niche for a sentry on its right-hand side.

Santuario Nurágico di Santa Vittoria

Località Santa Vittoria • Daily 9am–7pm, closes around 5pm in winter • €4 • ☎ 0782 806 156, ⊛ santavittoriaserri.it

A significant nuraghic site lies south of Ísili, reached from the village of **Serri**, 8km down the SS128, from where it's signposted another 4km northwest. Scattered around the country church of Santa Vittoria, the extensive ruins of the **Santuario Nurágico di Santa Vittoria**, dating from the end of the second millennium BC, have thrown up a rich assortment of nuraghic finds, including some of the most eye-catching *bronzetti* on display in Cágliari's archeological museum (see p.62).

The settlement was built around a sacred well and a temple, and the various remains strewn across the area include a circular assembly room, a grand oval festival area (*recinto delle feste*) and numerous habitations. The sacred well (*pozzo*) is the most complete survival, its thirteen basalt steps making a precisely carved descent to the spring. Regular pilgrimages and gatherings are thought to have taken place here, a tradition perpetuated by the two-day harvest **festival** that nowadays centres on the church of Santa Vittoria around September 11.

ARRIVAL AND DEPARTURE
ÍSILI

By train Ísili's train station is at the southern end of town (there's another station to the north), served by infrequent ARST-run services.

Destinations Belvì-Aritzo (mid-June to mid-Sept; Tues only; 2hr 15min); Monserrato, Cágliari (Mon–Sat 3 daily; 1hr 30min); Désulo-Tonara (mid-June to mid-Sept; Tues only; 2hr 25min); Láconi (mid-June to mid-Sept; Tues only;

50min); Mandas (Mon–Sat 5 daily; 20min); Sórgono (mid-June to mid-Sept; Tues only; 3hr).

By bus ARST buses stop on Corso Vittorio Emanuele.

Destinations Cágliari (2–4 daily; 1hr 40min–2hr); Láconi (Mon–Sat 5–8 daily, Sun 2 daily; 20–35min); Mandas (2 daily; 25min).

ACCOMMODATION AND EATING

Del Sole Corso Vittorio Emanuele 124 ☎ 0782 802 371, ⓦ hoteldelsole.com. The most convenient of Ísili's hotels is this two-star at the western end of town near the museum, with simple, modern rooms and a pool table. The ristorante-pizzeria here is also a good spot for a bite, with – unusual so far inland – a good choice of seafood at moderate prices. Tues–Sat 12.30–2.30pm & 7.30–10.30pm, Sun 7.30–10.30pm; **€50**

The eastern coast

Nuoro province's **eastern seaboard** is highly developed around the resorts of **Posada** and **Orosei**, but further south it preserves its rugged beauty, virtually untouched apart from the isolated **Cala Golone**. Farther down, the province of Ogliastra shares the same terrain of mountains and sea, with pockets of holiday activity on the coast at **Santa Maria Navarrese** and around the port of **Arbatax**, while a foray 20km west of here will give you a taste of the mountains at the village of **Lanusei**.

The **beaches** along this coast are some of Sardinia's wildest, including some extremely swim-worthy stretches around **Cala Liberotto**. The coast around Cala Gonone is also studded with isolated sandy coves, most of them inaccessible by road, and there are more beaches to the south around Santa Maria Navarrese and Arbatax.

GETTING AROUND   THE EASTERN COAST

By car The SS125 runs parallel to the eastern coast, taking in some magnificent scenery en route to Arbatax and beyond. You'll need your wits about you on some stretches, though traffic tends to be light in these parts.

By train Arbatax and Tortolì (the provincial capital) are on the narrow-gauge Trenino Verde line (see p.271) that operates in summer only, following an inland route to Mandas (which has frequent connections with Cágliari); the full journey from the coast to Cágliari takes around seven hours.

By bus Daily buses connect Cágliari and Nuoro with Tortolì, some of them also going on to Santa Maria Navarrese and Arbatax.

8

Posada

Northeast of Nuoro, the SS131dir highway follows the course of two river valleys, passing close to the inland town of **Siniscola**, the main centre of the rich agricultural land around here. The main road reaches the coast at **POSADA**, sited on a rise a little way inland, near the mouth of the river of the same name. Once a power-base for the surrounding districts, the town was prey to repeated attacks by seaborne raiders during the Middle Ages, and now only the ruins of its once impregnable castle – still commanding impressive views for miles around – attest to its former importance.

Castello della Fava

Via Eleonora d'Arborea • April–Sept daily 9am–dusk; Oct–March daily except Tues or Thurs 9am–1pm & 3–4pm • €3 • ☎ 347 480 1421

Reached by a brief climb up some steps above Piazza Eleonora d'Arborea in Posada's old town (drivers should leave their vehicles in the square or lower down), little

---

THE TALE OF THE BEAN

The Castello della Fava may owe its strange name – "**Bean Castle**" – to a colourful story. According to medieval legend, when besieged here by Turkish raiders, the *giudice* of Gallura took a homing pigeon, attached to it a message addressed to a fictitious army of rescuers, and forced the garrison's last remaining broad beans down its gullet. As planned, the Turks intercepted the bird, read the message and found the beans, concluding that not only was there an army on the way, but that the besieged Sards had plenty of provisions (enough to waste on pigeons, anyway) – and promptly withdrew. Scholars, however, are more in favour of an alternative explanation: *fava* may be a corruption of the Sard word *faedda*, meaning speak or voice – hence "the tower that sounds the alarm" when enemies are spotted.

survives of the **Castello della Fava** beyond a single oblong upright tower ringed by broken-down walls. Visitors must climb up four levels of wooden steps and iron rungs to reach the trapdoor at the top, but are rewarded by a sweeping panorama that takes in the citrus groves clustered around the coast and on the banks of the Posada river, the lagoons stretching south to the resort of La Caletta (see below) and Barbagia's inland peaks.

ARRIVAL AND DEPARTURE
POSADA

By bus ARST buses pull up in Via Véneto, in the lower town. Destinations La Caletta (4–11 daily; 15min); Nuoro (4–8 daily; 1hr 20min); Olbia (6–11 daily; 1hr 35min); Orosei (2 daily; 1hr 10min).

ACCOMMODATION

Il Castello Via Nazionale 3 ☎ 0784 854 572 or ☎ 349 146 8768. This B&B has three small en-suite rooms with Sard furnishings, wrought-iron beds and panoramic verandas where tasty breakfasts are served. German and English are spoken. Closed mid-Oct to April. No credit cards. €70

Sa Rocca Piazza Eleonora d'Arborea ☎ 0784 854 139, ⓦ hotelsarocca.it. Right below the castle in the old centre, this small three-star hotel/restaurant offers slightly outdated but functional rooms, some with great views. Breakfast costs €7 per person extra. There are more striking views from the restaurant, which serves good pasta, pizzas and seafood dishes at higher-than-average prices. Daily 12.30–2.30pm & 7.30–10.30pm; closed mid-Oct to mid-April. €65

The coast to Orosei

South of Posada, the coast is dotted with small holiday centres – **La Caletta**, **Santa Lucia** and **Cala Liberotto** – none of them with much in the way of character or even shops, but with a plentiful supply of bars, pizzerias and hotels, while the long tracts of pinewoods shelter a scattering of villas and **campsites**. The big draw, of course, is the almost unbroken line of **beaches**, from which sailing and windsurfing are available in summer. It's one of Sardinia's most enticing stretches, the fine white sands often backed by dunes and pinewoods, and overlooked by ruined Spanish watchtowers. Twelve kilometres north of Cala Liberotto, Sardinia's easternmost point, **Capo Comino**, is a wild and desolate spot of jagged rocks and abundant *macchia*.

Orosei

South of Cala Liberotto, the SS125 tracks away from the sea for 12km before crossing the Cedrino river, thick with reeds, to the town of **OROSEI**, the main centre of the **Baronia** region. Though it now stands 3km from the coast in a flat and fertile zone planted with vines and citrus groves, medieval accounts of Turkish raids suggest that Orosei was a significant harbour before the silting up of the river pushed back the shore. The town certainly shows signs of a prosperous past, in the many fine Spanish *palazzi* scattered around its interesting old quarter, and in its splendid ecclesiastical architecture, much of it constructed in the local grey-black basalt.

Piazza del Pópolo

A stroll through the old town's streets will at some point take in Orosei's central **Piazza del Pópolo**, the focus of a group of medieval buildings including the church of **San Giácomo**, whose cluster of tiled cupolas and campanile is fronted by a plain white Neoclassical facade at the top of a flight of steps.

Piazza Sas Ánimas and around

From Piazza del Popolo, take a right turn from Via Nazionale to reach **Piazza Sas Ánimas**, holding the sorely neglected remains of a fourteenth-century castle that was later used as a gaol – hence its name **Castello Prigione Vecchia** (or Sa Prejone Vezza);

it's usually open to the public on summer evenings (June–Sept Tues–Sat 8–11pm). Next to it stands the pretty **chiesa delle Ánime**, constructed in 1718 of rough brick and stonework with a tiled cupola and a handsome portal.

A brief walk from here (and well signposted) lie two more churches worth a glance: **San Gavino**, on the eastern edge of town, and the ruin of **San Sebastiano**, in a cobbled alley draped with bougainvillea on the western side.

Sant'Antonio

Piazza Sant'Antonio • Daily 8am–noon & 4–7pm

Foremost among the monuments in the rest of the town are the church and towers of **Sant'Antonio**, entered through an ogival arch at the bottom of Via Caduti in Guerra. The church precincts include a cobbled space surrounded by *muristenes*, temporary pilgrims' dwellings (known as *cumbessias* elsewhere in Sardinia), in the centre of which stands a Pisan tower converted into a private residence.

ARRIVAL AND INFORMATION   OROSEI

By bus Orosei has daily ARST-run bus connections with Nuoro and some other centres, plus a summer service along the coast operated by Deplano.

Destinations Dorgali (1–3 daily; 30min); Nuoro (Mon–Sat 9–12 daily, Sun 1–2 daily; 55min); Olbia (1–2 daily; 2hr 50min); Posada (1–2 daily; 1hr 15min).

Tourist information The Pro Loco is on Piazza del Pópolo

(Easter–Sept Mon–Sat 9am–1pm & 4–8pm; ☏ 0784 998 367, ⓦ orosei-proloco.com). There's also a tourist office in the town hall in Via Santa Veronica (Mon 9am–2pm & 3.30–6.30pm, Tues–Fri 9am–2pm; ☏ 0784 996 930, ⓦ oroseiturismo.it). Pick up walking itineraries of the old quarter or ask about guided tours at either.

ACCOMMODATION AND EATING

Cala Ginepro Viale Cala Ginepro ☏ 0784 91 017, ⓦ campingcalaginepro.com. Most of the local campsites are north of Orosei, including this well-organized place, right on the sea with its own private beach. You can rent caravans (€38.50), two-bed "tuculs" (cabins, €77) and four-person bungalows (€153). Closed Nov–March. Pitches **€34.50**

★ **Mannois** Via Angioy 32 ☏ 0784 991 040, ⓦ mannois .it. This boutique-style *albergo diffuso* has rooms spread between different buildings in Orosei's historic centre. It's all immaculately designed, and the main building has a courtyard garden where guests take breakfast. There's a bus

service to a private beach. **€110**

Su Barchile Via Mannu ☏ 0784 98 879, ⓦ wsubarchile .it. Family-run three-star with comfortable rooms and home-made pastries and jam for breakfast. The long-established and highly regarded restaurant (open to all) offers a small but delectable menu of Sard specialities such as *makkarrones de busa* and *porcetto* cooked in myrtle, plus a formidable array of seafood dishes, and it has an outdoor terrace. First courses cost €11–17, mains €16–25. Service can be slow. Daily 12.30–3pm & 7.30–10.30pm. **€120**

Dorgali and around

Centre of a region renowned for its **Cannonau** wines, the small inland town of **DORGALI** has also established a reputation for its craftwork. Apart from a couple of significant attractions in the neighbourhood, the **handicrafts shops** are the main reason to stop here, though you could also visit the town's small archeological museum.

Museo Archeologico

Via Lamármora • Daily 9.30am–1pm & 3–6pm • €3 • ☏ 349 442 5552

Below the school on the corner of Via Vittorio Emanuele, Dorgali's **Museo Archeologico** has a low-key collection of relics and minerals unearthed in the area, displayed in three rooms. Finds from the Neolithic age are contained in the first of these; the second shows nuraghic items, many of them found at the site of Serra Orrios (see p.298); the third concentrates on the Punic, Roman and medieval periods, including a good collection of coins, and amphoras and anchors retrieved from the sea.

The Grotta di Ispinígoli

SS125, 5km north of Dorgali • Daily: April, May & Oct 10am–1pm & 3–6pm; June & Sept 10am–6pm; July & Aug 10am–7pm; last tour 1hr before closing • €7.50 • ☎ 0784 96 243 (Pro Loco, Dorgali)

The **Grotta di Ispinígoli**, signposted off the main road between Dorgali and Orosei, is a deep cave containing a mind-bending collection of stalagmites and stalactites, dominated by one 38m column that appears to hold the whole lot up. Traces of some distant human presence have been found within – jewels, amphorae and bones, probably dating from Phoenician times. The local name for the cave, *Abisso delle Vérgini* ("Abyss of the Virgins"), probably owes more to popular imagination than to fact, but it is likely that such an impressive natural phenomenon would have attracted some kind of religious ritual. The 45min **tours** inside the grotto leave daily on the hour.

Serra Orrios

Off SS129, 10km northwest of Dorgali • Daily: April–June & Sept 9am–1pm & 3–6pm; July & Aug 9am–2pm & 4–7pm; Oct–March 9am–1pm & 2–5pm; last tour 1hr before closing • €6 • ☎ 338 834 1618

Though lacking a *nuraghe* as such, the nuraghic site of **Serra Orrios** makes a fascinating stop, vividly illustrating how a typical community of that era was organized. The remains of the village lie on a small plain surrounded by olive trees and overlooked by the peaks of Monte Albo to the north, located within a long, walled enclosure at the end of a 600m track through an olive grove.

Entered through a lintelled portal, the extensive **site** consists chiefly of the closely packed circular walls of the seventy-odd village buildings, about 2m high and separated by paths. Among them are two rectangular temples labelled "Tempietto A" and "Tempietto B", the first of which lies within a round walled area and is thought to have been used by visiting pilgrims. Tempietto B was probably the villagers' centre of worship – a long building surrounded by a wall, with a doorway at one end topped by a curved slab and a low bench running along the inside. All in all, it's an attractive site to wander around; guides provide a commentary in Italian or English, but are mainly there to keep you off the walls. Before setting off, it's worth examining the diagram near the entrance showing how the village must once have appeared. There's a bar and *paninoteca* on the site.

The Flumineddu valley

South of Dorgali lies the **Flumineddu valley**, one of Sardinia's last truly untouched tracts. The SS125 affords bird's-eye views of this majestic mountain landscape, largely devoid of human life, at the bottom of which lies the Gorroppu canyon (see box opposite). The SS125 continues into the neighbouring Codula di Luna valley at the **Genna Silana** pass (1017m), a departure point for walking expeditions in the area.

ARRIVAL AND DEPARTURE · DORGALI AND AROUND

By bus All services to and from Dorgali are operated by ARST, apart from a daily summer service to Olbia, Cala Gonone and places between run by Deplano.

Destinations Cala Gonone (Mon–Sat 7–14 daily, Sun 4–11; 25min); Nuoro (Mon–Sat 7–9 daily, Sun 3–5; 50min); Olbia (Mon–Sat 2–6 daily, Sun 1–5 daily; 2hr 50min); Oliena (Mon–Sat 7–9 daily, Sun 3–5; 25min); Orosei (Mon–Sat 2–7 daily, Sun 1–5 daily; 25min).

INFORMATION AND ACTIVITIES

Pro Loco Via Lamármora 108 (Mon–Fri 9am–1pm & 4–7pm; ☎ 0784 96 243, ⓦ dorgali.it).

Excursions One of the best local outfits for trekking and tours around the local archeological sites is Ghivine, Via Lamármora 69e (☎ 0784 96 721 or ☎ 338 834 1618,

ⓦ ghivine.com), staffed by friendly young guides and specializing in walking, caving and climbing trips, with accommodation options. The Pro Loco office has a complete list of excursion companies.

A HIKE IN THE GOLA DI GORROPPU

The **Gola di Gorroppu** (Gorroppu, or Gorrupu, canyon), one of the deepest and most spectacular in southern Europe, with walls reaching over 200m high, can be walked for much of its length between April and October. If you're considering it, however, you should find out the state of the **Flumineddu river** which bores through it; large sections of the gorge may be flooded, requiring specialist skills and even dinghies to negotiate. When conditions are good, there's little possibility of losing the way, but the walk can also be undertaken accompanied by a guide. The entire excursion will take a minimum of three hours, its length depending on how far up the gorge you want – or are able – to reach.

Unless you're with a guide, you'll need your own transport to get to the **start of the trail**, which can be approached from **Dorgali**. From the Circonvallazione that bypasses the town to the west, take the side road signposted for the *Sant'Elene* hotel (southwards). Past the hotel, take the left-hand turn, slightly descending, then take the middle road at the subsequent three-way fork. About 5km from Dorgali, you'll pass the chiesa di Buoncammino on your right. After a farther 4km, the unsurfaced road becomes increasingly bumpy before crossing the Flumineddu river. Take the left turn, signposted Gorroppu, and you'll soon come to the **car park** and seasonal **ticket office** (tickets are €5), beyond which you must proceed on foot.

This point can also be reached from Campo Base Gorropu, a visitor centre 12km south of the Cala Gonone turning on the SS125, though this involves a very steep descent on foot taking around one and a half hours. Alternatively, you might choose to make use of a Jeep service (April to mid-Nov €10 each way; ☏389 420 8595).

Following the **track** southwards, parallel to the river, take the left-hand fork after a few minutes, which dips before beginning a gentle ascent. Passing in and out of woods, and alongside copious growths of lentisk, myrtle, wild cyclamen and other plants of the *macchia*, the path – occasionally indicated by green arrows – follows the course of the river on its left. About one and a half hours after setting out, you'll finally descend to the **river**. This idyllic spot, with glades of oleander shading the rocky pools on all sides and the sheer walls of the gorge rising dramatically above, makes a good place for a pause. There's usually water here, even in high summer, and in winter it can be torrential.

To enter the *gola*, remain on the right side of the river, keeping as high as possible. The path will eventually become clear and once you're in the canyon there's no straying from the route, with high rock walls on either side. Much of the time it's simply a matter of negotiating the boulders, usually not unduly difficult, though some parts are challenging and demand concentration. Where **rockfalls** have blocked the way, look out for lengths of rope secured to the rock, which you can use to haul yourself up; these are occasionally marked with green paint.

How far you go, of course, depends on your perseverance and stamina. The total walkable length is about 8km, though you'd need **equipment** and a **guide** to go so far, and with expert help you could even reach the village of Urzulei and beyond. Even for shorter distances, some form of head protection is advisable. The biggest danger is of slipping on the smooth surfaces of the rocks – particularly when these are wet – so don't attempt the walk in shoes lacking a secure grip and ankle support.

ACCOMMODATION AND EATING

S'Adde Via Concordia 38 ☏0784 94 412, ⌨hotelsadde .it. Fairly basic lodging, very central but in a peaceful spot signposted above Via Lamármora. The en-suite rooms come with a/c and wi-fi, and some have fridges. The restaurant is worth sampling for its homely country dishes (mains are around €12), including good gluten-free options. Daily 12.30–2.30pm & 7.30–10pm; closed Mon in winter. **€110**

★ **Sant'Elene** Località Sant'Elene ☏0784 94 572, ⌨albergosantelene.it. Set on a quiet and secluded hillside 3km south of town (and invisible until you reach it), this classic mountain hotel has good-size rooms – though few with views. It's a good choice for anyone tackling the Gola di Gorroppu, located close to the start of the route. There's a great restaurant here, too, where you can dine on lip-smacking Sardinian specialities and enjoy the grand panorama from its veranda. A three-course meal should cost €20–30. The hotel is also signposted off the SS125. Daily 12.30–3pm & 7–10.30pm; closed Mon in winter. **€60**

Cala Gonone and around

A couple of kilometres south out of Dorgali, a left turn from the SS125 brings
you into a tunnel through the mountain wall, from which the road corkscrews
down through groves of cork to an azure bay. Beautifully sited at the base of the
900m-high mountains, **CALA GOLONE** was once a tiny settlement huddled around
a harbour, until recently accessible only by boat. Now hotels and villas dominate
the scene, though these have not entirely spoilt the sense of isolation, even in
summer, when the place positively hums. Abundant activities are offered, most
popular of which are the numerous boat excursions to the various secluded coves
up and down the coast.

The port and town beach

Cala Gonone's sheltered **port** is crowded with pleasure craft, with kiosks on the quay
hawking boat tours to the beaches (see box opposite) and dinghy rentals. Backed by
a busy beach promenade, a curve of sand extends south from here, culminating in
a full-size **beach** at the end of Lungomare Palmasera.

Beaches out of town

The town beach is convenient and will do for a dip, but it's a poor substitute for the
beaches farther afield, most reachable on boat tours from the port. However, **south of
Cala Gonone**, you can also reach one of the best beaches on foot from Cala Fuili, the
rocky cove at the southern end of Viale del Bue Marino. From here, a rough track leads
parallel to the sea for nearly 4km to **Cala Luna**. It's fairly level, but very stony, so you
need more than sandals (and there's no water along the way, so carry at least a litre).
The path is signposted with painted green arrows and white arrows chiselled into the
rock. The walk might take one and a half to two hours – if you don't feel like returning
on foot, jump on one of the boats shuttling back to the port (frequent in summer; €9).

    North of town, a car or bike would do for the pair of idyllic swimming places at
Spiaggia Cartoe and **Spiaggia Osalla**, reachable from the narrow road dug out of the
mountains that eventually connects up with the SS125 (and also from Orosei). Osalla
is about twenty minutes by car, Cartoe a little less.

Nuraghe Mannu

Località Nuraghe Mannu • Daily: April 9am–noon & 3–6pm; May, June & Sept 9am–noon & 4–7pm; July & Aug 9am–noon & 5–9pm;
Oct 10am–1pm & 3–6pm; last entry 1hr before closing • €3

Signposted left off the main road leading up to the SS125, **Nuraghe Mannu** lies at the
end of a 3km rocky track (not recommended for laden cars). On a ledge over the bay,
with a ravine to one side, it's a marvellous site, one of Sardinia's few nuraghic structures
to be built right by the sea, and affording magnificent views. The topless main tower
has steps off to one side, and niches in the central chamber. All around lie the traces of
dwellings, some paved, and mostly dating from much later times – there's evidence that
the site was occupied as recently as the Middle Ages.

Acquario

Via la Favorita • Daily: March Sat & Sun 10am–6pm; April 9am–noon & 3–6pm; May–July & Sept daily 10am–6pm; Aug daily
10am–8pm; Oct Tues–Sun 10am–6pm; last entry 1hr before closing • €10, with family discounts available • ☎ 0784 920 052,
ⓦ acquariocalagonone.it

A kilometre south of the centre, Cala Gonone's **Acquario** is probably not what
you came here to see, but it makes a good, family-friendly change from the beach.
In 24 tanks, the aquarium concentrates on sea-life – fauna and flora – from the
Golfo di Orosei, but includes a few tropical species too. You'll see dogfish sharks,
as well as some of the fish (snapper, grouper and mullet) you might find on a menu.
It's a modern, well-designed attraction, and a good chance to get a closer look at the
under-sea eco-system hereabouts. Feeding time is at 3pm.

BOAT TRIPS FROM CALA GONONE

From Cala Gonone's port, numerous operators offer a range of **boat trips** to the truly spectacular swimming spots dotted along the cliffy coast hereabouts. Between April and October, the most popular trips ply between the town and the remote inlets of **Cala Luna** and **Cala Sisine**, respectively 6km and 11km to the south. Return tickets for these cost €20–35, and departures are frequent. There are plenty of even more secluded beaches to visit, while other cruises explore some of the area's deep grottoes. The most famous of these is the **Grotta del Bue Marino** (€20 return, including the entrance charge of €8), which counts among Sardinia's most spectacular caves. The luminescent gallery is filled with remarkable natural sculptures resembling organ pipes, wedding cakes and even human heads – one of them is known as "Dante" for its fondly imagined likeness of the poet. The grotto is also famous as the last refuge in Italian waters of the Mediterranean monk seal, or "sea ox" (*bue marino*); the last of these creatures disappeared some years ago. **Night visits** are also occasionally available.

A **minicruise** of the coast – typically heading south for around two hours as far as Arco di Goloritzè or Spiaggia Aguglia for diving and swimming, then returning with stops at Cala Mariolu, Cala Biriola, Cala Sisine, Cala Luna and Grotta del Bue Marino – can also be booked from the quayside agencies, for around €35. Boats depart from 9am, returning at around 6pm. Note that food and refreshments are not available at the remoter beaches, so you should carry your own water at least. General **information** on all of these can be obtained from the Nuovo Consorzio Trasporti Maríttimi at the port (📞0784 93 305, 🌐calagononecrociere.it). For longer trips, book the day before, and take a sun hat and water.

ARRIVAL AND DEPARTURE

CALA GONONE

8

By bus ARST buses pull up above the centre on Viale Bue Marino – handy for those with hotels nearby or camping – and again by the port on Via Marco Polo. Deplano buses connecting Cala Gonone with Olbia airport also stop on Viale Bue Marino.

Destinations Dorgali (Mon–Sat 7–14 daily, Sun 4–11 daily; 20min); Nuoro (Mon–Sat 5–7 daily, Sun 3–5 daily; 1hr 10min); Olbia airport (June–Sept 4 daily; 2hr 10min); Oliena (Mon–Sat 5–7 daily, Sun 2–4; 50min).

INFORMATION AND ACTIVITIES

Tourist office Viale Bue Marino, opposite bus stop (daily: April & Oct 9am–3pm; May, June & Sept 9am–1pm & 3–7pm; July & Aug 9.30am–7pm; 📞0784 93 696, 🌐dorgali.it). See also 🌐dorgali.eu.

Bike and boat rental Bikes, scooters, kayaks and dinghies can be rented from Prima Sardegna, Lungomare Palmasera 32 (📞0784 93 367); bikes are around €24 for 24hr, scooters €48 and single kayaks €30. Kiosks at the port, such as Noleggio Malù (📞348 765 3503 or 📞349 878 3317), also offer boat rental: a simple motor-driven dinghy (*gommone*) in high season costs around €120 for a day; fuel costs an extra €20–40.

Diving Argonauta Diving Club, Via dei Lecci 10 (📞0784 93 046, 🌐argonauta.it) and Dimensione Mare, Via Colombo 8 (📞334 803 5686) arrange dives and snorkelling tours for all abilities, with equipment to rent. Two dives including gear will cost around €75.

Excursions Prima Sardegna (see above) offers a drop-off/pick-up service for hikers, and also – together with Dolmen, Via Vasco da Gama 18 (📞0784 93 260, 🌐sardegnadascoprire.it) and Centro Escursioni in Sardegna, Viale Colombo (📞349 672 7750, 🌐escursioniinsardegna.com) – organizes walking, biking, 4WD and boat excursions.

ACCOMMODATION

Cala Luna Lungomare Palmasera 📞0784 93 133, 🌐calaluna.net. At the south end of the seaside strip, this bougainvillea-covered holiday hotel has direct access to the beach, modern art on the walls and a great roof terrace, where the restaurant is located. The comfortable rooms have satellite TV and internet access, and some, costing extra, have balconies overlooking the sea. Closed Nov–March. **€110**

Ichnos Via delle Conchiglie 5 📞328 001 4014,

🌐bbichnos.com. Unspectacular but central and good-value B&B just 30m from the lungomare. The three rooms are very simple and a bit dark, but they have a/c and separate entrances from the shady patio where breakfast is served. No credit cards. **€70**

⭐ **L'Oasi** Via Lorca 📞0784 93 111, 🌐loasihotel.it. This small, modern *pensione* occupies a lofty site above the town, with breathtaking views and an air of pampered seclusion. Spacious rooms, landscaped gardens and fine dining are added advantages. The port is just 5min away along a steep short cut. There's a week's minimum stay in Aug, three days at other times. Closed late Nov to March. **€105**

★ **Miramare** Piazza Giardini 12 ☏ 0784 93 140, ⊕ htlmiramare.it. Central, modern hotel, offering smart, modern and spacious rooms, the best having large sea-facing balconies. There's a sun terrace with a great view, a fine restaurant with outdoor seating and wi-fi in the lobby. Service is professional and friendly. Closed mid-Oct to March. **€120**

Píccolo Viale Colombo 32 ☏ 0784 93 235, ⊕ piccolo hotelcalagonone.it. The resort's cheapest hotel – and one of few to stay open all year – is centrally located about 50m up from the port. Rooms are fairly basic, all with small en-suite bathrooms, and some have views through pine trees to the sea. **€60**

Pop Piazza del Porto ☏ 0784 93 185, ⊕ hotelpop.it. Right in front of the port, this modern hotel open all year has rooms with small balconies, most with sea views. It could do with a bit of pepping up, but the staff are friendly, there's a lively restaurant (see below) and the hotel's speedboat can whisk you to secluded sandy coves. **€98**

CAMPING

Camping Cala Gonone Via Collodi ☏ 0784 93 165, ⊕ campingcalagonone.it. This campsite lies in the pine-woods above the resort, a brief walk from the bus stop and tourist office, and 300m up from the seafront. Caravans (€46) and chalets (€70) can be rented, and a pool and tennis court are available in summer, but it can get very crowded. Closed Nov–March. Pitches **€34**

EATING AND DRINKING

★ **Al Porto** Piazza del Porto ☏ 0784 93 185. This friendly restaurant attached to the *Pop Hotel* offers a huge menu (try the *ravioli di mare*), with first courses at €5–16, second courses €12–20, and there are usually set-price menus. It gets packed out in summer. Daily noon–11pm.

Aquarius Lungomare Palmasera 34 ☏ 0784 93 428. On the seafront, with a few outdoor tables, *Aquarius* has some of the best fish in town and it's also good for pizza and ice cream. Try the *angelottos* – ravioli with spinach and cheese. First courses are €10–15, mains around €15, and fixed-price menus are €26. March–Oct daily noon–3pm & 7.30–11pm.

★ **Bue Marino** Via Vespucci 8 ☏ 0784 920 078. On a hotel rooftop above the port, you can soak up the wonderful vista while relishing fresh fish and meat dishes (€9–12 for firsts, €11–15 for mains), pizzas and a good wine list. The restaurant also has an off-street terrace which serves snacks at lunchtime and cocktails in the evening – very romantic. April to mid-Oct daily 12.30–2.30pm & 6.30–11pm.

Il Cormorano Via Vespucci ☏ 0784 93 601. Pleasant trattoria opposite the port with a terrace for dining alfresco. The good fixed-price menus may include *tagliolini della casa* – fresh pasta with artichokes, tomatoes, shrimps and *calamari*. There's a tourist menu for €24, otherwise starters are €7–11, mains €12–18. April to mid-Oct daily noon–2.30pm & 6.30–11pm; closed Mon in April, May & Oct.

Il Pescatore Via Acquadolce 7 ☏ 0784 93 174. Gourmet

seafood parlour on the seafront, a bit pricey but worth it for the lobster pasta, linguini and clams and grilled fish platters. You can eat alfresco in summer. Tourist menus are €25 and €30; otherwise reckon on around €40 for a full meal. April–Oct daily noon–3pm & 7.30–11pm.

La Poltrona Località Iscrittiorè ☏ 0784 93 414. This place specializes in "zero-kilometres" ingredients (ie strictly local and seasonal), but its marvellous terrace and wonderful views also pull in the punters. The pizzas, fresh pasta and meat and fish dishes are all first class – expect to pay €25–35 for a full meal. You'll need a car to get here: it's up by the Centro Sportivo, 2km from the port. March–Oct Mon 6.30–11pm, Tues–Sun 12.30–3pm & 6.30–11pm.

Roadhouse Blues Lungomare Palmasera ☏ 0784 93 187. Overlooking the sea, this groovy bar-restaurant has a rock'n'roll theme, with "Led Zeppelin" and "Hendrix" among the pizzas listed (around €8). The menu extends from burgers to red snapper Sardinian style, and cocktails and beers are served until late. Daily 7am–midnight, closed mid-Nov to mid-Dec.

Su Recreu Piazza Andrea Doria ☏ 0784 93 135. Up from the port, this café-bar serves the town's best ice cream as well as healthy breakfasts, smoothies, sandwiches and grills till late (tourist menus are €15–20). There's live salsa music on summer evenings. Mid-March to early Nov daily 8am–late.

DIRECTORY

Internet *Iris Café*, Viale Colombo, has free wi-fi, and terminals for €4/hr (March–Oct daily 7am–midnight, closes 2am in summer).

Laundrette Via Cala Luna (always open); €5 per wash (soap included), €5 for drying.

Pharmacy Viale Colombo 36 (Mon–Sat 9am–1pm &

4.30–8pm, June–Sept also open Sun).

Post office Via Cala Luna (Mon–Fri 8.15am–1.45pm, Sat 8.15am–12.45pm).

Supermarket Crai, Via Vasco de Gama (Mon–Sat 8am–1pm & 4.30–8pm.

Santa Maria Navarrese

Following the SS125 south, a turn-off 5km south of Baunei descends sharply to the sea and the minor resort of **SANTA MARIA NAVARRESE**. A calm, picturesque place for ten months of the year, backed by greenery and set against a mountain backdrop, it gets extremely busy in high summer when the nearby beaches draw thousands of visitors. The main **beach** is right in front of the town, facing two isles punctuating the horizon, with umbrellas and deckchairs available for €12 per day. Many, however, prefer the broader expanses south of town, backed by pines and embellished by reddish granite outcrops, for example **Lido delle Rose**.

From the bijou **port** north of the centre, at the end of Via Lungomare, boat **excursions** around the Golfo di Orosei depart in summer (around €35 per person).

ARRIVAL AND INFORMATION

By bus Santa Maria has frequent ARST connections with Tortolì, the main transport hub for the region.
Destinations Dorgali (1 daily; 1hr 35min); Nuoro (Mon–Sat 4 daily, Sun 2 daily; 2hr 25min); Tortolì (Mon–Sat 11–16 daily, Sun 7 daily; 15min).
Tourist office Piazza Principessa di Navarra (May–Sept

daily 10am–1pm & 5–8pm, also 9–11pm in July & Aug; Oct–April Tues & Thurs 10am–1pm; ☎0782 615 330, ⓦturinforma.it). In summer, the office transfers to a kiosk on the seafront, in front of the piazza. For the whole Ogliastra region, see ⓦturismo.ogliastra.it.

ACCOMMODATION

Nicoletta Via Lungomare 1 ☎0782 614 045, ⓦhotelnicoletta.info. Stylish and select hotel in the resort's centre, close to the beach. There are antique trimmings in its bright, clean rooms, and breakfast can be taken on a patio. Closed late Oct to late April. **€100**
★ **Ostello Bellavista** Via Pedra Longa ☎0782 614

039, ⓦostelloinogliastra.com. Though it's officially a hostel, this is actually more like an informal lodge, where each of the clean white doubles has a bathroom, sea view (rooms with balconies cost extra) and free wi-fi. Its biggest selling point is its wonderful position, on a height above Santa Maria's port. Breakfasts are good, too. **€74**

EATING

Il Pozzo Viale Plammas ☎0782 615 039. You'll find a good range of pizzas here, as well as a regular menu that includes such local dishes as fish ravioli (€9) and *seppie arrosto* (roast cuttlefish, €11). In summer, you can eat on the veranda across the road. Daily 12.30–3pm & 7.30–11pm; closed Mon Nov–Easter.

Sa Cadrea Località Sa Cadrea ☎0782 615 112. Just across from the hostel and sharing the same awesome views, this pub-restaurant has filling panini, salads and ice creams, as well as more substantial main courses (€12–16). June–Sept daily noon–3am.

Arbatax and around

TORTOLÌ, an unremarkable inland town that is one of the two capitals of Ogliastra province (along with Lanusei), is worth a stop mainly for its bus connections, banks and shops, but the port of **ARBATAX**, 5km east at the end of the long Via Virgilio, makes a more alluring base from which to explore the nearby **beaches**. The best ones are south of the centre in the **Porto Frailis** district, home to a cluster of hotels and restaurants, and there's another series of broad sand and rock beaches at **Lido Orri**, 4km farther down, accessible from the SS125. All the usual facilities are available in summer – bars, deckchairs and watersports.

Arbatax itself amounts to little more than a few bars and restaurants, and of course the docks from which ferries ply to Genoa and Civitavecchia. You'll see some of the striking red-tinted rocks for which the area is famous in a cove just south of the port, and **boat tours** for the premier beaches of the Golfo di Orosei to the north are advertised at the quayside in summer, including the sublime sandy cove of **Cala Mariolu** and the Grotta del Bue Marino (see box, p.301).

ARRIVAL AND DEPARTURE

By ferry Tirrenia (☎ 892 123, ⊛ tirrenia.it) runs a regular ferry service to the mainland from Arbatax, sometimes via Cágliari or Olbia. The Tirrenia office is near the port at Via Venezia 10 (☎ 0782 667 067). A general travel agent operates out of the same office.

Destinations Civitavecchia (2 weekly; 11hr); Genoa (2 weekly; 17hr–22hr 30min).

By train Between mid-June and mid-Sept, the narrow-gauge Trenino Verde line follows a scenic inland route to Lanusei and Mandas, from where you can change for a faster train to Cágliari; the full journey from the coast to Cágliari takes around 7hr. The station is by the port. Note

GETTING AROUND

By car Local rental companies include Europcar at Via Tirso 37, Tortolì (☎ 0782 620 090, ⊛ europcar.it).

By bus Without your own vehicle, you can make use of the hourly local bus service that links Arbatax and Tortolì (not Sun), also taking in Porto Frailis and Lido Orrì between

ARBATAX AND AROUND

that all services run from mid-June to mid-Sept daily except Tues.

Destinations Lanusei (2–3 daily; 1hr 5min–1hr 20min); Mandas (2 daily; 5hr 15min); Tortolì (2–3 daily; 10min).

By bus Buses to Santa Maria Navarrese, Cágliari and Nuoro leave from Tortolì, connected to Arbatax by local buses (see below).

Destinations from Tortolì Arbatax (Mon–Sat 1–2 hourly; 10–25min); Cágliari (2–4 daily; 3hr); Dorgali (Mon–Sat 1 daily; 1hr 50min); Lanusei (Mon–Sat 8–9 daily, Sun 1 daily; 45min); Nuoro (2–3 daily; 1hr 30min–2hr 40min); Santa Maria Navarrese (Mon–Sat 11–16 daily, Sun 7 daily; 15min).

mid-June and mid-Sept. Buses stop almost opposite the Tirrenia office on the road to the port (tickets €1 from the nearby bar), and at the port. The last service is at 9pm (midnight June–Sept).

ACCOMMODATION

Entula Via Sindaco Lorrai 2, Porto Frailis ☎ 0782 667 811 or ☎ 329 348 1855, ⊛ entula.com. Modern B&B 600m from the beach and close to good restaurants, with spacious, a/c rooms and a small garden. Apartments are also available. No credit cards. Closed Dec & Jan. **€60**

Telis Porto Frailis ☎ 0782 667 140, ⊛ wcampingtelis .com. Close to the beach and shaded by eucalyptus and mimosa trees, this campsite has efficient, modern facilities

(including two pools), and bungalows (€106) and caravans (€96) to rent. Pitches **€32**

Vecchio Mulino Via Parigi ☎ 0782 664 041, ⊛ hotel ilvecchiomulino.it. This small hotel set amid trees and plants has a calm, rustic feel, solidly furnished rooms with wi-fi and good breakfasts. It's off Viale Europa, about a kilometre from the beach at Porto Frailis. **€110**

EATING

Il Faro Porto Frailis ☎ 0782 667 499. There are a few restaurants in Arbatax itself, but you're better off heading to this place by the beach, offering a good choice of grilled fish and a lively atmosphere. Mains are €12–15. Easter–Sept daily 12.30–2.30pm & 5.30–10.30pm; Oct–March 12.30–2.30pm.

La Baia Via dei Portoghesi, Porto Frailis ☎ 0782 667

808. In a backstreet a few mins from the beach, this trattoria has three dining areas including a terrace, but still gets very crowded. The menu features delicious *antipasti*, including *polpette di pesce* (fish-balls), and crusty pizzas in three sizes. Starters cost €9–12, mains €12–15. April–Oct daily 12.30–3pm & 7.30–11pm; Nov–March Sat & Sun 12.30–3pm & 7.30–10.30pm.

Lanusei and around

To sample the more traditional culture of the mountainous interior of Ogliastra province, it's only necessary to take a 25-minute drive or bus ride west out of Tortolì up the squiggly SS198 to **LANUSEI**, an attractive mountain village (590m) with a lively old centre. There are good walks in the area, the woods, rivers and lakes offering a cool respite from the coastal heat. Six kilometres west on the SS198, the **Parco Archeologico Selene** holds the remains of a nuraghic village and burial site amid a thick forest of holm oaks and chestnuts at an altitude of 960m.

ARRIVAL AND DEPARTURE

By train Lanusei is a stop on the summer-only Mandas–Arbatax line, the station only minutes away from the centre. All services run daily except Tues from mid-June to

LANUSEI

mid-Sept only.

Destinations Arbatax (2–3 daily; 1hr 5min); Mandas (2 daily; 4hr); Tortolì (2–3 daily; 55min).

By bus The village is connected with Nuoro (Mon–Sat 3 daily, Sun 1 daily; 1hr 15min) and Tortolì (Mon–Sat 8–9 daily, Sun 1 daily; 45min) by ARST buses. There's a stop in Piazza Marcia.

ACCOMMODATION

★ **La Nuova Luna** Via Indipendenza ☎ 0782 41 051, ⓦ lanuovaluna.it. On a narrow lane off the main Via Umberto I, this excellent hostel has beds in modern, clean rooms, and a large common area with a gigantic fireplace. There's a bar, kitchen and washing machines, and the friendly staff have heaps of information on the area. Closed Nov–Feb. Dorms €18, doubles €40

8

ROMAN REMAINS, NORA

Contexts

307 History

315 Sardinian wildlife

319 Books

322 Italian

History

Sardinia's position at the centre of the Mediterranean has ensured that for most of its history it has been subject both to the great power struggles which convulsed this inland sea and prey to pirates for whom the island's exposed shores were an irresistible target. Only in remote prehistory did the island appear to enjoy relative freedom from external interference.

Prehistoric times

No one can say where the first Sards came from, though rival legends suggest they were the followers of Sardus, son of Heracles, or the descendants of the Libyan Shardana people. The earliest phase of the island's development is also the most intriguing, with mysterious remnants still dotting the landscape. Though recent discoveries indicate the presence of communities in the Paleolithic era, the first traces of human settlement go back to before 6000 BC, when a hunting and pastoral society lived in grottoes, creating tools and weapons of flint and obsidian and crudely decorated ceramic bowls.

The Bonu Ighinu, Ozieri and Bonnanaro cultures

In the fourth millennium BC, a more advanced culture appeared, called **Bonu Ighinu** after the grotto 11km northwest of Bonorva where their most significant remains have been found. The people of this society seem to have inhabited villages of huts and practised more advanced systems of agriculture. Finds show that they had trading links with Corsica, southern Italy and the south of France, while statuettes suggest a cult based on a mother-goddess.

Between around 3400 and 2700 BC, Sardinia's **Ozieri culture** achieved dominance in the island (also called the San Michele culture, after the grotto of San Michele at Ozieri, its first important settlement). This was a significantly advanced society of hunters, shepherds and farmers, who worked copper as well as flint, obsidian and ceramics. Their cult of the dead was also much developed; bodies were interred in caves cut into rock that were often decorated and came to be called *domus de janas* ("fairy houses") by later generations. The earliest remains at one of Sardinia's most important sites, the sanctuary of Monte d'Accoddi, near Porto Torres, can be attributed to the Ozieri culture in around 3000 BC.

The **Bonnanaro culture**, which held sway during the first centuries of the second millennium, seems to have attained a lower level of artistic achievement, and has left few surviving fragments.

The nuraghic culture

Sardinia's **Bonnanaro culture** was overshadowed by the emerging **nuraghic culture**, which has yielded the most ubiquitous and imposing remains of any of Sardinia's historical phases, and which survived until the third century BC or later. The first nuraghic phase, between about 1800 and 1500 BC, overlapped in many respects with the preceding cultures, including the use of *domus de janas* and menhirs. The second,

3400–2700 BC	1800–900 BC	900–800 BC
The Ozieri (or San Michele) culture holds sway, responsible for the first development of the sanctuary of Monte d'Accoddi	Sardinia's nuraghic culture flourishes, leaving a legacy of around seven thousand stone towers scattered around the island	Phoenicians begin trading in Sardinia, establishing colonies and exploiting the mineral reserves

lasting until around 1200 BC, saw the development of the **nuraghic towers** and the *tombe dei giganti* – "giants' tombs", or collective burial chambers. During the third phase (1200–900 BC), the nuraghic towers became elaborate complexes sheltering sizeable villages, such as those at Su Nuraxi and Santu Antine, while **sacred wells** indicate the existence of a water cult.

The nuraghic culture reached its apogee between the tenth and eighth centuries BC, cultivating at home and trading abroad. Its fate was sealed, however, when Sardinia became embroiled in the commercial and military rivalries of other Mediterranean powers. The last nuraghic phase is characterized by an increasing engagement with these external forces, even as the indigenous people were producing sophisticated *bronzetti*, bronze statuettes that have provided invaluable insights into **nuraghic society**, suggesting a tribal and highly stratified social organization comprising an aristocracy, priests, warriors, artisans, shepherds and farmers. These and other artefacts reveal the extent of the mercantile network of which Sardinia formed a part, encompassing Italy, North Africa and Spain.

Phoenicians and Carthaginians

From the eastern Mediterranean, **Phoenicians** first began trading in Sardinia around 900 BC, and soon established peaceful commercial bases at Cágliari (Karalis); Bythia and Nora, southwest of Cágliari; Monte Sirai and Sant'Antíoco (Sulki, or Sulcis), farther west; and Tharros, near Oristano. The Phoenicians were also attracted by the island's mineral resources – as was every subsequent group of invaders and settlers.

From the sixth century BC, the main protagonists were the much more warlike **Carthaginians**, whose capital, Carthage, was across the Mediterranean near present-day Tunis, and for whom the island was of crucial strategic importance in their rivalry with the Greek cities of Italy. Intent on drawing Sardinia into their sphere of influence, the Carthaginians took over and expanded the main Phoenician settlements, and almost all traces of the Phoenician presence were eradicated.

The Romans

Carthaginian expansion in Sardinia was arrested by the need to confront the growing power of **Rome**, which in 259 BC turned against Sardinia itself. The Sards – now in league with Carthage – struggled fiercely against the new aggressors, at first with some success, but the inevitable defeat occurred in 232 BC, followed five years later by the establishment of the Roman *provincia* of Sardinia and Corsica.

Resistance continued, however, and towards the end of the **Second Punic War** between Rome and Carthage (218–202 BC), a concerted attempt to shake off the Roman yoke was organized under **Ampsicora**, a Sard of Carthaginian culture who suffered a crushing defeat at Cornus, north of Oristano, in 216 BC. Other revolts followed, including one in 177 BC when twelve thousand of the islanders were slaughtered and many more sent away as slaves to the mainland. The survivors of these rebellions, and others who refused to bow to the Romans, fled into the impenetrable central and eastern mountains of the interior, where they retained their independence in an area called Barbaria by the Romans, and known today as Barbagia.

600–500 BC	227 BC	450–534 AD
The Carthaginians establish a military presence in Sardinia, taking over the Phoenician settlements	Having overcome the combined Sard and Carthaginian forces, the Romans establish the *provincia* of Sardinia and Corsica	Following the Roman withdrawal, Sardinia is a prey to raids by Vandals and other marauders, and a Byzantine administration is established in Cágliari

Under **Roman occupation**, Sardinia was bled of its resources – minerals and agricultural produce mainly, especially grain – and heavily taxed, without any great benefit to its people. Although the island was rewarded for supporting Julius Caesar in Rome's civil war of 49–45 BC, little was done over seven centuries to instil Roman values or develop the island.

The attitude of the Romans towards the island was summed up in the use they found for it as a **place of exile** for "undesirable elements", including four thousand Jews sent by Emperor Tiberius, and early Christian subversives, who helped to spread the gospel. Apart from some impressive ruins at Nora and Tharros, there are few **Roman remains** on the island. The most notable are at Porto Torres, seat of an important colony (Turris Libyssonis); the baths at Fordongianus (Forum Traiani), east of Oristano; the Tempio di Antas in the Iglesiente, which shows the integration of Roman and Sardinian cults; and the amphitheatre at Cágliari. Rome's most lasting contribution was perhaps the strong Latin element that can still be heard in the Sard dialect today.

Byzantine rule and the Giudicati

With the eclipse of the Roman empire in the fifth century AD, Sardinia became vulnerable to barbarian raids and plundering that reached far inland. For a short period the island was held by the Vandals, then after 534 AD, by the **Byzantines**. It was too remote an outpost of Byzantium to benefit greatly, though the island was given some protection from the incursions of Goths and Lombards.

One survival of Byzantine rule was the division of the island into **giudicati**, a system which was to endure right through the Middle Ages. There were four main *giudicati*: Cágliari, Arborea (around Oristano), Torres in the northwest and Gallura in the northeast, each a small kingdom with an elected king – originally a judge, or *giudice*. In practice, however, these were the preserve of local oligarchies, and the island was left to its own devices, increasingly prey to raids from the new **Muslim** empires of North Africa and Spain, which were to continue sporadically from the eighth century for over a thousand years. Fear of death or slavery at the hands of the corsairs was a fact of life in Sardinia throughout this period, and had the long-term effect of depopulating the island's coasts. Another reason for the move inland was the increasing prevalence of **malaria** on the coasts and lowlands, the result of neglected irrigation works, deforestation and the silting-up of rivers. The combination of marauders and malaria led to the gradual abandonment of much crop cultivation in the lowlands in favour of sheep and livestock farming in the safe highland pastures of the interior.

Pisa and Genoa in Sardinia

The Arab threat was not confined to local attacks: larger forces occupied Cágliari in 720 and further inroads were made in 752. In 1015 a substantial force from the Arab emirate in Spain landed and threatened to take over the entire island; the pope encouraged the Italian mercantile republics of **Pisa** and **Genoa** to intervene, and together they succeeded in ousting the invading army. The Pisans and Genoans themselves, however, proved harder to dislodge, and from this time on Sardinia was increasingly open to trading and political links with mainland Italy.

1015	1326	1392
Arab forces attempt to occupy Sardinia, leading to the intervention of the republics of Pisa and Genoa	The Aragonese prise Cágliari from the Pisans, a significant step in the Spanish efforts to conquer Sardinia	Eleonora d'Arborea institutes the Carta de Logu, which forms the basis of Sardinia's laws until 1817

The influence of **monastic orders** from Italy and Provence also grew during this period; granted special privileges on the island, they played an important part in restoring decayed irrigation works and industries such as salt extraction. They also influenced artistic and architectural currents: the Benedictine Vittorini, for example, were as instrumental in diffusing Romanesque building styles in the south of Sardinia as the Tuscans and Lombards were in the island's north.

By lending their support in the various conflicts between the *giudicati*, the rival cities of Pisa and Genoa began to take an increasingly active role. The driving forces were **individual families** rather than the cities themselves: the Visconti in Logudoro; the della Gherardesca in Iglésias; the Malaspina in Bosa; and the Doria dynasty with a power base in Castelsardo. In the northern *giudicato* of Torres, the influence of **Pisan merchants** can be seen in a string of churches such as San Gavino in Porto Torres, Santa Trinità di Saccárgia and San Pietro di Sorres (both southeast of Sássari). Farther south, Pisan power centred on Cágliari, where the defences built around that city's citadel still stand, but by the end of the thirteenth century, the balance had swung entirely in the favour of Genoa.

The struggle against Aragon

Around the turn of the fourteenth century, a new player appeared on the scene: the Iberian kingdom of **Aragon**, that had recently taken possession of Sicily. In 1297, Pope Boniface VIII managed to persuade James II to give up the Aragonese claim to Sicily in return for rights over the newly created kingdom of Sardinia and Corsica. The title was a mere formality, however, since Aragon was very far from asserting any control over the island, and the struggle to do so lasted more than a century. The campaign proved easier in the south of the island, with Cágliari taken from the Pisans in 1326; in the north, the biggest obstacle was the Doria family – of whom the king of Aragon was nominally feudal overlord – and there was continual fighting between Aragonese forces and an alliance of Sards, Genoans and the mixed-blood aristocracy.

The islanders' cause was led by the *giudicato* of Arborea, and championed in particular by **Eleonora d'Arborea** (see box, p.142), a warrior queen who granted Sardinia its first written code of laws which remained in force for the next four centuries. Eleonora succeeded in stemming the Aragonese advance, but after her death in 1404 Sardinian resistance crumbled. Following a decisive victory at Sanluri in 1409, the Aragonese finally triumphed.

The Spanish in power

Following the unification of the kingdoms of Aragon and Castile in 1479, Sardinia became a colony of a united Spain. Although this was an unusually peaceful period in the island's history, the three centuries of **Spanish rule** in Sardinia were not accompanied by any significant improvement in the lot of most Sards, and there were few attempts to develop or even maintain the infrastructure. Government was entrusted to viceroys uninterested in the island's welfare, trading links with the Italian mainland were cut, and Spain's shift of focus to its profitable Atlantic empire left Sardinia on the margins.

1410–1478	1626–34	1718
Consolidation of the Aragonese conquest – Sardinia becomes a peripheral part of the Spanish empire	Universities are founded in Cágliari and Sássari	Following the War of the Spanish Succession, the island is ceded to the Piedmontese House of Savoy and becomes part of the Kingdom of Sardinia

The Spanish introduced a **feudal system** under which the land was parcelled up and distributed among Catalan-Aragonese nobles who enjoyed absolute powers within their domains. However, these men rarely lived on the island, and day-to-day governance was left in the hands of local officials. Spanish influence was strongest in the cities, which absorbed elements of Catalan Gothic and later Baroque architecture. On the coasts, the most visible contribution was the series of defensive towers that still line Sardinia's shores, providing at least some warning of attacks from North African corsairs, who remained a constant threat. The Spanish king (and Holy Roman Emperor) **Charles V** attempted to end these destructive assaults by assembling huge fleets in 1535 and 1541, with which he hoped to extirpate the raiders from their lairs in Tunis and Algiers. But these armadas had only short-term success, and Charles and his successor Philip II were too preoccupied with their far-flung empire to devote much time to the island's welfare.

Throughout this period, Sardinia was hard hit by the malaria rife in all but the highest points of the island. In addition to this, plague swept the island in the 1650s, killing possibly 25 percent of the population, while the famine of 1680–81 is thought to have accounted for around eighty thousand deaths. More positively, universities were founded in Cágliari in 1626 and Sássari in 1634, encouraging the growth of a professional class.

The Kingdom of Sardinia

As Spain's power declined, events elsewhere in Europe began to impinge on Sardinia. During the War of the Spanish Succession in 1701–13, Cágliari was bombarded by an English fleet in 1708 and briefly occupied. The ensuing negotiations led to the island being ceded first to Austria, then, in 1718, to the Piedmontese **House of Savoy**, a duchy on the French-Italian border. The united possessions of Vittorio Amedeo II of Savoy became the new **Kingdom of Sardinia**.

Social unrest

Although Sardinia's Savoy period is associated with the beginnings of reconstruction, reforms did not take place quickly enough to stem the simmering discontent engendered by high expectations. The frustration manifested itself in a variety of forms during the **eighteenth century**. *Banditismo* – the factional fighting, clan warfare, robbery and kidnapping that had always existed in the rural interior – assumed chronic proportions, while the forced adoption of Italian as the language of government alienated an aristocracy for whom Spanish was the mother tongue.

For the majority of Sardinia's population, the chief problems included the low level of **education**, with schools dominated by the Church and illiteracy almost universal; the island's continued vulnerability to seaborne attacks; and Sardinia's very sparse population. The government attempted to solve the last of these by a poorly organized and ultimately unsuccessful attempt to introduce **foreign colonies** to the island. The most deep-rooted cause of Sard hostility to the new ruling elite, however, was the continuing existence of the feudal system.

Matters came to a head in the wake of the **French Revolution**, when the general turmoil prevailing in Europe exposed the drawbacks inherent in the island's links to

1794–1796	1836–43	1861
Revolts in Cágliari provoke uprisings across the island against the Savoy regime	Abolition of the feudal system, leading to wide-ranging rural reforms	Sardinia joins the new Kingdom of Italy

NELSON'S FINEST ISLAND

During the fifteen months he spent hovering around the coasts of Sardinia in his pursuit of the French fleet – an operation that culminated in the Battle of Trafalgar in 1805 – **Admiral Horatio Nelson** expressed an interest in the island as a potential base. "God knows," he wrote in his dispatches home, "if we could possess one island, Sardinia, we should want neither Malta, nor any other: this which is the finest island in the Mediterranean, possesses harbours fit for arsenals, and of a capacity to hold our navy, within 24 hours' sail of Toulon…"

the Piedmont regime. The House of Savoy's quarrels became Sardinia's, and in 1793 French troops succeeded in occupying the island of San Pietro, while another force which included the young **Napoleon Bonaparte** was repulsed at La Maddalena, as was a fleet which bombarded Cágliari. Though the Savoy king rewarded his Piedmontese officials for their part in the rout, the role of the islanders was unacknowledged. What rankled even more was the refusal of the royal court to respond to a delegation from Sardinia bearing the *Cinque Domande*, or "Five Demands", which called for a full constitutional reform, including the restoration of ancient privileges and the regular convocation of an island parliament.

Between 1794 and 1796 an **insurrection** in Cágliari forced the viceroy and his entourage to take flight, and full-scale revolts subsequently broke out all over Sardinia, which ended with Sássari being taken by the rebels. At their head was **Giovanni Maria Angioy**, an aristocrat whose anti-feudal stance made him popular among the peasants, but whose increasingly radical demands for a Sardinian republic alienated the more moderate elements. In 1796 Angioy was driven out of Sardinia and died in exile in Paris, leaving behind a name that has been given to streets and squares throughout the island. His followers were savagely persecuted by the Piedmontese.

The beginnings of reform

The most noteworthy Savoyard kings in the **nineteenth century** were Carlo Felice (1821–31), who did much to modernize the island's infrastructure, not least by building the Carlo Felice highway – today the SS131 – that runs the length of the island from Cágliari to Porto Torres, and Carlo Alberto (1831–49), responsible for the final **abolition of the feudal system** in 1836–43. Although this led to a bitter conflict over the introduction of enclosures to demarcate private land in the mountains – thereby restricting the ancient liberty of shepherds to wander freely in search of fresh pasturage – it was an essential prelude to rural reform.

Unified Italy

The Kingdom of Sardinia came to an end in 1861, when Vittorio Emanuele II, son of Carlo Alberto, became king (1861–78) of the newly unified Italy. The island had played a significant role in the Risorgimento (the struggle for nationhood) by providing a base from which **Giuseppe Garibaldi** embarked on both his major expeditions.

Sardinia's problems entered a new phase. Adjusting to its role as part of a modern nation-state became the central theme of the next century or so – some would argue up to and including the present. Matters weren't helped by the fact that colonial attitudes

1921	1928	1943
The Partito Sardo d'Azione is founded to campaign for regional autonomy	Arborea is built as part of Mussolini's regeneration programme, followed ten years later by Carbónia	Cágliari suffers intense bombardment during World War II

towards the island persisted, while its natural resources were ruthlessly plundered (accounting for much of the deforestation still evident today) and wages remained low. Agriculture also suffered, leading to soaring unemployment, which in turn fuelled widespread banditry. There was little money available to tackle the root causes of the problem, and although there was a degree of political reform, by the end of the nineteenth century voting rights were still only available to less than five percent of the island's population.

Nonetheless, Sardinia contributed notably to both world wars, with the Sássari Brigade in particular achieving lasting distinction during **World War I**, albeit at a heavy cost. The experience of war radicalized many Sards, and elections based on universal suffrage in 1920 and 1921 saw the creation of the **Partito Sardo d'Azione**, or Sardinian Action Party, whose manifesto demanded autonomy.

Fascism and World War II

Ironically, Sardinia had to wait for a ruthless centralizing dictatorship before real changes began to make themselves felt. **Benito Mussolini**, the Italian Fascist leader who came to power in 1922, saw the backward island as fertile ground for his social and economic experiments, particularly in the context of his drive for Italian self-sufficiency. In the 1920s and 1930s the Fascist government initiated a series of schemes which led to genuine improvements: the island's many rivers were harnessed and dammed to provide irrigation and power, land was drained and made fertile, agricultural colonies were set up, and the new towns of Carbónia, Arborea and Fertilia were founded – though the industrial projects were mostly failures. The island suffered badly during **World War II**: in 1943 Cágliari endured some of the heaviest bombing of all Italian cities, with 75 percent of its houses destroyed. Traumatized, the island awoke to a postwar era in which nothing seemed to have changed – once more, it felt itself to be a second-class member of the Italian state, subject to a remote bureaucracy and irrelevant legislation. As before, attempts to force the island to integrate into the new centralized, bureaucratic Italy gave rise to a host of resentments.

An attempt to offset this was made in 1948, when the *regione* of Sardinia was granted **autonomy**, allowing the regional government direct control over such fields as transport, tourism, police, industry and agriculture. Two years later, the central government's fund to speed up the development of the South of Italy, the Cassa per il Mezzogiorno, was extended to Sardinia, and the island began to receive hefty injections of capital investment. Perhaps more significantly, through the intervention of the US Rockefeller Foundation, Sardinia was saturated with enough **DDT** in the years immediately following World War II to rid it once and for all of malaria.

Sardinia today

The success of this combined effort to haul Sardinia up from a peripheral, third-world status is apparent everywhere, and some areas of Sardinian life are as streamlined and sophisticated as anywhere on the mainland. Visitors to the island today will recognize a piece of Italy – the same shops, cars and language – to the extent that it is growing ever harder to distinguish "the real Sardinia" underneath the Italian gloss.

1948	1962	2008
Sardinia is granted regional autonomy	A consortium led by the Aga Khan begins to develop what would become known as the Costa Smeralda, opening up the island to tourism	US naval base on La Maddalena archipelago closes after 35 years

However, the island's transformation would have taken a different course were it not for two initiatives that had lasting effects on its economy and infrastucture. In 1962, the Italian parliament finally authorized a **programme of industrialization**, which led to the introduction of heavy-duty petrochemical plants completely at odds with the island's traditional activities. In the same year, a consortium of investors led by the Aga Khan began to develop the **Costa Smeralda** as an elite jet-setters' enclave, opening up the tourist industry and giving Sardinia a new role which has been largely embraced by the locals, bringing a degree of wealth to a substantial section of the population.

The awakening of the island's tourist potential has gone hand in hand with a new appreciation of Sardinia's **traditional culture**, a re-evaluation of its language and folklore and a corresponding pride in Sard identity. On the minus side, the island has suffered the usual pitfalls of tourist economies everywhere – namely, poorly regulated construction and the degradation of the natural environment in pursuit of short-term profit.

Still, with its relatively prosperous population of 1.6 million, Sardinia today seems comfortable enough with its modern role. Despite a simmering resentment towards the centralized bureaucracy and the Italian state in general, overall there is satisfaction with Sardinia's place within Italy and the European Union, while the main party campaigning in the long term for complete independence, the Partito Sardo d'Azione, is too marginal to exert much influence except at a local level.

Sardinia's modern profile is represented by such individuals as **Renato Soru**, born in Sanluri in 1957, founder and chairman of Milan-based internet service provider Tiscali, and president of the *regione di Sardegna* 2004–2009 at the head of a Centre-Left coalition. The image of Sardinia as a playboy's playground, on the other hand, is illustrated by the antics of **Silvio Berlusconi**, ex-prime minister of Italy, famous for the lavish entertainments he hosted in his sumptuous villas on the Costa Smeralda. The shameless devotion to *la dolce vita* embodied by this millionaire's resort appears ever more incongruous in the context of the dire financial plight that has gripped Italy – and Europe – since 2009, which has resulted in a significant drop in tourist revenue for the islanders.

Sardinian wildlife

In common with all islands, Sardinia has that element of uniqueness that arises from isolation, in which plants and animals evolve differently from those on the mainland. Many species are found only here, or are shared with neighbouring Corsica, while the proximity of Africa gives the local fauna and flora a distinct, almost tropical character. In addition, Sardinia's location on a key bird-migration route between Africa and Europe accounts for the seasonal visitations of a number of bird species.

Sardinia's island ecology also means that a number of species present on the mainland are absent here – notably poisonous snakes, but also wolves, otters and moles. Those species which are present display a brilliant diversity, linked to the range of different terrains – mountain, forest, plain and coast – that exist within a relatively limited area, and to the typically Mediterranean climate, which keeps rainfall between 600mm (24 inches) on the plains to 990mm (39 inches) in the mountains.

Habitats

Sardinia boasts a significant proportion of Italy's **lagoons** and **wetlands**, as well as extensive areas of **maquis** (Mediterranean scrub), remnant **forests**, hot **plains** and high **mountains**. The overwhelming presence of mountains accounts for the island's numerous **rivers**, of which the Tirso and Flumendosa are the most important.

Lagoons

In ornithological terms, the **lagoons** (*stagni*) and wetlands are perhaps the most important feature of the island. Sardinia still has 130 square kilometres of protected lagoons, constituting 25 percent of all the lagoons located within Italy. Those in Sardinia are internationally designated both for their importance during migration time and for the presence of rare breeding birds.

The richest *stagni* are to be found in the vicinity of Oristano and Cágliari, where it is common to spot flocks of pink **flamingos**; they have long used both of these areas as a stop-off on their migrations between Africa and the Carmargue region of France, though they have also started nesting and breeding in lagoon areas throughout the island. The range of wetland species here is remarkable – most notably **black-winged stilt** (the "cavalier of Italy", named for its extraordinary leggy appearance), spoonbill, crane, avocet, cattle egret, tern, cormorant, glossy ibis, white-headed duck, osprey, pratincole, purple gallinule, ferruginous duck, marsh harrier and Andouin's gull.

In winter, there are large numbers of **ducks** and **cormorants**, their V-shaped skeins a prominent feature in the skies, not to mention numerous waders and wheeling flocks of **lapwings**. The spring and autumn migrations see significant numbers of passage

---

WHEN TO WATCH WILDLIFE

Timing is essential, for wildlife watchers in Sardinia. A visit in spring or autumn is best for viewing bird migrations and the flowering of plants and shrubs, many of which bloom first in spring and again in autumn, after the summer drought. In winter, there's less to see in higher terrain but the lowlands, particularly around lagoons, still shelter a range of waders and other aquatic birdlife.

birds, and this is a good time to see the **curlew sandpiper**, **Caspian tern**, **short-toed eagle** and **red-footed falcon**.

The area around Oristano has the island's best-protected lagoons, not least those on the Sinis peninsula, where the flatlands around the lakeside town of Cabras have the Pauli e Sali reserve, sheltering reeds and a wide range of waterfowl. The nearby Stagno di Sale Porcus is the place to see the extremely rare **European crane**. Another general feature of these wetlands are the reed beds, home to **great reed**, **fan-tailed** and **Cetti's warbler**s and hunted over by the fast, acrobatic **hobby**.

Coastal zones

In coastal areas, **Aleppo** and **maritime palms** lend a tropical feel, while the long **sand dunes** on the west coast of the provinces of Carbónia-Iglésias, Medio-Campidano and Oristano create a more arid environment, notably around Piscinas and Is Arenas. **Turtles** use these and other remote beaches to lay eggs.

Sardinia's eastern coast is mainly cliffy and undeveloped, the mountains ending in a sheer rocky wall of limestone. Capo di Monte Santu, at the southern end of the Gulf of Orosei, hosts a significant colony of the highly unusual **Eleonora's falcon**, a "semi-colonial" nesting falcon named after Sardinia's medieval warrior queen who decreed that she alone was permitted to hunt with it. Only found in the Mediterranean, this large migratory falcon is one of Europe's rarest and most enigmatic raptors, with long, thin, speedily vibrating wings, and is most often seen in autumn, since the species breeds late to feed its young on autumn-passage birds, catching its prey on the wing.

The Gulf of Orosei is also important as the last home of the monk or **Mediterranean seal** (in Italian *bue marino*, or "sea ox"). Sadly, it's either already extinct or facing extinction, with at best only a handful of individuals remaining scattered in the coves and grottoes of this rocky coast.

Off the Stintino peninsula in the northwest, the island of Asinara, now a national park, is most famous for the unique and diminutive **albino ass**. Some of these tiny creatures can also be found south of the peninsula on the massive cliffs of Capo Caccia, where they share the Prigionette reserve with **wild boars** as well as **griffon vultures** – Italy's largest colony of these immense creatures is to be found here and a few kilometres further south on the desolate Alghero–Bosa coast. A short distance north of Alghero, Sardinia's only natural lake, Lago di Baratz, has a species of **freshwater tortoise** and a system of pine-covered dunes and maritime *macchia*.

Plains and plateaus

Sardinia's **plains** are among the flatlands being agriculturally "improved" across much of Europe, but here they still shelter a range of flora and fauna. The island's most extensive plain is in the Campidano region, between Cágliari and Oristano, home to the **little bustard**, a turkey-like creature that was once much hunted by aristocratic falcons. The whole bustard family is endangered in much of Europe, but Sardinia is one of the few places where this particular member is expanding and flourishing in the mosaics of pasture particularly favoured by this species. The plains are also a rich habitat for **partridge**, **bunting**, **woodchat** and **shrike**, while the vividly colourful exotics – **roller**, **hoopoe** and **bee-eater** – are all found here. Springtime is the best time to visit, when the *macchia* and grasslands are a riot of colour.

East of Campidano, La Marmilla is characterized by odd-looking, bare hummocks and a series of high tablelands virtually empty of human developments, where **asphodel**, euphorbia, poppies, lavender, buttercups and daisies form a brilliant tapestry. The largest of these high basalt **plateaus** is the Giara di Gésturi, holding a concentration of the island's most interesting plants, including a number of rare species of **orchid**. Sheltering a range of wildlife including hares, boars and foxes, the plateau is also the principal habitat of Sardinia's famous *cavallini* – miniature **wild horses** whose origins are shrouded in mystery and which are notoriously difficult to spot.

A CHECKLIST OF SARDINIAN WILDLIFE SITES

Alghero–Bosa coast Home to Italy's largest colony of griffon vultures. See p.187.

Capo Figari Mouflons have been reintroduced on this cape and on the offshore islet of Figarolo. See p.240.

Caprera Dense *macchia* and woods, where sea and land birds nest. See p.254.

Foresta di Minniminni and Monte dei Sette Fratelli Rugged terrain sheltering deer, boar, wildcat and various birds of prey. See p.130.

Gennargentu This thickly forested central mountain range has boar and – more visibly – wild pigs. See p.287.

Giara di Gésturi A high basalt plateau famous as the island's main habitat of the miniature wild horses (*cavallini*); it's also a good place to see rare species of orchid. See p.125.

Monte Arcosu The Sardinian stag (*cervo sardo*) and other forest fauna, as well as a range of predatory birds, can be spotted here. See p.84.

Piscinas High dune system where esparto grasses and even wild lilies take root in the sands. See p.109.

Le Prigionette This reserve has wild boar and griffon vultures, though these are more common farther south, on the Alghero–Bosa coast. See p.184.

San Pietro The island's western cliffs are the habitat for rare sea birds and falcons. See p.97.

Sinis The dunes, marshes and lagoons here shelter reeds and a huge range of aquatic birdlife, including the European crane. See p.148.

Supramonte Wild goats clamber the slopes of this desolate massif, and eagles and other raptors circle above. See pp.280–282.

Tavolara The sheer cliffs of this island shelter peregrine falcons and storm petrels among other rare birds. See p.238.

The macchia

Sardinia's rocky slopes are everywhere covered with a thick layer of Mediterranean **maquis** (in Italian, *macchia*). This invasive scrub flourishes after fire or the felling of forests and also colonizes abandoned cultivated land. Tangled, heavily scented and richly colourful, *macchia* includes **juniper**, **lentisk**, **myrtle** and **arbutus** (strawberry tree); **heather** and the yellow-flowering **broom** and **gorse** are also common, as are the pink and white petals of the **cistus** family. Leaves here are often thick and gummy to help prevent water loss, and the shrubs are intermingled with herbs and flowers and orchids in more open patches.

Near the coast, the *macchia* has a more typically maritime selection of plants, while in the drier areas it is interspersed with **prickly pear** cactus (introduced from Mexico by the Spanish), the fruit of which ("Indian fig") is considered a delicacy. The typical **warblers** here – **Sardinian**, **Marmora's**, **subalpine**, **spectacled** and **Dartford** – are all of interest to those more familiar with northern European species. At night one can hear the calls of the **Scops owl** and the echoing, warm, low churring of the **nightjar** intermingling with the cicadas.

Mountain and woodland areas

As the altitude increases, the shrub layer gives way to taller **woodland** where trees such as cork and holm oak start to appear. Here, the richly lyrical **blackcap** and the **Orphean warbler** become more predominant as the thickening canopy shades out the *macchia*. Traditional olive groves and fruit orchards are very important for a number of bird species, the most important of which is the rare **wryneck**. Alder and the pink blossom of oleander may mark the line of water-courses, often totally dried out in summer, while on the more established streams the semi-aquatic **dipper** can sometimes be seen. Woodland is also one of the favoured habitats of the **Barbary partridge** – apart from Gibraltar, Sardinia is the only place in Europe where this species can be found. Outside reserves like Le Prigionette, however, you'll be lucky to glimpse one, just as you'll need luck and patience to spot the rare **Sardinian salamander**.

Sardinia has the highest level of **forest** cover of all the Italian regions. **Cork oak** trees stretch from Gallura to the northern Barbagia (the central zone of mountains), providing one of Europe's main sources of cork – the plantations are particularly thick around the village of Calangianus. The **holm oak** is another tree ubiquitous on the island: the Gennargentu mountains and the Abbasanta plateau near Oristano hold the remnants of a holm oak forest that once covered much of Sardinia, and at Sas Badas and Su Lidone on the Supramonte massif are remains of an ancient forest that has never been felled, its gnarled specimens numbering among the last remaining examples in Europe. The island even has a **petrified forest** near Soddi on the shore of Lake Omodeo, the result of a primeval volcanic eruption.

Higher up in the mountains, where the chiming of sheep- and goat-bells is a constant accompaniment, the species in the tree line change, with the appearance of **bay oaks** and **maples** whose red leaves provide a blaze of colour in autumn, and scattered clumps of **holly** and **yew** – residual vegetation from a cooler era. The **jay** is common here, while **goshawks** and **peregrine falcons** prey on the **wood pigeons**; rarer species include **golden eagles** and **Bonelli's eagles**. Towards the summits of the mountains, the forests largely disappear and are replaced by grassland, scattered **junipers** and **dwarf palm trees** beautifully contorted by the mistral wind.

Many species of rare and unique mountain plants are to be found in the Gennargentu, but pride of place goes to the **peony** whose blooming announces the arrival of spring. A notable mammal to be found in this terrain is the **Sardinian stag**, a few hundred of which have survived here and in the forests around Cágliari, for example Monte Arcosu, in the mountains of Sulcis – also the place to see **martens**, **wildcats** and **boar**.

Mouflon, or long-horned wild sheep, are now found only in the mountains of Sardinia, and on Corsica and Cyprus. You'll have to penetrate quite far into the deep and rugged valleys to glimpse examples of this extraordinary animal, perched on high ledges with enormous, regally curved horns. Lower down, the groves of hazel, almond, walnut and chestnut carpeting the slopes of the interior are grazed by both wild *cinghiali* (boar) and the more domesticated pig – which in many cases has interbred with its wild cousin. Although Sardinia's wild boar are hunted for both sport and their meat, numbers have not declined significantly in recent years.

Sardinians are unreconstructed **hunters**, and will shoot at anything that moves. It is not uncommon to come across heavily armed hunting parties trailing through the *macchia*, though European public opinion is having an impact on reducing the destructive effects of this "sport", and the provision of protected areas is increasing.

Books

Surprisingly little has been written about Sardinia, though the island has provided the inspiration for a small number of outstanding works. Titles marked ★ are particularly recommended.

TRAVEL, MUSIC AND FOOD

Giuliano Bugialli *Foods of Sicily and Sardinia*. Recipes and background on familiar – and less well-known – Sard dishes, beautifully illustrated.

★ **D.H. Lawrence** *Sea and Sardinia*. Lawrence's six-day journey through Sardinia in 1921 did not give the island much of a chance, and his account bristles with impatience and irritation. Travelling up from Cágliari to Nuoro and Olbia in the company of the "Queen Bee" (Frieda Lawrence), his highly personal travelogue alternates between disgust and rapture, though it sparkles with closely observed cameos.

Bernard Lortat-Jacob *Sardinian Chronicles*. Examines the music of the island through twelve vignettes of locals

who continue to practise the tradition of choral singing. CD included.

Amelie Posse-Brázdová *Sardinian Sideshow*. Translated from the Swedish in 1932, this light-hearted memoir relates the experiences of the protagonist and her Middle-European companions in exile during World War I in Alghero. Illuminating mainly for its descriptions of the island in the days before package tourism.

★ **Alan Ross** *The Bandit on the Billiard Table*. Well-written account of a journey through Sardinia in the 1950s, full of sympathetic descriptions of people and places; informative and readable, if a little old-fashioned.

SARDINIAN FILMS

Sardinia has no distinctive **film-making** tradition, although a few directors have taken advantage of its landscape. The following lists the most notable films associated with the island.

Banditi a Orgosolo (*Bandits of Orgosolo*, directed by Vittorio de Seta, 1961). This film capitalized on the publicity given to kidnapping and violence as practised by the outlaws living in the hills around the village of Orgósolo, outside Nuoro. The first feature film of this Sicilian-born director, made with minimal technical and financial facilities, it was enthusiastically received at the 1961 Venice Film Festival, but has disappeared almost without trace now.

Disamistade (directed by Gianfranco Cabiddu, 1988). Focusing on the conflicts between old ways and modern life, this tells the story of a young man in the 1950s who returns to the island and is forced to conform to traditional practices by now alien to him.

Il Deserto Rosso (*Red Desert*, directed by Michelangelo Antonioni, 1965). Filmed on Budelli – one of the Maddalena Islands – and responsible for propelling its *spiaggia rosa* or "pink beach" to instant fame, the movie has since sunk into obscurity.

Il Figlio di Bakùnin (directed by Gianfranco Cabiddu, 1997). This film by *Disamistade's* director is based on the book *Bakunin's Son*

by Sergio Atzeni (see p.320). Set in a mining community, it describes the plight of a shoemaker's son in the context of Sardinia's postwar history. Both films had a limited release.

Padre Padrone (directed by Paolo and Vittorio Taviani, 1977). This is the most famous film to come out of Sardinia, and the island's rugged mountain backdrops are used to full effect. All the same, the film, which was based on the autobiography of the writer Gavino Ledda (see p.320), was hated by Sards for giving a negative portrayal of the island, even if its main theme is chiefly an exploration of a boy's relationship with his tyrannical father. The cruelty and bleak poverty of the shepherds' society is perhaps overplayed, but it's a strongly atmospheric piece, the first film to win both the Palme d'Or and International Critics' Prize at Cannes, and for years *de rigueur* viewing at Communist Party gatherings. Roberto Rossellini, head of the Cannes jury, declared that the film "embodies everything which is most impressive, vigorous and coherent, and most daring, socially and artistically, in the Italian cinema".

WALKING, CYCLING AND DIVING

Paddy Dillon *Walking in Sardinia: 50 Walks in Sardinia's Mountains* This Cicerone guide ignores large areas of the island, but has excellent info on walks in the Ogliastra region, Supramonte and the Gennargenu range. There's lots of practical material on transport and the language, too.

Peter Herold, Amos Cardia and Davide Deidda *Mountain Bike Sardinia*. Seventy rides in the south and centre of the island, with clear overviews, detailed descriptions, maps and photos – it's well produced, but pricey.

★ **Walter Iwersen and Elisabeth van de Wetering** *Sardinia* (Rother Walking Guides). This excellent recent update is the best hiking guide to the island, with 63 walks lucidly described, each with a colour map (1:25,000, 1:50,000 or 1:75,000) and photographs, and downloadable GPS coordinates.

Egidio Trainito *Sardinia Diving Guide*. Lavishly illustrated guide outlining Sardinia's principal underwater ecosystems and describing 31 dives, with details of marine life and wrecks. Maps and diagrams show the sites, while photos help to identify fish and other sea life. Shortcomings include poor translation, some serious omissions regarding dive centres and background and unhelpful artwork.

HISTORY AND ARCHEOLOGY

★ **Rainer Pauli** *Sardegna*. Digestible survey of the archeological and historical sites of Sardinia, and an excellent handbook for anyone keen to deepen their knowledge of the island. It has not yet appeared in an English version, though copious photos, drawings and diagrams aid understanding.

Robert H. Tykot and Tamsey Andrews *Sardinia in the Mediterranean: A Footprint in the Sea*. Comprehensive (and highly expensive) study of Sardinian archeology that covers Paleolithic and Neolithic cultures and nuraghic, Phoenician, Punic, Greek and Roman settlements on the island.

Gary S. Webster *A Prehistory of Sardinia, 2300–500 BC*. Heavyweight academic tome bringing together all the research on Sardinian prehistory, with particular attention given to nuraghic society.

SARDINIAN LITERATURE

Sergio Atzeni *Bakunin's Son*. The portrait of a man conveyed through interviews with those who knew him. Though there is a disjointed and unfinished feel about the book, it develops into an engaging, multi-layered narrative. Atzeni drowned while swimming in 1995, and the book, published in 1991, was adapted as a film in 1997.

★ **Grazia Deledda** *After the Divorce, Cosima, Elias Portolu, La Madre, Canne al Vento*. Grazia Deledda's Sardinia is a raw place of instinct and passion, which she evokes in her simple, unsentimental tales set around her home town of Nuoro. In *After the Divorce* (1902), she writes of the grim sense of exclusion from the tribal mores prevailing in the village of Orlei, where the main protagonist is driven to betray her husband who has been convicted of murder. *Cosima* is an autobiographical novel published posthumously, vividly evoking the struggles of a Nuorese girl with literary aspirations. *Elias Portolu* (1900) relates the moral and social dilemmas of a convict returned to his rigid shepherds' society. *La Madre* (1920) deals with the frustrated love of a village priest and the efforts of his mother to dissuade him from giving up his vocation in order to follow his passion. *Canne al Vento* (1913), translated as *Reeds in the Wind*, tells of the decline of three noble spinster sisters, the guilt-ridden, unpaid servant who looks after them and the numerous local characters who inhabit this densely superstitious society. Deledda's writing is full of what D.H. Lawrence called "uncontaminated human instinct" and "the indescribable tang of the people of the island, not yet absorbed into the world". She won the Nobel Prize for Literature in 1926. Interested readers should search for the biography written by one of her translators, Martha King: *Grazia Deledda, A Legendary Life*.

Giuseppe Dessi *Il Disertore*. Published in 1961, "The Deserter" narrates the tale of a young Sardinian shepherd who, sent to fight in World War I, flees from the front after killing his captain in a fit of rage, and returns to Sardinia. Other works by Dessi include *Paese d'Ombre* ("Land of Shadows"), published in 1972 and winner of the Strega Prize that year.

Gavino Ledda *Padre Padrone*. Though best known outside Italy as a film (see box, p.319), this autobiographical novel from 1975 is the most famous literary work to have come out of Sardinia in recent times. Dragged out of school to tend sheep, Ledda (b.1938) was illiterate until the age of 20, when he entered the army and started on a journey of self-education. *Padre Padrone*, the story of his turbulent upbringing in the mountains and eventual rebellion against his sadistic father, was followed by other books, but none enjoyed the same success.

Emilio Lussu *Marcia su Roma e dintorni*. First published in 1933, "March on Rome" is an autobiographical account by a leading Sardinian republican politician of resistance to Fascism in Sardinia between 1918 and 1930, narrated with humour and evocative descriptions of the island.

★ **Salvatore Satta** *The Day of Judgement*. A respected jurist, Salvatore Satta wrote this classic over several years, though it was not published until after his death in 1975. Like Deledda's work, it is set in Nuoro, peopled by a procession of theatrical characters who seem to inhabit a bleak dreamscape of a long-dead past. The book lacks much in

SARDINIAN MUSIC AND DANCE

Music and dance are taken extremely seriously in Sardinia. You're bound to encounter both at any of the numerous festivals taking place in the island throughout the year, as well as at concerts and recitals in squares, parks and even archeological sites. It comes in a diversity of forms, though the island is probably best known for unaccompanied harmony singing. Most singing groups fall into one of two camps: the **coros** (choral), usually dedicated to liturgical song, with any number of participants, and the **tenores**, four-part male groups singing mainly secular material. The latter groups in particular have made quite an impact internationally in recent years, the most famous being **Tenores di Bitti** (see p.279). The four voices of a *tenores* group are said to imitate the typical sounds of the rural shepherds' society: "bassu" (bass, from the cow), "contra" (contralto, from the sheep), "mesu oche" (*mezza voce*, from the sound of the wind) and "oche" (*voce*, the human voice). Almost all vocal groups are male, though it is possible to hear women's voices in groups such as **Actores Alidos**, creating quite a different sound.

Festivals are also a good place to see **traditional instruments** being played, for example the *launeddas*, a simple, polyphonic triple pipe made from reed. **Efisio Melis** and **Antonio Lara** established themselves in the 1930s as the greatest players in this genre. You'll also see the more versatile accordion, or *organetto*, whose most famous living exponent is **Totore Chessa**, a light-fingered virtuoso.

There's no specific Sardinian rock music scene – radio and TV are dominated by mainstream Italian chart music, with a smattering of British and American hits. Local singer **Elena Ledda** has dabbled in pop while retaining specifically Sard elements in her music, especially in more recent recordings. The island has a higher profile in the field of jazz, reflected in the number of jazz festivals taking place, usually in summer. One of the best is at Berchidda, west of Olbia, in which the trumpeter **Paolo Fresu** is closely involved. Fresu has long been known on the Italian and European jazz circuit, though without accentuating the Sard connection in his work. **Antonello Salis** is another musician with an international reputation – an idiosyncratic pianist and accordionist who has worked with Billy Cobham, Pat Metheny and others.

Accordion, drum, tambourine, guitar and *launeddas* are the usual accompaniments to Sardinian **dancing**, a curiously twitchy spectacle in which the feet perform a constant fast rhythm while the rest of the body remains still. The group of men and women might have to sustain the synchronized movement for a long time, exercising flawless control during the elaborate sequences – definitely worth catching if you get the chance, at many of the island's festivals.

AN INTRODUCTION TO SARDINIA'S MUSIC – SOME SAMPLE RECORDINGS

Actores Alidos *Canti delle Donne Sarde* (2005)
Totore Chessa *Organittos* (2000)
Paolo Fresu *Sonos E Memoria* (2001)
Paolo Fresu & Ralph Towner *Chiaroscuro* (2009)
Elena Ledda *Amargura* (2005)

Efisio Melis and Antonio Lara *Launeddas* (2001)
Antonello Salis *Pianosolo* (2006)
Tenores di Bitti *S'Amore E Mama* (1996)
Various artists *Music of Sardinia* (2005)

the way of narrative, but powerfully evokes a lost world, set in the remotest recesses of Sardinia's impoverished interior. **Flavio Soriga** *Diavoli di Nuraiò, Neropioggia* and *Sardinia Blues*. First published in 2000, Soriga represents a new generation of Sard writers, his stories and novels (so far untranslated into English) peopled by intellectuals, tourists, druggies, Bohemians and aristocrats – a refreshing antidote to the world described in Sardinia's established literary canon. Seek out too his "counter-guide" to the island of Sardinia, *Sardinia Blues*.

Italian

The ability to speak European languages other than Italian is increasingly widespread in Sardinia. You'll often find the staff in museums, tourist offices and hotels, as well as guides, able to communicate in English, and students in particular are frequently willing to show off their knowledge. Outside the tourist areas, however, few people know more than some simple words and phrases – more often than not culled from pop songs or computer programs.

Anyone interested in Sardinia and the Sards will find their experience greatly enriched by learning a few basic phrases of **Italian**. Even if only a very superficial knowledge from a phrasebook is gained, just the ability to ask for a glass of water will make you feel less helpless. In any case, it's one of the easiest European languages to learn, especially if you already have a smattering of French or Spanish, which are grammatically similar. Keep your ears open on buses and trains, pick up a local newspaper and tune into a bit of TV or radio in your hotel room – and you'll be surprised how much you subconsciously absorb. When speaking, enunciate everything with maximum clarity, as mumbled or fumbled pronunciation often leads to misunderstanding.

All Italian words are **stressed** on the penultimate syllable unless an **accent** denotes otherwise, although in practice accents are often left out. Thus, Cágliari and Sássari are pronounced with the accent on the first syllable. Note that the ending **-ia** or **-ie** counts as two syllables, hence *trattoria* is stressed on the i. We've put accents in, throughout the text and below, wherever it isn't immediately obvious how a word should be pronounced: for example, in *Maríttima*, the accent is on the first i; conversely *Olbia* should theoretically have an accent on the **o**. Other words where we've omitted accents are common ones (like *Isola*, stressed on the I), some names (*Domenico*, *Vittorio*), and words that are stressed similarly in English, such as *archeologico* and *Repubblica*.

Lastly, it's pleasantly surprising how much can be communicated by the use of body language alone – gestures, gesticulations, facial expressions and miming – an art at which Italians are supremely adept.

Pronunciation

The rules of **pronunciation** are easy, since every word is spoken exactly as it's written: you articulate each syllable of every word – the louder and clearer the better. Double consonants – two s's or two p's, for example – are individually articulated, ie pronounced more forcefully than if they are single. The letter "h" is not aspirated at all, as in "hour". The only difficulties you're likely to encounter are the few consonants that change their pronunciation according to the letters following:

LINGUISTIC ETIQUETTE

To avoid making unnecessary gaffes, it's worth noting some elementary guidelines. When **speaking to strangers**, the third person is the polite form (ie *Lei* instead of *Tu* for "you"); using the second person is a mark of disrespect or ignorance. Likewise, "ciao" is only used informally to acquaintances; to others use *buongiorno* or *buonasera* for "hallo"; you may also hear *salve*, a sort of semi-formal greeting. When saying "goodbye", use *arrivederci* or (more formally) *arrivederla*. It's also worth remembering that Italians use "please" and "thank you" far less frequently than we do: it's all implied in the tone, though if you're in doubt, err on the polite side.

PHRASEBOOKS AND DICTIONARIES

The best **phrasebook** is the Rough Guides' own *Italian Phrasebook* (£5.99/$8.99), which has a large but accessible vocabulary, a detailed menu reader and useful dialogues. Collins also publishes a comprehensive series: its *Gem* or *Pocket* dictionaries are fine for travelling purposes, while its *Concise* dictionary is adequate for most language needs.

---

c before **a**, **o** or **u** is hard, as in **c**at; before **e** or **i** it is pronounced as in **ch**urch, while **ch** before the same vowels is hard.

The same goes for **g** – soft before **e** and **i**, as in **g**entle; hard when followed by **a**, **o** or **u**, or by an **h**, as in **g**arlic.

gn has the ni sound of o**ni**on.

gl in Italian is softened to something like li in English, as in vermi**li**on.

sci or **sce** are pronounced as in **sh**eet and **sh**elter respectively.

The Sard dialect

Italy has been a separate state for only a little over 140 years, and each of the regions of Italy speaks its own **local dialect** which has only very recently taken second place to "standard" Italian. But in informal family or social circles, it's often still the dialect that is instinctively spoken.

In Sardinia, isolated in the middle of the Mediterranean, the parlance is distinct enough to be classified as a separate language, while every area of the island, almost every village, has its own **dialect** or at least variation – as you might expect in a place that is both mountainous and, from ancient times, poorly integrated. These local strains will incorporate a concoction of ingredients according to each area's particular historical circumstances. Thus on the isle of San Pietro off the southwest coast of Sardinia, a strong **Genoan** dialect is spoken, owing to its settlement by a colony of Ligurians, invited by King Carlo Emanuele III in 1737. At around the same time there was a wave of immigration from Corsica into the northern region of Gallura, which still retains a dialect close to that spoken in the southern parts of Sardinia's sister island. And the people of Alghero still speak a variety of **Spanish Catalan** – over six hundred years after the Aragonese king made the town his main base in northern Sardinia and flooded it with Catalonians. Visitors there will find Catalan street names in the old quarter, though it's often difficult to distinguish in speech.

The influence of **Spanish** permeates all the island's various dialects – hardly surprising in a place that was a Spanish colony for three centuries. The evidence is also on maps, where you will see examples like *riu* used for a river, where the Italian would be *fiume*. Sard dialects also have large infusions of **Latin**, a residue of the much older Roman occupation. "House", for example, in Italian *casa*, is called *domus* in areas of Sardinia, the same as Latin. The words for "the" in northern Sardinia – *su* and *sa* in the singular, *sos* and *sas* in the plural – are derived from the Latin noun-endings. In the south of the island, "the" is *is*, from the Latin *ipse*. Again, you'll find copious examples on the maps.

SOME SARDINIAN DIALECT WORDS

abba	water	**genna**	gate
bruncu	peak, protuberance or promontory	**giara**	plateau
		mannu	big
cala	inlet, beach	**pranu**	plain
domus de janas	"fairy houses" – the name given to prehistoric burial chambers	**riu**	river
		sa (pl. sas)	the (feminine)
		scala	steep path
		serra	chain of mountains
flumineddu	river	**su (pl. sos)**	the (masculine)

The region which has the greatest preponderance of Latin in its dialect is Logudoro, in the island's northwestern quarter; its inhabitants boast of speaking the purest form of *sardo*, which in effect means the form least corrupted by later influences.

Added to the innate **insularity** of islanders, Sards have a particular reputation for being *isolani*, meaning that they are not only insular but a closed and introspective people, with little interest in anything beyond immediate concerns. Whether or not this is still true today, the trait has influenced – and been influenced by – the local variations in speech. Within the artificially imposed provincial boundaries, Sardinia is a conglomerate of diverse regions – Campidano, Arborea, Logudoro, Gallura, the Iglesiente and Barbagia, to name but the principal ones – each with distinct traditions and a fierce awareness of their differences from one another. The use of dialect became not just a colloquial mode of speech, but also a symbol of **local solidarity**, enabling Sards to identify each other according to the particular area of the island they inhabit, just by listening.

The result of this linguistic confusion is that Italian has become the best means for people of different areas of the island to communicate effectively, and it has been learned, as a foreign language is learned, to perfection. Indeed, it is claimed that Sards speak the most correct form of Italian anywhere. Television, of course, has also played its part in diffusing standard Italian.

BASIC ITALIAN TERMS AND PHRASES

NUMBERS

one	uno	one hundred	cento
two	due	one hundred and one	centouno
three	tre	two hundred	duecento
four	quattro	one thousand	mille
five	cinque	two thousand	duemila
six	sei	three thousand	tremila
seven	sette	one million	un milione
eight	otto		
nine	nove	**DAYS AND MONTHS**	
ten	dieci	Monday	lunedì
eleven	undici	Tuesday	martedì
twelve	dodici	Wednesday	mercoledì
thirteen	tredici	Thursday	giovedì
fourteen	quattordici	Friday	venerdì
fifteen	quindici	Saturday	sábato
sixteen	sedici	Sunday	domenica
seventeen	diciasette		
eighteen	diciotto	January	gennaio
nineteen	dicianove	February	febbraio
twenty	venti	March	marzo
twenty-one	ventuno	April	aprile
twenty-two	ventidue	May	maggio
thirty	trenta	June	giugno
thirty-one	trentuno	July	luglio
thirty-two	trentadue	August	agosto
forty	quaranta	September	settembre
forty-one	quarantuno	October	ottobre
fifty	cinquanta	November	novembre
sixty	sessanta	December	dicembre
seventy	settanta		
eighty	ottanta	**USEFUL PHRASES**	
		Good morning	Buongiorno
ninety	novanta	Good afternoon/evening	Buona sera

Good night	Buona notte	first name	primo nome
Hello/Goodbye	Ciao (informal; when speaking to strangers use the phrases above)	surname	cognome

ACCOMMODATION

Goodbye	Arrivederci (formal)	hotel	albergo
Yes	Sì	Is there a hotel nearby?	C'è un albergo qui vicino?
No	No	Do you have a room…?	Ha una cámera…?
Please	Per favore		
Thank you (very much)	Grázie (molte/mille grazie)	for one/two/ three people	per una persona, due/ tre persone
You're welcome	Prego	for one/two/ three nights	per una notte, due/ tre notti
Alright/That's OK	Va bene		
How are you? (informal/formal)	Come stai/sta?	for one/two weeks	per una settimana/ due settimane
I'm fine	Bene	with a double bed	con un letto matrimoniale
Do you speak English?	Parla inglese?	with a shower/bath	con una doccia/un bagno
I don't understand	Non capisco	with a balcony	con una terrazza
I haven't understood	Non ho capito	with air-conditioning	con aria condizionata
I don't know	Non lo so	hot/cold water	acqua calda/fredda
Excuse me/Sorry	Scusa (informal)	How much is it?	Quanto costa?
Excuse me/Sorry	Scusi/mi scusi (formal)	It's expensive	È caro
Excuse me	Permesso (in a crowd)	Is breakfast included?	È compresa la prima colazione?
I'm sorry	Mi dispiace		
I'm here on holiday	Sono qui in vacanza	Do you have anything cheaper?	Ha niente che costa di meno?
I live in…	Abito a…		
today	oggi	full/half-board	pensione completa/ mezza pensione
tomorrow	domani		
day after tomorrow	dopodomani	Can I see the room?	Posso vedere la cámera?
yesterday	ieri	I'll take it	La prendo
now	adesso	I'd like to book a room	Vorrei prenotare una cámera
later	più tardi		
Wait a minute!	Aspetta!	I have a booking	Ho una prenotazione
in the morning	di mattina	Can we camp here?	Possiamo fare il campeggio qui?
in the afternoon	nel pomeriggio		
in the evening	di sera	Is there a campsite nearby?	C'è un camping qui vicino?
here/there	qui/lì	tent	tenda
good/bad	buono/cattivo	cabin	cabina
big/small	grande/píccolo	youth hostel	ostello per la gioventù
cheap/expensive	económico/caro		

QUESTIONS AND DIRECTIONS

early/late	presto/ritardo	Where? (Where is/are…?)	Dove? (Dov'è/Dove sono?)
hot/cold	caldo/freddo	When?	Quando?
near/far	vicino/lontano	What? (What is it?)	Cosa? (Cos'è?)
vacant/occupied	líbero/occupato	How much/many?	Quanto/Quanti?
quickly/slowly	velocemente/lentamente	Why?	Perché?
slowly/quietly	piano	It is/There is (Is it?/Is there…?)	È/c'è (è/c'è…?)
with/without	con/senza		
more/less	più/meno	What time is it?	Che ora è/ Che ore sono?
enough, no more	basta	How do I get to…?	Come arrivo a…?
Mr…	Signor…	How far is it to…?	Quant'è lontano a…?
Mrs…	Signora…	Can you give me a lift to…?	Mi può dare un passaggio a…?
Miss…	Signorina… (il signore, la signora, la signorina when speaking about someone else)	Can you tell me when to get off?	Può dirmi quando devo scéndere?

What time does it open?	A che ora apre?	Next stop, please	La próssima fermata,
What time does it close?	A che ora chiude?		per favore
How much does it cost (...do they cost?)	Quanto costa? (Quanto costano?)	**DRIVING**	
What is it called in Italian?	Come si chiama in italiano?	parking	parcheggio
left/right	sinistra/destra	no parking	divieto di sosta/sosta
Go straight ahead	Sempre diritto		vietata
Turn to the right/left	Gira a destra/sinistra	one-way street	senso único
		no entry	senso vietato
TRANSPORT		slow down	rallentare
aeroplane	aereo	road closed/up	strada chiusa/guasta
local bus	autobus	no through road	vietato il tránsito
long-distance bus	pullman	no overtaking	vietato il sorpasso
train	treno	crossroads	incrocio
car	mácchina	speed limit	límite di velocità
taxi	taxi	traffic light	semáforo
bicycle	bicicletta		
ferry	traghetto	**SOME SIGNS**	
ship	nave	entrance/exit	entrata/uscita
hitch-hiking	autostop	free entrance	ingresso líbero
on foot	a piedi	gentlemen/ladies	signori/signore
bus station	autostazione	wc	gabinetto, bagno
railway station	stazione ferroviaria	vacant/engaged	líbero/occupato
ferry terminal	stazione maríttima	open/closed	aperto/chiuso
port	porto	arrivals/departures	arrivi/partenze
a ticket to...	un biglietto a...	closed for restoration	chiuso per restauro
one-way/return	solo andata/andata e ritorno	closed for holidays	chiuso per ferie
		pull/push	tirare/spíngere
Can I book a seat?	Posso prenotare un posto?	out of order	guasto
		drinking water	acqua potábile
What time does it leave?	A che ora parte?	to let	affitasi
When is the next bus/ train/ferry to...?	Quando parte il próssimo pullman/treno/traghetto per...?	platform	binario
		cash desk	cassa
		go/walk	avanti
Where does it leave from?	Da dove parte?	stop/halt	alt
Which platform?	Da quale binario parte?	customs	dogana
Do I have to change?	Devo cambiare?	do not touch	non toccare
How many kilometres is it?	Quanti chilómetri sono?	danger	perícolo
How long does it take?	Quanto ci vuole?	beware	attenzione
What number bus is it to...?	Que número di autobus per...?	first aid	pronto soccorso
		ring the bell	suonare il campanello
Where's the road to...?	Dov'è la strada a...?	no smoking	vietato fumare

ITALIAN FOOD TERMS

BASICS AND SNACKS

aceto	vinegar	gelato	ice cream
aglio	garlic	grissini	bread sticks
biscotti	biscuits	maionese	mayonnaise
burro	butter	marmellata	jam
caramelle	sweets	olio	oil
cioccolato	chocolate	olive	olives
focaccia	oven-baked bread snack	pane	bread
formaggio	cheese	pane integrale	wholemeal bread
frittata	omelette	panino	bread roll/sandwich
		patatine	crisps/potato chips

patatine fritte	chips	frutti di mare	seafood; usually mussels, prawns, squid and clams
pepe	pepper		
pizzetta	slice of pizza to take away	funghi	mushrooms; tinned, sliced button mushrooms unless it specifies fresh mushrooms, either funghi freschi or porcini
riso	rice		
sale	salt		
uova	eggs		
yogurt	yoghurt		
zúcchero	sugar		
zuppa	soup	margherita	cheese and tomato
		marinara	tomato and garlic

ANTIPASTI AND STARTERS

antipasto misto	mixed cold meats, seafood and cheese (plus a mix of other things in this list)	napoletana	tomato, anchovy and olive oil (often mozzarella, too)
		quattro formaggi	"four cheeses", usually mozzarella, fontina, gorgonzola and gruyère
caponata	mixed aubergine, olives, tomatoes	quattro stagioni	"four seasons"; the toppings split into four separate sections, usually including ham, peppers, onion, mushrooms, artichokes, olives, egg, etc.
caprese	tomato and mozzarella cheese salad		
insalata di mare	seafood salad (usually squid, octopus and prawn)		
insalata di riso	rice salad	romana	anchovy and olives
melanzane alla parmigiana	fried aubergine in tomato sauce with parmesan cheese		

THE FIRST COURSE (*IL PRIMO*)

SOUPS

brodo	clear broth
minestra	any light soup
minestrone	thick vegetable soup
pasta e fagioli	pasta soup with beans
pastina in brodo	pasta pieces in clear broth
stracciatella	broth with egg

mortadella	salami-type cured meat with white nuggets of fat; in Sardinia, often with pistachios
pancetta	bacon
peperonata	grilled green, red or yellow peppers stewed in olive oil
pomodori ripieni	stuffed tomatoes
prosciutto	ham
salame	salami
salmone/tonno/ pesce spada affumicato	smoked salmon/tuna/ swordfish

PASTA

cannelloni	large tubes of pasta, stuffed
farfalle	literally "bow"-shaped pasta; the word also means "butterflies"
fettuccine	narrow pasta ribbons
gnocchi	small potato and dough dumplings
lasagne	lasagne
maccheroni	macaroni (tubular pasta)
pappardelle	pasta ribbons
pasta al forno	pasta baked with minced meat, eggs, tomato and cheese
penne	smaller version of *rigatoni*
ravioli	ravioli
rigatoni	large, grooved tubular pasta

PIZZAS

biancaneve	"snow white" mozzarella and oregano
calzone	folded pizza with cheese, ham and tomato
capricciosa	literally "capricious"; topped with whatever they've got in the kitchen, usually including baby artichoke, ham and egg
cardinale	ham and olives
diávolo	spicy, with hot salami or Italian sausage

risotto	cooked rice dish, with sauce
spaghetti	spaghetti
spaghettini	thin spaghetti
tagliatelle	pasta ribbons, another word for *fettuccine*
tortellini	small rings of pasta, stuffed with meat or cheese
vermicelli	very thin spaghetti (literally "little worms")

THE SAUCE (SALSA)

aglio e olio (e peperoncino)	tossed in garlic and olive oil (and hot chillies)
amatriciana	cubed pork and tomato sauce (originally from Rome)
arrabbiata	tomato sauce spiced with chillies
bolognese	meat sauce
burro e salvia	butter and sage
carbonara	cream, ham and beaten egg
frutta di mare	seafood
funghi	mushroom
panna	cream
pesto	ground basil, pine nut, garlic and pecorino sauce
pomodoro	tomato sauce
puttanesca	"whorish"; tomato, anchovy, olive oil and oregano
ragù	meat sauce
vóngole (veraci)	clam and tomato sauce (fresh clams in shells, usually served with oil and herbs)

THE SECOND COURSE (IL SECONDO): MEAT (CARNE)

agnello	lamb
ásino	ass, donkey
bistecca	steak
capretto	young goat
cavallo	horse
cervello	brain
cinghiale	wild boar
coniglio	rabbit
costolette/cotolette	cutlets/chops
fegatini	chicken livers
fégato	liver
involtini	anything sliced, rolled and stuffed
lepre	hare
lingua	tongue
lumache	snails
maiale	pork
manzo	beef
montone	mutton
monzette	snails
ossobuco	shin of veal
pollo	chicken
polpette	meatballs
rognoni	kidneys
salsiccia	sausage
saltimbocca	veal with ham
scaloppina	escalope (of veal)
spezzatino	stew
tacchino	turkey
trippa	tripe
vitello	veal

FISH (PESCE) AND SHELLFISH (CROSTACEI)

Note that *surgelati* or *congelati* written on the menu next to a dish means "frozen" – it often applies to tuna, swordfish, squid and prawns.

acciughe	anchovies
anguilla	eel
aragosta	lobster
arselle	clams
baccalà	dried salted cod
bottarga	salted and dried eggs of mullet and tuna
calamari	squid
céfalo	grey mullet
cozze	mussels
dáttile	razor clams
déntice	dentex (like sea bass)
gamberetti	shrimps
gámberi	prawns
granchio	crab
merluzzo	cod
múggine	mullet
orata	gilthead
óstriche	oysters
pesce spada	swordfish
polpo/pólipo	octopus
ricci di mare	sea urchins
rospo	monkfish
sampiero	John Dory
sárago	bream
sarde	sardines
seppie	cuttlefish
sgombro	mackerel
sógliola	sole

spígola	sea bass
tonno	tuna
triglie	red mullet
trota	trout
vóngole	clams

VEGETABLES (*CONTORNI*) AND SALAD (*INSALATA*)

aspáragi	asparagus
basílico	basil
bróccoli	broccoli
cápperi	capers
carciofi	artichokes
carciofini	artichoke hearts
carotte	carrots
cavolfiori	cauliflower
cávolo	cabbage
ceci	chickpeas
cetriolo	cucumber
cipolla	onion
fagioli	beans
fagiolini	green beans
finocchio	fennel
funghi	mushrooms
insalata verde/mista	green salad/mixed salad
melanzane	aubergine/eggplant
orígano	oregano
patate	potatoes
peperoni	peppers
piselli	peas
pomodori	tomatoes
radicchio	red chicory
spinaci	spinach
zucca	pumpkin
zucchini	courgettes

DESSERTS (*DOLCI*)

amaretti	macaroons
gelato	ice cream
macedonia	fruit salad
torta	cake, tart
zabaglione	dessert made with eggs, sugar and Marsala wine
zuppa inglese	trifle

CHEESE

caciocavallo	a type of dried, mature mozzarella cheese
dolce sardo	dry, hard shepherds' cheese, often going into sandwiches
fiore sardo	sheep's cheese frequently used in cooking
fontina	mild northern Italian cheese used in cooking and in rolls
gorgonzola	soft, strong, blue-veined cheese
grana	hard cheese often used instead of *parmigiano* on pastas and soups
mozzarella	soft white cheese, traditionally made from buffalo's milk
parmigiano	parmesan cheese
pecorino	sheep's cheese, either *romano* or *sardo*, both from Sardinia
provolone	cheese with grooved rind, either mild or strong
ricotta	soft white cheese made from ewe's milk, used in sweet or savoury dishes

FRUIT AND NUTS

albicocche	apricots
ananas	pineapple
anguria/coccómero	water melon
arance	oranges
banane	bananas
cacchi	persimmons
ciliegie	cherries
fichi	figs
fichi d'India	prickly pears
frágole	strawberries
limone	lemon
mándorle	almonds
mele	apples
melone	melon
néspole	medlars
pere	pears
pesche	peaches
pignoli	pine nuts
pistacchio	pistachio nut
prugne	plums
uva	grapes

COOKING TERMS AND USEFUL WORDS

affumicato	smoked
arrosto	roast
ben cotto	well done
bollito/lesso	boiled
alla brace	barbecued
brasato	cooked in wine
cotto	cooked (not raw)
crudo	raw

al dente	firm, not overcooked
ai ferri	grilled without oil
al forno	baked
fritto	fried
grattugiato	grated
alla griglia	grilled
al marsala	cooked with Marsala wine
milanese	fried in egg and breadcrumbs
pizzaiola	cooked with tomato sauce
ripieno	stuffed
sangue	rare
allo spiedo	on the spit
stracotto	braised, stewed
surgelato	frozen
in úmido	stewed
al vapore	steamed

SARDINIAN SPECIALITIES: STARTERS, BREADS AND CHEESES

sa burrida	bits of dogfish boiled and marinated in garlic, parsley, walnuts and vinegar
culurgiones	ravioli stuffed with potato, cheese, garlic and mint
malloreddus	gnocchetti, or pasta shaped in little shells, with various toppings, for example, *alla campidanese*, a spicy sausage sauce
fainè	chickpea pizza to a Genoan recipe served plain, or with onion, sausage or anchovy (not usually available in summer)
sa frégula	couscous-type semolina pasta, either in a meat stock or dry with mussels or clams
pane carasau	crisp wafer bread, often served with olive oil and salt to add flavour
pane frattau	carasau bread soaked in tomato sauce with pecorino and an egg, typically from Mamoiada
spianadas	soft round bread from the Logudoro district, often served with sausages

zuppa/suppa cuata	bread, cheese and tomato soup

SARDINIAN SPECIALITIES: MAIN COURSES

aragosta catalana	lobster in sauce as served in Alghero
cashcà	couscous-type wheat semolina steamed with meat, vegetables or fish as prepared in Carloforte on San Pietro
sa córdula	roasted or barbecued sheep's entrails
cuscus	a version of North African couscous, a speciality of the island of San Pietro, usually served with a fish and vegetable sauce
fritto misto	a standard seafood dish; deep-fried prawns and calamari rings in batter
fritto di pesce	as above but also with other fried fish, like sardines and whitebait
giogghe	snails boiled and then fried with garlic, parsley and paprika
gran premio	horsemeat steak
grigliata di pesce	a mixed fish grill, usually quite substantial and expensive
sa merca	salted mullet from the Cabras lagoon, cooked in herbs
monzette	small snails roasted with salt, a speciality of Sássari; the rarer giogghe are boiled, then fried slowly with garlic, parsley and paprika
panadas	pastry rolls filled with meat, fish and vegetables, or all three, originating in Assémini, near Cágliari
pécora in capotta	mutton boiled with vegetables, garlic and rosemary, typical of the Nuoro area
porceddu/porcheddu	young pig roasted whole on a spit with myrtle leaves

stufato di capretto	chunks of kid casseroled with wine, artichokes and saffron
zuppa di pesce	a big dish of mixed fish in rich wine-based soup
zuppa gallurese	"Galluran soup" made from layers of bread and fresh cheese, soaked with meat broth and baked in the oven until golden and fluffy

SWEETS AND DESSERTS

aranciatte/aranzada	very sweet confection, available from Nuoro, made with almonds, oranges and honey
pardulas/casadinas	cheese-based pastries flavoured with saffron, vanilla and the peel of citrus fruit
seadas/sebadas	fried ricotta-filled pastry bubbles soaked in honey
torrone	crystallized almonds and honey, the best from the Barbagia villages of Tonara and Aritzo

DRINKS

acqua minerale	mineral water
aranciata	orangeade
bicchiere	glass
birra	beer
bottiglia	bottle
caffè	coffee
cioccolata calda	hot chocolate
ghiaccio	ice
granita	iced coffee/fruit drink
latte	milk
limonata	lemonade
selz	soda water
spremuta	fresh fruit juice
spumante	sparkling wine
succo di frutta	concentrated fruit juice, sometimes sugared
tè	tea
tónico	tonic water
vino	wine
rosso	red
bianco	white
rosato	rosé
secco	dry
dolce	sweet
caraffa	caraffe, usually a litre
litro	litre
mezzo	half litre
quarto	quarter litre
Salute!	Cheers!

Glossary

affittacámere literally rooms to rent, in practice a slightly larger B&B

agriturismo rural B&B, usually with restaurant

anfiteatro amphitheatre

artigianato handicrafts, made by an *artigiano* ("artisan")

autostazione bus station

belvedere look-out point

cappella chapel

castello castle

cattedrale cathedral

centro centre

chiesa church (*chiesa matrice/madre*, main "mother" church)

comune an administrative area; also, the local council or the town hall

corso avenue/boulevard

duomo cathedral

entrata entrance

festa festival (plural *feste*)

fiume river

giudicato medieval administrative territory headed by a *giúdice* (literally, a judge)

golfo gulf

lago lake

largo square (like piazza)

lungomare seafront promenade or road

macchia *maquis*, or Mediterranean scrub

mare sea

mercato market

mezzo veloce/unità veloce high-speed ferry

municipio town hall

palazzo palace, mansion or block (of flats)

parco park

passeggiata the customary early evening walk

piano a plain (also "slowly", "gently")

piazza square

pineta pinewood

Pro Loco a local tourist office, usually run by the town hall and with limited hours

sagra festival or special feast, usually an agricultural or religious event

santuario sanctuary
spiaggia beach
stazione station (train station, *stazione ferroviaria*; bus
  station, *autostazione*; ferry terminal, *stazione maríttima*)
strada road/street
tabacchino tobacconist's shop, often selling
  newspapers, stamps and bus tickets too

teatro theatre
tempio temple
torre tower
traghetto ferry
uscita exit
via road (always used with name; as Via Roma)
zona zone

ART AND ARCHITECTURE

apse domed recess at the altar end of a church
architrave the lowest part of the entablature
atrium forecourt, usually of a Roman house
campanile belltower
capital top of a column
Catalan-Gothic hybrid form of architecture, mixing
  elements from fifteenth-century Spanish and
  Northern European building styles
cavea the seating section in a theatre
cella sanctuary of a temple
cupola dome
decumanus the main street in a Roman town
entablature the part of the building above the capital
  on a classical building
ex-voto decorated tablet or other small item designed
  as thanksgiving to a saint or deity
hypogeum underground vault, often used as an early
  Christian church

loggia roofed gallery or balcony
nave central space in a church, usually flanked
  by aisles
polyptych painting or carving on several joined
  wooden panels
portico the covered entrance to a building
Punic Carthaginian/Phoenician
putti cherubs (singular *putto*), as portrayed in
  paintings and sculpture
retablo painted wood panel, usually in a church
stele (plural *stelae*) inscribed stone slab
thermae baths, usually elaborate buildings in
  Roman villas
tholos a dome-shaped tomb, usually associated with
  the Greek Mycenaean period
triptych painting or carving on three joined
  wooden panels

ACRONYMS

ACI Italian Automobile Club
CAI Club Alpino Italiano (Italian climbing club)
FS Italian state railways, now also called Trenitalia
IVA Imposta Valore Aggiunto (VAT)
PD Partito Democrático

PSd'Az Partito Sardo d'Azione (Sardinian Action Party)
RAI the Italian state TV and radio network
SP Strada Provinciale (a minor road, eg SP70)
SS Strada Statale (a main highway, eg SS195)

Small print and index

333 Small print

335 About the author

336 Index

342 Map symbols

A ROUGH GUIDE TO ROUGH GUIDES

Published in 1982, the first Rough Guide – to Greece – was a student scheme that became a publishing phenomenon. Mark Ellingham, a recent graduate in English from Bristol University, had been travelling in Greece the previous summer and couldn't find the right guidebook. With a small group of friends he wrote his own guide, combining a highly contemporary, journalistic style with a thoroughly practical approach to travellers' needs.

The immediate success of the book spawned a series that rapidly covered dozens of destinations. And, in addition to impecunious backpackers, Rough Guides soon acquired a much broader readership that relished the guides' wit and inquisitiveness as much as their enthusiastic, critical approach and value-for-money ethos.

These days, Rough Guides include recommendations from budget to luxury and cover more than 200 destinations around the globe, as well as producing an ever-growing range of eBooks and apps.

Visit **roughguides.com** to see our latest publications.

Rough Guide credits

Editor: Melissa Graham
Layout: Nikhil Agarwal
Cartography: Rajesh Chhibber
Picture editor: Michelle Bhatia
Proofreader: Jennifer Speake
Managing editor: Monica Woods
Assistant editor: Dipika Dasgupta
Photographer: Roger d'Olivere Mapp
Production: Charlotte Cade
Cover design: Nicole Newman, Nikhil Agarwal

Editorial assistant: Olivia Rawes
Senior pre-press designer: Dan May
Design director: Scott Stickland
Travel publisher: Joanna Kirby
Digital travel publisher: Peter Buckley
Operations coordinator: Helen Blount
Publishing director (Travel): Clare Currie
Commercial manager: Gino Magnotta
Managing director: John Duhigg

Publishing information

This fifth edition published June 2013 by
Rough Guides Ltd,
80 Strand, London WC2R 0RL
11, Community Centre, Panchsheel Park,
New Delhi 110017, India
Distributed by the Penguin Group
Penguin Books Ltd,
80 Strand, London WC2R 0RL
Penguin Group (USA)
375 Hudson Street, NY 10014, USA
Penguin Group (Australia)
250 Camberwell Road, Camberwell,
Victoria 3124, Australia
Penguin Group (NZ)
67 Apollo Drive, Mairangi Bay, Auckland 1310,
New Zealand
Penguin Group (South Africa)
Block D, Rosebank Office Park, 181 Jan Smuts Avenue,
Parktown North, Gauteng, South Africa 2193
Rough Guides is represented in Canada by Tourmaline
Editions Inc. 662 King Street West, Suite 304, Toronto,
Ontario M5V 1M7
Printed in Malaysia by Vivar Printing Sdn Bhd

© Robert Andrews, 2013
Maps © Rough Guides
No part of this book may be reproduced in any form
without permission from the publisher except for the
quotation of brief passages in reviews.
344pp includes index
A catalogue record for this book is available from the
British Library
ISBN: 978-1-40936-379-8
The publishers and authors have done their best to
ensure the accuracy and currency of all the information
in **The Rough Guide to Sardinia**, however, they
can accept no responsibility for any loss, injury, or
inconvenience sustained by any traveller as a result of
information or advice contained in the guide.
1 3 5 7 9 8 6 4 2

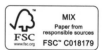

MIX
Paper from
responsible sources
FSC
www.fsc.org   FSC™ C018179

Help us update

We've gone to a lot of effort to ensure that the fifth edition of **The Rough Guide to Sardinia** is accurate and up-to-date. However, things change – places get "discovered", opening hours are notoriously fickle, restaurants and rooms raise prices or lower standards. If you feel we've got it wrong or left something out, we'd like to know, and if you can remember the address, the price, the hours, the phone number, so much the better.

Please send your comments with the subject line "**Rough Guide Sardinia Update**" to ❸ mail@uk.roughguides .com. We'll credit all contributions and send a copy of the next edition (or any other Rough Guide if you prefer) for the very best emails.

Find more travel information, connect with fellow travellers and book your trip on ⓦ roughguides.com

ABOUT THE AUTHOR

With family roots in Sicily, **Robert Andrews** divides his time between the UK and Italy – particularly the south and the islands. He has also written guides on Devon and Cornwall, Somerset and his home city of Bristol.

Acknowledgements

Mille grazie to Melissa Graham for exemplary, eagle-eyed, constructive and sensitive editing, to Monica Woods for expertly steering the project through the straits, and to Michelle Bhatia for picking the right pics. Huge thanks are also due to Mario Zizi of Casa Solotti (Nuoro) for his constant kindness, to Luigi Palmas and family of AeR Bundes Jack (Cágliari) for friendly welcomes, to Peter and Anne of the Lemon House B&B (Lotzorai, Ogliastra) for taking the time to send me tips, to the helpful and efficient staff at the tourist offices of Nuoro, Cala Gonone, Olbia and Alghero, to Carolyn and Mark for tackling some of the nitty-gritties and keeping me fed, and to QBC for staunch support and inspirations.

Readers' letters

Thanks to all the readers who have taken the time to write in with comments and suggestions (and apologies if we've inadvertently omitted or misspelt anyone's name):

Arezou Azad; Sharmila Bagse; Richard Budden; Peter & Anne Herold; David Leonard; Charles Norrie; Elinor Payne; Claudia Rizzini; Christen K. Thomsen & Odense C; Manus Walsh.

Photo credits

All photos © Rough Guides except the following:
(Key: t-top; c-centre; b-bottom; l-left; r-right)

p.1 SuperStock: Tips Images (t)
p.2 Corbis: Katja Kreder (c)
p.4 SuperStock (t)
p.7 SuperStock (b)
p.8 Alamy Images: CuboImages srl (c)
p.9 SuperStock: Cubo Images (t); Yadid Levy (b)
p.11 SuperStock: Cubo Images (t)
p.12 Corbis: Guido Cozzi (b)
p.13 Corbis: Giacomo Altamira/Demotix (t); SuperStock: Renault Philippe (b)
p.14 Alamy Images: Andy Christiani (t); SuperStock: Cubo Images (b)
p.15 Fotolia: Alessio Orrù (c); Getty Images: Bruno Morandi (t); SuperStock: Prisma (b)
p.16 Corbis: David Sutherland (b); Getty Images: Ken Gillham/Robert Harding (c)
p.17 Getty Images: Noemí Galera Ribera/Flickr RF (tr); Doug Pearson (tl); SuperStock: Claudio Ciabochi (br)
p.18 Getty Images: Danita Delimont/Gallo Images (t)
p.20 SuperStock: JTB Photo (t)
pp.52–53 Getty Images: John Miller/Robert Harding World Imagery (c)

p.55 Corbis: Ann Johansson (t)
p.65 Alamy Images: CuboImages srl (b); Getty Images: Danita Delimont/Gallo Images (t)
pp.78–79 SuperStock: Pablo Méndez/age fotostock (c)
p.93 SuperStock (t)
pp.110–111 SuperStock: imagebroker.net (c)
pp.134–135 Corbis: Giacomo Altamira/Demotix (c)
pp.164–165 Corbis: Ocean (c)
pp.198–199 SuperStock: Philippe Michel (c)
p.211 Corbis: Bruno Morandi (c)
pp.226–227 SuperStock (c)
p.229 SuperStock: Yadid Levy (t)
p.269 imagebroker/Alamy
p.285 Corbis: Bruno Morandi (t)
p.306 Paul Shawcross/Alamy

Front cover Maddalena archipelago © Canali Pietro/SIME-4Corners Images
Back cover Chia bay © Slow Images/Getty (t); Duomo de San Nicola, Sássari © Ellen Rooney/Axiom (bl); Piazza Yenne, Cágliari © Alberto Rossi/Axiom (br)

Index

Maps are marked in grey

A

accommodation................30–32
Aga Khan.................................241
Aggius.....................................264
agriturismi 31
ALGHERO.....................169–180
Alghero...............................170
Alghero Old Town.............172
  accommodation.....................176
  activities................................175
  Aquarium...............................174
  arriving..................................174
  bars.......................................178
  bastioni 174
  Bastione della Maddalena....172
  Cattedrale..............................171
  clubs......................................178
  entertainment........................179
  festivals..................................179
  getting around.......................175
  Giardini Púbblici....................171
  history....................................169
  information.............................175
  Museo Diocesano...................172
  Palazzo Carcassona................173
  Palazzo d'Albis.......................171
  Palazzo Machin......................173
  parking...................................175
  Piazza Cívica..........................171
  Piazza Sulis............................174
  port..174
  Porta a Mare..........................171
  restaurants.............................177
  San Francesco........................173
  San Michele............................173
  shopping................................179
  Torre di Porta Terra................171
  Torre di San Giovanni.............174
  Torre Sulis..............................174
  tours......................................175
  Via Carlo Alberto....................173
  Via Príncipe Umberto.............173
  walls......................................174
  waterfront..............................174
Ampsicora...................162, 308
Anghelu Ruju......................184
Angioy, Giovanni Maria........312
Anglona......................216–221
Antonioni, Michelangelo........255
apartments............................31
Aragon..................................310
Arbatax.................................303
Arborea.................................154
archeological sites...............49
Arcipelago di La
  Maddalena....................251
Árdara...................................222
Argentiera.............................185
Aritzo....................................289

Arzachena.....................244, 246
Asinara...................................197
Atza, Antonio........................189
Atzeni, Sergio.................319, 320

B

B&Bs..31
Baia di Malfatano....................88
Baia Sardinia..........................244
Baja di Conte.........................184
banditry.........................264, 287
Barbagia Belvì..............287–291
Barbagia Ollolai...........282–286
Barcelo, Joan...........................63
bars...36
Barúmini.....................122–124
beer..36
Belvì......................................288
Berchidda..............................263
Berlinguer, Enrico..................203
Berlusconi, Silvio...................314
Bitti.......................................279
Bonaparte, Napoleon.....255, 312
Bonelli's eagle............294, 318
Bonifica di Arborea................154
Bonnanaro culture.................307
Bonu Ighinu culture...............307
books..........................319–321
BOSA...........................187–194
Bosa...........................188–189
  accommodation.....................192
  arriving..................................191
  Bosa Marina...........................191
  Casa Deriu.............................188
  Castello Malaspina.................190
  Cattedrale..............................188
  Chiesa del Cármine................189
  Corso Vittorio Emanuele........188
  festivals..................................193
  getting around.......................191
  history....................................187
  Nostra Signora di Regnos
    Altos...................................190
  Piazza Costituzione................188
  restaurants and bars..............192
  Sa Costa.................................189
  San Pietro..............................190
  Sas Conzas.............................190
  Temo river..............................190
Brigata Sássari................117, 205
bronzetti 62, 204, 294, 308
Bruncu Spina.........................288
Budelli...................................255
Buggerru................................108
Bulzi......................................221
Burcei....................................130
Burgos...................................280

buses
  from the UK and Ireland...........24
  in Sardinia...............................28
Bythia.....................................87

C

Cabras....................................149
CÁGLIARI.......................54–77
Cágliari.........................56–57
Cágliari, Castello quarter.... 59
Cágliari, greater.................. 54
  accommodation.......................73
  airport....................................71
  Anfiteatro Romano..................68
  Antico Palazzo di Città...........61
  arriving....................................71
  banks......................................77
  bars..75
  Bastione San Remy.................60
  Bonaria...................................70
  buses......................................71
  Casa di Tigellio.......................69
  Castello.............................58–63
  Cattedrale...............................60
  Cavità di Via Vittorio Veneto 69
  Cittadella dei Musei................62
  Cripta di Santa Restituta.........67
  Cripta di Sant'Efisio................68
  entertainment.........................75
  Exma......................................70
  Festa di Sant'Efisio.................67
  festivals..................................76
  Galleria Comunale d'Arte........63
  Galleria Rifugio Don Bosco.....69
  getting around........................72
  history..............................56–58
  Il Ghetto.................................60
  information.............................72
  Marina..............................64, 66
  Marina Píccola........................71
  markets..................................76
  Mostra di Cere Anatomiche.....63
  Museo Archeologico................62
  Museo d'Arte Siamese.............63
  Museo del Duomo...................61
  Museo Sant'Eulalia.................64
  Orto Botánico.........................68
  Orto dei Cappuccini................69
  Palazzo Comunale..................64
  Palazzo Regio.........................61
  parking...................................72
  Piazza Yenne..........................66
  Pinacoteca.............................63
  Poetto....................................70
  port..71
  restaurants.............................74
  San Michele............................68
  San Saturnino.........................69
  San Sepolcro.....................64, 66
  Sant'Anna...............................66

Sant'Efisio 67
Sant'Eulalia 64
Santa Restituta 67
Santuario di Bonaria 70
shopping 76
Stampace 66–68
theatres 75
Torre dell'Elefante 60
Torre San Pancrazio 62
Trenino Verde 71
Villanova 69
Cala di Volpe 242
Cala Domestica 108
Cala Gonone **300–302**
Cala Liberotto 296
Cala Luna 300
Cala Regina 127
Cala Sapone 95
Cala Sinzias 129
Cala Sisine 301
Cala Su Pallosu 153
Calangianus 265
Calasetta 96
Calvino, Italo 68
Campidano **116–119**
**Campidano, La Marmilla and
   Sarrabus** **114–115**
camping 32
Cannigione 247
Capo Carbonara 127
Capo Ceraso 238
Capo Coda Cavallo 238
Capo Comino 296
Capo d'Orso 248
Capo Falcone 197
Capo Ferrato 129
Capo Figari 240
Capo Frasca 109
Capo Mannu 153
Capo Marargiu 187
Capo Pécora 109
Capo Sa Sturaggia 153
Capo Sándalo 99
Capo Spartivento 87
Capo Sperone 95
Capo Testa 257
Capo Teulada 88
Capoterra 84
Caprera 254
Capula, Giovanni 60, 62, 190
car rental 29
Carbónia **100–102**
Carloforte 98
Carnival 38, 76, 146, 161, 179,
   193, 262, 284
Carta de Logu 139, 142
Carthaginians 57, 138, 152,
   162, 232, 308
Castel Doria 222
Castello di Acquafredda 104
Castello di Eleonora
   d'Arborea 117
Castello di Medusa 157
Castello di Monreale 118
CASTELSARDO **216–220**

accommodation 219
arrival 219
Castello 217
information 219
Museo dell'Intreccio
   Mediterraneo 217
Porto di Frigianu 217
restaurants 220
Sant'Antonio Ábate 218
Santa Maria delle Grazie 217
Castiadas 129
Catalans 169
Cavaro, Michele 61, 66
Cavaro, Pietro 63, 66, 140, 144
Cervantes, Miguel de 62
Charles V ... 68, 169, 171, 217, 311
chemists 47
Chia 87
Chiaramonti 221
children, travelling with 44
churches 49
Cima, Gaetano 140
cinema 319
Ciusa, Francesco 63, 273, 274
climate 10
climbing 42
Coaquaddus 95
Coddu Vecchiu 246
coffee 35
Constantine, Emperor 159
consulates
   foreign 46, 77
   Italian 46
cooking, Sardinian 32
coral 179
cork 265
Cornus 162
Cossiga, Francesco 203
Costa del Sud 88
Costa Rei 129
Costa Smeralda **241–243**
Costa Verde 109
costs 44
credit cards 49
crime 45
Cúglieri 162
cuisine 32
currency 48
cycling 42

Alghero 175
Budelli 255
Cala Gonone 301
Palau 249
Porto Conte 184
Santa Teresa Gallura 258
San Teodoro 239
Stintino 196
doctors 47
Dolianova 125
Dolmen Ladas 265
dolmens 265
Dorgali **297–299**
Doria, Andrea 169
Doria, Brancaleone 142, 217
Dragut 233
drinks **35–37**
driving
   from the UK and Ireland 24
   in Sardinia 28–30
drugs 46

E

Easter celebrations 39, 76, 105,
   161, 179, 193, 216, 280
Efisius 67, 85
El Greco 242
electricity 46
embassies 46
emergencies 45
etiquette 41
Eurostar 22, 26

F

fainè 210
farm stays 31
fassonis 148, 149, 153,
   157, 217
Ferragosto 39, 41, 49, 179, 259
ferries
   from France 25
   from Ireland 24
   from mainland Italy 24–25
   from the UK 24
   operators 26
   to/from Arbatax 24, 304
   to/from Calasetta 96
   to/from Corsica 25, 30, 258
   to/from Golfo Aranci 25, 240
   to/from La Maddalena 252
   to/from Olbia 24–25, 235
   to/from Porto Torres 24–25, 215
   to/from Santa Teresa
      Gallura 25, 258
Ferry routes **23**
Fertilia 182
festivals **38–41**
   Carnival 38, 76, 146, 161, 179,
      193, 262, 284
   Corsa degli Scalzi, San Salvatore ... 151
   Creuza de Mà, San Pietro 99

D

d'Annunzio, Gabriele 117
d'Arborea, Eleonora 117, 142,
   143, 187, 217, 280, 310, 316
dance 321
de Seta, Vittorio 283
Deledda, Grazia 273, 276, 320
dentists 47
Dessi, Giuseppe 320
dialect 98, 122, 169, 323
disabled travellers 51
diving 43

Easter celebrations.......... 39, 76, 105, 161, 179, 193, 216, 280
Ferragosto 39, 41, 49, 179, 259
Festa dei Santi Cosma e Damiano, Bosa.....................................193
Festa dei Santi Pietro e Paolo, Bosa.....................................193
film festival, Tavolara 238
Girotonno, San Pietro................97, 99
I Candelieri, Iglésias.......................105
I Candelieri, Sássari 39, 41, 207
jazz festival, Berchidda..................263
La Cavalcata, Sássari 40, 207
Li 'Agghiani, Aggius.......................264
Lunissanti, Castelsardo 216
Madonna degli Angeli, Castelsardo.............................216
Musica sulle Bocche, Santa Teresa Gallura....................................259
Nit de Sant Miquel, Alghero 179
Posidonia, San Pietro.......................99
Regata della Vela Latina, Stintino...195
S'Ardia horse race, Sédilo.............159
Sa Carapigna, Aritzo......................290
Sa Sartiglia, Oristano 39, 146
Sagra degli Agrumi, Muravera 40, 132
Sagra dei Pescatori, Alghero........179
Sagra del Pesce, Santa Teresa Gallura....................................259
Sagra del Redentore, Nuoro....41, 278
Sagra della Madonna del Rimedio, Ozieri....................................223
Sagra delle Castagne, Aritzo........290
Sagra di Nostra Signora di Regnos Altos, Bosa.............................193
Sagra di Santa Maria del Mare, Bosa.....................................193
San Giovanni, Fonni.......................288
San Giovanni Battista, Villanova Monteleone...........................186
San Lussorio....................................280
San Pietro..99
San Símplicio, Olbia 237
Sant'Agostino, Alghero..................179
Sant'Agostino, Olbia......................237
Sant'Antíoco......................................95
Sant'Antonio Abate, Mamoiada ... 284
Sant'Efisio, Cágliari 40, 67
Santa Giusta...................................154
Santa Lucia, Olbia 237
Santa Sabina...................................194
Su Tuva, Macomer 194
Time in Jazz, Berchidda 263
Figuera, Joan 63
films...319
flag...6
flights
    booking online...........................25
    from Australia...........................21
    from Canada..............................21
    from the Italian mainland..........22
    from New Zealand......................21
    from South Africa......................22
    from the UK and Ireland............21
    from US......................................21
Floris, Carmelo...............................274
Fonni..287
Fontanamare...................................107
Fonti Rinaggiu................................261

food and drink 32–37
Fordongianus................................155
Foresta di Burgos...........................280
Foresta di Minniminni...................130
Fresu, Paolo...........................263, 321
fuel..28
Funtana Bona.................................283
Funtanazza.....................................109

G

Gallura 228–265
Gallura 230–231
Garibaldi, Giuseppe........254, 312
gas...28
Gavoi...286
gay travellers...................................46
Genna Silana.................................298
Gennargentu massif ... 287–291
Genoa...309
Gerrei...126
Gésturi...124
Gherardesca, Ugolino della....104, 161
Ghilarza...158
Giara di Gésturi.............................125
giudicati...........................139, 309
glossary..331
Gola di Gorroppu 299
Golfo Aranci...................................239
Golfo di Arzachena.............. 244, 246–249
Golfo di Cágliari.............................127
Golfo di Gonnesa...........................108
Golfo di Saline 248
Golfo di Teulada.............................. 88
Gonnesa...107
Gorroppu Gorge.............................299
Gramsci, Antonio............................158
griffon vultures.................. 187, 316
Grotta del Bue Marino............301
Grotta di Ispinigoli.........................298
Grotta di Nettuno............ 180, 182
Grotta Su Mannau...........................107
Gúspini...109

H

handicrafts......................... 218, 272
Hanno..232
Hassan Aga....................................169
health...46
hiking...43
history.......................... 307–314
hitching..30
holidays..49
horseriding 43, 155
hostels..31
hotels...30
House of Savoy...............................203

I

ice cream...33
IGLÉSIAS 103–107
Iglésias..................................... 103
    accommodation.......................105
    arrival......................................105
    Castello Salvaterra..................103
    Duomo....................................104
    festivals...................................105
    history.....................................104
    information..............................105
    Monteponi...............................106
    Museo delle Arti Minerarie..........106
    Piazza Município 103, 104
    Piazza Sella...................... 103, 104
    restaurants..............................106
    San Francesco..........................105
    Santa Maria delle Grazie...........105
Iglesiente......................... 103–109
Ingurtosu.......................................109
insurance..47
internet...48
Is Arenas............................. 153, 162
Is Aruttas.......................................152
Is Borroccus...................................294
Is Zuddas... 88
Ísili 293–295
Isola dei Cávoli..............................127
Isola Piana.....................................100
Italy, unification of 312

J

James II of Aragon 203
Joyce, James..................................217

K

kidnapping......................................287
kitesurfing.................................43, 250

L

La Bobba...100
La Caletta, Nuoro province 296
La Caletta, San Pietro island....100
La Licciola......................................257
La Marmilla 119–125
La Marmilla and Sarrabus, Campidano.............. 114–115
La Marmorata..................................257
La Mattanza.................................. 97
La Pelosa...197
La Prigiona......................................246
La Punta..100
La Speranza 186, 187
La Valle della Luna..........................264
Láconi........................... 291–293

Laerru..221
Lago del Temo.........................186
Lago di Baratz........................185
Lago di Coghinas....................263
Lago di Liscia..........................265
Lago di San Sebastiano.........294
Lago Omodeo..........................158
Laguna di Nora.........................86
Lamármora, Alberto di............62
language 322–332
Lanusei.....................................304
Las Plassas.................... 120, 122
laundry..48
Lawrence, D. H.........4, 54, 60, 271, 291, 319
Lazzaretto................................184
Le Bombarde............................183
Le Prigionette.........................184
Le Saline (Stintino)................196
Ledda, Gavino................. 319, 320
lesbian travellers......................46
Li Lolghi..................................246
Li Muri....................................246
Lido di Capoterra......................84
Lido Orri..................................303
Lilliu, Giovanni.......................123
Liscia di Vacca........................242
Logudoro...................... 222–225
Lu Bagnu..................................219
Luras.......................................265
Lussu, Emilio...........................320

M

Macomer...................................194
MADDALENA ISLANDS
.... 250–255
Maddalena archipelago 251
accommodation...........................253
Budelli..255
Cala Coticcio...............................254
Cala Gavetta................................252
Cala Lunga..................................253
Caprera.......................................254
Compendio Garibaldino.............254
getting around............................253
getting there...............................252
information.................................253
La Maddalena.....................251–254
Madonnetta.................................253
Museo Archeologico Navale........252
Punt Tegge.................................253
restaurants.................................254
Santa Maria Maddalena...............252
Santo Stéfano.............................255
Spalmatore.................................253
Spargi..255
Spiaggia Rosa.............................255
Teialone.....................................254
tours...253
Madonna di Bonaria...................70
Maestro di Castelsardo....124, 218
mail..48
Mainas, Antioco....63, 66, 105, 144

Mal di Ventre............................153
Maladroxia.................................95
Malaspina family......................187
Mamoiada........................ 284, 286
Mamuthones............................284
Manca, Mauro..........................273
Mandriola................................153
maps..48
Marazzino................................257
Marceddi..................................155
Marghinotti, Giovanni 66
Mari Ermi.................................153
Mariano II 139, 140, 142
Mariano IV 142, 280
Marina di Arborea....................154
Marina di Arbus.......................109
Marina di Sorso.......................213
Marina di Torre Grande 150
Mártiri Turritani.......................214
Masua......................................108
Mates, Joan................................63
meals.................................33–35
media, the.................................. 37
Melia, Melkiorre 189
menhirs...........................89, 292
Mesina, Graziano......................283
Milis...157
mining......................................106
mobile phones...........................49
Molara......................................238
money...48
Monte Arcosu............................84
Monte d'Accoddi......................215
Monte dei Sette Fratelli..........130
Monte Ferru..............................161
Monte Limbara.........................263
Monte Mandriolo......................238
Monte Ortobene.......................276
Monte San Giovanni................283
Monte Sirai...............................102
Monte Spada.............................288
Monte Tíscali............................281
Monteleone Rocca Doria........186
Montes.....................................283
Montessu...................................89
Montevécchio..........................109
Morandi, Giorgio....................... 63
motorbikes.................................42
murals.............................116, 283
Muravera 131–133
Museo e Tenuta Vitivinicola...185
museums....................................49
music............................. 279, 321
Mussolini, Benito....100, 139, 182, 313
Mussolinia................................154
Muto di Gallura........................265

N

Nébida.....................................108
Nelson, Horatio 252, 312
newspapers 37

Nivola, Costantino.......... 273, 286
Nora....................................84–87
Northwest coast................. 168
NUORO 271–278
Nuoro 272
accommodation...........................277
arriving.......................................276
bars..278
Casa di Grazia Deledda...............273
Duomo.......................................274
information.................................277
Monte Ortobene.........................276
Museo Archeologico...................274
Museo d'Arte Nuoro...................273
Museo della Vita e delle Tradizioni
Sarde.....................................275
Museo Tribu...............................274
Piazza Satta................................273
restaurants.................................277
Sagra del Redentore...................278
San Carlo...................................273
Santa Maria della Solitúdine........276
Nuoro province 271–302
Nuoro and Ogliastra
provinces 270
Nuraghe Albucciu.....................244
Nuraghe Arrubiu......................126
Nuraghe Asoru.........................130
Nuraghe di Genna Maria........120
Nuraghe di Palmavera.............183
Nuraghe di Santa Barbara......194
Nuraghe Is Paras.....................294
Nuraghe Izzana.......................264
Nuraghe Losa...........................159
Nuraghe Maiori........................261
Nuraghe Mannu.......................300
Nuraghe Paddaggiu 219
Nuraghe Ruju..........................194
Nuraghe Santu Antine.............224
nuraghic culture 62, 120, 122, 126, 130, 157, 159, 183, 194, 204, 219, 224, 244, 246, 261, 279, 281, 294, 298, 300, 307

O

Ogliastra province 303–305
Ogliastra and Nuoro
provinces.......................... 270
OLBIA 232–237
Olbia 233
accommodation...........................236
airport.......................................235
arriving.......................................235
Corso Umberto...........................232
festivals......................................237
history.......................................232
information.................................236
Municipio...................................232
Museo Archeologico...................234
Pittulongu..................................235
restaurants and bars...................236
Sa Testa.....................................234
San Paolo...................................234
San Símplicio.............................234

Oliena............................ 280–282
Olzai, Mastro di........................ 63
opening hours.......................... 49
Orani....................................286
Orgósolo..............................282
ORISTANO 140–148
Oristano.............................. 141
  accommodation....................145
  Antiquarium Arborense 143
  arriving................................144
  bars....................................148
  buses.............................144, 145
  Casa di Eleonora....................143
  Duomo................................143
  information...........................145
  parking...............................144
  Piazza Eleonora d'Arborea........140
  pinacoteca...........................144
  Portixedda...........................143
  restaurants...........................145
  Sa Sartiglia...........................146
  San Francesco........................140
  Santa Chiara..........................143
  shopping..............................148
  Torre di Mariano II..........140, 142
Oristano province....... 136–163
Oristano province.............. 138
Orosei..................................296
Orune...................................279
outdoor activities 42
Ozieri...................................223
Ozieri culture...................223, 307

P

package holidays....................... 22
Padre Padrone 319, 320
Palau....................................248
Pan di Zúcchero......................108
Parco Archeologico Selene....304
Partito Sardo d'Azione............313
Pater Babay...........................107
Paulilátino.............................158
Pedro IV of Aragon.................169
Perdas de Fogu........................ 95
petrol 28
pharmacies............................. 47
Phoenicians 56, 138, 152, 308
Piana....................................197
pinneddas 123, 157
Pisa......................................309
Pisan churches........154, 220, 222,
  223, 225, 234
Pisano, Andrea.......................104
Pisano, Nino...............140, 143
Piscinas................................109
pizzas.................................... 33
Platamona.............................213
police.................................... 45
population................................6
Portixeddu............................109
Porto Cervo...........................242
Porto Conte...........................184
Porto Corallo.........................132

Porto Ferro.............................185
Porto Frailis....................303, 304
Porto Istana...........................238
Porto Pino.............................. 88
Porto Pollo.............................250
Porto Pozzo...........................257
Porto Quadro.........................257
Porto Rotondo........................240
Porto San Paolo......................238
Porto Taverna.........................238
Porto Teulada.......................... 88
PORTO TORRES............. 213–216
  accommodation....................216
  Antiquarium Turritano............214
  arriving................................215
  Basilica di San Gavino 214
  ferries..................................215
  history.................................213
  information...........................216
  Monte d'Accoddi....................215
  Palazzo di Re Bárbaro..............215
  restaurants and bars................216
  Roman bridge........................215
Portoscuso............................100
Portovesme...........................100
Portu Tramatzu........................ 88
Posada..................................295
post offices............................. 48
prehistory..............................307
public holidays......................... 49
Pula...............................84–87
Punta Balistreri......................263
Punta della Volpe 240
Punta Falcone........................257
Punta La Mármora...................288
Putzu Idu..............................153

R

radio..................................... 38
rail travel 22–24, 26, 27
rainfall................................... 10
Rena Maiore...........................257
restaurants.......................33–35
riding..............................43, 155
Roccia dell'Elefante................218
Romagna, Giovanni Ciusa 274,
  276
Romangia..............................214
Romans 57, 139, 152, 155, 156,
  162, 232, 308

S

Sa Mesa Lunga 153
sailing.................................... 43
Samugheo.............................156
San Giovanni di Sinis...............151
San Leonardo de Siete
  Fuentes...............................161
San Michele culture.................223

San Nicolò Gerrei....................126
San Pantaleo..........................241
San Pietro di Sorres.................225
San Pietro island.............97–100
San Pietro, Sant'Antíoco
  and...................................... 91
San Salvatore.........................150
San Sperate...........................116
San Teodoro...........................239
San Vito................................131
Sanluri..................................117
Sant'Anna Arresi...................... 88
Sant'Antíoco di Bisarcio..........223
Sant'Antíoco island 90–96
Sant'Antíoco and San
  Pietro 91
SANT'ANTÍOCO TOWN 90–95
  accommodation...................... 94
  acropolis.............................. 92
  arriving................................ 94
  catacombs............................ 91
  festivities............................. 95
  Forte Su Pisu......................... 94
  information............................ 94
  Museo Archeologico............... 92
  Museo Etnográfico................. 94
  necropolis............................ 92
  restaurants........................... 95
  Sant'Antíoco, basilica.............. 91
  tophet................................. 92
  Villaggio ipogeo.................... 92
  zona archeologica.................. 92
Sant'Antonio di Gallura 265
Sant'Efisio.......................67, 85
Sant'Ignazio da Láconi 292
Santa Caterina di Pittinuri 162
Santa Cristina........................157
Santa Giusta..........................153
Santa Lucia............................296
Santa Margherita di Pula 86
Santa Maria (Tratalias) 89
Santa Maria Navarrese............303
Santa Sabina..........................194
SANTA TERESA DI
  GALLURA................... 255–260
Santa Teresa di Gallura...... 256
  accommodation....................258
  arriving................................258
  bars....................................259
  beaches.......................255, 257
  boat tours.............................258
  entertainment.......................259
  ferries..................................258
  festivals...............................259
  information...........................258
  port....................................255
  restaurants...........................259
  Rena Bianca..........................255
  Torre Spagnola.......................256
Santadi.................................. 89
Santissima Trinità di
  Saccargia.....................211, 222
Santo Stéfano........................255
Santu Lussurgiu 160
Santuario Nurágico di Santa
  Vittoria................................294
Sarcidano 291–295

Sard dialect 323
Sárdara 118
Sardinia, autonomy 313
Sardinia, Kingdom of 311
Sarrabus 127–131
**Sarrabus, Campidano and
   La Marmilla 114–115**
SÁSSARI 200–212
Sássari 204
Sássari and around 202
Sássari old quarter 206
   accommodation 209
   arriving 209
   bars 212
   Casa di Re Enzo 205
   Casa Farris 205
   Corso Vittorio Emanuele 205
   Duomo di San Nicola 205
   festivals 207
   Fonte Rosello 207
   Frumentaria 207
   history 203
   information 209
   medieval walls 208
   Museo della Brigata Sássari 205
   Museo Sanna 203–205
   Palazzo d'Usini 207
   Palazzo della Giustizia 203
   Palazzo della Provincia 203
   Palazzo Ducale 205
   Palazzo Giordano 203
   Piazza Italia 203
   Piazza Tola 207
   restaurants 210, 212
   Sant'Antonio Abate 208
   Santa Maria di Betlem 208
   shopping 212
   Teatro Cívico 205
   Via Roma 203
   Via Turritana 207
Satta, Salvatore 274, 320
Satta, Sebastiano 273
Saturninus 69
Savoy, House of 170, 311
Sciola, Pinuccio 116
Scipio, Lucius Cornelius 232
Sédilo 159
Sédini 221
Segni, Antonio 203
Serpentara 127
Serra Orrios 298
Serri 294
Sette Fratelli 130
shopping 43
Silanus 194
Sinis peninsula 148–153
smoking 32
Solanas 127
Sórgono 291
Soriga, Flavio 321
Sorso 214
Soru, Renato 314
Southwest Sardinia 82–83

Spanish in Sardinia, The
   .... 169, 187, 203, 310
Spargi 255
special diets 34
speed limits 29
Spiaggia Cartoe 300
Spiaggia Osalla 300
Stagno de Sale Porcus 153
Stagno di Marceddi 155
Stagno di S'Ena Arrubia 154
Stagno di Santa Caterina 90
Stagno di Santa Giusta 153
Stintino 195
Su Archittu 162
Su Gologone 281
Su Gunventeddu 85
Su Nuraxi 122
Su Tempiesu 279
Sulcis 84–102
Supramonte 280–282
surfing 153
Susini, Clemente 63, 118

T

Tavolara 238
telephones 49
temperatures 10
Tempietto Malchittu 244
Témpio di Antas 107
Tempio Pausania 261–263
Tenores di Bitti 279, 321
Tergu 220
Terralba 154
Terrazzu 89
Teulada 88
Tharros 151
Thomas, Rafael 63
time 50
tipping 35
Tíscali 281
toilets 50
Tonara 290
Torralba 224
Torre dei Corsari 109
Torre delle Stelle 127
Tortolì 303
tour operators 25
tourist offices 50
trains 22–24, 26, 27
Tratalias 89
travel agents 25
Trenino Verde 71, 191, 209
Tuerredda 88
Tuili 124
Turas 191
TV 38
Tyndale, John 232

U

Uta 116

V

Valle dei Nuraghi 224
Valle Lanaittu 281
vegans 34
vegetarians 34
vendettas 265, 283
Vernaccia 157
Vici, Michele Busiri 242
Vignola 257
Villanova Monteleone 186
Villanovaforru 119
Villaputzu 131
villas 31
Villasimius 127–129
visas 46
Vittorio Emanuele I 254

W

walking 43
walks 131, 281, 299
water 36
watersports 43
weather 10
websites 51
wells, sacred ... 158, 234, 279, 294
wildlife 315–318
windsurfing 43
   Le Bombarde 183
   Marina di Torre Grande 150
   Poetto 71
   Porto Conte 184
   Porto Pollo 250
   San Teodoro 239
   Santa Teresa di Gallura 259
wine 36, 37
World War I 313
World War II 313

Y

youth hostels 31

Z

Zumbo, Gaetano 118

Map symbols

The symbols below are used on maps throughout the book

✦	Point of interest	▲	Tower	✉	Post office
⌒	Mountain range	♟	Museum	⊞	Hospital
▲	Mountain peak	✝	Church (regional maps)	– –	Ferry route
⌒	Cave	✈	Airport		Church (town maps)
�	Archeological site	★	Bus stop		Building
∴	Ruins	ⓘ	Information office		Park
⋀⋀	Spring/spa	@	Internet café/access		Beach
♔	Castle	⛺	Campsite		Cemetery
P	Parking	🏛	Monument		

Listings key

■	Accommodation
●	Restaurants
■	Bar/café/venue
●	Shop

ROUGH GUIDES

SO NOW WE'VE TOLD YOU HOW TO MAKE THE MOST OF YOUR TIME, WE WANT YOU TO STAY SAFE AND COVERED WITH OUR FAVOURITE TRAVEL INSURER

WorldNomads.com
keep travelling safely

GET AN ONLINE QUOTE
roughguides.com/insurance

RECOMMENDED BY
ROUGH GUIDES

MAKE THE MOST OF YOUR TIME ON EARTH™

ROUGH GUIDES

MAKE THE MOST OF YOUR GADGETS

roughguides.com/downloads

kindle

THE ROUGH GUIDE to
Vietnam

ROUGH GUIDES SNAPSHOT
FRANCE
Corsica

Central
America
BIG TRIP
WHAT TO SEE • WHERE TO GO • WHAT TO DO

Multi-Touch

FROM
ANDROID
TO **iPADS** TO
SOCIAL MEDIA

BOOKS | EBOOKS | APPS

MAKE THE MOST OF YOUR TIME ON EARTH™